PostgreSQL

PostgreSQL

A comprehensive guide to building, programming, and administering PostgreSQL databases

---

Korry Douglas
Susan Douglas

Sams Publishing, 201 West 103rd Street, Indianapolis, Indiana 46290

PostgreSQL

FIRST EDITION: February 2003

International Standard Book Number: 0-7357-1257-3

Library of Congress Catalog Card Number: 2001098750

06 05 04 03   7 6 5 4 3 2 1

Interpretation of the printing code: The rightmost double-digit number is the year of the book's printing; the rightmost single-digit number is the number of the book's printing. For example, the printing code 03-1 shows that the first printing of the book occurred in 2003.

Printed in the United States of America

Trademarks

Warning and Disclaimer

Acquisitions Editors
Stephanie Wall
Elise Walter

Development Editors
Chris Zahn
Paul DuBois

Managing Editor
Charlotte Clapp

Senior Project Editor
Lori Lyons

Copy Editor
Linda Seifert

Senior Indexer
Cheryl Lenser

Proofreader
Nancy Sixsmith

Composition
Stacey DeRome

Cover Designer
Alan Clements

Contents At a Glance

Table of Contents

About the Authors

Korry Douglas is the Director of Research and Development for Appx Software. Over the last two decades, he has worked on the design and implementation of a number of high-level, high-productivity languages and development environments. His products interface with many relational (and non-relational) databases. Working with so many different database products (Oracle, Sybase, SQL Server, DB2, PostgreSQL, MySQL, MSQL) has given him a broad understanding of the commonalities of, and differences between, databases.

Susan Douglas is the President and CEO of Conjectrix, Inc., a software company specializing in database technologies and security tools. Consulting to the end-user community has given her widespread database experience and a real appreciation for high-quality programs and flexible tools powerful enough to handle data well and intuitive enough to actually use.

Korry and his wife (and best friend) Susan raise horses in rural Virginia. Both are natives of the Pacific Northwest, but prefer the sunshine and open spaces offered by Virginia. They both telecommute, preferring to spend as much time as possible with their 200 or so animal friends (who never complain about buggy code, inelegant design, or poor performance). Susan is an avid equestrienne; Korry gets to clean the barn.

About the Technical Reviewers

These reviewers contributed their considerable hands-on expertise to the entire development process for *PostgreSQL*. As the book was being written, these dedicated professionals reviewed all the material for technical content, organization, and flow. Their feedback was critical to ensuring that *PostgreSQL* fits our reader's need for the highest-quality technical information.

Barry Stinson graduated from Louisiana State University in 1995 with a Master's Degree in Music Composition. During his tenure there, he was fortunate enough to help design the Digital Arts studio with Dr. Stephen David Beck. Designing a full-fledged music and graphic-arts digital studio afforded him exposure to a diverse set of unique computing systems—particularly those from NeXT, SGI, and Apple.

It was during this time that he discovered Linux, and subsequently PostgreSQL, both of which were still in an early stage of development.

After graduation, Barry set up his own consulting company, Silicon Consulting, which is based in Lafayette, LA. Over the years, he has worked as a consultant for many companies throughout southern Louisiana.

Increasingly, much of the work that Barry has done over the years has centered on databases. In the time from his original exposure to Postgre95—to its present form as PostgreSQL—an amazing amount of development has taken place on open-source database systems.

The rise of high-quality and open-sourced computing systems that have taken place recently has produced a renaissance in the high-tech industry. However, according to his girlfriend Pamela, his continued insistence to rely on renegade operating systems, such as Linux, has only served to strengthen the unruly aspects already present in his personality. Barry is the author of New Riders *PostgreSQL Essential Reference*.

Peter Eisentraut, from Dresden, Germany, became involved with PostgreSQL development in 1999 when he needed to scratch the proverbial itch. (The result is the tab-completion in the psql client.) He has since worked in many areas of the PostgreSQL code, reviewed several PostgreSQL books, and contributed to other open-source projects. In his spare time he likes to study human languages and plans to ride his bicycle to the places where those languages are spoken.

About the Development Editor

This reviewer brought his gift for writing clear, understandable technical prose to this book in his role as Development Editor.

Paul DuBois is a writer, database administrator, and leader in the open-source community. He is the author of the best-selling *MySQL*, and *MySQL and Perl for the Web*, for New Riders Publishing, and *MySQL Cookbook*, *Using csh and tcsh*, and *Software Portability with imake* for O'Reilly and Associates.

Acknowledgments

Thank you to our technical reviewers, Peter Eisentraut and Barry Stinson, and to Paul DuBois for his developmental reviewing. We appreciate their many hours spent poring through manuscripts exposing technical inaccuracies and poor grammar. Their knowledge and expertise have been invaluable.

Thank you to the staff at New Riders, especially Chris Zahn, Elise Walter, and Stephanie Wall for keeping this project manageable, on time, and on course. The help and support they have provided has made this book possible.

We would especially like to thank the developers of PostgreSQL for the years of development spent producing an excellent database. Without their devotion to the project, it wouldn't have evolved into the masterpiece we all know today.

Most of the books that we read are dedicated to various household members for the long hours devoted to their writing project rather than to family life. Instead, we have enjoyed the long hours of R&D spent together, interspersed with screaming (during breaks, on the Roller Coasters at King's Dominion—not at each other).

We Want to Hear from You

As the reader of this book, you are our most important critic and commentator. We value your opinion and want to know what we're doing right, what we could do better, what areas you'd like to see us publish in, and any other words of wisdom you're willing to pass our way.

You can email or write me directly to let me know what you did or didn't like about this book—as well as what we can do to make our books stronger.

Please note that I cannot help you with technical problems related to the topic of this book, and that due to the high volume of mail I receive, I might not be able to reply to every message.

When you write, please be sure to include this book's title and author, as well as your name and contact information. I will carefully review your comments and share them with the author and editors who worked on the book.

Email: opensource@samspublishing.com
Mail: Mark Taber
Associate Publisher
Sams Publishing
201 West 103rd Street
Indianapolis, IN 46290 USA

Reader Services

For more information about this book or others from Sams Publishing, visit our Web site at www.samspublishing.com. Type the ISBN (excluding hyphens) or the title of the book in the Search box to find the book you're looking for.

Preface

These days, it seems that most discussion of open-source software centers on the idea that you should not have to tie your future to the whim of some giant corporation. People say that open-source software is better than proprietary software because it is developed and maintained by the users instead of a faceless company out to lighten your wallet.

I think that the real value in free software is education. I have never learned anything by reading my own code[1]. On the other hand, it's a rare occasion when I've looked at code written by someone else and haven't come away with another tool in my toolkit. People don't think alike. I don't mean that people disagree with each other; I mean that people solve problems in different ways. Each person brings a unique set of experiences to the table. Each person has his own set of goals and biases. Each person has his own interests. All these things will shape the way you think about a problem. Often, I'll find myself in a heated disagreement with a colleague only to realize that we are each correct in our approach. Just because I'm right, doesn't mean that my colleague can't be right as well.

Open-source software is a great way to learn. You can learn about programming. You can learn about design. You can learn about debugging. Sometimes, you'll learn how *not* to design, code, or debug; but that's a valuable lesson too. You can learn small things, such as how to cache file descriptors on systems where file descriptors are a scarce and expensive resource, or how to use the `select()` function to implement fine-grained timers. You can learn big things, like how a query optimizer works or how to write a parser, or how to develop a good memory management strategy.

PostgreSQL is a great example. I've been using databases for the last two decades. I've used most of the major commercial databases: Oracle, Sybase, DB2, and MS SQL Server. With each commercial database, there is a wall of knowledge between *my* needs and the *vendor's* need to protect his intellectual property. Until I started exploring open-source databases, I had an incomplete understanding of how a database works. Why was this particular feature implemented that way? Why am I getting poor performance when I try this? That's a neat feature; I wonder how they did that? Every commercial database tries to expose a small piece of its inner workings. The `explain` statement will show you why the database makes its optimization decisions. But, you only get to see what the vendor wants you to see. The vendor isn't trying to hide things from you (in most cases), but without complete access to the source code, they have to pick and choose how to expose information in a meaningful way. With open source software, you can dive deep into the source code and pull out all the information you need. While writing this book,

1. Maybe I should say that I have never learned anything *new* by reading my own code. I've certainly looked at code that I've written and wondered what I was thinking at the time, learning that I'm not nearly as clever as I had remembered. Oddly enough, those who have read my code have reached a similar conclusion.

I've spent a lot of time reading through the PostgreSQL source code. I've added a lot of my own code to reveal *more* information so that I could explain things more clearly. I can't do that with a commercial database.

There are gems of brilliance in most open-source projects. In a well-designed, well-factored project, you will find designs and code that you can use in your own projects. Many open source projects are starting to split their code into reusable libraries. The Apache Portable Runtime is a good example. The Apache Web server runs on many diverse platforms. The Apache development team saw the need for a layer of abstraction that would provide a portable interface to system functions such as shared memory and network access. They decided to factor the portability layer into a library separate from their main project. The result is the Apache Portable Runtime - a library of code that can be used in *other* open-source projects (such as PostgreSQL).

Some developers hate to work on someone else's code. I love working on code written by another developer——I always learn something from the experience. I strongly encourage you to dive into the PostgreSQL source code. You will learn from it. You might even decide to contribute to the project.

Introduction

PostgreSQL is a relational database with a long history. In the late 1970s, the University of California at Berkeley began development of PostgreSQL's ancestor—a relational database known as Ingres. Relational Technologies turned Ingres into a commercial product. Relational Technologies became Ingres Corporation and was later acquired by Computer Associates. Around 1986, Michael Stonebraker from UC Berkeley led a team that added object-oriented features to the core of Ingres; the new version became known as Postgres. Postgres was again commercialized; this time by a company named Illustra, which became part of the Informix Corporation. Andrew Yu and Jolly Chen added SQL support to Postgres in the mid-90s. Prior versions had used a different, Postgres-specific query language known as Postquel. In 1996, many new features were added, including the MVCC transaction model, more adherence to the SQL92 standard, and many performance improvements. Postgres once again took on a new name: PostgreSQL.

Today, PostgreSQL is developed by an international group of open-source software proponents known as the PostgreSQL Global Development group. PostgreSQL is an open-source product—it is not proprietary in any way. Red Hat has recently commercialized PostgreSQL, creating the Red Hat Database, but PostgreSQL itself will remain free and open-source.

PostgreSQL Features

PostgreSQL has benefited well from its long history. Today, PostgreSQL is one of the most advanced database servers available. Here are a few of the features found in a standard PostgreSQL distribution:

- Object-relational—In PostgreSQL, every table defines a class. PostgreSQL implements inheritance between tables (or, if you like, between classes). Functions and operators are polymorphic.
- Standards compliant—PostgreSQL syntax implements most of the SQL92 standard and many features of SQL99. Where differences in syntax occur, they are most often related to features unique to PostgreSQL.
- Open source—An international team of developers maintains PostgreSQL. Team members come and go, but the core members have been enhancing PostgreSQL's performance and feature set since at least 1996. One advantage to PostgreSQL's open-source nature is that talent and knowledge can be recruited as needed. The fact that this team is international ensures that PostgreSQL is a product that can be used productively in *any* natural language, not just English.

- Transaction processing—PostgreSQL protects data and coordinates multiple concurrent users through full transaction processing. The transaction model used by PostgreSQL is based on multi-version concurrency control (MVCC). MVCC provides much better performance than you would find with other products that coordinate multiple users through table-, page-, or row-level locking.
- Referential integrity—PostgreSQL implements complete referential integrity by supporting foreign and primary key relationships as well as triggers. Business rules can be expressed *within* the database rather than relying on an external tool.
- Multiple procedural languages—Triggers and other procedures can be written in any of several procedural languages. Server-side code is most commonly written in PL/pgSQL, a procedural language similar to Oracle's PL/SQL. You can also develop server-side code in Tcl, Perl, even `bash` (the open-source Linux/Unix shell).
- Multiple-client APIs—PostgreSQL supports the development of client applications in many languages. This book describes how to interface to PostgreSQL from C, C++, ODBC, Perl, PHP, Tcl/Tk, and Python.
- Unique data types—PostgreSQL provides a variety of data types. Besides the usual numeric, string, and date types, you will also find geometric types, a Boolean data type, and data types designed specifically to deal with network addresses.
- Extensibility—One of the most important features of PostgreSQL is that it can be extended. If you don't find something that you need, you can usually add it yourself. For example, you can add new data types, new functions and operators, and even new procedural and client languages. There are many contributed packages available on the Internet. For example, Refractions Research, Inc. has developed a set of geographic data types that can be used to efficiently model spatial (GIS) data.

What Versions Does This Book Cover?

This book has been in progress for almost a year and the PostgreSQL development team has not been idle during that year. When I started working on this book, PostgreSQL version 7.1.2 was on the streets. About half way through, PostgreSQL version 7.2 was released and the development team had started working on new features for version 7.3.

Fortunately, the PostgreSQL developers try *very* hard to maintain forward compatibility—new features tend not to break existing applications. This means that all the 7.1.2 and 7.2 features discussed in this book should still be available and substantially similar in later versions of PostgreSQL. I have tried to avoid talking about features that have not been released at the time of writing—where I *have* mentioned future developments, I will point them out.

Who Is This Book For?

If you are already using PostgreSQL, you should find this book a useful guide to some of the features that you might be less familiar with. The first part of the book provides an introduction to SQL and PostgreSQL for the new user. You'll also find information that shows how to obtain and install PostgreSQL on a Unix/Linux host, as well as on Microsoft Windows.

If you are developing an application that will store data in PostgreSQL, the second part of this book will provide you with a great deal of information relating to PostgreSQL programming. You'll find information on both server-side and client-side programming in a variety of languages.

Every database needs occasional administrative work. The final part of the book should be of help if you are a PostgreSQL administrator, or a developer or user that needs to do occasional administration. You will also find information on how to secure your data against inappropriate use.

Finally, if you are trying to decide *which* database to use for your current project (or for future projects), this book should provide all the information you need to evaluate whether PostgreSQL will fit your needs.

What Topics Does This Book Cover?

PostgreSQL is a *huge* product. It's not easy to find the right mix of topics when you are trying to fit everything into a single book. This book is divided into three parts.

The first part, "General PostgreSQL Use," is an introduction and user's guide for PostgreSQL. Chapter 1, "Introduction to PostgreSQL and SQL" covers the basics—how to obtain and install PostgreSQL (if you are running Linux, chances are you already have PostgreSQL and it may be installed). The first chapter also provides a gentle introduction to SQL and discusses the sample database we'll be using throughout the book. Chapter 2, "Working with Data in PostgreSQL," describes the many data types supported by a standard PostgreSQL distribution; you'll learn how to enter values (literals) for each data type, what kind of data you can store with each type, and how those data types are combined into expressions. Chapter 3, "PostgreSQL SQL Syntax and Use," fills in some of the details we glossed over in the first two chapters. You'll learn how to create new databases, new tables and indexes, and how PostgreSQL keeps your data safe through the use of transactions. Chapter 4, "Performance," describes the PostgreSQL optimizer. I'll show you how to get information about the decisions made by the optimizer, how to decipher that information, and how to influence those decisions.

Part II, "Programming with PostgreSQL," is all about PostgreSQL programming. In Chapter 5, "Introduction to PostgreSQL Programming," we start off by describing the options you have when developing a database application that works with PostgreSQL (and there are a *lot* of options). Chapter 6, "Extending PostgreSQL," briefly describes how to extend PostgreSQL by adding new functions, data types, and operators. Chapter 7, "PL/pgSQL describes the PL/pgSQL language. PL/pgSQL is a server-based procedural language. Code that you write in PL/pgSQL executes *within* the PostgreSQL server and has very fast access to data. Each chapter in the remainder of the programming section deals with a client-based API. You can connect to a PostgreSQL server using a number of languages. I show you how to interface to PostgreSQL using C, C++, ecpg,

ODBC, JDBC, Perl, PHP, Tcl/Tk, and Python. Chapters 8 through 17 all follow the same pattern: you develop a series of client applications in a given language. The first client application shows you how to establish a connection to the database (and how that connection is represented by the language in question). The next client adds error checking so that you can intercept and react to unusual conditions. The third client in each chapter demonstrates how to process SQL commands from within the client. The final client wraps everything together and shows you how to build an interactive query processor using the language being discussed. Even if you program in only one or two languages, I would encourage you to study the other chapters in this section. I think you'll find that looking at the same application written in a variety of languages will help you understand the philosophy followed by the PostgreSQL development team, and it's a great way to start learning a new language.

The final part of this book (Part III, "PostgreSQL Administration") deals with administrative issues. The final four chapters of this book show you how to perform the occasional duties required of a PostgreSQL administrator. In the first two chapters, Chapter 18, "Introduction to PostgreSQL Administration," and Chapter 19, "PostgreSQL Administration," you'll learn how to start up, shut down, back up, and restore a server. In Chapter 20, "Internationalization and Localization," you will learn how PostgreSQL supports internationalization and localization. PostgreSQL understands how to store and process a variety of single-byte and multi-byte character sets including Unicode, ASCII, and Japanese, Chinese, Korean, and Taiwan EUC. Finally, in Chapter 21, "Security," I'll show you how to secure your data against unauthorized uses (and unauthorized users).

I

General PostgreSQL Use

1

Introduction to PostgreSQL and SQL

POSTGRESQL IS AN OPEN SOURCE, CLIENT/SERVER, relational database. PostgreSQL offers a unique mix of features that compare well to the major commercial databases such as Sybase, Oracle, and DB2. One of the major advantages to PostgreSQL is that it is open source—you can see the source code for PostgreSQL. PostgreSQL is not owned by any single company. It is developed, maintained, broken, and fixed by a group of volunteer developers around the world. You don't have to buy PostgreSQL—it's free. You won't have to pay any maintenance fees (although you can certainly find commercial sources for technical support).

PostgreSQL offers all the usual features of a relational database plus quite a few unique features. PostgreSQL offers inheritance (for you object-oriented readers). You can add your own data types to PostgreSQL. (I know—some of you are probably thinking that you can do that in your favorite database.) Most database systems allow you to give a new name to an existing type. Some systems allow you to define composite types. With PostgreSQL, you can add new *fundamental* data types. PostgreSQL includes support for geometric data types such as `point`, `line segment`, `box`, `polygon`, and `circle`. PostgreSQL uses indexing structures that make geometric data types *fast*. PostgreSQL can be *extended*—you can build new functions, new operators, and new data types in the language of your choice. PostgreSQL is built around client/server architecture. You can build client applications in a number of different languages, including C, C++, Java, Python, Perl, TCL/Tk, and others. On the server side, PostgreSQL sports a powerful procedural language, PL/pgSQL (okay, the language is sportier than the name). You can *add* procedural languages to the server. You will find procedural languages supporting Perl, TCL/Tk, and even the `bash` shell.

A Sample Database

Throughout this book, I'll use a simple example database to help explain some of the more complex concepts. The sample database represents some of the data storage and retrieval requirements that you might encounter when running a video rental store. I won't pretend that the sample database is useful for any real-world scenarios; instead, this database will help us explore how PostgreSQL works and should illustrate many PostgreSQL features.

To begin with, the sample database (which is called *movies*) contains three kinds of records: customers, tapes, and rentals.

Whenever a customer walks into our imaginary video store, you will consult your database to determine whether you already know this customer. If not, you'll add a new record. What items of information should you store for each customer? At the very least, you will want to record the customer's name. You will want to ensure that each customer has a unique identifier—you might have two customers named "Danny Johnson," and you'll want to keep them straight. A name is a poor choice for a unique identifier—names might not be unique, and they can often be spelled in different ways. ("Was that Danny, Dan, or Daniel?") You'll assign each customer a unique customer ID. You might also want to store the customer's birth date so that you know whether he should be allowed to rent certain movies. If you find that a customer has an overdue tape rental, you'll probably want to phone him, so you better store the customer's phone number. In a real-world business, you would probably want to know much more information about each customer (such as his home address), but for these purposes, you'll keep your storage requirements to a minimum.

Next, you will need to keep track of the videos that you stock. Each video has a title and a distributor—you'll store those. You might own several copies of the same movie and you will certainly have many movies from the same distributor, so you can't use either one for a unique identifier. Instead, you'll assign a unique ID to each video.

Finally, you will need to track rentals. When a customer rents a tape, you will store the customer ID, tape ID, and rental date.

Notice that you won't store the customer name with each rental. As long as you store the customer ID, you can always retrieve the customer name. You won't store the movie title with each rental, either—you can find the movie title by its unique identifier.

At a few points in this book, we might make changes to the layout of the sample database, but the basic shape will remain the same.

Basic Database Terminology

Before we get into the interesting stuff, it might be useful to get acquainted with a few of the terms that you will encounter in your PostgreSQL life. PostgreSQL has a long history—you can trace its history back to 1977 and a program known as Ingres. A lot has changed in the relational database world since 1977. When you are breaking ground with a new product (as the Ingres developers were), you don't have the luxury of using standard, well-understood, and well-accepted terminology—you have to make it up as you go along. Many of the terms used by PostgreSQL have synonyms (or at least close analogies) in today's relational marketplace. In this section, I'll show you a few of the terms that you'll encounter in this book and try to explain how they relate to similar concepts in other database products.

- **Database**

  A *database* is a named collection of tables. (see *table*). A database can also contain views, indexes, sequences, data types, operators, and functions. Other relational database products use the term *catalog*.

- **Command**

  A *command* is a string that you send to the server in hopes of having the server do something useful. Some people use the word *statement* to mean *command*. The two words are very similar in meaning and, in practice, are interchangeable.

- **Query**

  A *query* is a type of command that retrieves data from the server.

- **Table (relation, file, class)**

  A *table* is a collection of rows. A table usually has a name, although some tables are temporary and exist only to carry out a command. All the rows in a table have the same shape (in other words, every row in a table contains the same set of columns). In other database systems, you may see the terms `relation`, `file`, or even `class`—these are all equivalent to a table.

- **Column (field, attribute)**

  A *column* is the smallest unit of storage in a relational database. A column represents one piece of information about an object. Every column has a name and a data type. Columns are grouped into rows, and rows are grouped into tables. In Figure 1.1, the shaded area depicts a single column.

  The terms *field* and *attribute* have similar meanings.

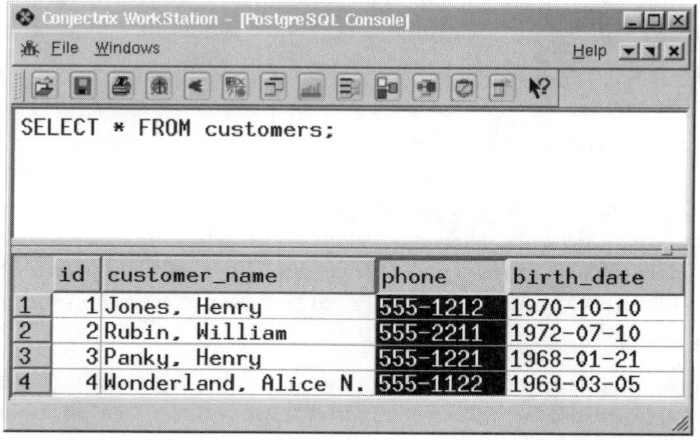
Conjectrix WorkStation - [PostgreSQL Console]
File Windows
Help
SELECT * FROM customers;
id customer_name phone birth_date
1 1 Jones, Henry 555-1212 1970-10-10
2 2 Rubin, William 555-2211 1972-07-10
3 3 Panky, Henry 555-1221 1968-01-21
4 4 Wonderland, Alice N. 555-1122 1969-03-05

Figure 1.1 A column (highlighted).

- **Row (record, tuple)**

  A *row* is a collection of column values. Every row in a table has the same shape (in other words, every row is composed of the same set of columns). If you are trying to model a real-world application, a row represents a real-world object. For example, if you are running an auto dealership, you might have a `vehicles` table. Each row in the `vehicles` table represents a car (or truck, or motorcycle, and so on). The kinds of information that you store are the same for all `vehicles` (that is, every car has a color, a vehicle ID, an engine, and so on). In Figure 1.2, the shaded area depicts a row.

  You may also see the terms *record* or *tuple*—these are equivalent to a row.

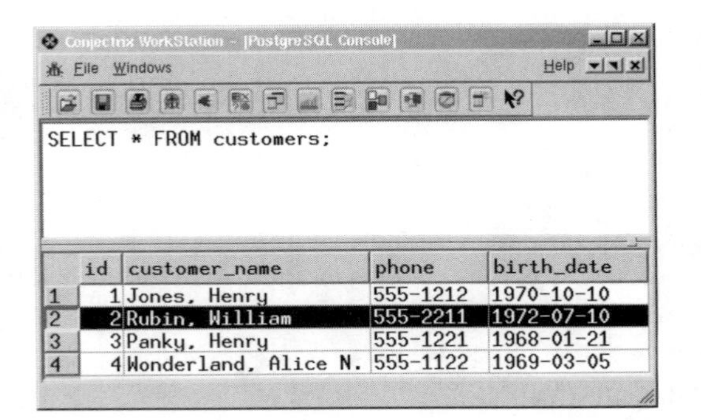

Figure 1.2 A row (highlighted).

- **View**

  A *view* is an alternative way to present a table (or tables). You might think of a view as a "virtual" table. A view is (usually) defined in terms of one or more tables. When you create a view, you are not storing more data, you are instead creating a different way of looking at existing data. A view is a useful way to give a name to a complex query that you may have to use repeatedly.

- **Client/server**

  PostgreSQL is built around a *client/server* architecture. In a client/server product, there are at least two programs involved. One is a client and the other is a server. These programs may exist on the same host or on different hosts that are connected by some sort of network. The server offers a service; in the case of PostgreSQL, the server offers to store, retrieve, and change data. The client asks a server to perform work; a PostgreSQL client asks a PostgreSQL server to serve up relational data.

- **Client**

  A *client* is an application that makes requests of the PostgreSQL server. Before a client application can talk to a server, it must connect to a postmaster (see `postmaster`) and establish its identity. Client applications provide a user interface and can be written in many languages. Chapters 8 through 17 will show you how to write a client application.

- **Server**

  The PostgreSQL *server* is a program that services commands coming from client applications. The PostgreSQL server has no user interface—you can't talk to the server directly, you must use a client application.

- **Postmaster**

  Because PostgreSQL is a client/server database, something has to listen for connection requests coming from a client application. That's what the `postmaster` does. When a connection request arrives, the `postmaster` creates a new server process in the host operating system.

- **Transaction**

  A *transaction* is a collection of database operations that are treated as a unit. PostgreSQL guarantees that all the operations within a transaction complete or that none of them complete. This is an important property—it ensures that if something goes wrong in the middle of a transaction, changes made before the point of failure will not be reflected in the database. A transaction usually starts with a `BEGIN` command and ends with a `COMMIT` or `ROLLBACK` (see the next entries).

- **Commit**

  A *commit* marks the successful end of a transaction. When you perform a commit, you are telling PostgreSQL that you have completed a unit of operation and that all the changes that you made to the database should become permanent.

- **Rollback**

  A *rollback* marks the *un*successful end of a transaction. When you roll back a transaction, you are telling PostgreSQL to discard any changes that you have made to the database (since the beginning of the transaction).

- **Index**

  An *index* is a data structure that a database uses to reduce the amount of time it takes to perform certain operations. An index can also be used to ensure that duplicate values don't appear where they aren't wanted. I'll talk about indexes in Chapter 4, "Query Optimization."

- **Result set**

  When you issue a query to a database, you get back a *result set*. The result set contains all the rows that satisfy your query. A result set may be empty.

Prerequisites

Before I go much further, let's talk about installing PostgreSQL. Chapters 19, "PostgreSQL Administration," and 21, "Security," discuss PostgreSQL installation in detail, but I'll show you a typical installation procedure here.

When you install PostgreSQL, you can start with prebuilt binaries or you can compile PostgreSQL from source code. In this chapter, I'll show you how to install PostgreSQL on a Linux host starting from prebuilt binaries. If you decide to install PostgreSQL from source code, many of the steps are the same. I'll show you how to build PostgreSQL from source code in Chapter 19, "General PostgreSQL Administration."

Installing PostgreSQL on a Windows host is a bit more complex. The PostgreSQL server is written for Unix (and Unix-like) hosts. You can run a PostgreSQL server on a Windows host, but you have to install a Unix-like environment (Cygwin) first. If you only want to install PostgreSQL client applications under Windows, you don't need Cygwin.

Chapter 19, "General PostgreSQL Administration," covers the installation procedure required for Windows.

Installing PostgreSQL Using an RPM

The easiest way to install PostgreSQL is to use a prebuilt RPM package. *RPM* is the *Red Hat Package Manager*. It's a software package designed to install (and manage) other software packages. If you choose to install using some method other than RPM, consult the documentation that comes with the distribution you are using.

PostgreSQL is distributed as a collection of RPM packages—you don't have to install all the packages to use PostgreSQL. Table 1.1 lists the RPM packages available as of release 7.1.3.

Table 1.1 **PostgreSQL RPM Packages as of Release 7.1.3**

Package	Description
postgresql	Clients, libraries, and documentation
postgresql-server	Programs (and data files) required to run a server
postgresql-devel	Files required to create new client applications
postgresql-odbc	ODBC driver for PostgreSQL
postgresql-jdbc	JDBC driver for PostgreSQL
postgresql-tk	Tk client and pgaccess
postgresql-tcl	Tcl client and PL/Tcl
postgresql-perl	Perl client library and PL/Perl
postgresql-python	PygreSQL library
postgresql-test	Regression test suite for PostgreSQL
postgresql-libs	Shared libraries for client applications
postgresql-docs	Extra documentation not included in the postgresql base package
postgresql-contrib	Contributed software

Don't worry if you don't know which of these you need; I'll explain most of the packages in later chapters. You can start working with PostgreSQL by downloading the postgresql, postgresql-libs, and postgresql-server packages. The actual files (at the `www.postgresql.org` web site) have names that include a version number: `postgresql-libs-7.1.3-1PGDG.i386.rpm`, for example.

I strongly recommend creating an empty directory, and then downloading the PostgreSQL packages into that directory. That way you can install all the PostgreSQL packages with a single command.

After you have downloaded the desired packages, use the `rpm` command to perform the installation procedure. You must have superuser privileges to install PostgreSQL.

To install the PostgreSQL packages, `cd` into the directory that contains the package files and issue the following command:

```
# rpm -ihv *.rpm
```

The `rpm` command installs all the packages in your current directory. You should see results similar to what is shown in Figure 1.3.

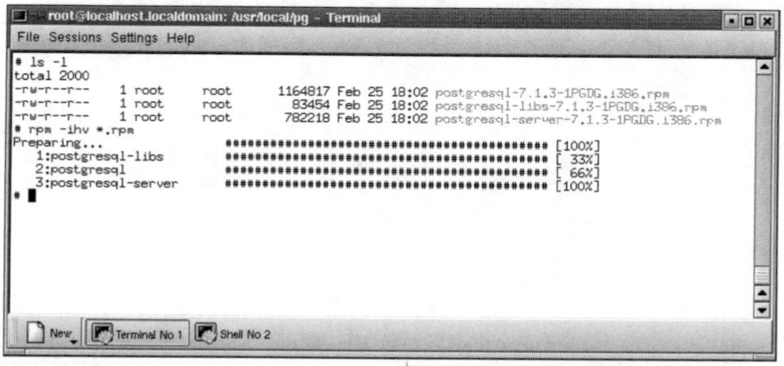

```
# ls -l
total 2000
-rw-r--r--    1 root     root     1164817 Feb 25 18:02 postgresql-7.1.3-1PGDG.i386.rpm
-rw-r--r--    1 root     root       83454 Feb 25 18:02 postgresql-libs-7.1.3-1PGDG.i386.rpm
-rw-r--r--    1 root     root      782218 Feb 25 18:02 postgresql-server-7.1.3-1PGDG.i386.rpm
# rpm -ihv *.rpm
Preparing...                ########################################### [100%]
   1:postgresql-libs        ########################################### [ 33%]
   2:postgresql             ########################################### [ 66%]
   3:postgresql-server      ########################################### [100%]
#
```

Figure 1.3 Using the `rpm` command to install PostgreSQL.

The RPM installer should have created a new user (named `postgres`) for your system. This user ID exists so that all database files accessed by PostgreSQL can be owned by a single user.

Each RPM package is composed of many files. You can view the list of files installed for a given package using the `rpm -ql` command:

```
# rpm -ql postgresql-server
/etc/rc.d/init.d/postgresql
/usr/bin/initdb
/usr/bin/initlocation
...
/var/lib/pgsql/data
# rpm -ql postgresql-libs
/usr/lib/libecpg.so.3
/usr/lib/libecpg.so.3.2.0
/usr/lib/libpgeasy.so.2
...
/usr/lib/libpq.so.2.1
```

At this point (assuming that everything worked), you have installed PostgreSQL on your system. Now it's time to create a database to play, er, work in.

While you have superuser privileges, issue the following commands:

```
# su - postgres
bash-2.04$ echo $PGDATA
/var/lib/pgsql/data
bash-2.04$ initdb
```

The first command (`su - postgres`) changes your identity from the OS superuser (root) to the PostgreSQL superuser (`postgres`). The second command (`echo $PGDATA`) shows you where the PostgreSQL data files will be created. The final command creates the two prototype databases (`template0` and `template1`).

You should get output that looks like that shown in Figure 1.4.

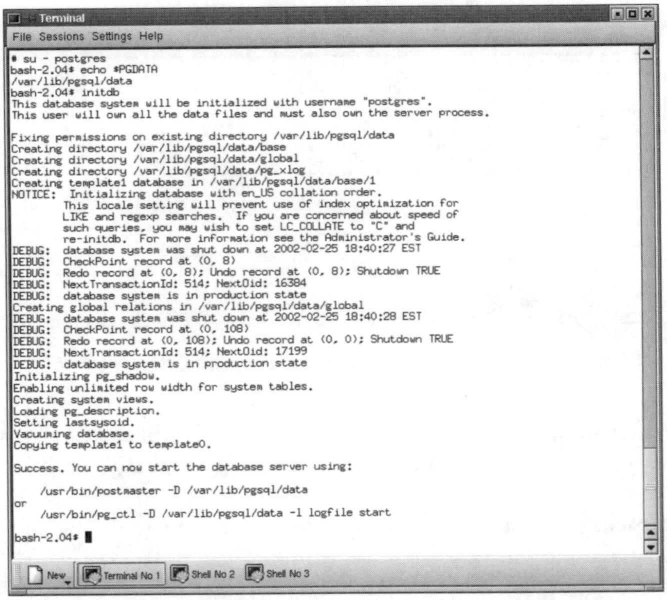

```
# su - postgres
bash-2.04$ echo $PGDATA
/var/lib/pgsql/data
bash-2.04$ initdb
This database system will be initialized with username "postgres".
This user will own all the data files and must also own the server process.

Fixing permissions on existing directory /var/lib/pgsql/data
Creating directory /var/lib/pgsql/data/base
Creating directory /var/lib/pgsql/data/global
Creating directory /var/lib/pgsql/data/pg_xlog
Creating template1 database in /var/lib/pgsql/data/base/1
NOTICE:  Initializing database with en_US collation order.
        This locale setting will prevent use of index optimization for
        LIKE and regexp searches.  If you are concerned about speed of
        such queries, you may wish to set LC_COLLATE to "C" and
        re-initdb.  For more information see the Administrator's Guide.
DEBUG:  database system was shut down at 2002-02-25 18:40:27 EST
DEBUG:  CheckPoint record at (0, 8)
DEBUG:  Redo record at (0, 8); Undo record at (0, 8); Shutdown TRUE
DEBUG:  NextTransactionId: 514; NextOid: 16384
DEBUG:  database system is in production state
Creating global relations in /var/lib/pgsql/data/global
DEBUG:  database system was shut down at 2002-02-25 18:40:28 EST
DEBUG:  CheckPoint record at (0, 108)
DEBUG:  Redo record at (0, 108); Undo record at (0, 0); Shutdown TRUE
DEBUG:  NextTransactionId: 514; NextOid: 17199
DEBUG:  database system is in production state
Initializing pg_shadow.
Enabling unlimited row width for system tables.
Creating system views.
Loading pg_description.
Setting lastsysoid.
Vacuuming database.
Copying template1 to template0.

Success. You can now start the database server using:

    /usr/bin/postmaster -D /var/lib/pgsql/data
or
    /usr/bin/pg_ctl -D /var/lib/pgsql/data -l logfile start

bash-2.04$
```

Figure 1.4 Creating the prototype databases using `initdb`.

You now have two empty databases named `template0` and `template1`. You really should not create new tables in either of these databases—a template database contains all the data required to create other databases. In other words, `template0` and `template1` act as prototypes for creating other databases. Instead, let's create a database that you *can* play in. First, start the `postmaster` process. The `postmaster` is a program that listens for connection requests coming from client applications. When a connection request arrives, the `postmaster` starts a new server process. You can't do anything in PostgreSQL without a `postmaster`. Figure 1.5 shows you how to get the `postmaster` started.

After starting the `postmaster`, use the `createdb` command to create the `movies` database (this is also shown in Figure 1.5). Most of the examples in this book take place in the `movies` database.

```
bash-2.04$ pg_ctl -l logfile start
postmaster successfully started
bash-2.04$ createdb movies
CREATE DATABASE
bash-2.04$
```

Figure 1.5 Creating a new database with `createdb`.

Notice that I used the `pg_ctl` command to start the `postmaster`[1].

The `pg_ctl` program makes it easy to start and stop the `postmaster`. To see a full description of the `pg_ctl` command, enter the command **`pg_ctl --help`**. You will get the output shown in Figure 1.6.

```
bash-2.04$ pg_ctl --help
pg_ctl is a utility to start, stop, restart, and report the status
of a PostgreSQL server.

Usage:
  pg_ctl start   [-w] [-D DATADIR] [-s] [-l FILENAME] [-o "OPTIONS"]
  pg_ctl stop    [-W] [-D DATADIR] [-s] [-m SHUTDOWN-MODE]
  pg_ctl restart [-w] [-D DATADIR] [-s] [-m SHUTDOWN-MODE] [-o "OPTIONS"]
  pg_ctl status  [-D DATADIR]

Common options:
  -D DATADIR             Location of the database storage area
  -s                     Only print errors, no informational messages
  -w                     Wait until operation completes
  -W                     Do not wait until operation completes
(The default is to wait for shutdown, but not for start or restart.)

If the -D option is omitted, the environment variable PGDATA is used.

Options for start or restart:
  -l FILENAME            Write (or append) server log to FILENAME.  The
                         use of this option is highly recommended.
  -o OPTIONS             Command line options to pass to the postmaster
                         (PostgreSQL server executable)
  -p PATH-TO-POSTMASTER  Normally not necessary

Options for stop or restart:
  -m SHUTDOWN-MODE       May be 'smart', 'fast', or 'immediate'

Shutdown modes are:
  smart                  Quit after all clients have disconnected
  fast                   Quit directly, with proper shutdown
  immediate              Quit without complete shutdown; will lead
                         to recovery run on restart

Report bugs to <pgsql-bugs@postgresql.org>.
bash-2.04$
```

Figure 1.6 `pg_ctl` options.

1. You can also arrange for the `postmaster` to start whenever you boot your computer, but the exact instructions vary depending on which operating system you are using. See the *PostgreSQL Administrator's Guide*, Section 3.3 for more information.

If you use a recent RPM file to install PostgreSQL, the two previous steps (`initdb` and `pg_ctl start`) can be automated. If you find a file named `postgresql` in the `/etc/rc.d/init.d` directory, you can use that shell script to initialize the database and start the `postmaster`. The `/etc/rc.d/init.d/postgresql` script can be invoked with any of the command-line options shown in Table 1.2.

Table 1.2 **/etc/rc.d/init.d/postgresql Options**

Option	Description
`start`	Start the `postmaster`
`stop`	Stop the `postmaster`
`status`	Display the process ID of the `postmaster` if it is running
`restart`	Stop and then start the `postmaster`
`reload`	Force the `postmaster` to reread its configuration files without performing a full restart

At this point, you should use the `createuser` command to tell PostgreSQL which users are allowed to access your database. Let's allow the user '`bruce`' into our system (see Figure 1.7).

```
bash-2.04$ pg_ctl --help
pg_ctl is a utility to start, stop, restart, and report the status
of a PostgreSQL server.

Usage:
  pg_ctl start   [-w] [-D DATADIR] [-s] [-l FILENAME] [-o "OPTIONS"]
  pg_ctl stop    [-W] [-D DATADIR] [-s] [-m SHUTDOWN-MODE]
  pg_ctl restart [-w] [-D DATADIR] [-s] [-m SHUTDOWN-MODE] [-o "OPTIONS"]
  pg_ctl status  [-D DATADIR]

Common options:
  -D DATADIR             Location of the database storage area
  -s                     Only print errors, no informational messages
  -w                     Wait until operation completes
  -W                     Do not wait until operation completes
(The default is to wait for shutdown, but not for start or restart.)

If the -D option is omitted, the environment variable PGDATA is used.

Options for start or restart:
  -l FILENAME            Write (or append) server log to FILENAME.  The
                         use of this option is highly recommended.
  -o OPTIONS             Command line options to pass to the postmaster
                         (PostgreSQL server executable)
  -p PATH-TO-POSTMASTER Normally not necessary

Options for stop or restart:
  -m SHUTDOWN-MODE       May be 'smart', 'fast', or 'immediate'

Shutdown modes are:
  smart                  Quit after all clients have disconnected
  fast                   Quit directly, with proper shutdown
  immediate              Quit without complete shutdown; will lead
                         to recovery run on restart

Report bugs to <pgsql-bugs@postgresql.org>.
bash-2.04$ createuser bruce
Shall the new user be allowed to create databases? (y/n) y
Shall the new user be allowed to create more new users? (y/n) y
CREATE USER
bash-2.04$
```

Figure 1.7 Creating a new PostgreSQL user.

That's it! You now have a PostgreSQL database up and running.

Connecting to a Database

Assuming that you have a copy of PostgreSQL up and running, it's pretty simple to connect to the database. Here is an example:

```
$ psql -d movies
Welcome to psql, the PostgreSQL interactive terminal.

Type:  \copyright for distribution terms
       \h for help with SQL commands
       \? for help on internal slash commands
       \g or terminate with semicolon to execute query
       \q to quit

movies=# \q
```

The `psql` program is a text-based interface to a PostgreSQL database. When you are running `psql`, you won't see a graphical application—no buttons or pictures or other bells and whistles, just a text-based interface. Later, I'll show you another client application that does provide a graphical interface (`pgaccess`).

`psql` supports a large collection of command-line options. To see a summary of the options that you can use, type **`psql --help`**:

```
$ psql --help
This is psql, the PostgreSQL interactive terminal.

Usage:
  psql [options] [dbname [username]]

Options:
  -a              Echo all input from script
  -A              Unaligned table output mode (-P format=unaligned)
  -c <query>      Run only single query (or slash command) and exit
  -d <dbname>     Specify database name to connect to (default: korry)
  -e              Echo queries sent to backend
  -E              Display queries that internal commands generate
  -f <filename>   Execute queries from file, then exit
  -F <string>     Set field separator (default: "|") (-P fieldsep=)
  -h <host>       Specify database server host (default: domain socket)
  -H              HTML table output mode (-P format=html)
  -l              List available databases, then exit
  -n              Disable readline
  -o <filename>   Send query output to filename (or |pipe)
  -p <port>       Specify database server port (default: hardwired)
  -P var[=arg]    Set printing option 'var' to 'arg' (see \pset command)
  -q              Run quietly (no messages, only query output)
  -R <string>     Set record separator (default: newline) (-P recordsep=)
```

```
-s               Single step mode (confirm each query)
-S               Single line mode (newline terminates query)
-t               Print rows only (-P tuples_only)
-T text          Set HTML table tag options (width, border) (-P tableattr=)
-U <username>    Specify database username (default: Administrator)
-v name=val      Set psql variable 'name' to 'value'
-V               Show version information and exit
-W               Prompt for password (should happen automatically)
-x               Turn on expanded table output (-P expanded)
-X               Do not read startup file (~/.psqlrc)
```

For more information, type **`\?`** (for internal commands) or **`\help`** (for SQL commands) from within `psql`, or consult the `psql` section in the PostgreSQL manual, which accompanies the distribution and is also available at `http://www.postgresql.org`. Report bugs to `pgsql-bugs@postgresql.org`.

The most important options are `-U <user>`, `-d <dbname>`, `-h <host>`, and `-p <port>`.

The `-U` option allows you to specify a username other than the one you are logged in as. For example, let's say that you are logged in to your host as user *bruce* and you want to connect to a PostgreSQL database as user *sheila*. This `psql` command makes the connection (or at least tries to):

```
$ whoami
bruce
$ psql -U sheila -d movies
```

Impersonating Another User

The `-U` option may or may not allow you to impersonate another user. Depending on how your PostgreSQL administrator has configured database security, you might be prompted for *sheila*'s password; if you don't know the proper password, you won't be allowed to impersonate her. (Chapter 21, "Security," discusses security in greater detail.) If you don't provide `psql` with a username, it will assume the username that you used when you logged in to your host.

You use the `-d` option to specify to which database you want to connect. If you don't specify a database, PostgreSQL will assume that you want to connect to a database whose name is your username. For example, if you are logged in as user *bruce*, PostgreSQL will assume that you want to connect to a database named `bruce`.

The `-d` and `-U` are not strictly required. The command line for `psql` should be of the following form:

```
psql [options] [dbname [username]]
```

If you are connecting to a PostgreSQL server that is running on the host that you are logged in to, you probably don't have to worry about the `-h` and `-p` options. If, on the other hand, you are connecting to a PostgreSQL server running on a different host, use the `-h` option to tell `psql` which host to connect to. You can also use the `-p` option to specify a TCP/IP port number—you only have to do that if you are connecting to a server that uses a nonstandard port (PostgreSQL usually listens for client connections on TCP/IP port number 5432). Here are a few examples:

```
$ # connect to a server waiting on the default port on host 192.168.0.1
$ psql -h 192.168.0.1

$ # connect to a server waiting on port 2000 on host arturo
$ psql -h arturo -p 2000
```

If you prefer, you can specify the database name, host name, and TCP/IP port number using environment variables rather than using the command-line options. Table 1.3 lists some of the `psql` command-line options and the corresponding environment variables.

Table 1.3 `psql` **Environment Variables**

Command-Line Option	Environment Variable	Meaning
`-d <dbname>`	`PGDATABASE`	Name of database to connect to
`-h <host>`	`PGHOST`	Name of host to connect to
`-p <port>`	`PGPORT`	Port number to connect to
`-U <user>`	`PGUSER`	PostgreSQL Username

A (Very) Simple Query

At this point, you should be running the `psql` client application. Let's try a *very* simple query:

```
$ psql -d movies
Welcome to psql, the PostgreSQL interactive terminal.

Type:  \copyright for distribution terms
       \h for help with SQL commands
       \? for help on internal slash commands
       \g or terminate with semicolon to execute query
       \q to quit

movies=# SELECT user;
 current_user
---------------
 korry
(1 row)

movies=# \q

$
```

Let's take a close look at this session. First, you can see that I started the `psql` program with the `-d movies` option—this tells `psql` that I want to connect to the `movies` database.

After greeting me and providing me with a few crucial hints, `psql` issues a prompt: `movies=#`. `psql` encodes some useful information into the prompt, starting with the name of the database that I am currently connected to (`movies` in this case). The character that follows the database name can vary. A `=` character means that `psql` is waiting for me to start a command. A `-` character means that `psql` is waiting for me to complete a command (`psql` allows you to split a single command over multiple lines. The first line is prompted by a `=` character; subsequent lines are prompted by a `-` character). If the prompt ends with a `(` character, you have entered more opening parentheses than closing parentheses.

You can see the command that I entered following the prompt: `SELECT user;`. Each SQL command starts with a verb—in this case, `SELECT`. The verb tells PostgreSQL what you want to do and the rest of the command provides information specific to that command. I am executing a `SELECT` command. `SELECT` is used to retrieve information from the database. When you execute a `SELECT` command, you have to tell PostgreSQL what information you are interested in. I want to retrieve my PostgreSQL user ID so I `SELECT user`. The final part of this command is the semicolon (`;`)—each SQL command must end with a semicolon.

After I enter the `SELECT` command (and press the `Return` key), `psql` displays the results of my command:

```
current_user
---------------
 korry
(1 row)
```

When you execute a `SELECT` command, `psql` starts by displaying a row of column headers. I have selected only a single column of information so I see only a single column header (each column header displays the name of the column). Following the row of column headers is a single row of separator characters (dashes). Next comes zero or more rows of the data that I requested. Finally, `psql` shows a count of the number of data rows displayed.

I ended this session using the `\q` command.

Tips for Interacting with PostgreSQL

The `psql` client has a lot of features that will make your PostgreSQL life easier.

Besides PostgreSQL commands (`SELECT`, `INSERT`, `UPDATE`, `CREATE TABLE`, and so on), `psql` provides a number of internal commands (also known as *meta-commands*). PostgreSQL commands are sent to the server, meta-commands are processed by `psql` itself. A meta-command begins with a backslash character (`\`). You can obtain a list of all the meta-commands using the `\?` meta-command:

```
movies=# \?
 \a               toggle between unaligned and aligned mode
 \c[onnect] [dbname|- [user]]
                  connect to new database (currently 'movies')
```

```
  \C <title>     table title
  \copy ...      perform SQL COPY with data stream to the client machine
  \copyright     show PostgreSQL usage and distribution terms
  \d <table>     describe table (or view, index, sequence)
  \d{t|i|s|v}    list tables/indices/sequences/views
  \d{p|S|l}      list permissions/system tables/lobjects
  \da            list aggregates
  \dd [object]   list comment for table, type, function, or operator
  \df            list functions
  \do            list operators
  \dT            list data types
  \e [file]      edit the current query buffer or [file]
                 with external editor
  \echo <text>   write text to stdout
  \encoding <encoding>  set client encoding
  \f <sep>       change field separator
  \g [file]      send query to backend (and results in [file] or |pipe)
  \h [cmd]       help on syntax of sql commands, * for all commands
  \H             toggle HTML mode (currently off)
  \i <file>      read and execute queries from <file>
  \l             list all databases
  \lo_export, \lo_import, \lo_list, \lo_unlink
                 large object operations
  \o [file]      send all query results to [file], or |pipe
  \p             show the content of the current query buffer
  \pset <opt>    set table output
                   <opt> = {format|border|expanded|fieldsep|
                   null|recordsep|tuples_only|title|tableattr|pager}
  \q             quit psql
  \qecho <text>  write text to query output stream (see \o)
  \r             reset (clear) the query buffer
  \s [file]      print history or save it in [file]
  \set <var> <value>  set internal variable
  \t             show only rows (currently off)
  \T <tags>      HTML table tags
  \unset <var>   unset (delete) internal variable
  \w <file>      write current query buffer to a <file>
  \x             toggle expanded output (currently off)
  \z             list table access permissions
  \! [cmd]       shell escape or command
movies=#
```

The most important meta-commands are `\?` (meta-command help), and `\q` (quit). The `\h` (SQL help) meta-command is also very useful. Notice that unlike SQL commands, meta-commands don't require a terminating semicolon, which means that meta-commands must be entered entirely on one line. In the next few sections, I'll show you some of the other meta-commands.

Creating Tables

Now that you have seen how to connect to a database and issue a simple query, it's time to create some sample data to work with.

Because you are pretending to model a movie-rental business (that is, a video store), you will create tables that model the data that you might need in a video store. Start by creating three tables: `tapes`, `customers`, and `rentals`.

The `tapes` table is simple: For each videotape, you want to store the name of the movie, the distributor, and a unique identifier (remember that you may have more than one copy of any given movie, so the movie name is not sufficient to uniquely identify a specific tape).

Here is the command you should use to create the `tapes` table:

```
CREATE TABLE tapes (
        tape_id      CHARACTER(8) UNIQUE,
        title        CHARACTER VARYING(80),
        distributor CHARACTER VARYING(80)
);
```

Let's take a close look at this command.

The verb in this command is `CREATE TABLE`, and its meaning should be obvious—you want to create a table. Following the `CREATE TABLE` verb is the name of the table (`tapes`) and then a comma-separated list of column definitions, enclosed within parentheses.

Each column in a table is defined by a name and a data type. The first column in `tapes` is named `tape_id`. Column names (and table names) must begin with a letter or an underscore character[2] and should be 31 characters or fewer[3]. The `tape_id` column is created with a data type of `CHARACTER(8)`. The data type you define for a column determines the set of values that you can put into that column. For example, if you want a column to hold numeric values, you should use a numeric data type; if you want a column to hold date (or time) values, you should use a date/time data type. `tape_id` holds alphanumeric values (a mixture of numbers and letters), so I chose a character data type, with a length of eight characters.

The `tape_id` column is defined as `UNIQUE`. The word `UNIQUE` is not a part of the data type—the data type is `CHARACTER(8)`. The keyword '`UNIQUE`' specifies a *column constraint*. A column constraint is a condition that must be met by a column. In this case, each row in the `tapes` table must have a unique `tape_id`. PostgreSQL supports a variety of column constraints (and table constraints). I'll cover constraints in Chapter 2, "Working with Data in PostgreSQL."

2. You can begin a column or table name with nonalphabetic characters, but you must enclose the name in double quotes. You have to quote the name not only when you create it, but each time you reference it.

3. You can increase the maximum identifier length beyond 31 characters if you build PostgreSQL from a source distribution. If you do so, you'll have to remember to increase the identifier length each time you upgrade your server, or whenever you migrate to a different server.

The `title` and `distributor` columns are both defined as `CHARACTER VARYING(80)`. The difference between `CHARACTER(n)` and `CHARACTER VARYING(n)` is that a `CHARACTER(n)` column is fixed-length—it will always contain a fixed number of characters (namely, *n* characters). A `CHARACTER VARYING(n)` column can contain a maximum of *n* characters. I'll mention here that `CHARACTER(n)` can be abbreviated as `CHAR(n)`, and `CHARACTER VARYING(n)` can be abbreviated as `VARCHAR(n)`. I chose `CHAR(8)` as the data type for `tape_id` because I know that a `tape_id` will always contain exactly eight characters, never more and never less. Movie titles (and distributor names), on the other hand, are not all the same length, so I chose `VARCHAR(80)` for those columns. A fixed length data type is a good choice when the data that you store is in fact fixed length; and in some cases, fixed length data types can give you a performance boost. A variable length data type saves space (and often gives you better performance) when the data that you are storing is not all the same length and can vary widely.

I'll be discussing PostgreSQL data types in detail in Chapter 2. Let's move on to creating the other tables in this example database.

The `customers` table is used to record information about each customer for the video store.

```
CREATE TABLE customers (
        customer_id   INTEGER UNIQUE,
        customer_name VARCHAR(50),
        phone         CHAR(8),
        birth_date    DATE,
        balance       NUMERIC(7,2)
);
```

Each customer will be assigned a unique `customer_id`. Notice that `customer_id` is defined as an `INTEGER`, whereas the identifier for a `tape` was defined as a `CHAR(8)`. A `tape_id` can contain alphabetic characters, but a `customer_id` is entirely numeric[4].

I've used two other data types here that you may not have seen before: `DATE` and `NUMERIC`. A `DATE` column can hold date values (century, year, month, and day). PostgreSQL offers other date/time data types that can store different date/time components. For example, a `TIME` column can store time values (hours, minutes, seconds, and microseconds). A `TIMESTAMP` column gives you both date and time components—centuries through microseconds.

A `NUMERIC` column, obviously, holds numeric values. When you create a `NUMERIC` column, you have to tell PostgreSQL the total number of digits that you want to store and the number of fractional digits (that is, the number of digits to right of the decimal point). The `balance` column contains a total of seven digits, with two digits to the right of the decimal point.

4. The decision to define `customer_id` as an `INTEGER` was arbitrary. I simply wanted to show a few more data types here.

Now, let's create the rentals table:

```
CREATE TABLE rentals (
        tape_id     CHARACTER(8),
        customer_id INTEGER,
        rental_date DATE
);
```

When a customer comes in to rent a tape, you will add a row to the rentals table to record the transaction. There are three pieces of information that you need to record for each rental: the tape_id, the customer_id, and the date that the rental occurred. Notice that each row in the rentals table refers to a customer (customer_id) and a tape (tape_id). In most cases, when one row refers to another row, you want to use the same data type for both columns.

> **What Makes a Relational Database Relational?**
>
> Notice that the each row in the rentals table refers to a row in the customer table (and a row in the tapes table). In other words, there is a relationship between rentals and customers and a relationship between rentals and tapes. The relationship between two rows is established by including an identifier from one row within the other row. Each row in the rentals table refers to a customer by including the customer_id. That's the heart of the relational database model—the relationship between two entities is established by including the unique identifier of one entity within the other.

Viewing Table Descriptions

At this point, you've defined three tables in the movies database: tapes, customers, and rentals. If you want to view the table definitions, you can use the \d meta-command in psql (remember that a meta-command is not really a SQL command, but a command understood by the psql client). The \d meta-command comes in two flavors: If you include a table name (\d customers), you will see the definition of that table; if you don't include a table name, \d will show you a list of all the tables defined in your database.

```
$ psql -d movies
Welcome to psql, the PostgreSQL interactive terminal.

Type:  \copyright for distribution terms
       \h for help with SQL commands
       \? for help on internal slash commands
       \g or terminate with semicolon to execute query
       \q to quit
```

```
movies=# \d
         List of relations
   Name    | Type  |     Owner
-----------+-------+---------------
 customers | table | bruce
 rental    | table | bruce
 tapes     | table | bruce
(3 rows)

movies=# \d tapes
                Table "tapes"
  Attribute  |         Type          | Modifier
-------------+-----------------------+----------
 tape_id     | character(8)          |
 title       | character varying(80) |
 distributor | character varying(80) |
Index: tapes_tape_id_key

movies=# \d customers
              Table "customers"
  Attribute  |         Type          | Modifier
-------------+-----------------------+----------
 customer_id | integer               |
 name        | character varying(50) |
 phone       | character(8)          |
 birth_date  | date                  |
 balance     | numeric(7,2)          |
Index: customers_customer_id_key

movies=# \d rentals
           Table "rentals"
  Attribute  |     Type     | Modifier
-------------+--------------+----------
 tape_id     | character(8) |
 customer_id | integer      |
 rental_date | date         |

movies=#
```

I'll point out a few things about the `\d` meta-command.

Notice that for each column in a table, the `\d` meta-command returns three pieces of information: the column name (or `Attribute`), the data type, and a `Modifier`.

The data type reported by the `\d` meta-command is spelled-out; you won't see `char(n)` or `varchar(n)`, you'll see `character(n)` and `character varying(n)` instead.

The `Modifier` column shows additional column attributes. The most commonly encountered modifiers are `NOT NULL` and `DEFAULT ...`. The `NOT NULL` modifier appears when you create a *mandatory* column—mandatory means that each row in the table must have a value for that column. The `DEFAULT ...` modifier appears when you create a column with a *default* value: A default value is inserted into a column when you don't specify a value for a column. If you don't specify a default value, PostgreSQL inserts the special value `NULL`. I'll discuss `NULL` values and default values in more detail in Chapter 2.

You might have noticed that the listing for the `tapes` and `customers` tables show that an index has been created. PostgreSQL automatically creates an index for you when you define `UNIQUE` columns. An index is a data structure that PostgreSQL can use to ensure uniqueness. Indexes are also used to increase performance. I'll cover indexes in more detail in Chapter 3, "PostgreSQL SQL Syntax and Use."

Adding New Records to a Table

The two previous sections showed you how to create some simple tables and how to view the table definitions. Now let's see how to insert data into these tables.

Using the INSERT Command

The most common method to get data into a table is by using the `INSERT` command. Like most SQL commands, there are a number of different formats for the `INSERT` command. Let's look at the simplest form first:

```
INSERT INTO table VALUES ( expression [,...] );
```

A Quick Introduction to Syntax Diagrams

In many books that describe a computer language (such as SQL), you will see *syntax diagrams*. A syntax diagram is a precise way to describe the syntax for a command. Here is an example of a simple syntax diagram:

```
INSERT INTO table VALUES ( expression [,...] );
```

In this book, I'll use the following conventions:

- Words that are presented in uppercase must be entered literally, as shown, except for the case. When you enter these words, it doesn't matter if you enter them in uppercase, lowercase, or mixed case, but the spelling must be the same. SQL keywords are traditionally typed in uppercase to improve readability, but the case does not really matter otherwise.
- A lowercase italic word is a placeholder for user-provided text. For example, the *`table`* placeholder shows where you would enter a table name, and *`expression`* shows where you would enter an expression.
- Optional text is shown inside a pair of square brackets (`[]`). If you include optional text, don't include the square brackets.
- Finally, `,...` means that you can repeat the previous component one or more times, separating multiple occurrences with commas.

So, the following `INSERT` commands are (syntactically) correct:

```
INSERT INTO states VALUES ( 'WA', 'Washington' );
INSERT INTO states VALUES ( 'OR' );
```

This command would not be legal:

```
INSERT states VALUES ( 'WA' 'Washington' );
```

There are two problems with this command. First, I forgot to include the `INTO` keyword (following `INSERT`). Second, the two values that I provided are not separated by a comma.

When you use an `INSERT` statement, you have to provide the name of the table and the values that you want to include in the new row. The following command inserts a new row into the `customers` table:

```
INSERT INTO customers VALUES
(
  1,
  'William Rubin',
  '555-1212',
  '1970-12-31',
  0.00
);
```

This command creates a single row in the `customers` table. Notice that you did not have to tell PostgreSQL how to match up each value with a specific column: In this form of the `INSERT` command, PostgreSQL assumes that you listed the values in column order. In other words, the first value that you provide will be placed in the first column, the second value will be stored in the second column, and so forth. (The ordering of columns within a table is defined when you create the table.)

If you don't include one (or more) of the trailing values, PostgreSQL will insert default values for those columns. The default value is typically `NULL`.

Notice that I have included single-quotes around some of the data values. Numeric data should not be quoted; most other data types must be. In Chapter 2, I'll cover the literal value syntax for each data type.

In the second form of the `INSERT` statement, you include a list of columns *and* a list of values:

```
INSERT INTO table ( column [,...] ) VALUES ( expression [,...] );
```

Using this form of `INSERT`, I can specify the order of the column values:

```
INSERT INTO customers
(
   name, birth_date, phone, customer_id, balance
)
```

```
VALUES
(
  'William Rubin',
  '1970-12-31',
  '555-1212',
  1,
  0.00
);
```

As long as the column *values* match up with the order of the column *names* that you specified, everybody's happy.

The advantage to this second form is that you can omit the value for any column (at least any column that allows NULLs). If you use the first form (without column names), you can only omit values for trailing columns. You can't omit a value in the middle of the row because PostgreSQL can only match up column values in left to right order.

Here is an example that shows how to `INSERT` a customer who wasn't willing to give you his date of birth:

```
INSERT INTO customers
(
   name, phone, customer_id, balance
)
VALUES
(
  'William Rubin',
  '555-1212',
  1,
  0.00
);
```

This is equivalent to either of the following statements:

```
INSERT INTO customers
(
   name, birth_date, phone, customer_id, balance
)
VALUES
(
  'William Rubin',
  NULL,
  '555-1212',
  1,
  0.00
);
```

or

```
INSERT INTO customers VALUES
(
  1,
  'William Rubin',
  '555-1212',
  NULL,
  0.00
);
```

There are two other forms for the `INSERT` command. If you want to create a row that contains only default values, you can use the following form:

```
INSERT INTO table DEFAULT VALUES;
```

Of course, if any of the columns in your table are `unique`, you can only insert a single row with default values.

The final form for the `INSERT` statement allows you to insert one or more rows based on the results of a query:

```
INSERT INTO table ( column [,...] ) SELECT query;
```

I haven't really talked extensively about the `SELECT` statement yet (that's in the next section), but I'll show you a simple example here:

```
INSERT INTO customer_backup SELECT * from customers;
```

This `INSERT` command copies every row in the `customers` table into the `customer_backup` table. It's unusual to use `INSERT...SELECT...` to make an exact copy of a table (in fact, there are easier ways to do that). In most cases, you will use the `INSERT...SELECT...` command to make an altered version of a table; you might add or remove columns or change the data using expressions.

Using the COPY Command

If you need to load a lot of data into a table, you might want to use the `COPY` command. The `COPY` command comes in two forms. `COPY ... TO` writes the contents of a table into an external file. `COPY ... FROM` reads data from an external file into a table.

Let's start by exporting the `customers` table:

```
COPY customers TO '/tmp/customers.txt';
```

This command copies every row in the `customers` table into a file named '`/tmp/customers.txt`'. Take a look at the customers.txt file:

```
1       Jones, Henry    555-1212        1970-10-10      0.00
2       Rubin, William  555-2211        1972-07-10      15.00
3       Panky, Henry    555-1221        1968-01-21      0.00
4       Wonderland, Alison      555-1122        1980-03-05      3.00
```

If you compare the file contents with the definition of the customers table:

```
movies=# \d customers
               Table "customers"
  Attribute  |         Type          | Modifier
-------------+-----------------------+----------
 customer_id | integer               |
 name        | character varying(50) |
 phone       | character(8)          |
 birth_date  | date                  |
 balance     | numeric(7,2)          |
Index: customers_customer_id_key
```

You can see that the columns in the text form match (left-to-right) with the columns defined in the table: The leftmost column is the `customer_id`, followed by `name`, `phone`, and so on. Each column is separated from the next by a tab character and each row ends with an invisible newline character. You can choose a different column separator (with the `DELIMITERS '`*`delimiter`*`'` option), but you can't change the line terminator. That means that you have to be careful editing a `COPY` file using a DOS (or Windows) text editor because most of these editors terminate each line with a carriage-return/newline combination. That will confuse the `COPY ... FROM` command when you try to import the text file.

The inverse of `COPY ... TO` is `COPY ... FROM`. `COPY ... FROM` imports data from an external file into a PostgreSQL table. When you use `COPY ... FROM`, the format of the text file is very important. The easiest way to find the correct format is to export a few rows using `COPY ... TO`, and then examine the text file.

If you decide to create your own text file for use with the `COPY ... FROM` command, you'll have to worry about a lot of details like proper quoting, column delimiters, and such. Consult the PostgreSQL reference documentation for more details.

Installing the Sample Database

If you want, you can download a sample database from this book's web site: `http://www.conjectrix.com/pgbook`.

After you have downloaded the bookdata.tar.gz file, you can unpack it with either of the following commands:

```
$ tar -zxvf bookdata.tar.gz
```

or

```
$ gunzip -c bookdata.tar.gz | tar -xvf -
```

The bookdata.tar.gz file contains a number of files and will unpack into your current directory. After unpacking, you will see a subdirectory for each chapter (okay, for most chapters—not all chapters include sample code or sample data).

You can use the chapter1/load_sample.sql file to create and populate the three tables that I have discussed (`tapes`, `customers`, and `rentals`). To use the load_sample.sql file, execute the following command:

```
$ psql -d movies -f chapter1/load_sample.sql
```

This command drops the `tapes`, `customers`, and `rentals` tables (if they exist), creates them, and adds a few sample rows to each one.

Retrieving Data from the Sample Database

At this point, you should have a sample database (movies) that contains three tables (`tapes`, `customers`, and `rentals`) and a few rows in each table. You know how to get data *into* a table; now let's see how to view that data.

The `SELECT` statement is used to retrieve data from a database. `SELECT` is the most complex statement in the SQL language, and the most powerful. Using `SELECT`, you can retrieve entire tables, single rows, a group of rows that meet a set of constraints, combinations of multiple tables, expressions, and more. To help you understand the basics of the `SELECT` statement, I'll try to break it down into each of its forms and move from the simple to the more complex.

SELECT Expression

In its most simple form, you can use the `SELECT` statement to retrieve one or more values from a set of predefined functions. You've already seen how to retrieve your PostgreSQL user id:

```
movies=# select user;
 current_user
---------------
 korry
(1 row)

movies=# \q
```

Other values that you might want to see are

```
  select 5;            -- returns the number 5 (whoopee)
  select sqrt(2.0);    -- returns the square root of 2
  select timeofday();-- returns current date/time
  select now();        -- returns time of start of transaction
  select version();    -- returns the version of PostgreSQL you are using

  select now(), timeofday();
```

Commenting

The -- characters introduce a comment—any text that follows is ignored.

The previous example shows how to SELECT more than one piece of information—just list all the values that you want, separated by commas.

The PostgreSQL User's Guide contains a list of all the functions that are distributed with PostgreSQL. In Chapter 2, I'll show you how to combine columns, functions, operators, and literal values into more complex expressions.

SELECT * FROM Table

You probably won't use the first form of the SELECT statement very often—it just isn't very exciting. Moving to the next level of complexity, let's see how to retrieve data from one of the tables that you created earlier:

```
movies=# SELECT * FROM customers;
 id |     customer_name      |  phone   | birth_date | balance
----+------------------------+----------+------------+---------
  3 | Panky, Henry           | 555-1221 | 1968-01-21 |    0.00
  1 | Jones, Henry           | 555-1212 | 1970-10-10 |    0.00
  4 | Wonderland, Alice N.   | 555-1122 | 1969-03-05 |    3.00
  2 | Rubin, William         | 555-2211 | 1972-07-10 |   15.00
(4 rows)
```

When you write a SELECT statement, you have to tell PostgreSQL what information you are trying to retrieve. Let's take a closer look at the components of this SELECT statement.

Following the SELECT keyword, you specify a list of the columns that you want to retrieve. I used an asterisk (*) here to tell PostgreSQL that we want to see *all* the columns in the customers table.

Next, you have to tell PostgreSQL which table you want to view; in this case, you want to see the customers table.

Now let's look at the results of this query. A SELECT statement returns a *result set*. A result set is a table composed of all the rows and columns (or *fields*) that you request. A result set may be empty.

You asked PostgreSQL to return all the columns in the customers table—notice that the columns are displayed (from left to right) in the order that you specified when you created the table. You may have noticed that the rows are returned in an (apparently) arbitrary order. That's an important thing to keep in mind: Unless you specifically request that PostgreSQL return rows in a particular order, you won't be able to predict which rows will come first[5]. This is a performance feature; if you don't care about row ordering, let PostgreSQL return the rows in the fastest possible way.

5. Okay, some people probably *could* predict the order in which the rows will appear. Those people have *way* too much free time and consider a propeller to be fashionable headwear. They are also very good at inducing sleep.

SELECT Single-Column FROM Table

If you don't want to view all of the columns from a table, you can replace the * (following the SELECT keyword) with the name of a column:

```
movies=# SELECT title FROM tapes;
     title
---------------
 The Godfather
 The Godfather
 Casablanca
 Citizen Kane
 Rear Window
(5 rows)
```

Again, the rows are presented in an arbitrary order. But this time you see only a single column. You may have noticed that "The Godfather" appears twice in this list. That happens because our imaginary video store owns two copies of that movie. I'll show you how to get rid of duplicates in a moment.

SELECT Column-List FROM Table

So far, you have seen how to select all the columns in a table and how to select a single column. Of course, there is a middle ground—you can select a list of columns:

```
movies=# SELECT customer_name, birth_date FROM customers;
    customer_name     | birth_date
----------------------+------------
 Jones, Henry         | 1970-10-10
 Rubin, William       | 1972-07-10
 Panky, Henry         | 1968-01-21
 Wonderland, Alice N. | 1969-03-05
(4 rows)
```

Instead of naming a single column after the SELECT keyword, you can provide a column-separated list of column names. Column names can appear in any order, and the results will appear in the order you specify.

SELECT Expression-List FROM Table

In addition to selecting columns, you can also select expressions. Remember, an expression is a combination of columns, functions, operators, literal values, and other expressions that will evaluate to a single value. Here is an example:

```
movies=# SELECT
movies-#     customer_name,
movies-#     birth_date,
movies-#     age( birth_date )
```

```
movies-# FROM customers;
    customer_name      | birth_date |              age
-----------------------+------------+------------------------------
 Jones, Henry          | 1970-10-10 | 31 years 4 mons 3 days 01:00
 Rubin, William        | 1972-07-10 | 29 years 7 mons 3 days 01:00
 Panky, Henry          | 1968-01-21 | 34 years 23 days
 Wonderland, Alice N.  | 1969-03-05 | 32 years 11 mons 8 days
(4 rows)
```

In this example, I've selected two columns and an expression. The expression `age( birth_date )` is evaluated for each row in the table. The `age()` function subtracts the given date from the current date[6].

Selecting Specific Rows

The preceding few sections have shown you how to specify which columns you want to see in a result set. Now let's see how to choose only the rows that you want.

First, I'll show you to how to eliminate duplicate rows; then I'll introduce the `WHERE` clause.

SELECT [ALL | DISTINCT | DISTINCT ON]

In an earlier example, you selected the titles of all the videotapes owned by your video store:

```
movies=# SELECT title from tapes;
     title
---------------
 The Godfather
 The Godfather
 Casablanca
 Citizen Kane
 Rear Window
(5 rows)
```

Notice that "The Godfather" is listed twice (you own two copies of that video). You can use the `DISTINCT` clause to filter out duplicate rows:

```
movies=# SELECT DISTINCT title FROM tapes;
     title
---------------
 Casablanca
 Citizen Kane
 Rear Window
 The Godfather
(4 rows)
```

6. Technically, the `age()` function subtracts the given timestamp (date+time) from the current date and time.

You now have a single row with the value "The Godfather." Let's see what happens when you add the `tape_id` back into the previous query:

```
movies=# SELECT DISTINCT title, tape_id FROM tapes;
     title     | tape_id
---------------+----------
 Casablanca    | MC-68873
 Citizen Kane  | OW-41221
 Rear Window   | AH-54706
 The Godfather | AB-12345
 The Godfather | AB-67472
(5 rows)
```

We're back to seeing "The Godfather" twice. What happened? The `DISTINCT` clause removes duplicate rows, not duplicate column values; and when the tape IDs are added to the result, the rows containing "The Godfather" are no longer identical.

If you want to filter rows that have duplicate values in one (or more) columns, use the `DISTINCT ON()` form:

```
movies=# SELECT DISTINCT ON (title) title, tape_id FROM tapes;
     title     | tape_id
---------------+----------
 Casablanca    | MC-68873
 Citizen Kane  | OW-41221
 Rear Window   | AH-54706
 The Godfather | AB-12345
(4 rows)
```

Notice that one of the "The Godfather" rows has been omitted from the result set. If you don't include an `ORDER BY` clause (I'll cover that in a moment), you can't predict which row in a set of duplicates will be included in the result set.

You can list multiple columns (or expressions) in the `DISTINCT ON()` clause.

The WHERE Clause

The next form of the `SELECT` statement includes the `WHERE` clause. Here is the syntax diagram for this form:

```
SELECT expression-list FROM table WHERE conditions
```

Using the `WHERE` clause, you can filter out rows that you don't want included in the result set. Let's see a simple example. First, here is the complete `customers` table:

```
movies=# SELECT * FROM customers;
 id |    customer_name     |  phone   | birth_date | balance
----+----------------------+----------+------------+---------
  1 | Jones, Henry         | 555-1212 | 1970-10-10 |    0.00
  2 | Rubin, William       | 555-2211 | 1972-07-10 |   15.00
  3 | Panky, Henry         | 555-1221 | 1968-01-21 |    0.00
  4 | Wonderland, Alice N. | 555-1122 | 1969-03-05 |    3.00
(4 rows)
```

Now pick out only those customers who owe you some money:

```
movies=# SELECT * FROM customers WHERE balance > 0;
 id |     customer_name      |  phone   | birth_date | balance
----+----------------------+----------+------------+---------
  2 | Rubin, William       | 555-2211 | 1972-07-10 |   15.00
  4 | Wonderland, Alice N. | 555-1122 | 1969-03-05 |    3.00
(2 rows)
```

In this example, I've used a single condition to restrict the rows included in the result set: `balance > 0`.

When PostgreSQL executes a `SELECT` statement, it evaluates the `WHERE` clause as it processes each row. If all the conditions specified by the `WHERE` clause are met, the row will be included in the result set (if a row meets all the conditions in the `WHERE` clause, the row *satisfies* the `WHERE` clause).

Here is an example that is slightly more complex:

```
movies=# SELECT customer_name, phone FROM customers
movies-#   WHERE
movies-#     ( balance = 0 )
movies-#     AND
movies-#     ( AGE( birth_date ) < '34 years' )
movies-# ;
 customer_name |  phone
---------------+----------
 Jones, Henry  | 555-1212
(1 row)
```

In this query, I've specified two conditions, separated by an `AND` operator. The conditions are: `balance = 0` and `AGE( birth_date ) < '34 years'`[7]. As before, PostgreSQL reads each row in the `customers` table and evaluates the `WHERE` clause. If a given row is to be included in the result set, it must satisfy two constraints—`balance` must be equal to zero *and* the customer must be younger than 34 years of age. If either of these conditions is false for a given row, that row will not be included in the result set.

`AND` is one of the *logical operators* supported by PostgreSQL. A logical operator is used to combine *logical expressions*. A logical expression is an expression that evaluates to `TRUE`, `FALSE`, or unknown (`NULL`). The other two logical operators are `OR` and `NOT`.

Let's see how the `OR` operator works:

```
movies=# SELECT id, customer_name, balance, AGE(birth_date)
movies-# FROM customers
movies-#   WHERE
movies-#     ( balance = 0 )
movies-#     OR
```

7. I'll show you how to format various date/time related values in Chapter 2.

```
movies-#      ( AGE( birth_date ) < '30 years' )
movies-# ;
 id | customer_name   | balance |              age
----+-----------------+---------+-----------------------------
  1 | Jones, Henry    |    0.00 | 31 years 4 mons 5 days 01:00
  2 | Rubin, William  |   15.00 | 29 years 7 mons 5 days 01:00
  3 | Panky, Henry    |    0.00 | 34 years 25 days
(3 rows)
```

The OR operator evaluates to `TRUE` if *either* (or both) of the conditions is `TRUE`. The first row (`id = 1`) is included in the result set because it satisfies the first condition (`balance = 0`). It is included even if it *does not* satisfy the second condition. The second row (`id = 2`) is included in the result set because it satisfies the second condition, but not the first. You can see the difference between `AND` and `OR`. A row satisfies the `AND` operator if both conditions are `TRUE`. A row satisfies the `OR` operator if either condition is `TRUE` (or if both are `TRUE`).

The NOT operator is simple:

```
movies=# SELECT * FROM customers
movies-# WHERE
movies-#      NOT ( balance = 0 )
movies-# ;
 id |     customer_name      | phone    | birth_date | balance
----+------------------------+----------+------------+---------
  2 | Rubin, William         | 555-2211 | 1972-07-10 |   15.00
  4 | Wonderland, Alice N.   | 555-1122 | 1969-03-05 |    3.00
(2 rows)
```

`NOT` evaluates to `TRUE` if its operand is `FALSE` and evaluates to `FALSE` if its operand is `TRUE`. The `NOT` operator inverts (or reverses) a test. Without the `NOT` operator, the previous example would have returned all `customers` where the `balance` column was equal to zero. With the `NOT` operator, you get the other rows instead.

One other point that I should mention about the `WHERE` clause. Just because you mention a column in the `WHERE` clause does not mean that you have to include the column in the result set. For example:

```
movies=# SELECT id, customer_name FROM customers
movies-#   WHERE
movies-#      balance != 0
movies-# ;
 id |    customer_name
----+----------------------
  2 | Rubin, William
  4 | Wonderland, Alice N.
(2 rows)
```

This example also shows a more common alternative to the NOT operator. The != operator means "*is not equal to*." The != operator is not an exact replacement for NOT—it can only be used to check for inequality, whereas NOT is used to reverse the sense of any logical expression.

NULL Values

Sometimes when you add data to a table, you find that you don't know what value you should include for a column. For example, you may encounter a customer who does not want to provide you with his or her birthday. What value should be recorded in the birth_date column for that customer? You don't really want to make up an answer—you want a date value that means "unknown." This is what the NULL value is for. NULL usually means that you don't know what value should be entered into a column, but it can also mean that a column does not apply. A NULL value in the birth_date column certainly means that we don't know a customer's birth_date, not that birth_date does not apply[8]. On the other hand, you might want to include a rating column in the tapes table. A NULL value in the rating column might imply that the movie was produced before ratings were introduced and therefore the rating column does not apply.

Some columns should not allow NULL values. In most cases, it would not make sense to add a customer to your customers table unless you know the customer's name. Therefore, the customer_name column should be mandatory (in other words, customer_name should not allow NULL values).

Let's drop and re-create the customers table so that you can tell PostgreSQL which columns should allow NULL values:

```
movies=# DROP TABLE customers;
DROP
movies=# CREATE TABLE customers (
movies-#        customer_id   INTEGER UNIQUE NOT NULL,
movies-#        name          VARCHAR(50)    NOT NULL,
movies-#        phone         CHAR(8),
movies-#        birth_date    DATE,
movies-#        balance       DECIMAL(7,2)
movies-#);
CREATE
```

The NOT NULL modifier tells PostgreSQL that the customer_id and name columns are mandatory. If you don't specify NOT NULL, PostgreSQL assumes that a column is optional. You can include the keyword NULL to make your choices more obvious:

```
movies=# DROP TABLE customers;
DROP
movies=# CREATE TABLE customers (
movies-#        customer_id   INTEGER UNIQUE NOT NULL,
```

8. I am making the assumption that the customers for your video store have actually been born. For some of you, that may not be a valid assumption.

```
movies-#        name          VARCHAR(50)    NOT NULL,
movies-#        phone         CHAR(8)        NULL,
movies-#        birth_date    DATE           NULL,
movies-#        balance       DECIMAL(7,2)   NULL
movies-#);
CREATE
```

Notice that a column of *any* data type can support NULL values.

The NULL value has a unique property that is often the source of much confusion. NULL is not equal to *any value*, not even itself. NULL is not less than any value, and NULL is not greater than any value. Let's add a customer with a NULL balance:

```
movies=# INSERT INTO customers
movies-#   VALUES
movies-#   (
movies(#      5, 'Funkmaster, Freddy', '555-FUNK', NULL, NULL
movies(#   )
movies-# ;
```

Now we have five customers:

```
movies=# SELECT * FROM customers;
 id |     customer_name      |  phone   | birth_date | balance
----+----------------------+----------+------------+---------
  1 | Jones, Henry           | 555-1212 | 1970-10-10 |    0.00
  2 | Rubin, William         | 555-2211 | 1972-07-10 |   15.00
  3 | Panky, Henry           | 555-1221 | 1968-01-21 |    0.00
  4 | Wonderland, Alice N.   | 555-1122 | 1969-03-05 |    3.00
  5 | Funkmaster, Freddy     | 555-FUNK |            |
(5 rows)
```

One of these customers has a NULL balance. Let's try a few queries:

```
movies=# SELECT * FROM customers WHERE balance > NULL;
 id | customer_name | phone | birth_date | balance
----+---------------+-------+------------+---------
(0 rows)
```

This query did not return any rows. You might think that it should have customer number 2 (Rubin, William); after all, 15.00 is surely greater than 0. But remember, NULL is not equal to, greater than, or less than any other value. NULL is not the same as zero. Rather than using relational operators ('=', '!=', '<', or '>'), you should use either the IS or IS NOT operator.

```
movies=# SELECT * FROM customers WHERE balance IS NULL;
 id |    customer_name    |  phone   | birth_date | balance
----+--------------------+----------+------------+---------
  6 | Funkmaster, Freddy | 555-FUNK |            |
(1 row)
```

```
movies=# SELECT * FROM customers WHERE balance IS NOT NULL;
 id |    customer_name     |  phone   | birth_date | balance
----+----------------------+----------+------------+---------
  1 | Jones, Henry         | 555-1212 | 1970-10-10 |    0.00
  2 | Rubin, William       | 555-2211 | 1972-07-10 |   15.00
  3 | Panky, Henry         | 555-1221 | 1968-01-21 |    0.00
  4 | Wonderland, Alice N. | 555-1122 | 1969-03-05 |    3.00
(4 rows)
```

The NULL value introduces another complication. If NULL is not greater than, equal to, or less than any other value, what would 'NULL + 4' mean? Is NULL + 4 greater than NULL? It can't be because that would imply that NULL is less than NULL + 4 and, by definition, NULL can't be less than another value. What does all this mean? It means that you can't do math with a NULL value.

```
movies=# SELECT id, customer_name, balance, balance+4 FROM customers;
 id |    customer_name     | balance | ?column?
----+----------------------+---------+----------
  1 | Jones, Henry         |    0.00 |     4.00
  2 | Rubin, William       |   15.00 |    19.00
  3 | Panky, Henry         |    0.00 |     4.00
  4 | Wonderland, Alice N. |    3.00 |     7.00
  5 | Funkmaster, Freddy   |         |
(5 rows)
```

This query shows what happens when you try to perform a mathematical operation using NULL. When you try to add '4' to NULL, you end up with NULL.

The NULL value complicates logic operators as well. Most programmers are familiar with two-valued logic operators (that is, logic operators that are defined for the values TRUE and FALSE). When you add in NULL values, the logic operators become a bit more complex. Tables 1.4, 1.5, and 1.6 show the truth tables for each logical operator.

Table 1.4 **Truth Table for Three-Valued** AND **Operator**

a	b	a AND b
TRUE	TRUE	TRUE
TRUE	FALSE	FALSE
TRUE	NULL	NULL
FALSE	FALSE	FALSE
FALSE	NULL	FALSE
NULL	NULL	NULL

Source: *PostgreSQL User's Guide*

Table 1.5 **Truth Table for Three-Valued `OR` Operator**

a	b	a OR b
TRUE	TRUE	TRUE
TRUE	FALSE	TRUE
TRUE	NULL	TRUE
FALSE	FALSE	FALSE
FALSE	NULL	NULL
NULL	NULL	NULL

Source: *PostgreSQL User's Guide*

Table 1.6 **Truth Table for Three-Valued `NOT` Operator**

a	NOT a
TRUE	FALSE
FALSE	TRUE
NULL	NULL

Source: *PostgreSQL User's Guide*

I don't mean to scare you away from the `NULL` value—it's very useful and often necessary—but you do have to understand the complications that it introduces.

The ORDER BY Clause

So far, all the queries that you have seen return rows in an arbitrary order. You can add an `ORDER BY` clause to a `SELECT` command if you need to impose a predictable ordering. The general form of the `ORDER BY` clause is[9]

```
ORDER BY expression [ ASC | DESC ] [, ...]
```

The `ASC` and `DESC` terms mean ascending and descending, respectively. If you don't specify `ASC` or `DESC`, PostgreSQL assumes that you want to see results in ascending order. The *`expression`* following `ORDER BY` is called a *sort key*.

9. PostgreSQL supports another form for the `ORDER BY` clause: `ORDER BY expression [ USING operator ] [, ...]`. This might seem a little confusing at first. When you specify `ASC`, PostgreSQL uses the < operator to determine row ordering. When you specify `DESC`, PostgreSQL uses the > operator. The second form of the `ORDER BY` clause allows you to specify an alternative operator.

Let's look at a simple example:

```
movies=# SELECT * FROM customers ORDER BY balance;
 id |     customer_name      |  phone   | birth_date | balance
----+------------------------+----------+------------+---------
  1 | Jones, Henry           | 555-1212 | 1970-10-10 |    0.00
  3 | Panky, Henry           | 555-1221 | 1968-01-21 |    0.00
  4 | Wonderland, Alice N.   | 555-1122 | 1969-03-05 |    3.00
  2 | Rubin, William         | 555-2211 | 1972-07-10 |   15.00
  5 | Funkmaster, Freddy     | 555-FUNK |            |
(5 rows)
```

You can see that this `SELECT` command returns the result set in ascending order of the `balance` column. Here is the same query, but in descending order:

```
movies=# SELECT * FROM customers ORDER BY balance DESC;
 id |     customer_name      |  phone   | birth_date | balance
----+------------------------+----------+------------+---------
  2 | Rubin, William         | 555-2211 | 1972-07-10 |   15.00
  4 | Wonderland, Alice N.   | 555-1122 | 1969-03-05 |    3.00
  1 | Jones, Henry           | 555-1212 | 1970-10-10 |    0.00
  3 | Panky, Henry           | 555-1221 | 1968-01-21 |    0.00
  5 | Funkmaster, Freddy     | 555-FUNK |            |
(5 rows)
```

This time, the largest balance is first, followed by successively smaller values.

You may have noticed something odd about how the `ORDER BY` clause handles the customer named Freddy Funkmaster. Recall from the previous section that `NULL` cannot be compared to other values. By its very nature, the `ORDER BY` clause must compare values. PostgreSQL resolves this issue with a simple rule: `NULL` values always sort last. For ascending sorts, `NULL` is considered greater than all other values. For descending sorts, `NULL` is considered less than all other values. Note that starting with PostgreSQL version 7.2, `NULL` is always considered larger than all other values when evaluating an `ORDER BY` clause.

You can include multiple sort keys in the `ORDER BY` clause. The following query sorts `customers` in ascending `balance` order, and then in descending `birth_date` order:

```
movies=# SELECT * FROM customers ORDER BY balance, birth_date DESC;
 id |     customer_name      |  phone   | birth_date | balance
----+------------------------+----------+------------+---------
  1 | Jones, Henry           | 555-1212 | 1970-10-10 |    0.00
  3 | Panky, Henry           | 555-1221 | 1968-01-21 |    0.00
  4 | Wonderland, Alice N.   | 555-1122 | 1969-03-05 |    3.00
  2 | Rubin, William         | 555-2211 | 1972-07-10 |   15.00
  5 | Funkmaster, Freddy     | 555-FUNK |            |
(5 rows)
```

When an ORDER BY clause contains multiple sort keys, you are telling PostgreSQL how to break ties. You can see that customers 1 and 3 have the same value (0.00) in the balance column—you have asked PostgreSQL to order rows using the balance column. What happens when PostgreSQL finds two rows with the same balance? When two sort key values are equal, PostgreSQL moves to the next sort key to break the tie. If two sort key values are not equal, sort keys with a lower precedence are ignored. So, when PostgreSQL finds that customers 1 and 3 have the same balance, it moves to the birth_date column to break the tie.

If you don't have a sort key with a lower precedence, you won't be able to predict the ordering of rows with duplicate sort key values.

You can include as many sort keys as you like.

LIMIT and OFFSET

Occasionally, you will find that you want to answer a question such as "Who are my top 10 salespeople?" In most relational databases, this is a difficult question to ask. PostgreSQL offers two extensions that make it easy to answer "Top *n*" or "Bottom *n*"-type questions. The first extension is the LIMIT clause. The following query shows the two customers who owe you the most money:

```
movies=# SELECT * FROM customers ORDER BY balance DESC LIMIT 2;
 id |     customer_name      |  phone   | birth_date | balance
----+-----------------------+----------+------------+---------
  2 | Rubin, William        | 555-2211 | 1972-07-10 |   15.00
  4 | Wonderland, Alice N.  | 555-1122 | 1969-03-05 |    3.00
(2 rows)
```

You can see here that I used an ORDER BY clause so that the rows are sorted such that the highest balances appear first—in most cases, you won't use a LIMIT clause without also using an ORDER BY clause. Let's change this query a little—this time we want the top five customers who have a balance over $10:

```
movies=# SELECT * FROM customers
movies-#   WHERE
movies-#     balance >= 10
movies-#   ORDER BY balance DESC
movies-#   LIMIT 5;
 id | customer_name  |  phone   | birth_date | balance
----+----------------+----------+------------+---------
  2 | Rubin, William | 555-2211 | 1972-07-10 |   15.00
(1 row)
```

This example shows that the LIMIT clause won't always return the number of rows that were specified. Instead, LIMIT returns *no more than* the number of rows that you request. In this sample database, you have only one customer who owes you more than $10.

The second extension is the `OFFSET` *n* clause. The `OFFSET` *n* clause tells PostgreSQL to skip the first *n* rows of the result set. For example:

```
movies=# SELECT * FROM customers ORDER BY balance DESC OFFSET 1;
 id |     customer_name      |  phone   | birth_date | balance
----+----------------------+----------+------------+---------
  4 | Wonderland, Alice N. | 555-1122 | 1969-03-05 |    3.00
  1 | Jones, Henry         | 555-1212 | 1970-10-10 |    0.00
  3 | Panky, Henry         | 555-1221 | 1968-01-21 |    0.00
  5 | Funkmaster, Freddy   | 555-FUNK |            |
(4 rows)
```

In this case, we are viewing all the `customers` *except* the customer with the greatest `balance`. It's common to use `LIMIT` and `OFFSET` together:

```
movies=# SELECT * FROM customers
movies-#    ORDER BY balance DESC LIMIT 2 OFFSET 1;
 id |     customer_name      |  phone   | birth_date | balance
----+----------------------+----------+------------+---------
  4 | Wonderland, Alice N. | 555-1122 | 1969-03-05 |    3.00
  1 | Jones, Henry         | 555-1212 | 1970-10-10 |    0.00
(2 rows)
```

Formatting Column Results

So far, you have seen how to tell PostgreSQL which rows you want to view, which columns you want to view, and the order in which the rows should be returned. Let's take a short side-trip here and learn how to change the appearance of the values that you select.

Take a look at the following query:

```
movies=# SELECT id, customer_name, balance, balance+4 FROM customers;
 id |     customer_name      | balance | ?column?
----+----------------------+---------+----------
  1 | Jones, Henry         |    0.00 |     4.00
  2 | Rubin, William       |   15.00 |    19.00
  3 | Panky, Henry         |    0.00 |     4.00
  4 | Wonderland, Alice N. |    3.00 |     7.00
  5 | Funkmaster, Freddy   |         |
(5 rows)
```

PostgreSQL inserts two lines of text between your query and the result set. These two lines are (obviously) column headings. You can see that the header for each of the first three columns contains the name of the column. What about the last column? When you `SELECT` an expression, PostgreSQL uses "`?column?`" for the field header[10].

10. Actually, if you `SELECT` a function (such as `AGE()` or `SQRT()`), PostgreSQL will use the name of the function for the field header.

You can change field headers using the AS clause:

```
movies=# SELECT id, customer_name,
movies-#        balance AS "Old balance",
movies-#        balance + 4 AS "New balance"
movies-#   FROM customers;
 id |     customer_name     | Old balance | New balance
----+-----------------------+-------------+-------------
  1 | Jones, Henry          |        0.00 |        4.00
  2 | Rubin, William        |       15.00 |       19.00
  3 | Panky, Henry          |        0.00 |        4.00
  4 | Wonderland, Alice N.  |        3.00 |        7.00
  5 | Funkmaster, Freddy    |             |
(5 rows)
```

Notice that you can provide a field header for table columns as well as for expressions. If you rename a field and the query includes an ORDER BY clause that refers to the field, the ORDER BY should use the new name, not the original one:

```
movies=# SELECT id, customer_name,
movies-#        balance AS "Old balance",
movies-#        balance + 4 AS "New balance"
movies-#   FROM customers
movies-#   ORDER BY "Old balance";
 id |     customer_name     | Old balance | New balance
----+-----------------------+-------------+-------------
  1 | Jones, Henry          |        0.00 |        4.00
  3 | Panky, Henry          |        0.00 |        4.00
  4 | Wonderland, Alice N.  |        3.00 |        7.00
  2 | Rubin, William        |       15.00 |       19.00
  5 | Funkmaster, Freddy    |             |
(5 rows)
```

This section explained how to change the column headers for a SELECT command. You can also change the appearance of the data values. In the next section, I'll show you a few examples using date values for illustration.

Working with Date Values

PostgreSQL supports six basic date, time, and date/time data types, as shown in Table 1.7. I'll use the term *temporal* to cover date, time, and date/time data types.

Table 1.7 **PostgreSQL Temporal Data Types**

Data Type Name	Type of Data Stored	Earliest Date/Time	Latest Date/Time
TIMESTAMP	Date/Time	4713 BC	1465001 AD
TIMESTAMP WITH TIME ZONE	Date/Time	1903 AD	2037 AD

Table 1.7 **Continued**

Data Type Name	Type of Data Stored	Earliest Date/Time	Latest Date/Time
INTERVAL	Interval	–178000000 years	178000000 years
DATE	Date	4713 BC	32767 AD
TIME	Time	00:00:00.00	23:59:59.99
TIME WITH TIME ZONE	Time	00:00:00.00+12	23:59:59.99–12

I'll cover the details of the date/time data types in Chapter 2. You have already seen two of these temporal data types. The customers table contains a DATE column (birth_date):

```
movies=# \d customers
               Table "customers"
   Attribute   |         Type          | Modifier
---------------+-----------------------+----------
 id            | integer               | not null
 customer_name | character varying(50) | not null
 phone         | character(8)          |
 birth_date    | date                  |
 balance       | numeric(7,2)          |
Index: customers_id_key

movies=# SELECT customer_name, birth_date FROM customers;
    customer_name     | birth_date
----------------------+------------
 Jones, Henry         | 1970-10-10
 Rubin, William       | 1972-07-10
 Panky, Henry         | 1968-01-21
 Wonderland, Alice N. | 1969-03-05
 Funkmaster, Freddy   |
(5 rows)
```

You've also seen the INTERVAL data type—the AGE() function returns an INTERVAL:

```
movies=# SELECT customer_name, AGE( birth_date ) FROM customers;
    customer_name     |              age
----------------------+------------------------------
 Jones, Henry         | 31 years 4 mons 8 days 01:00
 Rubin, William       | 29 years 7 mons 8 days 01:00
 Panky, Henry         | 34 years 28 days
 Wonderland, Alice N. | 32 years 11 mons 13 days
 Funkmaster, Freddy   |
(5 rows)
```

Date/time values are usually pretty easy to work with, but there is a complication that you need to be aware of. Let's say that I need to add a new customer:

```
movies=# INSERT INTO customers
movies-#   VALUES
movies-#   (
movies-#     7, 'Gull, Jonathon LC', '555-1111', '02/05/1984', NULL
movies-#   );
```

This customer has a `birth_date` of `'02/05/1984'`—does that mean "February 5th 1984", or "May 2nd 1984"? How does PostgreSQL know which date I meant? The problem is that a date such as '`02/05/1984`' is ambiguous—you can't know which date this string represents without knowing something about the context in which it was entered. `'02/05/1984'` is ambiguous. `'May 02 1984'` is unambiguous.

PostgreSQL enables you to enter and display dates in a number of formats—some date formats are ambiguous and some are unambiguous. The `DATESTYLE` runtime variable tells PostgreSQL how to format dates when displaying data and how to interpret ambiguous dates that you enter.

The `DATESTYLE` variable can be a little confusing. `DATESTYLE` is composed of two parts. The first part, called the convention, tells PostgreSQL how to interpret ambiguous dates. The second part, called the display format, determines how PostgreSQL displays date values. The convention controls date input and the display format controls date output.

Let's talk about the display format first. PostgreSQL supports four different display formats. Three of the display formats are unambiguous and one is ambiguous.

The default display format is named `ISO`. In `ISO` format, dates always appear in the form '`YYYY-MM-DD`'. The next display format is `GERMAN`. In `GERMAN` format, dates always appear in the form '`DD.MM.YYYY`'. The `ISO` and `GERMAN` formats are unambiguous because the format never changes. The `POSTGRES` format is also unambiguous, but the display format can vary. PostgreSQL needs a second piece of information (the convention) to decide whether the month should appear before the day (`US` convention) or the day should appear before the month (`European` convention). In `POSTGRES` format, date values display the day-of-the-week and month name in abbreviated text form; for example '`Wed May 02 1984`' (`US`) or '`Wed 02 May 1984`' (`European`).

The final display format is `SQL`. `SQL` format is ambiguous. In `SQL` format, the date 'May 02 1984' is displayed as '`05/02/1984`' (`US`), or as '`02/05/1984`'(`European`).

Table 1.8 `DATESTYLE` **Display Formats**

Display Format	`US` **Convention**	`European` **Convention**
`ISO`	1984-05-02	1984-05-02
`GERMAN`	02.05.1984	02.05.1984
`POSTGRES`	Wed May 02 1984	Wed 02 May 1984
`SQL`	05/02/1984	02/05/1984

As I mentioned earlier, the ISO and GERMAN display formats are unambiguous. In ISO format, the month always precedes the day. In GERMAN format, the day always precedes the month. If you choose POSTGRES or SQL format, you must also specify the order in which you want the month and day components to appear. You can specify the desired display format and month/day ordering (that is, the convention) in the DATESTYLE runtime variable:

```
movies=# SET DATESTYLE TO 'US,ISO';               -- 1984-05-02
movies=# SET DATESTYLE TO 'US,GERMAN';            -- 02.05.1984
movies=# SET DATESTYLE TO 'US,POSTGRES';          -- Wed May 02 1984
movies=# SET DATESTYLE TO 'US,SQL';               -- 05/02/1984

movies=# SET DATESTYLE TO 'EUROPEAN,ISO';         -- 1984-05-02
movies=# SET DATESTYLE TO 'EUROPEAN,GERMAN';      -- 02.05.1984
movies=# SET DATESTYLE TO 'EUROPEAN,POSTGRES';    -- Wed 02 May 1984
movies=# SET DATESTYLE TO 'EUROPEAN,SQL';         -- 02/05/1984
```

The convention part of the DATESTYLE variable determines how PostgreSQL will make sense of the date values that you enter. The convention also affects the ordering of the month and day components when displaying a POSTGRES or SQL date. Note that you are not restricted to entering date values in the format specified by DATESTYLE. For example, if you have chosen to display dates in 'US,SQL' format, you can still enter date values in any of the other formats.

Recall that the ISO and GERMAN date formats are unambiguous—the ordering of the month and day components is predefined. A date entered in POSTGRES format is unambiguous as well—you enter the name of the month so it cannot be confused with the day. If you choose to enter a date in SQL format, PostgreSQL will look to the first component of DATESTYLE (that is, the convention) to determine whether you want the value interpreted as a US or a European date. Let's look at a few examples.

```
movies=# SET DATESTYLE TO 'US,ISO';
movies=# SELECT CAST( '02/05/1984' AS DATE );
 1984-02-05

movies=# SET DATESTYLE TO 'EUROPEAN,ISO';
movies=# SELECT CAST( '02/05/1984' AS DATE );
 1984-05-02
```

In this example, I've asked PostgreSQL to display dates in ISO format, but I've entered a date in an ambiguous format. In the first case, you can see that PostgreSQL interpreted the ambiguous date using US conventions (the month precedes the day). In the second case, PostgreSQL uses European conventions to interpret the date.

Now let's see what happens when I enter an unambiguous date:

```
movies=# SET DATESTYLE TO 'US,ISO';
SET VARIABLE
movies=# SELECT CAST( '1984-05-02' AS DATE );
 1984-05-02
```

```
movies=# SET DATESTYLE TO 'EUROPEAN,ISO';
SET VARIABLE
movies=# SELECT CAST( '1984-05-02' AS DATE );
 1984-05-02
```

This time, there can be no confusion—an `ISO`-formatted date is always entered in '`YYYY-MM-DD`' format. PostgreSQL ignores the convention.

So, you can see that I can enter date values in many formats. If I choose to enter a date in an ambiguous format, PostgreSQL uses the convention part of the current `DATESTYLE` to interpret the date. I can also use `DATESTYLE` to control the display format.

Matching Patterns

In the previous two sections, you took a short detour to learn a little about how to format results. Now let's get back to the task of *producing* the desired results.

The `WHERE` clause is used to restrict the number of rows returned by a `SELECT` command[11]. Sometimes, you don't know the exact value that you are searching for. For example, you may have a customer ask you for a film, but he doesn't remember the exact name, although he knows that the film has the word "Citizen" in the title. PostgreSQL provides two features that make it possible to search for partial alphanumeric values.

LIKE and NOT LIKE

The `LIKE` operator provides simple pattern-matching capabilities. `LIKE` uses two special characters that indicate the unknown part of a pattern. The underscore (_) character matches any single character. The percent sign (`%`) matches any sequence of zero or more characters. Table 1.9 shows a few examples.

Table 1.9 **Pattern Matching with the `LIKE` Operator**

String	Pattern	Result
The Godfather	%Godfather%	Matches
The Godfather	%Godfather	Matches
The Godfather	%Godfathe_	Matches
The Godfather	____ Godfather	Matches
The Godfather	Godfather%	Does not match
The Godfather	_Godfather	Does not match
The Godfather: Part II	%Godfather	Does not match

11. Technically, the `WHERE` clause constrains the set of rows affected by a `SELECT`, `UPDATE`, or `DELETE` command. I'll show you the `UPDATE` and `DELETE` commands a little later.

Now let's see how to use the LIKE operator in a SELECT command:

```
movies=# SELECT * FROM tapes WHERE title LIKE '%Citizen%';
 tape_id  |         title         | duration
----------+-----------------------+----------
 OW-41221 | Citizen Kane          |
 KJ-03335 | American Citizen, An  |
(2 rows)
```

The LIKE operator is case-sensitive:

```
movies=# SELECT * FROM tapes WHERE title LIKE '%citizen%';
 tape_id | title | duration
---------+-------+----------
(0 rows)
```

If you want to perform case-insensitive pattern matching, use the ILIKE operator:

```
movies=# SELECT * FROM tapes WHERE title ILIKE '%citizen%';
 tape_id  |         title         | duration
----------+-----------------------+----------
 OW-41221 | Citizen Kane          |
 KJ-03335 | American Citizen, An  |
(2 rows)
```

You can, of course, combine LIKE and ILIKE with the NOT operator to return rows that do not match a pattern:

```
movies=# SELECT * FROM tapes WHERE title NOT ILIKE '%citizen%';
 tape_id  |     title     |   duration
----------+---------------+--------------
 AB-12345 | The Godfather |
 AB-67472 | The Godfather |
 MC-68873 | Casablanca    |
 AH-54706 | Rear Window   |
 OW-42200 | Sly           | 01:36
 OW-42201 | Stone         | 4 days 01:36
(6 rows)
```

Pattern Matching with Regular Expressions

The LIKE and ILIKE operators are easy to use, but they aren't very powerful. Fortunately, PostgreSQL lets you search for data using *regular expressions*. A regular expression is a string that specifies a pattern. The language that you use to create regular expressions is far more powerful than the LIKE and ILIKE operators. You have probably used regular expressions before; programs such as *grep*, *awk*, and the Unix (and DOS) shells use regular expressions.

The LIKE and ILIKE operators define two pattern-matching characters; the regular expression operator defines far more. First, the character "." within a regular expression operates in the same way as the "_" character in a LIKE pattern: it matches any single character. The characters ".*" in a regular expression operate in the same way as the "%" character in a LIKE pattern: they match zero or more occurrences of any single character.

Notice that in a regular expression, you use two characters to match a sequence of characters, whereas you use a single character in a LIKE pattern. The regular expression ".*" is actually two regular expressions combined into one complex expression. As I mentioned earlier, the "." character matches any single character. The "*" character matches zero or more occurrences of the pattern that precedes it. So, ".*" means to match any single character, zero or more times. There are three other repetition operators: The "+" character matches one or more occurrences of the preceding pattern, and the "?" character matches zero or one occurrence of the preceding pattern. If you need to get really fancy (I never have), you can use the form "{x[,y]}" to match at least x and no more than y occurrences of the preceding pattern.

You can also search for things other than ".". For example, the character "^" matches the beginning of a string and "$" matches the end. The regular expression syntax even includes support for character classes. The pattern "[:upper:]*[:digit:]" will match any string that includes zero or more uppercase characters followed by a single digit.

The "|" character gives you a way to search for a string that matches either of two patterns. For example, the regular expression "(^God)|.*Donuts.*" would match a string that either starts with the string "God" or includes the word "Donuts".

Regular expressions are extremely powerful, but they can get awfully complex. If you need more information, Chapter 4 of the PostgreSQL User's Manual provides an exhaustive reference to the complete regular expression syntax.

Table 1.10 shows how to construct regular expressions that match the same strings matched by the LIKE patterns in shown in Table 1.9.

Table 1.10 **Pattern Matching with Regular Expressions**

String	Pattern	Result
The Godfather	.*Godfather	Matches
The Godfather	.*Godfather.*	Matches
The Godfather	.*Godfathe.	Matches
The Godfather	... Godfather	Matches
The Godfather	Godfather.*	Does not match
The Godfather	.Godfather	Does not match
The Godfather: Part II	.*Godfather	Does not match

Aggregates

PostgreSQL offers a number of aggregate functions. An *aggregate* is a collection of things—you can think of an aggregate as the set of rows returned by a query. An aggregate function is a function that operates on an aggregate (nonaggregate functions operate on a single row within an aggregate). Most of the aggregate functions operate on a single value extracted from each row—this is called an *aggregate expression*.

COUNT()

`COUNT()` is probably the simplest aggregate function. `COUNT()` returns the number of objects in an aggregate. The `COUNT()` function comes in four forms:

- `COUNT(*)`
- `COUNT(` *`expression`* `)`
- `COUNT( ALL` *`expression`* `)`
- `COUNT( DISTINCT` *`expression`* `)`

In the first form, `COUNT(*)` returns the number of rows in an aggregate:

```
movies=# SELECT * FROM customers;
 id |    customer_name     |  phone   | birth_date | balance
----+----------------------+----------+------------+---------
  1 | Jones, Henry         | 555-1212 | 1970-10-10 |    0.00
  2 | Rubin, William       | 555-2211 | 1972-07-10 |   15.00
  3 | Panky, Henry         | 555-1221 | 1968-01-21 |    0.00
  4 | Wonderland, Alice N. | 555-1122 | 1969-03-05 |    3.00
  5 | Funkmaster, Freddy   | 555-FUNK |            |
  7 | Gull, Jonathon LC    | 555-1111 | 1984-02-05 |
  8 | Grumby, Jonas        | 555-2222 | 1984-02-21 |
(7 rows)

movies=# SELECT COUNT(*) FROM customers;
 count
-------
     7
(1 row)

movies=# SELECT COUNT(*) FROM customers WHERE id < 5;
 count
-------
     4
(1 row)
```

You can see from this example that the `COUNT(*)` function pays attention to the `WHERE` clause. In other words, `COUNT(*)` returns the number of rows that filter through the `WHERE` clause; that is, the number of rows in the aggregate.

In the second form, COUNT(*expression*) returns the number of non-NULL values in the aggregate. For example, you might want to know how many customers have a non-NULL balance:

```
movies=# SELECT COUNT( balance ) FROM customers;
 count
-------
     4
(1 row)

movies=# SELECT COUNT(*) - COUNT( balance )  FROM customers;
 ?column?
----------
        3
(1 row)
```

The first query returns the number of non-NULL balances in the customers table. The second query returns the number of NULL balances.

The third form, COUNT(ALL *expression*) is equivalent to the second form. PostgreSQL includes the third form for completeness; it complements the fourth form.

COUNT(DISTINCT *expression*) returns the number of distinct non-NULL values in the aggregate.

```
movies=# SELECT DISTINCT balance FROM customers;
 balance
---------
    0.00
    3.00
   15.00

(4 rows)

movies=# SELECT COUNT( DISTINCT balance ) FROM customers;
 count
-------
     3
(1 row)
```

You might notice a surprising result in that last example. The first query returns the distinct balances in the customers table. Notice that PostgreSQL tells you that it returned four rows—there are four distinct values. The second query returns a count of the distinct balances—it says that there are only three.

Is this a bug? No, both queries returned the correct information. The first query includes the NULL value in the result set. COUNT(), and in fact all the aggregate functions (except for COUNT(*)), ignore NULL values.

SUM()

The `SUM( expression )` function returns the sum of all the values in the aggregate expression. Unlike `COUNT()`, you can't use `SUM()` on entire rows[12]. Instead, you usually specify a single column:

```
movies=# SELECT SUM( balance ) FROM customers;
  sum
-------
 18.00
(1 row)
```

Notice that the `SUM()` function expects an expression. The name of a numeric column is a valid expression. You can also specify an arbitrarily complex expression as long as that expression results in a numeric value.

You can also `SUM()` an aggregate of `intervals`. For example, the following query tells you how long it would take to watch all the tapes in your video store:

```
movies=# SELECT SUM( duration ) FROM tapes;
     sum
--------------
 4 days 03:12
(1 row)
```

AVG()

The `AVG( expression )` function returns the average of an aggregate expression. Like `SUM()`, you can find the average of a numeric aggregate or an `interval` aggregate.

```
movies=# SELECT AVG( balance ) FROM customers;
     avg
--------------
 4.5000000000
(1 row)

movies=# SELECT AVG( balance ) FROM customers
movies-#   WHERE balance IS NOT NULL;
     avg
--------------
 4.5000000000
(1 row)
```

12. Actually, you can `SUM(*)`, but it probably doesn't do what you would expect. `SUM(*)` is equivalent to `COUNT(*)`.

These queries demonstrate an important point: the aggregate functions completely ignore rows where the aggregate expression evaluates to NULL. The aggregate produced by the second query explicitly omits any rows where the balance is NULL. The aggregate produced by the first query implicitly omits NULL balances. In other words, the following queries are equivalent:

```
SELECT AVG( balance ) FROM customers;
SELECT AVG( balance ) FROM customers WHERE balance IS NOT NULL;
SELECT SUM( balance ) / COUNT( balance ) FROM customers;
```

But these queries are *not* equivalent:

```
SELECT AVG( balance ) FROM customers;
SELECT SUM( balance ) / COUNT( * ) FROM customers;
```

Why not? Because COUNT(*) counts all rows whereas COUNT(balance) omits any rows where the balance is NULL.

MIN() and MAX()

The MIN(*expression*) and MAX(*expression*) functions return the minimum and maximum values, respectively, of an aggregate expression. The MIN() and MAX() functions can operate on numeric, date/time, or string aggregates:

```
movies=# SELECT MIN( balance ), MAX( balance ) FROM customers;
 min  |  max
------+-------
 0.00 | 15.00
(1 row)

movies=# SELECT MIN( birth_date ), MAX( birth_date ) FROM customers;
    min     |    max
------------+------------
 1968-01-21 | 1984-02-21
(1 row)

movies=# SELECT MIN( customer_name ), MAX( customer_name )
movies-#   FROM customers;
        min         |         max
--------------------+---------------------
 Funkmaster, Freddy | Wonderland, Alice N.
(1 row)
```

Other Aggregate Functions

In addition to COUNT(), SUM(), AVG(), MIN(), and MAX(), PostgreSQL also supports the STDDEV(*expression*) and VARIANCE(*expression*) aggregate functions. These last two aggregate functions compute the standard deviation and variance of an aggregate, two common statistical measures of variation within a set of observations.

Grouping Results

The aggregate functions are useful for summarizing information. The result of an aggregate function is a single value. Sometimes, you really want an aggregate function to apply to each of a number of subsets of your data. For example, you may find it interesting to compute some demographic information about your customer base. Let's first look at the entire customers table:

```
movies=# SELECT * FROM customers;
 id |     customer_name      |   phone   | birth_date | balance
----+----------------------+----------+------------+---------
  1 | Jones, Henry          | 555-1212 | 1970-10-10 |    0.00
  2 | Rubin, William        | 555-2211 | 1972-07-10 |   15.00
  3 | Panky, Henry          | 555-1221 | 1968-01-21 |    0.00
  4 | Wonderland, Alice N. | 555-1122 | 1969-03-05 |    3.00
  5 | Funkmaster, Freddy    | 555-FUNK |            |
  7 | Gull, Jonathon LC     | 555-1111 | 1984-02-05 |
  8 | Grumby, Jonas         | 555-2222 | 1984-02-21 |
(7 rows)
```

Look at the birth_date column—notice that you have customers born in three distinct decades (four if you count NULL as a decade):

```
movies=# SELECT DISTINCT( EXTRACT( DECADE FROM birth_date ))
movies-#   FROM customers;
 date_part
-----------
       196
       197
       198

(4 rows)
```

The EXTRACT() function extracts a date component from a date/time value. The DECADE component looks a little strange, but it makes sense to know whether the decade of the '60s refers to the 1960s or the 2060s, now that we are past Y2K.

Now that you know how many decades are represented in your customer base, you might next want to know how many customers were born in each decade. The GROUP BY clause helps answer this kind of question:

```
movies=# SELECT COUNT(*), EXTRACT( DECADE FROM birth_date )
movies-#   FROM customers
movies-#   GROUP BY  EXTRACT( DECADE FROM birth_date );
 count | date_part
-------+-----------
     2 |       196
     2 |       197
     2 |       198
     1 |
(4 rows)
```

The GROUP BY clause is used with aggregate functions. PostgreSQL sorts the result set by the GROUP BY expression and applies the aggregate function to each group.

There is an easier way to build this query. The problem with this query is that you had to repeat the EXTRACT(DECADE FROM birth_date) phrase. Instead, you can use the AS clause to name the decade field, and then you can refer to that field by name in the GROUP BY clause:

```
movies=# SELECT COUNT(*), EXTRACT( DECADE FROM birth_date ) AS decade
movies-#   FROM customers
movies-#   GROUP BY decade;
 count | decade
-------+--------
     2 |    196
     2 |    197
     2 |    198
     1 |
(4 rows)
```

If you don't request an explicit ordering, the GROUP BY clause will cause the result set to be sorted by the GROUP BY fields. If you want a different ordering, you can use the ORDER BY clause with GROUP BY. The following query shows how many customers you have for each decade, sorted by the count:

```
movies=# SELECT
movies-#   COUNT(*) as "Customers",
movies-#   EXTRACT( DECADE FROM birth_date ) as "Decade"
movies-#  FROM customers
movies-#   GROUP BY "Decade"
movies-#   ORDER BY "Customers";
 Customers | Decade
-----------+--------
         1 |
         2 |    196
         2 |    197
         2 |    198
(4 rows)
```

The NULL decade looks a little funny in this result set. You have one customer (Freddy Funkmaster) who was too vain to tell you when he was born. You can use the HAVING clause to eliminate aggregate groups:

```
movies=# SELECT COUNT(*), EXTRACT( DECADE FROM birth_date ) as decade
movies-#   FROM customers
movies-#   GROUP BY decade
movies-#   HAVING EXTRACT( DECADE FROM birth_date ) IS NOT NULL;
```

```
 count | decade
-------+--------
     2 |    196
     2 |    197
     2 |    198
(3 rows)
```

You can see that the `HAVING` clause is similar to the `WHERE` clause. The `WHERE` clause determines which rows are included in the aggregate, whereas the `HAVING` clause determines which *groups* are included in the result set.

Multi-Table Joins

So far, all the queries that you've seen involve a single table. Most databases contain multiple tables and there are relationships between these tables. This sample database has an example:

```
movies=# \d rentals

            Table "rentals"
  Attribute  |     Type      | Modifier
-------------+---------------+----------
 tape_id     | character(8)  | not null
 rental_date | date          | not null
 customer_id | integer       | not null
```

Here's a description of the `rentals` table from earlier in this chapter:

> "When a customer comes in to rent a tape, we will add a row to the `rentals` table to record the transaction. There are three pieces of information that we need to record for each rental: the `tape_id`, the `customer_id`, and the date that the rental occurred. Notice that each row in the rentals table refers to a customer (`customer_id`) and a tape (`tape_id`)."

You can see that each row in the `rentals` table refers to a tape (`tape_id`) and to a customer (`customer_id`). If you `SELECT` from the rentals table, you can see the tape ID and customer ID, but you can't see the movie title or customer name. What you need here is a *join*. When you need to retrieve data from multiple tables, you *join* those tables.

PostgreSQL (and all relational databases) supports a number of join types. The most basic join type is a *cross-join* (or Cartesian product). In a cross join, PostgreSQL joins each row in the first table to each row in the second table to produce a result table. If you are joining against a third table, PostgreSQL joins each row in the intermediate result with each row in the third table.

Let's look at an example. We'll cross-join the `rentals` and `customers` tables. First, I'll show you each table:

```
movies=# SELECT * FROM rentals;
 tape_id  | rental_date | customer_id
----------+-------------+-------------
 AB-12345 | 2001-11-25  |           1
 AB-67472 | 2001-11-25  |           3
 OW-41221 | 2001-11-25  |           1
 MC-68873 | 2001-11-20  |           3
(4 rows)

movies=# SELECT * FROM customers;
 id |     customer_name      |  phone   | birth_date | balance
----+------------------------+----------+------------+---------
  1 | Jones, Henry           | 555-1212 | 1970-10-10 |    0.00
  2 | Rubin, William         | 555-2211 | 1972-07-10 |   15.00
  3 | Panky, Henry           | 555-1221 | 1968-01-21 |    0.00
  4 | Wonderland, Alice N.   | 555-1122 | 1969-03-05 |    3.00
  5 | Funkmaster, Freddy     | 555-FUNK |            |
  7 | Gull, Jonathon LC      | 555-1111 | 1984-02-05 |
  8 | Grumby, Jonas          | 555-2222 | 1984-02-21 |
(7 rows)
```

Now I'll join these tables. To perform a cross-join, we simply list each table in the `FROM` clause:

```
movies=# SELECT rentals.*, customers.id, customers.customer_name
movies-#   FROM rentals, customers;
 tape_id  | rental_date | customer_id | id |     customer_name
----------+-------------+-------------+----+----------------------
 AB-12345 | 2001-11-25  |           1 |  1 | Jones, Henry
 AB-12345 | 2001-11-25  |           1 |  2 | Rubin, William
 AB-12345 | 2001-11-25  |           1 |  3 | Panky, Henry
 AB-12345 | 2001-11-25  |           1 |  4 | Wonderland, Alice N.
 AB-12345 | 2001-11-25  |           1 |  5 | Funkmaster, Freddy
 AB-12345 | 2001-11-25  |           1 |  7 | Gull, Jonathon LC
 AB-12345 | 2001-11-25  |           1 |  8 | Grumby, Jonas
 AB-67472 | 2001-11-25  |           3 |  1 | Jones, Henry
 AB-67472 | 2001-11-25  |           3 |  2 | Rubin, William
 AB-67472 | 2001-11-25  |           3 |  3 | Panky, Henry
 AB-67472 | 2001-11-25  |           3 |  4 | Wonderland, Alice N.
 AB-67472 | 2001-11-25  |           3 |  5 | Funkmaster, Freddy
 AB-67472 | 2001-11-25  |           3 |  7 | Gull, Jonathon LC
 AB-67472 | 2001-11-25  |           3 |  8 | Grumby, Jonas
 OW-41221 | 2001-11-25  |           1 |  1 | Jones, Henry
 OW-41221 | 2001-11-25  |           1 |  2 | Rubin, William
```

```
 OW-41221 | 2001-11-25  |           1 |  3 | Panky, Henry
 OW-41221 | 2001-11-25  |           1 |  4 | Wonderland, Alice N.
 OW-41221 | 2001-11-25  |           1 |  5 | Funkmaster, Freddy
 OW-41221 | 2001-11-25  |           1 |  7 | Gull, Jonathon LC
 OW-41221 | 2001-11-25  |           1 |  8 | Grumby, Jonas
 MC-68873 | 2001-11-20  |           3 |  1 | Jones, Henry
 MC-68873 | 2001-11-20  |           3 |  2 | Rubin, William
 MC-68873 | 2001-11-20  |           3 |  3 | Panky, Henry
 MC-68873 | 2001-11-20  |           3 |  4 | Wonderland, Alice N.
 MC-68873 | 2001-11-20  |           3 |  5 | Funkmaster, Freddy
 MC-68873 | 2001-11-20  |           3 |  7 | Gull, Jonathon LC
 MC-68873 | 2001-11-20  |           3 |  8 | Grumby, Jonas
(28 rows)
```

You can see that PostgreSQL has joined each row in the `rentals` table to each row in the `customers` table. The `rentals` table contains four rows; the `customers` table contains seven rows. The result set contains 4 × 7 or 28 rows.

Cross-joins are rarely useful—they usually don't represent real-world relationships.

The second type of join, the *inner-join*, is very useful. An inner-join starts with a cross-join, and then throws out the rows that you don't want. Take a close look at the results of the previous query. Here are the first seven rows again:

```
 tape_id  | rental_date | customer_id | id |    customer_name
----------+-------------+-------------+----+----------------------
 AB-12345 | 2001-11-25  |           1 |  1 | Jones, Henry
 AB-12345 | 2001-11-25  |           1 |  2 | Rubin, William
 AB-12345 | 2001-11-25  |           1 |  3 | Panky, Henry
 AB-12345 | 2001-11-25  |           1 |  4 | Wonderland, Alice N.
 AB-12345 | 2001-11-25  |           1 |  5 | Funkmaster, Freddy
 AB-12345 | 2001-11-25  |           1 |  7 | Gull, Jonathon LC
 AB-12345 | 2001-11-25  |           1 |  8 | Grumby, Jonas
     .          .               .      .        .
     .          .               .      .        .
     .          .               .      .        .
```

These seven rows were produced by joining the first row in the `rentals` table:

```
 tape_id  | rental_date | customer_id
----------+-------------+-------------
 AB-12345 | 2001-11-25  |           1
```

with each row in the `customers` table. What is the real-world relationship between a `rentals` row and a `customers` row? Each row in the `rentals` table contains a customer ID. Each row in the `customers` table is uniquely identified by a customer ID. So, given a `rentals` row, we can find the corresponding `customers` row by searching for a customer where the customer ID is equal to `rentals.customer_id`. Looking back at the previous query, you can see that the meaningful rows are those `WHERE customers.id = rentals.customer_id`.

Qualifying Column Names

Notice that this WHERE clause mentions two columns with similar names (customer_id and id). You may find it helpful to qualify each column name by prefixing it with the name of the corresponding table, followed by a period. So, customers.id refers to the id column in the customers table and rentals.customer_id refers to the customer_id column in the rentals table. Adding the table qualifier is *required* if a command involves two columns with identical names, but is useful in other cases.

Now you can construct a query that will show us all of the rentals and the names of the corresponding customers:

```
movies=# SELECT rentals.*, customers.id, customers.customer_name
movies-#   FROM rentals, customers
movies-#   WHERE customers.id = rentals.customer_id;
 tape_id  | rental_date | customer_id | id | customer_name
----------+-------------+-------------+----+---------------
 AB-12345 | 2001-11-25  |           1 |  1 | Jones, Henry
 OW-41221 | 2001-11-25  |           1 |  1 | Jones, Henry
 AB-67472 | 2001-11-25  |           3 |  3 | Panky, Henry
 MC-68873 | 2001-11-20  |           3 |  3 | Panky, Henry
(4 rows)
```

To execute this query, PostgreSQL could start by creating the cross-join between all the tables involved, producing an intermediate result table. Next, PostgreSQL could throw out all the rows that fail to satisfy the WHERE clause. In practice, this would be a poor strategy: Cross-joins can get very large quickly. Instead, the PostgreSQL query optimizer analyzes the query and plans an execution strategy to minimize execution time. I'll cover query optimization in Chapter 4, "Query Optimization."

Join Types

We've seen two join types so far: cross-joins and inner-joins. Now we'll look at *outer-joins*. An outer-join is similar to an inner-join: a relationship between two tables is established by correlating a column from each table.

In an earlier section, you wrote a query that answered the question: "Which customers are currently renting movies?" How would you answer the question: "Who are my customers and which movies are they currently renting?" You might start by trying the following query:

```
movies=# SELECT customers.*, rentals.tape_id
movies-#   FROM customers, rentals
movies-#   WHERE rentals.customer_id = customers.id;
 id | customer_name |  phone   | birth_date | balance | tape_id
----+---------------+----------+------------+---------+----------
  1 | Jones, Henry  | 555-1212 | 1970-10-10 |    0.00 | AB-12345
  1 | Jones, Henry  | 555-1212 | 1970-10-10 |    0.00 | OW-41221
  3 | Panky, Henry  | 555-1221 | 1968-01-21 |    0.00 | AB-67472
  3 | Panky, Henry  | 555-1221 | 1968-01-21 |    0.00 | MC-68873
(4 rows)
```

Well, that didn't work. This query showed you which customers are currently renting movies (and the movies that they are renting). What we really want is a list of *all* customers and, if a customer is currently renting any movies, all the movies rented. This is an outer-join. An outer-join preserves all the rows in one table (or both tables) regardless of whether a matching row can be found in the second table.

The syntax for an outer-join is a little strange. Here is an example:

```
movies=# SELECT customers.customer_name, rentals.tape_id
movies-#   FROM customers LEFT OUTER JOIN rentals
movies-#   ON customers.id = rentals.customer_id;
    customer_name      | tape_id
----------------------+----------
 Jones, Henry          | AB-12345
 Jones, Henry          | OW-41221
 Rubin, William        |
 Panky, Henry          | AB-67472
 Panky, Henry          | MC-68873
 Wonderland, Alice N.  |
 Funkmaster, Freddy    |
 Gull, Jonathon LC     |
 Grumby, Jonas         |
(9 rows)
```

This query is a *left outer-join*. Why left? Because you will see each row from the left table (the table to the left of the LEFT OUTER JOIN phrase). An inner-join would list only two customers ("Jones, Henry" and "Panky, Henry")—the other customers have no rentals.

A RIGHT OUTER JOIN preserves each row from the right table. A FULL OUTER JOIN preserves each row from both tables.

The following query shows a list of all customers, all tapes, and any rentals:

```
movies=# SELECT customers.customer_name, rentals.tape_id, tapes.title
movies-#   FROM customers FULL OUTER JOIN rentals
movies-#     ON customers.id = rentals.customer_id
movies-#   FULL OUTER JOIN tapes
movies-#     ON tapes.tape_id = rentals.tape_id;
    customer_name      | tape_id  |         title
----------------------+----------+----------------------
 Jones, Henry          | AB-12345 | The Godfather
 Panky, Henry          | AB-67472 | The Godfather
                       |          | Rear Window
                       |          | American Citizen, An
 Panky, Henry          | MC-68873 | Casablanca
 Jones, Henry          | OW-41221 | Citizen Kane
 Rubin, William        |          |
 Wonderland, Alice N.  |          |
 Funkmaster, Freddy    |          |
 Gull, Jonathon LC     |          |
```

```
 Grumby, Jonas          |           |
                        |           | Sly
                        |           | Stone
(13 rows)
```

UPDATE

Now that you've seen a number of ways to view your data, let's see how to modify (and delete) existing data.

The `UPDATE` command modifies data in one or more rows. The general form of the `UPDATE` command is

```
UPDATE table SET column = expression [, ...] [WHERE condition]
```

Using the `UPDATE` command is straightforward: The `WHERE` clause (if present) determines which rows will be updated and the `SET` clause determines which columns will be updated (and the new values).

You might have noticed in earlier examples that one of the tapes had a duration of `'4 days, 01:36'`—that's obviously a mistake. You can correct this problem with the `UPDATE` command as follows:

```
movies=# UPDATE tapes SET duration = '4 hours 36 minutes'
movies-#   WHERE tape_id = 'OW-42201';
UPDATE 1

movies=# SELECT * FROM tapes;
 tape_id  |         title         | duration
----------+-----------------------+----------
 AB-12345 | The Godfather         |
 AB-67472 | The Godfather         |
 MC-68873 | Casablanca            |
 OW-41221 | Citizen Kane          |
 AH-54706 | Rear Window           |
 OW-42200 | Sly                   | 01:36
 KJ-03335 | American Citizen, An  |
 OW-42201 | Stone Cold            | 04:36
(8 rows)
```

Using the `UPDATE` command, you can update all the rows in the table, a single row, or a set of rows—it all depends on the `WHERE` clause. The `SET` clause in this example updates a single column in all the rows that satisfy the `WHERE` clause. If you want to update multiple columns, list each assignment, separated by commas:

```
movies=# UPDATE tapes
movies-#   SET duration = '1 hour 52 minutes', title = 'Stone Cold'
movies-#   WHERE tape_id = 'OW-42201';
UPDATE 1
```

```
movies=# SELECT * FROM tapes;
 tape_id  |        title         | duration
----------+----------------------+----------
 AB-12345 | The Godfather        |
 AB-67472 | The Godfather        |
 MC-68873 | Casablanca           |
 OW-41221 | Citizen Kane         |
 AH-54706 | Rear Window          |
 OW-42200 | Sly                  | 01:36
 KJ-03335 | American Citizen, An |
 OW-42201 | Stone Cold           | 01:52
(8 rows)
```

The UPDATE statement displays the number of rows that were modified. The following UPDATE will modify three of the seven rows in the customers table:

```
movies=# SELECT * FROM customers;
 id |    customer_name     |  phone   | birth_date | balance
----+----------------------+----------+------------+---------
  1 | Jones, Henry         | 555-1212 | 1970-10-10 |    0.00
  2 | Rubin, William       | 555-2211 | 1972-07-10 |   15.00
  3 | Panky, Henry         | 555-1221 | 1968-01-21 |    0.00
  4 | Wonderland, Alice N. | 555-1122 | 1969-03-05 |    3.00
  5 | Funkmaster, Freddy   | 555-FUNK |            |
  7 | Gull, Jonathon LC    | 555-1111 | 1984-02-05 |
  8 | Grumby, Jonas        | 555-2222 | 1984-02-21 |
(7 rows)

movies=# UPDATE customers
movies-#   SET balance = 0
movies-#   WHERE balance IS NULL;
UPDATE 3
movies=# SELECT * FROM customers;
 id |    customer_name     |  phone   | birth_date | balance
----+----------------------+----------+------------+---------
  1 | Jones, Henry         | 555-1212 | 1970-10-10 |    0.00
  2 | Rubin, William       | 555-2211 | 1972-07-10 |   15.00
  3 | Panky, Henry         | 555-1221 | 1968-01-21 |    0.00
  4 | Wonderland, Alice N. | 555-1122 | 1969-03-05 |    3.00
  5 | Funkmaster, Freddy   | 555-FUNK |            |    0.00
  7 | Gull, Jonathon LC    | 555-1111 | 1984-02-05 |    0.00
  8 | Grumby, Jonas        | 555-2222 | 1984-02-21 |    0.00
(7 rows)
```

DELETE

Like UPDATE, the DELETE command is simple. The general format of the DELETE command is

```
DELETE FROM table [ WHERE condition ]
```

The DELETE command removes all rows that satisfy the (optional) WHERE clause. Here is an example:

```
movies=# SELECT * FROM tapes;
 tape_id  |        title          | duration
----------+-----------------------+----------
 AB-12345 | The Godfather         |
 AB-67472 | The Godfather         |
 MC-68873 | Casablanca            |
 OW-41221 | Citizen Kane          |
 AH-54706 | Rear Window           |
 OW-42200 | Sly                   | 01:36
 KJ-03335 | American Citizen, An  |
 OW-42201 | Stone Cold            | 01:52
(8 rows)
movies=# BEGIN WORK;
BEGIN
movies=# DELETE FROM tapes WHERE duration IS NULL;
DELETE 6
movies=# SELECT * FROM tapes;
 tape_id  |   title    | duration
----------+------------+----------
 OW-42200 | Sly        | 01:36
 OW-42201 | Stone Cold | 01:52
(2 rows)

movies=# ROLLBACK;
ROLLBACK
```

Before we executed the DELETE command, there were eight rows in the tapes table, and six of these tapes had a NULL duration.

You can see that the DELETE statement returns the number of rows deleted ("DELETE 6"). After the DELETE statement, only two tapes remain.

If you omit the WHERE clause in a DELETE command, PostgreSQL will delete *all* rows. Similarly, forgetting the WHERE clause for an UPDATE command updates all rows. Be careful!

A (Very) Short Introduction to Transaction Processing

You might have noticed two new commands in this example. The `BEGIN WORK` and `ROLLBACK` commands are used for *transaction processing*. A transaction is a group of commands. Usually, a transaction includes one or more table modifications (`INSERT`s, `DELETE`s, and `UPDATE`s).

`BEGIN WORK` marks the beginning of a transaction. Inside of a transaction, any changes that you make to the database are temporary changes. There are two ways to mark the end of a transaction: `COMMIT` and `ROLLBACK`. If you `COMMIT` a transaction, you are telling PostgreSQL to write all the changes made within the transaction into the database—in other words, when you `COMMIT` a transaction, the changes become permanent. When you `ROLLBACK` a transaction, all changes made within the transaction are discarded.

You can see that transactions are handy in that you can discard your changes if you change your mind. But transactions are important for another reason. PostgreSQL guarantees that all the modifications in a transaction will complete, or none of them will complete. The classic example of the importance of this property is to pretend that you are transferring money from one bank account to another. This transaction might be written in two steps. The first step is to subtract an amount from the first account. The second step is to add the amount to the second account. Now consider what would happen if your system crashed after completing the first step, but before the second step. Somehow, you've lost money! If you wrap these steps in a transaction, PostgreSQL promises that the first step will be rolled back if the second step fails (actually, the transaction will be rolled back unless you perform a `COMMIT`).

I'll cover the transaction processing features of PostgreSQL in great detail in Chapter 3.

Creating New Tables Using CREATE TABLE...AS

Let's turn our attention to something completely different. Earlier in this chapter, you learned how to use the `INSERT` statement to store data in a table. Sometimes, you want to create a new table based on the results of a `SELECT` command. That's exactly what the `CREATE TABLE...AS` command is designed to do.

The format of `CREATE TABLE...AS` is

```
CREATE [ TEMPORARY | TEMP ] TABLE table [ (column [, ...] ) ]
  AS select_clause
```

When you execute a `CREATE TABLE...AS` command, PostgreSQL automatically creates a new table. Each column in the new table corresponds to a column returned by the `SELECT` clause. If you include the `TEMPORARY` (or `TEMP`) keyword, PostgreSQL will create a temporary table. This table is invisible to other users and is destroyed when you end your PostgreSQL session. A temporary table is useful because you don't have to remember to remove the table later—PostgreSQL takes care of that detail for you.

Let's look at an example. A few pages earlier in the chapter, you created a complex join between the customers, rentals, and tapes tables. Let's create a new table based on that query so you don't have to keep entering the same complex query[13]:

```
movies=# CREATE TABLE info AS
movies-#   SELECT customers.customer_name, rentals.tape_id, tapes.title
movies-#     FROM customers FULL OUTER JOIN rentals
movies-#       ON customers.id = rentals.customer_id
movies-#     FULL OUTER JOIN tapes
movies-#       ON tapes.tape_id = rentals.tape_id;
SELECT
movies=# SELECT * FROM info;
    customer_name      | tape_id  |        title
----------------------+----------+----------------------
 Jones, Henry          | AB-12345 | The Godfather
 Panky, Henry          | AB-67472 | The Godfather
                       |          | Rear Window
                       |          | American Citizen, An
 Panky, Henry          | MC-68873 | Casablanca
 Jones, Henry          | OW-41221 | Citizen Kane
 Rubin, William        |          |
 Wonderland, Alice N.  |          |
 Funkmaster, Freddy    |          |
 Gull, Jonathon LC     |          |
 Grumby, Jonas         |          |
                       |          | Sly
                       |          | Stone Cold
(13 rows)
```

This is the same complex query that you saw earlier. I'll point out a few things about this example. First, notice that the SELECT command selected three columns (customer_name, tape_id, title)—the result table has three columns. Next, you can create a table using an arbitrarily complex SELECT command. Finally, notice that the TEMPORARY keyword is not included; therefore, info is a permanent table and is visible to other users.

What happens if you try to create the info table again?

```
movies=# CREATE TABLE info AS
movies-#   SELECT customers.customer_name, rentals.tape_id, tapes.title
movies-#     FROM customers FULL OUTER JOIN rentals
movies-#       ON customers.id = rentals.customer_id
movies-#     FULL OUTER JOIN tapes
movies-#       ON tapes.tape_id = rentals.tape_id;
ERROR:  Relation 'info' already exists
```

13. Some readers are probably thinking, "Hey, you should use a *view* to do that!" You're right, you'll soon see that I just needed a bad example.

As you might expect, you receive an error message because the `info` table already exists. `CREATE TABLE...AS` will not automatically drop an existing table. Now let's see what happens if you include the `TEMPORARY` keyword:

```
movies=# CREATE TEMPORARY TABLE info AS
movies-#   SELECT * FROM tapes;
SELECT
movies=# SELECT * FROM info;
 tape_id  |         title         | duration
----------+-----------------------+----------
 AB-12345 | The Godfather         |
 AB-67472 | The Godfather         |
 MC-68873 | Casablanca            |
 OW-41221 | Citizen Kane          |
 AH-54706 | Rear Window           |
 OW-42200 | Sly                   | 01:36
 KJ-03335 | American Citizen, An  |
 OW-42201 | Stone Cold            | 01:52
(8 rows)
```

This time, the `CREATE TABLE...AS` command succeeded. When I `SELECT` from `info`, I see a copy of the `tapes` table. Doesn't this violate the rule that I mentioned earlier ("`CREATE TABLE...AS` will not automatically drop an existing table")? Not really. When you create a temporary table, you are hiding any permanent table of the same name—the original (permanent) table still exists. Other users will still see the permanent table. If you `DROP` the temporary table, the permanent table will reappear:

```
movies=# SELECT * FROM info;
 tape_id  |         title         | duration
----------+-----------------------+----------
 AB-12345 | The Godfather         |
 AB-67472 | The Godfather         |
 MC-68873 | Casablanca            |
 OW-41221 | Citizen Kane          |
 AH-54706 | Rear Window           |
 OW-42200 | Sly                   | 01:36
 KJ-03335 | American Citizen, An  |
 OW-42201 | Stone Cold            | 01:52
(8 rows)

movies=# DROP TABLE info;
DROP
movies=# SELECT * FROM info;
    customer_name     | tape_id  |         title
----------------------+----------+---------------------
 Jones, Henry         | AB-12345 | The Godfather
 Panky, Henry         | AB-67472 | The Godfather
```

```
                        |          | Rear Window
                        |          | American Citizen, An
 Panky, Henry           | MC-68873 | Casablanca
 Jones, Henry           | OW-41221 | Citizen Kane
 Rubin, William         |          |
 Wonderland, Alice N.   |          |
 Funkmaster, Freddy     |          |
 Gull, Jonathon LC      |          |
 Grumby, Jonas          |          |
                        |          | Sly
                        |          | Stone Cold
(13 rows)
```

Using VIEW

In the previous section, I used the `CREATE TABLE...AS` command to create the `info` table so that you didn't have to type in the same complex query over and over again. The problem with that approach is that the `info` table is a snapshot of the underlying tables at the time that the `CREATE TABLE...AS` command was executed. If any of the underlying tables change (and they probably will), the `info` table will be out of synch.

Fortunately, PostgreSQL provides a much better solution to this problem—the view. A *view* is a named query. The syntax you use to create a view is nearly identical to the `CREATE TABLE...AS` command:

```
CREATE VIEW view AS select_clause;
```

Let's get rid of the `info` table and replace it with a view:

```
movies=# DROP TABLE info;
DROP
movies=# CREATE VIEW info AS
movies-#   SELECT customers.customer_name, rentals.tape_id,tapes.title
movies-#     FROM customers FULL OUTER JOIN rentals
movies-#       ON customers.id = rentals.customer_id
movies-#     FULL OUTER JOIN tapes
movies-#       ON tapes.tape_id = rentals.tape_id;
CREATE
```

While using `psql`, you can see a list of the views in your database using the \dv meta-command:

```
movies=# \dv
      List of relations
 Name | Type |     Owner
------+------+---------------
 info | view | bruce
(1 row)
```

You can see the definition of a view using the `\d view-name` meta-command:

```
movies=# \d info
                    View "info"
   Attribute    |         Type          | Modifier
----------------+-----------------------+----------
 customer_name  | character varying(50) |
 tape_id        | character(8)          |
 title          | character varying(80) |
View definition: SELECT customers.customer_name,
                        rentals.tape_id, tapes.title
                 FROM (( customers FULL JOIN rentals
                   ON ((customers.id = rentals.customer_id)))
                 FULL JOIN tapes
                   ON ((tapes.tape_id = rentals.tape_id)));
```

You can `SELECT` from a view in exactly the same way that you can `SELECT` from a table:

```
movies=# SELECT * FROM info WHERE tape_id IS NOT NULL;
 customer_name | tape_id  |     title
---------------+----------+---------------
 Jones, Henry  | AB-12345 | The Godfather
 Panky, Henry  | AB-67472 | The Godfather
 Panky, Henry  | MC-68873 | Casablanca
 Jones, Henry  | OW-41221 | Citizen Kane
(4 rows)
```

The great thing about a view is that it is always in synch with the underlying tables. Let's add a new `rentals` row:

```
movies=# INSERT INTO rentals VALUES( 'KJ-03335', '2001-11-26', 8 );
INSERT 38488 1
```

and then repeat the previous query:

```
movies=# SELECT * FROM info WHERE tape_id IS NOT NULL;
 customer_name | tape_id  |        title
---------------+----------+----------------------
 Jones, Henry  | AB-12345 | The Godfather
 Panky, Henry  | AB-67472 | The Godfather
 Grumby, Jonas | KJ-03335 | American Citizen, An
 Panky, Henry  | MC-68873 | Casablanca
 Jones, Henry  | OW-41221 | Citizen Kane
(5 rows)
```

To help you understand how a view works, you might imagine that the following sequence of events occurs each time you SELECT from a view:

1. PostgreSQL creates a temporary table by executing the SELECT command used to define the view.
2. PostgreSQL executes the SELECT command that you entered, substituting the name of temporary table everywhere that you used the name of the view.
3. PostgreSQL destroys the temporary table.

This is not what actually occurs under the covers, but it's the easiest way to think about views.

Unlike other relational databases, PostgreSQL treats all views as *read-only*—you can't INSERT, DELETE, or UPDATE a view.

To destroy a view, you use the DROP VIEW command:

```
movies=# DROP VIEW info;
DROP
```

Summary

This chapter has given you a gentle introduction to PostgreSQL. You have seen how to install PostgreSQL on your system and how to configure it for use. You've also created a sample database that you'll use throughout the rest of this book.

In the next chapter, I'll discuss the many PostgreSQL data types in more depth, and I'll give you some guidelines for choosing between them.

2

Working with Data in PostgreSQL

When you create a table in PostgreSQL, you specify the type of data that you will store in each column. For example, if you are storing a customer name, you will want to store alphabetic characters. If you are storing a customer's birth date, you will want to store values that can be interpreted as dates. An account balance would be stored in a numeric column.

Every value in a PostgreSQL database is defined within a data type. Each data type has a name (`NUMERIC`, `TIMESTAMP`, `CHARACTER`, and so on) and a range of valid values. When you enter a value in PostgreSQL, the data that you supply must conform to the syntax required by the type. PostgreSQL defines a set of functions that can operate on each data type: You can also define your own functions. Every data type has a set of *operators* that can be used with values of that type. An operator is a symbol used to build up complex expressions from simple expressions. You're already familiar with arithmetic operators such as + (addition) and – (subtraction). An operator represents some sort of computation applied to one or more operands. For example, in the expression `5 + 3`, + is the operator and `5` and `3` are the operands. Most operators require two operands, some require a single operand, and others can function in either context. An operator that works with two operands is called a binary operator. An operator that works with one operand is called a unary operator.

You can convert most values from one data type to another. I'll describe type conversion at the end of this chapter.

This chapter explores each of the data types built into a standard PostgreSQL distribution (yes, you can also define your own custom data types). For each type, I'll show you the range of valid values, the syntax required to enter a value of that type, and a list of operators that you can use with that type.

Each section includes a table showing which operators you can use with a specific data type. For example, in the discussion of character data types, you will see that the string concatenation operator (||) can be used to append one string value to the end of another string value. The operator table in that section shows that you use the string concatenation operator to join two CHARACTER values, two VARCHAR values, or two TEXT values. What the table does *not* show is that you can use the string concatenation operator to append an INTEGER value to the end of a VARCHAR. PostgreSQL automatically converts the INTEGER value into a string value and then applies the || operator. It's important to keep this point in mind as you read through this chapter—the operator tables don't show all possible combinations, only the combinations that don't require type conversion.

Later in this chapter, I'll give a brief description of the process that PostgreSQL uses to decide whether an operator (or function) is applicable, and if so, which values require automatic type conversion. For a detailed explanation of the process, see Chapter 5 of the *PostgreSQL User's Guide*.

Besides the operators listed in this section, PostgreSQL offers a huge selection of functions that you can call from within expressions. For a complete, up-to-date list of functions, see the *PostgreSQL User's Guide* that came with your copy of PostgreSQL.

NULL Values

No discussion of data types would be complete without talking about NULL values. NULL is not really a data type, but rather a value that can be held by *any* data type. A column (or other expression) of any given data type can hold all permissible values for that type, or it can hold no value. When a column has no value, it is said to be NULL. For example, a column of type SMALLINT can hold values between –32768 and +32767: it can also be NULL. A TIME column can hold values from midnight to noon, but a TIME value can also be NULL.

NULL values represent missing, unknown, or *not-applicable* values. For example, let's say that you want to add a membership_expiration_date to the customers table. Some customers might be permanent members—their memberships will never expire. For those customers, the membership_expiration_date is not applicable and should be set to NULL. You may also find some customers who don't want to provide you with their birth dates. The birth_date column for these customers should be NULL.

In one case, NULL means *not applicable*. In the other case, NULL means *don't know*. A NULL membership_expiration_date does not mean that you don't know the expiration date, it means that the expiration date does not apply. A NULL birth_date does not mean that the customer was never born(!); it means that the date of birth is unknown.

Of course, when you create a table, you can specify that a given column cannot hold NULL values (NOT NULL). When you do so, you aren't affecting the data type of the column; you're just saying that NULL is not a legal value for that particular column. A column that prohibits NULL values is *mandatory*; a column that allows NULL values is *optional*.

You may be wondering how a data type could hold all values legal for that type, plus one more value. The answer is that PostgreSQL knows whether a given column is NULL not by looking at the column itself, but by first examining a NULL indicator (a single bit) stored separately from the column. If the NULL indicator for a given row/column is set to TRUE, the data stored in the row/column is meaningless. This means that a data row is composed of values for each column plus an array of indicator bits—one bit for each optional column.

Character Values

There are three character (or, as they are more commonly known, string) data types offered by PostgreSQL. A string value is just that—a string of zero or more characters. The three string data types are `CHARACTER(n)`, `CHARACTER VARYING(n)`, and `TEXT`.

A value of type `CHARACTER(n)` can hold a fixed-length string of *n* characters. If you store a value that is shorter than *n*, the value is padded with spaces to increase the length to exactly *n* characters. You can abbreviate `CHARACTER(n)` to `CHAR(n)`. If you omit the "`(n)`" when you create a CHARACTER column, the length is assumed to be 1.

The `CHARACTER VARYING(n)` type defines a variable-length string of at most *n* characters. `VARCHAR(n)` is a synonym for `CHARACTER VARYING(n)`. If you omit the "`(n)`" when creating a `CHARACTER VARYING` column, you can store strings of any length in that column.

The last string type is `TEXT`. A `TEXT` column is equivalent to a `VARCHAR` column without a specified length—a `TEXT` column can store strings of any length.

Syntax for Literal Values

A *string value* is a sequence of characters surrounded by single quotes. Each of the following is a valid string value:

```
'I am a string'
'3.14159265'
''
```

The first example is obviously a string value. `'3.14159265'` is also a string value—at first glance it may look like a numeric value but that fact it is surrounded by single quotes tells you that it is really a string. The third example (`''`) is also a valid string: It is the string composed of zero characters (that is, it has a length of zero). It is important to understand that an empty string is not the same as a `NULL` value. An empty string means that you have a known value that just happens to be empty, whereas `NULL` implies that the value is unknown. Consider, for example, that you are storing an employee name in your database. You might create three columns to hold the complete name: `first_name`, `middle_name`, and `last_name`. If you find an employee whose `middle_name` is `NULL`, that should imply that the employee might have a middle name, but you don't know what it is. On the other hand, if you find an employee who has no middle name, you should store that `middle_name` as an empty string. Again, `NULL` implies that you don't have a piece of information; an empty string means that you do have the information, but it just happens to be empty.

If a string is delimited with single quotes, how do you represent a string that happens to include a single quote? There are three choices. First, you can embed a single quote within a string by entering two adjacent quotes. For example, the string "Where's my car?" could be entered as:

```
'Where''s my car?'
```

The other alternatives involve an *escape* character. An escape is a special character that tells PostgreSQL that the character (or characters) following the escape is to be interpreted as a directive instead of as a literal value. In PostgreSQL, the escape character is the backslash (`\`). When PostgreSQL sees a backslash in a string literal, it discards the backslash and interprets the following characters according to the following rules:

```
\b is the backspace character
\f is the form feed character
\r is the carriage-return character
\n is the newline character
\t is the tab character
```

`\xxx` (where *xxx* is an octal number) means the character whose ASCII value is *xxx*.

If any character, other than those mentioned, follows the backslash, it is treated as its literal value. So, if you want to include a single quote in a string, you can *escape* the quote by preceding it with a backslash:

```
'Where\'s my car?'
```

Or you can embed a single quote (or any character) within a string by escaping its ASCII value (in octal), as in

```
'Where\047s my car?'
```

To summarize, here are the three ways that you can embed a single quote within a string:

```
'It''s right where you left it'
'It\'s right where you left it'
'It\047s right where you left it'
```

Supported Operators

PostgreSQL offers a large number of string operators. One of the most basic operations is string concatenation. The concatenation operator (`||`) is used to combine two string values into a single `TEXT` value. For example, the expression

```
'This is ' || 'one string'
```

will evaluate to the value: `'This is one string'`. And the expression

```
'The current time is ' || now()
```

will evaluate to a `TEXT` value such as, `'The current time is 2002-01-01 19:45:17-04'`.

PostgreSQL also gives you a variety of ways to compare string values. All comparison operators return a `BOOLEAN` value; the result will be `TRUE`, `FALSE`, or `NULL`. A comparison operator will evaluate to `NULL` if either of the operands are `NULL`.

The equality (=) and inequality (<>) operators behave the way you would expect—two strings are equal if they contain the same characters (in the same positions); otherwise, they are not equal. You can also determine whether one string is greater than or less than another (and of course, greater than or equal to and less than or equal to).

Table 2.1[1] shows a few sample string comparisons.

Table 2.1 **Sample String Comparisons**

	Operator (θ)					
`Expression`	<	<=	=	<>	>=	>
`'string' θ 'string'`	FALSE	TRUE	TRUE	FALSE	TRUE	FALSE
`'string1' θ 'string'`	FALSE	FALSE	FALSE	TRUE	TRUE	TRUE
`'String1' θ 'string'`	TRUE	TRUE	FALSE	TRUE	FALSE	FALSE

You can also use pattern-matching operators with string values. PostgreSQL defines eight pattern-matching operators, but the names are a bit contrived and not particularly intuitive.

Table 2.2 contains a summary of the string operators.

The first set of pattern-matching operators is related to the `LIKE` keyword. `~~` is equivalent to `LIKE`. The `~~*` operator is equivalent to `ILIKE`—it is a case-insensitive version of `LIKE`. `!~~` and `!~~*` are equivalent to `NOT LIKE` and `NOT ILIKE`, respectively.

The second set of pattern-matching operators is used to match a string value against a `regular expression` (`regular expressions` are described in more detail in Chapter 1, "Introduction to PostgreSQL and SQL"). The naming convention for the `regular expression` operators is similar to that for the `LIKE` operators—`regular expression` operators are indicated with a single tilde and `LIKE` operators use two tildes. The `~` operator compares a string against a regular expression (returning `True` if the string satisfies the regular expression). `~*` compares a string against a regular expression, ignoring differences in case. The `!~` operator returns `False` if the string value matches the regular expression (and returns `True` if the string satisfies the regular expression). The `!~*` operator returns `False` if the string value matches the regular expression, ignoring differences in case, and returns `True` otherwise.

1. You might find the format of this table a bit confusing at first. In the first column, I use the 'θ' character to represent any one of the operators listed in the remaining columns. So, the first row of the table tells you that `'string' < 'string'` evaluates to `FALSE`, `'string' <= 'string'` evaluates to `TRUE`, `'string' = 'string'` evaluates to `TRUE`, and so forth. I'll use the 'θ' character throughout this chapter to indicate an operator.

Table 2.2 **String Operators**

Operator	Meaning	Case Sensitive?
`||`	Concatenation	*Not* applicable
`~`	Matches regular expression	Yes
`~~`	Matches `LIKE` expression	Yes
`~*`	Matches regular expression	No
`~~*`	Matches `LIKE` expression	No
`!~`	Does not match regular expression	Yes
`!~~`	Does not match `LIKE` expression	Yes
`!~*`	Does not match regular expression	No
`!~~*`	Does not match `LIKE` expression	No

Type Conversion Operators

There are two important operators that you should know about before we go much further—actually it's one operator, but you can write it two different ways.

The `CAST()` operator is used to convert a value from one data type to another. There are two ways to write the `CAST()` operator:

```
CAST(expression AS type)
expression::type
```

No matter which way you write it, the `expression` is converted into the specified `type`. Of course, not every value *can* be converted into every type. For example, the expression `CAST( 'abc' AS INTEGER )` results in an error (specifically, '`pg_atoi: error in "abc": can't parse "abc"`') because '`abc`' obviously can't be converted into an integer.

Most often, your casting requirements will come in either of two forms: you will need to `CAST()` a string value into some other type, or you will need to convert between related types (for example, `INTEGER` into `NUMERIC`). When you `CAST()` a string value into another data type, the string must be in the form required by the literal syntax for the target data type. Each of the following sections describes the literal syntax required by each type. When you convert between related data types, you may gain or lose precision. For example, when you convert from a fractional numeric type into an integer type, the value is rounded:

```
movies=# SELECT CAST( CAST( 12345.67 AS FLOAT8 ) AS INTEGER );
 ?column?
----------
    12346
```

Numeric Values

PostgreSQL provides a variety of numeric data types. Of the six numeric types, four are exact (`SMALLINT`, `INTEGER`, `BIGINT`, `NUMERIC(p, s)`) and two are approximate (`REAL`, `DOUBLE PRECISION`).

Three of the four exact numeric types (`SMALLINT`, `INTEGER`, and `BIGINT`) can store only integer values. The fourth (`NUMERIC(p, s)`) can accurately store any value that fits within the specified number (*p*) of digits.

The approximate numeric types, on the other hand, cannot store all values exactly. Instead, an approximate data type stores an approximation of a real number. The `DOUBLE PRECISION` type, for example, can store a total of 15 significant digits, but when you perform calculations using a `DOUBLE PRECISION` value, you can run into rounding errors. It's easy to see this problem:

```
movies=# select 2000.3 - 2000.0;
    ?column?
-------------------
 0.299999999999955
(1 row)
```

Size, Precision, and Range-of-Values

The four *exact* data types can accurately store any value within a type-specific range. The exact numeric types are described in Table 2.3.

Table 2.3 **Exact Numeric Data Types**

Type Name	Size in Bytes	Minimum Value	Maximum Value
`SMALLINT`	2	–32768	+32767
`INTEGER`	4	–2147483648	+2147483647
`BIGINT`	8	–9223372036854775808	+9223372036854775807
`NUMERIC(p,s)`	11+(*p*/2)	No limit	No limit

The `NUMERIC(p,s)` data type can accurately store any number that fits within the specified number of digits. When you create a column of type `NUMERIC(p,s)`, you can specify the total number of decimal digits (p) and the number of fractional digits (s). The total number of decimal digits is called the *precision*, and the number of fractional digits is called the *scale*.

Table 2.3 shows that there is no limit to the values that you can store in a `NUMERIC(p,s)` column. In fact, there is a limit (normally 1,000 digits), but you can adjust the limit by changing a symbol and rebuilding your PostgreSQL server from source code.

The two approximate numeric types are named `REAL` and `DOUBLE PRECISION`. Table 2.4 shows the size and range for each of these data types.

Table 2.4 **Approximate Numeric Data Types**

Type Name	Size in Bytes	Range
`REAL`	4	6 decimal digits
`DOUBLE PRECISION`	8	15 decimal digits

The numeric data types are also known by other names. For example, INT2 is synonymous with SMALLINT. Alternate names for the numeric data types are shown in Table 2.5.

Table 2.5 **Alternate Names for Numeric Data Types**

Common Name	Synonyms
SMALLINT	INT2
INTEGER	INT, INT4
BIGINT	INT8
NUMERIC(p,s)	DECIMAL(p,s)
REAL	FLOAT, FLOAT4
DOUBLE PRECISION	FLOAT8

SERIAL, BIGSERIAL and Sequences

Besides the numeric data types already described, PostgreSQL supports two "advanced" numeric types: SERIAL and BIGSERIAL. A SERIAL column is really an unsigned INTEGER whose value automatically increases (or decreases) by a defined increment as you add new rows. Likewise, a BIGSERIAL is a BIGINT that increases in value. When you create a BIGSERIAL or SERIAL column, PostgreSQL will automatically create a SEQUENCE for you. A SEQUENCE is an object that generates sequence numbers for you. I'll talk more about SEQUENCEs later in this chapter.

Syntax for Literal Values

When you need to enter a numeric literal, you must follow the formatting rules defined by PostgreSQL. There are two distinct styles for numeric literals: integer and fractional (the PostgreSQL documentation refers to fractional literals as floating-point literals).

Let's start by examining the format for fractional literals. Fractional literals can be entered in any of the following forms[2]:

```
[-]digits.[digits][E[+|-]digits]
[-][digits].digits[E[+|-]digits]
[-]digits[+|-]digits
```

Here are some examples of valid fractional literals:

```
3.14159
2.0e+15
0.2e-15
4e10
```

2. Syntax diagrams are described in detail in Chapter 1.

A numeric literal that contains only digits is considered to be an integer literal:

```
[-]digits
```

Here are some examples of valid integer literals:

```
-100
55590332
9223372036854775807
-9223372036854775808
```

A fractional literal is always considered to be of type DOUBLE PRECISION. An integer literal is considered to be of type INTEGER, unless the value is too large to fit into an integer—in which case, it will be promoted to type NUMERIC or REAL.

Supported Operators

PostgreSQL supports a variety of arithmetic, comparison, and bit-wise operators for the numeric data types.

Table 2.6 **Arithmetic Operators for Integers**

Data Types	Valid Operators (θ)
INT2 θ INT2	+ - * / %
INT2 θ INT4	+ - * / %
INT4 θ INT2	+ - * / %
INT4 θ INT4	+ - * / %
INT4 θ INT8	+ - * /
INT8 θ INT4	+ - * /
INT8 θ INT8	+ - * / %

Table 2.7 **Arithmetic Operators for Floats**

Data Types	Valid Operators (θ)
FLOAT4 θ FLOAT4	* + - /
FLOAT4 θ FLOAT8	* + - /
FLOAT8 θ FLOAT4	* + - /
FLOAT8 θ FLOAT8	* + - / ^

You use the comparison operators to determine the relationship between two numeric values. PostgreSQL supports the usual operators: <, <=, <> (not equal), =, >, and >=. You can use the comparison operators with all possible combinations of the numeric data types (some combinations will require type conversion).

PostgreSQL also provides a set of *bit-wise* operators that you can use with the integer data types. Bit-wise operators work on the individual bits that make up the two operands.

The easiest way to understand the bit-wise operators is to first convert your operands into binary notation—for example:

```
decimal 12 = binary 00001100
decimal  7 = binary 00000111
decimal 21 = binary 00010101
```

Next, let's look at each operator in turn.

The `AND` (`&`) operator compares corresponding bits in each operand and produces a `1` if both bits are `1` and a `0` otherwise—for example:

```
00001100 &     00000111 &
00010101       00010101
--------       --------
00000100       00000101
```

The `OR` (`|`) operator compares corresponding bits in each operand and produces a `1` if either (or both) bit is `1` and a `0` otherwise—for example:

```
00001100 |     00000111 |
00010101       00010101
--------       --------
00011101       00010111
```

The `XOR` (`#`) operator is similar to `OR`. `XOR` compares corresponding bits in each operand, and produces a `1` if either bit, but not both bits, is `1`, and produces a `0` otherwise.

```
00001100 #     00000111 #
00010101       00010101
--------       --------
00011001       00010010
```

PostgreSQL also provides two *bit-shift* operators.

The left-shift operator (<<) shifts the bits in the first operand *n* bits to the left, where *n* is the second operand. The leftmost *n* bits are discarded, and the rightmost *n* bits are set to 0. A left-shift by *n* bits is equivalent to multiplying the first operand by 2^n—for example:

```
00001100 << 2(decimal) = 00110000
00010101 << 3(decimal) = 10101000
```

The right-shift operator (>>) shifts the bits>)>>)> in the first operand *n* bits to the right, where *n* is the second operand. The rightmost *n* bits are discarded, and the leftmost *n* bits are set to 0. A right-shift by *n* bits is equivalent to dividing the first operand by 2^n:

```
00001100 >> 2(decimal) = 00000011
00010101 >> 3(decimal) = 00000010
```

The final bit-wise operator is the binary NOT (~). Unlike the other bit-wise operators, NOT is a unary operator—it takes a single operand. When you apply the NOT operator to a value, each bit in the original value is toggled: ones become zeroes and zeroes become ones—for example:

```
~00001100 = 11110011
~00010101 = 11101010
```

Table 2.8 shows the data types that you can use with the bit-wise operators.

Table 2.8 **Bit-Wise Operators for Integers**

<table>
<tr><th>Data Types</th><th>Valid Operators (θ)</th></tr>
<tr><td>INT2 θ INT2</td><td># & | << >></td></tr>
<tr><td>INT4 θ INT4</td><td># & | << >></td></tr>
<tr><td>INT8 θ INT4</td><td><< >></td></tr>
<tr><td>INT8 θ INT8</td><td># & |</td></tr>
</table>

Date/Time Values

PostgreSQL supports four basic temporal data types plus a couple of extensions that deal with time zone issues.

The DATE type is used to store dates. A DATE value stores a century, year, month and day.

The TIME data type is used to store a time-of-day value. A TIME value stores hours, minutes, seconds, and microseconds. It is important to note that a TIME value does not contain a time zone—if you want to include a time zone, you should use the type TIME WITH TIME ZONE. TIMETZ is a synonym for TIME WITH TIME ZONE.

The TIMESTAMP data type combines a DATE and a TIME, storing a century, year, month, day, hour, minutes, seconds, and microseconds. Unlike the TIME data type, a TIMESTAMP *does* include a time zone. If, for some reason, you want a date/time value that does not include a time zone, you can use the type TIMESTAMP WITHOUT TIME ZONE.

The last temporal data type is the INTERVAL. An INTERVAL represents a span of time. I find that the easiest way to think about INTERVAL values is to remember that an INTERVAL stores some (possibly large) number of seconds, but you can group the seconds into larger units for convenience. For example, the CAST('1 week' AS INTERVAL) is equal to CAST('604800 seconds' AS INTERVAL), which is equal to CAST('7 days' AS INTERVAL)—you can use whichever format you find easiest to work with.

Table 2.9 lists the size and range for each of the temporal data types.

Table 2.9 **Temporal Data Type Sizes and Ranges**

Data Type	Size (in bytes)	Range
`DATE`	4	`01-JAN-4713 BC` `31-DEC-32767 AD`
`TIME [ WITHOUT TIME ZONE ]`	4	`00:00:00.00` `23:59:59.99`
`TIME WITH TIME ZONE`	4	`00:00:00.00+12` `23:59:59.00-12`
`TIMESTAMP [ WITH TIME ZONE ]`	8	`14-DEC-1901` `18-JAN-2038`
`TIMESTAMP WITHOUT TIME ZONE`	8	`14-DEC-1901` `18-JAN-2038`
`INTERVAL`	12	`-178000000 YEARS` `+178000000 YEARS`

The data types that contain a time value (`TIME`, `TIME WITH TIME ZONE`, `TIMESTAMP`, `TIMESTAMP WITH TIME ZONE`, and `INTERVAL`) have microsecond precision. The `DATE` data type has a precision of one day.

Syntax for Literal Values

I covered date literal syntax pretty thoroughly in Chapter 1; see the section titled "Working with Date Values."

You may recall from Chapter 1 that date values can be entered in many formats, and you have to tell PostgreSQL how to interpret ambiguous values. Fortunately, the syntax for `TIME`, `TIMESTAMP`, and `INTERVAL` values is much more straightforward.

A `TIME` value stores hours, minutes, seconds, and microseconds. The syntax for a `TIME` literal is

```
hh:mm[:ss[.μμμ ]][AM|PM]
```

where *hh* specifies the hour, *mm* specifies the number of minutes past the hour, *ss* specifies the number of seconds, and μμμ specifies the number of microseconds. If you include an `AM` or `PM` indicator, the *hh* component must be less than or equal to 12; otherwise, the hour can range from 0 to 24.

Entering a `TIME WITH TIME ZONE` value is a bit more complex. A `TIME WITH TIME ZONE` value is a `TIME` value, plus a time zone. The time zone component can be specified in two ways. First, you can include an offset (in minutes and hours) from UTC:

```
hh:mm[:ss[.μμμ ]][AM|PM][{+|-}HH[:MM]]
```

where *HH* is the number of hours and *MM* is the number of minutes distant from UTC. Negative values are considered to be west of the prime meridian, and positive values are east of the prime meridian.

You can also use a standard time zone abbreviation (such as `UTC`, `PDT`, or `EST`) to specify the time zone:

`hh:mm[:ss[.µµµ ]] [AM|PM] [ZZZ]`

Table 2.10 shows all the time zone abbreviations accepted by PostgreSQL version 7.1.3.

Table 2.10 **PostgreSQL Time Zone Names**

Names	Offset	Description
`IDLW`	–12:00	International Date Line West
`NT`	–11:00	Nome Time
`AHST`		Alaska/Hawaii Standard Time
`CAT`	–10:00	Central Alaska Time
`HST`		Hawaii Standard Time
`YST`		Yukon Standard Time
`HDT`	–09:00	Alaska/Hawaii Daylight Time
`AKST`		Alaska Standard Time
`YDT`		Yukon Daylight Time
`PST`	–08:00	Pacific Standard Time
`AKDT`		Alaska Daylight Time
`MST`		Mountain Standard Time
`PDT`	–07:00	Pacific Daylight Time
`CST`	–06:00	Central Standard Time
`MDT`		Mountain Daylight Time
`EST`		Eastern Standard Time
`CDT`	–05:00	Central Daylight Time
`ACT`		Atlantic/Porto Acre Standard Time
`AST`		Atlantic Standard Time (Canada)
`EDT`	–04:00	Eastern Daylight Time
`ACST`		Atlantic/Porto Acre Summer Time
`NFT, NST`	–03:30	Newfoundland Standard Time
`ADT`	–03:00	Atlantic Daylight Time
`AWT`		Atlantic War Time
`NDT`	–02:30	Newfoundland Daylight Time
`SET`	–01:00	Seychelles Time
`WAT`		West Africa Time
`GMT`		Greenwich Mean Time
`UCT`		Universal Time Coordinated

Table 2.10 **Continued**

Names	Offset	Description
UT	+00:00	Universal Time
WET		Western Europe Time
ZULU, Z		Zulu
BST		British Summer Time
CET		Central European Time
DNT		Dansk Normal Time
FST		French Summer Time
MET	+01:00	Middle Europe Time
MEWT		Middle Europe Winter Time
MEZ		Middle Europe Zone
NOR		Norway Standard Time
WETDST		Western Europe Daylight Savings Time
SWT		Swedish Winter Time
EET		Eastern Europe (USSR Zone 1)
IST		Israel
SST		Swedish Summer Time
METDST		Middle Europe Daylight Time
MEST	+02:00	Middle Europe Summer Time
FWT		French Winter Time
CETDST		Central European Daylight Savings Time
CEST		Central European Savings Time
BDST		British Double Standard Time
BT		Baghdad Time
HMT	+03:00	Hellas Mediterranean Time
EETDST		Eastern Europe Daylight Savings Time
IT	+03:30	Iran Time
JT	+07:30	Java Time
WAST	+07:00	West Australian Standard Time
AWST		West Australian Standard Time
CCT	+08:00	China Coast Time
WST		West Australian Standard Time
WADT		West Australian Daylight Time
MT	+08:30	Moluccas Time
JST		Japan Standard Time(USSR Zone 8)
KST	+09:00	Korea Standard Time
WDT		West Australian Daylight Time
AWSST		Australia Western Summer Standard Time
ACST		Australia Central Standard Time

Table 2.10 **Continued**

Names	Offset	Description
CAST	+09:30	Australia Central Standard Time
SAST		South Australian Standard Time
AEST		Australia Eastern Standard Time
EAST	+10:00	Australia Eastern Standard Time
GST		Guam Standard Time (USSR Zone 9)
LIGT		Melbourne
SADT	+10:30	South Australian Daylight Time
CADT		Central Australia Daylight Savings Time
ACSST		Central Australia Summer Standard Time
AESST	+11:00	Australia Eastern Summer Standard Time
IDLE		International Date Line East
NZST	+12:00	New Zealand Standard Time
NZT		New Zealand Time
NZDT	+13:00	New Zealand Daylight Time

I mentioned earlier in this section that an `INTERVAL` value represents a time span. I also mentioned than an `INTERVAL` stores some number of seconds. The syntax for an `INTERVAL` literal allows you to specify the number of seconds in a variety of units.

The format of an `INTERVAL` value is

```
quantity unit [quantity unit ...] [AGO]
```

The *`unit`* component specifies a number of seconds, as shown in Table 2.11. The *`quantity`* component acts as a multiplier (and may be fractional). If you have multiple *`quantity unit`* groups, they are all added together. The optional phrase `AGO` will cause the `INTERVAL` to be negative.

Table 2.11 `INTERVAL` **Units**

Description	Seconds	Unit Names
Microsecond[3]	.000001	us, usec, usecs, useconds, microsecon, microsecond
Millisecond[3]	.001	ms, msecs, mseconds, millisecon, millisecond
Second	1	s, sec, secs, second, seconds
Minute	60	m, min, mins, minute, minutes
Hour	3600	h, hr, hrs, hours
Day	86400	d, day, days
Week	604800	w, week, weeks
Month (30 days)	2592000	mon, mons, month, months

Table 2.11 **Continued**

Description	Seconds	Unit Names
Year	31557600	`y, yr, yrs, year, years`
Decade	315576000	`dec, decs, decade, decades`
Century	3155760000	`c, cent, century, centuries`
Millennium	31557600000	`mil, mils, millennia, millennium`

[3] `millisecond` and `microsecond` can be used only in combination with another date/time component. For example, `CAST( '1 SECOND 5000 MSEC' AS INTERVAL )` results in an interval of six seconds.

You can use the `EXTRACT( EPOCH FROM` *`interval`* `)` function to convert an `INTERVAL` into a number of seconds. A few sample `INTERVAL` values are shown in Table 2.12. The Display column shows how PostgreSQL would format the Input Value for display. The `EPOCH` column shows the value that would be returned by extracting the `EPOCH` from the Input Value.

Table 2.12 **Sample `INTERVAL` Values**

Input Value	Display	EPOCH
`.5 minutes`	`00:00:30`	30
`22 seconds 1 msec`	`00:00:22.00`	22.001
`22.001 seconds`	`00:00:22.00`	22.001
`10 centuries 2 decades`	`1020 years`	32188752000
`1 week 2 days 3.5 msec`	`9 days 00:00:00.00`	777600.0035

Supported Operators

There are two types of operators that you can use with temporal values: arithmetic operators (addition and subtraction) and comparison operators.

You can add an `INT4`, a `TIME`, or a `TIMETZ` to a `DATE`. When you add an `INT4`, you are adding a number of days. Adding a `TIME` or `TIMETZ` to a `DATE` results in a `TIMESTAMP`. Table 2.13 lists the valid data type and operator combinations for temporal data types. The last column in Table 2.14 shows the data type of the resulting value.

Table 2.13 **Arithmetic Date/Time Operators**

Data Types	Valid Operators (θ)	Result Type
`DATE θ DATE`	`-`	`INTEGER`
`DATE θ TIME`	`+`	`TIMESTAMP`
`DATE θ TIMETZ`	`+`	`TIMESTAMP WITH TIMEZONE`
`DATE θ INT4`	`+ -`	`DATE`

Table 2.13 **Continued**

Data Types	Valid Operators (θ)	Result Type
TIME θ DATE	+	TIMESTAMP
TIME θ INTERVAL	+ -	TIME
TIMETZ θ DATE	+	TIMESTAMP WITH TIMEZONE
TIMETZ θ INTERVAL	+ -	TIMETZ
TIMESTAMP θ TIMESTAMP	-	INTERVAL
TIMESTAMP θ INTERVAL	+ -	TIMESTAMP WITH TIMEZONE
INTERVAL θ TIME	+	TIME WITHOUT TIMEZONE

Table 2.14 shows how each of the arithmetic operators behave when applied to date/time values.

Table 2.14 **Arithmetic Date/Time Operator Examples**

Example	Result
'23-JAN-2003'::DATE - '23-JAN-2002'::DATE	365
'23-JAN-2003'::DATE + '2:35 PM'::TIME	2003-01-23 14:35:00
'23-JAN-2003'::DATE + '2:35 PM GMT'::TIMETZ	2003-01-23 09:35:00-05
'23-JAN-2003'::DATE + 2::INT4	2003-01-25
'2:35 PM'::TIME + '23-JAN-2003'::DATE	2003-01-23 14:35:00
'2:35 PM'::TIME + '2 hours 5 minutes'::INTERVAL	16:40:00
'2:35 PM EST'::TIMETZ + '23-JAN-2003'::DATE	2003-01-23 14:35:00-05
'2:35 PM EST'::TIMETZ + '2 hours 5 minutes'::INTERVAL	16:40:00-05
'23-JAN-2003 2:35 PM EST'::TIMESTAMP - '23-JAN-2002 1:00 PM EST'::TIMESTAMP	365 days 01:35

Table 2.14 **Continued**

Example	Result

`'23-JAN-2003 2:35 PM EST'::TIMESTAMP`
`+`
`'3 days 2 hours 5 minutes'::INTERVAL`
	`2003-01-26 16:40:00-05`

`'2 hours 5 minutes'::INTERVAL`
`+`
`'2:34 PM'::TIME`
	`16:39:00`

Using the temporal comparison operators, you can determine the relationship between to date/time values. For purposes of comparison, an earlier date/time value is considered to be *less than* a later date/time value.

Table 2.15 shows how you can combine the various temporal types with comparison operators.

Table 2.15 **Date/Time Comparison Operators**

Data Types	Valid Operators (θ)
`date θ date`	`< <= <> = >= >`
`time θ time`	`< <= <> = >= >`
`timetz θ timetz`	`< <= <> = >= >`
`timestamp θ timestamp`	`< <= <> = >= >`

Boolean (Logical) Values

PostgreSQL supports a single Boolean (or logical) data type: `BOOLEAN` (`BOOLEAN` can be abbreviated as `BOOL`).

Size and Valid Values

A `BOOLEAN` can hold the values `TRUE`, `FALSE`, or `NULL`, and consumes a single byte of storage.

Syntax for Literal Values

Table 2.16 shows the alternate spellings for `BOOLEAN` literals.

Table 2.16 **BOOLEAN Literal Syntax**

Common Name	Synonyms
`TRUE`	`true, 't', 'y', 'yes', 1`
`FALSE`	`false, 'f', 'n', 'no', 0`

Supported Operators

The only operators supported for the BOOLEAN data type are the logical operators shown in Table 2.17:

Table 2.17 **Logical Operators for BOOLEAN**

Data Types	Valid Operators (θ)
BOOLEAN θ BOOLEAN	AND OR NOT

I covered the AND, OR, and NOT operators in Chapter 1. For a complete definition of these operators, see Tables 1.3, 1.4, and 1.5.

Geometric Data Types

PostgreSQL supports six data types that represent two-dimensional geometric objects. The most basic geometric data type is the POINT—as you might expect, a POINT represents a point within a two-dimensional plane.

A POINT is composed of an x-coordinate and a y-coordinate—each coordinate is a DOUBLE PRECISION number.

The LSEG data type represents a two-dimensional line segment. When you create a LSEG value, you specify two points—the starting POINT and the ending POINT.

A BOX value is used to define a rectangle—the two points that define a box specify opposite corners.

A PATH is a collection of an arbitrary number of POINTs that are connected. A PATH can specify either a closed path or an open path. In a closed path, the beginning and ending points are considered to be connected, and in an open path, the first and last points are not connected. PostgreSQL provides two functions to force a PATH to be either open or closed: POPEN() and PCLOSE(). You can also specify whether a PATH is open or closed using special literal syntax (described later).

A POLYGON is similar to a closed PATH. The difference between the two types is in the supporting functions.

A center POINT and a (DOUBLE PRECISION) floating-point radius represent a CIRCLE.

Table 2.18 summarizes the geometric data types.

Table 2.18 **Geometric Data Types**

Type	Meaning	Defined By
POINT	2D point on a plane	x- and y-coordinates
LSEG	Line segment	Two points
BOX	Rectangle	Two points
PATH	Open or closed path	*n* points
POLYGON	Polygon	*n* points
CIRCLE	Circle	Center point and radius

Syntax for Literal Values

When you enter a value for geometric data type, keep in mind that you are working with a list of two-dimensional points (except in the case of a `CIRCLE`, where you are working with a `POINT` and a radius).

A single `POINT` can be entered in either of the following two forms:

```
'( x, y )'
' x, y '
```

The `LSEG` and `BOX` types are constructed from a pair of `POINTs`. You can enter a pair of `POINTs` in any of the following formats:

```
'(( x1, y1 ), ( x2, y2 ))'
'( x1, y1 ), ( x2, y2 )'
'x1, y1, x2, y2'
```

The `PATH` and `POLYGON` types are constructed from a list of one or more `POINTs`. Any of the following forms is acceptable for a `PATH` or `POLYGON` literal:

```
'(( x1, y1 ), ..., ( xn, yn ))'
'( x1, y1 ), ...,  ( xn, yn )'
'( x1, y1, ..., xn, yn )'
'x1, y1, ..., xn, yn'
```

You can also use the syntax `'[( x1, y1 ), ..., ( xn, yn )]'` to enter a `PATH` literal: A `PATH` entered in this form is considered to be an open `PATH`.

A `CIRCLE` is described by a central point and a floating point radius. You can enter a `CIRCLE` in any of the following forms:

```
'< ( x, y ), r >'
'(( x, y ), r )'
'( x, y ), r'
'x, y, r'
```

Notice that the surrounding single quotes are required around all geometric literals—in other words, geometric literals are entered as string literals. If you want to create a geometric value from individual components, you will have to use a geometric conversion function. For example, if you want to create a `POINT` value from the results of some computation, you would use:

```
POINT( 4, 3*height )
```

The `POINT( DOUBLE PRECISION x, DOUBLE PRECISION y )` function creates a `POINT` value from two `DOUBLE PRECISION` values. There are similar functions that you can use to create any geometric type starting from individual components. Table 2.19 lists the conversion functions for geometric types.

Table 2.19 **Type Conversion Operators for the Geometric Data Types**

Result Type	Meaning
POINT	POINT(DOUBLE PRECISION *x*, DOUBLE PRECISION *y*)
LSEG	LSEG(POINT p1, POINT p2)
BOX	BOX(POINT p1, POINT p2)
PATH	PATH(POLYGON poly)
POLYGON	POLYGON(PATH path)
	POLYGON(BOX b) yields a 12-point polygon
	POLYGON(CIRCLE c) yields a 12-point polygon
	POLYGON(INTEGER n, CIRCLE c) yields an *n* point polygon
CIRCLE	CIRCLE(BOX *b*)
	CIRCLE(POINT *radius*, DOUBLE PRECISION *point*)

Sizes and Valid Values

Table 2.20 lists the size of each geometric data type.

Table 2.20 **Geographic Data Type Storage Requirements**

Type	Size (in bytes)
POINT	16 (2 * sizeof DOUBLE PRECISION)
LSEG	32 (2 * sizeof POINT)
BOX	32 (2 * sizeof POINT)
PATH	4+(32*number of points)[4]
POLYGON	4+(32*number of points)[4]
CIRCLE	24 (sizeof POINT + sizeof DOUBLE PRECISION)

[4] The size of a PATH or POLYGON is equal to 4 + (sizeof LSEG * number of segments).

Supported Operators

PostgreSQL features a large collection of operators that work with the geometric data types. I've divided the geometric operators into two broad categories (transformation and proximity) to make it a little easier to talk about them.

Using the transformation operators, you can translate, rotate, and scale geometric objects. The + and - operators translate a geometric object to a new location. Consider Figure 2.1, which shows a BOX defined as BOX(POINT(3,5), POINT(1,2)).

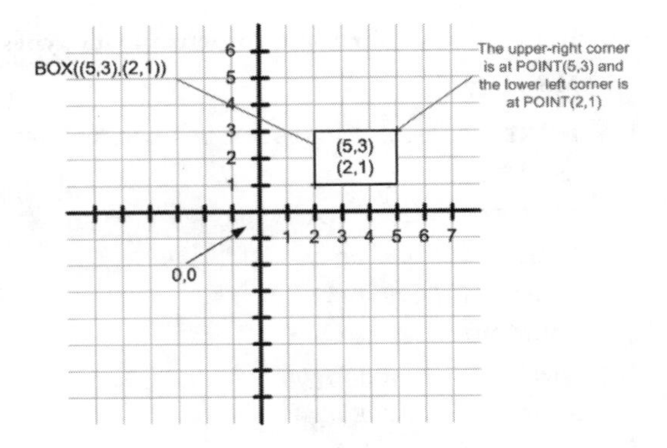

Figure 2.1 BOX(POINT(3,5), POINT(1,2)).

If you use the + operator to add the `POINT( 2,1 )` to this `BOX`, you end up with the object shown in Figure 2.2.

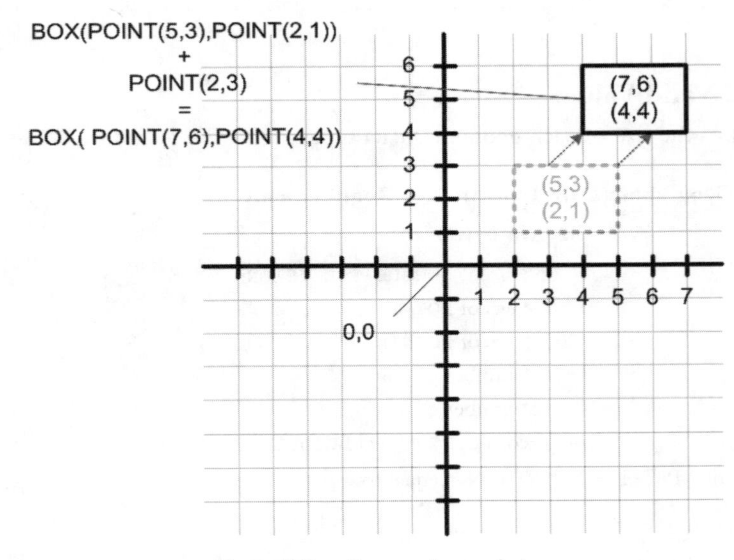

Figure 2.2 Geometric translation.

You can see that the x-coordinate of the `POINT` is added to each of the x-coordinates in the `BOX`, and the y-coordinate of the `POINT` is added to the y-coordinates in the `BOX`. The `-` operator works in a similar fashion: the x-coordinate of the `POINT` is subtracted from the x-coordinates of the `BOX`, and the y-coordinate of the `POINT` is subtracted from each y-coordinate in the `BOX`.

Using the + and - operators, you can move a POINT, BOX, PATH, or CIRCLE to a new location. In each case, the *x*-coordinate in the second operand (a POINT), is added or subtracted from each *x*-coordinate in the first operand, and the *y*-coordinate in the second operand is added or subtracted from each *y*-coordinate in the first operand.

The multiplication and division operators (* and /) are used to scale and rotate. The multiplication and division operators treat the operands as points in the complex plane. Let's look at some examples.

Figure 2.3 shows the result of multiplying BOX(POINT(3,2),POINT(1,1)) by POINT(2,0).

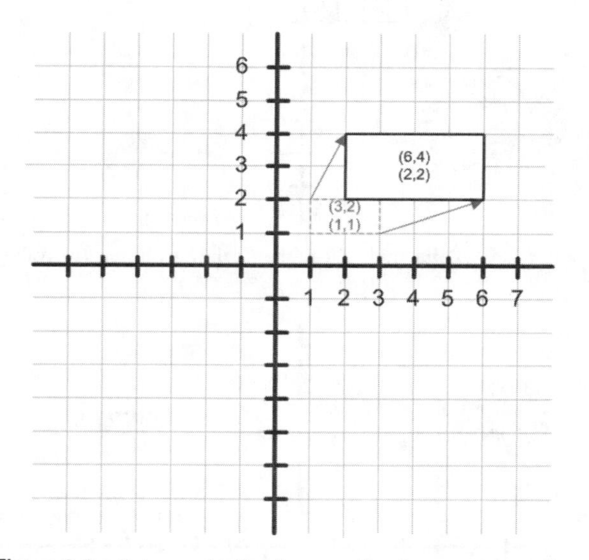

Figure 2.3 Point multiplication—scaling by a positive value.

You can see that each coordinate in the original box is multiplied by the *x*-coordinate of the point, resulting in BOX(POINT(6,4),POINT(2,2)). If you had multiplied the box by POINT(0.5,0), you would have ended up with BOX(POINT(1.5,1),POINT(0.5,0.5)). So the effect of multiplying an object by POINT(*x*,0) is that each coordinate in the object moves away from the origin by a factor *x*. If *x* is negative, the coordinates move to the other side of the origin, as shown in Figure 2.4.

You can see that the *x*-coordinate controls scaling. The y-coordinate controls rotation. When you multiply any given geometric object by POINT(0,*y*), each point in the object is rotated around the origin. When *y* is equal to 1, each point is rotated counterclockwise by 90° about the origin. When *y* is equal to –1, each point is rotated –90° about the origin (or 270°). When you rotate a point without scaling, the length of the line segment drawn between the point and origin remains constant, as shown in Figure 2.5.

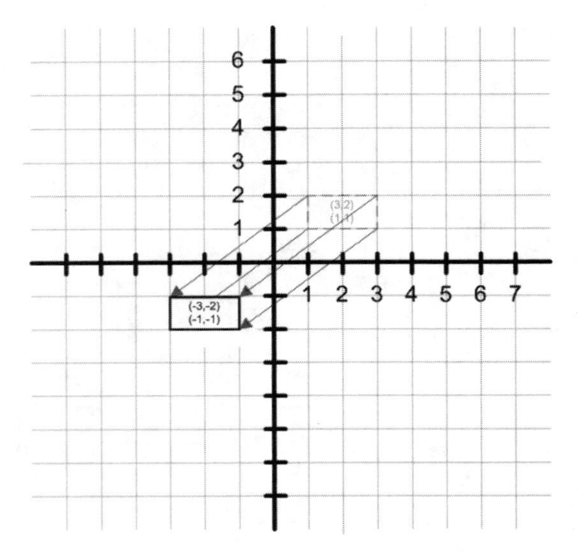

Figure 2.4 Point multiplication—scaling by a negative value.

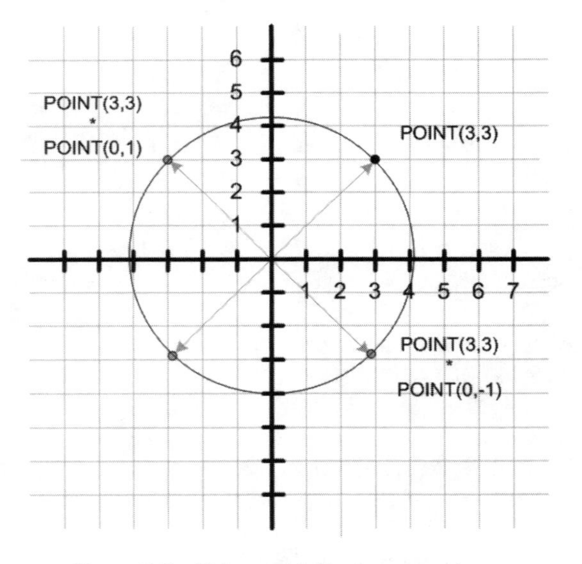

Figure 2.5 Point multiplication—rotation.

You can combine rotation and scaling into the same operation by specifying non-zero values for both the x- and y-coordinates. For more information on using complex numbers to represent geometric points, see `http://www.clarku.edu/~djoyce/complex`.

Table 2.21 shows the valid combinations for geometric types and geometric operators.

Table 2.21 **Transformation Operators for the Geometric Types**

Data Types	Valid Operators (θ)
POINT θ POINT	* + - /
BOX θ POINT	* + - /
PATH θ POINT	* + - /
CIRCLE θ POINT	* + - /

The proximity operators allow you to determine the spatial relationships between two geometric objects.

First, let's look at the three containment operators. The ~ operator evaluates to TRUE if the left operand contains the right operand. The @ operator evaluates to TRUE if the left operand is contained within the right operand. The ~= returns TRUE if the left operand is the same as the right operand—two geographic objects are considered identical if the points that define the objects are identical (two circles are considered identical if the radii and center points are the same).

The next two operators are used to determine the distance between two geometric objects.

The ## operator returns the closest point between two objects. You can use the ## operator with the following operand types shown in Table 2.22.

Table 2.22 **Closest-Point Operators**

Operator	Description
LSEG$_a$ ## BOX$_b$	Returns the point in BOX$_b$ that is closest to LSEG$_a$
LSEG$_a$ ## LSEG$_b$	Returns the point in LSEG$_b$ that is closest to LSEG$_a$
POINT$_a$ ## BOX$_b$	Returns the point in BOX$_b$ that is closest to POINT$_a$
POINT$_a$ ## LSEG$_b$	Returns the point in LSEG$_b$ that is closest to POINT$_a$

The distance (<->) operator returns (as a DOUBLE PRECISION number) the distance between two geometric objects. You can use the distance operator with the operand types in Table 2.23.

Table 2.23 **Distance Operators**

Operator	Description (or Formula)
BOX$_a$ <-> BOX$_b$	(@@ BOX$_a$) <-> (@@ BOX$_b$)
CIRCLE$_a$ <-> CIRCLE$_b$	(@@ CIRCLE$_a$) <-> (@@ CIRCLE$_b$) - (radius$_a$ + radius$_b$)

Table 2.23 **Continued**

Operator	Description (or Formula)
$CIRCLE_a$ <-> $POLYGON_b$	0 if any point in $POLYGON_b$ is inside $CIRCLE_a$ otherwise, distance between center of $CIRCLE_a$ and closest point in $POLYGON_b$
$LSEG_a$ <-> BOX_b	(LSEG ## BOX) <-> (LSEG ## (LSEG ## BOX))
$LSEG_a$ <-> $LSEG_b$	Distance between closest points (0 if $LSEG_a$ intersects $LSEG_b$)
$PATH_a$ <-> $PATH_b$	Distance between closest points
$POINT_a$ <-> BOX_b	$POINT_a$ <-> ($POINT_a$ ## BOX_b)
$POINT_a$ <-> $CIRCLE_b$	$POINT_a$ <-> ((@@ $CIRCLE_b$) - $CIRCLE_b$ radius)
$POINT_a$ <-> $LSEG_b$	$POINT_a$ <-> ($POINT_a$ ## $LSEG_b$)
$POINT_a$ <-> $PATH_b$	Distance between $POINT_a$ and closest points
$POINT_a$ <-> $POINT_b$	SQRT(($POINT_a$.x - $POINT_b$.x)^2 + ($POINT_a$.y - $POINT_b$.y)^2)

Next, you can determine the spatial relationships between two objects using the left-of (<<), right-of(>>), below (<^), and above (>^) operators.

There are three overlap operators. && evaluates to TRUE if the left operand overlaps the right operand. The &> operator evaluates to TRUE if the leftmost point in the first operand is left of the rightmost point in the second operand. The &< evaluates to TRUE if the rightmost point in the first operand is right of the leftmost point in the second operand.

The intersection operator (#)returns the intersecting points of two objects. You can find the intersection of two BOXes, or the intersection of two LSEGs. The intersection of two BOXes evaluates to a BOX. The intersection of two LSEGs evaluates to a single POINT.

Finally, the ?# operator evaluates to TRUE if the first operand intersects with or overlaps the second operand.

The final set of geometric operators determines the relationship between a line segment and an axis, or the relationship between two line segments.

The ?- operator evaluates to TRUE if the given line segment is horizontal (that is, parallel to the x-axis). The ?| operator evaluates to TRUE if the given line segment is vertical (that is, parallel to the y-axis). When you use the ?- and ?| operators with a line segment, they function as prefix unary operators. You can also use the ?- and ?| operators as infix binary operators (meaning that the operator appears between two values), in which case they operate as if you specified two points on a line segment.

The ?-| operator evaluates to TRUE if the two operands are perpendicular. The ?|| operator evaluates to TRUE if the two operands are parallel. The perpendicular and parallel operators can be used only with values of type LSEG.

The final geometric operator (@@) returns the center point of an LSEG, PATH, BOX, POLYGON, or CIRCLE.

Table 2.24 **Proximity Operators for the Geometric Types**

Data Types	Valid Operators (θ)
POINT θ POINT	<-> << <^ >> >^ ?- ?| @
POINT θ LSEG	## <-> @
POINT θ BOX	## <-> @
POINT θ PATH	<-> @
POINT θ POLYGON	@
POINT θ CIRCLE	<-> @
LSEG θ LSEG	# ## < <-> <= <> = > >= ?# ?-| ?||
LSEG θ BOX	## <-> ?# @
BOX θ POINT	* + - /
BOX θ BOX	# && &< &> < <-> << <= <^ = > >= >> >^ ?# @ ~ ~=
PATH θ POINT	* + - / ~
PATH θ PATH	+ < <-> <= = > >= ?#
POLYGON θ POINT	~
POLYGON θ POLYGON	&& &< &> <-> >> << @ ~ ~=
CIRCLE θ POINT	* + - / ~
CIRCLE θ POLYGON	<->
CIRCLE θ CIRCLE	&& &< &> > <-> << <= <> <^ = > >= >> >^ @ ~ ~=

Table 2.25 summarizes the names of the proximity operators for geometric types.

Table 2.25 **Geometric Proximity Operator Names**

Data Types	Valid Operators (θ)
#	Intersection or point count(for polygons)
##	Point of closest proximity
<->	Distance Between
<<	Left of?
>>	Right of?
<^	Below?
>^	Above?
&&	Overlaps
&>	Overlaps to left
&<	Overlaps to right
?#	Intersects or overlaps
@	Contained in
~	Contains
~=	Same as

Table 2.25 **Continued**

Data Types	Valid Operators (θ)
?-	Horizontal
?|	Vertical
?-|	Perpendicular
?||	Parallel
@@	Center

Object IDs (OID)

An OID is a 32-bit, positive whole number. Every row[5] in a PostgreSQL database contains a unique identifier[6]—the object ID (or OID). Normally, the OID column is hidden. You can see the OID for a row by including the OID column in a the target list of a SELECT statement:

```
movies=# SELECT OID, * FROM customers;
  oid  | id |    customer_name     |  phone   | birth_date | balance
-------+----+----------------------+----------+------------+---------
 38333 |  1 | Jones, Henry         | 555-1212 | 1970-10-10 |    0.00
 38334 |  2 | Rubin, William       | 555-2211 | 1972-07-10 |   15.00
 38335 |  3 | Panky, Henry         | 555-1221 | 1968-01-21 |    0.00
 38386 |  5 | Funkmaster, Freddy   | 555-FUNK |            |
 38392 |  7 | Gull, Jonathon LC    | 555-1111 | 1984-02-05 |
 38393 |  8 | Grumby, Jonas        | 555-2222 | 1984-02-21 |
 38336 |  4 | Wonderland, Alice N. | 555-1122 | 1969-03-05 |    3.00
```

You can create a column of type OID if you want to explicitly refer to another object (usually a row in another table). Think back to the rentals table that you developed in Chapter 1. Each row in the rentals table contains a tape_id, a customer_id, and a rental date. The rentals table currently looks like this:

```
movies=# \d rentals
            Table "rentals"
  Attribute   |     Type     | Modifier
--------------+--------------+----------
 tape_id      | character(8) | not null
 rental_date  | date         | not null
 customer_id  | integer      | not null
```

5. By default, all tables are created such that every row contains an OID. You can omit the object IDs using the WITHOUT OIDS clause of the CREATE TABLE command.

6. The PostgreSQL documentation warns that object IDs are currently unique within a database cluster; but in a future release, an OID may be unique only within a single table.

```
movies=# SELECT * FROM rentals;
 tape_id  | rental_date | customer_id
----------+-------------+-------------
 AB-12345 | 2001-11-25  |           1
 AB-67472 | 2001-11-25  |           3
 OW-41221 | 2001-11-25  |           1
 MC-68873 | 2001-11-20  |           3
 KJ-03335 | 2001-11-26  |           8
(5 rows)
```

Each value in the `tape_id` column refers to a row in the `tapes` table. Each value in the `customer_id` column refers to a row in the `customers` table. Rather than storing the `tape_id` and `customer_id` in the `rentals` table, you could store `OID`s for the corresponding rows. The following `CREATE TABLE ... AS` command creates a new table, `rentals2`, that is equivalent to the original `rentals` table:

```
movies=# CREATE TABLE rentals2 AS
movies-#   SELECT
movies-#     t.oid AS tape_oid, c.oid AS customer_oid, r.rental_date
movies-#   FROM
movies-#     tapes t, customers c, rentals r
movies-#   WHERE
movies-#     t.tape_id = r.tape_id
movies-#        AND
movies-#     c.id = r.customer_id;
```

This statement (conceptually) works as follows. First, you retrieve a row from the `rentals` table. Next, you use the `rentals.customer_id` column to retrieve the matching `customers` row and the `rentals.tape_id` column to retrieve the matching `tapes` row. Finally, you store the `OID` of the `customers` row and the `OID` of the `tapes` row (and the `rental_date`) in a new `rentals2` row.

Now, when you `SELECT` from the rentals2 table, you will see the object IDs for the `customers` row and the `tapes` row:

```
movies=# SELECT * FROM rentals2;
 tape_oid | customer_oid | rental_date
----------+--------------+-------------
    38337 |        38333 | 2001-11-25
    38338 |        38335 | 2001-11-25
    38394 |        38393 | 2001-11-26
    38339 |        38335 | 2001-11-20
    38340 |        38333 | 2001-11-25
```

You can re-create the data in the original table by joining the corresponding customers and tapes records, based on their respective OIDs:

```
movies=# SELECT t.tape_id, r.rental_date, c.id
movies-#   FROM
movies-#     tapes t, rentals2 r, customers c
movies-#   WHERE
movies-#     t.oid = r.tape_oid AND
movies-#     c.oid = r.customer_oid
movies-#   ORDER BY t.tape_id;

tape_id  | rental_date | id
----------+-------------+----
 AB-12345 | 2001-11-25  |  1
 AB-67472 | 2001-11-25  |  3
 KJ-03335 | 2001-11-26  |  8
 MC-68873 | 2001-11-20  |  3
 OW-41221 | 2001-11-25  |  1
(5 rows)
```

Here are a couple of warnings about using OIDs in your own tables.

The first concern has to do with backups. The standard tool for performing a backup of a PostgreSQL database is pg_dump. By default, pg_dump will *not* archive OIDs. This means that if you back up a table that contains an OID column (referring to another object) and then restore that table from the archive, the relationships between objects will be lost, unless you remembered to tell pg_dump to archive OIDs. This happens because when you restore a row from the archive, it might be assigned a *different* OID.

The second thing you should consider when using OIDs is that they offer no real performance advantages. If you are coming from an Oracle or Sybase environment, you might be thinking that an OID sounds an awful lot like a ROWID. It's true that an OID and a ROWID provide a unique identifier for a row, but that is where the similarity ends. In an Oracle environment, you can use a ROWID as the fastest possible way to get to a specific row. A ROWID encodes the location (on disk) of the row that it belongs to—when you retrieve a row by ROWID, you can bypass any index[7] searches and go straight to the data. An OID is just a 32-bit number—you can create an index on the OID column, but you could also create an index on any other (unique) column to achieve the same results. In fact, the only time that it might make sense to use an OID to identify a row is when the primary key[7] for a table is very long.

Finally, I should point out that OIDs can wrap. In an active database cluster, it's certainly possible that 4 billion objects can be created. That doesn't mean that all 4 billion objects

7. Don't be too concerned if you aren't familiar with the concept of indexes or primary keys, I'll cover each of those topics a bit later.

have to exist at the same time, just that 4 billion OIDs have been created since the cluster was created. When the OID generator wraps, you end up with duplicate values. This may sound a little far-fetched, but it does happen and it is not easy to recover from. There really is no good reason to use an OID as a primary key—use SERIAL (or BIGSERIAL) instead.

Syntax for Literal Values

The format in which you enter literal OID values is the same that you would use for unsigned INTEGER values. An OID literal is simply a sequence of decimal digits.

Size and Valid Values

As I mentioned earlier, an OID is an unsigned 32-bit (4-byte) integer. An OID column can hold values between 0 and 4294967295. The value 0 represents an invalid OID.

Supported Operators

You can compare two OID values, and you can compare an OID value against an INTEGER value. Table 2.26 shows which operators you can use with the OID data type.

Table 2.26 **OID Operators**

Data Types	Valid Operators
OID θ OID	< <= <> = >= >
OID θ INT4	< <= <> = >= >
INT4 θ OID	< <= <> = >= >

BLOBs

Most database systems provide a data type that can store raw data, and PostgreSQL is no exception. I use the term *raw data* to mean that the database doesn't understand the structure or meaning of a value. In contrast, PostgreSQL *does* understand the structure and meaning of other data types. For example, when you define an INTEGER column, PostgreSQL knows that the bytes of data that you place into that column are supposed to represent an integer value. PostgreSQL knows what an integer is—it can add integers, multiply them, convert them to and from string form, and so on. Raw data, on the other hand, is just a collection of bits—PostgreSQL can't infer any meaning in the data.

PostgreSQL offers the type BYTEA for storing raw data. A BYTEA column can theoretically hold values of any length, but it appears that the maximum length is 1GB.

The size of a BYTEA value is 4 bytes plus the actual number of bytes in the value.

Syntax for Literal Values

Entering a `BYTEA` value can be a little tricky. A `BYTEA` literal is entered as a string literal: It is just a string of characters enclosed within single quotes. Given that, how do you enter a `BYTEA` value that includes a single quote? If you look back to the discussion of string literal values (earlier in this chapter), you'll see that you can include *special characters* in a string value by escaping them. In particular, a single quote can by escaped in one of three ways:

- Double up the single quotes (`'This is a single quote'''`)
- Precede the single quote with a backslash (`'This is a single quote \''`)
- Include the octal value of the character instead (`'This is a single quote \047'`)

There are two other characters that you must escape when entering `BYTEA` literals. A byte whose value is zero (not the character `0`, but the null byte) must be escaped, and the backslash character must be escaped. You can escape any character using the "`\\`*ddd*" form (where *ddd* is an octal number). You can escape any printable character using the "`\\`*c*" form. So, if you want to store a `BYTEA` value that includes a zero byte, you could enter it like this:

```
'This is a zero byte \\000'
```

If you want to store a BYTEA value that includes a backslash, you can enter it in either of the following forms:

```
'This is a backslash \\\\'
'This is also a backslash \\134'
```

If you compare these rules to the rules for quoting string literals, you'll notice that `BYTEA` literals require twice as many backslash characters. This is a quirk of the design of the PostgreSQL parser. `BYTEA` literals are processed by two different parsers. The main PostgreSQL parser sees a `BYTEA` literal as a string literal (gobbling up the first set of backslash characters). Then, the `BYTEA` parser processes the result, gobbling up the second set of backslash characters.

So, if you have a `BYTEA` value such as `This is a backslash \`, you quote it as `'This is a backslash \\\\'`. After the string parser processes this string, it has been turned into `'This is a backslash \\'`. The `BYTEA` parser finally transforms this into `This is a backslash \`.

Supported Operators

PostgreSQL offers a single `BYTEA` operator: concatenation. You can append one `BYTEA` value to another `BYTEA` value using the concatenation (||) operator.

Note that you can't compare two `BYTEA` values, even for equality/inequality. You can, of course, convert a `BYTEA` value into another value using the `CAST()` operator, and that opens up other operators.

Large-Objects

The BYTEA data type is currently limited to storing values no larger than 1GB. If you need to store values larger than will fit into a BYTEA column, you can use large-objects. A *large-object* is a value stored *outside* of a table. For example, if you want to store a photograph with each row in your tapes table, you would add an OID column to hold a *reference* to the corresponding large-object:

```
movies=# ALTER TABLE tapes ADD COLUMN photo_id OID;
ALTER
```

Each value in the photo_id column refers to an entry in the pg_largeobject system table. PostgreSQL provides a function that will load an external file (such as a JPEG file) into the pg_largeobject table:

```
movies=# INSERT INTO tapes VALUES
movies-# (
movies(#   'AA-55892',
movies(#   'Casablanca',
movies(#   lo_import('/tmp/casablanca.jpg' )
movies(# );
```

The lo_import() function loads the named file into pg_largeobject and returns an OID value that refers to the large-object. Now when you SELECT this row, you see the OID, not the actual bits that make up the photo:

```
movies=# SELECT * FROM tapes WHERE title = 'Casablanca';
 tape_id  |   title    | photo_id
----------+------------+----------
 MC-68873 | Casablanca |   510699
```

If you want to write the photo back into a file, you can use the lo_export() function:

```
movies=# SELECT lo_export( 510699, '/tmp/Casablanca.jpg' );
 lo_export
-----------
         1
(1 row)
```

To see all large-objects in the current database, use psql's \lo_list metacommand:

```
movies=# \lo_list
    Large objects
   ID    | Description
--------+-------------
 510699 |
(1 row)
```

You can remove large-objects from your database using the `lo_unlink()` function:

```
movies=# SELECT lo_unlink( 510699 );
 lo_unlink
-----------
         1
(1 row)

movies=# \lo_list
  Large objects
 ID | Description
----+-------------
(0 rows)
```

How do you get to the actual bits behind the reference `OID`? You can't—at least not with `psql`. Large-object support must be built into the client application that you are using. `psql` is a text-oriented tool and has no way to display a photograph, so the best that you can do is to look at the raw data in the `pg_largeobject` table. A few client applications, such as the Conjectrix Workstation, do support large-objects and can interpret the raw data properly, in most cases.

Network Address Data Types

PostgreSQL supports three data types that are designed to hold network addresses, both IP[8] (logical) and MAC[9] (physical) addresses. I don't think there are many applications that require the storage of an IP or MAC address, so I won't spend too much time describing them. The *PostgreSQL User's Guide* contains all the details that you might need to know regarding network data types.

MACADDR

The `MACADDR` type is designed to hold a MAC address. A MAC address is a hardware address, usually the address of an ethernet interface.

CIDR

The `CIDR` data type is designed to hold an IP network address. A `CIDR` value contains an IP network address and an optional netmask (the netmask determines the number of meaningful bits in the network address).

8. IP stands for Internet Protocol, the substrate of the Internet.

9. The acronym *MAC* stands for one or more of the following: Machine Address Code, Media Access Control, or Macaroni And Cheese.

INET

An INET value can hold the IP address of a network or of a network host. An INET value contains a network address and an optional netmask. If the netmask is omitted, it is assumed that the address identifies a single host (in other words, there is no discernible network component in the address).

Note that an INET value can represent a network or a host, but a CIDR is designed to represent the address of a network.

Syntax for Literal Values

The syntax required for literal network values is shown in Table 2.27.

Table 2.27 **Literal Syntax for Network Types**

Type	Syntax	Examples
INET	*a.b.c.d[/e]*	192.168.0.1
		192.168.150.0/26
		130.155.16.1/20
CIDR	a[.b[.c[.d]]][/e]	192.168.0.0/16
		192.168/16
MACADDR	*xxxxxx:xxxxxx*	0004E2:3695C0
	xxxxxx-xxxxxx	0004E2-3695C0
	xxxx.xxxx.xxxx	0004.E236.95C0
	xx-xx-xx-xx-xx-xx	00-04-E2-36-95-C0
	xx:xx:xx:xx:xx:xx	00:04:E2:36:95:C0

An INET or CIDR value consumes 12 bytes of storage. A MACADDR value consumes 6 bytes of storage.

Supported Operators

PostgreSQL provides comparison operators that you can use to compare two INET values, two CIDR values, or two MACADDR values. The comparison operators work by first checking the common bits in the network components of the two addresses; then, if those are equal, the address with the greatest number of netmask bits is considered the largest value. If the number of bits in the netmask is equal (and the network components of the addresses are equal), then the entire address is compared. The net effect (pun intended) is that 192.168.0.22/24 is considered greater than 192.168.0.22/20.

When you are working with two INET (or CIDR) values, you can also check for containership. Table 2.28 describes the network address operators.

Table 2.28 **Network Address Operators**

Operator	Meaning
$\texttt{INET}_1 < \texttt{INET}_2$ $\texttt{CIDR}_1 < \texttt{CIDR}_2$ $\texttt{MACADDR}_1 < \texttt{MACADDR}_2$	True if operand_1 is less than operand_2
$\texttt{INET}_1 <= \texttt{INET}_2$ $\texttt{CIDR}_1 <= \texttt{CIDR}_2$ $\texttt{MACADDR}_1 <= \texttt{MACADDR}_2$	True if operand_1 is less than or equal to operand_2
$\texttt{INET}_1 <> \texttt{INET}_2$ $\texttt{CIDR}_1 <> \texttt{CIDR}_2$ $\texttt{MACADDR}_1 <> \texttt{MACADDR}_2$	True if operand_1 is not equal to operand_2
$\texttt{INET}_1 = \texttt{INET}_2$ $\texttt{CIDR}_1 = \texttt{CIDR}_2$ $\texttt{MACADDR}_1 = \texttt{MACADDR}_2$	True if operand_1 is equal to operand_2
$\texttt{INET}_1 >= \texttt{INET}_2$ $\texttt{CIDR}_1 >= \texttt{CIDR}_2$ $\texttt{MACADDR}_1 >= \texttt{MACADDR}_2$	True if operand_1 is greater than or equal to operand_2
$\texttt{INET}_1 > \texttt{INET}_2$ $\texttt{CIDR}_1 > \texttt{CIDR}_2$ $\texttt{MACADDR}_1 > \texttt{MACADDR}_2$	True if operand_1 is greater than operand_2
$\texttt{INET}_1 << \texttt{INET}_2$ $\texttt{CIDR}_1 << \texttt{CIDR}_2$	TRUE if operand_1 is contained within operand_2
$\texttt{INET}_1 <<= \texttt{INET}_2$ $\texttt{CIDR}_1 <<= \texttt{CIDR}_2$	True if operand_1 is contained within operand_2 or if operand_1 is equal to operand_2
$\texttt{INET}_1 >> \texttt{INET}_2$ $\texttt{CIDR}_1 >> \texttt{CIDR}_2$	True if operand_1 contains operand_2
$\texttt{INET}_1 >>= \texttt{INET}_2$ $\texttt{CIDR}_1 >>= \texttt{CIDR}_2$	True if operand_1 contains operand_2 or if operand_1 is equal to operand_2

Sequences

One problem that you will most likely encounter in your database life is the need to generate unique identifiers. We've already seen one example of this in the `customers` table—the `customer_id` column is nothing more than a unique identifier. Sometimes, an entity that you want to store in your database will have a naturally unique identifier. For example, if you are designing a database to track employee information (in the U.S.), a Social Security number might make a good identifier. Of course, if you employ people who are not U.S. citizens, the Social Security number scheme will fail. If you are tracking information about automobiles, you might be tempted to use the license plate number as a unique identifier. That would work fine until you needed to track autos in more than one state. The VIN (or Vehicle Identification Number) is a naturally unique identifier.

Quite often, you will need to store information about an entity that has no naturally unique ID. In those cases, you are likely to simply assign a unique number to each entity. After you have decided to create a uniquifier[10], the next problem is coming up with a sequence of unique numbers.

PostgreSQL offers help in the form of a `SEQUENCE`: A `SEQUENCE` is an object that automatically generates sequence numbers. You can create as many `SEQUENCE` objects as you like: Each `SEQUENCE` has a unique name.

Let's create a new `SEQUENCE` that you can use to generate unique identifiers for rows in your `customers` table. You already have a few customers, so start the sequence numbers at 10:

```
movies=# CREATE SEQUENCE customer_id_seq START 10;
CREATE
```

The "`\ds`" command (in `psql`) shows you a list of the `SEQUENCE` objects in your database:

```
movies=# \ds
           List of relations
      Name       |   Type   | Owner
-----------------+----------+------
 customer_id_seq | sequence | korry
(1 row)
```

Now, let's try using this `SEQUENCE`. PostgreSQL provides a number of functions that you can call to make use of a `SEQUENCE`: The one that you are most interested in at the moment is the `nextval()` function. When you call the `nextval()` function, you provide (in the form of a string) the name of the `SEQUENCE` as the only argument.

For example, when you `INSERT` a new row in the `customers` table, you want PostgreSQL to automatically assign a unique `customer_id`:

```
movies=# INSERT INTO
movies-#    customers( customer_id, customer_name )
movies-#  VALUES
movies-#  (
movies-#    nextval( 'customer_id_seq' ), 'John Gomez'
movies-#  );

movies=# SELECT * FROM customers WHERE customer_name = 'John Gomez';
 customer_id | customer_name | phone | birth_date | balance
-------------+---------------+-------+------------+--------
          10 | John Gomez    |       |            |
(1 row)
```

10. I'm not sure that "uniquifier" is a real word, but I've used it for quite some time and it sure is a lot easier to say than "disambiguator."

You can see that the SEQUENCE (customer_id_seq) generated a new customer_id, starting with the value that you requested. You can use the currval() function to find the value that was just generated by your server process:

```
movies=# SELECT currval( 'customer_id_seq' );
 currval
---------
      10
```

The complete syntax for the CREATE SEQUENCE command is

```
CREATE SEQUENCE name
  [ INCREMENT increment ]
  [ MINVALUE min ]
  [ MAXVALUE max ]
  [ START start_value ]
  [ CACHE cache_count ]
  [ CYCLE ]
```

Notice that the only required item is the name.

The INCREMENT attribute determines the amount added to generate a new sequence number. This value can be positive or negative, but not zero. Positive values cause the sequence numbers to increase in value as they are generated (that is, 0, 1, 2, and so on). Negative values cause the sequence numbers to decrease in value (that is, 3, 2, 1, 0, and so on).

The MINVALUE and MAXVALUE attributes control the minimum and maximum values (respectively) for the SEQUENCE.

What happens when a SEQUENCE has reached the end of its valid range? You get to decide: If you include the CYCLE attribute, the SEQUENCE will wrap around. For example, if you create a cyclical SEQUENCE with MINVALUE 0 and MAXVALUE 3, you will retrieve the following sequence numbers: 0, 1, 2, 3, 0, 1, 2, 3, ... If you don't include the CYCLE attribute, you will see: 0, 1, 2, 3, error: reached MAXVALUE.

The START attribute determines the first sequence number generated by a SEQUENCE. The value for the START attribute must be within the MINVALUE and MAXVALUE range.

The default values for most of the SEQUENCE attributes depend on whether the INCREMENT is positive or negative. The default value for the INCREMENT attribute is 1. If you specify a negative INCREMENT, the MINVALUE defaults to –2147483647, and MAXVALUE defaults to –1. If you specify a positive INCREMENT, MINVALUE defaults to 1, and MAXVALUE defaults to 2147483647. The default value for the START attribute is also dependent on the sign of the INCREMENT. A positive INCREMENT defaults the START value to the MINVALUE attribute. A negative INCREMENT defaults the START value to the MAXVALUE attribute.

Remember, these are the defaults—you can choose any meaningful combination of values that you like (within the valid range of a BIGINT).

The default SEQUENCE attributes are summarized in Table 2.29.

Table 2.29 **Sequence Attributes**

Attribute Name	Default Value
INCREMENT	1
MINVALUE	INCREMENT > 0 ? 1 INCREMENT < 0 ? –2147483647
MAXVALUE	INCREMENT > 0 ? 2147483647 INCREMENT < 0 ? –1
START	INCREMENT > 0 ? MINVALUE INCREMENT < 0 ? MAXVALUE
CACHE	1
CYCLE	False

The CACHE attribute is a performance-tuning parameter; it determines how many sequence numbers are generated and held in memory. In most cases, you can simply use the default value (1). If you suspect that sequence number generation is a bottleneck in your application, you might consider increasing the CACHE attribute, but be sure to read the warning in the PostgreSQL documentation (see the CREATE SEQUENCE section).

You can view the attributes of a SEQUENCE by treating it as a table and selecting from it[11]:

```
movies=# SELECT
movies-#   increment_by, max_value, min_value, cache_value, is_cycled
movies-# FROM
movies-#   customer_id_seq;

 increment_by | max_value | min_value | cache_value | is_cycled
--------------+-----------+-----------+-------------+-----------
            1 |         3 |         0 |           1 | f
```

PostgreSQL provides three functions that work with SEQUENCEs. I described the nextval() and currval() functions earlier; nextval() generates (and returns) a new value from a SEQUENCE, and currval() retrieves the most-recently generated value. You can reset a SEQUENCE to any value between MINVALUE and MAXVALUE by calling the setval() function—for example:

11. There are four other columns in a SEQUENCE, but they hold bookkeeping information required to properly maintain the SEQUENCE.

```
movies=# SELECT nextval( 'customer_id_seq' );
ERROR:  customer_id_seq.nextval: reached MAXVALUE (3)

movies=# SELECT setval( 'customer_id_seq', 0 );
 setval
--------
      0
(1 row)

movies=# SELECT nextval( 'customer_id_seq' );
 nextval
---------
       1
```

Now that you know how SEQUENCEs work in PostgreSQL, let's revisit the SERIAL data type. I mentioned earlier in this chapter that a SERIAL is really implemented as a SEQUENCE (see the "SERIAL, BIGSERIAL, and Sequences" sidebar). Remember that a SERIAL provides an automatically increasing (or decreasing) unique identifier. That sounds just like a SEQUENCE, so what's the difference? A SEQUENCE is a standalone object, whereas SERIAL is a data type that you can assign to a column.

Let's create a new table that contains a SERIAL column:

```
movies=# CREATE TABLE serial_test ( pkey SERIAL, payload INTEGER );

NOTICE:  CREATE TABLE will create implicit
         sequence 'serial_test_pkey_seq' for
         SERIAL column 'serial_test.pkey'
NOTICE:  CREATE TABLE/UNIQUE will create implicit
         index 'serial_test_pkey_key' for table 'serial_test'
CREATE
```

The CREATE TABLE command is normally silent. When you create a table with a SERIAL column, PostgreSQL does a little extra work on your behalf. First, PostgreSQL creates a SEQUENCE for you. The name of the SEQUENCE is based on the name of the table and the name of the column. In this case, the SEQUENCE is named serial_test_pkey_seq. Next, PostgreSQL creates a unique index. We haven't really talked about indexes yet: for now, know that a unique index on the pkey column ensures that you have no duplicate values in that column. PostgreSQL performs one more nicety for you when you create a SERIAL column. The \d command (in psql) shows you this last step:

```
movies=# \d serial_test
                              Table "serial_test"
 Attribute | Type    |                        Modifier
-----------+---------+--------------------------------------------------
 pkey      | integer | not null default nextval('serial_test_pkey_seq')
 payload   | integer |
Index: serial_test_pkey_key
```

PostgreSQL has created a default value for the pkey column. A column's default value is used whenever you insert a row but omit a value for that column. For example, if you execute the command `INSERT INTO serial_test( payload ) VALUES( 24307 );`, you have not provided an explicit value for the pkey column. In this case, PostgreSQL evaluates the default value for pkey and inserts the resulting value. Because the default value for pkey is a call to the `nextval()` function, each new row is assigned a new (unique) sequence number.

Arrays

One of the unique features of PostgreSQL is the fact that you can define a column to be an array. Most commercial database systems require that a single column within a given row can hold no more than one value. With PostgreSQL, you aren't bound by that rule—you can create columns that store multiple values (of the same data type).

The customers table defined in Chapter 1 contained a single balance column. What change would you have to make to the database if you wanted to store a month-by-month balance for each customer, going back at most 12 months? One alternative would be to create a separate table to store monthly balances. The primary key of the cust_balance might be composed of the customer_id and the month number (either 0–11 or 1–12, whichever you found more convenient)[12]. This would certainly work, but in PostgreSQL, it's not the only choice.

You know that there are never more than 12 months in a year and that there are never fewer than 12 months in a year. Parent/child relationships are perfect when the parent has a variable number of children, but they aren't always the most convenient choice when the number of child records is fixed.

Instead, you could store all 12 monthly balance values inside the customers table. Here is how you might create the customers table using an array to store the monthly balances:

```
CREATE TABLE customers (
        customer_id       INTEGER UNIQUE,
        customer_name     VARCHAR(50),
        phone             CHAR(8),
        birth_date        DATE,
        balance           DECIMAL(7,2),
        monthly_balances DECIMAL(7,2)[12]
);
```

12. The relationship between the customers table and the cust_balance is called a *parent/child* relationship. In this case, the customers table is the parent and cust_balance is the child. The primary key of a child table is composed of the parent key plus a uniquifier (that is, a value, such as the month number, that provides a unique identifier within a group of related children).

Notice that I have added a new column named `monthly_balances`—this is an array of 12 `DECIMAL` values. I'll show you how to put values into an array in a moment.

You can define an array of *any* data type: the built-in types, user-defined types, even other arrays. When you create an array of arrays, you are actually creating a multidimensional array. For example, if we wanted to store month-by-month balances for the three previous years, I could have created the `monthly_balances` field as

```
monthly_balances DECIMAL(7,2)[3][12]
```

This would give you three arrays of 12-element arrays.

There is no limit to the number of members in an array. There is also no limit to the number of dimensions in a multidimensional array.

Now, let's talk about inserting and updating array values. When you want to insert a new row into the `customers` table, you provide values for each member in the `monthly_balances` array as follows:

```
INSERT INTO customers
(
customer_id, customer_name, phone, birth_date, balance, monthly_balances
)
VALUES
(
   8,
   'Wink Wankel',
   '555-1000',
   '1988-12-25',
   0.00,
   '{1,2,3,4,5,6,7,8,9,10,11,12}'
);
```

To `INSERT` values into an array, you enclose all the array elements in single quotes and braces ({}) and separate multiple elements with a comma.

Inserting values into a multidimensional array is treated as if you were inserting an array of arrays. For example, if you had a table defined as

```
CREATE TABLE arr
(
   pkey  serial,
   val   int[2][3]
);
```

you would INSERT a row as

```
INSERT INTO arr( val ) VALUES( '{ {1,2,3}, {4,5,6} }' );
```

Looking back at the `customers` table now; if you `SELECT` the row that you `INSERTed`, you'll see:

```
movies=# \x
Expanded display is on.

movies=# SELECT
movies-#    customer_name, monthly_balances
movies-#  FROM customers
movies-#  WHERE id = 8;
-[ RECORD 1 ]----+-----------------------------------
id               | 8
customer_name    | Wink Wankel
phone            | 555-1000
birth_date       | 1988-12-25
monthly_balances | {1.00,2,3,4,5,6,7,8,9,10,11,12.00}
```

To make this example a little more readable in book form, I have used `psql`'s `\x` command to rearrange the display format here. I have also edited out some of the trailing zeroes in the `monthly_balances` column.

You can retrieve specific elements within an array:

```
movies=# SELECT
movies-#    customer_name, monthly_balances[3]
movies-#  FROM customers
movies-#  WHERE id = 8;
 customer_name | monthly_balances
---------------+------------------
 Wink Wankel   |             3.00
(1 row)
```

Or you can ask for a range[13] of array elements:

```
movies=# SELECT
movies-#    customer_name, monthly_balances[1:3]
movies-#  FROM customers
movies-#  WHERE id = 8;
 customer_name |     monthly_balances
---------------+-----------------------
 Wink Wankel   |  {"1.00","2.00","3.00"}
(1 row)
```

13. The PostgreSQL documentation refers to a contiguous range of array elements as a *slice*.

The index for an array starts at `1` by default. I'll show you how to change the range of an index in a moment.

You can use an array element in any situation where you can use a value of the same data type. For example, you can use an array element in a `WHERE` clause:

```
movies=# SELECT
movies-#     customer_name, monthly_balances[1:3]
movies-# FROM customers
movies-# WHERE monthly_balances[1] > 0;
 customer_name |    monthly_balances
---------------+------------------------
 Wink Wankel   | {"1.00","2.00","3.00"}
(1 row)
```

There are three ways to `UPDATE` an array. If you want to `UPDATE` all elements in an array, simply `SET` the array to a new value:

```
movies=# UPDATE customers SET
movies-#   monthly_balances = '{12,11,10,9,8,7,6,5,4,3,1}'
movies-# WHERE customer_id = 8;
```

If you want to `UPDATE` a single array element, simply identify the element:

```
movies=# UPDATE customers SET monthly_balances[1] = 22;
```

Finally, you can `UPDATE` a contiguous range of elements:

```
movies=# UPDATE customers SET monthly_balances[1:3] = '{11,22,33}';
```

Now, there are a few odd things you should know about arrays in PostgreSQL.

First, the array bounds that you specify when you create a column are optional. I don't just mean that you can omit an array bound when you create a column (although you can), I mean that PostgreSQL won't enforce any limits that you try to impose. For example, you created the `monthly_balances` column as a 12-element array. PostgreSQL happily lets you put a value into element 13, 14, or 268. The `array_dims()` function tells the upper and lower bounds of an array value:

```
movies=# SELECT array_dims( monthly_balances ) FROM customers
movies-#   WHERE
movies-#     customer_id = 8;

array_dims
------------
 [1:12]
```

You can increase the size of an array by updating values adjacent to those that already exist[14]. For example, the `monthly_balances` column for customer 8 (Wink Wankel) contains 12 elements, numbered 1 through 12. You can add new elements at either end of the range (array subscripts can be negative):

```
movies=# UPDATE customers SET
movies-#    monthly_balances[13] = 13
movies-#  WHERE
movies-#    customer_id = 8;
UPDATE 1

movies=# SELECT array_dims( monthly_balances ) FROM customers
movies-#  WHERE
movies-#    customer_id = 8;
 array_dims
------------
 [1:13]

movies=# UPDATE customers SET
movies-#    monthly_balances[-1:0] = '{ -1, 0 }'
movies-#  WHERE
movies-#    customer_id = 8;
UPDATE 1

movies=# SELECT array_dims( monthly_balances ) FROM customers
movies-#   WHERE
movies=#     customer_id = 8;
array_dims
------------
 [-1:13]
```

Note that you can expand an array only by updating elements that are directly adjacent to the existing elements. For example, customer number 8 now contains elements –1:13. We can't add an element 15 without first adding element 14:

```
movies=# UPDATE customers SET
movies-#   monthly_balances[15] = 15
movies-# WHERE
movies-#   customer_id = 8;
ERROR:  Invalid array subscripts
```

14. The PostgreSQL documentation warns that you can't expand a multidimensional array.

Next, the syntax for inserting or updating array values is a bit misleading. Let's say that you want to insert a new row in your `customers` table, but you only want to provide a balance for month number 3:

```
movies=# INSERT INTO customers
movies-# ( customer_id, customer_name, monthly_balances[3] )
movies-# VALUES
movies-# ( 9, 'Samuel Boney', '{300}' );
```

This appears to work, but there is danger lurking here. Let's go back and retrieve the data that you just inserted:

```
movies=# SELECT customer_name, monthly_balances[3]
movies-#   FROM customers
movies-#   WHERE
movies-#     customer_id = 9;
 customer_name | monthly_balances
---------------+------------------
 Samuel Boney  |
```

Where'd the data go? If you `SELECT` all array elements, the data is still there:

```
movies=# SELECT customer_name, monthly_balances
movies-#   FROM customers
movies-#   WHERE
movies-#     customer_id = 9;
 customer_name | monthly_balances
---------------+------------------
 Samuel Boney  | {"300"}
```

The `array_dims()` function gives you a pretty good hint:

```
movies=# SELECT array_dims( monthly_balances ) FROM customers
movies-#   WHERE
movies-#     customer_id = 9;

array_dims
------------
 [1:1]
```

According to `array_dims()`, the high and low subscript values are both `1`. You explicitly `INSERT`ed the value `300` into array element 3, but PostgreSQL (silently) decided to place it into element one anyway. This seems a bit mysterious to me, but that's how it works.

The final oddity concerns how PostgreSQL handles `NULL` values and arrays. An array can be `NULL`, but an individual element cannot—you can't have an array in which some elements are NULL and others are not. Furthermore, PostgreSQL silently ignores an attempt to UPDATE an array member to NULL:

```
movies=# SELECT customer_name, monthly_balances
movies-#   FROM
movies-#     customers
movies-#   WHERE
movies-#     customer_id = 8;
-[ RECORD 1 ]----+----------------------------------
id               | 8
customer_name    | Wink Wankel
phone            | 555-1000
birth_date       | 1988-12-25
monthly_balances | {1.00,2,3,4,5,6,7,8,9,10,11,12.00}

movies=# UPDATE customers SET
movies-#   monthly_balances[1] = NULL
movies-# WHERE
movies-#   customer_id = 8;
UPDATE 1
```

You won't get any error messages when you try to change an array element to NULL, but a SELECT statement will show that the UPDATE had no effect:

```
movies=# SELECT customer_name, monthly_balances
movies-#   FROM
movies-#     customers
movies-#   WHERE
movies-#     customer_id = 8;
-[ RECORD 1 ]----+----------------------------------
id               | 8
customer_name    | Wink Wankel
phone            | 555-1000
birth_date       | 1988-12-25
monthly_balances | {1.00,2,3,4,5,6,7,8,9,10,11,12.00}
```

If you keep these three oddities in mind, arrays can be very useful. Remember, though, that an array is not a substitute for a child table. You should use an array only when the number of elements is fixed by some real-world constraint (12 months per year, 7 days per week, and so on).

Column Constraints

When you create a PostgreSQL table, you can define column constraints[15]. A *column constraint* is a rule that must be satisfied whenever you insert or update a value in that column.

15. You can also define table constraints. A table constraint applies to the table as a whole, not just a single column. We'll discuss table constraints in Chapter 3.

It's very important to understand that when you define a column constraint, PostgreSQL won't ever let your table get into a state in which the constraints are not met. If you try to INSERT a value that violates a constraint, the insertion will fail. If you try to UPDATE a value in such a way that it would violate a constraint, the modification will be rejected.

You can also define constraints that establish relationships between two tables. For example, each row in the rentals table contains a tape_id (corresponding to a row in the tapes table). You could define a constraint to tell PostgreSQL that the rentals.tape_id column REFERENCES the tapes.tape_id column. I'll discuss the implications of a REFERENCES constraint in a moment.

Needless to say, column constraints are a very powerful feature.

NULL/NOT NULL

Let's start with the most basic column constraints: NULL and NOT NULL. You've already seen some examples of the NOT NULL constraint (in Chapter 1):

```
CREATE TABLE customers (
        customer_id   INTEGER UNIQUE NOT NULL,
        name          VARCHAR(50)    NOT NULL,
        phone         CHAR(8),
        birth_date    DATE,
        balance       DECIMAL(7,2)
);
```

I have specified that the customer_id and name columns are NOT NULL. The meaning of a NOT NULL constraint is pretty clear: The column is not allowed to contain a NULL value[16]. If you try to INSERT a NULL value into the customer_id or name columns, you will receive an error:

```
INSERT INTO customers VALUES
(
    11,
    NULL,
    '555-1984',
    '10-MAY-1980',
    0
);

ERROR:  ExecAppend: Fail to add null value in not null
                    attribute customer_name
```

16. A column that has been defined to be NOT NULL is also known as a *mandatory* column. A column that can accept NULL values is said to be *optional*.

You'll also get an error if you try to UPDATE either column in such a way that the result would be NULL:

```
UPDATE customers SET customer_name = NULL WHERE customer_id = 1;

ERROR:  ExecReplace: Fail to add null value in not null
                     attribute customer_name
```

The opposite of NOT NULL is NULL. You can explicitly define a NULL constraint, but it really doesn't function as a constraint. A NULL constraint does not force a column to contain *only* NULL values (that would be pretty pointless). Instead, a NULL constraint simply tells PostgreSQL that NULL values are allowed in a particular column. If you don't specify that a column is mandatory, it is considered optional.

UNIQUE

The UNIQUE constraint ensures that a column will contain unique values; that is, there will be no duplicate values in the column. If you look back to the previous section, you'll see that you specified that the customer_id column should be UNIQUE. If you try to INSERT a duplicate value into a UNIQUE column, you will receive an error message:

```
movies=# SELECT * FROM customers;

 customer_id |     customer_name      |  phone   | birth_date | balance
-------------+------------------------+----------+------------+--------
           1 | Jones, Henry           | 555-1212 | 1970-10-10 |    0.00
           2 | Rubin, William         | 555-2211 | 1972-07-10 |   15.00
           3 | Panky, Henry           | 555-1221 | 1968-01-21 |    0.00
           4 | Wonderland, Alice N.   | 555-1122 | 1969-03-05 |    3.00

movies=# INSERT INTO customers VALUES
movies-# (
movies-#    1,
movies-#    'John Gomez',
movies-#    '555-4272',
movies-#    '1982-06-02',
movies-#    0.00
movies-# );

ERROR:  Cannot insert a duplicate key into unique
        index customers_customer_id_key
```

When you create a UNIQUE column, PostgreSQL will ensure that an index exists for that column. If you don't create one yourself, PostgreSQL will create one for you. We'll talk more about indexes in Chapter 3.

PRIMARY KEY

Almost every table that you create will have one column (or possibly a set of columns) that uniquely identifies each row. For example, each tape in the tapes table is uniquely identified by its tape_id. Each customer in your customers table is identified by a UNIQUE customer_id. In relational database lingo, the set of columns that act to identify a row is called the *primary key*.

Quite often, you will find that a table has more than one unique column. For example, a table holding employee information might have an employee_id column and a social_security_number (SSN) column. You could argue that either of these would be a reasonable primary key. The employee_id would probably be the better choice for at least three reasons. First, you are likely to refer to an employee record in other tables (for example, withholdings and earnings)—an employee_id is (most likely) shorter than an SSN. Second, an SSN is considered private information, and you don't want to expose an employee's SSN to everyone who has access to one of the related files. Third, it is entirely possible that some of your employees may not have Social Security numbers (they may not be U.S. citizens)—you can't define a column as the PRIMARY KEY if that column allows NULL values.

PostgreSQL provides a constraint, PRIMARY KEY, that you can use to define the primary key for a table. Practically speaking, identifying a column (or a set of columns) as a PRIMARY KEY is the same as defining the column to be NOT NULL and UNIQUE. But the PRIMARY KEY constraint does offer one advantage over NULL and UNIQUE: documentation. When you create a PRIMARY KEY, you are stating that the columns that comprise the key should be used when you need to refer to a row in that table. Each row in the rentals table, for example, contains a reference to a tape (rentals.tape_id) and a reference to a customer (rentals.customer_id). You should define the customers.customer_id column as the primary key of the customers table:

```
CREATE TABLE customers (
        customer_id   INTEGER PRIMARY KEY,
        name          VARCHAR(50)    NOT NULL,
        phone         CHAR(8),
        birth_date    DATE,
        balance       DECIMAL(7,2)
);
```

You should also define the tapes.tape_id column as the primary key of the tapes table:

```
CREATE TABLE tapes (
        tape_id     CHARACTER(8) PRIMARY KEY,
        title       CHARACTER VARYING(80)
);
```

Now, let's look at the other half of the equation: the REFERENCES constraint.

REFERENCES

A *foreign key* is a column (or group of columns) in one table that refers to a row in another table. Usually, but not always, a foreign key refers to the primary key of another table.

The REFERENCES constraint tells PostgreSQL that one table refers to another table (or more precisely, a foreign key in one table refers to the primary key of another). Let's look at an example:

```
CREATE TABLE rentals (
        tape_id     CHARACTER(8) REFERENCES tapes,
        customer_id INTEGER      REFERENCES customers,
        rental_date DATE
);
```

I've now defined `rentals.tape_id` and `rentals.customer_id` to be foreign keys. In this example, the `rentals.tape_id` column is also called a *reference* and the `tapes.tape_id` column is called the *referent*.

There are a few implications to the REFERENCES constraint that you will need to consider. First, the REFERENCES constraint is a *constraint*: PostgreSQL does not allow you to change the database in such a way that the constraint would be violated. You cannot add a `rentals` row that refers to a nonexistent tape (or to a nonexistent customer):

```
movies=# SELECT * FROM tapes;
 tape_id  |     title
----------+---------------
 AB-12345 | The Godfather
 AB-67472 | The Godfather
 MC-68873 | Casablanca
 OW-41221 | Citizen Kane
 AH-54706 | Rear Window

movies=# INSERT INTO rentals VALUES
movies-# (
movies(#     'OW-00000',
movies(#     1,
movies(#     '2002-02-21'
movies(# );
ERROR:  <unnamed> referential integrity violation -
             key referenced from rentals not found in tapes
```

The next thing to consider is that you cannot (normally) DELETE a referent—doing so would violate the REFERENCES constraint:

```
movies=# SELECT * FROM rentals;
 tape_id  | customer_id | rental_date
----------+-------------+------------
 AB-12345 |           1 | 2001-11-25
 AB-67472 |           3 | 2001-11-25
```

```
 OW-41221 |           1 | 2001-11-25
 MC-68873 |           3 | 2001-11-20
(4 rows)

movies=# DELETE FROM tapes WHERE tape_id = 'AB-12345';
ERROR:  <unnamed> referential integrity violation -
                  key in tapes still referenced from rentals
```

Sometimes, it's not appropriate for a `REFERENCES` constraint to block the deletion of a referent. You can specify the action that PostgreSQL should take when the referent is deleted. The default action (also known as `NO ACTION` and `RESTRICT`) is to prevent the deletion of a referent if there are still any references to it. The next alternative, `CASCADE`, deletes all rows that refer to a value when the referent is deleted. The final two choices break the link between the reference and the referent: `SET NULL` updates any references to `NULL` whenever a referent is deleted, whereas `SET DEFAULT` updates any references to their default values when a referent is deleted.

If you want to specify one of the alternatives, you would use the following syntax when you create the `REFERENCES` constraint:

```
REFERENCES table [ (column) ] ON DELETE
     NO ACTION | RESTRICT | CASCADE | SET NULL | SET DEFAULT
```

By default, a `REFERENCES` constraint also prevents you from changing data in such a way that the constraint would be violated. You can use the `ON UPDATE` clause to relax the constraint a little, much the same as the `ON DELETE` clause.

The syntax required for `ON UPDATE` is

```
REFERENCES table [ (column) ] ON UPDATE
    NO ACTION | RESTRICT | CASCADE | SET NULL | SET DEFAULT
```

There is a subtle difference between the `ON UPDATE` clause and `ON DELETE` clause. When you `DELETE` a referent, the entire row disappears, so the behavior of the `ON DELETE` clause is obvious. When you `UPDATE` a referent row, you may change values other than the referent column(s). If you `UPDATE` a referent row, but you don't update the referent column, you can't introduce a constraint violation, so the `ON UPDATE` action doesn't come into play. If you *do* change the referent column, the `ON UPDATE` action is triggered.

The `NO ACTION` and `RESTRICT` actions simply prevent a constraint violation—this is identical to the `ON DELETE` clause. The `CASCADE` action causes all references to be updated whenever a referent changes. `SET NULL` and `SET DEFAULT` actions work the same for `ON UPDATE` as for `ON DELETE`.

CHECK()

By defining a `CHECK()` constraint on a column, you can tell PostgreSQL that any values inserted into that column must satisfy an arbitrary Boolean expression. The syntax for a `CHECK()` constraint is

```
[CONSTRAINT constraint-name] CHECK( boolean-expression )
```

For example, if you want to ensure that the customer_balance column is a positive value, but less than $10,000.00, you might use the following:

```
CREATE TABLE customers
(
        customer_id   INTEGER UNIQUE,
        customer_name VARCHAR(50),
        phone         CHAR(8),
        birth_date    DATE,
        balance       DECIMAL(7,2)
           CONSTRAINT invalid_balance
           CHECK( balance > 0 AND balance < 10000 )
);
```

Now, if you try to INSERT an invalid value into the customer_balance table, you'll cause an error:

```
INSERT INTO customers VALUES
(
  10,
  'John Smallberries',
  '555-8426',
  '1970-JAN-02',
  20000
);

ERROR:  ExecAppend: rejected due to CHECK constraint invalid_balance
```

Expression Evaluation and Type Conversion

Now that you have seen all the standard PostgreSQL data types, it's time to talk about how you can combine values of different types into complex expressions.

First, you should understand than an expression represents a value. In a well-designed language, you can use an expression anywhere you can use a value. An expression can be as simple as a single value: 3.14159 is an expression. A complex expression is created by combining two simple expressions with an operator. An operator is a symbol that represents some sort of operation to be applied to one or two operands. For example, the expression "customer_balance * 1.10" uses the multiplication operator (*) to multiply customer_balance by 1.10. In this example, customer_balance is the left operand, * is the operator, and 1.10 is the right operand. This expression combines two different kinds of values: customer_balance is (presumably) a column in one of your tables; whereas 1.10 is a literal value (informally called a constant). You can combine column values, literal values, function results, and other expressions to build complex expressions.

Most operators (such as `*`, `+`, and `<`) require two operands: these are called *binary operators*. Other operators (such as `!!`, the factorial operator) work with a single value: these are called *unary operators*[17]. Some operators (such as `-`) can function as either.

For some expressions, particularly those expressions that mix data types, PostgreSQL must perform implicit type conversions[18]. For example, there is no predefined operator that allows you to add an `INT2` to a `FLOAT8`. PostgreSQL can convert the `INT2` into a `FLOAT8` before performing the addition, and there *is* an operator that can add two `FLOAT8` values. Every computer language defines a set of rules[19] that govern automatic type conversion; PostgreSQL is no exception.

PostgreSQL is rather unique in its depth of support for user-defined data types. In most RDBMSs, you can define new data types, but you are really just providing a different name for an existing data type (although you might be able to constrain the set of legal values in the new type). With PostgreSQL, you can add new data types that are not necessarily related to the existing data types. When you add a new data type to PostgreSQL, you can also define a set of operators that can operate on the new type. Each operator is implemented as an operator function; usually, but not necessarily, written in C. When you use an operator in an expression, PostgreSQL must find an operator function that it can use to evaluate the expression. The point of this short digression is that although most languages can define a static set of rules governing type conversion, the presence of user-defined data types requires a more dynamic approach. To accommodate user-defined data types, PostgreSQL consults a table named `pg_operator`. Each row in the `pg_operator` contains an operator name (such as + or #), the operand data types, and the data type of the result. For example, (in PostgreSQL version 7.1.2) there are 31 rows in `pg_operator` that describe the + operator: One row describes the + operator when applied to two `POINT` values, another row describes the + operator when applied to two `INTERVAL` values, and a third row describes the + operator when applied to an `INT2` and an `INT4`.

You can see the complete list of operators using the "`\do`" command in the `psql` query tool.

When searching for an operator function, PostgreSQL first searches the `pg_operator` table for an operator that exactly matches data types involved in the expression. For example, given the expression:

```
CAST( 1.2 AS DECIMAL ) + CAST( 5 AS INTEGER )
```

17. You may also see the terms *dyadic* (meaning two-valued) and *monadic* (meaning single-valued). These terms have the distinct advantage that you will never have to worry about accidentally saying "urinary operator" in polite company.

18. A type conversion that is automatically provided by PostgreSQL is called a *coercion*. A type conversion caused explicitly by the programmer (using the `CAST()` or '`::`' operator) is called a *cast*.

19. A given language might simply prohibit automatic type conversion, but most languages try to help out the programmer a bit.

PostgreSQL searches for a function named '+' that takes a `DECIMAL` value as the left operand and an `INTEGER` value as right operand. If it can't find a function that meets those criteria, the next step is to determine whether it can coerce one (or both) of the values into a different data type. In our example, PostgreSQL could choose to convert either value: The `DECIMAL` value could be converted into an `INTEGER`, or the `INTEGER` value could be converted into a `DECIMAL`. Now we have *two* operator functions to choose from: One function can add two `DECIMAL` values and the other can add two `INTEGER` values. If PostgreSQL chooses the `INTEGER + INTEGER` operator function, it will have to convert the `DECIMAL` value into an `INTEGER`—this will result in loss of precision (the fractional portion of the `DECIMAL` value will be rounded to the nearest whole number). Instead, PostgreSQL will choose the `DECIMAL + DECIMAL` operator, coercing the `INTEGER` value into a `DECIMAL`.

So to summarize, PostgreSQL first looks for an operator function in which the operand types exactly match the expression being evaluated. If it can't find one, PostgreSQL looks through the list of operator functions that could be applied by coercing one (or both) operands into a different type. If type coercion would result in more than one alternative, PostgreSQL tries to find the operator function that will maintain the greatest precision.

The process of selecting an operator function can get complex and is described more fully in Chapter 5 of the *PostgreSQL User's Guide*.

Table 2.30 lists the type conversion functions supplied with a standard PostgreSQL distribution.

Table 2.30 **Explicit Type Conversion Functions**

Result Type	Source Type
BOX	CIRCLE, POLYGON
DATE	TIMESTAMPTZ, DATE, TEXT
INTERVAL	INTERVAL, TEXT, TIME
LSEG	BOX
MACADDR	TEXT
NUMERIC	BIGINT, SMALLINT, INTEGER, REAL, DOUBLE PRECISION
OID	TEXT
PATH	POLYGON
POINT	PATH, LSEG, BOX, POLYGON, CIRCLE
POLYGON	PATH, CIRCLE, BOX
TEXT	INET, DOUBLE PRECISION, NAME, OID, SMALLINT, INTEGER, INTERVAL, TIMESTAMP WITH TIME ZONE, TIME WITH TIME ZONE, TIME, BIGINT, DATE, MACADDR, CHAR, REAL
TIME	TEXT, TIME, TIMESTAMP WITH TIME ZONE, INTERVAL

Creating Your Own Data Types

PostgreSQL allows you to create your own data types. This is not unique among relational database systems, but PostgreSQL's depth of support is unique. In other RDBMSs, you can define one data type in terms of another (predefined) data type. For example, you might create a new numeric data type to hold an employee's age, with valid values between 18 and 100. This is still a numeric data type—you must define the new type as a subset of an existing type.

With PostgreSQL, you can create entirely new types that have no relationship to existing types. When you define a custom data type (in PostgreSQL), you determine the syntax required for literal values, the format for internal data storage, the set of operators supported for the new type, and the set of (predefined) functions that can operate on values of that type.

There are a number of contributed packages that add new data types to the standard PostgreSQL distribution. For example, the PostGIS project (`http://postgis.refractions.net`) adds geographic data types based on specifications produced by the Open GIS Consortium. The `/contrib` directory of a standard PostgreSQL distribution contains a cube data type as well as an implementation of ISBN/ISSN (International Standard Book Number/International Standard Serial Number) data types.

Creating a new data type is too advanced for this chapter. If you are interested in defining a new data type, see Chapter 6, "Extending PostgreSQL."

Summary

As you can see, PostgreSQL offers a data type to fit almost every need. In this chapter, I've described each data type included in a standard PostgreSQL distribution. The syntax for literal values may seem a bit contrived for some of the data types, but the fact that PostgreSQL allows you to define new data types requires a few concessions (fortunately, very few).

I've listed all the standard operators in this chapter because they are a bit under-documented in the *PostgreSQL User's Guide*. Functions, on the other hand, are well documented (as well as constantly changing)—refer to Chapter 4 of the *PostgreSQL User's Guide* for an up-to-date list of functions.

In Chapter 3, "PostgreSQL SQL Syntax and Use," we'll explore a variety of topics that should round out your knowledge of PostgreSQL from the perspective of a user. Later chapters will cover PostgreSQL programming and PostgreSQL administration.

3

PostgreSQL SQL Syntax and Use

THE FIRST TWO CHAPTERS EXPLORED THE BASICS OF the SQL language and looked at the data types supported by PostgreSQL. This chapter covers a variety of topics that should round out your knowledge of PostgreSQL.

We'll start by looking at the rules that you have to follow when choosing names for tables, columns, indexes, and such. Next, you'll see how to create, destroy, and view PostgreSQL databases. In Chapter 1, "Introduction to PostgreSQL and SQL," you created a few simple tables; in this chapter, you'll learn all the details of the `CREATE TABLE` command. I'll also talk about indexes. I'll finish up by talking about transaction processing and locking. If you are familiar with Sybase, DB2, or Microsoft SQL Server, I think you'll find that the locking model used by PostgreSQL is a refreshing change.

PostgreSQL Naming Rules

When you create an object in PostgreSQL, you give that object a name. Every table has a name, every column has a name, and so on. PostgreSQL uses a single type to define all object names: the `name` type.

A value of type `name` is a string of 31 or fewer characters[1]. A `name` must start with a letter or an underscore; the rest of the string can contain letters, digits, and underscores.

If you examine the entry corresponding to `name` in the pg_type table, you will find that a `name` is really 32 characters long. Because the `name` type is used internally by the PostgreSQL engine, it is a null-terminated string. So, the maximum length of `name` value is 31 characters. You can enter more than 31 characters for an object name, but PostgreSQL stores only the first 31 characters.

1. You can increase the length of the `name` data type by changing the value of the `NAMEDATALEN` symbol before compiling PostgreSQL.

Both SQL and PostgreSQL reserve certain words and normally, you cannot use those words to name objects. Examples of reserved words are

```
ANALYZE
BETWEEN
CHARACTER
INTEGER
CREATE
```

You cannot create a table named `INTEGER` or a column named `BETWEEN`. A complete list of reserved words can be found in Appendix B of the *PostgreSQL User's Guide*.

If you find that you need to create an object that does not meet these rules, you can enclose the name in double quotes. Wrapping a name in quotes creates a quoted identifier. For example, you could create a table whose name is `"3.14159"`—the double quotes are required, but are not actually a part of the name (that is, they are not stored and do not count against the 31-character limit). When you create an object whose name must be quoted, you have to include the quotes not only when you create the object, but every time you refer to that object. For example, to select from the table mentioned previously, you would have to write

```
SELECT filling, topping, crust FROM "3.14159";
```

Here are a few examples of both valid and invalid names:

```
my_table        -- valid
my_2nd_table    -- valid
échéanciers     -- valid: accented and non-Latin letters are allowed
"2nd_table"     -- valid: quoted identifier
"create table" -- valid: quoted identifier
"1040Forms"     -- valid: quoted identifier
2nd_table       -- invalid: does not start with a letter or an underscore
```

Quoted names are case-sensitive. `"1040Forms"` and `"1040FORMS"` are two distinct names. Unquoted names are converted to lowercase, as shown here:

```
movies=# CREATE TABLE FOO( BAR INTEGER );
CREATE
movies=# CREATE TABLE foo( BAR INTEGER );
ERROR: Relation 'foo' already exists
movies=# \d
            List of relations
       Name        | Type  |     Owner
-------------------+-------+---------------
 1040FORMS         | table | bruce
 1040Forms         | table | sheila
 customers         | table | bruce
 distributors      | table | bruce
 foo               | table | bruce
```

```
rentals          | table | bruce
returns          | table | John Whorfin
tapes            | table | bruce
(6 rows)
```

The names of all objects must be unique within some scope. Every database must have a unique name; the name of a table must be unique within the scope of a single database[2], and column names must be unique within a table. The name of an index must be unique within a database.

Creating, Destroying, and Viewing Databases

Before you can do anything else with a PostgreSQL database, you must first create the database. Before you get too much further, it might be a good idea to see where a database fits into the overall scheme of PostgreSQL. Figure 3.1 shows the relationships between clusters, databases, and tables.

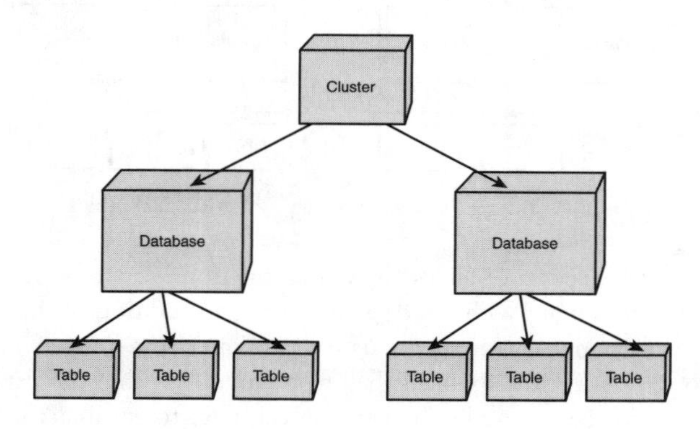

Figure 3.1 Clusters, databases, and tables.

At the highest level of the PostgreSQL storage hierarchy is the *cluster*. A cluster is a collection of databases. Each cluster exists within a single directory tree, and the entire cluster is serviced by a single `postmaster`[3]. A cluster is not named—there is no way to refer to a cluster within PostgreSQL, other than by contacting the `postmaster` servicing that cluster. The `$PGDATA` environment variable should point to the root of the cluster's directory tree.

Three system tables are shared between all databases in a cluster: `pg_group` (the list of user groups), `pg_database` (the list of databases within the cluster), and `pg_shadow` (the list of valid users).

2. PostgreSQL version 7.3 introduces a new naming context, the *schema*. Table names must be unique within a schema.

3. The `postmaster` is the program that listens for connection requests from client applications. When a connection request is received (and the user's credentials are authenticated), the `postmaster` starts a new server process that inherits the client connection.

Each cluster contains one or more databases. Every database has a name that must follow the naming rules described in the previous section. Database names must be unique within a cluster. A database is a collection of tables, data types, functions, operators, views, indexes, and so on.

Starting with release 7.3, there is a new level in the PostgreSQL hierarchy—the schema. Figure 3.2 shows the 7.3 hierarchy.

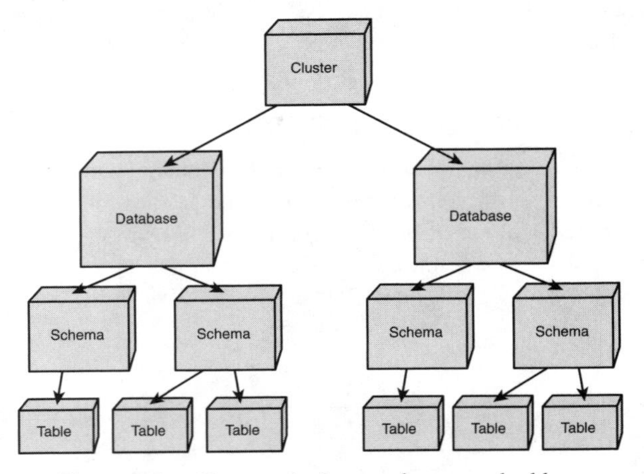

Figure 3.2 Clusters, databases, schemas and tables.

A *schema* is a named collection of tables (as well as functions, data types, and operators). The schema name must be unique within a database. With the addition of the schema, table names, function names, index names, type names, and operators must be unique within the schema. Prior to release 7.3, these objects had to be unique within the database. A schema exists primarily to provide a naming context. You can refer to an object in any schema within a single database by prefixing the object name with `schema-name`. For example, if you have a schema named `bruce`, you can create a table within that schema as

```
CREATE TABLE bruce.ratings ( ... );
SELECT * FROM bruce.ratings;
```

Each connection has a schema search path. If the object that you are referring to is found on the search path, you can omit the schema name. However, because table names are no longer required to be unique within a database, you may find that there are two tables with the same name within your search path (or a table may not be in your search path at all). In those circumstances, you can include the schema name to remove any ambiguity.

To view the schema search path, use the command `SHOW SEARCH_PATH`:

```
movies=# SHOW SEARCH_PATH;
search_path
--------------
 $user,public
(1 row)
```

The default search path, shown here, is `$user,public`. The `$user` part equates to your PostgreSQL user name. For example, if I connect to `psql` as user `bruce`, my search path is `bruce,public`. If a schema named `bruce` does not exist, PostgreSQL will just ignore that part of the search path and move on to the schema named `public`. To change the search path, use `SET SEARCH_PATH TO`:

```
movies=# SET SEARCH_PATH TO 'bruce','sheila','public';
SET
```

New schemas are created with the `CREATE SCHEMA` command and destroyed with the `DROP SCHEMA` command:

```
movies=# CREATE SCHEMA bruce;
CREATE SCHEMA

movies=# CREATE TABLE bruces_table( pkey INTEGER );
CREATE TABLE

movies=# \d
      List of relations
 Name            | Schema | Type  | Owner
-----------------+--------+-------+-------
 bruces_table    | bruce  | table | bruce
 tapes           | public | table | bruce
(2 rows)

movies=# DROP SCHEMA bruce;
ERROR:  Cannot drop schema bruce because other objects depend on it
        Use DROP ... CASCADE to drop the dependent objects too

movies=# DROP SCHEMA bruce CASCADE;
NOTICE:  Drop cascades to table bruces_table
DROP SCHEMA
```

Notice that you won't be able to drop a schema that is not empty unless you include the `CASCADE` clause. Schemas are a new feature that should appear in version 7.3. Schemas are *very* useful. At many sites, you may need to keep a "development" system and a "production" system. You might consider keeping both systems in the same database, but in separate schemas. Another (particularly clever) use of schemas is to separate financial data by year. For example, you might want to keep one year's worth of data per schema. The table names (`invoices`, `sales`, and so on) remain the same across all schemas, but the schema name reflects the year to which the data applies. You could then refer to data for 2001 as FY2001.invoices, FY2001.sales, and so on. The data for 2002 would be stored in FY2002.invoices, FY2002.sales, and so on. This is a difficult problem to solve without schemas because PostgreSQL does not support cross-database access. In other words, if you are connected to database `movies`, you can't access tables stored in another database. Starting with PostgreSQL 7.3, you can keep all your data in a single database and use schemas to partition the data.

Creating New Databases

Now let's see how to create a new database and how to remove an existing one.

The syntax for the CREATE DATABASE command is

```
CREATE DATABASE database-name
    [ WITH [ OWNER    [=] {username|DEFAULT} ]
           [ TEMPLATE [=] {template-name|DEFAULT} ]
           [ ENCODING [=] {encoding|DEFAULT} ] ]
           [ LOCATION [=] {'path'|DEFAULT} ]
```

As I mentioned earlier, the `database-name` must follow the PostgreSQL naming rules described and must be unique within the cluster.

If you don't include the `OWNER=username` clause or you specify `OWNER=DEFAULT`, you become the owner of the database. If you are a PostgreSQL superuser, you can create a database that will be owned by another user using the `OWNER=username` clause. If you are not a PostgreSQL superuser, you can still create a database if you have the `CREATEDB` privilege, but you cannot assign ownership to another user. Chapter 19, "General PostgreSQL Administration," describes the process of defining user privileges.

The `TEMPLATE=template-name` clause is used to specify a *template* database. A *template* defines a starting point for a database. If you don't include a `TEMPLATE=template-name` or you specify `TEMPLATE=DEFAULT`, the database named `template1` is copied to the new database. All tables, views, data types, functions, and operators defined in the template database are duplicated into the new database. If you add objects (usually functions, operators, and data types) to the `template1` database, those objects will be propagated to any new databases that you create based on `template1`. You can also trim down a template database if you want to reduce the size of new databases. For example, you might decide to remove the geometric data types (and the functions and operators that support that type) if you know that you won't need them. Or, if you have a set of functions that are required by your application, you can define the functions in the `template1` database and all new databases will automatically include those functions. If you want to create an *as-distributed* database, you can use `template0` as your template database. The `template0` database is the starting point for `template1` and contains only the standard objects included in a PostgreSQL distribution. You should not make changes to the `template0` database, but you can use the `template1` database to provide a site-specific set of default objects.

You can use the `ENCODING=character-set` clause to choose an encoding for the string values in the new database. An *encoding* determines how the bytes that make up a string are interpreted as characters. For example, specifying `ENCODING=SQL_ASCII` tells PostgreSQL that characters are stored in ASCII format, whereas `ENCODING=ISO-8859-8` requests ECMA-121 Latin/Hebrew encoding. When you create a database, all characters stored in that database are encoded in a single format. When a client retrieves data, the client/server protocol automatically converts between the database encoding and the encoding being used by the client. Chapter 20, "Internationalization/Localization," discusses encoding schemes in more detail.

The last option for the `CREATE DATABASE` command is the `LOCATION=`*`path`* clause. In most cases, you will never have to use the `LOCATION` option, which is good because it's a little strange.

If you do have need to use an alternate location, you will probably want to specify the location by using an environment variable. The environment variable must be known to the `postmaster` processor at the time the `postmaster` is started and it should contain an absolute pathname.

The `LOCATION=`*`path`* clause can be confusing. The *`path`* might be specified in three forms:

- The path contains a `/`, but does not begin with a `/`—this specifies a relative path
- The path begins with a `/`—this specifies an absolute path
- The path does not include a `/`

Relative locations are not allowed by PostgreSQL, so the first form is invalid.

Absolute paths are allowed only if you defined the C/C++ preprocessor symbol "`ALLOW_ABSOLUTE_DBPATHS`" at the time you compiled your copy of PostgreSQL. If you are using a prebuilt version of PostgreSQL, the chances are pretty high that this symbol was *not* defined and therefore absolute paths are not allowed.

So, the only form that you can rely on in a standard distribution is the last—a path that does not include any "`/`" characters. At first glance, this may look like a relative path that is only one level deep, but that's not how PostgreSQL sees it. In the third form, the path must be the *name* of an environment variable. As I mentioned earlier, the environment variable must be known to the `postmaster` processor at the time the `postmaster` is started, and it should contain an absolute pathname. Let's look at an example:

```
$ export PG_ALTERNATE=/bigdrive/pgdata
$ initlocation PG_ALTERNATE
$ pg_ctl restart -l /tmp/pg.log -D $PGDATA
...
$ psql -q -d movies
movies=# CREATE DATABASE bigdb WITH LOCATION=PG_ALTERNATE;
...
```

First, I've defined (and exported) an environment variable named `PG_ALTERNATE`. I've defined `PG_ALTERNATE` to have a value of `/bigdrive/pgdata`—that's where I want my new database to reside. After the environment variable has been defined, I need to initialize the directory structure—the `initlocation` script will take care of that for me. Now I have to restart the `postmaster` so that it can see the `PG_ALTERNATE` variable. Finally, I can start `psql` (or some other client) and execute the `CREATE DATABASE` command specifying the `PG_ALTERNATE` environment variable.

This all sounds a bit convoluted, and it is. The PostgreSQL developers consider it a security risk to allow users to create databases in arbitrary locations. Because the `postmaster` must be started by a PostgreSQL administrator, only an administrator can choose where databases can be created. So, to summarize the process:

1. Create a new environment variable and set it to the path where you want new databases to reside.
2. Initialize the new directory using the `initlocation` application.
3. Stop and restart the `postmaster`.
4. Now, you can use the environment variable with the `LOCATION=`*`path`* clause.

createdb

The `CREATE DATABASE` command creates a new database from within a PostgreSQL client application (such as `psql`). You can also create a new database from the operating system command line. The `createdb` command is a shell script that invokes psql for you and executes the `CREATE DATABASE` command for you. For more information about `createdb`, see the *PostgreSQL Reference Manual* or invoke `createdb` with the `--help` flag:

```
$ createdb --help
createdb creates a PostgreSQL database.

Usage:
  createdb [options] dbname [description]

Options:
  -D, --location=PATH          Alternative place to store the database
  -T, --template=TEMPLATE      Template database to copy
  -E, --encoding=ENCODING      Multibyte encoding for the database
  -h, --host=HOSTNAME          Database server host
  -p, --port=PORT              Database server port
  -U, --username=USERNAME      Username to connect as
  -W, --password               Prompt for password
  -e, --echo                   Show the query being sent to the backend
  -q, --quiet                  Don't write any messages

By default, a database with the same name as the current user is created.

Report bugs to <pgsql-bugs@postgresql.org>.
```

Dropping a Database

Getting rid of an old database is easy. The `DROP DATABASE` command will delete all of the data in a database and remove the database from the cluster.

For example:

```
movies=# CREATE DATABASE redshirt;
CREATE DATABASE
movies=# DROP DATABASE redshirt;
DROP DATABASE
```

There are no options to the `DROP DATABASE` command; you simply include the name of the database that you want to remove. There *are* a few restrictions. First, you must own the database that you are trying to drop, or you must be a PostgreSQL superuser. Next, you cannot drop a database from within a transaction block—you cannot roll back a `DROP DATABASE` command. Finally, the database must not be in use, even by you. This means that before you can drop a database, you must connect to a different database (`template1` is a good candidate). An alternative to the `DROP DATABASE` command is the `dropdb` shell script. `dropdb` is simply a wrapper around the `DROP DATABASE` command; see the *PostgreSQL Reference Manual* for more information about `dropdb`.

Viewing Databases

Using `psql`, there are two ways to view the list of databases. First, you can ask `psql` to simply display the list of databases and then exit. The `-l` option does this for you:

```
$ psql -l
     List of databases
   Name    |    Owner
-----------+---------------
 template0 | postgres
 template1 | postgres
 movies    | bruce
(3 rows)
$
```

From within psql, you can use the `\l` or `\l+` meta-commands to display the databases within a cluster:

```
movies=# \l+
                  List of databases
   Name    |     Owner     |        Description
-----------+---------------+--------------------------
 template0 | postgres      |
 template1 | postgres      | Default template database
 movies    | bruce         | Virtual Video database
 (3 rows)
```

Creating New Tables

The previous section described how to create and drop databases. Now let's move down one level in the PostgreSQL storage hierarchy and talk about creating and dropping tables.

You've created some simple tables in the first two chapters; it's time to talk about some of the more advanced features of the `CREATE TABLE` command. Here is the command that you used to create the `customers` table:

```
CREATE TABLE customers (
        customer_id   INTEGER UNIQUE,
        customer_name VARCHAR(50),
        phone         CHAR(8),
        birth_date    DATE,
        balance       DECIMAL(7,2)
);
```

This command creates a *permanent* table named `customers`. A table name must meet the naming criteria described earlier in this chapter. When you create a table, PostgreSQL automatically creates a new data type[4] with the same name as the table. This means that you can't create a table whose name is the same as an existing data type.

When you execute this command, the `customers` table is created in the database that you are connected to. If you are using PostgreSQL 7.3 or later, the `customers` table is created in the first schema in your search path. (If you are using a version older than 7.3, your copy of PostgreSQL does not support schemas). If you want the table to be created in some other schema, you can prefix the table name with the schema qualifier, for example:

```
CREATE TABLE joes_video.customers( ... );
```

The new table is owned by you. You can't give ownership to another user at the time you create the table, but you can change it later using the `ALTER TABLE...OWNER TO` command (described later).

Temporary Tables

I mentioned earlier that the `customers` table is a permanent table. You can also create *temporary* tables. A permanent table persists after you terminate your PostgreSQL session; a temporary table is automatically destroyed when your PostgreSQL session ends. Temporary tables are also local to your session, meaning that other PostgreSQL sessions can't see temporary tables that you create. Because temporary tables are local to each session, you don't have to worry about colliding with the name of a table created by another session.

4. This seems to be a holdover from earlier days. You can't actually *do* anything with this data type.

If you create a temporary table with the same name as a permanent table, you are effectively *hiding* the permanent table. For example, let's create a temporary table that hides the permanent `customers` table:

```
CREATE TEMPORARY TABLE customers (
        customer_id   INTEGER UNIQUE,
        customer_name VARCHAR(50),
        phone         CHAR(8),
        birth_date    DATE,
        balance       DECIMAL(7,2)
);
```

Notice that the only difference between this command and the command that you used to create the permanent `customers` table is the `TEMPORARY` keyword[5]. Now you have two tables, each named `customers`. If you now `SELECT` from or `INSERT` into the `customers` table, you will be working with the temporary table. Prior to version 7.3, there was no way to get back to the permanent table except by dropping the temporary table:

```
movies=# SELECT * FROM customers;
 customer_id |     customer_name     |  phone   | birth_date | balance
-------------+----------------------+----------+------------+---------
           1 | Jones, Henry         | 555-1212 | 1970-10-10 |    0.00
           2 | Rubin, William       | 555-2211 | 1972-07-10 |   15.00
           3 | Panky, Henry         | 555-1221 | 1968-01-21 |    0.00
           4 | Wonderland, Alice N. | 555-1122 | 1969-03-05 |    3.00
           8 | Wink Wankel          | 555-1000 | 1988-12-25 |    0.00
(5 rows)

movies=# CREATE TEMPORARY TABLE customers
movies-# (
movies(#   customer_id   INTEGER UNIQUE,
movies(#   customer_name VARCHAR(50),
movies(#   phone         CHAR(8),
movies(#   birth_date    DATE,
movies(#   balance       DECIMAL(7,2)
movies(#   );
CREATE

movies=# SELECT * FROM customers;
 customer_id |     customer_name     |  phone   | birth_date | balance
-------------+----------------------+----------+------------+---------
(0 rows)
```

5. You can abbreviate `TEMPORARY` to `TEMP`.

```
movies=# DROP TABLE customers;
DROP

movies=# SELECT * FROM customers;
 customer_id |     customer_name      |  phone   | birth_date | balance
-------------+------------------------+----------+------------+---------
           1 | Jones, Henry           | 555-1212 | 1970-10-10 |    0.00
           2 | Rubin, William         | 555-2211 | 1972-07-10 |   15.00
           3 | Panky, Henry           | 555-1221 | 1968-01-21 |    0.00
           4 | Wonderland, Alice N.   | 555-1122 | 1969-03-05 |    3.00
           8 | Wink Wankel            | 555-1000 | 1988-12-25 |    0.00
(5 rows)
```

Starting with release 7.3, you can access the permanent table by including the name of the schema where the permanent table resides.

A temporary table is like a scratch pad. You can use a temporary table to accumulate intermediate results. Quite often, you will find that a complex query can be formulated more easily by first extracting the data that interests you into a temporary table. If you find that you are creating a given temporary table over and over again, you might want to convert that table into a view. See the section titled "Using Views" in Chapter 1, "Introduction to PostgreSQL and SQL," for more information about views.

Table Constraints

In Chapter 2 we explored the various constraints that you can apply to a column: `NOT NULL`, `UNIQUE`, `PRIMARY KEY`, `REFERENCES`, and `CHECK()`. You can also apply constraints to a table as a whole or to groups of columns within a table.

First, let's look at the `CHECK()` constraint. The syntax for a `CHECK()` constraint is

```
[CONSTRAINT constraint-name] CHECK( boolean-expression )
```

When you define a `CHECK()` constraint for a table, you are telling PostgreSQL that any insertions or updates made to the table must satisfy the *`boolean-expression`* given within the constraint. The difference between a column constraint and a table constraint is that a column constraint should refer only to the column to which it relates. A table constraint can refer to any column in the table.

For example, suppose that you had an `orders` table to track customer orders:

```
CREATE TABLE orders
(
    customer_number    INTEGER,
    part_number        CHAR(8),
    quantity_ordered   INTEGER,
    price_per_part     DECIMAL(7,2)
);
```

You could create a table-related CHECK() constraint to ensure that the extended price (that is, quantity_ordered times price_per_part) of any given order is at least $5.00:

```
CREATE TABLE orders
(
    customer_number     INTEGER,
    part_number         CHAR(8),
    quantity_ordered    INTEGER,
    price_per_part      DECIMAL(7,2),

    CONSTRAINT verify_minimum_order
     CHECK (( price_per_part * quantity_ordered) >= 5.00::DECIMAL )
);
```

Each time a row is inserted into the orders table (or the quantity_ordered or price_per_part columns are updated), the verify_minimum_order constraint is evaluated. If the expression evaluates to FALSE, the modification is rejected. If the expression evaluates to TRUE or NULL, the modification is allowed.

You may have noticed that a table constraint looks very much like a column constraint. PostgreSQL can tell the difference between the two types by their placement within the CREATE TABLE statement. A column constraint is placed *within* a column definition—after the column's data type and before the comma. A table constraint is listed *outside* of a column definition. The only tricky spot is a table constraint that follows the last column definition; you normally would not include a comma after the last column. If you want a constraint to be treated as a table constraint, be sure to include a comma following the last column definition. At the moment, PostgreSQL does not treat table constraints and column constraints differently, but in a future release it may.

Each of the table constraint varieties is related to a type of column constraint.

The UNIQUE table constraint is identical to the UNIQUE column constraint, except that you can specify that a group of columns must be unique. For example, here is the rentals table as currently defined:

```
CREATE TABLE rentals
(
    tape_id     CHARACTER(8),
    customer_id INTEGER,
    rental_date DATE
);
```

Let's modify this table to reflect the business rule that any given tape cannot be rented twice on the same day:

```
CREATE TABLE rentals
(
```

```
    tape_id      CHARACTER(8),
    customer_id INTEGER,
    rental_date DATE,

    UNIQUE( rental_date, tape_id )

);
```

Now when you insert a row into the `rentals` table, PostgreSQL will ensure that there are no other rows with the same combination of `rental_date` and `tape_id`. Notice that I did not provide a constraint name in this example; constraint names are optional.

The `PRIMARY KEY` table constraint is identical to the `PRIMARY KEY` column constraint, except that you can specify that the key is composed of a group of columns rather than a single column.

The `REFERENCES` table constraint is similar to the `REFERENCES` column constraint. When you create a `REFERENCES` column constraint, you are telling PostgreSQL that a column value in one table refers to a row in another table. More specifically, a `REFERENCES` column constraint specifies a relationship between two columns. When you create a `REFERENCES` table constraint, you can relate a group of columns in one table to a group of columns in another table. Quite often, you will find that the unique identifier for a table (that is, the `PRIMARY KEY`) is composed of multiple columns. Let's say that the Virtual Video Store is having great success and you decide to open a second store. You might want to consolidate the data for each store into a single database. Start by creating a new table:

```
CREATE TABLE stores
(
    store_id      INTEGER PRIMARY KEY,
    location      VARCHAR
);
```

Now, change the definition of the `customers` table to include a `store_id` for each customer:

```
CREATE TABLE customers (
        store_id       INTEGER REFERENCES stores( store_id ),
        customer_id    INTEGER UNIQUE,
        customer_name VARCHAR(50),
        phone          CHAR(8),
        birth_date     DATE,
        balance        DECIMAL(7,2),

        PRIMARY KEY( store_id, customer_id )
);
```

The store_id column in the customers table refers to the store_id column in the stores table. Because store_id is the primary key to the stores table, you could have written the REFERENCES constraint in either of two ways:

```
store_id INTEGER REFERENCES stores( store_id )
```

or

```
store_id INTEGER REFERENCES stores
```

Also, notice that the primary key for this table is composed of two columns: store_id and customer_id. I can have two customers with the same customer_id as long as they have different store_ids.

Now you have to change the rentals table as well:

```
CREATE TABLE rentals
(
    store_id    INTEGER,
    tape_id     CHARACTER(8),
    customer_id INTEGER,
    rental_date DATE,

    UNIQUE( rental_date, tape_id )
    FOREIGN KEY( store_id, customer_id ) REFERENCES customers
);
```

The customers table has a two-part primary key. Each row in the rentals table refers to a row in the customers table, so the FOREIGN KEY constraint must specify a two-part foreign key. Again, because foreign key refers to the primary key of the customers table, I can write this constraint in either of two forms:

```
FOREIGN KEY( store_id, customer_id )
  REFERENCES customers( store_id, customer_id )
```

or

```
FOREIGN KEY( store_id, customer_id )
 REFERENCES customers
```

Now that I have the referential integrity constraints defined, they will behave as described in the *Column Constraints* section of Chapter 2, "Working with Data in PostgreSQL." Remember, a table constraint functions the same as a column constraint, except that table constraints can refer to more than one column.

Dropping Tables

Dropping a table is much easier than creating a table. The syntax for the DROP TABLE command is

```
DROP TABLE table-name [, ...];
```

If you are using PostgreSQL 7.3 or later, you can qualify the table name with a schema. For example, here is the command to destroy the `rentals` table:

```
DROP TABLE rentals;
```

If the `rentals` table existed in some schema other than your current schema, you would qualify the table name:

```
DROP TABLE sheila.rentals;
```

You can destroy a table only if you are the table's owner or if you are a PostgreSQL superuser. Notice that I used the word *destroy* here rather than *drop*. It's important to realize that when you execute a `DROP TABLE` command, you are destroying all the data in that table.

PostgreSQL has a nice feature that I have not seen in other databases: You can roll back a `DROP TABLE` command. Try the following experiment. First, let's view the contents of the `tapes` table:

```
movies=# SELECT * FROM tapes;
 tape_id  |     title     | dist_id
----------+---------------+---------
 AB-12345 | The Godfather |       1
 AB-67472 | The Godfather |       1
 MC-68873 | Casablanca    |       3
 OW-41221 | Citizen Kane  |       2
 AH-54706 | Rear Window   |       3
(5 rows)
```

Now, start a multistatement transaction and destroy the `tapes` table:

```
movies=# BEGIN WORK;
BEGIN

movies=# DROP TABLE tapes;
NOTICE:  DROP TABLE implicitly drops referential integrity trigger
         from table "rentals"
NOTICE:  DROP TABLE implicitly drops referential integrity trigger
         from table "distributors"
NOTICE:  DROP TABLE implicitly drops referential integrity trigger
         from table "distributors"
DROP
```

If you try to `SELECT` from the `tapes` table, you'll find that it has been destroyed:

```
movies=# SELECT * FROM tapes;
ERROR:  Relation "tapes" does not exist
```

If you `COMMIT` this transaction, the table will permanently disappear; let's `ROLLBACK` the transaction instead:

```
movies=# ROLLBACK;
ROLLBACK
```

The ROLLBACK threw out all changes made since the beginning of the transaction, including the DROP TABLE command. You should be able to SELECT from the tapes table again and see the same data that was there before:

```
movies=# SELECT * FROM tapes;
 tape_id  |     title     | dist_id
----------+---------------+---------
 AB-12345 | The Godfather |       1
 AB-67472 | The Godfather |       1
 MC-68873 | Casablanca    |       3
 OW-41221 | Citizen Kane  |       2
 AH-54706 | Rear Window   |       3
(5 rows)
```

This is a *very* nice feature. You can roll back CREATE TABLE, DROP TABLE, CREATE VIEW, DROP VIEW, CREATE INDEX, DROP INDEX, and so on. I'll discuss transactions a bit later in this chapter. For now, I'd like to point out a few details that I glossed over in the previous example. You may have noticed that the DROP TABLE command produced a few NOTICES.

```
movies=# DROP TABLE tapes;
NOTICE:  DROP TABLE implicitly drops referential integrity trigger
         from table "rentals"
NOTICE:  DROP TABLE implicitly drops referential integrity trigger
         from table "distributors"
NOTICE:  DROP TABLE implicitly drops referential integrity trigger
         from table "distributors"
DROP
```

When you drop a table, PostgreSQL will automatically DROP any indexes defined for that table as well as any triggers or rules. If other tables refer to the table that you dropped (by means of a REFERENCE constraint), PostgreSQL will automatically drop the constraints in the other tables. However, any *views* that refer to the dropped table will not be removed—a view can refer to many tables and PostgreSQL would not know how to remove a single table from a multitable SELECT.

Inheritance

Another PostgreSQL feature that is uncommon in relational database systems is *inheritance*. Inheritance is one of the foundations of the object-oriented programming paradigm. Using inheritance, you can define a hierarchy of related data types (in PostgreSQL, you define a hierarchy of related tables). Each layer in the inheritance hierarchy represents a *specialization* of the layer above it[6].

6. We'll view an inheritance hierarchy with the most general type at the top and the most specialized types at the bottom.

Let's look at an example. The Virtual Video database defines a table that stores information about the tapes that you have in stock:

```
movies=# \d tapes
 Column  |         Type          | Modifiers
---------+-----------------------+-----------
 tape_id | character(8)          | not null
 title   | character varying(80) |
 dist_id | integer               |
Primary key: tapes_pkey
```

For each tape, you store the `tape_id`, `title`, and `distributor id`. Let's say that you decide to jump into the twenty-first century and rent DVDs as well as videotapes. You *could* store DVD records in the `tapes` table, but a tape and a DVD are not really the same thing. Let's create a new table that defines the characteristics common to both DVDs and videotapes:

```
CREATE TABLE video
(
  video_id        CHARACTER(8) PRIMARY KEY,
  title           VARCHAR(80),
  dist_id         INTEGER
);
```

Now, create a table to hold the DVDs. For each DVD you have in stock, you want to store everything in the `video` table plus a `region_id` and an array of `audio_tracks`. Here is the new table definition:

```
movies=# CREATE TABLE dvds
movies-# (
movies(#   region_id    INTEGER,
movies(#   audio_tracks VARCHAR[]
movies(# ) INHERITS ( video );
```

Notice the last line in this command: You are telling PostgreSQL that the `dvds` table *inherits from* the `video` table. Now let's `INSERT` a new DVD:

```
movies=# INSERT INTO dvds VALUES
movies=# (
movies(#   'ASIN-750',                        -- video_id
movies(#   'Star Wars - The Phantom Menace', -- title
movies(#   3,                                 -- dist_id
movies(#   1,                                 -- region_id
movies(#   '{English,Spanish}'                -- audio_tracks
movies(# );
```

Now, if you SELECT from the dvds table, you'll see the information that you just inserted:

```
title_id |              title              | dist_id | region |    audio_tracks
---------+---------------------------------+---------+--------+-----------------
ASIN-750 | Star Wars - The Phantom Menace |       3 |      1 | {English,Spanish}
```

At this point, you might be thinking that the INHERITS clause did nothing more than create a row template that PostgreSQL copied when you created the dvds table. That's not the case. When we say that dvds inherits from video, we are not simply saying that a DVD is *like* a video, we are saying that a DVD *is* a video. Let's SELECT from the video table now; remember, you haven't explicitly inserted any data into the video table, so you might expect the result set to be empty:

```
movies=# SELECT * FROM video;
 video_id |              title              | dist_id
----------+---------------------------------+--------
 ASIN-750 | Star Wars - The Phantom Menace |       3
(1 row)
```

A DVD is a video. When you SELECT from the video table, you see only the columns that comprise a video. When you SELECT from the dvds table, you see all the columns that comprise a DVD. In this relationship, you say that the dvd table *specializes*[7] the more general video table.

If you are using a version of PostgreSQL older than 7.2, you must code this query as SELECT * FROM video* to see the DVD entries. Starting with release 7.2, SELECT will include descendent tables and you have to say SELECT * FROM ONLY video to suppress descendents.

You now have a new table to track your DVD inventory; let's go back and redefine the tapes table to fit into the inheritance hierarchy. For each tape, we want to store a video_id, a title, and a distributor_id. This is where we started: the video table already stores all this information. You should still create a new table to track videotapes—at some point in the future, you may find information that relates to a videotape, but not to a DVD:

```
movies=# CREATE TABLE tapes ( ) INHERITS( video );
CREATE
```

This CREATE TABLE command creates a new table identical in structure to the video table. Each row in the tapes table will contain a video_id, a title, and a dist_id. Insert a row into the tapes table:

```
movies=# INSERT INTO tapes VALUES
movies-# (
movies(#   'ASIN-8YD',
movies(#   'Flight To Mars(1951)',
movies(#   3
movies(# );
INSERT
```

7. Object-oriented terminology defines many different phrases for this inheritance relationship: specialize/generalize, subclass/superclass, and so on. Choose the phrase that you like.

When you SELECT from the tapes table, you should see this new row:

```
movies=# SELECT * FROM tapes;
 title_id |        title         | dist_id
----------+----------------------+--------
 ASIN-8YD | Flight To Mars(1951) |       3
(1 row)
```

And because a tape *is* a video, you would also expect to see this row in the video table:

```
movies=# SELECT * FROM video;
 video_id |             title              | dist_id
----------+--------------------------------+--------
 ASIN-750 | Star Wars - The Phantom Menace |       3
 ASIN-8YD | Flight To Mars(1951)           |       3
(2 rows)
```

Now here's the interesting part. A DVD is a video—any row that you add to the dvds table shows up in the video table. A tape is a video—any row that you add to the tapes table shows up in the video table. But a DVD is *not* a tape (and a tape is *not* a DVD). Any row that you add to the dvds table will *not* show up in the tapes table (and vice versa).

If you want a list of all the tapes you have in stock, you can SELECT from the tapes table. If you want a list of all the DVDs in stock, SELECT from the dvds table. If you want a list of all videos in stock, SELECT from the videos table.

In this example, the inheritance hierarchy is only two levels deep. PostgreSQL imposes no limit to the number of levels that you can define in an inheritance hierarchy. You can also create a table that inherits from *multiple* tables—the new table will have all the columns defined in the more general tables.

I should caution you about two problems with the current implementation of inheritance in PostgreSQL. First, indexes are not shared between parent and child tables. On one hand, that's good because it gives you good performance. On the other hand, that's bad because PostgreSQL uses an index to guarantee uniqueness. That means that you could have a videotape and a DVD with the same video_id. Of course, you can work around this problem by encoding the type of video in the video_id (for example, use a T for tapes and a D for DVDs). But PostgreSQL won't give you any help in fixing this problem. The other *potential* problem with inheritance is that triggers are not shared between parent and child tables. If you define a trigger for the topmost table in your inheritance hierarchy, you will have to remember to define the same trigger for each descendant.

We have redefined some of the example tables many times in the past few chapters. In a real-world environment, you probably won't want to throw out all your data each time you need to make a change to the definition of an existing table. Let's explore a better way to alter a table.

ALTER TABLE

Now that you have a video table, a dvds table, and a tapes table, let's add a new column to all three tables that you can use to record the rating of the video (PG, G, R, and so on).

You could add the rating column to the tapes table and to the dvds table, but you really want the rating column to be a part of every video. The ALTER TABLE ... ADD COLUMN command adds a new column for you, leaving all the original data in place:

```
movies=# ALTER TABLE video ADD COLUMN rating VARCHAR;
ALTER
```

Now, if you look at the definition of the video table, you will see the new column:

```
movies=# \d video
                Table "video"
  Column  |         Type          | Modifiers
----------+-----------------------+-----------
 title_id | character(8)          | not null
 title    | character varying(80) |
 dist_id  | integer               |
 rating   | character varying     |
Primary key: video_pkey
```

After the ALTER TABLE command completes, each row in the video table has a new column; the value of every rating column will be NULL. Because you have changed the definition of a video, and a DVD is a video, you might expect that the dvds table will also contain a rating column:

```
movies=# \d dvds
                      Table "dvds"
    Column    |         Type          |     Modifiers
--------------+-----------------------+-------------------
 title_id     | character(8)          | not null
 title        | character varying(80) |
 dist_id      | integer               |
 region       | integer               |
 audio_tracks | character varying[]   |
 rating       | character varying(8)  |
```

Similarly, the tapes table will also inherit the new rating column:

```
movies=# \d dvds
                   Table "tapes"
  Column  |         Type          |     Modifiers
----------+-----------------------+-------------------
 title_id | character(8)          | not null
 title    | character varying(80) |
 dist_id  | integer               |
 rating   | character varying(8)  |
```

The ALTER TABLE command is useful when you are in the development stages of a project. Using ALTER TABLE, you can add new columns to a table, define default values, rename columns (and tables), add and drop constraints, and transfer ownership. The capabilities of the ALTER TABLE command seem to grow with each new release, see the *PostgreSQL Reference Manual* for more details.

Adding Indexes to a Table

Most of the tables that you have created so far have no indexes. An index serves two purposes. First, an index can be used to guarantee uniqueness. Second, an index provides quick access to data (in certain circumstances).

Here is the definition of the customers table that you created in Chapter 1:

```
CREATE TABLE customers (
        customer_id   INTEGER UNIQUE,
        customer_name VARCHAR(50),
        phone         CHAR(8),
        birth_date    DATE,
        balance       DECIMAL(7,2)
);
```

When you create this table, PostgreSQL will display a rather terse message:

```
NOTICE:  CREATE TABLE / UNIQUE will create implicit index
'customers_customer_id_key' for table 'customers'
```

What PostgreSQL is trying to tell you here is that even though you didn't explicitly ask for one, an index has been created on your behalf. The implicit index is created so that PostgreSQL has a quick way to ensure that the values that you enter into the customer_id column are unique.

Think about how you might design an algorithm to check for duplicate values in the following list of names:

Grumby, Jonas	Poole, Frank
Hinkley, Roy	Morbius, Edward
Wentworth, Eunice	Farman, Jerry
Floyd, Heywood	Stone, Jeremy
Bowman, David	Dutton, Charles
Dutton, Charles	Manchek, Arthur

A first attempt might simply start with the first value and look for a duplicate later in the list, comparing Grumby, Jonas to Hinkley, Roy, then Wentworth, Eunice, and so on. Next, you would move to the second name in the list and compare Hinkley, Roy to Wentworth, Eunice, then Floyd, Heywood, and so on. This algorithm would certainly work, but it would turn out to be slow as the list grew longer. Each time you add a new name to the list, you have to compare it to every other name already in the list.

A better solution would be to first sort the list:

Bowman, David
Dutton, Charles
Dutton, Charles
Farman, Jerry
Floyd, Heywood
Grumby, Jonas
Hinkley, Roy
Manchek, Arthur
Morbius, Edward
Poole, Frank
Stone, Jeremy
Wentworth, Eunice

After the list is sorted, it's easy to check for duplicates—any duplicate values appear next to each other. To check the sorted list, you start with the first name, `Bowman, David` and compare it to the second name, `Dutton, Charles`. If the second name is not a duplicate of the first, you know that you won't find any duplicates later in the list. Now when you move to the second name on the list, you compare it to the third name—now you can see that there is a duplicate. Duplicate values appear next to each other after the list is sorted. Now when you add a new name to the list, you can stop searching for duplicate values as soon as you encounter a value that sorts after the name you are adding.

An index is similar in concept to a sorted list, but it's even better. An index provides a quick way for PostgreSQL to find data within a range of values. Let's see how an index can help narrow a search. First, let's assign a number to each of the names in the sorted list, just for easy reference (I've removed the duplicate value):

1 Bowman, David
2 Dutton, Charles
3 Farman, Jerry
4 Floyd, Heywood
5 Grumby, Jonas
6 Hinkley, Roy
7 Manchek, Arthur
8 Morbius, Edward
9 Poole, Frank
10 Stone, Jeremy
11 Wentworth, Eunice

Now let's build a (simplistic) index. The English alphabet contains 26 letters— split this roughly in half and choose to keep track of where the "Ms" start in the list. In this list, names beginning with an `M` start at entry number 7. Keep track of this pair (M,7) and call it the *root* of your index.

1	Bowman, David
2	Dutton, Charles
3	Farman, Jerry
4	Floyd, Heywood
5	Grumby, Jonas
6	Hinkley, Roy
7	Manchek, Arthur
8	Morbius, Edward
9	Poole, Frank
10	Stone, Jeremy
11	Wentworth, Eunice

M(root) →

Figure 3.3 One-level index.

Now when you insert a new name, `Tyrell, Eldon`, you start by comparing it to the root. The root of the index tells you that names starting with the letter `M` are found starting at entry number 7. Because the list is sorted, and you know that `Tyrell` will sort after `M`, you can start searching for the insertion point at entry 7, skipping entries 1 through 6. Also, you can stop searching as soon as you encounter a name that sorts later than `Tyrell`.

As your list of names grows, it would be advantageous to add more levels to the index. The letter `M` splits the alphabet (roughly) in half. Add a second level to the index by splitting the range between `A` and `M` (giving you `G`), and splitting the range between `M` and `Z` (giving you `T`).

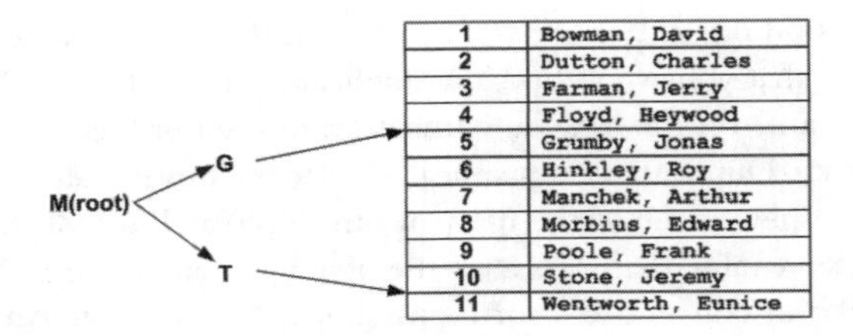

Figure 3.4 Two-level index.

Now when you want to add `Tyrell, Eldon` to the list, you compare `Tyrell` against the root and find that `Tyrell` sorts later than `M`. Moving to the next layer of the index, you find that `Tyrell` sorts later than `T`, so you can jump straight to slot number 11 and insert the new value.

You can see that you can add as many index levels as you need. Each level divides the parent's range in half, and each level reduces the number of names that you have to search to find an insertion point[8].

Using an index is similar in concept to the way you look up words in a dictionary. If you have a dictionary handy, pull it off the shelf and take a close look at it. If it's like my dictionary, it has those little thumb-tab indentations, one for each letter of the alphabet. If I want to find the definition of the word "polyglot," I'll find the thumb-tab labeled "*P*" and start searching about halfway through that section. I know, because the dictionary is sorted, that "polyglot" won't appear in any section prior to "P" and it won't appear in any section following "P." That little thumb-tab saves a lot of searching.

You also can use an index as a quick way to check for uniqueness. If you are inserting a new name into the index structure shown earlier, you simply search for the new name in the index. If you find it in the index, it is obviously a duplicate.

8. Technically speaking, the index diagrams discussed here depict a *clustered* index. In a clustered index, the leaf nodes in the index tree are the data rows themselves. In a *non-clustered* index, the leaf nodes are actually row pointers—the rows are not kept in sorted order. PostgreSQL does not support clustered indexes. I've diagrammed the index trees in clustered form for clarity. A clustered index provides fast, sequential access along one index path, but it is *very* expensive to maintain.

I mentioned earlier that PostgreSQL uses an index for two purposes. You've seen that an index can be used to search for unique values. But how does PostgreSQL use an index to provide faster data access?

Let's look at a simple query:

```
SELECT * FROM characters WHERE name >= 'Grumby' AND name < 'Moon';
```

Now assume that the list of names that you worked with before is actually a table named `characters` and you have an index defined for the `name` column:

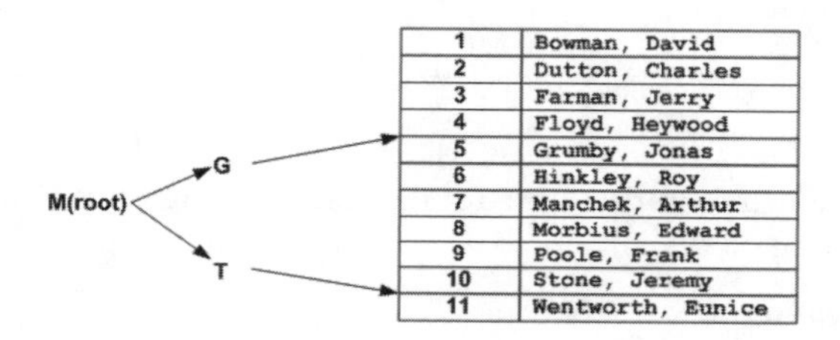

Figure 3.5 Two-level index (again).

When PostgreSQL parses through the `SELECT` statement, it notices that you are constraining the result set to a *range* of names and that you have an index on the `name` column. That's a convenient combination. To satisfy this statement, PostgreSQL can use the index to start searching at entry number 5. Because the rows are already sorted, PostgreSQL can stop searching as soon as it finds the first entry greater than "Moon" (that is, the search ends as soon as you hit entry number 8). This kind of operation is called a *partial index scan*.

Think of how PostgreSQL would process this query if the rows were *not* indexed. It would have to start at the beginning of the table and compare each row against the constraints; PostgreSQL can't terminate the search without processing every row in the table. This kind of operation is called a *full table scan*, or *table scan*.

Because this kind of index can access data in sorted order, PostgreSQL can use such an index to avoid a sort that would otherwise be required to satisfy an `ORDER BY` clause.

In these examples, we are working with small tables, so the performance difference between a full table scan and an indexed range read is negligible. As tables become larger, the performance difference can be huge. Chapter 4, "Query Optimization," discusses how the PostgreSQL query optimizer chooses when it is appropriate to use an index.

PostgreSQL actually supports several kinds of indexes. The previous examples show how a B-Tree index works[9]. Another type of index is the Hash index. A Hash index uses a technique called *hashing* to evenly distribute keys among a number of *hash buckets*. Each key value added to a hash index is run through a hashing function. The result of a hashing function is a bucket number. A simplistic hashing function for string values might

9. The "B" in B-Tree stands for "Balanced." A *balanced tree* is a type of data structure that retains its performance characteristics even in the face of numerous insertions and deletions. The most important feature of a B-Tree is that it takes about the same amount of time to find any given record.

sum the ASCII value of each character in the string and then compute the sum modulo the number of buckets to get the result. In C, you might write this function as

```
int hash_string( char * key, int bucket_count )
{
    int hash = 0;
    int i;

    for( i = 0; i < strlen( key ); i++ )
        hash = hash + key[i];

    return( hash % bucket_count );
}
```

Let's run each of the names in the `characters` table through this function to see what kind of numbers you get back (I've used a `bucket_count` of 5):

hash_string() Value	Name
1	Grumby, Jonas
2	Hinkley, Roy
3	Wentworth, Eunice
4	Floyd, Heywood
4	Bowman, David
3	Dutton, Charles
3	Poole, Frank
0	Morbius, Edward
0	Farman, Jerry
0	Stone, Jeremy
4	Manchek, Arthur

The numbers returned don't really have any intrinsic meaning, they simply serve to distribute a set of keys amongst a set of buckets.

Now let's reformat this table so that the contents are grouped by bucket number:

Bucket Number	Bucket Contents
0	Morbius, Edward
	Farman, Jerry
	Stone, Jeremy
1	Grumby, Jonas
2	Hinkley, Roy

Bucket Number	Bucket Contents
3	Wentworth, Eunice
	Dutton, Charles
	Poole, Frank
4	Floyd, Heywood
	Bowman, David
	Manchek, Arthur

You can see that the hash function (`hash_string()`) did a respectable job of distributing the names between the five hash buckets. Notice that we did not have to assign a unique hash value to each key—hash keys are seldom unique. The important feature of a good hash function is that it distributes a set of keys fairly evenly. Now that you have a Hash index, how can you use it? First, let's try to insert a new name: `Lowell, Freeman`. The first thing you do is run this name through your `hash_string()` function, giving you a hash value of 4. Now you know that if `Lowell, Freeman` is already in the index, it will be in bucket number 4; all you have to do is search that one bucket for the name you are trying to insert.

There are a couple of important points to note about Hash indexes.

First, you may have noticed that each bucket can hold many keys. Another way to say this is that each key does not have a unique hash value. If you have too many collisions (that is, too many keys hashing to the same bucket), performance will suffer. A good hash function distributes keys evenly between all hash buckets.

Second, notice that a hash table is not sorted. The name `Floyd, Heywood` hashes to bucket 4, but `Farman, Jerry` hashes to bucket 0. Consider the `SELECT` statement that we looked at earlier:

```
SELECT * FROM characters WHERE name >= 'Grumby' AND name < 'Moon';
```

To satisfy this query using a Hash index, you have to read the entire contents of each bucket. Bucket 0 contains one row that meets the constraints (`Farman, Jerry`), bucket 2 contains one row, and bucket 4 contains one row. A Hash index offers no advantage to a range read. A Hash index is good for searches based on equality. For example, the `SELECT` statement

```
SELECT * FROM characters WHERE name = 'Grumby, Jonas';
```

can be satisfied simply by hashing the string that you are searching for. A Hash index is also useful when you are joining two tables where the join constraint is of the form *`table1-column = table2-column`*[10]. A Hash read cannot be used to avoid a sort required to satisfy an `ORDER BY` clause.

10. This type of join is known as an *equi-join*.

PostgreSQL supports two other types of index structures: the R-Tree index and the GiST index. An R-Tree index is best suited for indexing spatial (that is, geometric or geographic) data. A GiST index is a B-Tree index that can be extended by defining new query predicates[11]. More information about GiST indexes can be found at `http://gist.cs.berkeley.edu/`.

Tradeoffs

The previous section showed that PostgreSQL can use an index to speed the process of searching for data within a range of values (or data with an exact value). Most queries (that is, `SELECT` commands) in PostgreSQL include a `WHERE` clause to limit the result set. If you find that you are often searching for results based on a range of values for a specific column or group of columns, you might want to consider creating an index that covers those columns.

However, you should be aware that an index represents a performance tradeoff. When you create an index, you are trading read performance for write performance. An index can significantly reduce the amount of time it takes to retrieve data, but it will also *increase* the amount of time it takes to `INSERT`, `DELETE`, and `UPDATE` data. Maintaining an index introduces substantial overhead when you modify the data within a table.

You should consider this tradeoff when you feel the need to add a new index to a table. Adding an index to a table that is updated frequently will certainly slow the updates. A good candidate for an index is a table that you `SELECT` from frequently but seldom update. A customer list, for example, doesn't change often (possibly several times each day), but you probably query the customer list frequently. If you find that you often query the customer list by phone number, it would be beneficial to index the phone number column. On the other hand, a table that is updated frequently, but seldom queried, such as a transaction history table, would be a poor choice for an index.

Creating an Index

Now that you have seen what an index can do, let's look at the process of adding an index to a table. The process of creating a new index can range from simple to somewhat complex.

Let's add an index to the `rentals` table. Here is the structure of the rentals table for reference:

```
CREATE TABLE rentals
(
        tape_id      CHARACTER(8) REFERENCES tapes,
        customer_id  INTEGER REFERENCES customers,
        rental_date  DATE
);
```

11. A *predicate* is a test. A simple predicate is the less-than operator (<). An expression such as `a < 5` tests whether the value of `a` is less than `5`. In this expression, `<` is the predicate and it is called the *less-than* predicate. Other predicates are `=`, `>`, `>=`, and so on.

The syntax for a simple CREATE INDEX command is

```
CREATE [UNIQUE] INDEX index-name ON table-name( column [,...] );
```

You want to index the rental_date column in the rentals table:

```
CREATE INDEX rentals_rental_date ON rentals ( rental_date );
```

You haven't specified any optional information in this command (I'll get to the options in a moment), so PostgreSQL creates a B-Tree index named rentals_rental_date. PostgreSQL considers using this whenever it finds a WHERE clause that refers to the rental_date column using the <, <=, =, >=, or > operator. This index also can be used when you specify an ORDER BY clause that sorts on the rental_date column.

Multicolumn Indexes

A B-Tree index (or a GiST index) can cover more than one column. Multicolumn indexes are usually created when you have many values on the second column for each value in the first column. For example, you might want to create an index that covers the rental_date and tape_id columns—you have many different tapes rented on any given date. PostgreSQL can use multicolumn indexes for selection or for ordering. When you create a multicolumn index, the order in which you name the columns is important. PostgreSQL can use a multicolumn index when you are selecting (or ordering by) a prefix of the key. In this context, a *prefix* may be the entire key or a leading portion of the key. For example, the command SELECT * FROM rentals ORDER BY rental_date could not use an index that covers tape_id plus rental_date, but it could use an index that covers rental_date plus tape_id.

The *index-name* must be unique within the database: You can't have two indexes with the same name, even if they are defined on different tables. New rows are indexed as they are added, and deleted rows are removed. If you change the rental_date for a given row, the index will be updated automatically. If you have any data in the rentals table, each row will be included in the index.

Indexes and NULL Values

Earlier, I mentioned that an index includes a pointer for every row in a table. That statement isn't 100% accurate. PostgreSQL will not index NULL values. This is an important point. Because an index will never include NULL values, it cannot be used to satisfy the ORDER BY clause of a query that returns all rows in a table. For example, if you define an index covering the phone column in the customers table, that index would not include rows where phone was NULL. If you executed the command SELECT * FROM customers ORDER BY phone, PostgreSQL would have to perform a full table scan and then sort the results. If PostgreSQL tried to use the phone index, it would not find all rows. If the phone column were defined as NOT NULL, then PostgreSQL *could* use the index to avoid a sort. Or, if the SELECT command included the clause WHERE phone NOT NULL, PostgreSQL could use the index to satisfy the ORDER BY clause. An index that covers an optional (for example, NULLs-allowed) column will not be used to speed table joins, either.

If you don't specify an index type when creating an index, you'll get a B-Tree index. Let's change the `rentals_rental_date` index into a Hash index. First, drop the original index:

```
DROP INDEX rentals_rental_date;
```

Then you can create a new index:

```
CREATE INDEX rentals_rental_date ON rentals USING HASH ( rental_date );
```

The only difference between this `CREATE INDEX` command and the previous one is that I have included a `USING` clause. You can specify `USING BTREE` (which is the default), `USING HASH`, `USING RTREE`, or `USING GIST`.

This index cannot be used to satisfy an `ORDER BY` clause. In fact, this index can be used only when `rental_date` is compared using the = operator.

I dropped the B-Tree index before creating the Hash index, but that is not strictly necessary. It is perfectly valid (but unusual) to have two or more indexes that cover the same column, as long as the indexes are uniquely named. If we had both a B-Tree index and a Hash index covering the `rental_date` column, PostgreSQL could use the Hash index for = comparisons and the B-Tree index for other comparisons.

Functional Indexes and Partial Indexes

Now let's look at two variations on the basic index types: functional indexes and partial indexes.

A column-based index catalogs column values. A functional index (or more precisely a function-valued index) catalogs the values returned by a given function. This might be easiest to understand by looking at an example. Each row in the `customers` table contains a phone number. You can use the exchange[12] portion of the phone number to determine whether a given customer is located close to your store. For example, you may know that the 555, 556, and 794 exchanges are within five miles of your virtual video store. Let's create a function that extracts the exchange from a phone number:

```
--  exchange_index.sql
--
CREATE OR REPLACE FUNCTION get_exchange( CHARACTER )
  RETURNS CHARACTER AS '

  DECLARE
    result              CHARACTER(3);
  BEGIN

    result := SUBSTR( $1, 1, 3 );

    return( result );
  END;
' LANGUAGE 'plpgsql' WITH ( ISCACHABLE );
```

12. In the U.S., a phone number is composed of an optional three-digit area code, a three-digit exchange, and a four-digit...ummm, number.

Don't be too concerned if this looks a bit confusing, I'll cover the PL/pgSQL language in more detail in Chapter 7, "PL/pgSQL." This function (`get_exchange()`) accepts a single argument, presumably a phone number, and extracts the first three characters. You can call this function directly from `psql`:

```
movies=# SELECT customer_name, phone, get_exchange( phone )
movies-#   FROM customers;

    customer_name      |  phone   | get_exchange
-----------------------+----------+------------
 Jones, Henry          | 555-1212 | 555
 Rubin, William        | 555-2211 | 555
 Panky, Henry          | 555-1221 | 555
 Wonderland, Alice N.  | 555-1122 | 555
 Wink Wankel           | 555-1000 | 555
```

You can see that given a phone number, `get_exchange()` returns the first three digits. Now let's create a function-valued index that uses this function:

```
CREATE INDEX customer_exchange ON customers ( get_exchange( phone ));
```

When you insert a new row into a column-based index, PostgreSQL will index the values in the columns covered by that index. When you insert a new row into a *function-valued* index, PostgreSQL will call the function that you specified and then index the return value.

After the `customer_exchange` index exists, PostgreSQL can use it to speed up queries such as

```
SELECT * FROM customers WHERE get_exchange( phone ) = '555';
SELECT * FROM customers ORDER BY get_exchange( phone );
```

Now you have an index that you can use to search the customer list for all customers that are geographically close. Let's pretend that you occasionally want to send advertising flyers to those customers closest to you: you might never use the `customer_exchange` index for any other purpose. If you need the `customer_exchange` index for only a small set of customers, why bother maintaining that index for customers outside of your vicinity? This is where a *partial* index comes in handy. When you create an index, you can include a `WHERE` clause in the `CREATE INDEX` command. Each time you insert (or update) a row, the `WHERE` clause is evaluated. If a row satisfies the constraints of the `WHERE` clause, that row is included in the index; otherwise, the row is not included in the index. Let's `DROP` the `customer_exchange` index and replace it with a partial, function-valued index:

```
movies=# DROP INDEX customer_exchange;
DROP
movies=# CREATE INDEX customer_exchange
movies-#   ON customers ( get_exchange( phone ))
movies-#   WHERE
```

```
movies-#     get_exchange( phone ) = '555'
movies-#      OR
movies-#     get_exchange( phone ) = '556'
movies-#      OR
movies-#     get_exchange( phone ) = '794';
CREATE
```

Now the `customer_exchange` partial index contains entries only for customers in the 555, 556, or 794 exchange.

There are three performance advantages to a partial index:

- A partial index requires less disk space than a full index.
- Because fewer rows are cataloged in a partial index, the cost of maintaining the index is lower.
- When a partial index is used in a query, PostgreSQL will have fewer index entries to search.

Partial indexes and function-valued indexes are variations on the four basic index types. You can create a function-valued Hash index, B-Tree index, R-tree index, or GiST index. You can also create a partial variant of any index type. And, as you have seen, you can create partial function-valued indexes (of any type). A function-valued index doesn't change the organization of an index—just the values that are actually included in the index. The same is true for a partial index.

Getting Information About Databases and Tables

When you create a table, PostgreSQL stores the definition of that table in the system catalog. The system catalog is a collection of PostgreSQL tables. You can issue `SELECT` statements against the system catalog tables just like any other table, but there are easier ways to view table and index definitions.

When you are using the psql client application, you can view the list of tables defined in your database using the `\d` meta-command:

```
movies=# \d
             List of relations
       Name        | Type  |     Owner
-------------------+-------+---------------
 customers         | table | bruce
 distributors      | table | bruce
 rentals           | table | bruce
 returns           | table | John Whorfin
 tapes             | table | bruce
```

To see the detailed definition of a particular table, use the `\d` *`table-name`* meta-command:

```
movies=# \d tapes
                Table "tapes"
 Column  |          Type          | Modifiers
---------+-----------------------+-----------
 tape_id | character(8)           | not null
 title   | character varying(80) |
 dist_id | integer                |
Primary key: tapes_pkey
Triggers: RI_ConstraintTrigger_74939,
          RI_ConstraintTrigger_74941,
          RI_ConstraintTrigger_74953
```

You can also view a list of all indexes defined in your database. The `\di` meta-command displays indexes:

```
movies=# \di
                List of relations
           Name            | Type  |     Owner
---------------------------+-------+---------------
customers_pkey             | index | Administrator
distributors_pkey          | index | Administrator
tapes_pkey                 | index | Administrator
```

You can see the full definition for any given index using the `\d` *`index-name`* meta-command:

```
movies=# \d tapes
   Index "tapes_pkey"
 Column  |     Type
---------+--------------
 tape_id | character(8)
unique btree (primary key)
```

Table 3.1 shows a complete list of the system catalog-related meta-commands in `psql`:

Table 3.1 **System Catalog Meta-Commands**

Command	Result
`\d`	
`\dt`	List all tables
`\di`	List all indexes
`\ds`	List all sequences
`\dv`	List all views
`\dS`	List all PostgreSQL-defined tables
`\d table-name`	Show table definition

Table 3.1 **Continued**

Command	Result
`\d index-name`	Show index definition
`\d view-name`	Show view definition
`\d sequence-name`	Show sequence definition
`\dp`	List all privileges
`\dl`	List all large objects
`\da`	List all aggregates
`\df`	List all functions
`\df function-name`	List all functions with given name
`\do`	List all operators
`\do operator-name`	List all operators with given name
`\dT`	List all types
`\l`	List all databases in this cluster

Alternative Views (Oracle-Style Dictionary Views)

One of the nice things about an open-source product is that code contributions come from many different places. One such project exists to add Oracle-style dictionary views to PostgreSQL. If you are an experienced Oracle user, you will appreciate this feature. The orapgsqlviews project contributes Oracle-style views such as `all_views`, `all_tables`, `user_tables`, and so on. For more information, see `http://gborg.postgresql.org`.

Transaction Processing

Now let's move on to an important feature in any database system: transaction processing.

A *transaction* is a group of one or more SQL commands treated as a unit. PostgreSQL promises that all commands within a transaction will complete or that none of them will complete. If any command within a transaction does not complete, PostgreSQL will roll back all changes made within the transaction.

PostgreSQL makes use of transactions to ensure database consistency. Transactions are needed to coordinate updates made by two or more concurrent users. Changes made by a transaction are not visible to other users until the transaction is *committed*. When you commit a transaction, you are telling PostgreSQL that all the changes made within the transaction are logically complete, the changes should be made permanent, and the changes should be exposed to other users. When you roll back a transaction, you are telling PostgreSQL that the changes made within the transaction should be discarded and not made visible to other users.

To start a new transaction, execute a `BEGIN`[13] command. To complete the transaction and have PostgreSQL make your changes permanent, execute the `COMMIT` command. If you want PostgreSQL to revert all changes made within the current transaction, execute the `ROLLBACK` command.

It's important to realize that *all* SQL commands execute within a transaction. If you don't explicitly `BEGIN` a transaction, PostgreSQL will automatically execute each command within its own transaction.

Persistence

I used to think that single-command transactions were pretty useless: I was wrong. Single-command transactions are important because a single command can access multiple rows. Consider the following: Let's add a new constraint to the `customers` table.

```
movies=# ALTER TABLE customers ADD CONSTRAINT
movies-#   balance_exceeded CHECK( balance <= 50 );
```

This constraint ensures that no customer is allowed to have a balance exceeding $50.00. Just to prove that it works, let's try setting a customer's balance to some value greater than $50.00:

```
movies=# UPDATE CUSTOMERS SET balance = 100 where customer_id = 1;
ERROR:  ExecReplace: rejected due to CHECK constraint balance_exceeded
```

You can see that the `UPDATE` is rejected. What happens if you try to update more than one row? First, let's look at the data already in the `customers` table:

```
movies=# SELECT * FROM customers;
 customer_id |     customer_name      |  phone   | birth_date | balance
-------------+------------------------+----------+------------+---------
           1 | Jones, Henry           | 555-1212 | 1970-10-10 |    0.00
           2 | Rubin, William         | 555-2211 | 1972-07-10 |   15.00
           3 | Panky, Henry           | 555-1221 | 1968-01-21 |    0.00
           4 | Wonderland, Alice N.   | 555-1122 | 1969-03-05 |    3.00
           8 | Wink Wankel            | 555-1000 | 1988-12-25 |    0.00
(5 rows)
```

Now, try to `UPDATE` every row in this table:

```
movies=# UPDATE customers SET balance = balance + 40;
ERROR:  ExecReplace: rejected due to CHECK constraint balance_exceeded
```

This `UPDATE` command is rejected because adding $40.00 to the balance for `Rubin, William` violates the `balance_exceeded` constraint. The question is, were any of the `customers` updated before the error occurred? The answer is: probably. You don't really

13. `BEGIN` can also be written as `BEGIN WORK` or `BEGIN TRANSACTION`. `COMMIT` can also be written as `COMMIT WORK` or `COMMIT TRANSACTION`. `ROLLBACK` can also written as `ROLLBACK WORK` or `ROLLBACK TRANSACTION`.

know for sure because any changes made before the error occurred are rolled back. The net effect is that no changes were made to the database:

```
movies=# SELECT * FROM customers;
 customer_id |     customer_name      |  phone   | birth_date | balance
-------------+------------------------+----------+------------+---------
           1 | Jones, Henry           | 555-1212 | 1970-10-10 |    0.00
           2 | Rubin, William         | 555-2211 | 1972-07-10 |   15.00
           3 | Panky, Henry           | 555-1221 | 1968-01-21 |    0.00
           4 | Wonderland, Alice N.   | 555-1122 | 1969-03-05 |    3.00
           8 | Wink Wankel            | 555-1000 | 1988-12-25 |    0.00
(5 rows)
```

If some of the changes persisted while others did not, you would have to somehow find the persistent changes yourself and revert them. You can see that single-command transactions are far from useless. It took me awhile to learn that lesson.

What about multicommand transactions? PostgreSQL treats a multicommand transaction in much the same way that it treats a single-command transaction. A transaction is *atomic*, meaning that all the commands within the transaction are treated as a single unit. If any of the commands fail to complete, PostgreSQL reverts the changes made by other commands within the transaction.

Transaction Isolation

I mentioned earlier in this section that the changes made within a transaction are not visible to other users until the transaction is committed. To be a bit more precise, uncommitted changes made in one transaction are not visible to other transactions[14].

Transaction isolation helps to ensure consistent data within a database. Let's look at a few of the problems solved by transaction isolation.

Consider the following transactions:

User: `bruce`	**Time**	**User:** `sheila`
`BEGIN TRANSACTION`	T1	`BEGIN TRANSACTION`

`UPDATE customers`
`  SET balance = balance - 3`
`  WHERE customer_id = 2;`
	T2	

	T3	`SELECT SUM( balance )` `  FROM customers;`
	T4	`COMMIT TRANSACTION;`
`ROLLBACK TRANSACTION;`	T5	

14. This distinction is important when using (or developing) a client that opens two or more connections to the same database. Transactions are not shared between multiple connections. If you make an uncommitted change using one connection, those changes will not be visible to the other connection (until committed).

At time T1, bruce and sheila each begin a new transaction. bruce updates the balance for customer 3 at time T1. At time T3, sheila computes the SUM() of the balances for all customers, completing her transaction at time T4. At time T5, bruce rolls back his transaction, discarding all changes within his transaction. If these transactions were not isolated from each other, sheila would have an incorrect answer: Her answer was calculated using data that was rolled back.

This problem is known as the *dirty read* problem: without transaction isolation, sheila would read uncommitted data. The solution to this problem is known as READ COMMITTED. READ COMMITTED is one of the two transaction isolation levels supported by PostgreSQL. A transaction running at the READ COMMITTED isolation level is not allowed to read uncommitted data. I'll show you how to change transaction levels in a moment.

There are other data consistency problems that are avoided by isolating transactions from each other. In the following scenario, sheila will receive two different answers within the same transaction:

User: bruce	**Time**	**User:** sheila
`BEGIN TRANSACTION;`	T1	`BEGIN TRANSACTION;`

	T2	`SELECT balance`
		`FROM customers`
		`WHERE customer_id = 2;`

`UPDATE customers`
`SET balance = 20`
`WHERE customer_id = 2;`
	T3	

`COMMIT TRANSACTION;`	T4	

	T5	`SELECT balance`
		`FROM customers`
		`WHERE customer_id = 2;`

	T6	`COMMIT TRANSACTION;`

Again, bruce and sheila each start a transaction at time T1. At T2, sheila finds that customer 2 has a balance of $15.00. bruce changes the balance for customer 2 from $15.00 to $20.00 at time T3 and commits his change at time T4. At time T5, sheila executes the same query that she executed earlier in the transaction, but this time she finds that the balance is $20.00. In some applications, this isn't a problem; in others, this interference between the two transactions is unacceptable. This problem is known as the *non-repeatable read*.

Here is another type of problem:

User: `bruce`	**Time**	**User:** `sheila`
`BEGIN TRANSACTION;`	T1	`BEGIN TRANSACTION;`
	T2	`SELECT * FROM customers;`
`INSERT INTO customers VALUES`	T3	
`(`		
`6,`		
`'Neville, Robert',`		
`'555-9999',`		
`'1971-03-20',`		
`0.00`		
`);`		
`COMMIT TRANSACTION;`	T4	
	T5	`SELECT * FROM customers;`
	T6	`COMMIT TRANSACTION;`

In this example, `sheila` again executes the same query twice within a single transaction. This time, `bruce` has inserted a new row in between the `sheila`'s queries. Notice that this is not a case of a *dirty read*—`bruce` has committed his change before `sheila` executes her second query. At time T5, `sheila` finds a new row. This is similar to the non-repeatable read, but this problem is known as the *phantom read* problem.

The answer to both the non-repeatable read and the phantom read is the `SERIALIZABLE` transaction isolation level. A transaction running at the `SERIALIZABLE` isolation level is only allowed to see data committed before the transaction began.

In PostgreSQL, transactions usually run at the `READ COMMITTED` isolation level. If you need to avoid the problems present in `READ COMMITTED`, you can change isolation levels using the `SET TRANSACTION` command. The syntax for the `SET TRANSACTION` command is

```
SET TRANSACTION ISOLATION LEVEL { READ COMMITTED | SERIALIZABLE };
```

The `SET TRANSACTION` command affects only the current transaction (and it must be executed before the first DML[15] command within the transaction). If you want to change the isolation level for your session (that is, change the isolation level for future transactions), you can use the `SET SESSION` command:

```
SET SESSION CHARACTERISTICS AS
    TRANSACTION ISOLATION LEVEL { READ COMMITTED | SERIALIZABLE }
```

15. A DML (data manipulation language) command is any command that can update or read the data within a table. `SELECT`, `INSERT`, `UPDATE`, `FETCH`, and `COPY` are DML commands.

Multi-Versioning and Locking

Most commercial (and open-source) databases use *locking* to coordinate multiuser updates. If you are modifying a table, that table is locked against updates and queries made by other users. Some databases perform page-level or row-level locking to reduce contention, but the principle is the same—other users must wait to read the data you have modified until you have committed your changes.

PostgreSQL uses a different model called *multi-versioning*, or *MVCC* for short (locks are still used, but much less frequently than you might expect). In a multi-versioning system, the database creates a new copy of the rows you have modified. Other users see the original values until you commit your changes—they don't have to wait until you finish. If you roll back a transaction, other users are not affected—they did not have access to your changes in the first place. If you commit your changes, the original rows are marked as obsolete and other transactions running at the `READ COMMITTED` isolation level will see your changes. Transactions running at the `SERIALIZABLE` isolation level will continue to see the original rows. Obsolete data is not automatically removed from a PostgreSQL database. It is hidden, but not removed. You can remove obsolete rows using the `VACUUM` command. The syntax of the `VACUUM` command is

```
VACUUM [ VERBOSE ] [ ANALYZE ] [ table ]
```

I'll talk about the `VACUUM` command in more detail in the next chapter.

The MVCC transaction model provides for much higher concurrency than most other models. Even though PostgreSQL uses multiple versions to isolate transactions, it is still necessary to lock data in some circumstances.

Try this experiment. Open two `psql` sessions, each connected to the `movies` database. In one session, enter the following commands:

```
movies=# BEGIN WORK;
BEGIN
movies=# INSERT INTO customers VALUES
movies-#  ( 5, 'Manyjars, John', '555-8000', '1960-04-02', 0 );
INSERT
```

In the other session, enter these commands:

```
movies=# BEGIN WORK;
BEGIN
movies=# INSERT INTO customers VALUES
movies-#  ( 6, 'Smallberries, John', '555-8001', '1960-04-02', 0 );
INSERT
```

When you press the `Enter` (or `Return`) key, this `INSERT` statement completes immediately. Now, enter this command into the second session:

```
movies=# INSERT INTO customers VALUES
movies-#  ( 5, 'Gomez, John', '555-8000', '1960-04-02', 0 );
```

This time, when you press `Enter`, `psql` hangs. What is it waiting for? Notice that in the first session, you already added a customer whose `customer_id` is 5, but you have not yet committed this change. In the second session, you are also trying to insert a customer whose `customer_id` is 5. You can't have two customers with the same `customer_id` (because you have defined the `customer_id` column to be the unique `PRIMARY KEY`). If you commit the first transaction, the second session would receive a *duplicate value* error. If you roll back the first transaction, the second insertion will continue (because there is no longer a constraint violation). PostgreSQL won't know which result to give you until the transaction completes in the first session.

Summary

Chapter 1, "Introduction to PostgreSQL and SQL," showed you some of the basics of retrieving and modifying data using PostgreSQL. In Chapter 2, "Working with Data in PostgreSQL," you learned about the many data types offered by PostgreSQL. This chapter has filled in some of the scaffolding—you've seen how to create new databases, new tables, and new indexes. You've also seen how PostgreSQL solves concurrency problems through its multi-versioning transaction model.

The next chapter, Chapter 4, "Query Optimization," should help you understand how the PostgreSQL server decides on the fastest way to execute your SQL commands.

4

Performance

IN THE PREVIOUS THREE CHAPTERS, you have seen how to create new databases and tables. You have also seen a variety of ways to retrieve data. Inevitably, you will run into a performance problem. At some point, PostgreSQL won't process data as quickly as you would like. This chapter should prepare you for that situation—after reading this chapter, you'll have a good understanding of how PostgreSQL executes a query and what you can do to make queries run faster.

How PostgreSQL Organizes Data

Before you can really dig into the details of performance tuning, you need to understand some of the basic architecture of PostgreSQL.

You already know that in PostgreSQL, data is stored in tables and tables are grouped into databases. At the highest level of organization, databases are grouped into clusters—a cluster of databases is serviced by a postmaster.

Let's see how this data hierarchy is stored on disk. You can see all databases in a cluster using the following query:

```
perf=# SELECT datname, oid FROM pg_database;
  datname  |  oid
-----------+-------
 perf      | 16556
 template1 |     1
 template0 | 16555
```

From this list, you can see that I have three databases in this cluster. You can find the storage for these databases by looking in the `$PGDATA` directory:

```
$ cd $PGDATA
$ ls
base    pg_clog     pg_ident.conf  pg_xlog          postmaster.opts
global  pg_hba.conf PG_VERSION     postgresql.conf  postmaster.pid
```

The $PGDATA directory has a subdirectory named base. The base subdirectory is where your databases reside:

```
$ cd ./base
$ ls -l
total 12
drwx------    2 postgres pgadmin      4096 Jan 01 20:53 1
drwx------    2 postgres pgadmin      4096 Jan 01 20:53 16555
drwx------    3 postgres pgadmin      4096 Jan 01 22:38 16556
```

Notice that there are three subdirectories underneath $PGDATA/base. The name of each subdirectory corresponds to the oid of one entry in the pg_database table: the subdirectory named 1 contains the template1 database, the subdirectory named 16555 contains the template0 database, and the subdirectory named 16556 contains the perf database.

Let's look a little deeper:

```
$ cd ./1
$ ls
1247   16392  16408  16421  16429  16441  16449  16460  16472
1249   16394  16410  16422  16432  16442  16452  16462  16474
1255   16396  16412  16423  16435  16443  16453  16463  16475
1259   16398  16414  16424  16436  16444  16454  16465  16477
16384  16400  16416  16425  16437  16445  16455  16466  pg_internal.init
16386  16402  16418  16426  16438  16446  16456  16468  PG_VERSION
16388  16404  16419  16427  16439  16447  16457  16469
16390  16406  16420  16428  16440  16448  16458  16471
```

Again, you see a lot of files with numeric filenames. You can guess that these numbers also correspond to oids, but which oids? You know that you can store tables inside a database, so you can expect to find a match between these filenames and table oids. Let's go back into psql and look for the match:

```
$ psql -q -d template1
template1=# SELECT relname, oid FROM pg_class;
template1=# SELECT oid, relname FROM pg_class ORDER BY oid;
  oid  |              relname
-------+---------------------------------
  1247 | pg_type
  1249 | pg_attribute
  1255 | pg_proc
  1259 | pg_class
  1260 | pg_shadow
  1261 | pg_group
  1262 | pg_database
 16384 | pg_attrdef
 16386 | pg_relcheck
  ...  |    ...
```

The correspondence between filenames and table `oid`s is now obvious. Each table is stored in its own disk file and, in most cases, the name of the file is the `oid` of the table's entry in the `pg_class` table[1].

There are a two more columns in `pg_class` that might help explain PostgreSQL's storage structure:

```
perf=# SELECT relname, oid, relpages, reltuples FROM pg_class
perf-#   ORDER BY oid
   relname     | oid  | reltuples | relpages
--------------+------+-----------+----------
 pg_type       | 1247 |       143 |        2
 pg_attribute  | 1249 |       795 |       11
 pg_proc       | 1255 |      1263 |       31
 pg_class      | 1259 |       101 |        2
 pg_shadow     | 1260 |         1 |        1
 pg_group      | 1261 |         0 |        0
     ...       | ...  |       ... |      ...
```

The `reltuples` column tells you how many tuples are in each table. The `relpages` column shows how many *pages* are required to store the current contents of the table. How do these numbers correspond to the actual on-disk structures? If you look at the table files for a few tables, you'll see that there is a relationship between the size of the file and the number of `relpages` columns:

```
$ ls -l 1247 1249
-rw-------    1 postgres pgadmin     16384 Jan 01 20:53 1247
-rw-------    1 postgres pgadmin     90112 Jan 01 20:53 1249
```

The file named `1247` (`pg_type`) is 16384 bytes long and consumes two pages. The file named `1249` (`pg_attribute`) is 90122 bytes long and consumes 11 pages. A little math will show that 16384/2 = 8192 and 90122/11 = 8192: each page is 8192 (8K) bytes long. In PostgreSQL, all disk I/O is performed on a page-by-page basis[2]. When you select a single row from a table, PostgreSQL will read at least one page—it may read many pages if the row is large. When you update a single row, PostgreSQL will write the new version of the row at the end of the table and will mark the original version of the row as invalid.

1. The name of a table file is the same as the `oid` of the table's entry in `pg_class`. You can also derive the filename from the `pg_class.pg_relfilenode` column. Some tables are never stored on disk—those tables still have an entry in the `pg_class` table, but their `relfilenode` values are 0. The most reliable way to match a numeric filename to a table is to use the `pg_class.relfilenode` column; at present, `pg_class.relfilenode` is equal to `pg_class.oid`, but that is likely to change in future releases.

2. Actually, *most* disk I/O is performed on a page-by-page basis. Some configuration files and log files are accessed in other forms, but all table and index access is done in pages.

The size of a page is fixed at 8,192 bytes. You can increase or decrease the page size if you build your own copy of PostgreSQL from source, but all pages within a database will be the same size. The size of a row is *not* fixed—different tables will yield different row sizes. In fact, the rows within a single table may differ in size if the table contains variable length columns. Given that the page size is fixed and the row size is variable, it's difficult to predict exactly how many rows will fit within any given page.

The `perf` database and the `recalls` Table

The sample database that you have been using so far doesn't really hold enough data to show performance relationships. Instead, I've created a new database (named `perf`) that holds some large tables. I've downloaded the `recalls` database from the U.S. National Highway Traffic Safety Administration[3]. This database contains a single table with 39,241 rows. Here is the layout of the `recalls` table:

```
perf=# \d recalls
                 Table "recalls"
   Column     |          Type           | Modifiers
--------------+-------------------------+-----------
 record_id    | numeric(9,0)            |
 campno       | character(9)            |
 maketxt      | character(25)           |
 modeltxt     | character(25)           |
 yeartxt      | character(4)            |
 mfgcampno    | character(10)           |
 compdesc     | character(75)           |
 mgftxt       | character(30)           |
 bgman        | character(8)            |
 endman       | character(8)            |
 vet          | character(1)            |
 potaff       | numeric(9,0)            |
 ndate        | character(8)            |
 odate        | character(8)            |
 influenced   | character(4)            |
 mfgname      | character(30)           |
 rcdate       | character(8)            |
 datea        | character(8)            |
 rpno         | character(3)            |
 fmvss        | character(3)            |
 desc_defect  | character varying(2000) |
 con_defect   | character varying(2000) |
 cor_action   | character varying(2000) |
Indexes: recall_record_id
```

Notice that there is only one index and it covers the `record_id` column.

3. This data (`ftp://ftp.nhtsa.dot.gov/rev_recalls/`) is in the form of a flat ASCII file. I had to import the data into my `perf` database.

The `recalls` table in the `perf` database contains 39,241 rows in 4,412 pages:

```
perf=# SELECT relname, reltuples, relpages, oid FROM pg_class
perf-#   WHERE relname = 'recalls';
 relname | reltuples | relpages |  oid
---------+-----------+----------+-------
 recalls |     39241 |     4412 | 96409
```

Given that a page is 8,192 bytes long, you would expect that the file holding this table (`$PGDATA/base/16556/96409`) would be 36,143,104 bytes long:

```
$ ls -l $PGDATA/base/16556/96409
-rw-------    1 postgres pgadmin  36143104 Jan 01 23:34 96409
```

Figure 4.1 shows how the `recalls` table might look on disk. (Notice that the rows are not sorted—they appear in the approximate order of insertion.)

Page 1

record_id	campno	maketxt	...	cor_action
42009	02E009000	NXT	...	Nexl will remove the...
13621	82E018000	CATERPILLAR	...	The Dealer will inspect...
42010	02E010000	NEXL	...	Next will notify its custom...
35966	99E039000	APC	...	APS will replace these...
42011	02E010000	NEXL	...	Nexl will notify its custom...
12927	81T009000	HERCULES	...	Tires will be replaced,...
42012	02E010000	NEXL	...	Nexl will notify its custom...
35974	99E039000	APC	...	APS will replace these...

Page 2

record_id	campno	maketxt	...	cor_action
42013	02E010000	NEXT	...	Nexl will notify its custom...
13654	82T014000	GOODYEAR	...	The Dealer will replace all...
42014	02E010000	NXT	...	Nexl will notify its custom...
35133	99E018000	D	...	Dealers will inspect their...
42005	02E009000	NEXL	...	Nexl will remove the...
12924	81T008000	NANKANG	...	Defective tires will be...
41467	01X003000	BRITAX	...	Customers will receive a...
35131	99E017000	MERITOR	...	Meritor will inspect and...

...

Page 4412

record_id	campno	maketxt	...	cor_action
42054	02V074002	PONTIAC	...	Dealers will properly tight...
41863	02V044000	HYUNDAI	...	Dealers will inspect the ...
42139	02V095000	INTERNATIONAL	...	Dealers will inspect the ...
41926	02V065000	COUNTRY COACH	...	Dealers will replace the...
42138	02V095000	INTERNATIONAL	...	Dealers will inspect the...
41927	02V065000	COUNTRY COACH	...	Dealers will replace the...
42140	02V095000	INTERNATIONAL	...	Dealers will inspect the...
41930	02V065000	COUNTRY COACH	...	Dealers will replace the...

Figure 4.1 The `recalls` table as it might look on disk.

If a row is too large to fit into a single 8K block[4], PostgreSQL will write part of the data into a *TOAST*[5] table. A TOAST table acts as an extension to a normal table. It holds values too large to fit *inline* in the main table.

Indexes are also stored in page files. A page that holds row data is called a *heap* page. A page that holds index data is called an *index* page. You can locate the page file that stores an index by examining the index's entry in the `pg_class` table. And, just like tables, it is difficult to predict how many index entries will fit into each 8K page[6]. If an index entry is too large, it is moved to an index TOAST table.

In PostgreSQL, a page that contains row data is a *heap block*. A page that contains index data is an *index block*. You will never find heap blocks and index blocks in the same page file.

Page Caching

Two of the fundamental performance rules in any database system are

- Memory access is fast; disk access is slow.
- Memory space is scarce; disk space is abundant.

Accordingly, PostgreSQL tries very hard to minimize disk I/O by keeping frequently used data in memory. When the first server process starts, it creates an in-memory data structure known as the *buffer cache*. The buffer cache is organized as a collection of 8K pages—each page in the buffer cache corresponds to a page in some page file. The buffer cache is shared between all processes servicing a given database.

When you select a row from a table, PostgreSQL will read the heap block that contains the row into the buffer cache. If there isn't enough free space in the cache, PostgreSQL will move some other block out of the cache. If a block being removed from the cache has been modified, it will be written back out to disk; otherwise. it will simply be discarded. Index blocks are buffered as well.

In the next section, you'll see how to measure the performance of the cache and how to change its size.

Summary

This section gave you a good overview of how PostgreSQL stores data on disk. With some of the fundamentals out of the way, you can move on to more performance issues.

4. PostgreSQL tries to store at least four rows per heap page and at least four entries per index page.

5. The acronym *TOAST* stands for "the oversized attribute storage technique."

6. If you want more information about how data is stored *inside* a page, I recommend the `pg_filedump` utility from Red Hat.

Gathering Performance Information

With release 7.2, the PostgreSQL developers introduced a new collection of performance-related system views. These views return two distinct kinds of information. The `pg_stat` views characterize the frequency and type of access for each table in a database. The `pg_statio` views will tell you how much physical I/O is performed on behalf of each table.

Let's look at each set of performance-related views in more detail.

The `pg_stat_all_tables` contains one row for each table in your database. Here is the layout of `pg_stat_all_tables`:

```
perf=# \d pg_stat_all_tables
      View "pg_stat_all_tables"
    Column     |  Type   | Modifiers
---------------+---------+-----------
 relid         | oid     |
 relname       | name    |
 seq_scan      | bigint  |
 seq_tup_read  | bigint  |
 idx_scan      | numeric |
 idx_tup_fetch | numeric |
 n_tup_ins     | bigint  |
 n_tup_upd     | bigint  |
 n_tup_del     | bigint  |
```

The `seq_scan` column tells you how many sequential (that is, table) scans have been performed for a given table, and `seq_tup_read` tells you how many rows were processed through table scans. The `idx_scan` and `idx_tup_fetch` columns tell you how many index scans have been performed for a table and how many rows were processed by index scans. The `n_tup_ins`, `n_tup_upd`, and `n_tup_del` columns tell you how many rows were inserted, updated, and deleted, respectively.

> **Query Execution**
>
> If you're not familiar with the terms "table scan" or "index scan," don't worry—I'll cover query execution later in this chapter (see "Understanding How PostgreSQL Executes a Query").

The real value in `pg_stat_all_tables` is that you can find out which tables in your database are most heavily used. This view does *not* tell you much disk I/O is performed against each table file, nor does it tell you how much time it took to perform the operations.

The following query finds the top 10 tables in terms of number of rows read:

```
SELECT relname, idx_tup_fetch + seq_tup_read AS Total
  FROM pg_stat_all_tables
  WHERE idx_tup_fetch + seq_tup_read != 0
  ORDER BY Total desc
  LIMIT 10;
```

Here's an example that shows the result of this query in a newly created database:

```
perf=# SELECT relname, idx_tup_fetch + seq_tup_read AS Total
perf-#   FROM pg_stat_all_tables
perf-#   WHERE idx_tup_fetch + seq_tup_read != 0
perf-#   ORDER BY Total desc
perf-#   LIMIT 10;

   relname     | total
---------------+-------
 recalls       | 78482
 pg_class      | 57425
 pg_index      | 20901
 pg_attribute  |  5965
 pg_proc       |  1391
```

It's easy to see that the `recalls` table is heavily used—you have read 78482 tuples from that table.

There are two variations on the `pg_stat_all_tables` view. The `pg_stat_sys_tables` view is identical to `pg_stat_all_tables`, except that it is restricted to showing system tables. Similarly, the `pg_stat_user_tables` view is restricted to showing only user-created tables.

You can also see how heavily each index is being used—the `pg_stat_all_indexes`, `pg_stat_user_indexes`, and `pg_stat_system_indexes` views expose index information.

Although the `pg_stat` view tells you how heavily each table is used, it doesn't provide any information about how much physical I/O is performed on behalf of each table. The second set of performance-related views provides that information.

The `pg_statio_all_tables` view contains one row for each table in a database. Here is the layout of `pg_statio_all_tables`:

```
perf=# \d pg_statio_all_tables

      View "pg_statio_all_tables"
     Column      |  Type   | Modifiers
-----------------+---------+-----------
 relid           | oid     |
 relname         | name    |
 heap_blks_read  | bigint  |
 heap_blks_hit   | bigint  |
 idx_blks_read   | numeric |
 idx_blks_hit    | numeric |
 toast_blks_read | bigint  |
 toast_blks_hit  | bigint  |
 tidx_blks_read  | bigint  |
 tidx_blks_hit   | bigint  |
```

This view provides information about heap blocks (heap_blks_read, heap_blks_hit), index blocks (idx_blks_read, idx_blks_hit), toast blocks (toast_blks_read, toast_blks_hit), and index toast blocks (tidx_blks_read, tidx_blks_hit). For each of these block types, pg_statio_all_tables exposes two values: the number of blocks read and the number of blocks that were found in PostgreSQL's cache. For example, the heap_blks_read column contains the number of heap blocks read for a given table, and heap_blks_hit tells you how many of those pages were found in the cache.

PostgreSQL exposes I/O information for each index in the pg_statio_all_indexes, pg_statio_user_indexes, and pg_statio_sys_indexes views.

Let's try a few examples and see how you can use the information exposed by pg_statio_all_tables.

I've written a simple utility (called timer) that makes it a little easier to see the statistical results of a given query. This utility takes a snapshot of pg_stat_all_tables and pg_statio_all_tables, executes a given query, and finally compares the new values in pg_stat_all_tables and pg_statio_all_tables. Using this utility, you can see how much I/O was performed on behalf of the given query. Of course, the database must be idle except for the query under test.

Execute this simple query and see what kind of I/O results you get:

```
$ timer "SELECT * FROM recalls;"

+-------------------------------+------------------------------+
|          SEQUENTIAL I/O       |            INDEXED I/O       |
| scans | tuples | heap_blks |cached| scans | tuples | idx_blks |cached|
+-------+--------+-----------+------+-------+--------+----------+------+
|   1   | 39241  |    4412   |   0  |   0   |    0   |     0    |   0  |
+-------+--------+-----------+------+-------+--------+----------+------+
```

This query retrieved 39241 rows in a single table scan. This scan read 4412 heap blocks from disk and found none in the cache. Normally, you would hope to see a cache ratio much higher than 4412 to 0! In this particular case, I had just started the postmaster so there were few pages in the cache and none were devoted to the recalls table. Now, try this experiment again to see if the cache ratio gets any better:

```
$ timer "SELECT * FROM recalls;"

+-------------------------------+------------------------------+
|          SEQUENTIAL I/O       |            INDEXED I/O       |
| scans | tuples | heap_blks |cached| scans | tuples | idx_blks |cached|
+-------+--------+-----------+------+-------+--------+----------+------+
|   1   | 39241  |    4412   |   0  |   0   |    0   |     0    |   0  |
+-------+--------+-----------+------+-------+--------+----------+------+
```

You get exactly the same results—no cache hits. Why not? We did not include an ORDER BY clause in this query so PostgreSQL returned the rows in (approximately) the order of insertion. When we execute the same query a second time, PostgreSQL starts reading at the beginning of the page file and continues until it has read the entire file. Because my cache is only 64 blocks in size, the first 64 blocks have been forced out of the cache by the time I get to the end of the table scan. The next time I execute the same query, the final 64 blocks are in the cache, but you are looking for the leading blocks. The end result is no cache hits.

Just as an experiment, try to increase the size of the cache to see if you can force some caching to take place.

The PostgreSQL cache is kept in a segment of memory shared by all backend processes. You can see this using the `ipcs -m` command[7]:

```
$ ipcs -m
------ Shared Memory Segments --------
key        shmid      owner      perms      bytes      nattch     status
0x0052e2c1 1409024    postgres   600        1417216    3
```

The shared memory segment contains more than just the buffer cache: PostgreSQL also keeps some bookkeeping information in shared memory. With 64 pages in the buffer cache and an 8K block size, you see a shared memory segment that is 1,417,216 bytes long. Let's increase the buffer cache to 65 pages and see what effect that has on the size of the shared memory segment. There are two ways that you can adjust the size of the cache. You could change PostgreSQL's configuration file (`$PGDATA/postgresql.conf`), changing the `shared_buffers` variable from 64 to 65. Or, you can override the `shared_buffers` configuration variable when you start the `postmaster`:

```
$ pg_ctl stop
waiting for postmaster to shut down......done
postmaster successfully shut down
$ #
$ # Note:  specifying -o "-B 65" is equivalent
$ #        to setting shared_buffers = 65 in
$ #        the $PGDATA/postgresql.conf file
$ #
$ pg_start -o "-B 65" -l /tmp/pg.log
postmaster successfully started
```

Now you can use the `ipcs -m` command to see the change in the size of the shared memory segment:

```
$ ipcs -m
------ Shared Memory Segments --------
key        shmid      owner      perms      bytes      nattch     status
0x0052e2c1 1409024    postgres   600        1425408    3
```

7. In case you are curious, the `key` value uniquely identifies a shared memory segment. The `key` is determined by multiplying the postmaster's port number by 1000 and then incrementing until a free segment is found. The `shmid` value is generated by the operating system (`key` is generated by PostgreSQL). The `nattach` column tells you how many processes are currently using the segment.

The shared memory segment increased from 1,417,216 bytes to 1,425,408 bytes. That's a difference of 8,192 bytes, which happens to be the size of a block. Now, let's increase our buffer count to 128 (twice the default):

```
$ pg_ctl stop
waiting for postmaster to shut down......done
postmaster successfully shut down
$ pg_start -o "-B 128" -l /tmp/pg.log
postmaster successfully started
$ ipcs -m
------ Shared Memory Segments --------
key        shmid      owner      perms      bytes      nattch     status
0x0052e2c1 1409024    postgres   600        1949696    3
```

If you do the math, you'll see that the difference in size of the shared memory segment between 64 buffers and 128 buffers is greater than 64 * 8192. The overhead in the shared memory segment is not fixed—it varies with the number of buffers.

Now, let's get back to the problem at hand. We want to find out if doubling the buffer count will result in more cache hits and therefore fewer I/O operations. Remember, a table scan on the `recalls` table resulted in 4,412 heap blocks read and 0 cache hits. Let's try the same query again and check the results:

```
$ timer "SELECT * FROM recalls;"

+----------------------------------+--------------------------------+
|          SEQUENTIAL I/O          |           INDEXED I/O          |
| scans | tuples | heap_blks |cached| scans | tuples | idx_blks |cached|
+-------+--------+-----------+------+-------+--------+----------+------+
|   1   | 39241  |      4412 |   0  |   0   |   0    |     0    |   0  |
+-------+--------+-----------+------+-------+--------+----------+------+
```

You have to run this query twice because you shut down and restarted the postmaster to adjust the cache size. When you shut down the postmaster, the cache is destroyed (you can use the `ipcs -m` command to verify this).

```
$ timer "SELECT * FROM recalls;"

+----------------------------------+--------------------------------+
|          SEQUENTIAL I/O          |           INDEXED I/O          |
| scans | tuples | heap_blks |cached| scans | tuples | idx_blks |cached|
+-------+--------+-----------+------+-------+--------+----------+------+
|   1   | 39241  |      4412 |   0  |   0   |   0    |     0    |   0  |
+-------+--------+-----------+------+-------+--------+----------+------+
```

Still the same results as before—PostgreSQL does not seem to buffer any of the data blocks read from the `recalls` table. Actually, each block *is* buffered as soon as it is read from disk; but as before, the blocks read at the beginning of the table scan are pushed out by the blocks read at the end of the scan. When you execute the same query a second time, you start at the beginning of the table and find that the blocks that you need are not in the cache.

You could increase the cache size to be large enough to hold the entire table (somewhere around 4412 + 64 blocks should do it), but that's a large shared memory segment, and if you don't have enough physical memory, your system will start to thrash.

Let's try a different approach. You have room for 128 pages in your buffer. The entire `recalls` table consumes 4412 pages. If you use the `LIMIT` clause to select a subset of the `recalls` table, you should see some caching. I'm going to lower the cache size back to its default of 64 pages before we start—my development system is memory-starved at the moment:

```
$ pg_ctl stop
waiting for postmaster to shut down......done
postmaster successfully shut down
$ pg_start -o "-B 64" -l /tmp/pg.log
postmaster successfully started
```

You know that it takes 4,412 pages to hold the 39,241 rows in `recalls`, which gives you an average of about 9 rows per page. We have 64 pages in the cache; let's assume that PostgreSQL needs half (32) of them for its own bookkeeping. So, you should ask for 9 * 32 (or 288) rows:

```
$ timer "SELECT * FROM recalls LIMIT 288;"

+----------------------------------+---------------------------------+
|          SEQUENTIAL I/O          |           INDEXED I/O           |
| scans | tuples | heap_blks |cached| scans | tuples | idx_blks |cached|
+-------+--------+-----------+------+-------+--------+----------+------+
|   1   |    289 |        40 |   0  |   0   |   0    |     0    |   0  |
+-------+--------+-----------+------+-------+--------+----------+------+
```

PostgreSQL read 40 heap blocks. If everything worked, those pages should still be in the cache. Let's run the query again:

```
$ timer "SELECT * FROM recalls LIMIT 288;"

+----------------------------------+---------------------------------+
|          SEQUENTIAL I/O          |           INDEXED I/O           |
| scans | tuples | heap_blks |cached| scans | tuples | idx_blks |cached|
+-------+--------+-----------+------+-------+--------+----------+------+
|   1   |    289 |        40 |  40  |   0   |   0    |     0    |   0  |
+-------+--------+-----------+------+-------+--------+----------+------+
```

Now you're getting somewhere. You read 40 heap blocks and found all 40 of them in the cache.

Dead Tuples

Now let's look at another factor that affects performance. Make a simple update to the `recalls` table:

```
perf=# UPDATE recalls SET potaff = potaff + 1;
UPDATE
```

This command increments the `potaff` column of each row in the `recalls` table. (Don't read too much into this particular `UPDATE`. I chose `potaff` simply because I needed an easy way to update every row.) Now, after restarting the database, go back and `SELECT` all rows again:

```
$ timer "SELECT * FROM recalls"

+-----------------------------------+-----------------------------------+
|          SEQUENTIAL I/O           |             INDEXED I/O           |
| scans | tuples | heap_blks |cached| scans | tuples | idx_blks |cached|
+-------+--------+-----------+------+-------+--------+----------+------+
|   1   |   39241|     8825  |  0   |   0   |   0    |    0     |  0   |
+-------+--------+-----------+------+-------+--------+----------+------+
```

That's an interesting result—you still retrieved 39,241 rows, but this time you had to read 8,825 pages to find them. What happened? Let's see if the `pg_class` table gives any clues:

```
perf=# SELECT relname, reltuples, relpages
perf-#   FROM pg_class
perf-#   WHERE relname = 'recalls';
 relname | reltuples | relpages
---------+-----------+----------
 recalls |     39241 |     4412
```

No clues there—`pg_class` still thinks you have 4,412 heap blocks in this table. Let's try counting the individual rows:

```
perf=# SELECT count(*) FROM recalls;
 count
-------
 39241
```

At least that gives you a consistent answer. But why does a simple update cause you to read twice as many heap blocks as before?

When you `UPDATE` a row, PostgreSQL performs the following operations:

1. The new row values are written to the table.
2. The old row is deleted from the table.
3. The deleted row *remains* in the table, but is no longer accessible.

This means that when you executed the statement "`UPDATE recalls SET potaff = potaff + 1`", PostgreSQL inserted 39,241 new rows and deleted 39,241 old rows. We now have 78,482 rows, half of which are inaccessible.

Why does PostgreSQL carry out an UPDATE command this way? The answer lies in PostgreSQL's MVCC (multiversion concurrency control) feature. Consider the following commands:

```
perf=# BEGIN WORK;
BEGIN
perf=# UPDATE recalls SET potaff = potaff + 1;
UPDATE
```

Notice that you have started a new transaction, but you have not yet completed it. If another user were to SELECT rows from the recalls table at this point, he *must* see the old values—you might roll back this transaction. In other database systems (such as DB2, Sybase, and SQL Server), the other user would have to wait until you either committed or rolled back your transaction before his query would complete. PostgreSQL, on the other hand, keeps the old rows in the table, and other users will see the original values until you commit your transaction. If you roll back your changes, PostgreSQL simply hides your modifications from all transactions.

When you DELETE rows from a table, PostgreSQL follows a similar set of rules. The deleted row remains in the table, but is hidden. If you roll back a DELETE command, PostgreSQL will simply make the rows visible again.

Now you also know the difference between a *tuple* and a *row*. A tuple is some version of a row.

You can see that these hidden tuples can dramatically affect performance—updating every row in a table doubles the number of heap blocks required to read the entire table.

There are at least three ways to remove dead tuples from a database. One way is to export all (visible) rows and then import them again using pg_dump and pg_restore. Another method is to use CREATE TABLE ... AS to make a new copy of the table, drop the original table, and rename the copy. The preferred way is to use the VACUUM command. I'll show you how to use the VACUUM command a little later (see the section "Table Statistics").

Index Performance

You've seen how PostgreSQL batches all disk I/O into 8K blocks, and you've seen how PostgreSQL maintains a buffer cache to reduce disk I/O. Let's find out what happens when you throw an index into the mix. After restarting the postmaster (to clear the cache), execute the following query:

```
$ timer "SELECT * FROM recalls ORDER BY record_id;"

+-----------------------------------+--------------------------------+
|          SEQUENTIAL I/O           |          INDEXED I/O           |
| scans | tuples | heap_blks |cached| scans | tuples | idx_blks |cached|
+-------+--------+-----------+------+-------+--------+----------+------+
|   0   |     0 |   26398   | 12843|   1   | 39241  |    146   |   0  |
+-------+--------+-----------+------+-------+--------+----------+------+
```

You can see that PostgreSQL chose to execute this query using an index scan (remember, you have an index defined on the `record_id` column). This query read 146 index blocks and found none in the buffer cache. You also processed 26,398 heap blocks and found 12,843 in the cache. You can see that the buffer cache helped the performance a bit, but you still processed over 26,000 heap blocks, and you need only 4,412 to hold the entire `recalls` table. Why did you need to read each heap block (approximately) five times?

Think of how the `recalls` table is stored on disk (see Figure 4.2).

Page 1

record_id	campno	maketxt	...	cor_action
42009	02E009000	NXT	...	Nexl will remove the...
13621	82E018000	CATERPILLAR	...	The Dealer will inspect...
42010	02E010000	NEXL	...	Next will notify its custom...
35966	99E039000	APC	...	APS will replace these...
42011	02E010000	NEXL	...	Nexl will notify its custom...
12927	81T009000	HERCULES	...	Tires will be replaced,...
42012	02E010000	NEXL	...	Nexl will notify its custom...
35974	99E039000	APC	...	APS will replace these...

Page 2

record_id	campno	maketxt	...	cor_action
42013	02E010000	NEXT	...	Nexl will notify its custom...
13654	82T014000	GOODYEAR	...	The Dealer will replace all...
42014	02E010000	NXT	...	Nexl will notify its custom...
35133	99E018000	D	...	Dealers will inspect their...
42005	02E009000	NEXL	...	Nexl will remove the...
12924	81T008000	NANKANG	...	Defective tires will be...
41467	01X003000	BRITAX	...	Customers will receive a...
35131	99E017000	MERITOR	...	Meritor will inspect and...

...

Page 4412

record_id	campno	maketxt	...	cor_action
42054	02V074002	PONTIAC	...	Dealers will properly tight...
41863	02V044000	HYUNDAI	...	Dealers will inspect the ...
42139	02V095000	INTERNATIONAL	...	Dealers will inspect the ...
41926	02V065000	COUNTRY COACH	...	Dealers will replace the...
42138	02V095000	INTERNATIONAL	...	Dealers will inspect the...
41927	02V065000	COUNTRY COACH	...	Dealers will replace the...
42140	02V095000	INTERNATIONAL	...	Dealers will inspect the...
41930	02V065000	COUNTRY COACH	...	Dealers will replace the...

Figure 4.2 The recalls table on disk.

Notice that the rows are not stored in `record_id` order. In fact, they are stored in order of insertion. When you create an index on the `record_id` column, you end up with a structure like that shown in Figure 4.3.

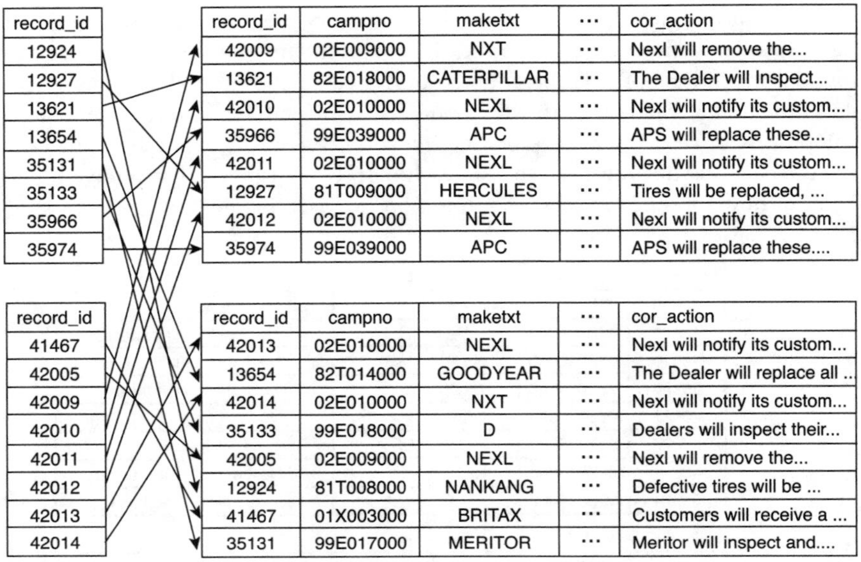

record_id
12924
12927
13621
13654
35131
35133
35966
35974

record_id	campno	maketxt	...	cor_action
42009	02E009000	NXT	...	Nexl will remove the...
13621	82E018000	CATERPILLAR	...	The Dealer will Inspect...
42010	02E010000	NEXL	...	Nexl will notify its custom...
35966	99E039000	APC	...	APS will replace these...
42011	02E010000	NEXL	...	Nexl will notify its custom...
12927	81T009000	HERCULES	...	Tires will be replaced, ...
42012	02E010000	NEXL	...	Nexl will notify its custom...
35974	99E039000	APC	...	APS will replace these....

record_id
41467
42005
42009
42010
42011
42012
42013
42014

record_id	campno	maketxt	...	cor_action
42013	02E010000	NEXL	...	Nexl will notify its custom...
13654	82T014000	GOODYEAR	...	The Dealer will replace all ..
42014	02E010000	NXT	...	Nexl will notify its custom...
35133	99E018000	D	...	Dealers will inspect their...
42005	02E009000	NEXL	...	Nexl will remove the...
12924	81T008000	NANKANG	...	Defective tires will be ...
41467	01X003000	BRITAX	...	Customers will receive a ...
35131	99E017000	MERITOR	...	Meritor will inspect and....

Figure 4.3 The `recalls` table structure after creating an index.

Consider how PostgreSQL uses the `record_id` index to satisfy the query. After the first block of the `record_id` index is read into the buffer cache, PostgreSQL starts scanning through the index entries. The first index entry points to a `recalls` row on heap block 2, so that heap block is read into the buffer cache. Now, PostgreSQL moves on to the second index entry—this one points to a row in heap block 1. PostgreSQL reads heap block 1 into the buffer cache, throwing out some other page if there is no room in the cache. Figure 4.2 shows a partial view of the `recalls` table: remember that there are actually 4,412 heap blocks and 146 index blocks needed to satisfy this query. It's the random ordering of the rows within the `recalls` table that kills the cache hit ratio.

Let's try reordering the `recalls` table so that rows are inserted in `record_id` order. First, create a work table with the same structure as `recalls`:

```
perf=# CREATE TABLE work_recalls AS
perf-#   SELECT * FROM recalls ORDER BY record_id;
SELECT
```

Then, drop the original table, rename the work table, and re-create the index:

```
perf=# DROP TABLE recalls;
DROP
perf=# ALTER TABLE work_recalls RENAME TO recalls;
ALTER
perf=# CREATE INDEX recalls_record_id ON recalls( record_id );
CREATE
```

At this point, you have the same data as before, consuming the same amount of space:

```
perf=# SELECT relname, relpages, reltuples FROM pg_class
perf-#   WHERE relname IN ('recalls', 'recalls_record_id' );
      relname       | relpages | reltuples
-------------------+----------+-----------
 recalls_record_id |      146 |     39241
 recalls           |     4422 |     39241
(2 rows)
```

After restarting the postmaster (again, this clears out the buffer cache so you get consistent results), let's re-execute the previous query:

```
$ timer "SELECT * FROM recalls ORDER BY record_id;"

+-----------------------------------+---------------------------------+
|         SEQUENTIAL I/O            |          INDEXED I/O            |
| scans | tuples | heap_blks |cached| scans | tuples | idx_blks |cached|
+-------+--------+-----------+------+-------+--------+----------+------+
|   0   |      0 |    4423   | 34818|   1   | 39241  |    146   |  0   |
+-------+--------+-----------+------+-------+--------+----------+------+
```

That made quite a difference. Before reordering, you read 26,398 heap blocks from disk and found 12,843 in the cache for a 40% cache hit ratio. After physically reordering the rows to match the index, you read 4,423 heap blocks from disk and found 34,818 in the cache for hit ratio of 787%. This makes a huge performance difference. Now as you read through each index page, the heap records appear next to each other; you won't be thrashing heap pages in and out of the cache. Figure 4.4 shows how the recalls table looks after reordering.

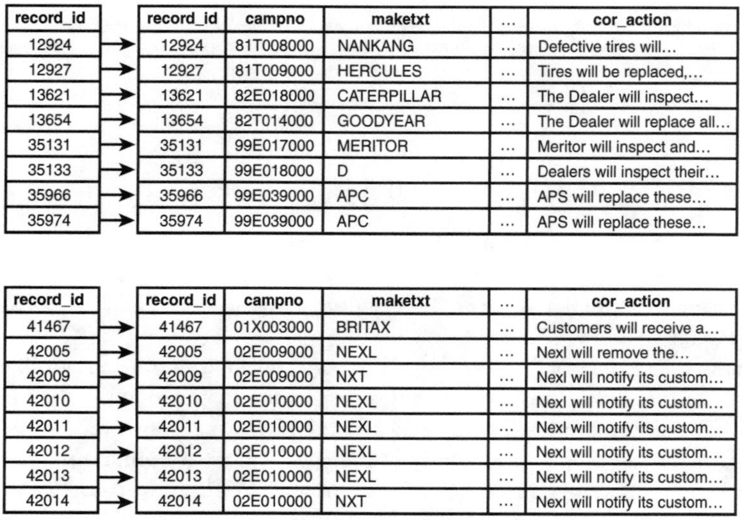

record_id		record_id	campno	maketxt	...	cor_action
12924	→	12924	81T008000	NANKANG	...	Defective tires will...
12927	→	12927	81T009000	HERCULES	...	Tires will be replaced,...
13621	→	13621	82E018000	CATERPILLAR	...	The Dealer will inspect...
13654	→	13654	82T014000	GOODYEAR	...	The Dealer will replace all...
35131	→	35131	99E017000	MERITOR	...	Meritor will inspect and...
35133	→	35133	99E018000	D	...	Dealers will inspect their...
35966	→	35966	99E039000	APC	...	APS will replace these...
35974	→	35974	99E039000	APC	...	APS will replace these...

record_id		record_id	campno	maketxt	...	cor_action
41467	→	41467	01X003000	BRITAX	...	Customers will receive a...
42005	→	42005	02E009000	NEXL	...	Nexl will remove the...
42009	→	42009	02E009000	NXT	...	Nexl will notify its custom...
42010	→	42010	02E010000	NEXL	...	Nexl will notify its custom...
42011	→	42011	02E010000	NEXL	...	Nexl will notify its custom...
42012	→	42012	02E010000	NEXL	...	Nexl will notify its custom...
42013	→	42013	02E010000	NEXL	...	Nexl will notify its custom...
42014	→	42014	02E010000	NXT	...	Nexl will notify its custom...

Figure 4.4 The recalls table on disk after reordering.

We reordered the `recalls` table by creating a copy of the table (in the desired order), dropping the original table, and then renaming the copy back to the original name. You can also use the `CLUSTER` command—it does exactly the same thing.

Understanding How PostgreSQL Executes a Query

Before going much further, you should understand the procedure that PostgreSQL follows whenever it executes a query on your behalf.

After the PostgreSQL server receives a query from the client application, the text of the query is handed to the *parser*. The parser scans through the query and checks it for syntax errors. If the query is syntactically correct, the parser will transform the query text into a *parse tree*. A parse tree is a data structure that represents the *meaning* of your query in a formal, unambiguous form.

Given the query

```
SELECT customer_name, balance FROM customers WHERE balance > 0 ORDER BY balance
```

the parser might come up with a parse tree structured as shown in Figure 4.5.

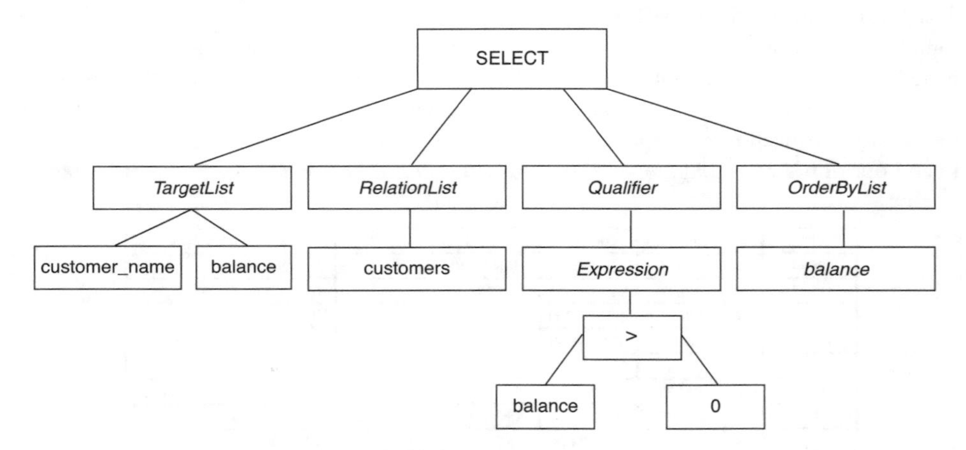

Figure 4.5 A sample parse tree.

After the parser has completed parsing the query, the parse tree is handed off to the planner/optimizer.

The planner is responsible for traversing the parse tree and finding all possible plans for executing the query. The plan might include a sequential scan through the entire table and index scans if useful indexes have been defined. If the query involves two or more tables, the planner can suggest a number of different methods for joining the tables. The execution plans are developed in terms of query operators. Each query operator transforms one or more *input sets* into an intermediate result set. The `Seq Scan` operator, for example, transforms an input set (the physical table) into a result set, filtering out any rows that don't meet the query constraints. The `Sort` operator produces a result set by reordering the input set according to one or more sort keys. I'll describe each of the query operators in more detail a little later. Figure 4.6 shows an example of a simple execution plan (it is a new example; it is *not* related to the parse tree in Figure 4.5).

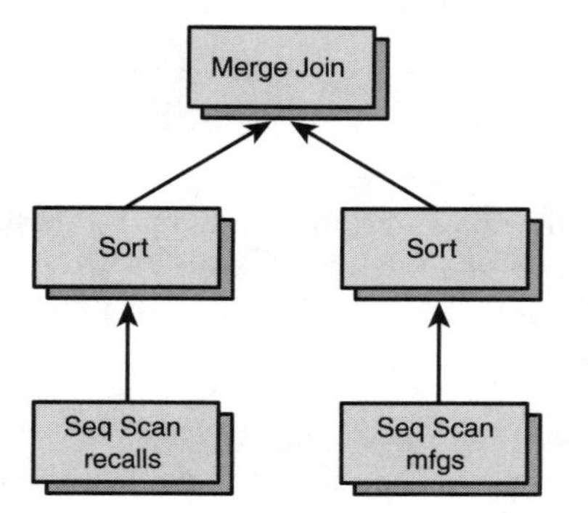

Figure 4.6 A simple execution plan.

You can see that complex queries are broken down into simple steps. The input set for a query operator at the bottom of the tree is usually a physical table. The input set for an upper-level operator is the result set of a lower-level operator.

When all possible execution plans have been generated, the optimizer searches for the least-expensive plan. Each plan is assigned an estimated execution cost. Cost estimates are measured in units of disk I/O. An operator that reads a single block of 8,192 bytes (8K) from the disk has a cost of one unit. CPU time is also measured in disk I/O units, but usually as a fraction. For example, the amount of CPU time required to process a single tuple is assumed to be $1/100^{th}$ of a single disk I/O. You can adjust many of the cost estimates. Each query operator has a different cost estimate. For example, the cost of a sequential scan of an entire table is computed as the number of 8K blocks in the table, plus some CPU overhead.

After choosing the (apparently) least-expensive execution plan, the query executor starts at the beginning of the plan and asks the topmost operator to produce a result set. Each operator transforms its input set into a result set—the input set may come from another operator lower in the tree. When the topmost operator completes its transformation, the results are returned to the client application.

EXPLAIN

The `EXPLAIN` statement gives you some insight into how the PostgreSQL query planner/optimizer decides to execute a query.

First, you should know that the `EXPLAIN` statement can be used only to analyze `SELECT`, `INSERT`, `DELETE`, `UPDATE`, and `DECLARE...CURSOR` commands.

The syntax for the EXPLAIN command is

```
EXPLAIN [ANALYZE][VERBOSE] query;
```

Let's start by looking at a simple example:

```
perf=# EXPLAIN ANALYZE SELECT * FROM recalls;
NOTICE:  QUERY PLAN:

Seq Scan on recalls  (cost=0.00..9217.41 rows=39241 width=1917)
                     (actual time=69.35..3052.72 rows=39241 loops=1)
Total runtime: 3144.61 msec
```

The format of the execution plan can be a little mysterious at first. For each step in the execution plan, EXPLAIN prints the following information:

- The type of operation required.
- The estimated cost of execution.
- If you specified EXPLAIN ANALYZE, the actual cost of execution. If you omit the ANALYZE keyword, the query is planned but not executed, and the actual cost is not displayed.

In this example, PostgreSQL has decided to perform a sequential scan of the recalls table (Seq Scan on recalls). There are many operations that PostgreSQL can use to execute a query. I'll explain the operation type in more detail in a moment.

There are three data items in the cost estimate. The first set of numbers (cost=0.00..9217.41) is an estimate of how "expensive" this operation will be. "Expensive" is measured in terms of disk reads. Two numbers are given: The first number represents how quickly the first row in the result set can be returned by the operation; the second (which is usually the most important) represents how long the entire operation should take. The second data item in the cost estimate (rows=39241) shows how many rows PostgreSQL expects to return from this operation. The final data item (width=1917) is an estimate of the width, in bytes, of the average row in the result set.

If you include the ANALYZE keyword in the EXPLAIN command, PostgreSQL will execute the query and display the *actual* execution costs.

Cost Estimates

I will remove the cost estimates from some of the EXPLAIN results in this chapter to make the plan a bit easier to read. Don't be confused by this—the EXPLAIN command will always print cost estimates.

This was a simple example. PostgreSQL required only one step to execute this query (a sequential scan on the entire table). Many queries require multiple steps and the EXPLAIN command will show you each of those steps. Let's look at a more complex example:

```
perf=# EXPLAIN ANALYZE SELECT * FROM recalls ORDER BY yeartxt;
NOTICE:  QUERY PLAN:

Sort (cost=145321.51..145321.51 rows=39241 width=1911)
     (actual time=13014.92..13663.86 rows=39241 loops=1)

  ->Seq Scan on recalls (cost=0.00..9217.41 rows=39241 width=1917)
                        (actual time=68.99..3446.74 rows=39241 loops=1)
Total runtime: 16052.53 msec
```

This example shows a two-step query plan. In this case, the first step is actually listed at the end of the plan. When you read a query plan, it is important to remember that each step in the plan produces an intermediate result set. Each intermediate result set is fed into the next step of the plan.

Looking at this plan, PostgreSQL first produces an intermediate result set by performing a sequential scan (`Seq Scan`) on the entire `recalls` table. That step should take about 9,217 disk page reads, and the result set will have about 39,241 rows, averaging 1,917 bytes each. Notice that these estimates are identical to those produced in the first example—and in both cases, you are executing a sequential scan on the entire table.

After the sequential scan has finished building its intermediate result set, it is fed into the next step in the plan. The final step in this particular plan is a sort operation, which is required to satisfy our `ORDER BY` clause[8]. The sort operation reorders the result set produced by the sequential scan and returns the final result set to the client application.

The `Sort` operation expects a single operand—a result set. The `Seq Scan` operation expects a single operand—a table. Some operations require more than one operand. Here is a join between the `recalls` table and the `mfgs` table:

```
perf=# EXPLAIN SELECT * FROM recalls, mfgs
perf-#   WHERE recalls.mfgname = mfgs.mfgname;
NOTICE:  QUERY PLAN:

Merge Join
  -> Sort
      -> Seq Scan on recalls
  ->  Sort
      -> Seq Scan on mfgs
```

If you use your imagination, you will see that this query plan is actually a tree structure, as illustrated in Figure 4.7.

8. An `ORDER BY` clause does not require a sort operation in all cases. The planner/optimizer may decide that it can use an index to order the result set.

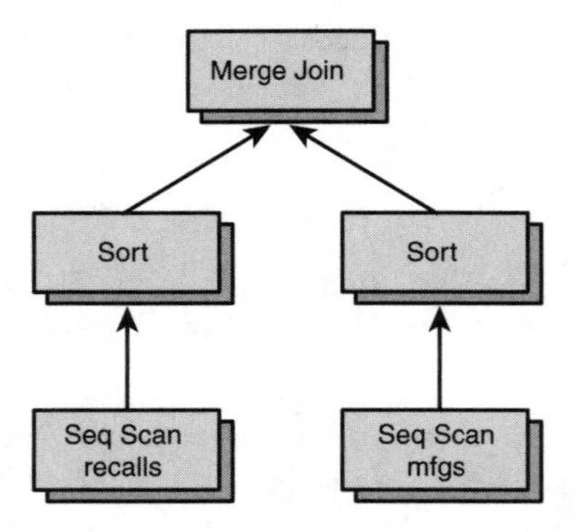

Figure 4.7 Execution plan viewed as a tree.

When PostgreSQL executes this query plan, it starts at the top of the tree. The `Merge Join` operation requires two result sets for input, so PostgreSQL must move down one level in the tree; let's assume that you traverse the left child first. Each `Sort` operation requires a single result set for input, so again the query executor moves down one more level. At the bottom of the tree, the `Seq Scan` operation simply reads a row from a table and returns that row to its parent. After a `Seq Scan` operation has scanned the entire table, the left-hand `Sort` operation can complete. As soon as the left-hand `Sort` operation completes, the `Merge Join` operator will evaluate its right child. In this case, the right-hand child evaluates the same way as the left-hand child. When both `Sort` operations complete, the `Merge Join` operator will execute, producing the final result set.

So far, you've seen three query execution operators in the execution plans. PostgreSQL currently has 19 query operators. Let's look at each in more detail.

Seq Scan

The `Seq Scan` operator is the most basic query operator. Any single-table query can be carried out using the `Seq Scan` operator.

`Seq Scan` works by starting at the beginning of the table and scanning to the end of the table. For each row in the table, `Seq Scan` evaluates the query constraints[9] (that is, the `WHERE` clause); if the constraints are satisfied, the required columns are added to the result set.

As you saw earlier in this chapter, a table can include dead (that is, deleted) rows and rows that may not be visible because they have not been committed. `Seq Scan` does not include dead rows in the result set, but it must read the dead rows, and that can be expensive in a heavily updated table.

9. The entire `WHERE` clause may not be evaluated for each row in the input set. PostgreSQL evaluates only the portions of the clause that apply to the given row (if any). For a single-table `SELECT`, the entire `WHERE` clause is evaluated. For a multi-table join, only the portion that applies to the given row is evaluated.

The cost estimate for a Seq Scan operator gives you a hint about how the operator works:

```
Seq Scan on recalls (cost=0.00..9217.41 rows=39241 width=1917)
```

The startup cost is always 0.00. This implies that the first row of a Seq Scan operator can be returned immediately and that Seq Scan does not read the entire table before returning the first row. If you open a cursor against a query that uses the Seq Scan operator (and no other operators), the first FETCH will return immediately—you won't have to wait for the entire result set to be materialized before you can FETCH the first row. Other operators (such as Sort) *do* read the entire input set before returning the first row.

The planner/optimizer chooses a Seq Scan if there are no indexes that can be used to satisfy the query. A Seq Scan is also used when the planner/optimizer decides that it would be less expensive (or just as expensive) to scan the entire table and then sort the result set to meet an ordering constraint (such as an ORDER BY clause).

Index Scan

An Index Scan operator works by traversing an index structure. If you specify a starting value for an indexed column (WHERE record_id >= 1000, for example), the Index Scan will begin at the appropriate value. If you specify an ending value (such as WHERE record_id < 2000), the Index Scan will complete as soon as it finds an index entry greater than the ending value.

The Index Scan operator has two advantages over the Seq Scan operator. First, a Seq Scan must read every row in the table—it can only remove rows from the result set by evaluating the WHERE clause for each row. Index Scan may not read every row if you provide starting and/or ending values. Second, a Seq Scan returns rows in table order, not in sorted order. Index Scan will return rows in index order.

Not all indexes are scannable. The B-Tree, R-Tree, and GiST index types can be scanned; a Hash index cannot.

The planner/optimizer uses an Index Scan operator when it can reduce the size of the result set by traversing a range of indexed values, or when it can avoid a sort because of the implicit ordering offered by an index.

Sort

The Sort operator imposes an ordering on the result set. PostgreSQL uses two different sort strategies: an in-memory sort and an on-disk sort. You can tune a PostgreSQL instance by adjusting the value of the sort_mem runtime parameter. If the size of the result set exceeds sort_mem, Sort will distribute the input set to a collection of sorted work files and then merge the work files back together again. If the result set will fit in sort_mem*1024 bytes, the sort is done in memory using the QSort algorithm.

A Sort operator never reduces the size of the result set—it does not remove rows or columns.

Unlike `Seq Scan` and `Index Scan`, the `Sort` operator must process the entire input set before it can return the first row.

The `Sort` operator is used for many purposes. Obviously, a `Sort` can be used to satisfy an `ORDER BY` clause. Some query operators require their input sets to be ordered. For example, the `Unique` operator (we'll see that in a moment) eliminates rows by detecting duplicate values as it reads through a sorted input set. `Sort` will also be used for some join operations, group operations, and for some set operations (such as `INTERSECT` and `UNION`).

Unique

The `Unique` operator eliminates duplicate values from the input set. The input set must be ordered by the columns, and the columns must be unique. For example, the following command

```
SELECT DISTINCT mfgname FROM recalls;
```

might produce this execution plan:

```
Unique
  ->  Sort
        ->  Seq Scan on recalls
```

The `Sort` operation in this plan orders its input set by the `mfgname` column. `Unique` works by comparing the unique column(s) from each row to the previous row. If the values are the same, the duplicate is removed from the result set.

The `Unique` operator removes only rows—it does not remove columns and it does not change the ordering of the result set.

`Unique` can return the first row in the result set before it has finished processing the input set.

The planner/optimizer uses the `Unique` operator to satisfy a `DISTINCT` clause. `Unique` is also used to eliminate duplicates in a `UNION`.

LIMIT

The `LIMIT` operator is used to limit the size of a result set. PostgreSQL uses the `LIMIT` operator for both `LIMIT` and `OFFSET` processing. The `LIMIT` operator works by discarding the first *x* rows from its input set, returning the next *y* rows, and discarding the remainder. If the query includes an `OFFSET` clause, *x* represents the offset amount; otherwise, *x* is zero. If the query includes a `LIMIT` clause, *y* represents the `LIMIT` amount; otherwise, *y* is at least as large as the number of rows in the input set.

The ordering of the input set is not important to the `LIMIT` operator, but it is usually important to the overall query plan. For example, the query plan for this query

```
perf=# EXPLAIN SELECT * FROM recalls LIMIT 5;
NOTICE: QUERY PLAN:

Limit (cost=0.00..0.10 rows=5 width=1917)
  -> Seq Scan on recalls (cost=0.00..9217.41 rows=39241 width=1917)
```

shows that the `LIMIT` operator rejects all but the first five rows returned by the `Seq Scan`. On the other hand, this query

```
perf=# EXPLAIN ANALYZE SELECT * FROM recalls ORDER BY yeartxt LIMIT 5;
NOTICE:  QUERY PLAN:


Limit (cost=0.00..0.10 rows=5 width=1917)
  ->Sort (cost=145321.51..145321.51 rows=39241 width=1911)
    ->Seq Scan on recalls (cost=0.00..9217.41 rows=39241 width=1917)
```

shows that the `LIMIT` operator returns the first five rows from an ordered input set.

The `LIMIT` operator never removes columns from the result set, but it obviously removes rows.

The planner/optimizer uses a `LIMIT` operator if the query includes a `LIMIT` clause, an `OFFSET` clause, or both. If the query includes only a `LIMIT` clause, the `LIMIT` operator can return the first row before it processes the entire set.

Aggregate

The planner/optimizer produces an `Aggregate` operator whenever the query includes an aggregate function. The following functions are aggregate functions: `AVG()`, `COUNT()`, `MAX()`, `MIN()`, `STDDEV()`, `SUM()`, and `VARIANCE()`.

`Aggregate` works by reading all the rows in the input set and computing the aggregate values. If the input set is not grouped, `Aggregate` produces a single result row. For example:

```
movies=# EXPLAIN SELECT COUNT(*) FROM customers;
Aggregate (cost=22.50..22.50 rows=1 width=0)
  -> Seq Scan on customers  (cost=0.00..20.00 rows=1000 width=0)
```

If the input set *is* grouped, `Aggregate` produces one result row for each group:

```
movies=# EXPLAIN
movies-#   SELECT COUNT(*), EXTRACT( DECADE FROM birth_date )
movies-#     FROM customers
movies-#     GROUP BY EXTRACT( DECADE FROM birth_date );
NOTICE:  QUERY PLAN:

Aggregate (cost=69.83..74.83 rows=100 width=4)
  -> Group (cost=69.83..72.33 rows=1000 width=4)
     -> Sort (cost=69.83..69.83 rows=1000 width=4)
        ->  Seq Scan on customers  (cost=0.00..20.00 rows=1000 width=4)
```

Notice that the row estimate of an ungrouped aggregate is always 1; the row estimate of a group aggregate is $1/10^{th}$ of the size of the input set.

Append

The Append operator is used to implement a UNION. An Append operator will have two or more input sets. Append works by returning all rows from the first input set, then all rows from the second input set, and so on until all rows from all input sets have been processed.

Here is a query plan that shows the Append operator:

```
perf=# EXPLAIN
perf-#   SELECT * FROM recalls WHERE mfgname = 'FORD'
perf-#     UNION
perf=#   SELECT * FROM recalls WHERE yeartxt = '1983';

Unique
  ->Sort
    ->Append
      ->Subquery Scan *SELECT* 1
        ->Seq Scan on recalls
      ->Subquery Scan *SELECT* 2
        ->Seq Scan on recalls
```

The cost estimate for an Append operator is simply the sum of cost estimates for all input sets. An Append operator can return its first row before processing all input rows.

The planner/optimizer uses an Append operator whenever it encounters a UNION clause. Append is also used when you select from a table involved in an inheritance hierarchy. In Chapter 3, "PostgreSQL SQL Syntax and Use," I defined three tables, as shown in Figure 4.8.

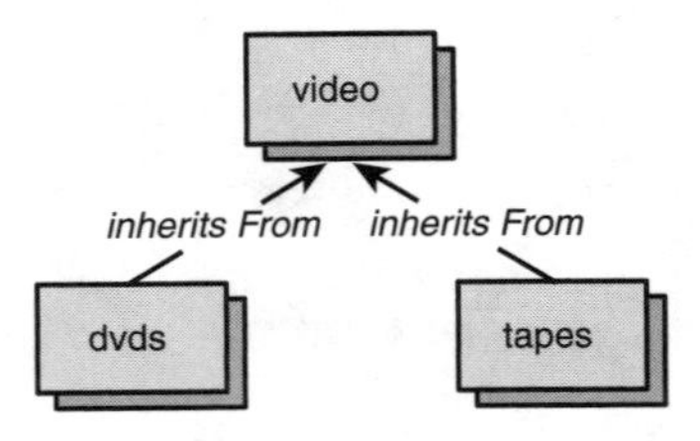

Figure 4.8 Inheritance hierarchy.

The dvds table inherits from video, as does the tapes table. If you SELECT from dvds or video, PostgreSQL will respond with a simple query plan:

```
movies=# EXPLAIN SELECT * FROM dvds;
  Seq Scan on dvds (cost=0.00..20.00 rows=1000 width=122)

movies=# EXPLAIN SELECT * FROM tapes;
  Seq Scan on tapes (cost=0.00..20.00 rows=1000 width=86)
```

Remember, because of the inheritance hierarchy, a dvd *is a* video and a tape *is a* video. If you SELECT from video, you would expect to see all dvds, all tapes, and all videos. The query plan reflects the inheritance hierarchy:

```
movies=# EXPLAIN SELECT * FROM video;

Result(cost=0.00..60.00 rows=3000 width=86)
  ->Append(cost=0.00..60.00 rows=3000 width=86)
    ->Seq Scan on video  (cost=0.00..20.00 rows=1000 width=86)
    ->Seq Scan on tapes video  (cost=0.00..20.00 rows=1000 width=86)
    ->Seq Scan on dvds video  (cost=0.00..20.00 rows=1000 width=86)
```

Look closely at the width clause in the preceding cost estimates. If you SELECT from the dvds table, the width estimate is 122 bytes per row. If you SELECT from the tapes table, the width estimate is 86 bytes per row. When you SELECT from video, all rows are expected to be 86 bytes long. Here are the commands used to create the tapes and dvds tables:

```
movies=# CREATE TABLE tapes ( ) INHERITS( video );

movies=# CREATE TABLE dvds
movies-# (
movies(#   region_id    INTEGER,
movies(#   audio_tracks VARCHAR[]
movies(# ) INHERITS ( video );
```

You can see that a row from the tapes table is identical to a row in the video table—you would expect them to be the same size (86 bytes). A row in the dvds table contains a video plus a few extra columns, so you would expect a dvds row to be longer than a video row. When you SELECT from the video table, you want all videos. PostgreSQL discards any columns that are not inherited from the video table.

Result

The Result operator is used in three contexts.

First, a Result operator is used to execute a query that does not retrieve data from a table:

```
movies=# EXPLAIN SELECT timeofday();
  Result
```

In this form, the Result operator simply evaluates the given expression(s) and returns the results.

Result is also used to evaluate the parts of a WHERE clause that don't depend on data retrieved from a table. For example:

```
movies=# EXPLAIN SELECT * FROM tapes WHERE 1 <> 1;
  Result
    ->Seq Scan on tapes
```

This might seem like a silly query, but some client applications will generate a query of this form as an easy way to retrieve the metadata (that is, column definitions) for a table.

In this form, the `Result` operator first evaluates the constant part of the `WHERE` clause. If the expression evaluates to `FALSE`, no further processing is required and the `Result` operator completes. If the expression evaluates to `TRUE`, `Result` will return its input set.

The planner/optimizer also generates a `Result` operator if the top node in the query plan is an `Append` operator. This is a rather obscure rule that has no performance implications; it just happens to make the query planner and executor a bit simpler for the PostgreSQL developers to maintain.

Nested Loop

The `Nested Loop` operator is used to perform a join between two tables. A `Nested Loop` operator requires two input sets (given that a `Nested Loop` joins two tables, this makes perfect sense).

`Nested Loop` works by fetching each from one of the input sets (called the *outer table*). For each row in the outer table, the other input (called the *inner table*) is searched for a row that meets the join qualifier.

Here is an example:

```
perf=# EXPLAIN
perf-#   SELECT * FROM customers, rentals
perf=#   WHERE customers.customer_id = rentals.customer_id;

Nested Loop
  -> Seq Scan on rentals
  -> Index Scan using customer_id on customers
```

The outer table is always listed first in the query plan (in this case, `rentals` is the outer table). To execute this plan, the `Nested Loop` operator will read each row[10] in the `rentals` table. For each `rentals` row, `Nested Loop` reads the corresponding `customers` row using an indexed lookup on the `customer_id` index.

A `Nested Loop` operator can be used to perform inner joins, left outer joins, and unions.

Because `Nested Loop` does not process the entire inner table, it can't be used for other join types (full, right join, and so on).

Merge Join

The `Merge Join` operator also joins two tables. Like the `Nested Loop` operator, `Merge Join` requires two input sets: an outer table and an inner table. Each input set must be ordered by the join columns.

10. Actually, `Nested Loop` reads only those rows that meet the query constraints.

Let's look at the previous query, this time executed as a `Merge Join`:

```
perf=# EXPLAIN
perf-#   SELECT * FROM customers, rentals
perf=#   WHERE customers.customer_id = rentals.customer_id;

Merge Join
  -> Sort
     -> Seq Scan on rentals
  -> Index Scan using customer_id on customers
```

`Merge Join` starts reading the first row from each table (see Figure 4.9).

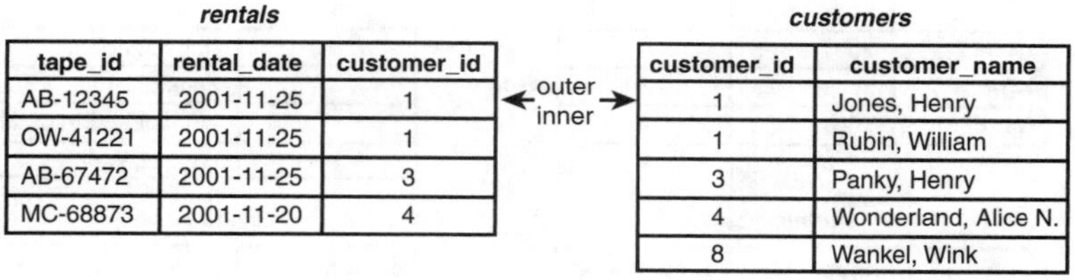

rentals

tape_id	rental_date	customer_id
AB-12345	2001-11-25	1
OW-41221	2001-11-25	1
AB-67472	2001-11-25	3
MC-68873	2001-11-20	4

customers

customer_id	customer_name
1	Jones, Henry
1	Rubin, William
3	Panky, Henry
4	Wonderland, Alice N.
8	Wankel, Wink

Figure 4.9 Merge Join—Step 1.

If the join columns are equal (as in this case), `Merge Join` creates a new row containing the necessary columns from each input table and returns the new row. `Merge Join` then moves to the next row in the outer table and joins it with the corresponding row in the inner table (see Figure 4.10).

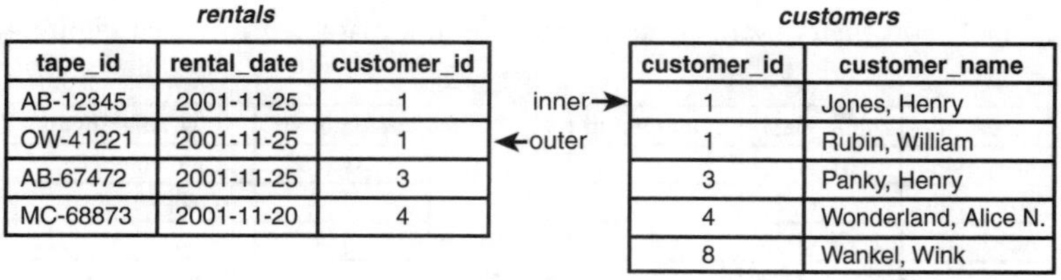

rentals

tape_id	rental_date	customer_id
AB-12345	2001-11-25	1
OW-41221	2001-11-25	1
AB-67472	2001-11-25	3
MC-68873	2001-11-20	4

customers

customer_id	customer_name
1	Jones, Henry
1	Rubin, William
3	Panky, Henry
4	Wonderland, Alice N.
8	Wankel, Wink

Figure 4.10 Merge Join—Step 2.

Next, `Merge Join` reads the third row in the outer table (see Figure 4.11).
Now `Merge Join` must advance the inner table twice before another result row can be created (see Figure 4.12).

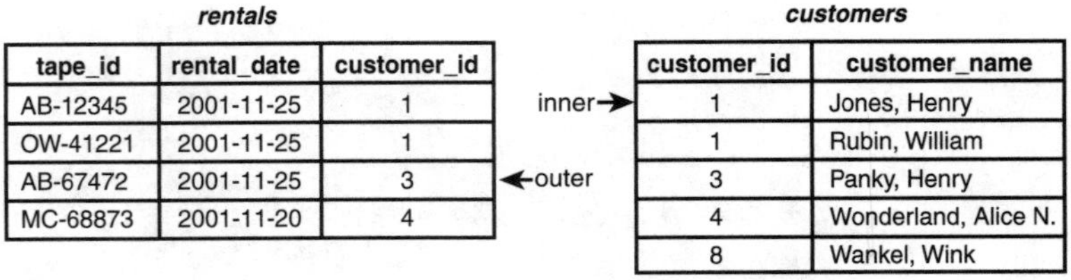

rentals

tape_id	rental_date	customer_id
AB-12345	2001-11-25	1
OW-41221	2001-11-25	1
AB-67472	2001-11-25	3
MC-68873	2001-11-20	4

inner→

←outer

customers

customer_id	customer_name
1	Jones, Henry
1	Rubin, William
3	Panky, Henry
4	Wonderland, Alice N.
8	Wankel, Wink

Figure 4.11 Merge Join—Step 3.

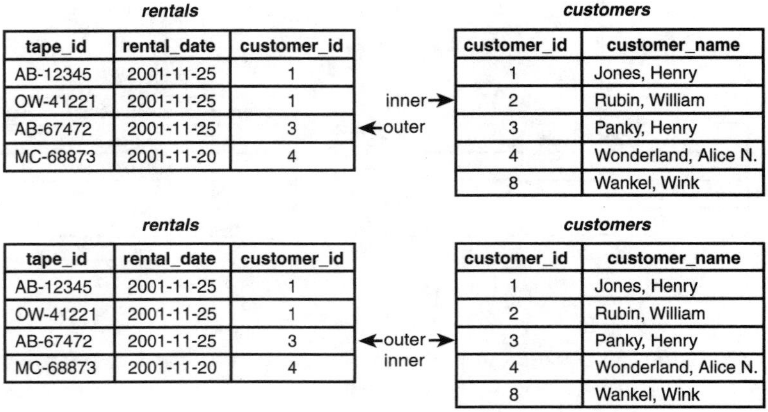

rentals

tape_id	rental_date	customer_id
AB-12345	2001-11-25	1
OW-41221	2001-11-25	1
AB-67472	2001-11-25	3
MC-68873	2001-11-20	4

inner→

←outer

customers

customer_id	customer_name
1	Jones, Henry
2	Rubin, William
3	Panky, Henry
4	Wonderland, Alice N.
8	Wankel, Wink

rentals

tape_id	rental_date	customer_id
AB-12345	2001-11-25	1
OW-41221	2001-11-25	1
AB-67472	2001-11-25	3
MC-68873	2001-11-20	4

←outer→
inner

customers

customer_id	customer_name
1	Jones, Henry
2	Rubin, William
3	Panky, Henry
4	Wonderland, Alice N.
8	Wankel, Wink

Figure 4.12 Merge Join—Step 4.

After producing the result row for `customer_id = 3`, `Merge Join` moves to the last row in the outer table and then advances the inner table to a matching row (see Figure 4.13).

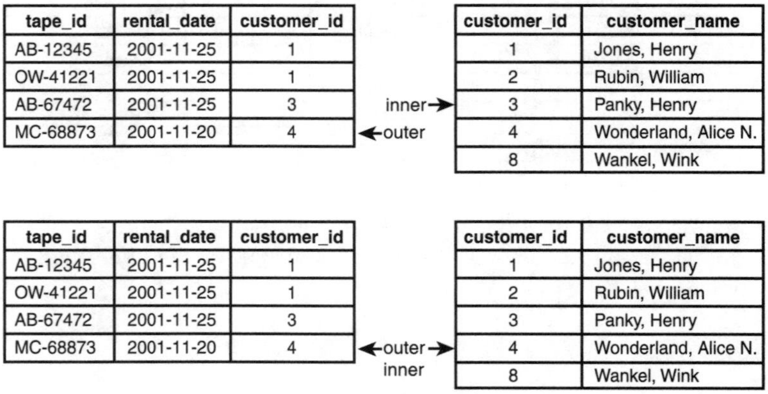

tape_id	rental_date	customer_id
AB-12345	2001-11-25	1
OW-41221	2001-11-25	1
AB-67472	2001-11-25	3
MC-68873	2001-11-20	4

inner→

←outer

customer_id	customer_name
1	Jones, Henry
2	Rubin, William
3	Panky, Henry
4	Wonderland, Alice N.
8	Wankel, Wink

tape_id	rental_date	customer_id
AB-12345	2001-11-25	1
OW-41221	2001-11-25	1
AB-67472	2001-11-25	3
MC-68873	2001-11-20	4

←outer→
inner

customer_id	customer_name
1	Jones, Henry
2	Rubin, William
3	Panky, Henry
4	Wonderland, Alice N.
8	Wankel, Wink

Figure 4.13 Merge Join—Step 5.

Merge Join completes by producing the final result row (customer_id = 4).

You can see that Merge Join works by walking through two sorted tables and finding matches—the trick is in keeping the pointers synchronized.

This example shows an *inner join*, but the Merge Join operator can be used for other join types by walking through the sorted input sets in different ways. Merge Join can do inner joins, outer joins, and unions.

Hash and Hash Join

The Hash and Hash Join operators work together. The Hash Join operator requires two input sets, again called the outer and inner tables. Here is a query plan that uses the Hash Join operator:

```
movies=# EXPLAIN
movies-#   SELECT * FROM customers, rentals
movies-#     WHERE rentals.customer_id = customers.customer_id;

Hash Join
  -> Seq Scan on customers
  -> Hash
       -> Seq Scan on rentals
```

Unlike other join operators, Hash Join does not require either input set to be ordered by the join column. Instead, the inner table is *always* a hash table, and the ordering of the outer table is not important.

The Hash Join operator starts by creating its inner table using the Hash operator. The Hash operator creates a temporary Hash index that covers the join column in the inner table.

Once the hash table (that is, the inner table) has been created, Hash Join reads each row in the outer table, hashes the join column (from the outer table), and searches the temporary Hash index for a matching value.

A Hash Join operator can be used to perform inner joins, left outer joins, and unions.

Group

The Group operator is used to satisfy a GROUP BY clause. A single input set is required by the Group operator,7 and it must be ordered by the grouping column(s).

Group can work in two distinct modes. If you are computing a grouped aggregate, Group will return each row in its input set, following each group with a NULL row to indicate the end of the group (the NULL row is for internal bookkeeping only, and it will not show up in the final result set). For example:

```
movies=# EXPLAIN
movies-#   SELECT COUNT(*), EXTRACT( DECADE FROM birth_date )
movies-#     FROM customers
movies-#     GROUP BY EXTRACT( DECADE FROM birth_date );
NOTICE:  QUERY PLAN:
```

```
Aggregate (cost=69.83..74.83 rows=100 width=4)
  -> Group (cost=69.83..72.33 rows=1000 width=4)
     -> Sort (cost=69.83..69.83 rows=1000 width=4)
       ->  Seq Scan on customers  (cost=0.00..20.00 rows=1000 width=4)
```

Notice that the row count in the `Group` operator's cost estimate is the same as the size of its input set.

If you are *not* computing a group aggregate, `Group` will return one row for each group in its input set. For example:

```
movies=# EXPLAIN
movies-#   SELECT EXTRACT( DECADE FROM birth_date ) FROM customers
movies-#     GROUP BY EXTRACT( DECADE FROM birth_date );

Group (cost=69.83..69,83 rows=100 width=4)
  -> Sort (cost=69.83..69.83 rows=1000 width=4)
         -> Seq Scan on customers  (cost=0.00..20.00 rows=1000 width=4)
```

In this case, the estimated row count is 1/10th of the `Group` operator's input set.

Subquery Scan and Subplan

A `Subquery Scan` operator is used to satisfy a `UNION` clause; `Subplan` is used for sub-selects. These operators scan through their input sets, adding each row to the result set. Each of these operators are used for internal bookkeeping purposes and really don't affect the overall query plan—you can usually ignore them.

Just so you know when they are likely to be used, here are two sample query plans that show the `Subquery Scan` and `Subplan` operators:

```
perf=# EXPLAIN
perf-#   SELECT * FROM recalls WHERE mfgname = 'FORD'
perf-#     UNION
perf=#   SELECT * FROM recalls WHERE yeartxt = '1983';

Unique
  ->Sort
    ->Append
      ->Subquery Scan *SELECT* 1
        ->Seq Scan on recalls
      ->Subquery Scan *SELECT* 2
        ->Seq Scan on recalls

movies=# EXPLAIN
movies-#   SELECT * FROM customers
movies-#     WHERE customer_id IN
movies-#       (
movies(#          SELECT customer_id FROM rentals
movies(#       );
NOTICE:  QUERY PLAN:
```

```
Seq Scan on customers  (cost=0.00..3.66 rows=2 width=47)
  SubPlan
    ->  Seq Scan on rentals  (cost=0.00..1.04 rows=4 width=4)
```

Tid Scan

The `Tid Scan` (tuple ID scan) operator is rarely used. A tuple is roughly equivalent to a row. Every tuple has an identifier that is unique within a table—this is called the tuple ID. When you select a row, you can ask for the row's tuple ID:

```
movies=# SELECT ctid, customer_id, customer_name FROM customers;
 ctid  | customer_id |    customer_name
-------+-------------+----------------------
 (0,1) |           1 | Jones, Henry
 (0,2) |           2 | Rubin, William
 (0,3) |           3 | Panky, Henry
 (0,4) |           4 | Wonderland, Alice N.
 (0,5) |           8 | Wink Wankel
```

The "`ctid`" is a special column (similar to the `oid`) that is automatically a part of every row. A tuple ID is composed of a block number and a tuple number within the block. All the rows in the previous sample are stored in block 0 (the first block of the table file). The `customers` row for "`Panky, Henry`" is stored in tuple 3 of block 0.

After you know a row's tuple ID, you can request that row again by using its ID:

```
movies=# SELECT customer_id, customer_name FROM customers
movies-#   WHERE ctid = '(0,3)';
 customer_id | customer_name
-------------+---------------
           3 | Panky, Henry
```

The tuple ID works like a bookmark. A tuple ID, however, is valid only within a single transaction. After the transaction completes, the tuple ID should not be used.

The `Tid Scan` operator is used whenever the planner/optimizer encounters a constraint of the form `ctid = `*`expression`* or *`expression`*` = ctid`.

The fastest possible way to retrieve a row is by its tuple ID. When you `SELECT` by tuple ID, the `Tid Scan` operator reads the block specified in the tuple ID and returns the requested tuple.

Materialize

The `Materialize` operator is used for some subselect operations. The planner/optimizer may decide that it is less expensive to materialize a subselect once than to repeat the work for each top-level row.

`Materialize` will also be used for some merge-join operations. In particular, if the inner input set of a `Merge Join` operator is not produced by a `Seq Scan`, an `Index`

Scan, a Sort, or a Materialize operator, the planner/optimizer will insert a Materialize operator into the plan. The reasoning behind this rule is not obvious—it has more to do with the capabilities of the other operators than with the performance or the structure of your data. The Merge Join operator is complex; one requirement of Merge Join is that the input sets must be ordered by the join columns. A second requirement is that the inner input set must be *repositionable*; that is, Merge Join needs to move backward and forward through the input set. Not all ordered operators can move backward and forward. If the inner input set is produced by an operator that is not repositionable, the planner/optimizer will insert a Materialize.

Setop (Intersect, Intersect All, Except, Except All)

There are four Setop operators: Setop Intersect, Setop Intersect All, Setop Except, and Setop Except All. These operators are produced only when the planner/optimizer encounters an INTERSECT, INTERSECT ALL, EXCEPT, or EXCEPT ALL clause, respectively.

All Setop operators require two input sets. The Setop operators work by first combining the input sets into a sorted list, and then groups of identical rows are identified. For each group, the Setop operator counts the number of rows contributed by each input set. Finally, each Setop operator uses the counts to determine how many rows to add to the result set.

I think this will be easier to understand by looking at an example. Here are two queries; the first selects all customers born in the 1960s:

```
movies=# SELECT * FROM customers
movies-#   WHERE EXTRACT( DECADE FROM birth_date ) = 196;
 customer_id |     customer_name      |   phone    | birth_date | balance
-------------+------------------------+----------+------------+---------
           3 | Panky, Henry           | 555-1221 | 1968-01-21 |    0.00
           4 | Wonderland, Alice N.   | 555-1122 | 1969-03-05 |    3.00
```

The second selects all customers with a balance greater than 0:

```
movies=# SELECT * FROM customers WHERE balance > 0;
 customer_id |     customer_name      |   phone    | birth_date | balance
-------------+------------------------+----------+------------+---------
           2 | Rubin, William         | 555-2211 | 1972-07-10 |   15.00
           4 | Wonderland, Alice N.   | 555-1122 | 1969-03-05 |    3.00
```

Now, combine these two queries with an INTERSECT clause:

```
movies=# EXPLAIN
movies-#  SELECT * FROM customers
movies-#    WHERE EXTRACT( DECADE FROM birth_date ) = 196
movies-#  INTERSECT
movies-#    SELECT * FROM customers WHERE balance > 0;
SetOp Intersect
  -> Sort
```

```
-> Append
   -> Subquery Scan *SELECT* 1
      -> Seq Scan on customers
    -> Subquery Scan *SELECT* 2
       -> Seq Scan on customers
```

The query executor starts by executing the two subqueries and then combining the results into a sorted list. An extra column is added that indicates which input set contributed each row:

```
 customer_id |     customer_name      | birth_date | balance | input set
-------------+------------------------+------------+---------+----------
           2 | Rubin, William         | 1972-07-10 |   15.00 | inner
           3 | Panky, Henry           | 1968-01-21 |    0.00 | outer
           4 | Wonderland, Alice N.   | 1969-03-05 |    3.00 | outer
           4 | Wonderland, Alice N.   | 1969-03-05 |    3.00 | inner
```

The `SetOp` operator finds groups of duplicate rows (ignoring the input set pseudo-column). For each group, `SetOp` counts the number of rows contributed by each input set. The number of rows contributed by the outer set is called `count(outer)`. The number of rows contributed by the inner result set is called `count(inner)`.

Here is how the sample looks after counting each group:

```
 customer_id |     customer_name      | birth_date | balance | input set
-------------+------------------------+------------+---------+----------
           2 | Rubin, William         | 1972-07-10 |   15.00 | inner
                               count(outer) = 0
                               count(inner) = 1
           3 | Panky, Henry           | 1968-01-21 |    0.00 | outer
                               count(outer) = 1
                               count(inner) = 0
           4 | Wonderland, Alice N.   | 1969-03-05 |    3.00 | outer
           4 | Wonderland, Alice N.   | 1969-03-05 |    3.00 | inner
                               count(outer) = 1
                               count(inner) = 1
```

The first group contains a single row, contributed by the inner input set. The second group contains a single row, contributed by the outer input set. The final group contains two rows, one contributed by each input set.

When `SetOp` reaches the end of a group of duplicate rows, it determines how many copies to write into the result set according to the following rules:

- `INTERSECT`—If `count(outer) > 0` and `count(inner) > 0`, write one copy of the row to the result set; otherwise, the row is not included in the result set.
- `INTERSECT ALL`—If `count(outer) > 0` and `count(inner) > 0`, write *n* copies of the row to the result set; where *n* is the greater `count(outer)` and `count(inner)`.

- `EXCEPT`—If `count(outer) > 0` and `count(inner) = 0`, write one copy of the row to the result set.
- `EXCEPT ALL`—If count(inner) >= count(outer), write *n* copies of the row to the result set; where *n* is `count(outer) - count(inner)`.

Table Statistics

You've seen all the operators that PostgreSQL can use to execute a query. Remember that the goal of the optimizer is to find the plan with the least overall expense. Each operator uses a different algorithm for estimating its cost of execution. The cost estimators need some basic statistical information to make educated estimates.

Table statistics are stored in two places in a PostgreSQL database: `pg_class` and `pg_statistic`.

The `pg_class` system table contains one row for each table defined in your database (it also contains information about views, indexes, and sequences). For any given table, the `pg_class.relpages` column contains an estimate of the number of 8KB pages required to hold the table. The `pg_class.reltuples` column contains an estimate of the number of tuples currently contained in each table.

Note that `pg_class` holds only estimates—when you create a new table, the `relpages` estimate is set to 10 pages and reltuples is set to 1000 tuples. As you `INSERT` and `DELETE` rows, PostgreSQL does *not* maintain the `pg_class` estimates. You can see this here:

```
movies=# SELECT * FROM tapes;
 tape_id  |     title     | dist_id
----------+---------------+---------
 AB-12345 | The Godfather |       1
 AB-67472 | The Godfather |       1
 MC-68873 | Casablanca    |       3
 OW-41221 | Citizen Kane  |       2
 AH-54706 | Rear Window   |       3
(5 rows)

movies=# CREATE TABLE tapes2 AS SELECT * FROM tapes;
SELECT
movies=# SELECT reltuples, relpages FROM pg_class
movies-#   WHERE relname = 'tapes2';
 reltuples | relpages
-----------+----------
      1000 |       10
```

Create the tapes2 table by duplicating the tapes table. You know that tapes2 really holds five tuples (and probably requires a single disk page), but PostgreSQL has not updated the initial default estimate.

There are three commands that you can use to update the pg_class estimates: VACUUM, ANALYZE, and CREATE INDEX.

The VACUUM command removes any dead tuples from a table and recomputes the pg_class statistical information:

```
movies=# VACUUM tapes2;
VACUUM
movies=# SELECT reltuples, relpages FROM pg_class WHERE relname = 'tapes2';
 reltuples | relpages
-----------+----------
         5 |        1
(1 row)
```

The pg_statistic system table holds detailed information about the data in a table. Like pg_class, pg_statistic is *not* automatically maintained when you INSERT and DELETE data. The pg_statistic table is not updated by the VACUUM or CREATE INDEX command, but it is updated by the ANALYZE command:

```
movies=# SELECT staattnum, stawidth, stanullfrace FROM pg_statistic
movies-#   WHERE starelid =
movies-#     (
movies(#       SELECT oid FROM pg_class WHERE relname = 'tapes2'
movies(#     );
 staattnum | stawidth | stanullfrac
-----------+----------+-------------
 (0 rows)

movies=# ANALYZE tapes;
ANALYZE

movies=# SELECT staattnum, stawidth, stanullfrace FROM pg_statistic
movies-#   WHERE starelid =
movies-#     (
movies(#       SELECT oid FROM pg_class WHERE relname = 'tapes2'
movies(#     );
 staattnum | stawidth | stanullfrac
-----------+----------+-------------
         1 |       12 |           0
         2 |       15 |           0
         3 |        4 |           0
(3 rows)
```

PostgreSQL defines a view (called pg_stats) that makes the pg_statistic table a little easier to deal with. Here is what the pg_stats view tells us about the tapes2 table:

```
movies=# SELECT attname, null_frac, avg_width, n_distinct FROM pg_stats
movies-#   WHERE tablename = 'tapes2';
 attname | null_frac | avg_width | n_distinct
---------+-----------+-----------+------------
 tape_id |         0 |        12 |         -1
 title   |         0 |        15 |       -0.8
 dist_id |         0 |         4 |       -0.6
(3 rows)
```

You can see that pg_stats (and the underlying pg_statistics table) contains one row for each column in the tapes2 table. The null_frac value tells you the percentage of rows where a given column contains NULL. In this case, there are no NULL values in the tapes2 table, so null_frac is set to 0 for each column. avg_width contains the average width (in bytes) of the values in a given column. The n_distinct value tells you how many distinct values are present for a given column. If n_distinct is positive, it indicates the actual number of distinct values. If n_distinct is negative, it indicates the percentage of rows that contain a distinct value. A value of –1 tells you that every row in the table contains a unique value for that column.

pg_stats also contains information about the actual values in a table:

```
movies=# SELECT attname, most_common_vals, most_common_freqs
movies-#   FROM pg_stats
movies-#   WHERE tablename = 'tapes2';
 attname | most_common_vals  | most_common_freqs
---------+-------------------+-------------------
 tape_id |                   |
 title   | {"The Godfather"} | {0.4}
 dist_id | {1,3}             | {0.4,0.4}
(3 rows)
```

The most_common_vals column is an array containing the most common values in a given column. The most_common_freqs value tells you how often each of the most common values appear. By default, ANALYZE stores the 10 most common values (and the frequency of those 10 values). You can increase or decrease the number of common values using the ALTER TABLE ... SET STATISTICS command.

Another statistic exposed by pg_stat is called histogram_bounds:

```
movies=#  SELECT attname, histogram_bounds FROM pg_stats
movies-#   WHERE tablename = 'tapes2';
 attname |                histogram_bounds
---------+------------------------------------------------
 tape_id | {AB-12345,AB-67472,AH-54706,MC-68873,OW-41221}
 title   | {Casablanca,"Citizen Kane","Rear Window"}
 dist_id |
(3 rows)
```

The histogram_bounds column contains an array of values for each column in your table. These values are used to partition your data into approximately equally sized chunks.

The last statistic stored in pg_stats is an indication of whether the rows in a table are stored in column order:

```
movies=# SELECT attname, correlation FROM pg_stats
movies-#   WHERE tablename = 'tapes2';
 attname | correlation
---------+-------------
 tape_id |         0.7
 title   |        -0.5
 dist_id |         0.9
(3 rows)
```

A correlation of 1 means that the rows are sorted by the given column. In practice, you will see a correlation of 1 only for brand new tables (whose rows happened to be sorted before insertion) or tables that you have reordered using the CLUSTER command.

Performance Tips

That wraps up the discussion of performance in PostgreSQL. Here are few tips that you should keep in mind whenever you run into an apparent performance problem:

- VACUUM and ANALYZE your database after any large change in data values. This will give the query optimizer a better idea of how your data is distributed.
- Use the CREATE TABLE AS or CLUSTER commands to cluster rows with similar key values. This makes an index traversal *much* faster.
- If you think you have a performance problem, use the EXPLAIN command to find out how PostgreSQL has decided to execute your query.
- You can influence the optimizer by disabling certain query operators. For example, if you want to ensure that a query is executed as a sequential scan, you can disable the Index Scan operator by executing the following command: "SET ENABLE_INDEX_SCAN TO OFF;". Disabling an operator does not guarantee that the optimizer won't use that operator—it just considers the operator to be much more expensive. The *PostgreSQL User Manual* contains a complete list of runtime parameters.
- You can also influence the optimizer by adjusting the relative costs for certain query operations. See the descriptions for CPU_INDEX_TUPLE_COST, CPU_OPERATOR_COST, CPU_TUPLE_COST, EFFECTIVE_CACHE_SIZE, and RANDOM_PAGE_COST in the *PostgreSQL User Manual*.
- Minimize network traffic by doing as much work as possible in the server. You will usually get better performance if you can filter data on the server rather than in the client application.

- One source of extra network traffic that might not be so obvious is metadata. If your client application retrieves 10 rows using a single `SELECT`, one set of metadata is sent to the client. On the other hand, if you create a cursor to retrieve the same set of rows, but execute 10 `FETCH` commands to grab the data, you'll also get 10 (identical) sets of metadata.
- Use server-side procedures (triggers and functions) to perform common operations. A server-side procedure is parsed, planned, and optimized the first time you use it, not every time you use it.

II

Programming with PostgreSQL

5

Introduction to PostgreSQL Programming

PostgreSQL is a client/server database. When you use PostgreSQL, there are at least two processes involved—the client and the server. In a client/server environment, the server provides a service to one or more clients. The PostgreSQL server provides data storage and retrieval services. A PostgreSQL client is an application that receives data storage and retrieval services from a PostgreSQL server. Quite often, the client and the server exist on different physical machines connected by a network. The client and server can also exist on a single host. As you will see, the client and the server do not have to be written in the same computer language. The PostgreSQL server is written in C; many client applications are written in other languages.

In this chapter, I'll introduce you to some of the concepts behind client/server programming for PostgreSQL. I'll also show you options you have for server-side programming languages and for client-side programming interfaces. I also discuss the basic structure of a PostgreSQL client application, regardless of which client-side language you choose. Finally, I explore the advantages and disadvantages of client-side versus server-side code.

Server-Side Programming

The task of programming for PostgreSQL falls into two broad categories: server-side programming and client-side programming.

Server-side code (as the name implies) is code that executes within a PostgreSQL server. Server-side code executes the same way regardless of which language was used to implement any given client. If the client and server are running on different physical hosts, all server-side code executes on the server machine and within the server process. If the client and server are running on the same machine, server-side code still runs within the server process. In most cases, server-side code is written in one of the procedural languages distributed with PostgreSQL.

PostgreSQL version 7.1 ships with three procedural languages: PL/pgSQL, PL/Tcl, and PL/Perl. Release 7.2 adds PL/Python to the mix.

You can use procedural languages to create functions that execute within the server. A *function* is a named sequence of statements that you can use within an SQL expression. When you write a function in a server-side language, you are extending the server. These server extensions are also known as *stored procedures.*

PL/pgSQL

If you have ever used a commercial database system—Oracle, Sybase, or SQL Server, for example—you have probably used a SQL-based procedural language. Oracle's procedural language is called PL/SQL; Sybase and SQL Server use TransactSQL. PL/pgSQL is very similar to these procedural languages.

PL/pgSQL combines the declarative nature of SQL commands with structures offered by other languages. When you create a PL/pgSQL function, you can declare local variables to store intermediate results. PL/pgSQL offers a variety of loop constructs (`FOR` loops, `WHILE` loops, and cursor iteration loops). PL/pgSQL gives you the capability to conditionally execute sections of code based on the results of a test. You can pass parameters to a PL/pgSQL function, making the function reusable. You can also invoke other functions from within a PL/pgSQL function.

Chapter 7, "PL/pgSQL," provides an in-depth description of PL/pgSQL.

Other Procedural Languages Supported by PostgreSQL

One of the more unusual aspects of PostgreSQL (compared to other database systems) is that you can write procedural code in more than one language. As noted previously, the standard distribution of PostgreSQL includes PL/pgSQL, PL/Perl, PL/Tcl, and, as of release 7.2, PL/Python.

The latter three languages each enable you to create stored procedures using a subset of the host language. PostgreSQL restricts each to a subset of the language to ensure that a stored procedure can't do nasty things to your environment.

Specifically, the PostgreSQL procedural languages are not allowed to perform I/O external to the database (in other words, you can't use a PostgreSQL procedural language to do anything outside of the context of the server). If you find that you need to affect your external environment, you can load an untrusted procedural language, but be aware that you will be introducing a security risk when you do so.

Because of space limitations, I won't be discussing procedural languages other than PL/pgSQL in this book. If you want to explore PL/Perl, PL/Tcl, or PL/Python, I would recommend that you find a good book about the base language and consult the PostgreSQL reference documentation for PostgreSQL-specific information.

When you install PostgreSQL from a standard distribution, none of the server-side languages are installed. You can pick and choose which languages you want to install in the server. If you don't use a given language, you can choose not to install it. I'll show you how to install server-side languages in Chapter 7.

You can see which languages are currently installed in your database server with the following query:

```
movies=# select * from pg_language;
 lanname  | lanispl | lanpltrusted | lanplcallfoid | lancompiler
----------+---------+--------------+---------------+-------------
 internal | f       | f            |             0 | n/a
 C        | f       | f            |             0 | /bin/cc
 sql      | f       | f            |             0 | postgres
(3 rows)
```

You can see that my server currently supports three languages: `internal`, `C`, and `sql`. The `lanispl` column tells us that none of these are considered to be procedural languages. You may be thinking that `C` should be considered a procedural language, but in this context a procedural language is one that can be installed and de-installed from the server. You can determine whether a language is trusted by examining the `lanpltrusted` column. A *trusted language* promises not to provide elevated privileges to a user. If a language is not a trusted language, only PostgreSQL superusers can create new function in that language.

Extending PostgreSQL Using External Languages

PostgreSQL-hosted procedural languages are not the only tools available for extending the server. You can also add extensions to a PostgreSQL server by creating custom data types, new functions, and new operators written in an external language (usually C or C++).

When you create procedural-language extensions, the source code (and the object-code, if any) for those functions is stored in tables within the database. When you create a function using an external language, the function is not stored in the database. Instead, it is stored in a shared-library that is linked into the server when first used.

You can find many PostgreSQL extensions on the web. For example, the PostGIS project adds a set of data types and supporting functions for dealing with geographic data. The `contrib` directory of a PostgreSQL distribution contains an extension for dealing with ISBNs and ISSNs.

In Chapter 6, "Extending PostgreSQL," I'll show you a few simple examples of how to add custom data types and functions written in C.

Client-Side APIs

When you want to build applications that access a PostgreSQL database, you use one (or more) of the client application programming interfaces (or APIs for short). PostgreSQL has a rich variety of APIs that support a number of programming languages.

PostgreSQL ships with the APIs shown in Table 5.1.

Table 5.1 **PostgreSQL Client APIs**

Interface Name	Supported Languages	Described In
`libpq`	C/C++	Chapter 8
`libpgeasy`	C/C++	Chapter 9
`libpq++`	C++	Chapter 10
`ecpg`	C/C++	Chapter 11
`ODBC`	C/C++	Chapter 12
`JDBC`	Java	Chapter 13
`Perl`	Perl	Chapter 14
`PHP`[1]	PHP	Chapter 15
`pgtcl`	TCL	Chapter 16
`PyGreSQL`	Python	Chapter 17
`pg.el`[1]	Emacs Lisp	Not covered

[1] The standard PostgreSQL distribution does not include the PHP or Emacs interfaces, but they are available separately on the web.

Table 5.1 is not all-inclusive. You can write PostgreSQL clients using languages not mentioned in Table 5.1. For example, Kylix (Borland's Pascal offering for Linux) offers a PostgreSQL interface. Also, many other languages (such as Microsoft Access and Visual Basic) provide access to PostgreSQL through the ODBC interface.

General Structure of Client Applications

This is a good time to discuss, in general terms, how a client application interacts with a PostgreSQL database. All the client APIs have a common structure, but the details vary greatly from language to language.

Figure 5.1 illustrates the basic flow of a client's interaction with a server.

An application begins interacting with a PostgreSQL database by establishing a connection.

Because PostgreSQL is a client/server database, some sort of connection must exist between a client application and a database server. In the case of PostgreSQL, client/server communication takes the form of a network link. If the client and server are on different systems, the network link is a TCP/IP socket. If the client and server are on the same system, the network link is either a Unix-domain socket or a TCP/IP connection. A Unix-domain socket is a link that exists entirely within a single host—the network is a logical network (rather than a physical network) within the OS kernel.

Regardless of whether you are connecting to a local server or a remote server, the API uses a set of properties to establish the connection. Connection properties are used to identify the server (a network port number and host address), the specific database that you want to connect to, your user ID (and password if required), and various debugging and logging options. Each API allows you to explicitly specify connection properties, but you can also use default values for some (or all) of the properties. I'll cover the defaulting mechanisms used by each API in later chapters.

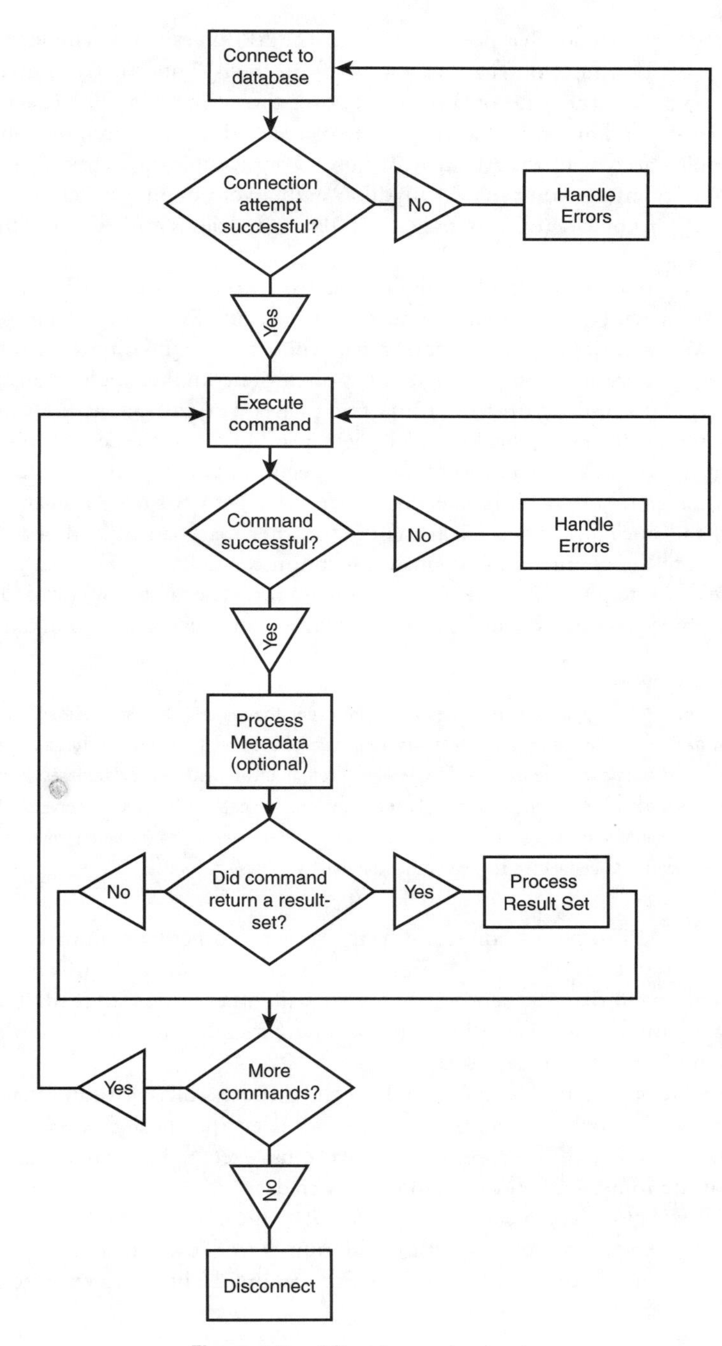

Figure 5.1 Client/server interaction.

After a server connection has been established, the API gives you a handle. A *handle* is nothing more than a chunk of data that you get from the API and that you give back to the API when you want to send or receive data over the connection. The exact form of a handle varies depending on the language that you are using (or more precisely, the data type of a handle varies with the API that you use). For example, in `libpq` (the C API), a handle is a void pointer—you can't do anything with a void pointer except to give it back to the API. In the case of `libpq++` and JDBC, a handle is embedded within a class.

After you obtain a connection handle from the API, you can use that handle to interact with the database. Typically, a client will want to execute SQL queries and process results. Each API provides a set of functions that will send a SQL command to the database. In the simplest case, you use a single function; more complex applications (and APIs) can separate command execution into two phases. The first phase sends the command to the server (for error checking and query planning) and the second phase actually carries out the command; you can repeat the execution phase as many times as you like. The advantage to a two-phase execution method is performance. You can parse and plan a command once and execute it many times, rather than parsing and planning every time you execute the command. Two-phase execution can also simplify your code by factoring the work required to generate a command into a separate function: One function can generate a command and a separate function can execute the command.

Two-Phase Execution

Even though some APIs support a two-phase execution model, the underlying PostgreSQL server does not. You will not gain any performance improvements using two-phase execution with PostgreSQL, but you will if your application uses a PostgreSQL-compatible API to communicate with other databases. If your client application uses a portable API (meaning an API that can communicate with database servers other than PostgreSQL), you might want to use a two-phase strategy so that you can realize a performance gain when your client application is connected to some other database.

After you use an API to send a command to the server, you get back three types of results. The first result that comes back from the server is an indication of success or failure—every command that you send to the server will either fail or succeed. If your command fails, you can use the API to retrieve an error code and a translation of that code into some form of textual message.

If the server tells you that the command executed successfully, you can retrieve the next type of result: metadata. Metadata is data about data. Specifically, *metadata* is information about the results of the command that you just executed. If you already know the format of the result set, you can ignore the metadata.

When you execute a command such as `INSERT`, `UPDATE`, or `DELETE`, the metadata returned by the server is simply a count of the number of rows affected by the command. Some commands return no metadata. For example, when you execute a

CREATE TABLE command, the only results that you get from the server are success or failure (and an error code if the command fails). When you execute a SELECT command, the metadata is more complex. Remember that a SELECT statement can return a set of zero or more rows, each containing one or more columns. This is called the *result set*. The metadata for a SELECT statement describes each of the columns in the result set.

Field Versus Column in Result Sets

When discussing a result set, the PostgreSQL documentation makes a distinction between a *field* and a *column*. A column comes directly from a table (or a view). A field is the result of a computation in the SELECT statement. For example, if you execute the command SELECT customer_name, customer_balance * 1.05 FROM customers, customer_name is a column in the result set and customer_balance * 1.05 is a field in the result set. The difference between a field and a column is mostly irrelevant and can be ignored; just be aware that the documentation uses two different words for the same meaning.

When the server sends result set metadata, it returns the number of rows in the result set and the number of fields. For each field in the result set, the metadata includes the field name, data type information, and the size of the field (on the server).

I should mention here that most client applications don't really need to deal with all the metadata returned by the server. In general, when you write an application you already know the structure of your data. You'll often need to know how many rows were returned by a given query, but the other metadata is most useful when you are processing ad-hoc commands—commands that are not known to you at the time you are writing your application.

After you process the metadata (if you need to), your application will usually process all the rows in the result set. If you execute a SELECT statement, the result set will include all the rows that meet the constraints of the WHERE clause (if any). In some circumstances, you will find it more convenient to DECLARE a cursor for the SELECT statement and then execute multiple FETCH statements. When you execute the DECLARE statement, you won't get metadata. However, as you execute FETCH commands, you are constructing a new result set for each FETCH and the server has to send metadata describing the resulting fields—that can be expensive.

After you have finished processing the result set, you can execute more commands, or you can disconnect from the server.

Choosing an Application Environment

When you choose an environment for your code, there are a number of issues to consider. To start with, you have to decide whether the feature that you want to build should be server-side code, client-side code, or a combination of both.

Server-Side Code

There are several advantages to adding functionality as server-side code.

The first consideration is performance. If you are creating an application that needs to access many rows of data, it will execute faster on the server. You won't have to send the data across the network to the client (network traffic is very expensive in terms of performance).

Next, you should consider code reuse. If you add a feature in the form of a server-side function, that feature can be used by *any* client application. You can also use server-side functions within SQL queries.

Another advantage to creating server-side functions is that you can use a server function as a trigger. A *trigger function* is executed whenever a particular condition occurs. For example, you can define a trigger that executes whenever a row is deleted from a particular table.

Finally, server-side code is portable. Any function that you write in a server-side procedural language runs on any platform that supports PostgreSQL. Of course, if you write a server-side function that requires specific server-side features (such as other functions or data types), those features must be installed in each server.

Client-Side Code

Client-side code is useful for building the user interface. You can't build a user interface using one of the server-side procedural languages—they execute within the context of the server and the server has no user interface.

One of the interesting things to note about the client APIs is that most of them are implemented using the `libpq` API (ODBC and JDBC are not). This means, for example, that if you are using `libpq++` from a C++ application and you call a member function of the `PgDatabase` class, it will be translated into one or more calls to the `libpq` library.

The ODBC and JDBC interfaces are not implemented using `libpq`. Instead, they talk directly to the backend database using the same network protocol as `libpq`. If you ever decide to implement your own client API, you can choose either method: implement your API in terms of `libpq` (or one of the other APIs), or talk directly to the server using the same underlying network protocol.

Mixing Server-Side and Client-Side Code

A particularly powerful strategy is to create an application using a mixture of client-side code and stored-procedures. Many commercial applications are shipped with two types of code. When you use one of these packages, you install a set of stored-procedures into the database; then you install external client applications that make use of the custom procedures.

This arrangement gives you all the advantages of server-side code (performance, portability, and reusability) plus the capability to create a pleasant user interface in the client.

Summary

This chapter discussed the options available to you when you create applications to work with PostgreSQL. With PostgreSQL, you can write client-side applications in a variety of languages and you can also choose between many server-side languages.

When you write an application that uses PostgreSQL, you have to decide whether you want to implement server-side code, client-side code, or a combination of both. I've explained some of the advantages and disadvantages of each approach. Personally, I prefer to mix server-side and client-side code so that I can realize the advantages offered by each.

The next few chapters describe in greater detail PL/pgSQL (server-side programming) and many of the client APIs.

6

Extending PostgreSQL

POSTGRESQL IS AN EXTENSIBLE DATABASE. You can add new functions, new operators, and custom data types to the PostgreSQL server.

In this chapter, I'll show you how to add two simple functions, a new data type, and a set of operators that work with the new type. The examples build on each other, so it would be a good idea to read this chapter in sequence rather than skipping around too much. The sample code used in this chapter was developed using PostgreSQL release 7.2. Release 7.3 introduces some new features that make it easier to write server extensions; I'll point out those features.

We'll start by adding a new function to the PostgreSQL server. The details are important, but the process is not difficult. After you know how to add one function to the server, it's easy to add others.

Extending the PostgreSQL Server with Custom Functions

An extension function is loaded into a running PostgreSQL server process as needed. If you don't actually use an extension, it will not be loaded. Extension functions must be created in the form of a dynamically loadable object module. In the Windows world, an extension is contained within a DLL. In the Linux/Unix environment, an extension is contained within a shared object module.

There are two phases to the process of adding an extension function to the PostgreSQL server. First, you create the extension function in the language of your choice, compiling it into a dynamic object module (`.dll` or `.so`). Next, tell the PostgreSQL server about the function. The `CREATE FUNCTION` command adds a new function to a database.

I'll show you two examples that should help clarify this process.

PostgreSQL and Portability

Some of the steps required to write a PostgreSQL extension function in C may seem rather odd at first. You may feel more comfortable with the process if you understand the problem that the PostgreSQL authors were trying to fix.

When you call a function in a typical C program, you know at the time you write your code how to call that function. You know how many arguments are required and you know the data type of each argument. If you provide an incorrect number of parameters or incorrect data types, it is highly likely that your program will crash. For example, the `fopen()` function (from the C Runtime Library) requires two parameters:

```
FILE * fopen( const char * filename, const char * mode )
```

If you omit the `mode` parameter or send a numeric data type instead of a pointer, your program will fail in some way.

Now, suppose that your program prompts the user for the name of a dynamic object module and the name of a function within that module. After you load the given module into your program, you have to call the named function. If you know which function the user will select, you can formulate your function call properly at the time you write your code. What happens if the user selects some other function that takes a completely different argument list? How can you formulate the function call if you don't know the parameter list? There is no portable way to do that, and PostgreSQL aims to be extremely portable.

So, the PostgreSQL authors decided to change the way you pass arguments to an extension function. Rather than declaring a separate *formal* parameter for each value passed to the function, PostgreSQL marshals all the arguments into a separate data structure and passes the address of the marshaled form to your extension. When you need to access function parameters, you get to them through the marshaled form.

This is similar in concept to the way the `main()` function of a C program behaves. You can't know, at the time you write the `main()` function, how many command-line parameters you will receive. (You might know how many parameters you *should* receive, but how many you *will* receive is not quite the same animal.) The startup routine on the C Runtime Library marshals the command-line arguments into a data structure (the `argv[]` array) and passes you the address of that structure. To find the actual values specified on the command line, you must use the data structure rather than formal parameters.

Older versions of PostgreSQL used a strategy that became less portable as operating systems advanced into the 64-bit arena. The old strategy is known as the "version-0 calling convention." The new strategy is called the "version-1 calling convention." PostgreSQL still supports both calling conventions, but you should stick to the version-1 convention for better portability.

For more information on the difference between the version-0 and version-1 conventions, see section 12 of the *PostgreSQL Programmer's Guide*.

There are two important consequences to the version-1 convention. First, all version-1 functions return the same data type: a `Datum`. A `Datum` is a sort of universal data type. Any PostgreSQL data type can be accessed through a `Datum`. PostgreSQL provides a set of macros that make it easy to work with `Datums`. Second, a version-1 function makes use of a set of macros to access function arguments. Every version-1 function is declared in the same way:

```
Datum function-name(PG_FUNCTION_ARGS);
```

As you read through the examples in this chapter, keep in mind that the PostgreSQL authors had to solve the portability problem.

The first example adds a simple function, named `filesize`, to the PostgreSQL server. Given the name of a file, it returns the size of the file (in bytes). If the file does not exist, cannot be examined, or is not a regular[1] file, this function returns `NULL`. You might find this function (and the `filelist()` function shown later) useful for performing system administration tasks from within a PostgreSQL application. After you have created the `filesize` function, you can call it like this:

```
movies=# SELECT filesize( '/bin/bash' );
 filesize
----------
   512668
```

We'll develop the `filesize` function in C.

The `filesize` function takes a single argument—a pathname in the form of a `TEXT` value. This function returns the size of the named file as an `INTEGER` value.

```
 1 /*
 2 ** Filename: filesize.c
 3 */
 4
 5 #include "postgres.h"
 6 #include "fmgr.h"
 7 #include <sys/stat.h>
 8
 9 PG_FUNCTION_INFO_V1(filesize);
10
11 Datum filesize(PG_FUNCTION_ARGS)
12 {
13     text * fileNameText = PG_GETARG_TEXT_P(0);
14     size_t fileNameLen  = VARSIZE( fileNameText ) - VARHDRSZ;
15     char * fileName     = (char *)palloc( fileNameLen + 1 );
16     struct stat statBuf;
17
18     memcpy( fileName, VARDATA( fileNameText ), fileNameLen );
19     fileName[fileNameLen] = '\0';
20
21     if( stat(fileName, &statBuf) == 0 && S_ISREG(statBuf.st_mode))
22     {
23        pfree( fileName );
24
25        PG_RETURN_INT32((int32)statBuf.st_size );
26     }
27     else
```

1. In this context, a file is considered "regular" if it is not a directory, named pipe, symbolic link, device file, or socket.

```
28      {
29         pfree( fileName );
30
31         PG_RETURN_NULL();
32      }
33 }
```

Lines 5 and 6 `#include` two header files supplied by PostgreSQL. These files (`postgres.h` and `fmgr.h`) provide data type definitions, function prototypes, and macros that you can use when writing extensions. The `<sys/stat.h>` file included at line 7 defines the layout of the `struct stat` object used by the `stat()` function (described later).

Line 9 uses the `PG_FUNCTION_INFO_V1()` to tell PostgreSQL that the function (`filesize()`) uses the version-1 calling convention.

At line 11, you see the signature used for all version-1 functions. The `filesize()` function returns a `Datum` and expects a single argument. `PG_FUNCTION_ARGS` is a preprocessor symbol that expands to declare a consistently named parameter. So, your function definition expands from this:

```
Datum filesize(PG_FUNCTION_ARGS)
```

to this:

```
Datum filesize( FunctionCallInfo fcinfo )
```

This might seem a little strange at first, but the version-1 argument accessor macros are written so that the single function argument must be named `fcinfo`.

At line 13, you create a variable of type `text`. `text` is one of the data types defined in the `postgres.h` header file (or in a file included by `postgres.h`). Whenever you write an extension function, you will be working with two sets of data types. Each function parameter (and the return value) will have a SQL data type and a C data type. For example, when you call the `filesize` function from within PostgreSQL, you pass a `TEXT` parameter: `TEXT` is the SQL data type. When you implement the `filesize` function in C, you receive a `text` value: `text` is the C data type. The name for the C data type is usually similar to the name of the corresponding SQL data type. For clarity, I'll refer to the PostgreSQL data types using uppercase letters and the C data types using lowercase letters.

Notice that a macro is vused to retrieve the address of the `TEXT` value. I mentioned earlier that an extension function must use macros to access parameters, and this is an example of such a macro. The `PG_GETARG_TEXT_P(`*n*`)` macro returns the *n*th parameter, which must be of type `TEXT`. The return value of `PG_GETARG_TEXT_P(`*n*`)` is of type `text`. There are many argument-accessor functions, each corresponding to a specific parameter type: `PG_GETARG_INT32(`*n*`)`, `PG_GETARG_BOOL(`*n*`)`, `PG_GETARG_OID(`*n*`)`, and so on. See the `fmgr.h` PostgreSQL header file for a complete list.

We'll be using the `stat()` function (from the C Runtime library) to find the size of a given file. `stat()` expects to find the pathname in the form of a null-terminated string. PostgreSQL has given you a `text` value, and `text` values are not null-terminated. You will need to convert `fileNameText` into a null-terminated string.

If `fileNameText` is not null-terminated, how do you know the length of the pathname? Let's take a peek at the definition of the `text` data type (from the `c.h` PostgreSQL header file):

```
struct varlena
{
    int32   vl_len;
    char    vl_data[1];
};

typedef struct varlena text;
```

You can see that a `text` value is defined by the `struct varlena` structure. The `vl_len` member tells you how many bytes are required to hold the entire structure. The characters that make up the text value start at the address of the `vl_data[0]` member. PostgreSQL supplies two macros that make it easy to work with variable-length data structures. The `VARHDRSZ` symbol contains the size of the fixed portion of a `struct varlena`. The `VARSIZE()` macro returns the size of the entire data structure. The `VARDATA()` macro returns a pointer to first byte of the `TEXT` value. The length of the `TEXT` value is `VARSIZE() - VARHDRSZ`. You store that length in the `fileNameLen` variable.

At line 15, you allocate enough space to hold a copy of the null-terminated string. The `palloc()` function is similar to `malloc()`: It allocates the requested number of bytes and returns a pointer to the new space. You should use `palloc()` and `pfree()` when you write extension functions rather than `malloc()` and `free()`. The `palloc()` and `pfree()` functions ensure that you can't create a memory leak in an extension function, which is something you *can* do if you use `malloc()` instead.

Lines 18 and 19 create a null-terminated copy of the `TEXT` value, and line 21 passes the null-terminated string to the `stat()` function. If the `stat()` function succeeds, it fills in the `statBuf` structure and returns 0.

If you succeeded in retrieving the file status information and the file is a regular file, free the null-terminated string (using `pfree()`) and return the file size. Notice that you must use a macro to translate the return value (an `int32`) into a `Datum`.

If the `stat()` function failed (or the file is not a regular file), you free the null-terminated string and return `NULL`. Again, you use a macro to produce the return value in the form of a `Datum`.

Now that you have crafted the `filesize` function, you need to compile it into a shared object module. You usually compile a C source file into a standalone executable program, but PostgreSQL expects to find the `filesize` function in a shared object module. The procedure for producing a shared object module is different for each compiler; section 12.5 of the *PostgreSQL Programmer's Guide* describes the process for a number of compilers. Here is the makefile that I've used to compile the filesize function using Red Hat Linux 7.2:

```
# File name: makefile
SERVER_INCLUDES += -I $(shell pg_config --includedir)
SERVER_INCLUDES += -I $(shell pg_config --includedir-server)

CFLAGS += -g $(SERVER_INCLUDES)

.SUFFIXES:      .so

.c.so:
        $(CC) $(CFLAGS) -fpic -c $<
        $(CC) $(CFLAGS) -shared -o $@ $(basename $<).o
```

To compile filesize using this makefile, you would issue the following command:

```
$ make -f makefile filesize.so
```

After the compile step is completed, you are left with a file named filesize.so in your current directory. The preferred location for a PostgreSQL extension can be found using the pg_config command:

```
$ pg_config --pkglibdir
/usr/local/pg721/lib/postgresql
```

You can copy the filesize.so file to this directory, but I prefer to create a symbolic link pointing back to my development directory instead. After an extension is completely debugged, I delete the symbolic link and copy the final version into the preferred location. To create a symbolic link, use the following command:

```
$ ln -s `pwd`/filesize.so `pg_config --pkglibdir`
```

At this point, you have a shared object module, but you still have to tell PostgreSQL about the function that you want to import into the server.

The CREATE FUNCTION command tells PostgreSQL everything it needs to know to call your function:

```
movies=# CREATE OR REPLACE FUNCTION
movies-#   filesize( TEXT ) RETURNS INTEGER AS
movies-#   'filesize.so', 'filesize' LANGUAGE 'C'
movies-#   WITH ( ISSTRICT );
CREATE
```

This command defines a function named filesize(TEXT). This function returns an INTEGER value. The function is written in C and can be found in the file filesize.so in the preferred extension directory. You can specify a complete pathname to the shared object module if you want to, but in most cases it's easier to just put it where PostgreSQL expects to find it, as I've done here. You can also omit the filename extension (the .so part), as long as you follow the shared object module-naming rules imposed by your host operating system.

I've defined `filesize()` as a *strict* function. The `ISSTRICT` attribute tells PostgreSQL that this function will always return `NULL` if any argument is `NULL`. If PostgreSQL knows that a function `ISSTRICT`, it can avoid calling the function with a `NULL` argument (again, a performance optimization). `ISSTRICT` makes it easier for you to implement your extension functions; you don't have to check for `NULL` arguments if you declare your functions to be `ISSTRICT`.

Syntax Change in PostgreSQL 7.3

The syntax for the `CREATE FUNCTION` command will change in PostgreSQL release 7.3. In releases 7.3 and later, you can use the keyword `STRICT` or the phrase `RETURNS NULL ON NULL INPUT` instead of including the `WITH(ISSTRICT)` clause.

Now you can call the function from within a PostgreSQL session:

```
movies=# SELECT filesize( '/bin/bash' );
 filesize
----------
   512668
(1 row)
movies=# SELECT filesize( 'non-existent file' );
 filesize
----------

(1 row)
```

Returning Multiple Values from an Extension Function

The second extension that you will add works well with the `filesize` function. Given the name of a directory, the `filelist` function returns a list of all files (and subdirectories) contained in that directory. The `filesize` function (from the previous example) returns a single value; `filelist` will return multiple rows. An extension function that can return multiple results is called a *set-returning function*, or SRF.

When you are finished creating this function, you can use it like this:

```
movies=# SELECT filelist( '/usr' );
  filelist
------------
 .
 ..
 bin
 dict
 etc
 games
 html
```

```
 include
 kerberos
 lib
 libexec
 local
 sbin
 share
 src
 tmp
 X11R6
(17 rows)
```

In this example, the user has invoked the `filelist` function only once, but 17 rows were returned. A SRF is actually called multiple times. In this case, the `filelist()` function is called 18 times. The first time through, `filelist()` does any preparatory work required and then returns the first result. For each subsequent call, `filelist()` returns another row until the result set is exhausted. On the 18th call, `filelist()` returns a status that tells the server that there are no more results available.

Like the `filesize` function, `filelist` takes a single argument; a directory name in the form of a `TEXT` value. This function returns a `SETOF TEXT` values.

```
 1 /*
 2 **  Filename:  filelist.c
 3 */
 4
 5 #include "postgres.h"
 6 #include "fmgr.h"
 7 #include "nodes/execnodes.h"
 8
 9 #include <dirent.h>
10
11 typedef struct
12 {
13   int               dir_ctx_count;
14   struct dirent ** dir_ctx_entries;
15   int               dir_ctx_current;
16 } dir_ctx;
17
18 PG_FUNCTION_INFO_V1(filelist);
19
```

`filelist.c` `#includes` four header files, the first three of which are supplied by PostgreSQL. `postgres.h` and `fmgr.h` provide data type definitions, function prototypes, and macros that you will need to create extensions. The `nodes/execnodes.h` header file defines a structure (`ReturnSetInfo`) that you need because `filelist` returns a set of values. You will use the `scandir()` function to retrieve the directory contents from the operating system. The fourth header file defines a few data types that are used by `scandir()`.

Line 11 defines a structure that keeps track of your progress. In the first invocation, you will set up a context structure (dir_ctx) that we can use for each subsequent call. The dir_ctx_count member indicates the number of files and subdirectories in the given directory. The dir_ctx_entries member is a pointer to an array of struct dirent structures. Each member of this array contains a description of a file or subdirectory. dir_ctx_current keeps track of the current position as you traverse the dir_ctx_entries array.

Line 18 tells PostgreSQL that filelist() uses the version-1 calling convention.

```
20 Datum filelist(PG_FUNCTION_ARGS)
21 {
22   FmgrInfo       * fmgr_info  = fcinfo->flinfo;
23   ReturnSetInfo  * resultInfo = (ReturnSetInfo *)fcinfo->resultinfo;
24   text           * startText  = PG_GETARG_TEXT_P(0);
25   int              len        = VARSIZE( startText ) - VARHDRSZ;
26   char           * start      = (char *)palloc( len+1 );
27   dir_ctx        * ctx;
28
29   memcpy( start, startText->vl_dat, len );
30   start[len] = '\0';
31
32   if( fcinfo->resultinfo == NULL )
33     elog(ERROR, "filelist: context does not accept a set result");
34
35   if( !IsA( fcinfo->resultinfo, ReturnSetInfo ))
36     elog(ERROR, "filelist: context does not accept a set result");
37
38   if( fmgr_info->fn_extra == NULL )
39   {
40     dir_ctx      * new_ctx;
41
42     fmgr_info->fn_extra = MemoryContextAlloc( fmgr_info->fn_mcxt,
43                                               sizeof( dir_ctx ));
44
45     new_ctx = (dir_ctx *)fmgr_info->fn_extra;
46
47     new_ctx->dir_ctx_count   = scandir( start,
48                                         &new_ctx->dir_ctx_entries,
49                                         NULL,
50                                         alphasort );
51     new_ctx->dir_ctx_current = 0;
52   }
53
54   ctx = (dir_ctx *)fmgr_info->fn_extra;
55
56   if( ctx->dir_ctx_count == -1 )
57   {
58     pfree( fmgr_info->fn_extra );
```

```
 59
 60     fmgr_info->fn_extra = NULL;
 61
 62     resultInfo->isDone = ExprEndResult;
 63
 64     PG_RETURN_NULL();
 65   }
 66
 67   if( ctx->dir_ctx_current < ctx->dir_ctx_count )
 68   {
 69     struct dirent * entry;
 70     size_t          nameLen;
 71     size_t          resultLen;
 72     text          * result;
 73
 74     entry     = ctx->dir_ctx_entries[ctx->dir_ctx_current];
 75     nameLen   = strlen( entry->d_name );
 76     resultLen = nameLen + VARHDRSZ;
 77
 78     result = (text *)palloc( resultLen );
 79
 80     VARATT_SIZEP( result ) = resultLen;
 81
 82     memcpy( VARDATA( result ), entry->d_name, nameLen );
 83
 84     resultInfo->isDone = ExprMultipleResult;
 85
 86 /*
 87 **  Advance to the next entry in our array of
 88 **  filenames/subdirectories
 89 */
 90     ctx->dir_ctx_current++;
 91
 92     PG_RETURN_TEXT_P( result );
 93   }
 94   else
 95   {
 96     free( ctx->dir_ctx_entries );
 97
 98     pfree( fmgr_info->fn_extra );
 99
100     fmgr_info->fn_extra = NULL;
101
102     resultInfo->isDone = ExprEndResult;
103
104     PG_RETURN_NULL();
105   }
106 }
```

Line 20 declares `filelist()` using the standard version-1 calling convention (remember, a version-1 function always returns a `Datum` and uses the `PG_FUNCTION_ARGS` preprocessor symbol as an argument list).

The C preprocessor translated line 20 into

```
Datum filesize( FunctionCallInfo fcinfo )
```

As you can see, you can access the single argument to `filesize()` through the variable `fcinfo`. All version-1 extension functions expect a `FunctionCallInfo` structure. Here is the definition of the `FunctionCallInfo` data type:

```
typedef struct FunctionCallInfoData
{
  FmgrInfo    *flinfo;      /* ptr to lookup info used for this call  */
  struct Node *context;     /* pass info about context of call        */
  struct Node *resultinfo;  /* pass or return extra info about result */
  bool        isnull;       /* true if result is NULL                 */
  short       nargs;        /* # arguments actually passed            */
  Datum       arg[FUNC_MAX_ARGS];     /* Function arguments           */
  bool        argnull[FUNC_MAX_ARGS]; /* T if arg[i] is NULL          */
} FunctionCallInfoData;
```

There is quite a bit of information in this structure. For now, you need to know about only two of the structure members; the rest of the members are manipulated using macros, so you should pretend that you don't see them. The two members that you are interested in are `flinfo` and `resultInfo`. The `flinfo` member points to a structure of type `FmgrInfo`. The `FmgrInfo` structure looks like this:

```
typedef struct FmgrInfo
{
  PGFunction  fn_addr;   /* function or handler to be called          */
  Oid         fn_oid;    /* OID of function (NOT of handler, if any) */
  short       fn_nargs;  /* 0..FUNC_MAX_ARGS, or -1 if variable arg  */
  bool        fn_strict; /* func. is "strict" (NULL in = NULL out)   */
  bool        fn_retset; /* func. returns a set (multiple calls)     */
  void       *fn_extra;  /* extra space for use by handler           */
  MemoryContext fn_mcxt; /* memory context to store fn_extra in      */
} FmgrInfo;
```

Look closely at the `FmgrInfo` and `FunctionCallInfo` structures. Why would you need two structures to represent a function call? The `FmgrInfo` function contains information about the *definition* of a function; in other words, the stuff you tell PostgreSQL in the `CREATE FUNCTION` command can be found in the `FmgrInfo` structure. The `FunctionCallInfo` structure represents a single invocation of a function. If you call the same function 20 times, you'll have 20 different `FunctionCallInfo` structures, each pointing to a single `FmgrInfo` structure. You can see the difference by comparing `FmgrInfo.fn_nargs` with `FunctionCallInfo.nargs`. `FmgrInfo.fn_nargs` tells you how many arguments were listed in the `CREATE FUNCTION` command; `FmgrInfo.fn_nargs` tells you how many arguments were passed to this particular invocation.

Line 23 declares a variable called `fmgr_info`; you'll use this to get to the `FmgrInfo` structure for this function. Line 24 declares a variable that you will use to get to the `ReturnSetInfo` structure. I'll describe the `ReturnSetInfo` structure in a moment.

Lines 24 through 30 turn the `text` argument into a null-terminated string. This is basically the same procedure you used in the `filesize()` function.

Lines 32 through 36 perform some sanity checks. It's possible to call the `filelist()` function in an inappropriate context. We know that `filelist()` returns multiple rows, so it makes sense to call that function as a target of a `SELECT` command. You could also call `filelist()` in the `WHERE` clause of a `SELECT` command, but that would be an inappropriate context (because of that multiple-row problem). When you write a function that returns a set of values, you should ensure that your function is being called in an appropriate context the way we do here.

Line 38 is where the interesting stuff starts. `fmgr_info->fn_extra` is a pointer that you can use for your own purposes; PostgreSQL doesn't do anything with this structure member except to provide for your use. The first time `filelist()` is called, the `fmgr_info->fn_extra` member is `NULL`. In each subsequent call, `fmgr_info->fn_extra` is equal to whatever you set it to in the previous call. Sounds like a great place to keep context information. Remember the `dir_ctx` structure you looked at earlier? That structure holds the information that you use to keep track of your progress as you walk through the array of file entries in a given directory.

At line 42, you know that `fmgr_info->fn_extra` is `NULL`: That implies that you have not yet started traversing a directory list. So, you allocate a `dir_ctx` structure and point `fmgr_info->fn_extra` to the new structure. The next time you are called, `fmgr_info->fn_extra` will point to the same `dir_ctx` structure (remember, there is only one `FmgrInfo` structure, regardless of how many times this function is called).

You may be thinking that I should have used `palloc()` to allocate the `dir_ctx` structure. In most extension functions, that is precisely what you should do. But in the case of an SRF, you want to allocate information related to the `FmgrInfo` structure in a different memory context[2], the context pointed to in the `fmgr_info` structure.

Lines 47 through 50 do the real grunt work. You use the `scandir()` function to create an array of `struct dirent` structures. Each element in this array (`new_ctx->dir_ctx_entries`) describes a file or subdirectory. The `scandir()` function expects four parameters. The first parameter is the name of the directory that you are interested in; you pass the null-terminated string (`start`) that you crafted earlier in this function. The second parameter is a bit complex—it's a pointer to a pointer to an array of

2. You can think of a *memory context* as a pool of memory. Unlike `malloc()`, the `MemoryContextAlloc()` function allocates memory from a specific pool (`malloc()` allocates all memory from the same pool). A memory context has lifetime (or scope). When the scope completes, all memory allocated within that scope is automatically released. The `palloc()` function is just a wrapper around `MemoryContextAlloc()`. The memory context used by `palloc()` is destroyed at the end of a transaction (or possibly sooner).

struct dirent structures. You know that your dir_ctx.dir_ctx_entries member is a pointer to an array of structures, so you pass the *address* of dir_ctx_entries and scandir() points dir_ctx_entries to the new array. The third parameter is a pointer to a structure. If you want to choose which files and subdirectories to include in the result set, you can write your own selection function and pass its address to scandir(). You want all files and subdirectories so you just pass in a NULL to tell scandir() not to filter the result set. The final scandir() parameter is a pointer to a comparison function. If you *don't* provide a comparison function, scandir() won't sort the result set. Use the alphasort function from the C Runtime Library—it's already written, and you aren't too concerned about performance here. For more information on scandir() and alphasort(), see the scandir() man page.

Finish initializing the dir_ctx structure by setting dir_ctx_current to zero. dir_ctx_current is incremented as you walk through the dir_ctx_entries. Now that the initialization is complete, you can return your first result. But first, a quick review. You know that PostgreSQL calls this function many times and it continues to call filelist() until you set resultInfo->isDone to ExprEndResult. You can detect the initial call to filelist() by the fact that fmgr_info->fn_extra is NULL. In the initial call, you allocate a context structure and point fmgr_info->fn_extra to the new structure; the next time that filelist() is called, fmgr_info->fn_extra will *not* be NULL, so you know that you can skip the initialization step. Next, populate the context structure by calling the scandir() function: scandir() allocates an array of struct dirent structures and gives you a pointer to that array.

Line 54 retrieves the address of your context structure from fmgr_info->fn_extra.

Lines 56 through 65 take care of the case where the scandir() function fails to return any directory entries. The scandir() function returns the number of directory entries retrieved—it returns –1 on failure.

The details in this section of code are important. First, you must free the context structure that you allocated in the initial call (using pfree()). You also set fmgr_info->fn_extra to NULL; if you forget this step, the next call to filelist() will find a stale context structure and won't reinitialize. Remember, there is one FunctionCallInfo structure for each invocation, but there is never more than one FmgrInfo structure; you'll get the same FmgrInfo structure each time filelist() is invoked. Line 62 tells PostgreSQL that you have reached the end of the result set and line 64 returns a NULL Datum.

Lines 67 through 93 take care of returning a single result to the caller.

Lines 74 through 82 create a text value from a null-terminated directory entry (actually, ignore most of the struct dirent structure and just return the name portion). You first allocate a new text structure using palloc(); then set the structure size and copy the directory entry name into place. Notice that you don't copy the null-terminator: A text value should not be null-terminated. At line 84, you tell PostgreSQL that you are returning a result and there may be more results, so keep calling. Next, you increment the array index so that the next call to filelist() will return the next directory entry. Finally, you return the directory entry to the caller in the form of a text value.

Notice that the context structure in this section of code has not been freed. You need to preserve the dir_ctx structure until you have processed the last directory entry.

You reach Lines 96 through 104 once you have returned all directory entries. This section is nearly identical to the code that deals with a scandir() failure (lines 58–64). In fact the only difference is that you have one more thing to clean up. When you called the scandir() function, it allocated an array of struct dirent structures using malloc(). You have to free() that array before you finish up.

That completes the C part of this function, now you have to compile it into a shared object module and tell PostgreSQL where to find it. You can use the same makefile that you used to compile the filesize function:

```
$ make -f makefile filelist.so
```

As before, you'll create a symbolic link between filelist.so and PostgreSQL's preferred package directory:

```
$ ln -s `pwd`/filelist.so `pg_config --pkglibdir`
```

Now the only thing remaining is to tell PostgreSQL about the new function:

```
movies=# CREATE FUNCTION filelist( TEXT )
movies-#   RETURNS SETOF TEXT
movies-#   AS 'filelist.so' LANGUAGE 'C';
CREATE
```

Now, let's call filelist() to see how it works:

```
movies=# SELECT filelist( '/usr' );
  filelist
------------
 .
 ..
 bin
 dict
 etc
 games
 html
 include
 kerberos
 lib
 libexec
 local
 sbin
 share
 src
 tmp
 X11R6
(17 rows)
```

Notice that the results appear in sorted order. The ordering comes because you used the `alphasort()` function when you called `scandir()`. If you don't care about the ordering, you can specify a `NULL` comparison function instead. Of course, we can ask PostgreSQL to order the data itself:

```
movies=# SELECT filelist( '/usr' ) ORDER BY filelist DESC;
  filelist
------------
 X11R6
 tmp
 src
 share
 sbin
 local
 libexec
 lib
 kerberos
 include
 html
 games
 etc
 dict
 bin
 ..
 .
 (17 rows)
```

You can see that adding useful extension functions to PostgreSQL is not too difficult (assuming that you are comfortable working in C). Now that you understand the mechanism for creating new functions, I'd like to turn your attention to the process of creating a new data type. When you add a new data type to PostgreSQL, you must create a few supporting extension functions, so be sure you understand the material covered so far.

New SRF Features in Version 7.3

PostgreSQL release 7.3 will introduce a friendlier SRF (set-returning-function) mechanism. As this chapter is being written, 7.3 has not been released yet, and the documentation does not include any mention of the new SRF mechanism. If you want more information, see the `contrib/tablefunc` directory in the source distribution and the `src/include/funcapi.h` header file. The code that I've shown in this chapter will still function in release 7.3, but you may find a few new features that make it easier to build complex SRFs.

Extending the PostgreSQL Server with Custom Data Types

The `customers` table in this sample application contains a column named `balance`. I've made the assumption that the values in the `balance` column are expressed in local currency (that is, U.S. dollars in the U.S., British pounds in the U.K.). This assumption serves us well until our corner video store opens a web site and starts accepting orders from foreign customers.

PostgreSQL doesn't have a predefined data type that represents a foreign currency value, so let's create one. You want to store three pieces of information for each foreign currency value: the name of the currency (pounds, dollars, drachma, and so on), the number of units, and the exchange rate at the time the foreign currency value was created. Call your new data type `FCUR` (Foreign Currency). After you have fully defined the `FCUR` data type, you can create tables with `FCUR` columns, enter and display `FCUR` values, convert between `FCUR` values and other numeric types, and use a few operators (`+`,`-`,`*`,`/`) to manipulate `FCUR` values.

Internal and External Forms

Before going much further, it is important to understand the difference between the external form of a value and the internal form.

The *external* form of a data type defines how the user enters a value and how a value is displayed to the user. For example, if you enter a numeric value, you might enter the characters `7218942`. If you enter these characters from a client that uses an ASCII encoding, you have entered the character values `37`, `32`, `31`, `38`, `39`, `34`, and `32` (in hexadecimal notation). The external form of a data type is used to interact with the user.

The *internal* form of a data type defines how a value is represented inside the database. The preceding numeric value from might be translated from the string `7218942` into the four-byte integer value `00 6E 26 FE` (again in hexadecimal notation). The internal form of a data type is used within the database.

Why have two forms? Most programming languages can deal with numeric values implicitly (that is, without requiring the *programmer* to implement simple arithmetic operations). For example, the C programming language defines a built-in data type named `int`. An `int` value can store integer (that is, whole) numbers within some range determined by the compiler. The C compiler knows how to add, subtract, multiply, and divide `int` values. A C programmer is not required to perform the bit manipulations himself; the compiler emits the code required to perform the arithmetic.

Most programmers share a common understanding of what it means to add two integer values. When you add two integer values, you expect the result to be the arithmetic sum of the values. Another way to state this is to say that the `+` operator, when applied to two integer operands, should return the arithmetic sum of the operands, most likely in the form of an integer.

What would you expect the result to be if you applied the + operator to two string values? If each string contained only a sequence of one or more digits, such as `'1' + '34'`, you might expect the result to be the string `'35'`. What would happen if you tried adding `'1' + 'red'`? That's pretty hard to predict. Because it is difficult to come up with a good *arithmetic* definition of the + operator when applied to strings, many programming languages define + to mean concatenation when applied to string operands. So, the expression `'1' + 'red'` would evaluate to the string `'1red'`.

So, to summarize a bit, the external form of a numeric value is a string of numeric digits, sign characters, and a radix point. When you choose the internal form for a numeric value, you want to choose a representation that makes it easy to define and implement mathematical operations.

You've already seen the external and internal form of the `TEXT` data type. The external form of a `TEXT` value is a string of characters enclosed in single quotes (the quotes are not part of the value; they just mark the boundaries of the value). If you need to include single quotes in a `TEXT` value, the external form defines a set of rules for doing so. The internal form of a `TEXT` value is defined by the `TEXT` data type. The `TEXT` structure contains a length and an array of characters.

Defining a Simple Data Type in PostgreSQL

Now that you understand the difference between internal and external forms, it should be obvious that PostgreSQL needs to convert values between these forms. When you define a new data type, you tell PostgreSQL how to convert a value from external form to internal form and from internal form to external form.

Let's create a simple type that mimics the built-in `TEXT` data type. Data type descriptions are stored in the `pg_type` system table. We are interested in three of the columns:

```
movies=# SELECT typinput, typoutput, typlen
movies-#   FROM pg_type
movies-#   WHERE typname = 'text';
 typinput | typoutput | typlen
----------+-----------+--------
 textin   | textout   |     -1
```

The `typinput` column tells you the name of the function that PostgreSQL uses to convert a `TEXT` value from external form to internal form; in this case, the function is named `textin`. The `typoutput` column contains the name of the function (`textout`) that PostgreSQL uses to convert from internal to external form. Finally, `typlen` specifies how much space is required to hold the internal form of a `TEXT` value. `TEXT` values are of variable length, so the space required to hold the internal form is also variable (–1 in this column means *variable length*). If `TEXT` were a fixed-length type, the `typlen` column would contain the number of bytes required to hold the internal form.

Now you have enough information to create a new data type. Here is the command that you'll use to create a type named `mytexttype`:

```
movies=# CREATE TYPE mytexttype
movies-# (
movies-#   INPUT=textin,
movies-#   OUTPUT=textout,
movies-#   INTERNALLENGTH=VARIABLE
movies-# );
```

The `INPUT=textin` clause tells PostgreSQL which function to call when it needs to convert a `mytexttype` value from external to internal form. The `OUTPUT=textout` clause tells PostgreSQL which function converts a `mytexttype` value from internal to external form. The final clause, `INTERNALLENGTH=VARIABLE`, tells PostgreSQL how much space is required to hold the internal form of a `mytexttype` value; you specify `VARIABLE` here to tell PostgreSQL that you are not defining a fixed length data type.

You have essentially cloned the `TEXT`[3] data type. Because you are using the same input and output functions as the `TEXT` type, the internal and external form of a `mytexttype` value is identical to the internal and external form of a `TEXT` value.

After you execute this `CREATE TYPE` command, you can use the `mytexttype` data type to create new columns:

```
movies=# CREATE TABLE myTestTable
movies-# (
movies(#   pkey  INTEGER,
movies(#   value  mytexttype
movies(# );
CREATE
```

You can also enter `mytexttype` values. Because you borrowed the `textin` and `textout` functions, you have to enter values according to the rules for a `TEXT` value:

```
movies=# INSERT INTO myTestTable
movies-#   VALUES ( 1, 'This is a mytexttype value in external form' );
```

Now, let's define a new data type from scratch.

3. You have created an *extremely* limited clone. At this point, you can enter and display `mytexttype` values, but you can't do anything else with them. You have not defined any operators that can manipulate `mytexttype` values.

Defining the Data Type in C

We'll start out by defining the internal form for an `FCUR` value. As I mentioned before, you want to store three pieces of information for each value: the name of the currency (dollars, euros, yen, and so on), the number of units, and the exchange rate at the time the value was created. Why do you need to store the exchange rate with each value? Because exchange rates vary over time, and you need to know the rate at the time the value is created.

Because you are going to use the C programming language to implement the required conversion functions, you need to define a structure[4] containing the three components. Here are the first few lines of the implementation file:

```
 1 /*
 2 **  File name: fcur.c
 3 */
 4
 5 #include "postgres.h"
 6 #include "fmgr.h"
 7
 8 typedef struct
 9 {
10     char     fcur_name[4];    /* Currency name     */
11     float4   fcur_units;      /* Units of currency    */
12     float4   fcur_xrate;      /* Exchange rate    */
13 } fcur;
14
15 static char * baseCurrencyName    = "US$";
16 static char * unknownCurrencyName = "???";
17
```

Start by `#including` the `postgres.h` and `fmgr.h` header files, just like you did for the earlier examples. The `fcur` structure defines the internal form for your `fcur` data type. Store the currency name (`fcur_name`) as a three- character, null-terminated string. The `fcur_units` member store the number of currency units as a floating-point number. The exchange rate is stored as a floating-point number in `fcur_xrate`.

At lines 15 and 16, you define two currency names. The `baseCurrencyName` is the name of the local currency. When the `fcur_name` of a value is equal to `baseCurrencyName`, the value is said to be *normalized*. A normalized value will always have an exchange rate (`fcur_xrate`) of `1.0`: One U.S. dollar always equals one U.S. dollar. The `unknownCurrencyName` is used when the user enters a value containing a number of units and an exchange rate, but fails to provide the currency name. We'll use each of these variables in a moment.

4. This is not necessarily the most efficient (or even realistic) way to store a foreign currency value, but it works well for purposes of illustration. In a real-world implementation, you would not want to store monetary values using floating-point data types because of their inherent lack of precision. You would also want more control over the format of the currency name.

Defining the Input and Output Functions in C

Now you will create the input and output functions for this data type. At this point, you have to decide what your external form will look like. You know that you need to deal with three components: the number of units, an optional exchange rate, and an optional currency name. You want the typical case (units only) to be easy to enter, so you will accept input in any of the following forms:

```
units
units(exchange-rate)
units(exchange-rate/currency-name)
```

If you see a number (and nothing else), assume that you have a number of units of the base currency. If you see a number followed by an open parenthesis, you will expect an exchange rate to follow. If the exchange rate is followed by a slash character, expect a currency name. Of course, we expect a closed parenthesis if we see an open one.

Table 6.1 shows a few valid `FCUR` external values (assuming that `baseCurrencyName` is "US$"):

Table 6.1 **Sample `FCUR` Values (in External Form)**

External Form	Meaning
`'1'`	1 U.S. dollar
`'1(.5)'`	1 unit of `unknownCurrencyName` with an exchange rate of 0.5
`'3(1/US$)'`	3 U.S. dollars
`'5(.687853/GPB)'`	5 British pounds with an exchange rate of .687853 Pounds per 1 U.S. dollar
`'10(7.2566/FRF)'`	10 French francs with an exchange rate of 7.2566 Francs per 1 U.S. dollar
`'1.52(1.5702/CA$)'`	1.52 Canadian dollars with an exchange rate of 1.5702 Canadian dollars per 1 U.S. dollar

The input function is named `fcur_in`, and it converts from external (`FCUR`) form to internal (`fcur`) form. This function expects a single parameter: a pointer to a null-terminated string containing the external form of an `fcur` value.

```
18 /*
19 **  Name: fcur_in()
20 **
21 **        Converts an fcur value from external form
22 **     to internal form.
23 */
24
25 PG_FUNCTION_INFO_V1(fcur_in);
26
```

```
27 Datum fcur_in(PG_FUNCTION_ARGS)
28 {
29     char  * src     = PG_GETARG_CSTRING(0);
30     char  * workStr = pstrdup( src );
31     char  * units   = NULL;
32     char  * name    = NULL;
33     char  * xrate   = NULL;
34     fcur  * result  = NULL;
35     char  * endPtr  = NULL;
36
37     /* strtok() will find all of the components for us */
38
39     units = strtok( workStr, "(" );
40     xrate = strtok( NULL, "/)" );
41     name  = strtok( NULL, ")" );
42
43     result = (fcur *)palloc( sizeof( fcur ));
44
45     memset( result, 0x00, sizeof( fcur ));
46
47     result->fcur_units = strtod( units, &endPtr );
48
49     if( xrate )
50     {
51         result->fcur_xrate = strtod( xrate, &endPtr );
52     }
53     else
54     {
55         result->fcur_xrate = 1.0;
56     }
57
58     if( name )
59     {
60         strncpy( result->fcur_name,
61                  name,
62                  sizeof( result->fcur_name ));
63     }
64     else
65     {
66        strncpy( result->fcur_name,
67                 unknownCurrencyName,
68                sizeof( result->fcur_name ));
69     }
70
71     PG_RETURN_POINTER( result );
72 }
73
```

Notice that this looks suspiciously similar to the extension functions you saw earlier in this chapter. In particular, `fcur_in()` returns a `Datum` and uses `PG_FUNCTION_ARGS` to declare the parameter list. This similarity exists because `fcur_in()` *is* an extension function, so everything that you already know about writing extension functions applies to this discussion as well.

You use the `strtok()` function (from the C Runtime Library) to parse out the external form. `strtok()` is a destructive function; it modifies the string that you pass to it. So the first thing you need to do in this function is to make a copy of the input string. Use the `pstrdup()` function to make the copy. `pstrdup()` is similar to the `strdup()` function from the C Runtime Library, except that the memory that holds the copy is allocated using `palloc()` and must be freed using `pfree()`. You use `pstrdup()` to avoid any memory leaks should you forget to clean up after yourself.

Lines 39, 40, and 41 parse the input string into three components. Remember, you will accept input strings in any of the following forms:

```
units
units(exchange-rate)
units(exchange-rate/currency-name)
```

The *units* component must be a string representing a floating-point number. You will use the `strtod()` runtime function to convert *units* into a `float4`, so the format of the input string must meet the requirements of `strtod()`. Here is an excerpt from the Linux `strtod()` man page that describes the required form:

```
The expected form of the string is optional leading  white
space  as  checked by isspace(3), an optional plus (``+'')
or minus sign (``-'') followed by  a  sequence  of  digits
optionally  containing  a decimal-point character, option-
ally followed by an exponent.  An exponent consists of  an
``E''  or  ``e'',  followed  by  an optional plus or minus
sign, followed by a non-empty sequence of digits.  If  the
locale  is  not  "C"  or "POSIX", different formats may be
used.
```

The optional *exchange-rate* component is also converted to a `float4` by `strtod()`.

The *currency-name* component is simply a three-character string. Values such as "US$" (U.S. dollar),"GPB" (British pound), and "CA$" (Canadian dollar) seem reasonable. In your sample data type, you won't do any validation on this string. In a real-world implementation, you would probably want to match the currency name with a table of valid (and standardized) spellings.

The first call to `strtok()` returns a null-terminated string containing all characters up to (but not including) the first `(` in `workStr`. If `workStr` doesn't contain a `(` character, `units` will contain the entire input string. The second call to `strtok()` picks out the optional *exchange-rate* component. The final call to `strtok()` picks out the optional *currency-name*.

After you have tokenized the input string into units, exchange rate, and currency name, you can allocate space for the internal form at line 43. Notice that `palloc()` is used here.

The rest of this function is pretty simple. You use `strtod()` to convert the units and exchange rate into the `fcur` structure. If the user didn't provide you with an exchange rate, assume that it must be 1.0. You finish building the `fcur` structure by copying in the first three characters of the currency name, or `unknownCurrencyName` if you didn't find a currency name in the input string.

Line 71 returns the `Datum` to the caller.

That's pretty simple! Of course, I omitted all the error-checking code that you would need in a real-world application.

Now, let's look at the output function. `fcur_out()` converts an `fcur` structure from internal to external form.

```
 74 /*
 75 **  Name: fcur_out()
 76 **
 77 **        Converts an fcur value from internal form
 78 **        to external form.
 79 */
 80
 81 PG_FUNCTION_INFO_V1(fcur_out);
 82
 83 Datum fcur_out(PG_FUNCTION_ARGS)
 84 {
 85     fcur  * src  = (fcur *)PG_GETARG_POINTER( 0 );
 86     char  * result;

 87     char    work[16+sizeof(src->fcur_name)+16+4];
 88
 89     sprintf( work, "%g(%g/%s)",
 90         src->fcur_units,
 91         src->fcur_xrate,
 92         src->fcur_name );
 93
 94     result = (char *)palloc( strlen( work ) + 1 );
 95
 96     strcpy( result, work );
 97
 98     PG_RETURN_CSTRING( result );
 99
100 }
101
```

This function is much shorter than the input function. That's typically the case because your code has far fewer decisions to make.

You format the `fcur` components into a work buffer at lines 89 through 92: `sprintf()` takes care of all the grunt work. Notice that you are formatting into an array of characters large enough to hold the largest result that you can expect (two 16-digit numbers, a function name, two parentheses, a slash, and a null terminator). Some of you might not like using a fixed-size buffer with `sprintf()`, use `snprintf()` if you have it and you are worried about buffer overflows.

After you have a formatted string, use `palloc()` to allocate the result string. (In case you were wondering, you format into a temporary buffer first so that you can allocate a result string of the minimum possible size.) At line 96, you copy the temporary string into the result string and then return that string at line 98.

I should point out an important consideration about the input and output functions that you have just written. It's *very* important that the format of the string produced by the output function match the format understood by the input function. When you back up a table using `pg_dump`, the archive contains the external form of each column. When you restore from the archive, the data must be converted from external form to internal form. If they don't match, you won't be able to restore your data.

Defining the Input and Output Functions in PostgreSQL

Now that you have created the input (external to internal) and output (internal to external) functions in C, you must compile them into a shared object module:

```
$ make -f makefile fcur.so
```

Next, create a symbolic link between `fcur.so` and PostgreSQL's preferred package directory so that PostgreSQL knows how to find out code:

```
$ ln -s `pwd`/fcur.so `pg_config --pkglibdir`
```

Now you can define the input and output functions in PostgreSQL:

```
movies=# CREATE OR REPLACE FUNCTION fcur_in( opaque )
movies-#   RETURNS opaque
movies-#   AS 'fcur.so' LANGUAGE 'C'
movies-#   WITH ( ISCACHABLE, ISSTRICT );
CREATE
movies=# CREATE OR REPLACE FUNCTION fcur_out( opaque )
movies-#   RETURNS opaque
movies-#   AS 'fcur.so' LANGUAGE 'C'
movies-#   WITH ( ISCACHABLE, ISSTRICT );
```

Notice that each of these functions expects an opaque parameter and returns an opaque value. You might be thinking that fcur_in() should take a null-terminated string and return a FCUR. That makes sense except for two minor problems: PostgreSQL doesn't have a SQL data type that represents a null-terminated string and PostgreSQL doesn't know anything about the FCUR data type yet. Okay, those aren't exactly *minor* problems. PostgreSQL helps you out a little here by letting you define these functions in terms of opaque. The opaque data type tells PostgreSQL that a SQL data type doesn't define the data that you are working with. One of the special properties of an opaque function is that you can't call it directly:

```
movies=# SELECT fcur_in( '5(1.3/GPB)' );
ERROR:  getTypeOutputInfo: Cache lookup of type 0 failed
```

This error message means, "don't try that again."

We've defined each of these functions with two additional attributes. The ISCACHABLE attribute tells PostgreSQL that calling this function twice with the same argument(s) is guaranteed to return the same result. If PostgreSQL knows that a function ISCACHABLE, it can optimize certain operations by computing the return value once and caching the result (hence the clever name).

> **CREATE_FUNCTION Syntax Change in 7.3**
>
> The syntax for the CREATE FUNCTION command will change in PostgreSQL release 7.3. In release 7.3, you can use the keyword IMMUTABLE instead of the WITH(ISCACHABLE) clause. See the *PostgreSQL Reference Manual* for more details.
>
> As I mentioned earlier in this chapter, the ISSRICT attribute tells PostgreSQL that this function always returns NULL if any argument is NULL.

Defining the Data Type in PostgreSQL

At this point, PostgreSQL knows about your input and output functions. Now you can tell PostgreSQL about your data type:

```
CREATE TYPE FCUR ( INPUT=fcur_in, OUTPUT=fcur_out, INTERNALLENGTH=12 );
```

This command creates a new data type (how exciting) named FCUR. The input function is named fcur_in, and the output function is named fcur_out. The INTERNAL-LENGTH=12 clause tells PostgreSQL how much space is required to hold the internal value. I computed this value by hand—just add up the size of each member of the fcur structure and be sure that you account for any pad bytes. The safest way to compute the INTERNALLENGTH is to use your C compiler's sizeof() operator.

Let's create a table that uses this data type and insert a few values:

```
movies=# CREATE TABLE fcur_test( pkey INT, val FCUR );
CREATE
movies=# INSERT INTO fcur_test VALUES( 1, '1' );
```

```
INSERT
movies=# INSERT INTO fcur_test VALUES( 2, '1(.5)' );
INSERT
movies=# INSERT INTO fcur_test VALUES( 3, '3(1/US$)' );
INSERT
movies=# INSERT INTO fcur_test VALUES( 4, '5(.687853/GBP)' );
INSERT
movies=# INSERT INTO fcur_test VALUES( 5, '10(7.2566/FRF)' );
INSERT
movies=# INSERT INTO fcur_test VALUES( 6, '1(1.5702/CA$)' );
INSERT
movies=# INSERT INTO fcur_test VALUES( 7, '1.5702(1.5702/CA$)' );
INSERT
```

Now let's see what those values look like when you retrieve them:

```
movies=# SELECT * FROM fcur_test;
 pkey |         val
------+--------------------
    1 | 1(1/???)
    2 | 1(0.5/???)
    3 | 3(1/US$)
    4 | 5(0.687853/GBP)
    5 | 10(7.2566/FRF)
    6 | 1(1.5702/CA$)
    7 | 1.5702(1.5702/CA$)
```

Not bad. The question marks are kind of ugly, but the data that you put in came back out.

At this point, you officially have a new data type. You can put values in and you can get values out. Let's add a few functions that make the FCUR type a little more useful.

It would be nice to know if two FCUR values represent the same amount of money expressed in your local currency. In other words, you want a function, fcur_eq, which you can call like this:

```
movies=# SELECT fcur_eq( '1', '1.5702(1.5702/CA$)' );
 fcur_eq
---------
 t
(1 row)

movies=# SELECT fcur_eq( '1', '3(1.5702/CA$)' );
 fcur_eq
---------
 f
(1 row)
```

The first call to `fcur_eq` tells you that 1.5702 Canadian dollars is equal to 1 U.S. dollar. The second call tells you that 3 Canadian dollars are *not* equal to 1 U.S. dollar.

To compare two `FCUR` values, you need to convert them into a common currency:

```
102 /*
103 **  Name: normalize()
104 **
105 **        Converts an fcur value into a normalized
106 **        double by applying the exchange rate.
107 */
108
109 static double normalize( fcur * src )
110 {
111     return( src->fcur_units / src->fcur_xrate );
112 }
```

The `normalize()` function converts a given `FCUR` value into our local currency. You can use `normalize()` to implement the `fcur_eq()` function:

```
115 /*
116 **  Name: fcur_eq()
117 **
118 **        Returns true if the two fcur values
119 **        are equal (after normalization), otherwise
120 **        returns false.
121 */
122
123 PG_FUNCTION_INFO_V1(fcur_eq);
124
125 Datum fcur_eq(PG_FUNCTION_ARGS)
126 {
127     fcur  * left     = (fcur *)PG_GETARG_POINTER(0);
128     fcur  * right    = (fcur *)PG_GETARG_POINTER(1);
129
130     PG_RETURN_BOOL( normalize( left ) == normalize( right ));
131 }
132
```

This function is straightforward. You normalize each argument, compare them using the C == operator, and return the result as a `BOOL Datum`. You declare this function as `ISSTRICT` so that you don't have to check for `NULL` arguments.

Now you can compile your code again and tell PostgreSQL about your new function (`fcur_eq()`):

```
$ make -f makefile fcur.so
$ psql -q
movies=# CREATE OR REPLACE FUNCTION fcur_eq( fcur, fcur )
```

```
movies-#   RETURNS bool
movies-#   AS 'fcur.so' LANGUAGE 'C'
movies-#   WITH ( ISCACHABLE, ISSTRICT );
```

Now you can call this function to compare any two FCUR values:

```
movies=# SELECT fcur_eq( '1', '1.5702(1.5702/CA$)' );
 fcur_eq
---------
 t
(1 row)

movies=# SELECT fcur_eq( '1', NULL );
 fcur_eq
---------

(1 row)
```

The fcur_eq function is nice, but you really want to compare FCUR values using the = operator. Fortunately, that's easy to do:

```
movies=# CREATE OPERATOR =
movies-# (
movies-#   leftarg    = FCUR,
movies-#   rightarg   = FCUR,
movies-#   procedure  = fcur_eq,
movies-#  );
```

This command creates a new operator named =. This operator has a FCUR value on the left side and a FCUR value on the right side. PostgreSQL calls the fcur_eq function whenever it needs to evaluate this operator.

Now you can evaluate expressions such as

```
movies=# SELECT * FROM fcur_test WHERE val = '1';
 pkey |        val
------+--------------------
    1 | 1(1/???)
    7 | 1.5702(1.5702/CA$)
(2 rows)
```

The operator syntax is much easier to read than the functional syntax. Let's go ahead and add the other comparison operators: <>, <, <=, >, and >=. They all follow the same pattern as the = operator: You normalize both arguments and then compare them as double values.

```
133 /*
134 **  Name: fcur_ne()
135 **
136 **        Returns true if the two fcur values
137 **        are not equal (after normalization),
138 **        otherwise returns false.
```

```
139 */
140
141 PG_FUNCTION_INFO_V1(fcur_ne);
142
143 Datum fcur_ne(PG_FUNCTION_ARGS)
144 {
145     fcur  * left     = (fcur *)PG_GETARG_POINTER(0);
146     fcur  * right    = (fcur *)PG_GETARG_POINTER(1);
147
148     PG_RETURN_BOOL( normalize( left ) != normalize( right ));
149 }
150
151 /*
152 **  Name: fcur_lt()
153 **
154 **        Returns true if the left operand
155 **        is less than the right operand.
156 */
157
158 PG_FUNCTION_INFO_V1(fcur_lt);
159
160 Datum fcur_lt(PG_FUNCTION_ARGS)
161 {
162     fcur  * left     = (fcur *)PG_GETARG_POINTER(0);
163     fcur  * right    = (fcur *)PG_GETARG_POINTER(1);
164
165     PG_RETURN_BOOL( normalize( left ) < normalize( right ));
166 }
167
168 /*
169 **  Name: fcur_le()
170 **
171 **        Returns true if the left operand
172 **        is less than or equal to the right
173 **        operand.
174 */
175
176 PG_FUNCTION_INFO_V1(fcur_le);
177
178 Datum fcur_le(PG_FUNCTION_ARGS)
179 {
180     fcur  * left     = (fcur *)PG_GETARG_POINTER(0);
181     fcur  * right    = (fcur *)PG_GETARG_POINTER(1);
182
183     PG_RETURN_BOOL( normalize( left ) <= normalize( right ));
184 }
185
```

```
186 /*
187 **  Name: fcur_gt()
188 **
189 **        Returns true if the left operand
190 **     is greater than the right operand.
191 */
192
193 PG_FUNCTION_INFO_V1(fcur_gt);
194
195 Datum fcur_gt(PG_FUNCTION_ARGS)
196 {
197     fcur  * left     = (fcur *)PG_GETARG_POINTER(0);
198     fcur  * right    = (fcur *)PG_GETARG_POINTER(1);
199
200     PG_RETURN_BOOL( normalize( left ) > normalize( right ));
201 }
202
203 /*
204 **  Name: fcur_ge()
205 **
206 **        Returns true if the left operand
207 **        is greater than or equal to the right operand.
208 */
209
210 PG_FUNCTION_INFO_V1(fcur_ge);
211
212 Datum fcur_ge(PG_FUNCTION_ARGS)
213 {
214     fcur  * left     = (fcur *)PG_GETARG_POINTER(0);
215     fcur  * right    = (fcur *)PG_GETARG_POINTER(1);
216
217     PG_RETURN_BOOL( normalize( left ) >= normalize( right ));
218 }
```

Now you can tell PostgreSQL about these functions:

```
movies=# CREATE OR REPLACE FUNCTION fcur_ne( fcur, fcur )
movies-#   RETURNS boolean
movies-#   AS 'fcur.so' LANGUAGE 'C'
movies-#   WITH( ISCACHABLE, ISSTRICT );
CREATE
movies=# CREATE OR REPLACE FUNCTION fcur_lt( fcur, fcur )
movies-#   RETURNS boolean
movies-#   AS 'fcur.so' LANGUAGE 'C'
movies-#   WITH( ISCACHABLE, ISSTRICT );
CREATE
movies=# CREATE OR REPLACE FUNCTION fcur_le( fcur, fcur )
movies-#   RETURNS boolean
```

```
movies-#   AS 'fcur.so' LANGUAGE 'C'
movies-#   WITH( ISCACHABLE, ISSTRICT );
CREATE
movies=# CREATE OR REPLACE FUNCTION fcur_gt( fcur, fcur )
movies-#   RETURNS boolean
movies-#   AS 'fcur.so' LANGUAGE 'C'
movies-#   WITH( ISCACHABLE, ISSTRICT );
CREATE
movies=# CREATE OR REPLACE FUNCTION fcur_ge( fcur, fcur )
movies-#   RETURNS boolean
movies-#   AS 'fcur.so' LANGUAGE 'C'
movies-#   WITH( ISCACHABLE, ISSTRICT );
CREATE
```

And you can turn each of these functions into an operator:

```
movies=# CREATE OPERATOR <>
movies-# (
movies-#   leftarg    = fcur,
movies-#   rightarg   = fcur,
movies-#   procedure  = fcur_ne,
movies-#   commutator = <>
movies-# );
CREATE

movies=# CREATE OPERATOR <
movies-# (
movies-#   leftarg    = fcur,
movies-#   rightarg   = fcur,
movies-#   procedure  = fcur_lt,
movies-#   commutator = >
movies-#);
CREATE

movies=# CREATE OPERATOR <=
movies-# (
movies-#   leftarg    = fcur,
movies-#   rightarg   = fcur,
movies-#   procedure  = fcur_le,
movies-#   commutator = >=
movies-# );
CREATE

movies=# CREATE OPERATOR >
movies-# (
movies-#   leftarg    = fcur,
movies-#   rightarg   = fcur,
```

```
movies-#   procedure  = fcur_gt,
movies-#   commutator = <
movies-# );
CREATE

movies=# CREATE OPERATOR >=
movies-# (
movies-#   leftarg    = fcur,
movies-#   rightarg   = fcur,
movies-#   procedure  = fcur_ge,
movies-#   commutator = <=
movies-#);
CREATE
```

Notice that there is a `commutator` for each of these operators. The `commutator` can help PostgreSQL optimize queries that involve the operator.

For example, let's say that you have an index that covers the `balance` column. With a `commutator`, the query

```
SELECT * FROM customers WHERE balance > 10 and new_balance > balance;
```

can be rewritten as

```
SELECT * FROM customers WHERE balance > 10 and balance < new_balance;
```

This allows PostgreSQL to perform a range scan using the `balance` index. The `commutator` for an operator is the operator that PostgreSQL can use to swap the order of the operands. For example, `>` is the commutator for `<` because if `x > y`, `y < x`. Likewise, `<` is the commutator for `>`. Some operators are `commutators` for themselves. For example, the `=` operator is a commutator for itself. If `x = y` is true, then `y = x` is also true.

There are other optimizer hints that you can associate with an operator. See the `CREATE OPERATOR` section of the *PostgreSQL Reference Manual* for more information.

I'll finish up this chapter by defining one more operator (addition) and two functions that extend the usefulness of the `FCUR` data type.

First, let's look at a function that adds two `FCUR` values:

```
259 /*
260 **  Name: fcur_add()
261 **
262 **        Adds two fcur values, returning the result
263 **     If the operands are expressed in the same
264 **     currency (and exchange rate), the result
265 **     will be expressed in that currency,
266 **        otherwise, the result will be in normalized
267 **     form.
268 */
269
270 PG_FUNCTION_INFO_V1(fcur_add);
271
```

```
272 Datum fcur_add(PG_FUNCTION_ARGS)
273 {
274     fcur * left   = (fcur *)PG_GETARG_POINTER(0);
275     fcur * right  = (fcur *)PG_GETARG_POINTER(1);
276     fcur * result;
277
278     result = (fcur *)palloc( sizeof( fcur ));
279
280     if( left->fcur_xrate == right->fcur_xrate )
281     {
282        if( strcmp( left->fcur_name, right->fcur_name ) == 0 )
283        {
284 /*
285 **   The two operands have a common currency - preserve
286 **   that currency by constructing a new fcur with the
287 **    same currency type.
288 */
289          result->fcur_xrate = left->fcur_xrate;
290          result->fcur_units = left->fcur_units + right->fcur_units;
291          strcpy( result->fcur_name, left->fcur_name );
292
293          PG_RETURN_POINTER( result );
294        }
295     }
296
297     result->fcur_xrate = 1.0;
298     result->fcur_units = normalize( left ) + normalize( right );
299     strcpy( result->fcur_name, baseCurrencyName );
300
301     PG_RETURN_POINTER( result );
302
303 }
```

This function returns a FCUR datum; at line 278, we use `palloc()` to allocate the return value. `fcur_add()` has a nice feature: If the two operands have a common currency and a common exchange rate, the result is expressed in that currency. If the operands are not expressed in a common currency, the result will be a value in local currency.

Lines 289 through 291 construct the result in a case where the operand currencies are compatible. If the currencies are not compatible, construct the result at lines 297 through 299.

Let's tell PostgreSQL about this function and make an operator (+) out of it:

```
movies=# CREATE OR REPLACE FUNCTION fcur_add( fcur, fcur )
movies-#   RETURNS fcur
movies-#   AS 'fcur.so' LANGUAGE 'C'
movies-#   WITH( ISCACHABLE, ISSTRICT );
```

```
CREATE
movies-# CREATE OPERATOR +
movies-# (
movies-#   leftarg    = fcur,
movies-#   rightarg   = fcur,
movies-#   procedure  = fcur_add,
movies-#   commutator = +
movies-# );
CREATE
```

Now, try it:

```
movies=# SELECT *, val + '2(1.5702/CA$)' AS result FROM fcur_test;
 pkey |         val          |       result
------+----------------------+--------------------
    1 | 1(1/???)             | 2.27372(1/US$)
    2 | 1(0.5/???)           | 3.27372(1/US$)
    3 | 3(1/US$)             | 4.27372(1/US$)
    4 | 5(0.687853/GBP)      | 8.54272(1/US$)
    5 | 10(7.2566/FRF)       | 2.65178(1/US$)
    6 | 1(1.5702/CA$)        | 3(1.5702/CA$)
    7 | 1.5702(1.5702/CA$)   | 3.5702(1.5702/CA$)
(7 rows)
```

Notice that the `result` values for rows 6 and 7 are expressed in Canadian dollars.

Creating other arithmetic operators for the `FCUR` type is simple. If the operands share a common currency (and exchange rate), the result should be expressed in that currency. I'll let you add the rest of the arithmetic operators.

The last two functions that I wanted to show you will convert `FCUR` values to and from `REAL` values. Internally, the `REAL` data type is known as a `float4`.

```
220 /*
221 **  Name: fcur_to_float4()
222 **
223 **        Converts the given fcur value into a
224 **        normalized float4.
225 */
226
227 PG_FUNCTION_INFO_V1(fcur_to_float4);
228
229 Datum fcur_to_float4(PG_FUNCTION_ARGS)
230 {
231     fcur * src = (fcur *)PG_GETARG_POINTER(0);
232
233     PG_RETURN_FLOAT4( normalize( src ));
234
235 }
```

The `fcur_to_float4()` function converts an `FCUR` value into a normalized `FLOAT4` (that is, `REAL`) value. There isn't anything fancy in this function; let `normalize()` do the heavy lifting.

```
237 /*
238 **  Name: float4_to_fcur()
239 **
240 **        Converts the given float4 value into an
241 **        fcur value
242 */
243
244 PG_FUNCTION_INFO_V1(float4_to_fcur);
245
246 Datum float4_to_fcur(PG_FUNCTION_ARGS)
247 {
248     float4  src    = PG_GETARG_FLOAT4(0);
249     fcur   * result = (fcur *)palloc( sizeof( fcur ));
250
251     result->fcur_units = src;
252     result->fcur_xrate = 1.0;
253
254     strcpy( result->fcur_name, baseCurrencyName );
255
256     PG_RETURN_POINTER( result );
257 }
```

The `float4_to_fcur()` function is a bit longer, but it's not complex. You allocate space for the `result` using `palloc()`; then create the `result` as a value expressed in your local currency.

When you tell PostgreSQL about these functions, you won't follow the same form that you have used in earlier examples:

```
movies=# CREATE OR REPLACE FUNCTION FCUR( FLOAT4 )
movies-#   RETURNS FCUR
movies-#   AS 'fcur.so','float4_to_fcur'
movies-#   LANGUAGE 'C'
movies-#   WITH( ISCACHABLE, ISSTRICT );
CREATE
```

Notice that the internal (C) name for this function is `float4_to_fcur()`, but the external (PostgreSQL) name is `FCUR`. PostgreSQL knows that the `FCUR` function can be used to implicitly convert a `FLOAT4` (or `REAL`) value into a `FCUR` value. PostgreSQL considers a function to be a conversion function if all the following are true:

- The name of the function is the same as the name of a data type.
- The function returns a value whose type is the same as the function's name.
- The function takes a single argument of some other data type.

You can see that the FCUR function meets these criteria. Let's create the FLOAT4 function along the same pattern:

```
movies=# CREATE OR REPLACE FUNCTION FLOAT4( FCUR )
movies-#   RETURNS FLOAT4
movies-#   AS 'fcur.so','fcur_to_float4'
movies-#   LANGUAGE 'C'
movies-#   WITH( ISCACHABLE, ISSTRICT );
CREATE
```

Now PostgreSQL knows how to convert between FLOAT4 values and FCUR values. Why is that so important? You can now use a FCUR value in any context in which a FLOAT4 value is allowed. If you haven't defined a particular function (or operator), PostgreSQL will implicitly convert the FCUR value into a FLOAT4 value and then choose the appropriate function (or operator).

> **CAST Functions**
>
> Starting with PostgreSQL release 7.3, you must explicitly create CAST functions. See the documentation for the CREATE CAST command in the release 7.3 *PostgreSQL Reference Manual* for more information.

For example, you have not defined a multiplication operator for your FCUR data type, but PostgreSQL knows how to multiply FLOAT4 values:

```
movies=# SELECT *, (val * 5) as "Result" FROM fcur_test;
 pkey |          val          |      Result
------+--------------------+------------------
    1 | 1(1/???)           |                5
    2 | 1(0.5/???)         |               10
    3 | 3(1/US$)           |               15
    4 | 5(0.687853/GBP)    | 36.3449764251709
    5 | 10(7.2566/FRF)     | 6.89027905464172
    6 | 1(1.5702/CA$)      | 3.18430781364441
    7 | 1.5702(1.5702/CA$) |                5
```

You can now multiply FCUR values. Notice that the Result column does not contain FCUR values. PostgreSQL converted the FCUR values into FLOAT4 values and then performed the multiplication. Of course, you can cast the result back to FCUR form. Here, we use the @ (absolute value) operator to convert from FCUR to FLOAT4 form and then cast the result back into FCUR form:

```
movies=# SELECT *, CAST( abs(val) AS FCUR ) FROM fcur_test;
 pkey |          val          |      fcur
------+--------------------+-----------------
    1 | 1(1/???)           | 1(1/US$)
    2 | 1(0.5/???)         | 2(1/US$)
    3 | 3(1/US$)           | 3(1/US$)
    4 | 5(0.687853/GBP)    | 7.269(1/US$)
```

```
    5 | 10(7.2566/FRF)       | 1.37806(1/US$)
    6 | 1(1.5702/CA$)        | 0.636862(1/US$)
    7 | 1.5702(1.5702/CA$) | 1(1/US$)
(7 rows)
```

Notice that all the result values have been normalized into your local currency.

Summary

I hope I've convinced you that adding new functions, operators, and data types is not a complex task. If you follow the rules that I've described in this chapter, you should be able to extend PostgreSQL to meet your specific needs. I encourage you to explore Open Source extensions, which you can find on the web. You might also consider contributing your extensions to the PostgreSQL community—if you need it, someone else probably needs it, too.

7

PL/pgSQL

PL/PGSQL (PROCEDURAL LANGUAGE/POSTGRESQL) is a language that combines the expressive power of SQL with the more typical features of a programming language. PL/pgSQL adds control structures such as conditionals, loops, and exception handling to the SQL language. When you write a PL/pgSQL function, you can include any and all SQL commands, as well as the procedural statements added by PL/pgSQL.

Functions written in PL/pgSQL can be called from other functions. You can also define a PL/pgSQL function as a *trigger*. A trigger is a procedure that executes when some event occurs. For example, you might want to execute a PL/pgSQL function that fires when a new row is added to a table—that's what a trigger is for. You can define triggers for the `INSERT`, `UPDATE`, and `DELETE` commands.

Installing PL/pgSQL

PostgreSQL can support a variety of procedural languages. Before you can use a procedural language, you have to install it into the database. Fortunately, this is a simple procedure.

The `createlang` shell script installs PL/pgSQL into a database. If you install PL/pgSQL in the `template1` database, it will automatically be installed in all databases created from that template. The format for `createlang` is

```
createlang plpgsql database-name
```

To install PL/pgSQL in the `movies` database, execute the following command:

```
$ createlang plpgsql movies
```

Notice that this is a command-line utility, not a `psql` command.

Language Structure

PL/pgSQL is termed a block-structured language. A *block* is a sequence of statements between a matched set of DECLARE/BEGIN and END statements. Blocks can be nested—meaning that one block can entirely contain another block, which in turn can contain other blocks, and so on. For example, here is a PL/pgSQL function:

```
 1 --
 2 -- my_factorial1.sql
 3 --
 4
 5 CREATE FUNCTION my_factorial(INTEGER) RETURNS INTEGER AS '
 6   DECLARE
 7     arg INTEGER;
 8   BEGIN
 9
10     arg := $1;
11
12     IF arg IS NULL OR arg < 0 THEN
13       RAISE NOTICE ''Invalid Number'';
14       RETURN NULL;
15     ELSE
16       IF arg = 1 THEN
17         RETURN 1;
18       ELSE
19         DECLARE
20           next_value INTEGER;
21         BEGIN
22
23           next_value := my_factorial(arg - 1) * arg;
24           RETURN next_value;
25         END;
26       END IF;
27     END IF;
28   END;
29 ' LANGUAGE 'plpgsql';
```

The body of my_factorial() is actually the string between the opening single quote (following the word AS) and the closing single quote (just before the word LANGUAGE).

This function contains two blocks of code. The first block starts at line 6 and ends at line 28. The second block, which is nested inside the first, starts at line 19 and ends at line 25. The first block is called an *outer* block because it contains the *inner* block.

I'll talk about variable declarations in more detail in a moment, but I want to point out a few things here. At line 7, you declare a variable named arg. This variable has a well-defined lifetime. arg comes into existence when the function reaches the first DECLARE statement and goes out of existence as soon as the function reaches the END statement at line 27. The lifetime of a variable is also referred to as its *scope*. You can refer to a variable in any statement within the block that defines the scope of the variable. If you try to refer to a variable outside of its scope, you will receive a compilation error. Remember that you have two (nested) blocks in this function: the outer block and the inner block. Variables declared in an outer block can be used in inner blocks, but the reverse is not true. At line 23 (which is in the inner block), you use the `arg` variable, which was declared in the outer block. The variable `next_value` is declared within the inner block: If you try to use `next_value` in the outer block, you'll get an error.

This function (`my_factorial()`) contains two blocks, one nested within the other. You can nest blocks as deeply as you need to. You can also define blocks that are not nested. Here is the `my_factorial()` function again, but this time, I've included a few more blocks:

```
 1 --
 2 -- my_factorial2.sql
 3 --
 4
 5 CREATE FUNCTION my_factorial(INTEGER) RETURNS INTEGER AS '
 6   DECLARE
 7     arg INTEGER;
 8   BEGIN
 9
10     arg := $1;
11
12     IF arg IS NULL OR arg < 0 THEN
13       BEGIN
14         RAISE NOTICE ''Invalid Number'';
15         RETURN NULL;
16       END;
17     ELSE
18       IF arg = 1 THEN
19         BEGIN
20           RETURN 1;
21         END;
22       ELSE
23         DECLARE
24           next_value INTEGER;
25         BEGIN
26           next_value := my_factorial(arg - 1) * arg;
27           RETURN next_value;
28         END;
29       END IF;
30     END IF;
31   END;
32 ' LANGUAGE 'plpgsql';
```

This version still has an outer block (lines 6 through 31), but you have multiple inner blocks: lines 13 through 16, lines 19 through 21, and lines 23 through 28. As I said earlier, variables declared in an outer block can be used in inner blocks but the reverse is not true. If you had declared any variables in the block starting at line 19, you could not use any of those variables past the end of the block (at line 21).

Notice that you can indicate the beginning of a block with a `DECLARE` statement or with a `BEGIN` statement. If you need to declare any variables within a block, you must include a `DECLARE` section. If you don't need any local variables within a block, the `DECLARE` section is optional (an empty `DECLARE` section is perfectly legal).

Quoting Embedded Strings

Take a close look at line 14 in the previous example:

```
RAISE NOTICE ''Invalid Number'';
```

You may have noticed that there are two single quotes at the start of the string `''Invalid Number''` and there are two single quotes at the end. You have to quote strings inside of a function this way because the body of a function is defined as a string. Of course, you can quote embedded strings using any of the three methods described in Chapter 2, "Working with Data in PostgreSQL." You could have written the embedded string in any of the three following forms:

```
RAISE NOTICE ''Invalid Number'';

RAISE NOTICE \'Invalid Number\';

RAISE NOTICE \047Invalid Number\047;
```

CREATE FUNCTION

Now, let's go back and look at the components of a function in more detail.

You define a new PL/pgSQL function using the `CREATE FUNCTION` command. The `CREATE FUNCTION` command comes in two forms. The first form is used for language interpreters that are embedded into the PostgreSQL server—PL/pgSQL functions fall into this category:

```
CREATE [OR REPLACE] FUNCTION name ( [ argtype [, ...] ] )
    RETURNS return_type
    AS 'definition'
    LANGUAGE langname
    [ WITH ( attribute [, ...] ) ]
```

The second form is used to define functions that are defined in an external language and compiled into a dynamically loaded object module:

```
CREATE [OR REPLACE] FUNCTION name ( [ argtype [, ...] ] )
    RETURNS return_type
```

```
AS 'obj_file', 'link_symbol'
LANGUAGE langname
[ WITH ( attribute [, ...] ) ]
```

I covered compiled functions in more detail in Chapter 6, "Extending PostgreSQL." For this chapter, I'll focus on the first form.

Each function has a name. However, the name alone is not enough to uniquely identify a PostgreSQL function. Instead, the function name and the data types of each argument (if any) are combined into a *signature*. A function's signature uniquely identifies the function within a database. This means that you can define many `my_factorial()` functions:

```
CREATE FUNCTION my_factorial( INTEGER )...
CREATE FUNCTION my_factorial( REAL )...
CREATE FUNCTION my_factorial( NUMERIC )...
```

Each of these functions is uniquely identified by its signature. When you call one of these functions, you provide the function name and an argument; PostgreSQL determines which function to use by comparing the data type of the arguments that you provide with the function signatures. If an exact match is found, PostgreSQL uses that function. If PostgreSQL can't find an exact match, it tries to find the closest match.

When you create a new function, you specify a list of arguments required by that function. In most programming languages, you would declare a name and a type for each function argument. In PL/pgSQL, you declare only the data type. The first argument is automatically named "`$1`", the second argument is named "`$2`", and so forth, up to a maximum of 16 arguments (I'll show you how to provide more meaningful names in a moment). You can use predefined data types and user-defined data types in a PL/pgSQL function.

It is important to remember that PL/pgSQL does *not* support default parameters. If you define a function that requires three parameters, you cannot call that function with fewer (or more) parameters. If you find that you need a function with a variable argument list, you can usually *overload* your function to obtain the same effect. When you overload a function, you define two (or more) functions with the same name but different argument lists. For example, let's define a function to compute the due date for a tape rental:

```
 1 --
 2 -- compute_due_date.sql
 3 --
 4
 5 CREATE FUNCTION compute_due_date(DATE) RETURNS DATE AS '
 6   DECLARE
 7
 8     due_date        DATE;
 9     rental_period   INTERVAL := ''7 days'';
10
11   BEGIN
```

```
12
13      due_date := $1 + rental_period;
14
15      RETURN due_date;
16
17    END;
18 ' LANGUAGE 'plpgsql';
```

This function takes a single parameter, a DATE value, and returns the date one week later. You might want a second version of this function that expects the rental date and a rental period:

```
20 -- compute_due_date.sql
21 --
22 CREATE FUNCTION compute_due_date(DATE, INTERVAL) RETURNS DATE AS '
23    BEGIN
24
25      RETURN( $1 + $2 );
26
27    END;
28 ' LANGUAGE 'plpgsql';
```

Now you have two functions named `compute_due_date()`. One function expects a `DATE` value, and the other expects a `DATE` value and an `INTERVAL` value. The first function `compute_due_date(DATE)`, provides the equivalent of a default parameter. If you call `compute_due_date()` with a single argument, the `rental_period` defaults to seven days.

I'd like to point out two things about the `compute_due_date(DATE, INTERVAL)` function.

First, a stylistic issue—the `RETURN` statement takes a single argument, the value to be returned to the caller. You can `RETURN` any expression that evaluates to the *return_type* of the function (we'll talk more about a function's *return_type* in a moment). I find it easier to read a `RETURN` statement if the expression is enclosed in parentheses (see line 25).

Second, you'll notice that I did not `DECLARE` any local variables. You can treat parameter variables just like any other variable—I used them in an expression in line 25. It's a rare occasion when you should settle for the automatic variable names supplied for function parameters. The name "`$1`" doesn't convey much meaning beyond telling you that this variable happens to be the first parameter. You should really provide a meaningful name for each parameter; this gives the reader some idea of what you intended to do with each parameter. Using the `ALIAS` statement, you can give a second, more meaningful, name to a parameter. Here is the `compute_due_date(DATE, INTERVAL)` function again, but this time I have given alternate names to the parameters:

```
20 -- compute_due_date.sql
21 --
22 CREATE FUNCTION compute_due_date(DATE, INTERVAL) RETURNS DATE AS '
23    DECLARE
```

```
24      rental_date     ALIAS FOR $1;
25      rental_period  ALIAS FOR $2;
26    BEGIN
27
28      RETURN( rental_date + rental_period );
29
30    END;
31 ' LANGUAGE 'plpgsql';
```

`ALIAS` gives you an alternate name for a parameter: you can still refer to an aliased parameter using the `$n` form, but I don't recommend it. Why bother to give a meaningful name to a parameter and then ignore it?

Every PL/pgSQL function must return a value, even if it only returns `NULL`. When you create a function, you must declare the data type of the return value. Our `compute_due_date()` functions return a value of type `DATE`. A value is returned from a function using the `RETURN` *`expression`* statement. Keep in mind that PL/pgSQL will try to convert the returned *`expression`* into the type that you specified when you created the function. If you tried to `RETURN( ''Bad Value'' )` from the `compute_due_date()` function, you would get an error (`Bad Date External Representation`). We'll see a special data type a little later (`OPAQUE`) that can be used only for trigger functions.

I'll skip over the function body[3] for the moment and look at the final component[4] required to define a new function. PostgreSQL functions can be written in a variety of languages. When you create a new function, the last component that you specify is the name of the language in which the body of the function is written. All the functions that you will see in this chapter are written in PL/pgSQL, which PostgreSQL knows as `LANGUAGE 'plpgsql'`.

DROP FUNCTION

Before you experiment much more with PL/pgSQL functions, it might be useful for you to know how to replace the definition of a function.

If you are using PostgreSQL 7.2 or later, you can use the `CREATE OR REPLACE FUNCTION ...` syntax. If a function with the same signature already exists, PostgreSQL will silently replace the old version of the function, otherwise, a new function is created.

3. The function body is everything between the `AS` keyword and the `LANGUAGE keyword`. The function body is specified in the form of a string.

4. When you create a function, you can also specify a set of optional *attributes* that apply to that function. These attributes tell PostgreSQL about the behavior of the function so that the query optimizer can know whether it can take certain shortcuts when evaluating the function. See the `CREATE FUNCTION` section in the *PostgreSQL Programmer's Guide* for more information.

If you are using a version of PostgreSQL older than 7.2, you will have to `DROP` the old function before you can create a new one. The syntax for the `DROP FUNCTION` command is

```
DROP FUNCTION name( [ argtype [, ...] ] );
```

Notice that you have to provide the complete signature when you drop a function; otherwise, PostgreSQL would not know which version of the function to remove.

Of course, you can use the `DROP FUNCTION` command to simply remove a function—you don't have to replace it with a new version.

Function Body

Now that you have an overview of the components of a PL/pgSQL function, let's look at the function body in greater detail. I'll start by showing you how to include documentation (that is, comments) in your PL/pgSQL functions. Next, I'll look at variable declarations. Finally, I'll finish up this section by describing the different kinds of statements that you can use inside of a PL/pgSQL function.

Comments

There are two comment styles in PL/pgSQL. The most frequently seen comment indicator is the double dash: `--`. A double dash introduces a comment that extends to the end of the current line. For example:

```
-- This line contains a comment and nothing else
DECLARE
    customer_id  INTEGER;      -- This is also a comment

--  due_date     DATE;         -- This entire line is a comment
                               -- because it begins with a '--'
```

PL/pgSQL understands C-style comments as well. A C-style comment begins with the characters `/*` and ends with the characters `*/`. A C-style comment can span multiple lines:

```
/*
    NAME: compute_due_date()

    DESCRIPTION:  This function will compute the due date for a tape
                  rental.

    INPUT:
                  $1 -- Date of original rental

    RETURNS:      A date indicating when the rental is due.
*/

CREATE FUNCTION compute_due_date( DATE ) RETURNS DATE
...
```

Choosing a comment style is purely a matter of personal preference. Of course, the person choosing the style may not be y ou—you may have to conform to coding standards imposed by your customer (and/or employer). I tend to use only the double-dash comment style in PL/pgSQL code. If I want to include a multiline comment, I start each line with a double dash:

```
----------------------------------------------------------------------
--  NAME: compute_due_date()
--
--  DESCRIPTION:  This function will compute the due date for a tape
--                rental.
--
--  INPUT:
--                $1 -- Date of original rental
--
--  RETURNS:      A date indicating when the rental is due.

CREATE FUNCTION compute_due_date( DATE ) RETURNS DATE
...
```

I find that the double-dash style looks a little cleaner.

Variables

The variable declarations that you've seen up to this point have all been pretty simple. There are actually five ways to introduce a new variable (or at least a new variable name) into a PL/pgSQL function.

- Each parameter defines a new variable (the name is automatically assigned, but you declare the data type).
- You can declare new variables in the `DECLARE` section of a block.
- You can create an alternate name for a function parameter using the `ALIAS` statement.
- You can define a new name for a variable (invalidating the old name) using the `RENAME` statement.
- The iterator variable for an integer-based `FOR` loop is automatically declared to be an integer.

Let's look at these variables one at a time.

Function Parameters

I mentioned earlier in this chapter that each parameter in a PL/pgSQL function is automatically assigned a name. The first parameter (in left-to-right order) is named `$1`, the second parameter is named `$2`, and so on. You define the data type for each parameter in the function definition—for example:

```
CREATE FUNCTION write_history( DATE, rentals )...
```

This function expects two parameters. The first parameter is named `$1` and is of type `DATE`. The second parameter is named `$2` and is of type `rentals`.

Notice that the `write_history()` function (in the preceding code line) expects an argument of type `rentals`. In the sample database, '`rentals`' is actually the name of a table. Inside of the `write_history()` function, you can use the `rentals` parameter (`$2`) as if it were a row in the `rentals` table. That means that you can work with `$2.tape_id`, `$2.customer_id`, and `$2.rental_date`.

When you call this function, you need to pass a row from the `rentals` table as the second argument—for example:

```
SELECT write_history( NOW(), rentals ) FROM rentals;
```

If you define a function that expects a row as a parameter, I would recommend ALIASing that parameter for the sake of readability. It's less confusing to see "`rentals.tape_id`" than "`$2.tape_id`".

DECLARE

The second way to introduce a new variable into a PL/pgSQL function is to list the variable in the `DECLARE` section of a block. The name of a nonparameter variable can include alphabetic characters (A–Z), underscores, and digits. Variable names must begin with a letter (A–Z or a–z) or an underscore. Names are case-insensitive: `my_variable` can also be written as `My_Variable`, and both still refer to the same variable.

The PL/pgSQL documentation mentions that you can force a variable name to be case-sensitive by enclosing it in double quotes—for example, `"pi"`. As of PostgreSQL 7.1.3, this does not seem to work. You *can* enclose a variable name within double quotes if you need to start the name with a digit.

Oddly enough, you can actually `DECLARE` a variable whose name starts with a '`$`', `$3` for example, but I wouldn't recommend it; I would expect that this feature (bug?) may be removed (fixed?) at some point in the future.

The complete syntax for a variable declaration is

```
var-name [CONSTANT] var-type [NOT NULL] [{ DEFAULT | := } expression];
```

Some of the examples in this chapter have declared variables using the most basic form:

```
due_date        DATE;
rental_period   INTERVAL := ''7 days'';
```

The first line creates a new variable named `due_date`. The data type of `due_date` is `DATE`. Because I haven't explicitly provided an initial value for `due_date`, it will be initialized to `NULL`.

The second line defines a new `INTERVAL` variable named `rental_period`. In this case, I *have* provided an initial value, so `rental_period` will be initialized to the `INTERVAL` value `'7 days'`. I could have written this declaration as

```
rental_period   INTERVAL DEFAULT ''7 days'';
```

In the `DECLARE` section of a block, `DEFAULT` is synonymous with '`:=`'.

The initializer expression must evaluate to a value of the correct type. If you are creating an INTEGER variable, the initializer expression must evaluate to an INTEGER value or to a type that can be coerced into an INTEGER value.

There are two things about the DECLARE section that you may find a bit surprising. First, you cannot use any of the function parameters in the initializer expression, even if you ALIAS them. The following is illegal:

```
CREATE FUNCTION compute_due_date(DATE) RETURNS DATE AS '
  DECLARE
    due_date  DATE := $1 + ''7 days''::INTERVAL;
     ...

ERROR: Parameter $1 is out of range
```

The second issue is that once you create a variable in a DECLARE section, you cannot use that variable later within the same DECLARE section. This means that you can't do something like

```
CREATE FUNCTION do_some_geometry(REAL) RETURNS REAL AS '
  DECLARE
    pi      CONSTANT REAL := 3.1415926535;
    radius           REAL := 3.0;
    diameter         REAL := pi * ( radius * radius );
     ...

ERROR: Attribute 'pi' not found
```

Notice in the previous example that I declared pi to be a 'CONSTANT REAL'. When you define a variable as CONSTANT, you prevent assignment to that variable. You must provide an initializer for a CONSTANT.

The final modifier for a variable declaration is NOT NULL. Defining a variable to be NOT NULL means that you will receive an error if you try to set that variable to NULL. You must provide an initializer when you create a NOT NULL variable[5].

Now you can put all these pieces together. The following declarations are identical in function:

```
pi CONSTANT REAL NOT NULL DEFAULT 3.1415926535;
pi CONSTANT REAL NOT NULL := 3.1415926535;
pi CONSTANT REAL := 3.1415926535;
```

Each declares a REAL variable named pi, with an initial value of 3.14159265. The NOT NULL clause is superfluous here because we have declared pi to be a constant and we have given it a non-null initial value; it's not a bad idea to include NOT NULL for documentation purposes.

5. This makes perfect sense if you think about it. If you don't provide an initializer, PL/pgSQL will initialize each variable to NULL—you can't do that if you have declared the variable to be NOT NULL.

Pseudo Data Types—%TYPE, %ROWTYPE, OPAQUE, and RECORD

When you create a PL/pgSQL variable, you must declare its data type. Before moving on to the ALIAS command, there are four *pseudo* data types that you should know about.

%TYPE lets you define one variable to be of the same type as another. Quite often, you will find that you need to temporarily store a value that you have retrieved from a table, or you might need to make a copy of a function parameter. Let's say that you are writing a function to process a rentals record in some way:

```
CREATE FUNCTION process_rental( rentals ) RETURNS BOOLEAN AS '
  DECLARE
   original_tape_id        CHAR(8);
   original_customer_id    INTEGER;
   original_rental_row     ALIAS FOR $1;

  BEGIN

   original_tape_id     := original_rental_row.tape_id;
   original_customer_id := original_rental_row.customer_id;
   ...
```

In this snippet, you are making a local copy of the rentals.tape_id and rentals.customer_id columns. Without %TYPE, you have to ensure that you use the correct data types when you declare the original_tape_id and original_customer_id variables. That might not sound like such a big deal now, but what about six months later when you decide that eight characters isn't enough to hold a tape ID?

Instead of doing all that maintenance work yourself, you can let PL/pgSQL do the work for you. Here is a much better version of the process_rental() function:

```
CREATE FUNCTION process_rental( rentals ) RETURNS BOOLEAN AS '
  DECLARE
   original_tape_id        rentals.tape_id%TYPE;
   original_customer_id    rentals.customer_id%TYPE;
   original_rental_row     ALIAS FOR $1;

  BEGIN

   original_tape_id     := original_rental_row.tape_id;
   original_customer_id := original_rental_row.customer_id;
   ...
```

By using %TYPE, I've told PL/pgSQL to create the original_tape_id variable using whatever type rentals.tape_id is defined to be. I've also created original_customer_id with the same data type as the rentals.customer_id column.

This is an extremely powerful feature. At first blush, it may appear to be just a simple timesaving trick that you can use when you first create a function. The real power behind %TYPE is that your functions become self-maintaining. If you change the data type of the rentals.tape_id column, the process_rentals() function will automatically inherit the change. You won't have to track down all the places where you have made a temporary copy of a tape_id and change the data types.

You can use the %TYPE feature to obtain the type of a column or type of another variable (as shown in the code that follows). You cannot use %TYPE to obtain the type of a parameter. Starting with PostgreSQL version 7.2, you can use %TYPE in the argument list for a function—for example:

```
CREATE FUNCTION process_rental( rentals, rentals.customer_id%TYPE )
 RETURNS BOOLEAN AS '
  DECLARE
   original_tape_id      rentals.tape_id%TYPE;
   original_customer_id  rentals.customer_id%TYPE;
   original_rental_row   ALIAS FOR $1;
   ...
```

%TYPE lets you access the data type of a column (or variable). %ROWTYPE provides similar functionality. You can use %ROWTYPE to declare a variable that has the same structure as a row in the given table. For example:

```
CREATE FUNCTION process_rental( rentals ) RETURNS BOOLEAN AS '
  DECLARE
   original_tape_id      rentals.tape_id%TYPE;
   original_customer_id  rentals.customer_id%TYPE;
   original_rental_row   rentals%ROWTYPE;
   ...
```

The original_rental_row variable is defined to have the same structure as a row in the rentals table. You can access columns in original_rental_row using the normal dot syntax: original_rental_row.tape_id, original_rental_row.rental_date, and so on.

Using %ROWTYPE, you can define a variable that has the same structure as a row in a specific table. A bit later in this chapter, I'll show you how to process dynamic queries (see the section "EXECUTE"); that is, a query whose text is not known at the time you are writing your function. When you are processing dynamic queries, you won't know which table to use with %ROWTYPE. The RECORD data type is used to declare a composite variable whose structure will be determined at execution time. I'll describe the RECORD type in more detail a bit later (see the section "Loop Constructs").

The final pseudo data type is OPAQUE. The OPAQUE type can be used only to define the return type of a function[6]. You cannot declare a variable (or parameter) to be of type OPAQUE. In fact, you can use OPAQUE only to define the return type of a trigger function (and a trigger function can return *only* an OPAQUE value). OPAQUE is a little strange. When you return an OPAQUE value, you return a row in the trigger's table. I'll talk about trigger functions later in this chapter (see the section "Triggers").

6. You *can* use OPAQUE to define the data type of a function argument, but not when you are creating a PL/pgSQL function. Remember, functions can be defined in a number of different languages.

ALIAS and RENAME

Now, let's move on to the next method that you can use to define a new variable, or a least a new name for an existing variable. You've already seen the `ALIAS` statement earlier in this chapter. The `ALIAS` statement creates an alternative name for a function parameter. You cannot `ALIAS` a variable that is not a function parameter. Using `ALIAS`, you can define any number of names that equate to a parameter:

```
CREATE FUNCTION foo( INTEGER ) RETURNS INTEGER AS '
  DECLARE
    param_1  ALIAS FOR $1;
    my_param ALIAS FOR $1;
    arg_1    ALIAS FOR $1;
  BEGIN
    $1 := 42;
    -- At this point, $1, param_1, my_param and arg_1
    -- are all set to 42.
   ...
```

The `RENAME` statement is similar to `ALIAS`; it provides a new name for an existing variable. Unlike `ALIAS`, `RENAME` invalidates the old variable name. You can `RENAME` any variable, not just function parameters. The syntax for the `RENAME` statement is

```
RENAME old-name TO new-name
```

Here is an example of the `RENAME` statement:

```
CREATE FUNCTION foo( INTEGER ) RETURNS INTEGER AS '
  DECLARE
    RENAME $1 TO param1;
  BEGIN
    ...
```

Important Note

The `RENAME` statement does not work in PostgreSQL versions 7.1.2 through at least 7.2.

`RENAME` and `ALIAS` can be used only within the `DECLARE` section of a block.

FOR Loop Iterator

So far, you have seen four methods for introducing a new variable or a new variable name. In each of the preceding methods, you explicitly declare a new variable (or name) in the `DECLARE` section of a block and the scope of the variable is the block in which it is defined. The final method is different.

One of the control structures that you will be looking at soon is the `FOR` loop. The `FOR` loop comes in two flavors—the first flavor is used to execute a block of statements some fixed number of times; the second flavor executes a statement block for each row returned by a query. In this section, I will talk only about the first flavor.

Here is an example of a `FOR` loop:

```
FOR i IN 1 .. 12 LOOP
  balance := balance + customers.monthly_balances[i];
END LOOP;
```

In this example, you have defined a loop that will execute 12 times. Each statement within the loop (you have only a single statement) will be executed 12 times. The variable `i` is called the *iterator* for the loop (you may also see the term *loop index* to describe the iterator). Each time you go through this loop, the iterator (`i`) is incremented by 1.

The iterator for an integer `FOR` loop is automatically declared for you. The type of the iterator is `INTEGER`. It is important to remember that the iterator for an integer `FOR` loop is a *new* variable. If you have already declared a variable with the same name as the iterator, the original variable will be hidden for the remainder of the loop. For example:

```
...
  DECLARE
    i REAL = 0;
    balance NUMERIC(9,2) = 0;
  BEGIN

    --
    -- At this point, i = 0
    --

    FOR i IN 1 .. 12 LOOP

      --
      -- we now have a new copy of i, it will vary from 1 to 12
      --

      balance := balance + customers.monthly_balances[i];
    END LOOP;

    --
    -- Now, if we access i, we will find that it is
    -- equal to 0 again
    --
```

Notice that while you are inside the loop, there are two variables named `i`—the inner variable is the loop iterator, and the outer variable was declared inside of this block. If you refer to `i` inside the loop, you are referring to the inner variable. If you refer to `i` outside the loop, you are referring to the outer variable. A little later, I'll show you how to access the outer variable from within the loop.

Now that you have seen how to define new variables, it's time to move on. This next section explains each type of statement that you can use in the body of a PL/pgSQL function.

PL/pgSQL Statement Types

At the beginning of this chapter, I said that PL/pgSQL adds a set of procedural constructs to the basic SQL language. In this next section, I'll examine the statement types added by PL/pgSQL. PL/pgSQL includes constructs for looping, exception and error handling, simple assignment, and conditional execution (that is, IF/THEN/ELSE). Although I don't describe them here, it's important to remember that you can also include any SQL command in a PL/pgSQL function.

Assignment

The most commonly seen statement in many programs is the assignment statement. Assignment lets you assign a new value to a variable. The format of an assignment statement should be familiar by now; you've already seen it in most of the examples in this chapter:

```
target := expression;
```

`target` should identify a variable, a function parameter, a column, or in some cases, a row. If `target` is declared as `CONSTANT`, you will receive an error. When PL/pgSQL executes an assignment statement, it starts by evaluating the *expression*. If *expression* evaluates to a value whose data type is not the same as the data type of `target`, PL/pgSQL will convert the value to the `target` type. (In cases where conversion is not possible, PostgreSQL will reward you with an error message.)

The *expression* is actually evaluated by the PostgreSQL server, not by PL/pgSQL. This means that *expression* can be any valid PostgreSQL expression. Chapter 2, "Working with Data in PostgreSQL," describes PostgreSQL expressions in more detail.

SELECT INTO

The assignment statement is one way to put data into a variable; `SELECT INTO` is another. The syntax for a `SELECT INTO` statement is

```
SELECT INTO destination [, ...] select-list FROM ...;
```

A typical `SELECT INTO` statement might look like this:

```
...
DECLARE
  customer    customers%ROWTYPE;
BEGIN
  SELECT INTO customer * FROM customers WHERE customer_id = 10;
...
```

When this statement is executed, PL/pgSQL sends the query "`SELECT * FROM customers WHERE customer_id = 10`" to the server. This query cannot return more than one row (if it *does* return more than one row, an error will occur). The results of the query are placed into the `customer` variable. Because I specified that `customer` is of type `customers%ROWTYPE`, the query must return a row shaped exactly like a `customers` row; otherwise, PL/pgSQL signals an error.

I could also SELECT INTO a list of variables, rather than into a single composite variable:

```
DECLARE
  phone    customers.phone%TYPE;
  name     customers.customer_name%TYPE:
BEGIN
  SELECT INTO name,phone
    customer_name, customers.phone FROM customers
    WHERE customer_id = 10;
...
```

Notice that I had to explicitly request customers.phone in this query. If I had simply requested phone, PL/pgSQL would have assumed that I really wanted to execute the query:

```
SELECT customer_name, NULL FROM customers where customer_id = 10;
```

Why? Because I have declared a local variable named phone in this function, and PL/pgSQL would substitute the current value of phone wherever it occurred in the query. Because phone (the local variable) is initialized to NULL, PL/pgSQL would have stuffed NULL into the query. You should choose variable names that don't conflict with column names, or fully qualify column name references.

Of course, you can also SELECT INTO a RECORD variable and the RECORD will adapt its shape to match the results of the query.

I mentioned earlier that the query specified in a SELECT INTO statement must return no more than one row. What happens if the query returns no data? The variables that you are selecting into are set to NULL. You can also check the value of the predefined variable FOUND (described later in this chapter) to determine whether a row was actually retrieved. A bit later in this chapter, you'll see the FOR-IN-SELECT loop that can handle an arbitrary number of rows (see the section "Loop Constructs").

Conditional Execution

Using the IF statement, you can conditionally execute a section of code. The most basic form of the IF statement is

```
IF expression THEN
  statements
END IF;
```

The *expression* must evaluate to a BOOLEAN value or to a value that can be coerced into a BOOLEAN value. If *expression* evaluates to TRUE, the *statements* between THEN and END IF are executed. If *expression* evaluates to FALSE or NULL, the *statements* are not executed.

Here are some sample IF statements:

```
IF ( now() > rentals.rental_date + rental_period ) THEN
   late_fee := handle_rental_overdue();
END IF;

IF ( customers.balance > maximum_balance ) THEN
    PERFORM customer_over_balance( customers );
    RETURN( FALSE );
END IF;
```

In each of these statements, the condition expression is evaluated by the PostgreSQL server. If the condition evaluates to TRUE, the statements between THEN and END IF are executed; otherwise, they are skipped and execution continues with the statement following the END IF.

You can also define a new block within the IF statement:

```
IF ( tapes.dist_id IS NULL ) THEN
  DECLARE
    default_dist_id CONSTANT integer := 0;
  BEGIN
    ...
  END;
END IF;
```

The obvious advantage to defining a new block within an IF statement is that you can declare new variables. It's usually a good idea to declare variables with the shortest possible scope; you won't pollute the function's namespace with variables that you need in only a few places, and you can assign initial values that may rely on earlier computations.

The next form of the IF statement provides a way to execute one section of code if a condition is TRUE and a different set of code if the condition is not TRUE. The syntax for an IF-THEN-ELSE statement is

```
IF expression THEN
  statements_1
ELSE
  statements_2
END IF;
```

In this form, *statements_1* will execute if *expression* evaluates to TRUE; otherwise, *statements_2* will execute. Note that *statements_2* will not execute if the *expression* is TRUE. Here are some sample IF-THEN-ELSE statements:

```
IF ( now() > rentals.rental_date + rental_period ) THEN
  late_fee := handle_rental_overdue();
ELSE
  late_fee := 0;
END IF;
```

```
IF ( customers.balance > maximum_balance ) THEN
  PERFORM customer_over_balance( customers );
  RETURN( FALSE );
ELSE
  rental_ok = TRUE;
END IF;
```

An IF-THEN-ELSE is *almost* equivalent to two IF statements—for example, the following

```
IF ( now() > rentals.rental_date + rental_period ) THEN
   statements_1
ELSE
   statements_2
END IF;
```

is nearly identical to

```
IF ( now() > rentals.rental_date + rental_period ) THEN
   statements_1
END IF;

IF ( now() <= rentals.rental_date + rental_period ) THEN
   statements_2
END IF;
```

The difference between these two scenarios is that using IF-THEN-ELSE, the condition expression is evaluated once; but using two IF statements, the condition expression is evaluated twice. In many cases, this distinction won't be important; but in some circumstances, the condition expression may have side effects (such as causing a trigger to execute), and evaluating the expression twice will double the side effects.

You can nest IF-THEN-ELSE statements:

```
IF ( today > compute_due_date( rentals )) THEN
  --
  --  This rental is past due
  --
  ...
ELSE
  IF ( today = compute_due_date( rentals )) THEN
    --
    --  This rental is due today
    --
    ...
  ELSE
    --
    -- This rental is not late and it's not due today
    --
    ...
  END IF;
END IF;
```

PostgreSQL version 7.2 supports a more convenient way to nest `IF-THEN-ELSE-IF` statements:

```
IF ( today > compute_due_date( rentals )) THEN
  --
  --  This rental is past due
  --
  ...
ELSIF ( today = compute_due_date( rentals )) THEN
  --
  --  This rental is due today
  --
  ...
ELSE
  --
  -- This rental is not late and it's not due today
  --
  ...
END IF;
```

The `ELSIF` form is functionally equivalent to a nested `IF-THEN-ELSE-IF` but you need only a single `END IF` statement. Notice that the spelling is `ELSIF`, not `ELSE IF`. You can include as many `ELSIF` sections as you like.

Loop Constructs

Next, let's look at the loop constructs offered by PL/pgSQL. Using a loop, you can repeat a sequence of statements until a condition occurs. The most basic loop construct is the `LOOP` statement:

```
[<<label>>]
LOOP
  statements
END LOOP;
```

In this form, the *`statements`* between `LOOP` and `END LOOP` are repeated until an `EXIT` or `RETURN` statement exits the loop. If you don't include an `EXIT` or `RETURN` statement, your function will loop forever. I'll explain the optional `<<`*`label`*`>>` in the section that covers the `EXIT` statement.

You can nest loops as deeply as you need:

```
1 row := 0;
2
3 LOOP
4   IF( row = 100 ) THEN
5     EXIT;
6   END IF;
7
```

```
 8    col := 0;
 9
10    LOOP
11      IF( col = 100 ) THEN
12        EXIT;
13      END IF;
14
15      PERFORM process( row, col );
16
17      col := col + 1;
18
19    END LOOP;
20
21    row := row + 1;
22 END LOOP;
23
24 RETURN( 0 );
```

In the preceding code snippet, there are two loops. Because the inner loop is completely enclosed within the outer loop, the inner loop executes each time the outer loop repeats. The statements in the outer loop execute 100 times. The statements in the inner loop (lines 10 through 19) execute 100 × 100 times.

The `EXIT` statement at line 5 causes the outer `LOOP` to terminate; when you execute that statement, execution continues at the statement following the `END LOOP` for the enclosing loop (at line 24). The `EXIT` statement at line 12 will change the point of execution to the statement following the `END LOOP` for the enclosing loop (at line 21).

I'll cover the `EXIT` statement in more detail in the next section.

The next loop construct is the `WHILE` loop. The syntax for a `WHILE` loop is

```
[<<label>>]
WHILE expression LOOP
  statements
END LOOP;
```

The `WHILE` loop is used more frequently than a plain `LOOP`. A `WHILE` loop is equivalent to

```
[<<label>>]
LOOP

  IF( NOT ( expression )) THEN
    EXIT;
  END IF;

  statements

END LOOP;
```

The condition *expression* must evaluate to a BOOLEAN value or to a value that can be coerced to a BOOLEAN. The *expression* is evaluated each time execution reaches the top of the loop. If *expression* evaluates to TRUE, the statements within the loop are executed. If *expression* evaluates to FALSE or NULL, execution continues with the statement following the END LOOP.

Here is the nested loop example again, but this time, I have replaced the IF tests with a WHILE loop:

```
 1 row := 0;
 2
 3 WHILE ( row < 100 ) LOOP
 4
 5   col := 0;
 6
 7   WHILE ( col < 100 ) LOOP
 8
 9     PERFORM process( row, col );
10
11     col := col + 1;
12
13   END LOOP;
14
15   row := row + 1;
16 END LOOP;
17
18 RETURN( 0 );
```

You can see that the WHILE loop is much neater and easier to understand than the previous form. It's also a lot easier to introduce a bug if you use a plain LOOP and have to write the IF tests yourself.

The third loop construct is the FOR loop. There are two forms of the FOR loop. In the first form, called the *integer-FOR* loop, the loop is controlled by an integer variable:

```
[<<label>>]
FOR iterator IN [ REVERSE ] start-expression .. end-expression LOOP
    statements
END LOOP;
```

In this form, the statements inside the loop are repeated while the *iterator* is less than or equal to *end-expression* (or greater than or equal to if the loop direction is REVERSE). Just before the first iteration of the loop, *iterator* is initialized to *start-expression*. At the bottom of the loop, *iterator* is incremented by 1 (or –1 if the loop direction is REVERSE); and if within the *end-expression*, execution jumps back to the first statement in the loop.

An integer-FOR loop is equivalent to:

```
[<<label>>]
DECLARE
   Iterator  INTEGER;
   increment INTEGER;
   end_value INTEGER;
BEGIN
  IF( loop-direction = REVERSE ) THEN
    increment := -1;
  ELSE
    increment := 1;
  END IF;

  iterator  := start-expression;
  end_value := end-expression;

  LOOP
    IF( iterator >= end_value ) THEN
      EXIT;
    END IF;

    statements

   iterator := iterator + increment;

  END LOOP;
END;
```

The start-expression and end-expression are evaluated once, just before the loop begins. Both expressions must evaluate to an INTEGER value or to a value that can be coerced to an INTEGER.

Here is the example code snippet again, this time written in the form of an integer-FOR loop:

```
 1 FOR row IN 0 .. 99 LOOP
 2
 3   FOR col in 0 .. 99 LOOP
 4
 5     PERFORM process( row, col );
 6
 8   END LOOP;
 9
10 END LOOP;
11
12 RETURN( 0 );
```

This version is more readable than the version that used a `WHILE` loop. All the information that you need in order to understand the loop construct is in the first line of the loop. Looking at line 1, you can see that this loop uses a variable named `row` as the iterator; and unless something unusual happens inside the loop, `row` starts at 0 and increments to 99.

There are a few points to remember about the `integer-FOR` loop. First, the *`iterator`* variable is automatically declared—it is defined to be an `INTEGER` and is local to the loop. Second, you can terminate the loop early using the `EXIT` (or `RETURN`) statement. Third, you can change the value of the *`iterator`* variable inside the loop (but I don't recommend it): Doing so can affect the number of iterations through the loop.

You can use this last point to your advantage. In PL/pgSQL, there is no way to explicitly specify a loop increment other than 1 (or –1 if the loop is `REVERSE`d). But you can change the effective increment by modifying the iterator within the loop. For example, let's say that you want to process only odd numbers inside a loop:

```
1 ...
2 FOR i IN 1 .. 100 LOOP
3   ...
4   i := i + 1;
5   ...
6 END LOOP;
7 ...
```

The first time you go through this loop, `i` will be initialized to 1. At line 4, you increment `i` to 2. When you reach line 6, the `FOR` loop will increment `i` to 3 and then jump back to line 3 (the first line in the loop). You can, of course, increment the loop iterator in whatever form you need. If you fiddle with the loop iterator, be sure to write yourself a comment that explains what you're doing.

The second form of the `FOR` loop is used to process the results of a query. The syntax for this form is

```
[<<label>>]
FOR iterator IN query LOOP
  statements
END LOOP;
```

In this form, which I'll call the `FOR-IN-SELECT` form, the *`statements`* within the loop are executed once for each row returned by the *`query`*. *`query`* must be a SQL `SELECT` command. Each time through the loop, *`iterator`* will contain the next row returned by the *`query`*. If the *`query`* does not return any rows, the `statements` within the loop will not execute.

The *`iterator`* variable must either be of type `RECORD` or of a `%ROWTYPE` that matches the structure of a row returned by the *`query`*. Even if the *`query`* returns a single column, the iterator must be a `RECORD` or a `%ROWTYPE`.

Here is a code snippet that shows the FOR statement:

```
 1 DECLARE
 2   rental   rentals%ROWTYPE;
 3 BEGIN
 4
 5   FOR rental IN SELECT * FROM rentals ORDER BY rental_date LOOP
 6     IF( rental_is_overdue( rental )) THEN
 7        PERFORM process_late_rental( rental );
 8     END IF;
 9   END LOOP;
10
11 END;
```

A %ROWTYPE *iterator* is fine if the *query* returns an entire row. If you need to retrieve a partial row, or you want to retrieve the result of a computation, declare the *iterator* variable as a RECORD. Here is an example:

```
 1 DECLARE
 2   my_record  RECORD;
 3 BEGIN
 4
 5 FOR my_record IN
 6   SELECT tape_id, compute_due_date(rentals) AS due_date FROM rentals
 7 LOOP
 8   PERFORM
 9     check_for_late_rental( my_record.tape_id, my_record.due_date );
10 END LOOP;
11
12 END;
```

A RECORD variable does not have a fixed structure. The fields in a RECORD variable are determined at the time that a row is assigned. In the previous example, you assign a row returned by the SELECT to the my_record RECORD. Because the query returns two columns, my_record will contain two fields: tape_id and due_date. A RECORD variable can change its shape. If you used the my_record variable as the iterator in a second FOR-IN-SELECT loop in this function, the field names within the RECORD would change. For example:

```
1 DECLARE
2   my_record  RECORD;
3 BEGIN
4
5   FOR my_record IN SELECT * FROM rentals LOOP
6     -- my_record now holds a row from the rentals table
7     -- I can access my_record.tape_id, my_record.rental_date, etc.
8   END LOOP;
9
```

```
10   FOR my_record IN SELECT * FROM tapes LOOP
11     -- my_record now holds a row from the tapes table
12     -- I can now access my_record.tape_id, my_record.title, etc.
13   END LOOP;
12 END;
```

You also can process the results of a dynamic query (that is, a query not known at the time you write the function) in a `FOR` loop. To execute a dynamic query in a `FOR` loop, the syntax is a bit different:

```
[<<label>>]
FOR iterator IN EXECUTE query-string LOOP
  statements
END LOOP;
```

Notice that this is nearly identical to a `FOR-IN` loop. The `EXECUTE` keyword tells PL/pgSQL that the following string may change each time the statement is executed. The *query-string* can be an arbitrarily complex expression that evaluates to a string value; of course, it must evaluate to a valid `SELECT` statement. The following function shows the `FOR-IN-EXECUTE` loop:

```
 1 CREATE OR REPLACE FUNCTION my_count( VARCHAR ) RETURNS INTEGER AS '
 2   DECLARE
 3     query            ALIAS FOR $1;
 4     count            INTEGER := 0;
 5     my_record        RECORD;
 6   BEGIN
 7     FOR my_record IN EXECUTE query LOOP
 8       count := count + 1;
 9     END LOOP;
10   RETURN count;
11   END;
12 ' LANGUAGE 'plpgsql';
```

EXIT

An `EXIT` statement (without any operands) terminates the enclosing block, and execution continues at the statement following the end of the block.

The full syntax for the `EXIT` statement is

```
EXIT [label] [WHEN boolean-expression];
```

All the `EXIT` statements that you have seen in this chapter have been simple `EXIT` statements. A simple `EXIT` statement unconditionally terminates the most closely nested block.

If you include `WHEN` *`boolean-expression`* in an `EXIT` statement, the `EXIT` becomes conditional—the `EXIT` occurs only if *`boolean-expression`* evaluates to `TRUE`—for example:

```
1 FOR i IN 1 .. 12 LOOP
2   balance := customer.customer_balances[i];
3   EXIT WHEN ( balance = 0 );
4   PERFORM check_balance( customer, balance );
5 END LOOP;
6
7 RETURN( 0 );
```

When execution reaches line 3, the `WHEN` expression is evaluated. If the expression evaluates to `TRUE`, the loop will be terminated and execution will continue at line 7.

This statement should really be named `EXIT...IF`. The `EXIT...WHEN` expression is not evaluated after each statement, as the name might imply.

Labels—EXIT Targets and Name Qualifiers

Now let's turn our attention to the subject of labels. A label is simply a string of the form

<<*label*>>

You can include a label prior to any of the following:

- A `DECLARE` section
- A `LOOP`
- A `WHILE` loop
- An integer `FOR` loop
- A `FOR...SELECT` loop

A label can perform two distinct functions. First, a label can be referenced in an `EXIT` statement—for example:

```
 1 <<row_loop>>
 2 FOR row IN 0 .. 99 LOOP
 3
 4   <<column_loop>>
 5   FOR col in 0 .. 99 LOOP
 6
 7     IF( process( row, col ) = FALSE ) THEN
 8       EXIT row_loop;
 9     END IF;
10
11   END LOOP;
12
13 END LOOP;
15
15 RETURN( 0 );
```

Normally, an `EXIT` statement terminates the most closely nested block (or loop). When you refer to a label in an `EXIT` statement, you can terminate more than one nested block. When PL/pgSQL executes the `EXIT` statement at line 8, it will terminate the `<<column_loop>>` block *and* the `<<row_loop>>` block. You can't `EXIT` a block unless it is active: In other words, you can't `EXIT` a block that has already ended or that has not yet begun.

The second use for a label has to do with variable scoping. Remember that an `integer-FOR` loop creates a new copy of the iterator variable. If you have already declared the iterator variable outside of the loop, you can't directly access it within the loop. Consider the following example:

```
1 <<func>>
2 DECLARE
3   month_num  INTEGER := 6;
4 BEGIN
5   FOR month_num IN 1 .. 12 LOOP
6     PERFORM compute_monthly_info( month_num );
7   END LOOP;
8 END;
```

Line 2 declares a variable named `month_num`. When execution reaches line 4, PL/pgSQL will create a second variable named `month_num` (and this variable will vary between 1 and 12). Within the scope of the new variable (between lines 4 and 6), any reference to `month_num` will refer to the new variable created at line 4. If you want to refer to the outer variable, you can qualify the name as `func.month_num`. In general terms, you can refer to any variable in a fully qualified form. If you omit the label qualifier, a variable reference refers to the variable with the shortest lifetime (that is, the most recently created variable).

RETURN

Every PL/pgSQL function must terminate with a `RETURN` statement. The syntax for a `RETURN` statement is

```
RETURN expression;
```

When a `RETURN` statement executes, four things happen:

1. The *`expression`* is evaluated and, if necessary, coerced into the appropriate data type. The `RETURN` type of a function is declared when you create the function. In the example "`CREATE FUNCTION func() RETURNS INTEGER ...`", the `RETURN` type is declared to be an `INTEGER`. If the `RETURN` *`expression`* does not evaluate to the declared `RETURN` type, PL/pgSQL will try to convert it to the required type.

2. The current function terminates. When a function terminates, all code blocks within that function terminate, and all variables declared within that function are destroyed.

3. The return value (obtained by evaluating *expression*) is returned to the caller. If the caller assigns the return value to a variable, the assignment completes. If the caller uses the return value in an expression, the caller uses the return value to evaluate the expression. If the function was called by a `PERFORM` statement, the return value is discarded.
4. The point of execution returns to the caller.

If you fail to return a value, you will receive an error (`control reaches end of function without RETURN`). You can include many `RETURN` statements in a function, but only one will execute: whichever `RETURN` statement is reached first.

PERFORM

A function written in PL/pgSQL can contain SQL commands intermingled with PL/pgSQL-specific statements. Remember, a SQL command is something like `CREATE TABLE`, `INSERT`, `UPDATE`, and so on; whereas PL/pgSQL adds procedural statements such as `IF`, `RETURN`, or `WHILE`. If you want to create a new table within a PL/pgSQL function, you can just include a `CREATE TABLE` command in the code:

```
CREATE FUNCTION process_month_end( ) RETURNS BOOLEAN AS '
  BEGIN
    ...
    CREATE TABLE temp_data ( ... );
    ...
    DROP TABLE temp_data;
    ...
  END;
' LANGUAGE 'plpgsql';
```

You can include *almost* any SQL command just by writing the command inline. The exception is the `SELECT` command. A `SELECT` command retrieves data from the server. If you want to execute a `SELECT` command in a PL/pgSQL function, you normally provide variables to hold the results:

```
DECLARE
  Customer    customers%ROWTYPE;
BEGIN
  ...
  SELECT INTO customer * FROM customers WHERE( customer_id = 1 );
  --
  -- The customer variable will now hold the results of the query
  --
  ...
END;
```

On rare occasions, you may need to execute a `SELECT` statement, but you want to ignore the data returned by the query. Most likely, the `SELECT` statement that you want to execute will have some side effect, such as executing a function. You can use the PERFORM statement to execute an arbitrary SELECT command without using the results. For example:

```
...
  PERFORM SELECT my_function( rentals ) FROM rentals;
...
```

You can also use PERFORM to evaluate an arbitrary expression, again discarding the results:

```
...
  PERFORM record_timestamp( timeofday() );
...
```

EXECUTE

The EXECUTE statement is similar to the PERFORM statement. Although the PERFORM statement evaluates a SQL expression and discards the results, the EXECUTE statement executes a *dynamic* SQL command, and then discards the results. The difference is subtle but important. When the PL/pgSQL processor compiles a PERFORM *expression* statement, the query plan required to evaluate the *expression* is generated and stored along with the function. This means that *expression* must be known at the time you write your function. The EXECUTE statement, on the other hand, executes a SQL statement that is *not* known at the time you write your function. You may, for example, construct the text of a SQL statement within your function, or you might accept a string value from the caller and then execute that string.

Here is a function that uses the EXECUTE command to time the execution of a SQL command:

```
 1 CREATE FUNCTION time_command( VARCHAR ) RETURNS INTERVAL AS '
 2  DECLARE
 3    beg_time  TIMESTAMP;
 4    end_time  TIMESTAMP;
 5  BEGIN
 6
 7    beg_time := timeofday( );
 8    EXECUTE $1;
 9    end_time := timeofday( );
10
11    RETURN( end_time - beg_time );
12  END;
13 ' LANGUAGE 'plpgsql';
```

You would call the time_command() function like this:

```
movies=# SELECT time_command( 'SELECT * FROM rentals' );
time_command
--------------
 00:00:00.82
(1 row)
```

With the EXECUTE statement, you can execute any SQL command (including calls to PL/pgSQL functions) and the results will be discarded, except for the side effects.

GET DIAGNOSTICS

PL/pgSQL provides a catch-all statement that gives you access to various pieces of result information: GET DIAGNOSTICS. Using GET DIAGNOSTICS, you can retrieve a count of the rows affected by the most recent UPDATE or DELETE command and the object-ID of the most recently inserted row. The syntax for the GET DIAGNOSTICS statement is

```
GET DIAGNOSTICS variable = [ROW_COUNT|RESULT_OID], ...;
```

ROW_COUNT is meaningless until you have executed an UPDATE or DELETE command. Likewise, RESULT_OID is meaningless until you execute an INSERT command.

Error Handling

Error handling is PL/pgSQL's weak point (actually, the problem is with PostgreSQL, not specifically with PL/pgSQL). Whenever the PostgreSQL server decides that something has "gone wrong," it aborts the current transaction and reports an error. That's it. You can't intercept the error in PL/pgSQL, you can't correct it and try again, and you can't even translate the error message into a more user-friendly format.

It seems likely that the error-handling mechanism in PostgreSQL will be improved in the future. At that point, you can probably expect PL/pgSQL to offer better ways to intercept and handle error conditions.

For now, you should try to write PL/pgSQL functions so that errors are headed off before they occur. For example, if your function needs to INSERT a row into a table with a UNIQUE constraint, you might want to check for a duplicate value before performing the INSERT.

RAISE

Even though PL/pgSQL doesn't offer a way to intercept errors, it does provide a way to generate an error: the RAISE statement. The syntax for a RAISE statement is

```
RAISE severity 'message' [, variable [...]];
```

The *severity* determines how far the error message will go and whether the error should abort the current transaction.

Valid values for *severity* are

- DEBUG—The message is written to the server's log file and otherwise ignored. The function runs to completion, and the current transaction is not affected.

- NOTICE—The message is written to the server's log file and sent to the client application. The function runs to completion, and the current transaction is not affected.
- EXCEPTION—The message is written to the server's log file, the function terminates, and the current transaction is aborted.

The *message* string must be a literal value—you can't use a PL/pgSQL variable in this slot, and you cannot include a more complex expression. If you need to include variable information in the error message, you can sneak it into the message by including a % character wherever you want the variable value to appear—for example:

```
rentals.tape_id := ''AH-54706'';
RAISE DEBUG ''tape_id = %'', rentals.tape_id;
```

When these statements are executed, the message `tape_id = AH-54706` will be written to the server's log file. For each (single) % character in the *message* string, you must include a *variable*. If you want to include a literal percent character in the message, write it as %%—for example:

```
percentage := 20;
RAISE NOTICE ''Top (%)%%'', percentage;
```

translates to `Top (20)%`.

The RAISE statement is useful for debugging your PL/pgSQL code; it's even better for debugging someone else's code. I find that the DEBUG severity is perfect for leaving evidence in the server log. When you ship a PL/pgSQL function to your users, you might want to leave a few RAISE DEBUG statements in your code. This can certainly make it easier to track down an elusive bug (remember, users *never* write down error messages, so you might as well arrange for the messages to appear in a log file). I use the RAISE NOTICE statement for interactive debugging. When I am first building a new PL/pgSQL function, the chances are *very* slim that I'll get it right the first time. (Funny, it doesn't seem to matter how trivial or complex the function is...) I start out by littering my code with RAISE NOTICE statements; I'll usually print the value of each function parameter as well as key information from each record that I SELECT. As it becomes clearer that my code is working, I'll either remove or comment out (using "--") the RAISE NOTICE statements. Before I send out my code to a victim, er, user, I'll find strategic places where I can leave RAISE DEBUG statements. The RAISE DEBUG statement is perfect for reporting things that should never happen. For example, because of the referential integrity that I built into the tapes, customers, and rentals tables, I should never find a rentals record that refers to a nonexistent customer. I'll check for that condition (a missing customer) and report the error with a RAISE DEBUG statement. Of course, in some circumstances, a missing customer should really trigger a RAISE EXCEPTION—if I just happen to notice the problem in passing and really doesn't affect the current function, I'll just note it with a RAISE DEBUG. So, the rule I follow is if the condition prevents further processing, I RAISE an EXCEPTION; if the condition should never happen, I RAISE a DEBUG message; if I am still developing my code, I RAISE a NOTICE.

Cursors

Direct cursor support is new in PL/pgSQL version 7.2. Processing a result set using a cursor is similar to processing a result set using a `FOR` loop, but cursors offer a few distinct advantages that you'll see in a moment.

You can think of a cursor as a name for a result set. You must declare a cursor variable just as you declare any other variable. The following code snippet shows how you might declare a cursor variable:

```
...
DECLARE
  rental_cursor       CURSOR FOR SELECT * FROM rentals;
...
```

`rental_cursor` is declared to be a cursor for the result set of the query `SELECT * FROM rentals`. When you declare a variable of type `CURSOR`, you must include a query. The cursor variable is said to be *bound* to this query, and the variable is a *bound* cursor variable.

Before you can use a bound cursor, you must open the cursor using the `OPEN` statement:

```
...
DECLARE
  rental_cursor       CURSOR FOR SELECT * FROM rentals;
BEGIN

   OPEN rental_cursor;

...
```

If you try to `OPEN` a cursor that is already open, you will receive an error message (`cursor "name" already in use`). If you try to `FETCH` (see the section that follows) from a cursor that has not been opened, you'll receive an error message (`cursor "name" is invalid`). When you use a cursor, you first `DECLARE` it, then `OPEN` it, `FETCH` from it, and finally `CLOSE` it, in that order. You can repeat the `OPEN`, `FETCH`, `CLOSE` cycle if you want to process the cursor results again.

FETCH

After a bound cursor has been opened, you can retrieve the result set (one row at a time) using the `FETCH` statement. When you fetch a row from a cursor, you have to provide one or more destination variables that PL/pgSQL can stuff the results into. The syntax for the `FETCH` statement is

```
FETCH cursor-name INTO destination [ , destination [...]];
```

The *destination* (or *destinations*) must match the shape of a row returned by the cursor. For example, if the cursor SELECTs a row from the rentals table, there are three possible destinations:

- A variable of type rentals%ROWTYPE
- Three variables: one of type rentals.tape_id%TYPE, one of type rentals.customer_id%TYPE, and the last of type rentals.rental_date%TYPE
- A variable of type RECORD

Let's look at each of these destination types in more detail.

When you FETCH into a variable of some %ROWTYPE, you can refer to the individual columns using the usual *variable.column* notation. For example:

```
...
DECLARE
  rental_cursor       CURSOR FOR SELECT * FROM rentals;
  rental              rentals%ROWTYPE;
BEGIN

   OPEN rental_cursor;

   FETCH rental_cursor INTO rental;
   --
   -- I can now access rental.tape_id,
   -- rental.customer_id, and rental.rental_date
   --
   IF ( overdue( rental.rental_date )) THEN
      ...
```

Next, I can FETCH into a comma-separated list of variables. In the previous example, the rental_cursor cursor will return rows that each contain three columns. Rather than fetching into a %ROWTYPE variable, I can declare three separate variables (of the appropriate types) and FETCH into those instead:

```
...
DECLARE
  rental_cursor       CURSOR FOR SELECT * FROM rentals;
  tape_id             rentals.tape_id%TYPE;
  customer_id         rentals.customer_id%TYPE;
  rental_date         rentals.rental_date%TYPE;
BEGIN

   OPEN rental_cursor;

   FETCH rental_cursor INTO tape_id, customer_id, rental_date;

   IF ( overdue( rental_date )) THEN
      ...
```

You are not required to use variables declared with %TYPE, but this is the perfect place to do so. At the time you create a function, you usually know which columns you will be interested in, and declaring variables with %TYPE will make your functions much less fragile in cases where the referenced column types might change.

You *cannot* combine composite variables and scalar variables in the same FETCH statement[7]:

```
...
DECLARE
  rental_cursor   CURSOR FOR SELECT *, now() - rental_date FROM rentals;
  rental          rentals%ROWTYPE;
  elapsed         INTERVAL;
  BEGIN

   OPEN rental_cursor;

   FETCH rental_cursor INTO rental, elapsed; -- WRONG! Can't combine
                                             -- composite and scalar
                                             -- variables in the same
                                             -- FETCH

   IF ( overdue( rental.rental_date )) THEN
      ...
```

The third type of destination that you can use with a FETCH statement is a variable of type RECORD. You may recall from earlier in this chapter that a RECORD variable is something of a chameleon—it adjusts to whatever kind of data that you put into it. For example, the following snippet uses the same RECORD variable to hold two differently shaped rows:

```
...
DECLARE
  rental_cursor   CURSOR FOR SELECT * FROM rentals;
  customer_cursor CURSOR FOR SELECT * FROM customers;
  my_data         RECORD;
BEGIN
   OPEN rental_cursor;
   OPEN customer_cursor;

    FETCH rental_cursor INTO my_data;
    --  I can now refer to:
    --      my_data.tape_id
    --      my_data.customer_id
    --      my_data.rental_date
```

7. This seems like a bug to me. You may be able to combine composite and scalar variables in a future release.

```
    FETCH customer_cursor INTO my_data;
    --  Now I can refer to:
    --      my_data.customer_id
    --      my_data.customer_name
    --      my_data.phone
    --      my_data.birth_date
    --      my_data.balance
  ...
```

After you have executed a FETCH statement, how do you know whether a row was actually retrieved? If you FETCH after retrieving the entire result, no error occurs. Instead, each PL/pgSQL function has an automatically declared variable named FOUND. FOUND is a BOOLEAN variable that is set by the PL/pgSQL interpreter to indicate various kinds of state information. Table 7.1 lists the points in time where PL/pgSQL sets the FOUND variable and the corresponding values.

Table 7.1 **FOUND Events and Values**

Event	Value
Start of each function	FALSE
Start of an integer-FOR loop	FALSE
Within an integer-FOR loop	TRUE
Start of a FOR...SELECT loop	FALSE
Within a FOR...SELECT loop	TRUE
Before SELECT INTO statement	FALSE
After SELECT INTO statement	TRUE (if rows are returned)
Before FETCH statement	FALSE
After FETCH statement	TRUE (if a row is returned)

So, you can see that FOUND is set to TRUE if a FETCH statement returns a row. Let's see how to put all the cursor related statements together into a single PL/pgSQL function:

```
...
DECLARE
  next_rental  CURSOR FOR SELECT * FROM rentals;
  rental       rentals%ROWTYPE;
BEGIN
  OPEN next_rental;

  LOOP
    FETCH next_rental INTO rental;
    EXIT WHEN NOT FOUND;
    PERFORM process_rental( rental );
  END LOOP;
```

```
  CLOSE next_rental;
END;
...
```

The first thing you do in this code snippet is OPEN the cursor. Next, you enter a LOOP that will process every row returned from the cursor. Inside of the LOOP, you FETCH a single record, EXIT the loop if the cursor is exhausted, and call another function (process_rental())if not. After the loop terminates, close the cursor using the CLOSE statement.

So far, it looks like a cursor loop is pretty much the same as a FOR-IN-SELECT loop. What else can you do with a cursor?

Parameterized Cursors

You've seen that you must provide a SELECT statement when you declare a CURSOR. Quite often, you'll find that you don't know the exact values involved in the query at the time you're writing a function. You can declare a *parameterized* cursor to solve this problem.

A parameterized cursor is similar in concept to a parameterized function. When you define a function, you can declare a set of parameters (these are called the *formal* parameters, or *formal arguments*); those parameters can be used within the function to change the results of the function. If you define a function without parameters, the function will always return the same results (unless influenced by global, external data). Each language imposes restrictions on where you can use a parameter within a function. In general, function parameters can be used anywhere that a value-yielding expression can be used. When you make a call to a parameterized function, you provide a value for each parameter: The values that you provide (these are called the *actual* parameters, or *actual arguments*) are substituted inside of the function wherever the formal parameters appear.

When you define a cursor, you can declare a set of formal parameters; those parameters can be used with the cursor to change the result set of the query. If you define a cursor without parameters, the query will always return the same result set, unless influenced by external data. PL/pgSQL restricts the places that you can use a parameter within a cursor definition. A cursor parameter can be used anywhere that a value-yielding expression can be used. When you open a cursor, you must specify values for each formal parameter. The actual parameters are substituted inside of the cursor wherever the formal parameters appear.

Let's look at an example:

```
1 ...
2 DECLARE
3   next_customer    CURSOR (ID INTEGER) FOR
4                       SELECT * FROM customers WHERE
5                       customer_id = ID;
6   customer         customers%ROWTYPE;
7   target_customer ALIAS FOR $1;
```

```
 8 BEGIN
 9
10   OPEN next_customer( target_customer );
11 ...
```

Lines 3, 4, and 5 declare a parameterized cursor. This cursor has a single formal parameter; an `INTEGER` named `ID`. Notice (at the end of line 5), that I have used the formal parameter within the cursor definition. When I open this cursor, I'll provide an INTEGER value for the `ID` parameter. The actual parameter that I provide will be substituted into the query wherever the formal parameter is used. So, if `target_customer` is equal to, say, 42, the cursor opened at line 10 will read:

```
SELECT * FROM customers WHERE customer_id = 42;
```

The full syntax for a cursor declaration is

```
variable-name CURSOR
    [ (param-name param-type [, param-name param-type ...] ) ]
  FOR select-query;
```

The full syntax for an `OPEN` statement is

```
OPEN cursor-name [ ( actual-param-value [, actual-param-value...] ) ];
```

You would parameterize a cursor for the same reasons that you would parameterize a function: you want the results to depend on the actual arguments. When you parameterize a cursor, you are also making the cursor more reusable. For example, I might want to process all the tapes in my inventory, but I want to process the tapes one distributor at a time. If I don't use a parameterized cursor, I have to declare one cursor for each of my distributors (and I have to know the set of distributors at the time I write the function). Using a parameterized cursor, I can declare the cursor once and provide different actual arguments each time I open the cursor:

```
 1 CREATE FUNCTION process_tapes_by_distributors( ) RETURNS INTEGER AS '
 2 DECLARE
 3 next_distributor  CURSOR FOR SELECT * FROM distributors;
 4 next_tape         CURSOR( ID ) CURSOR FOR
 5                       SELECT * FROM tapes WHERE dist_id = ID;
 6 dist              distributors%ROWTYPE;
 7 tape              tapes%ROWTYPE;
 8 count             INTEGER := 0;
 9 BEGIN
10   OPEN next_distributor;
11   LOOP
12     FETCH next_distributor INTO dist;
13     EXIT WHEN NOT FOUND;
14     OPEN next_tape( dist.distributor_id );
15     LOOP
16       FETCH next_tape INTO tape;
```

```
17       EXIT WHEN NOT FOUND;
18       PERFORM process_tape( dist, tape );
19       count := count + 1;
20     END LOOP;
21     CLOSE next_tape;
22   END LOOP;
23   CLOSE next_distributor;
24   RETURN( count );
25 END;
26 ' LANGUAGE 'plpgsql';
```

Notice that you can OPEN and CLOSE a cursor as often as you like. A cursor must be closed before it can be opened. Each time you open a parameterized cursor, you can provide new actual parameters.

Cursor References

Now, let's turn our attention to another aspect of cursor support in PL/pgSQL—cursor references.

When you declare a CURSOR variable, you provide a SELECT statement that is bound to the cursor. You can't change the text of the query after the cursor has been declared. Of course, you can parameterize the query to change the results, but the shape of the query remains the same: If the query returns rows from the tapes table, it will always return rows from the tapes table.

Instead of declaring a CURSOR, you can declare a variable to be of type REFCURSOR. A REFCURSOR is not actually a cursor, but a *reference* to a cursor. The syntax for declaring a REFCURSOR is

```
DECLARE
  ref-name REFCURSOR;
  ...
```

Notice that you do *not* specify a query when creating a REFCURSOR. Instead, a cursor is bound to a REFCURSOR at runtime. Here is a simple example:

```
 1 ...
 2 DECLARE
 3   next_rental CURSOR FOR SELECT * FROM rentals;
 4   next_tape   CURSOR FOR SELECT * FROM tapes;
 5   rental      rentals%ROWTYPE;
 6   tape        tape%ROWTYPE;
 7   next_row    REFCURSOR;
 8 BEGIN
 9   OPEN next_rental;
10   next_row := next_rental;
11   FETCH next_rental INTO rental;
12   FETCH next_row INTO rental;
13   CLOSE next_rental;
```

```
14
15   next_row := next_tape;
16   OPEN next_tape;
17   FETCH next_row  INTO tape;
18   CLOSE next_row;
19 ...
```

In this block, I've declared two cursors and one cursor reference. One of the cursors returns rows from the `rentals` table, and the other returns rows from the `tapes` table.

At line 9, the `next_rental` cursor opens. At line 10, I give a value to the `next_row` cursor reference. We now have two ways to access the `next_rental` cursor: through the `next_rental` cursor variable and through the `next_row` cursor reference. At this point, `next_row` *refers to* the `next_rental` cursor. You can see (at lines 11 and 12) that you can `FETCH` a row using either variable. Both `FETCH` statements return a row from the `rentals` table.

At line 14, the `next_row` cursor reference points to a different cursor. Now, when you `FETCH` from `next_row`, you'll get a row from the `tapes` table. Notice that you can point `next_row` to a cursor that has not yet been opened. You can `CLOSE` a cursor using a cursor reference, but you can't `OPEN` a cursor using a cursor reference.

Actually, you *can* open a cursor using a `REFCURSOR`; you just can't open a *named* cursor. When you declare a `CURSOR` variable, you are really creating a PostgreSQL cursor whose name is the same as the name of the variable. In the previous example, you created one cursor (not just a cursor variable) named `next_rental` and a cursor named `next_tape`. PL/pgSQL allows you to create anonymous cursors using `REFCURSOR` variables. An anonymous cursor is a cursor that doesn't have a name[8]. You create an anonymous cursor using the `OPEN` statement, a `REFCURSOR`, and a `SELECT` statement:

```
1 ...
2 DECLARE
3   next_row REFCURSOR;
4 BEGIN
5   OPEN next_row FOR SELECT * FROM customers;
6 ...
```

At line 5, you are creating an anonymous cursor and binding it to the `next_row` cursor reference. After an anonymous cursor has been opened, you can treat it like any other cursor. You can `FETCH` from it, `CLOSE` it, and lose it. That last part might sound a little fishy, so let me explain further. Take a close look at the following code fragment:

```
1 CREATE FUNCTION leak_cursors( INTEGER ) RETURNS INTEGER AS '
2   DECLARE
3    next_customer CURSOR FOR SELECT * FROM customers;
4      next_rental  REFCURSOR;
5     customer      customers%ROWTYPE;
```

8. An anonymous cursor does in fact have a name, but PostgreSQL constructs the name, and it isn't very reader-friendly. An anonymous cursor has a name such as `<unnamed cursor 42>`.

```
 6      rental          rentals%ROWTYPE;
 7      count           INTEGER := 0;
 8    BEGIN
 9
10     OPEN next_customer;
11
12     LOOP
13     FETCH next_customer INTO customer;
14     EXIT WHEN NOT FOUND;
15     OPEN next_rental FOR
16        SELECT * FROM rentals
17          WHERE rentals.customer_id = customer.customer_id;
18
19      LOOP
20      FETCH next_rental INTO rental;
21      EXIT WHEN NOT FOUND;
22
23      RAISE NOTICE ''customer_id = %, rental_date = %'',
24            customer.customer_id, rental.rental_date;
25
26       count := count + 1;
27      END LOOP;
28
29      next_rental := NULL;
30
31    END LOOP;
32     CLOSE next_customer;
33    RETURN( count );
34  END;
35 ' LANGUAGE 'plpgsql';
```

This function contains two loops: an outer loop that reads through the `customers` table and an inner loop that reads each rental for a given customer. The `next_customer` cursor is opened (at line 10) before the outer loop begins. The `next_rental` cursor is bound and opened (at lines 15, 16, and 17) just before the inner loop begins. After the inner loop completes, I set the `next_rental` cursor reference to `NULL` and continue with the outer loop. What happens to the cursor that was bound to `next_rental`? I didn't explicitly close the cursor, so it must remain open. After executing the assignment statement at line 29, I have no way to access the cursor again—remember, it's an anonymous cursor, so I can't refer to it by name. This situation is called a *resource leak*. A resource leak occurs when you create an object (in this case, a cursor) and then you lose all references to that object. If you can't find the object again, you can't free the resource. Avoid resource leaks; they're nasty and can cause performance problems. Resource leaks will also cause your code to fail if you run out of a resource (such as memory space). We can avoid the resource leak shown in this example by closing the `next_rental` before setting it to `NULL`.

You've seen what *not* to do with a cursor reference, but let's see what cursor references are really good for. The nice thing about a cursor reference is that you can pass the reference to another function, or you can return a reference to the caller. These are powerful features. By sharing cursor references between functions, you can factor your PL/pgSQL code into reusable pieces.

One of the more effective ways to use cursor references is to separate the code that processes a cursor from the code that creates the cursor. For example, you may find that we need a function to compute the total amount of money that we have received from a given customer over a given period of time. I might start by creating a single function that constructs a cursor and processes each row in that cursor:

```
...
  OPEN next_rental FOR
    SELECT * FROM rentals WHERE
      customer_id = $1 AND
      rental_date BETWEEN $2 AND $3;

  LOOP
    FETCH next_rental INTO rental
    -- accumulate rental values here
    ...
```

This is a good start, but it works only for a single set of conditions: a given customer and a given pair of dates. Instead, you can factor this one function into three separate functions.

The first function creates a cursor that, when opened, will return all `rentals` records for a given customer within a given period; the cursor is returned to the caller:

```
CREATE FUNCTION
select_rentals_by_customer_interval( INTEGER, DATE, DATE )
 RETURNS REFCURSOR AS '
  DECLARE
    next_rental  REFCURSOR;
  BEGIN
    OPEN next_rental FOR
      SELECT * FROM RENTALS WHERE
        customer_id = $1 AND
        rental_date BETWEEN $2 AND $3;
     RETURN( next_rental );
  END;
' LANGUAGE 'plpgsql';
```

The second function, given a cursor that returns `rentals` records, computes the total value of the `rentals` accessible through that cursor:

```
CREATE FUNCTION
compute_rental_value( REFCURSOR )
 RETURNS NUMERIC AS '
  DECLARE
    total        NUMERIC(7,2) := 0;
```

```
    rental      rentals%ROWTYPE;
    next_rental ALIAS FOR $1;
  BEGIN
    LOOP
      FETCH next_rental INTO rental;
      EXIT WHEN NOT FOUND;
      -- accumulate rental values here
      --
      -- pretend that this is a complex
      -- task which requires loads of amazingly
      -- clever code
      ...
    END LOOP;
    RETURN( total );
  END;
' LANGUAGE 'plpgsql';
```

The last function invokes the first two:

```
CREATE FUNCTION
compute_value_by_customer_interval( INTEGER, DATE, DATE )
 RETURNS NUMERIC AS '
  DECLARE
    curs  REFCURSOR;
    total NUMERIC(7,2);
  BEGIN
    curs  := select_rentals_by_customer_interval( $1, $2, $3 );
    total := compute_rental_value( curs );
    CLOSE curs;
    RETURN( total );
  END;
' LANGUAGE 'plpgsql';
```

The advantage to this approach is that you can construct a cursor using *different* selection criteria and call `compute_total_value()`. For example, you might want to compute the total values of all `rentals` of a given tape:

```
CREATE FUNCTION compute_tape_value( VARCHAR )
 RETURNS NUMERIC AS '
  DECLARE
    curs  REFCURSOR;
    total NUMERIC(7,2);
  BEGIN
    OPEN curs FOR SELECT * FROM rentals WHERE tape_id = $1;
    total := compute_rental_value( curs );
    CLOSE curs;
    RETURN( total );
  END;
' LANGUAGE 'plpgsql';
```

Triggers

So far, all the functions that defined in this chapter have been called explicitly, either by using a `SELECT function()` command or by using the function within an expression. You can also call certain PL/pgSQL functions automatically. A *trigger* is a function that is called whenever a specific event occurs in a given table. An `INSERT` command, `UPDATE` command, or `DELETE` command can cause a trigger to execute.

Let's look at a simple example. You currently have a `customers` table defined like this:

```
CREATE TABLE customers
(
      customer_id    integer primary key,
      customer_name  character varying(50) not null,
      phone          character(8),
      birth_date     date,
      balance        decimal(7,2)
);
```

You want to create a new table that you can use to archive any rows that are deleted from the `customers` table. You also want to archive any updates to the `customers` table. Name this table `customer_archive`:

```
CREATE TABLE customer_archive
(
  customer_id     integer,
  customer_name   character varying(50) not null,
  phone           character(8),
  birth_date      date,
  balance         decimal(7,2),
  user_changed    varchar,
  date_changed    date,
  operation       varchar
);
```

Each row in the `customer_archive` table contains a complete `customers` record plus a few pieces of information about the modification that took place.

Now, let's create a trigger function that executes whenever a change is made to a row in the `customers` table. A trigger function is a function that takes no arguments and returns a special data type—`OPAQUE`. (I'll talk more about the information returned by a trigger in a moment.)

```
CREATE FUNCTION archive_customer() RETURNS OPAQUE AS '
  BEGIN
     INSERT INTO customer_archive
        VALUES
        (
```

```
        OLD.customer_id,
        OLD.customer_name,
        OLD.phone,
        OLD.birth_date,
        OLD.balance,
        CURRENT_USER,
        now(),
              TG_OP
      );
    RETURN NULL;
  END;
' LANGUAGE 'plpgsql';
```

Notice that I am using a variable in this function that I have not declared: `OLD`. Trigger functions have access to several predefined variables that make it easier to find information about the context in which the trigger event occurred. The `OLD` variable contains a copy of the original row when a trigger is executed because of an `UPDATE` or `DELETE` command. The `NEW` variable contains a copy of the new row when a trigger is executed for an `UPDATE` or `INSERT` command.

When this trigger executes, it creates a new row in the `customer_archive()` table. The new row will contain a copy of the original `customers` row, the name of the user making the modification, the date that the modification was made, and the type of operation: `TG_OP` will be set to `'UPDATE'`, `'INSERT'`, or `'DELETE'`.

Table 7.2 contains a complete list of the predefined variables that you can use inside of a trigger function:

Table 7.2 **Predefined Trigger Variables**

Name	Type	Description
NEW	%ROWTYPE	New values (for UPDATE and INSERT)
OLD	%ROWTYPE	Old values (for UPDATE and DELETE)
TG_NAME	name	Name of trigger
TG_WHEN	text	BEFORE or AFTER
TG_LEVEL	text	ROW or STATEMENT[9]
TG_OP	text	INSERT, UPDATE, or DELETE
TG_RELID	oid	Object ID of trigger table
TG_RELNAME	name	Name of trigger table
TG_NARGS	integer	Count of the optional arguments given to the CREATE TRIGGER command
TG_ARGV[]	text[]	Optional arguments given to the CREATE TRIGGER command

[9] Statement triggers are not supported in PostgreSQL, so `TG_LEVEL` will always be set to `ROW`.

Now that you have created a function, you have to define it as a trigger function. The CREATE TRIGGER command associates a function with an event (or events) in a given table. Here is the command that you use for the archive_customer() function:

```
1 CREATE TRIGGER archive_customer
2   AFTER DELETE OR UPDATE
3   ON customers
4   FOR EACH ROW
5     EXECUTE PROCEDURE archive_customer();
```

This is a rather unwieldy command, so let's look at it one line at a time.

The first line tells PostgreSQL that you want to create a new trigger—each trigger has a name—in this case, archive_customer. Trigger names must be unique within each table (in other words, I can have two triggers named foo as long as the triggers are defined for two different tables). Inside the trigger function, the TG_NAME variable holds the name of the trigger.

Line 2 specifies the event (or events) that cause this trigger to fire. In this case, I want the trigger to occur AFTER a DELETE command or an UPDATE command. Altogether, PostgreSQL can fire a trigger BEFORE or AFTER an UPDATE command, an INSERT command, or a DELETE command. In the trigger function, TG_WHEN is set to either BEFORE or AFTER, and TG_OP is set to INSERT, UPDATE, or DELETE.

Line 3 associates this trigger with a specific table. This is not an optional clause; each trigger must be associated with a specific table. You can't, for example, define a trigger that will execute on every INSERT statement regardless of the table involved. You can use the TG_RELNAME variable in the trigger function to find the name of the associated table. TG_RELOID holds the object-ID (oid) of the table.

A single DELETE or UPDATE statement can affect multiple rows. The FOR EACH clause determines whether a trigger will execute once for each row or once for the entire statement. PostgreSQL does not support statement-level triggers at the moment, so the only choice is FOR EACH ROW. Inside of the trigger function, TG_LEVEL can contain either ROW or STATEMENT; but the only value currently implemented is ROW.

Line 5 finally gets around to telling PostgreSQL which function you actually want to execute when the specified events occur.

The full syntax for the CREATE TRIGGER command is

```
CREATE TRIGGER trigger-name
 [BEFORE | AFTER] [ INSERT | DELETE | UPDATE [OR ...]]
    ON table-name FOR EACH ROW
    EXECUTE PROCEDURE function-name [(args)];
```

Notice that the CREATE TRIGGER command allows you to specify optional arguments (indicated by *args* in the preceding syntax diagram). You can include a list of string literals when you create a trigger (any arguments that are not of string type are converted into strings). The arguments that you specify are made available to the trigger function through the TG_NARGS and TG_ARGV variables. TG_NARGS contains an integer count of the number of arguments. TG_ARGV contains an array of strings corresponding to the values that you specified when you created the trigger: `TG_ARGV[0]` contains the first argument, `TG_ARGV[1]` contains the second argument, and so on. You can use the optional trigger arguments to pass extra information that might help the trigger function know more about the context in which the trigger has executed. You might find this useful when using the same function as a trigger for multiple tables; although in most situations, the `TG_NAME`, `TG_RELNAME`, and `TG_OP` variables provide enough context information.

Summary

In this chapter, you've seen that PL/pgSQL provides a way for you to execute procedural code on the server. PL/pgSQL is not the only procedural language that you can use for server-side programming. The standard PostgreSQL distribution includes PL/perl, PL/python, and PL/tcl. You can also add functionality to the server using the Server Programming Interface. For more information on these features, refer to the *PostgreSQL Programmer's Guide*.

The next several chapters will describe the client-side programming interfaces included with PostgreSQL.

8

The PostgreSQL C API—libpq

A USER INTERACTS WITH A POSTGRESQL DATABASE by using an application, but how does an application interact with PostgreSQL? PostgreSQL provides a number of *application programming interfaces* (or APIs for short). Three of these APIs are designed to be used by applications written in C—libpq, libpgeasy, and ODBC. Each API has advantages and disadvantages. libpgeasy, for example, is very easy to use, but doesn't offer much flexibility. If your application uses the ODBC API, you gain portability at the cost of complexity.

Table 8.1 compares the three C-language APIs offered by PostgreSQL.

Table 8.1 **Comparison of C Language APIs for PostgreSQL**

API	Complexity	Flexibility	RDBMS Portability
libpq	Medium	Medium to high	PostgreSQL only
libpgeasy	Low	Low	PostgreSQL only
ODBC	Medium to high	High	Multiple database systems

Notice that an application that uses ODBC to connect to PostgreSQL can connect to other database systems as well.

In this chapter, I'll explain the libpq API. libpq is a set of functions that you can call from a C program to interact with a PostgreSQL server. In later chapters, I will cover libpgeasy and ODBC, as well as a few APIs designed for languages other than C.

The libpq API is used to implement most of the other client APIs. After you understand how to interact with a PostgreSQL server using libpq, you will find that most of the other APIs simply wrap up the libpq API in different flavors. For example, the libpgeasy API combines some of the more common libpq operations into a set of higher-level functions. The libpgeasy functions are easier to use, but you don't have quite as much power and flexibility as you would with a libpq application.

Prerequisites

When you write a client application using libpq, you'll need a C compiler. I'll assume that you have the GNU C compiler (gcc) installed and ready to use. I'll also assume that you have GNU make available, and I'll use that tool to actually invoke the compiler (and linker).

APIs that are used within a C application are usually made up of two components: a set of header files and an object code library.

The header files contain data type definitions and function prototypes (in other words, the header files *describe* the API to your C compiler). The object code library contains the actual implementation for each function contained in the API. When you use libpq, you will need to include the libpq-fe.h header file within your C code (using the #include directive). You will also need to link your program against the libpq object library.

Client 1—Connecting to the Server

Our first client is very simple—it connects to a server, disconnects, and then exits.

There are two sets of functions that you can use to connect to a PostgreSQL server: the simple form uses the PQconnectdb() function, whereas the more complex form uses PQconnectStart() and PQconnectPoll(). PQconnectdb() is easier to use because it is a *synchronous* function; when you call PQconnectdb(), your program will not continue until the connection attempt succeeds or fails. The PQconnectStart() and PQconnectPoll() functions give your application a way to connect to a server *asynchronously*. A call to PQconnectStart() returns immediately—it won't wait for the connection attempt to complete. The PQconnectPoll() function can be used to monitor the progress of a connection attempt started by PQconnectStart(). I use the synchronous form in this chapter:

```
/*
** File: client1.c
*/

#include "libpq-fe.h"

int main( void )
{
    PGconn * connection;

    connection = PQconnectdb( "" );

    PQfinish( connection);

    return( 0 );
}
```

client1.c starts by including a single header file: libpq-fe.h. The libpq-fe.h file defines the data types that we need to communicate with libpq. libpq-fe.h also contains function prototypes for the libpq API functions.

Connecting to a PostgreSQL database from libpq can be very simple. The PQconnectdb() function returns a handle to a connection object. PQconnectdb() is synchronous—it will not return to the caller until the connection attempt succeeds or fails. Here is the prototype for PQconnectdb():

```
extern PGconn *PQconnectdb(const char *conninfo);
```

PQconnectdb() takes a single argument—a pointer to a null-terminated connection string. A *connection string* is a list of zero or more connection attributes. For example, the connection string "dbname=accounting user=korry" specifies that we want to connect to a database named "accounting" as user "korry". Each option is of the form *keyword=value*. Multiple attributes are separated by whitespace.

Notice that I specified an empty connection string in this example. When PQconnectdb() finds an empty connection string, it connects to the default database using a default set of attributes. An empty string is not the same as a NULL pointer. Don't pass a NULL pointer to PQconnectdb() unless you want to see libpq (and your application) die a fiery death.

I'll describe connection attributes and their default values in more detail a bit later. When you call PQconnectdb(), you get back a pointer to a PGconn. PGconn is considered a handle. A *handle* is an opaque data type, meaning that there is something behind a PGconn pointer, but you can't see it. The information behind a handle is for "internal use only". The libpq library has access to the implementation details, but API users do not. A PGconn object represents a database connection within your application. You will use this object when you call other libpq functions.

Compiling the Client

Now let's compile client1.c and try to run it. You will use a simple makefile to drive the C compiler and linker. Here is the makefile you will use throughout this chapter—as you add new clients, you will just add new targets to the makefile:

```
## File: Makefile
##
##       Rules to create libpq sample applications

CPPFLAGS += -I/usr/local/pgsql/include
CFLAGS   += -g
LDFLAGS  += -g
LDLIBS   += -L/usr/local/pgsql/lib -lpq

client1:  client1.o
```

If you have installed PostgreSQL into a directory other than `/usr/local/pgsql`, you should substitute your directory names in the `makefile`.

To build `client1` with this `makefile`, you can use the following command:

```
$ make client1
cc -g -I/usr/local/pg721/include  -c -o client1.o client1.c
cc -g  client1.o -L/usr/local/pgsql/lib -lpq -o client1
$
```

The `client1` application doesn't expect any command-line parameters so you can run it like this:

```
$ ./client1
```

Using GNU `make` to Build libpq Applications

The `make` utility is used to perform the operations required to turn a source file (such as `client1.c`) into an application. `make` does two (extremely useful) things for you. First, `make` determines the minimum set of operations required to build an application. Second, `make` invokes the various preprocessors, compilers, and linkers to actually carry out minimum required operations.

The `make` utility learns how to build an application by consulting two sources of information. `make` has a huge collection of built-in rules that describe how to convert one type of file into another type of file. For example, `make` knows how convert a "`.c`" file into an executable. First, `make` converts a source file into a "`.o`" (object) module by asking the C compiler to compile the source file. Then, `make` converts the "`.o`" into an executable by invoking the linker.

The second information source that `make` uses is known as a `makefile` (probably because the file is usually named "`makefile`"—clever huh?). A `makefile` is a set of rules that define how to build your specific application (or applications). `makefiles` are usually written in terms of targets and prerequisites. A *target* is something that you want to build. A *prerequisite* is a file that the target depends on. In this case, you want to build an application named `client1`—that's your target. The prerequisite for your target is `client1.c`. The `makefile` rule that describes this relationship is "`client1:    client1.c`". This line is read as "`client1` depends on `client1.c`". When `make` sees this rule, it looks through its database of built-in rules to find a way to convert `client1.c` into `client1`. It finds the rule (or actually, rules) to perform this conversion, invokes the C compiler to produce `client1.o` from `client1.c`, and then invokes the linker to convert `client1.o` into the `client` executable.

The `makefile` that you will use for the examples in this chapter is a little more complex than the single rule that I just described.

The built-in rule that produces an object module (`.o`) from a C source file (`.c`) looks like this:

```
$(CC) -c $(CPPFLAGS) $(CFLAGS)
```

This command invokes the C compiler, passing it the command-line flags `-c`, `$(CPPFLAGS)`, and `$(CFLAGS)`. `$(CPPFLAGS)` and `$(CFLAGS)` are variables that you can modify within the `makefile`. To build a libpq application, you have to tell the C compiler how to find the PostgreSQL header files. You can do that by modifying the `$(CPPFLAGS)` variable:

```
CPPFLAGS += -I/usr/local/pgsql/include
```

If you want the C compiler to produce debuggable code, you can modify the `$(CFLAGS)` variable to include the `-g` flag:

```
CFLAGS += -g
```

Now when `make` invokes the C compiler to compile `client1.c`, the command will look like this:

```
cc -c -I/usr/local/pgsql/include -g -o client1.o client1.c
```

If the compiler does not find any serious errors in `client1.c`, you will end up with an object module named `client1.o`. Your target is not `client1.o`, but `client1`: client1.o is just an intermediate target. To build `client1` from `client1.o`, `make` will invoke the linker using the following built-in rule:

```
$(CC) $(LDFLAGS) prerequisite.o $(LOADLIBES) $(LDLIBS)
```

You want to link `client1.o` with the libpq library to produce `client1`. The libpq library is found in `/usr/local/pgsql/lib` on my system, so I'll tell `make` to include libpq by modifying `$(LDLIBS)`. I want debugging symbols in my executable, so I also will add the `-g` flag to `$(LDFLAGS)`:

```
LDLIBS += -L/usr/local/pgsql/lib -lpq
LDFLAGS += -g
```

The final command produced by `make` is

```
cc -g client1.o -L/usr/local/pgsql/lib -lpq -o client1
```

The complete `makefile` looks like this:

```
CPPFLAGS += -I/usr/local/pgsql/include
CFLAGS   += -g
LDFLAGS  += -g
LDLIBS   += -L/usr/local/pgsql/lib -lpq

client1:  client1.o
```

Identifying the Server

If you provide an empty connection string to `PQconnectdb()`, how does it find a database server? libpq uses a hierarchy of default values to decide which server to try to connect to.

The libpq library uses three different sources when trying to find each connection attribute.

First, the connection string (given to `PQconnectedb()`) can contain a set of `keyword=value` pairs.

Next, libpq looks for a set of specifically named environment variables. Each environment variable corresponds to one of the `keyword=value` pairs that you can use in the connection string.

Finally, libpq uses a set of values that are hard-wired into the library at build-time.

Table 8.2 shows how the keywords and environment variables correspond to each other.

Table 8.2 **Connection Attributes**

Connect-String Keyword	Environment Variable	Example
user	PGUSER	user=korry
password	PGPASSWORD	password=cows
dbname	PGDATABASE	dbname=accounting
host	PGHOST	host=jersey
hostaddr	PGHOSTADDR	hostaddr=127.0.0.1
port	PGPORT	port=5432

You can use the PQconndefaults() function to find the default value for each connection attribute.

```
 1 /*
 2 ** File: get_dflts.c
 3 */
 4
 5 #include <stdio.h>
 6 #include <libpq-fe.h>
 7
 8 int main( void )
 9 {
10   PQconninfoOption * d;
11   PQconninfoOption * start;
12 /*
13 **  Get the default connection attributes
14 */
15   start = d = PQconndefaults( );
16
17   while( d->keyword != NULL )
18   {
19     printf( "keyword  = %s\n", d->keyword  ? d->keyword  : "null" );
20     printf( "envvar   = %s\n", d->envvar   ? d->envvar   : "null" );
21     printf( "label    = %s\n", d->label    ? d->label    : "null" );
22     printf( "compiled = %s\n", d->compiled ? d->compiled : "null" );
23     printf( "val      = %s\n", d->val      ? d->val      : "null" );
24     printf( "\n" );
25
26     d++;
27   }
28
29 /*
30 **  Free up the memory that lipq allocated on our behalf
31 */
32
33   PQconninfoFree( start );
34
35   return( 0 );
```

When you call the `PQconndefaults()` function, you get back a pointer to the first member of an array of `PQconninfoOption` structures. Each structure contains (among other things) a keyword, the name of an environment variable, a hard-wired (or compiled-in) value, and a current value. If you iterate through the members of this array, you can recognize the end of the list by looking for a member where the `keyword` pointer is `NULL`.

You can compile this program by adding another entry to the `makefile` and then typing `make get_dflts`:

```
$ cat makefile
##
##  File:  Makefile
##
##         Rules for building libpq sample applications
##

CPPFLAGS += -I/usr/local/pgsql/include
CFLAGS   += -g
LDFLAGS  += -g
LDLIBS   += -L/usr/local/pgsql/lib -lpq

client1:    client1.o
get_dflts:  get_dflts.o


$ make get_dflts
cc -g -I/usr/local/pg721/include -c -o get_dflts.o get_dflts.c
cc -g  get_dflts.o -L/usr/local/pgsql/lib -lpq -o get_dflts
```

Running the `get_dflts` program on my system results in the following:

```
$ ./get_dflts
keyword  = authtype
envvar   = PGAUTHTYPE
label    = Database-Authtype
compiled =
val      =

keyword  = service
envvar   = PGSERVICE
label    = Database-Service
compiled = (null)
val      = (null)

keyword  = user
envvar   = PGUSER
label    = Database-User
```

```
compiled = (null)
val      = Administrator

keyword  = password
envvar   = PGPASSWORD
label    = Database-Password
compiled =
val      =

keyword  = dbname
envvar   = PGDATABASE
label    = Database-Name
compiled = (null)
val      = Administrator

keyword  = host
envvar   = PGHOST
label    = Database-Host
compiled = (null)
val      = (null)

keyword  = hostaddr
envvar   = PGHOSTADDR
label    = Database-Host-IPv4-Address
compiled = (null)
val      = (null)

keyword  = port
envvar   = PGPORT
label    = Database-Port
compiled = 5432
val      = 5432

keyword  = tty
envvar   = PGTTY
label    = Backend-Debug-TTY
compiled =
val      =

keyword  = options
envvar   = PGOPTIONS
label    = Backend-Debug-Options
compiled =
val      =
```

You can see that each `keyword` member corresponds to a `keyword` accepted by the `PQconnectdb()` function. You may have noticed that `PQconndefaults()` returned more connection attributes than are shown in Table 8.2. Some of the connection attributes are obsolete but still supported for compatibility with older clients. Some attributes are reserved for future use and are not fully supported. Other attributes exist for debugging purposes and are not normally used. If you stick to the connection attributes listed in Table 8.2, you should be safe.

Each connection parameter is computed from a sequence of default values, in the absence of explicitly specified values in the connection string.

For example, if you omit the `port` keyword from your `PQconnectdb()` connection string, libpq will look for an environment variable named `PGPORT`. If you have defined the `PGPORT` environment variable, libpq will use the value of that variable for the port; if not, a hard-wired (or compiled-in) value is used. In this case, the hard-wired port number is `5432`. (Compiled-in values are defined when the libpq object-code library is built from source code.) The default hierarchy works like this:

If the keyword is found in the connection string, the value is taken from the connection string, else

If the associated environment variable is defined, the value is taken from the environment variable, else

The hard-wired value is used.

The `user` and `dbname` parameters are treated a little differently—rather than using hard-wired values, the last default for the `user` parameter is your login name and the `dbname` parameter is copied from the `user` parameter. For example, if I am logged in (to my Linux operating system) as user `korry`, both `user` and `dbname` will default to `korry`. Of course, I can override the default `user` and `dbname` attributes using environment variables or explicit connect-string attributes.

Client 2—Adding Error Checking

The `client1.c` application discussed has a fundamental flaw—there is no way to tell whether the connection attempt was successful. This next program attempts a connection and displays an error message if the attempt fails:

```
1 /*
2 ** File: client2.c
3 */
4
5 #include <stdlib.h>
6 #include <libpq-fe.h>
7
8 int main( int argc, char * argv[] )
9 {
```

```
10   PGconn * connection;
11
12   if( argc != 2 )
13   {
14     printf( "usage  : %s \"connection-string\"\n", argv[0] );
15     printf( "example: %s \"user=myname password=cows\"\n", argv[0]);
16     exit( 1 );
17   }
18
19   if(( connection = PQconnectdb( argv[1] )) == NULL )
20   {
21     printf( "Fatal error - unable to allocate connection\n" );
22     exit( 1 );
23   }
24
25   if( PQstatus( connection ) != CONNECTION_OK )
26     printf( "%s\n", PQerrorMessage( connection ));
27   else
28     printf( "Connection ok, disconnecting\n" );
29
30   PQfinish( connection );
31
32   exit( 0 );
33
34 }
```

You can specify a connection string on the command line when you run this program. If you want to include more than one connection attribute, enclose the entire connection string in double quotes. For example:

```
$ ./client2 user=korry
Connection ok, disconnecting

$ ./client2 "user=korry password=cows"
Connection ok, disconnecting
```

I recommend that you run this program a few times, feeding it a variety of invalid connect strings so you become familiar with the error messages that you might receive when things go wrong. For example:

```
$ ./client2 host=badhost
connectDBStart() --  unknown hostname: badhost

$ ./client2 port=1000
connectDBStart() -- connect() failed: No such file or directory
        Is the postmaster running locally
        and accepting connections on Unix socket '/tmp/.s.PGSQL.1000'?
```

```
$ ./client2 badparameter
ERROR: Missing '=' after 'badparameter' in conninfo

$ ./client2 badparameter=1000
ERROR: Unknown conninfo option 'badparameter'
```

Viewing Connection Attributes

In the `get_dflts` application I showed you how to use the `PQconndefaults()` function to view the default connection attributes that will be used to establish a connection.

libpq also provides a number of functions that you can use to retrieve the *actual* connection attributes after you have a `PGconn` object. These functions are useful because in most situations, you won't explicitly specify every connection attribute. Instead, many (perhaps all) of the connection attributes will be defaulted for you.

`PQconnectdb()` will return a `PGconn` pointer in almost every case (only if libpq runs out of memory, `PQconnectdb()` will return a `NULL` pointer).

The following program attempts to make a connection and then print the set of connection parameters. I've modified `client2.c` to show the complete set of final connection parameters after a connection attempt. The new application is called `client2b`:

```
 1 /*
 2 ** File: client2b.c
 3 */
 4
 5 #include <stdlib.h>
 6 #include <libpq-fe.h>
 7
 8 static void show_connection_attributes( const PGconn * conn );
 9 static const char * check( const char * value );
10
11 int main( int argc, char * argv[] )
12 {
13   PGconn * connection;
14
15   if( argc != 2 )
16   {
17     printf( "usage  : %s \"connection-string\"\n", argv[0] );
18     printf( "example: %s \"user=myname password=cows\"\n", argv[0]);
19     exit( 1 );
20   }
21
22   if(( connection = PQconnectdb( argv[1] )) == NULL )
23   {
24     printf( "Fatal error - unable to allocate connection\n" );
25     exit( 1 );
26   }
27
```

```
28   if( PQstatus( connection ) != CONNECTION_OK )
29     printf( "%s\n", PQerrorMessage( connection ));
30   else
31     printf( "Connection ok\n" );
32
33   show_connection_attributes( connection );
34
35   PQfinish( connection );
36
37   exit( 0 );
38
39 }
40
41 static const char * check( const char * value )
42 {
43     if( value )
44     return( value );
45     else
46     return( "(null)" );
47 }
48
49 static void show_connection_attributes( const PGconn * c )
50 {
51   printf( "dbname   = %s\n", check( PQdb( c )));
52   printf( "user     = %s\n", check( PQuser( c )));
53   printf( "password = %s\n", check( PQpass( c )));
54   printf( "host     = %s\n", check( PQhost( c )));
55   printf( "port     = %s\n", check( PQport( c )));
56   printf( "tty      = %s\n", check( PQtty( c )));
57   printf( "options  = %s\n", check( PQoptions( c )));
58 }
```

Take a look at the `show_connection_attributes()` function (lines 49–58). Given a `PGconn` pointer, you can find the connection attributes that result after all the defaults are applied by calling `PQdb()`, `PQuser()`, and so on. In some cases, one of these functions returns a `NULL` pointer, so I wrapped each function invocation in a call to `check()` (lines 41–47) so you don't try to give any bad pointers to `printf()`.

Remember that `PQconnectdb()` returns a `PGconn` pointer even when a connection attempt fails; it is often instructive to see the final connection attributes for a failed connection attempt. Here are the results when I try to connect to a nonexistent database on my system:

```
$ ./client2b user=korry
FATAL 1:  Database "korry" does not exist in the system catalog.

dbname   = korry
user     = korry
```

```
password =
host     = (null)
port     = 5432
tty      =
options  =
```

In this case, I can see that libpq chose an invalid database name (defaulted from my username).

Client 3—Simple Processing—PQexec() and PQprint()

Now let's turn our attention to the task of processing a query. I'll start by showing a simple example—you'll connect to a database, execute a hard-wired query, process the results, clean up, and exit.

```
 1 /*
 2 ** File: client3.c
 3 */
 4
 5 #include <stdlib.h>
 6 #include <libpq-fe.h>
 7
 8 void process_query( PGconn * connection, const char * query_text )
 9 {
10   PGresult  *       result;
11   PQprintOpt        options = {0};
12
13   if(( result = PQexec( connection, query_text )) == NULL )
14   {
15     printf( "%s\n", PQerrorMessage( connection ));
16     return;
17   }
18
19   options.header    = 1;    /* Ask for column headers            */
20   options.align     = 1;    /* Pad short columns for alignment   */
21   options.fieldSep  = "|";  /* Use a pipe as the field separator */
22
23   PQprint( stdout, result, &options );
24
25   PQclear( result );
26 }
27
28 int main( int argc, char * argv[] )
29 {
30   PGconn * connection;
31
```

```
32   if( argc != 2 )
33   {
34     printf( "usage  : %s \"connection-string\"\n", argv[0] );
35     printf( "example: %s \"user=myname password=cows\"\n", argv[0]);
36     exit( 1 );
37   }
38
39   if(( connection = PQconnectdb( argv[1] )) == NULL )
40   {
41     printf( "Fatal error - unable to allocate connection\n" );
42     exit( 1 );
43   }
44
45   if( PQstatus( connection ) != CONNECTION_OK )
46     printf( "%s\n", PQerrorMessage( connection ));
47   else
48   {
49     process_query( connection, "SELECT * FROM rentals" );
50   }
51
52   PQfinish( connection );
53
54   exit( 0 );
55 }
```

The interesting part of this program is the `process_query()` function (lines 8–26). You start by calling `PQexec()`. This function is used to synchronously execute a query. (Like the connection API, there are two methods to execute a query: synchronous and asynchronous. I'll show you the asynchronous query functions later.) When you call `PQexec()`, you provide a connection object(a `PGconn` pointer) and a command-string. `PQexec()` returns a pointer to a `PGresult` object. A `PGresult` is similar to a `PGconn`—it is an opaque handle and you can query the object for different pieces of information (such as "Did my query succeed or fail?"). A `PGresult` object represents the results of a command. When you execute a query (as opposed to an `INSERT` command), the entire result set (including meta-data) of the query is accessible through the object. A `PGresult` object also provides access to any error messages that may result from executing a command.

I'm going to cheat here. Older versions of libpq provided a handy function called `PQprint()` that does all the dirty work required to print the results of a query. `PQprint()` is still included in libpq (at least as of version 7.2.1), but the online documentation says that the function is obsolete and is not supported. It's likely that `PQprint()` will not be removed from libpq, but you won't see too many new features added to is as new PostgreSQL releases appear.

I'll use `PQprint()` here because it is such a simple way to print a result set. Later, I'll show you how to produce much of the same functionality yourself.

Before you can call PQprint(), you must construct a PQprintOpt object. At line 11, you initialize the PQprintOpt object and then set the three members that you care about (header, align, and fieldSep) at lines 19–21. PQprint() requires three arguments: a FILE pointer (in this case, specify stdout), a PGresult pointer (returned from PQexec()), and a pointer to a PGprintOpt object. PQprint() formats the results of the query and prints them to the file that you specified. If the query fails, PQprint() will print an appropriate error message.

Remember that PQexec() returned a pointer to a PGresult object—you need to free that object because PQclear() will destroy a PGresult object.

When you are finished processing the result set, free the PGresult resources using PQclear() (see line 25). It's important to PQclear() all PGresult objects when you are done with them. When libpq executes a query on your behalf, the entire result set of the query is accessible through a PGresult object. That means that if you execute a query that returns 100,000 rows, the PGresult object will consume enough memory to hold all 100,000 rows.

Results Returned by PQexec()

Many client applications need to do more than just print column values. After executing a command, you can obtain a lot of information about the results of the command through the PGresult object returned by PQexec().

The most obvious piece of information that you can obtain from a PGresult pointer is whether your command succeeded or failed. If your command succeeded, PQresultStatus() will return either PGRES_COMMAND_OK or PGRES_TUPLES_OK. PGRES_TUPLES_OK means that you successfully executed a query and there are zero or more rows available for processing. PGRES_COMMAND_OK means that you successfully executed some command other than SELECT; an INSERT command for example. If your query causes an error, you will get back a result of PGRES_FATAL_ERROR or PGRES_NONFATAL_ERROR. (There are other values that PQresultStatus() can return; see the *PostgreSQL Programmer's Guide* for more information.) It's possible that PQexec() will return a NULL PGresult pointer if libpq runs out of memory—you should treat that as a PGRES_FATAL_ERROR.

If your command fails, you can use PQresultErrorMessage() to find the reason for failure. To call PQresultErrorMessage(), you pass the PGresult pointer that was returned by PQexec(). PQresultErrorMessage() returns a pointer to the null-terminated string containing the reason for failure (if you call PQresultErrorMessage() for a successful query, you'll get back a pointer to an empty string).

I'll modify the process_query() function from the previous example (client3.c) to show how to use PQresultStatus() and PQresultErrorMessage():

```
1 /*
2 ** File: client3b.c
3 */
```

```
 4
 5 #include <stdlib.h>
 6 #include <libpq-fe.h>
 7
 8 void process_query( PGconn * connection, const char * query_text )
 9 {
10   PGresult  *       result;
11
12   if(( result = PQexec( connection, query_text )) == NULL )
13   {
14     printf( "%s\n", PQerrorMessage( connection ));
15     return;
16   }
17
18   if(( PQresultStatus( result ) == PGRES_COMMAND_OK ) ||
19      ( PQresultStatus( result ) == PGRES_TUPLES_OK ))
20   {
21     PQprintOpt              options = {0};
22
23     options.header    = 1;    /* Ask for column headers            */
24     options.align     = 1;    /* Pad short columns for alignment  */
25     options.fieldSep  = "|";  /* Use a pipe as the field separator*/
26
27     PQprint( stdout, result, &options );
28
29   }
30   else
31   {
32     printf( "%s\n", PQresStatus( PQresultStatus( result )));
33     printf( "%s\n", PQresultErrorMessage( result ));
34
35   }
36
37   PQclear( result );
38 }
39
40 int main( int argc, char * argv[] )
41 {
42   PGconn * connection;
43
44   if( argc != 2 )
45   {
46     printf( "usage  : %s \"connection-string\"\n", argv[0] );
47     printf( "example: %s \"user=myname password=cows\"\n", argv[0]);
48     exit( 1 );
49   }
50
```

```
51   if(( connection = PQconnectdb( argv[1] )) == NULL )
52   {
53     printf( "Fatal error - unable to allocate connection\n" );
54     exit( 1 );
55   }
56
57   if( PQstatus( connection ) != CONNECTION_OK )
58     printf( "%s\n", PQerrorMessage( connection ));
59   else
60   {
61     process_query( connection, "SELECT * FROM rentals" );
62   }
63
64   PQfinish( connection );
65
66   exit( 0 );
67 }
```

At lines 18 and 19, check to see whether the command succeeded. If so, use `PQprint()` to print the result set just like you did in client3.c

If the command failed, tell the user what went wrong. Look closely at line 32. You are calling the `PQresultStatus()` function again, but this time around you call `PQresStatus()` with the return value. `PQresultStatus()` returns the command status in the form of an integer[1]. The `PQresStatus()` function translates a value returned by `PQresultStatus()` into a human-readable string.

At line 33, you call `PQresultErrorMessage()` to retrieve the text of the error message.

After you have successfully executed a query (that is, `PQresultStatus()` has returned either `PGRES_COMMAND_OK` or `PGRES_TUPLES_OK`), you are ready to process the actual results. There are three types of information that you can access through a `PGresult` object. You've already seen the first type of information: success or failure and an error message. The second type of information is metadata, or data about your data. We'll look at meta-data next. Finally, you can access the values returned by the command itself—the rows returned by a query or the `OID` of an affected row in the case of an `INSERT` or `UPDATE`.

First, I'll show you how to find the metadata for your query. libpq provides a number of functions that let you find information about the *kind* of data returned by your query. For example, the `PQntuples()` function tells you how many rows (or tuples) will be returned from your query.

The following function prints (most of) the metadata returned for a command:

```
1 void print_meta_data( PGresult * result )
2 {
3   int   col;
4
```

1. More precisely, `PQresultStatus()` returns a value of type `enum ExecStatusType`.

```
 5   printf( "Status: %s\n", PQresStatus( PQresultStatus( result )));
 6   printf( "Returned %d rows ", PQntuples( result ));
 7   printf( "with %d columns\n\n", PQnfields( result ));
 8
 9   printf( "Column Type TypeMod Size Name        \n" );
10   printf( "------ ---- ------- ---- -----------\n" );
11
12   for( col = 0; col < PQnfields( result ); col++ )
13   {
14     printf( "%3d    %4d %7d %4d %s\n",
15             col,
16             PQftype( result, col ),
17             PQfmod( result, col ),
18             PQfsize( result, col ),
19             PQfname( result, col ));
20   }
21 }
```

If you want to try this function, it is included in `client3c.c` in the sample code for this book. I won't show the complete application here because it is largely the same as `client3b.c`.

At line 5, you print the success/failure status from the given `PQresult` object. It uses the same `PQresStatus()` and `PQresultStatus()` functions described earlier, but I've included them in this example because they really do return metadata information.

At line 6, you use the `PQntuples()` function to retrieve the number of rows returned by the command. `PQntuples()` returns zero if the command was not a query. `PQntuples()` also returns zero if the command *was* a query, but the query happened to return zero rows in the result set. libpq does not consider it an error for a query to return zero rows. In fact, the `PQresult` object contains all the usual metadata even when a query does not return any rows.

The `PQnfields()` function (line 7) returns the number of columns in the result set. Line `PQntuples()`, `PQnfields()` returns zero for commands other than `SELECT`.

The naming convention for the metadata functions is a little confusing at first. `PQntuples()` returns the number of *rows* in the result set. `PQnfields()` returns the number of *columns* in the result set. A tuple is the same thing as a row. A field is the same thing as a column[2].

2. Technically speaking, a tuple is a *version* of a row. PostgreSQL uses a concurrency system known as multiversion concurrency control (MVCC). In MVCC, the database can contain multiple versions of the same row. There is also a slight difference between a field and a column. A column is stored in a table. A field is the result of an expression. A column is a valid expression, so a column can be considered a field, but a field is not necessarily a column.

At line 16, you call `PQftype()` to find the data type for a given column. The `PQftype()`, `PQfmod()`, and `PQfsize()` functions work together to tell you about the format of the data in a given column.

`PQftype()` returns a value of type `OID`. The value returned by `PQftype()` corresponds to the object-id (`OID`) of a row in the `pg_type` system table. (In Chapter 6, "Extending PostgreSQL," you learned that data type descriptions are stored in `pg_type`.) You can find the OIDs for predefined data types in the `catalog/pg_type.h` PostgreSQL header file. `PQfmod()` returns a value that, in theory, gives you more detailed information about a data type. The values returned by `PQfmod()` are type-specific and are not documented. You can use the `format_type()`[3] function to convert values returned by `PQftype()` and `PQfmod()` into a human-readable string. `PQfsize()` returns the number of bytes required to hold a value on the server. For variable-length data types, `PQfsize()` returns –1.

It turns out that the information returned by `PQftype()`, `PQfmod()`, and `PQfsize()` is not all that useful in most applications. In most cases, the field values returned to your application will be null-terminated strings. For example, if you `SELECT` a date column, the date values will be converted into string form before it gets to your application. The same is true for numeric values. It *is* possible to request raw data values (that is, values that have not been converted into string form). I'll show you how to do that a little later.

The last two metadata functions are `PQfname()` and `PQfnumber()`. `PQfname()` returns the name of the given column in the result set. `PQfnumber()` returns the column number of the named column.

Now that you know how to retrieve the metadata for a query, let's see how to actually retrieve the data. In this example, you'll replace the earlier calls to `PQprint()` with your own function.

```
 1 /*
 2 ** File: client3d.c
 3 */
 4
 5 #include <stdlib.h>
 6 #include <string.h>
 7 #include <libpq-fe.h>
 8
 9 #define MAX_PRINT_LEN       40
10
11 static char separator[MAX_PRINT_LEN+1];
12
13 void print_result_set( PGresult * result )
14 {
```

3. `format_type()` is *not* a libpq function. It is a server function that you can call from a `SELECT` command. For example, `SELECT format_type( atttpyid, atttypmod ) FROM pg_attribute`.

```
15   int           col;
16   int           row;
17   int              * sizes;
18
19 /*
20 **  Compute the size for each column
21 */
22   sizes = (int *)calloc( PQnfields( result ), sizeof( int ));
23
24   for( col = 0; col < PQnfields( result ); col++ )
25   {
26     int      len = 0;
27
28     for( row = 0; row < PQntuples( result ); row++ )
29     {
30       if( PQgetisnull( result, row, col ))
31         len = 0;
32       else
33         len = PQgetlength( result, row, col );
34
35       if( len > sizes[col] )
36         sizes[col] = len;
37     }
38
39     if(( len = strlen( PQfname( result, col ))) > sizes[col] )
40       sizes[col] = len;
41
42     if( sizes[col] > MAX_PRINT_LEN )
43       sizes[col] = MAX_PRINT_LEN;
44   }
45
46 /*
47 **  Print the field names.
48 */
49   for( col = 0; col < PQnfields( result ); col++ )
50   {
51     printf( "%-*s ", sizes[col], PQfname( result, col ));
52   }
53
54   printf( "\n" );
55
56 /*
57 **  Print the separator line
58 */
59   memset( separator, '-', MAX_PRINT_LEN );
60
```

```
61   for( col = 0; col < PQnfields( result ); col++ )
62   {
63     printf( "%*.*s ", sizes[col], sizes[col], separator );
64   }
65
66   printf( "\n" );
67
68 /*
69 **  Now loop through each of the tuples returned by
70 **  our query and print the results.
71 */
72   for( row = 0; row < PQntuples( result ); row++ )
73   {
74     for( col = 0; col < PQnfields( result ); col++ )
75     {
76       if( PQgetisnull( result, row, col ))
77         printf( "%*s", sizes[col], "" );
78       else
79         printf( "%*s ", sizes[col], PQgetvalue( result, row, col ));
80     }
81
82     printf( "\n" );
83
84   }
85   printf( "(%d rows)\n\n", PQntuples( result ));
86   free( sizes );
87 }
```

This function (`print_result_set()`) replaces your earlier use of `PQprint()`.

The real work in this function is finding the width of each column. For each column in the result set, you have to search through all rows, finding the widest value. At line 22, you allocate an array (`sizes[]`) of integers to hold the column widths. At lines 24 through 44, you fill in the `sizes[]` array. The `PQgetisnull()` function tells you whether a given column is `NULL` in the current row. If you find a `NULL` field, consider it to have a length of 0. Use the `PQgetlength()` function to find the length of each value.

Notice that we ensure that each column is wide enough to hold the column name. The limit to each column is `MAX_PRINT_LEN` characters. This is a rather arbitrary decision that you can certainly change.

After computing the column widths, you print the name of each column followed by a line of separator characters (lines 46 –66).

At lines 68 through 84, you loop through every row in the result set and print each column value. The `PQgetvalue()` function returns a pointer to the value for a given row and column. Because you have not requested a `BINARY` cursor (I'll talk about those soon), each data value comes to you in the form of a null-terminated string.

Finally, at line 86, you free up the resource that you allocated (`sizes[]`) and return.

```
 89 void process_query( PGconn * connection, const char * query_text )
 90 {
 91   PGresult  *       result;
 92
 93   if(( result = PQexec( connection, query_text )) == NULL )
 94   {
 95     printf( "%s\n", PQerrorMessage( connection ));
 96     return;
 97   }
 98
 99   if( PQresultStatus( result ) == PGRES_TUPLES_OK )
100   {
101     print_result_set( result );
102   }
103   else if( PQresultStatus( result ) == PGRES_COMMAND_OK )
104   {
105     printf( "%s", PQcmdStatus( result ));
106
107     if( strlen( PQcmdTuples( result )))
108       printf( " - %s rows\n\n", PQcmdTuples( result ));
109     else
110       printf( "\n\n" );
111   }
112   else
113   {
114       printf( "%s\n\n", PQresultErrorMessage( result ));
115   }
116
117   PQclear( result );
118 }
```

This function (`process_query()`) is not very complex. You execute the given command and print the results. If an error occurs, you use `PQerrorMessage()` or `PQresultErrorMessage()` to display an error message to the user. You call `PQerrorMessage()` if `PQexec()` fails to return a `PQresult` pointer, otherwise you call `PQresultErrorMessage()`.

If the command is successful, you need to decide whether it was a `SELECT` or some other type of command. If `PQresultStatus()` returns `PGRES_TUPLES_OK`, you know that the command was a query and you call `print_result_set()` to do the grunt work. If `PQresultStatus()` returns `PGRES_COMMAND_OK`, you know that some other command was executed. `PQcmdStatus()` tells you the name of the command that you just executed. You've probably noticed that when you execute a command (other than `SELECT`) in `psql`, the name of the command is echoed if the command succeeded—that's what `PQcmdStatus()` gives us. `PQcmdTuples()` tells us how many rows were affected by the command. `PQcmdTuples()` is meaningful for the `INSERT`, `UPDATE`, or `DELETE` command. For any other command, `PQcmdTuples()` returns a string of zero length.

Finish `process_query()` by freeing up the `PGresult` object and all the resources (that is, memory) managed by that object.

The `main()` function for `client3d.c` is the same as for `client3.c`:

```
117 int main( int argc, char * argv[] )
118 {
119   PGconn * connection;
120
121   if( argc != 2 )
122   {
123     printf( "usage  : %s \"connection-string\"\n", argv[0] );
124     printf( "example: %s \"user=myname password=cows\"\n", argv[0]);
125     exit( 1 );
126   }
127
128   if(( connection = PQconnectdb( argv[1] )) == NULL )
129   {
130     printf( "Fatal error - unable to allocate connection\n" );
131     exit( 1 );
132   }
133
134   if( PQstatus( connection ) != CONNECTION_OK )
135     printf( "%s\n", PQerrorMessage( connection ));
136   else
137     process_query( connection, "SELECT * FROM rentals" );
138
139   PQfinish( connection );
140
141   exit( 0 );
142 }
```

Now let's compile this client and run it:

```
$ make client3d
cc -g -I/usr/local/pg721/include  -c -o client3d.o client3d.c
cc -g  client1.o -L/usr/local/pgsql/lib -lpq -o client3

$ ./client3d "dbname=movies"
tape_id  rental_date customer_id
-------- ----------- -----------
AB-12345  2002-07-01           1
AB-67472  2002-07-01           3
OW-41221  2002-07-01           1
(3 rows)
```

Let's compare that with the output from client3:

```
$ ./client3 "dbname=movies"
tape_id |rental_date|customer_id
--------+-----------+-----------
AB-12345| 2002-07-01|          1
AB-67472| 2002-07-01|          3
OW-41221| 2002-07-01|          1
(3 rows)
```

Pretty similar—the only differences are in the vertical separator characters. Remember, client3 uses the `PQprint()` function (from the libpq library) to format the result set. In `client3d`, you did all of the hard work yourself.

Binary Cursors

Now let's look at another option for processing query results.

So far, every data value that was retrieved from the server has come to you in the form of a null-terminated string. When you store data in a PostgreSQL table, it is rarely, if ever, stored in the form of a null-terminated string. In Chapter 6, "Extending PostgreSQL," you explored the difference between the *external* form of a data value and the *internal* form. In short, the external form is meant to be "human-readable" and the internal form is meant to be "computer-friendly." The external form of an `INTEGER` value, "`521`" for example, is a series of numeric characters expressed in the encoding of the client application (in other words, you see the ASCII characters '`5`', '`2`', and '`1`' if you are using an ASCII client). The internal form of the same numeric value is a four-byte, binary-encoded integer. On an Intel-based system, this value is represented by the bits '`1000001001`' (leading zeroes suppressed). CPUs know how to deal with these binary-encoded values, but most people don't find that form very convenient.

When you retrieve `SELECT` values using libpq, you get the results in external form (and the external form is contained in a null-terminated string). The *disadvantage* to external form is that PostgreSQL must convert every value that it sends to you. That can be an expensive operation, especially if your application converts the external form back into internal form.

Instead of retrieving values from a `SELECT` command, you can utilize a `BINARY CURSOR`. A binary cursor is a cursor that does not convert the raw data to external form. When you call `PQgetvalue()` to retrieve values from a binary cursor, you get back a pointer to the internal form of the data.

A binary cursor is a strange beast. In all the other RDBMS systems that I have used (Oracle, Sybase, SQL Server, and so on), I tell the API which format I want the data to appear in on a column-by-column basis. The SQL commands that I send to the server are the same, regardless of the data format that I choose. Data conversion is an API issue, not a SQL issue. PostgreSQL takes a different approach. If I want raw (unconverted) data in PostgreSQL, I have to send a different set of commands to the server. All columns retrieved from a binary cursor are internal form—I can't pick and choose.

Let's see how you might convert a normal `SELECT` command into a binary cursor. You have been using the following command in most of the examples in this chapter:

```
SELECT * FROM rentals;
```

If you want to retrieve this data in internal form, you must execute the following commands:

```
BEGIN TRANSACTION;
  DECLARE mycursor BINARY CURSOR FOR SELECT * FROM rentals;
  FETCH ALL FROM mycursor;
END TRANSACTION;
```

The only command that returns any data values here is `FETCH ALL FROM mycursor`. When you fetch from `mycursor`, you will get three columns of data and each column will be in internal format.

Now you're probably wondering exactly what the internal form for each column will be. Table 8.3 shows the relationships between SQL data types and corresponding C data types.

Table 8.3 **Equivalent C Types for Built-In PostgreSQL Types**

SQL Type	C Type	Defined In
`abstime`	`AbsoluteTime`	utils/nabstime.h
`boolean`	`bool`	postgres.h (maybe compiler built-in)
`box`	`BOX*`	utils/geo_decls.h
`bytea`	`bytea*`	postgres.h
`"char"`	`char`	(compiler built-in)
`character`	`BpChar*`	postgres.h
`cid`	`CommandId`	postgres.h
`date`	`DateADT`	utils/date.h
`smallint (int2)`	`int2` or `int16`	postgres.h
`int2vector`	`int2vector*`	postgres.h
`integer (int4)`	`int4` or `int32`	postgres.h
`real (float4)`	`float4*`	postgres.h
`double precision (float8)`	`float8*`	postgres.h
`interval`	`Interval*`	utils/timestamp.h
`lseg`	`LSEG*`	utils/geo_decls.h
`name`	`Name`	postgres.h
`oid`	`Oid`	postgres.h
`oidvector`	`oidvector*`	postgres.h
`path`	`PATH*`	utils/geo_decls.h
`point`	`POINT*`	utils/geo_decls.h

Table 8.3 **Continued**

SQL Type	C Type	Defined In
`regproc`	`regproc`	postgres.h
`reltime`	`RelativeTime`	utils/nabstime.h
`text`	`text*`	postgres.h
`tid`	`ItemPointer`	storage/itemptr.h
`time`	`TimeADT`	utils/date.h
`time` with time zone	`TimeTzADT`	utils/date.h
`timestamp`	`Timestamp*`	utils/timestamp.h
`tinterval`	`TimeInterval`	utils/nabstime.h
`varchar`	`VarChar*`	postgres.h
`xid`	`TransactionId`	postgres.h

*(Source: *PostgreSQL Programmer's Guide*, Section 12.5)

Here is the definition of the `rentals` table:

```
movies=# \d rentals
            Table "rentals"
   Column     |      Type      | Modifiers
-------------+--------------+-----------
 tape_id      | character(8) |
 rental_date  | date         |
 customer_id  | integer      |
```

Given the mappings shown in Table 8.2, you would expect to find the `tape_id` column represented as a pointer to a `char[8]` array, the `rental_date` column as a pointer to a `DateADT`, and the `customer_id` column as a pointer to an `int32`; and in fact, that's what you get.

Most of the data type mappings are easy to understand. For example, the internal form for a `POINT` value is `POINT` structure. If you look in the `utils/geo_decls.h` header file, you will see that a `POINT` structure looks like this:

```
typedef struct
{
  double  x;
  double  y;
} Point;
```

That pretty much matches what you would expect. A few of the internal data types, particularly the date/time types, are more complex. A `DATE` value, for example, is represented by the `DateADT` type. The `utils/date.h` header file shows this definition for `DateADT`:

```
typedef int32 DateADT;
```

This tells you that a `DATE` value is stored as a 32-bit integer, but you don't know how to interpret the internal-form values. A bit of sleuthing through the PostgreSQL documentation, combined with some experimentation, shows that a `DateADT` value represents the number of days since 01-JAN-2000.

A good way to deal with internal date/time values is to not deal with internal date/time values. For example, rather than selecting the `rental_date` column from the `rentals` table, you could `SELECT DATE_PART( 'EPOCH', rental_date )`. The `DATE_PART( 'EPOCH', ...)` function returns the number of seconds since the Midnight of 01-JAN-1970. The return value will be of type `DOUBLE PRECISION` (internal form = `float8`). This way, you can avoid the `DateADT` type completely. You also have the added benefit that the value returned by `DATE_PART( 'EPOCH', ...)` just happens to match the standard Unix epoch, so you can use epoch-based date values with Unix library functions.

There is one other *gotcha* to watch out for when using binary cursors. Different CPUs use different byte orderings. For example, on an Intel CPU, the number `0x12345678` would be stored in memory as

```
78 65 43 21
```

whereas on a SPARC CPU, this number would be stored as

```
12 34 56 78
```

(SPARC format is called *big-endian* and Intel format is call *little-endian*.)

libpq will *not* convert between byte-orderings. If your data is hosted on a SPARC-based computer but you are reading internal values from within an Intel-hosted client, you must take care of the byte-ordering conversion yourself.

Client 4—An Interactive Query Processor

At this point, you should have a pretty good understanding of how to use many of the libpq functions. There are two other issues I want to explore in this chapter: processing multiple result sets and asynchronous operations. Before we get to those, let's convert the previous client application (`client3d`) into an interactive query processor. After you've done that, you will have a good example of why you need to consider multiple result sets and asynchronous processing.

The next client that we want to build connects to a database and prompts you for a SQL command. You send the command to the server and display the results. You repeat this cycle (prompt, execute, display) until you enter the command `quit`.

You've already seen most of the code in this application; you are building on the client3d application. The important difference between client3d and client4 is that you use the GNU `readline` library to prompt the user for multiple commands (in `client3d`, the command text was hard-coded).

```
1 /*
2 ** File:  client4.c
3 */
```

```
 4
 5 #include <stdlib.h>
 6 #include <string.h>
 7 #include <libpq-fe.h>
 8 #include <readline/readline.h>
 9 #include <readline/history.h>
10
11 typedef enum { FALSE, TRUE } bool;
```

Notice the two extra header files in this application. The `readline/readline.h` header file defines the interface to the GNU `readline` library. You may not be familiar with the name of the `readline` library; but if you are a Linux (or `bash`) user, you probably know the user interface that it provides. When you use the `readline` library in your application, your users can enter SQL commands *and* correct their typing errors. I don't know about you, but I type faster backward than I do forward—I hate using tools that don't let me correct typing mistakes.

The `readline/history.h` header file defines the interface to the GNU `history` library. `readline` and `history` work well together. The `history` library gives you an easy way to record SQL commands and recall them later.

I'll show you how to use `readline` and `history` a bit later.

```
13 #define MAX_PRINT_LEN       40
14
15 static char separator[MAX_PRINT_LEN+1];
16
17 void print_result_set( PGresult * result )
18 {
19   int          col;
20   int          row;
21   int            * sizes;
22
23 /*
24 ** Compute the size for each column
25 */
26   sizes = (int *)calloc( PQnfields( result ), sizeof( int ));
27
28   for( col = 0; col < PQnfields( result ); col++ )
29   {
30     int     len = 0;
31
32     for( row = 0; row < PQntuples( result ); row++ )
33     {
34       if( PQgetisnull( result, row, col ))
35         len = 0;
36       else
37         len = PQgetlength( result, row, col );
```

```
38
39        if( len > sizes[col] )
40          sizes[col] = len;
41      }
42
43      if(( len = strlen( PQfname( result, col ))) > sizes[col] )
44        sizes[col] = len;
45
46      if( sizes[col] > MAX_PRINT_LEN )
47        sizes[col] = MAX_PRINT_LEN;
48    }
49
50 /*
51 ** Print the field names.
52 */
53    for( col = 0; col < PQnfields( result ); col++ )
54    {
55      printf( "%-*s ", sizes[col], PQfname( result, col ));
56    }
57
58    printf( "\n" );
59
60 /*
61 ** Print the separator line
62 */
63    memset( separator, '-', MAX_PRINT_LEN );
64
65    for( col = 0; col < PQnfields( result ); col++ )
66    {
67      printf( "%*.*s ", sizes[col], sizes[col], separator );
68    }
69
70    printf( "\n" );
71
72 /*
73 ** Now loop through each of the tuples returned by
74 ** our query and print the results.
75 */
76    for( row = 0; row < PQntuples( result ); row++ )
77    {
78      for( col = 0; col < PQnfields( result ); col++ )
79      {
80        if( PQgetisnull( result, row, col ))
81          printf( "%*s", sizes[col], "" );
82        else
83          printf( "%*s ", sizes[col], PQgetvalue( result, row, col ));
84      }
```

```
 85
 86     printf( "\n" );
 87
 88   }
 89   printf( "(%d rows)\n\n", PQntuples( result ));
 90   free( sizes );
 91 }
 92
 93 void process_query( PGconn * connection, const char * query_text )
 94 {
 95   PGresult  *       result;
 96
 97   if(( result = PQexec( connection, query_text )) == NULL )
 98   {
 99     printf( "%s\n", PQerrorMessage( connection ));
100     return;
101   }
102
103   if( PQresultStatus( result ) == PGRES_TUPLES_OK )
104   {
105     print_result_set( result );
106   }
107   else if( PQresultStatus( result ) == PGRES_COMMAND_OK )
108   {
109     printf( "%s", PQcmdStatus( result ));
110
111     if( strlen( PQcmdTuples( result )))
112       printf( " - %s rows\n\n", PQcmdTuples( result ));
113     else
114       printf( "\n\n" );
115   }
116   else
117   {
118       printf( "%s\n\n", PQresultErrorMessage( result ));
119   }
120
121   PQclear( result );
122 }
```

The `print_result_set()` and `process_query()` functions in client4 are identical to those used in `client3d`. If you need a refresher on how these functions operate, look back to the previous example.

```
124 int main( int argc, char * argv[] )
125 {
126   PGconn   * connection;
```

```
127   char     * buf;
128
129
130   connection = PQconnectdb( argc > 1 ? argv[1] : "" );
131
132   if( connection == NULL )
133   {
134     printf( "Fatal error - unable to allocate connection\n" );
135     exit( EXIT_FAILURE );
136   }
137
138   if( PQstatus( connection ) == CONNECTION_OK )
139   {
140
141     using_history();
142     read_history( ".pg_history" );
143
144     while(( buf = readline( "-->" )) != NULL )
145     {
146       if( strncmp( buf, "quit", sizeof( "quit" ) - 1  ) == 0 )
147       {
148         break;
149       }
150       else
151       {
152         if(strlen( buf ) != 0 )
153         {
154           add_history( buf );
155           process_query( connection, buf );
156         }
157         free( buf );
158       }
159     }
160
161     err = write_history( ".pg_history" );
162
163   }
164   else
165   {
166     printf( "%s\n", PQerrorMessage( connection ));
167   }
168
169   PQfinish( connection );
170
171   exit( EXIT_SUCCESS );
172 }
```

The `main()` function differs significantly from client3d. The first change you might notice is how we handle command-line arguments. In previous examples, you were required to enter a connection string on the command-line. Now we are trying to be a bit more user-friendly, so the command-line argument is optional. If you provide a command-line argument, we assume that it is a connection string. If you don't, you pass an empty string to `PQconnectdb()` (see line 130) to indicate that you want to connect using default connection attributes.

The most significant change is the processing loop starting at line 141 and continuing through line 158. At line 141, you call a function named `using_history()` that initializes the GNU `history` library.

Just before exiting this application, you will call the `write_history()` function to write your command history to the `$PWD/.pg_history` file. The call to `read_history()` reads in any history records from previous invocations. Using `write_history()` and `read_history()`, you can maintain a command history across multiple invocations of client4. The `read_history()` and `write_history()` functions are part of the GNU `history` library.

At line 144, you prompt the user for a command using the `readline()` function. `readline()` is the primary function in the GNU `readline` library (no big surprise there). This function prints the prompt that provided (`-->`) and waits for you to enter a complete command. You can use the normal editing keys (backspace, left and right arrows, and so on) to correct typing errors. You can also use the up- and down-arrow keys to scroll through command history. (See the `readline` man page for a complete list of editing options.) `readline()` returns a pointer to the null-terminated command string entered by the user. `readline()` will return a `NULL` pointer if the user presses the end-of-file key (usually `Ctrl-D`).

Check for the `quit` command at line 146 and break out of the command-processing loop when you see it.

If you enter a non-blank command, you add the command to the history list and call `process_query()` to execute and display the results. You `free()` the buffer returned by `readline()` after you have finished processing the command.

At line 161, you write the history list to the `.pg_history` file. The next time you run this application, you will read the `.pg_history` file at startup.

This function finishes up by handling connection errors (at line 166), disconnecting from the server (line 166), and exiting.

You have to make a couple of minor changes to the `makefile` before you can build this application:

```
##
##  File:  Makefile
##
##         Rules for building libpq sample applications
##
```

```
INCLUDES  += -I/usr/local/pg721/include

CPPFLAGS  += $(INCLUDES)
CFLAGS    +=  -g

LDLIBS    += -L/usr/local/pgsql/lib -lpq
LDFLAGS   += -g

client1:         client1.o
get_dflts:       get_dflts.o

client4:         LDLIBS += -lreadline -ltermcap
client4:         client4.o
```

The last two lines tell make that you need to link `client4.o` against the `readline` (and `termcap`) libraries to build the `client4` application (`termcap` is required by the `readline` library).

Now let's build `client4` and test it:

```
$ make client4
cc -g -I/usr/local/pg721/include -c -o client4.o client4.c
cc -g client4.o -L/usr/local/pgsql/lib -lpq -lreadline -ltermcap -o client4

$ ./client4
-->SELECT * FROM rentals;
tape_id  rental_date customer_id
-------- ----------- -----------
AB-12345  2002-07-01           1
AB-67472  2002-07-01           3
OW-41221  2002-07-01           1
(3 rows)
-->quit
$
```

Go ahead and play around with `client4` a little. Try the editing keys; use the up-arrow key and down-arrow key to scroll through your history list. Notice that when you quit and reinvoke `client4`, you can recall the commands entered in the previous session[4].

Processing Multiple Result Sets

Now try an experiment. Run `client4` and enter two commands on the same line, terminating the first command with a semicolon:

```
$ client4 "dbname=movies"
-->SELECT * FROM tapes; SELECT * FROM rentals
tape_id  rental_date customer_id
```

4. If you find that your command history is *not* saved between sessions, it is probably because you don't have the permissions required to create the `.pg_history` file in your current directory.

```
-------- ----------- -----------
AB-12345  2002-07-03           1
AB-67472  2002-07-03           3
OW-41221  2002-07-03           1
(3 rows)
-->
```

Hmmm, there's a problem here. We executed two `SELECT` commands, but we only see the results of the last command.

This demonstrates a problem with the `PQexec()` function. `PQexec()` discards all result sets except for the last one.

Fortunately, it's not too difficult to fix this problem. Here is a replacement for the `process_query()` function that will correctly handle multiple result sets (this function appears in `client4b.c` in the sample source code):

```
 1 void process_query( PGconn * connection, const char * query_text )
 2 {
 3   PGresult  *       result;
 4
 5   if( PQsendQuery( connection, query_text ) == 0 )
 6   {
 7     printf( "%s\n", PQerrorMessage( connection ));
 8     return;
 9   }
10
11   while(( result = PQgetResult( connection )) != NULL )
12   {
13     if( PQresultStatus( result ) == PGRES_TUPLES_OK )
14     {
15       print_result_set( result );
16     }
17     else if( PQresultStatus( result ) == PGRES_COMMAND_OK )
18     {
19       printf( "%s", PQcmdStatus( result ));
20
21       if( strlen( PQcmdTuples( result )))
22         printf( " - %s rows\n", PQcmdTuples( result ));
23       else
24         printf( "\n" );
25     }
26     else
27     {
28       printf( "%s\n", PQresultErrorMessage( result ));
29     }
30
31     PQclear( result );
32   }
33 }
```

In this version of `process_query()`, you split the command-processing effort into two steps. First, you send the command string to the server using the `PQsendQuery()` function. `PQsendQuery()` returns immediately after queuing the command—it will not wait for results from the server. If `PQsendQuery()` cannot send the command string, it will return `0` and you can find the error message by calling `PQerrorMessage()`.

The second step starts at line 11. You call `PQgetResult()` to obtain a result set from the server. Notice that you invoke `PQgetResult()` within a loop. `PQgetResult()` returns one result set for each command in the command string and returns `NULL` when there are no more result sets to process. The `PQgetResult()` function returns a pointer to a `PGresult` object—we already know how to work with a `Pgresult`, so the rest of this function remains unchanged.

Now let's try to run this version (`client4b`):

```
$ client4b "dbname=movies"
-->SELECT * FROM tapes; SELECT * FROM rentals
tape_id  title
-------- -------------
AB-12345 The Godfather
AB-67472 The Godfather
MC-68873    Casablanca
OW-41221  Citizen Kane
AH-54706   Rear Window
(5 rows)

tape_id  rental_date customer_id
-------- ----------- -----------
AB-12345  2002-07-03           1
AB-67472  2002-07-03           3
OW-41221  2002-07-03           1
(3 rows)

-->quit
$
```

This time, you get the results that you would expect: one result set for each command.

Asynchronous Processing

In the previous section, I mentioned that the `PQsendQuery()` function will not wait for a result set to be returned by the server. That can be an important feature for certain applications, particularly graphical (GUI) applications. In a GUI application, your code must remain responsive to the user even if you are waiting for results from a long-running SQL command. If you use `PQexec()` in a GUI application, you will find that the screen will not repaint while waiting for server results. The `PQexec()` function (and in fact most of the libpq functions) is *synchronous*—the function will not return until the work has been completed.

In a GUI application, you need *asynchronous* functions, like `PQsendQuery()`. Things get a little more complex when you use asynchronous functions. Simply using `PQsendQuery()` is not enough to make your application responsive while waiting for results. Without doing some extra work, your application will still pause when you call the `PQgetResult()` function.

Here is a revised version of the `process_query()` function:

```
 1 void process_query( PGconn * connection, const char * query_text )
 2 {
 3   PGresult  *       result;
 4
 5   if( PQsendQuery( connection, query_text ) == 0 )
 6   {
 7     printf( "%s\n", PQerrorMessage( connection ));
 8     return;
 9   }
10
11   do
12   {
13     while( is_result_ready( connection ) == FALSE )
14     {
15       putchar( '.' );
16       fflush( stdout );
17     }
18     printf( "\n" );
19
20     if(( result = PQgetResult( connection )) != NULL )
21     {
22       if( PQresultStatus( result ) == PGRES_TUPLES_OK )
23       {
24         print_result_set( result );
25       }
26       else if( PQresultStatus( result ) == PGRES_COMMAND_OK )
27       {
28         printf( "%s", PQcmdStatus( result ));
29
30         if( strlen( PQcmdTuples( result )))
31           printf( " - %s rows\n", PQcmdTuples( result ));
32         else
33           printf( "\n" );
34       }
35       else
36       {
37         printf( "%s\n", PQresultErrorMessage( result ));
38       }
39       PQclear( result );
40     }
41   } while( result != NULL );
42 }
```

The important change to this version of `process_query()` starts at line 13. After sending the command to the server, you enter a loop that calls `is_result_ready()`. The `is_result_ready()` function waits for a result set to appear from the server. `is_result_ready()` will wait no longer than one second—if a result set is not ready within one second, `is_result_ready()` will return `FALSE`. You simulate normal GUI processing here by printing a "`.`" for every second that we wait. (Okay, that's a pretty cheap imitation of a GUI don't you think?)

Now let's look at the `is_result_ready()` function:

```
44 bool is_result_ready( PGconn * connection )
45 {
46     int              my_socket;
47     struct timeval   timer;
48     fd_set           read_mask;
49
50     if( PQisBusy( connection ) == 0 )
51       return( TRUE );
52
53     my_socket = PQsocket( connection );
54
55     timer.tv_sec  = (time_t)1;
56     timer.tv_usec = 0;
57
58     FD_ZERO( &read_mask );
59     FD_SET( my_socket, &read_mask );
60
61     if( select(my_socket + 1, &read_mask, NULL, NULL, &timer) == 0)
62     {
63       return( FALSE );
64     }
65     else if( FD_ISSET( my_socket, &read_mask ))
66     {
67       PQconsumeInput( connection );
68
69       if( PQisBusy( connection ) == 0 )
70         return( TRUE );
71       else
72         return( FALSE );
73     }
74     else
75     {
76       return( FALSE );
77     }
78 }
```

This is one of the most complex functions that we've seen in this chapter. You start (at line 50) by calling a the `PQisBusy()` function. `PQisBusy()` returns `0` if a result set is ready for processing, and `1` if not.

If you find that a result set is not ready, you have more work to do. It might help to understand the details to come if you have a quick overview of where you are heading.

When you connect to a PostgreSQL server, the connection is represented by a `PGconn` object. You know that a `PGconn` object is opaque—you can't look at the internals of the object to see what's inside. libpq provides one function that enables you to peek under the covers: `PQsocket()`. The `PQsocket()` returns the network socket that libpq uses to communicate with the server. We will use that socket to determine when data from the server becomes available.

Although server data is available it does *not* mean that a result set is ready. This is an important point. You may find that a single byte has been received from the server, but the result set is many megabytes in size. Once you know that *some* data is available, you have to let libpq peek at it. The `PQconsumeInput()` function (from libpq) reads all available server data and assembles it into a partial result set. After libpq has processed the available data, you can ask if an entire result set is ready for you.

That's the overview, now the details.

At line 53, you retrieve the client/server socket by calling `PQsocket()`. Remember, this is the socket that libpq uses to communicate with the server.

Next, you prepare to wait for data to become available from the server. At lines 55 and 56, set up a timer structure. You want to wait, at most, one second for data to become available from the server so you initialize the `timer` structure to indicate one second and zero microseconds. This is an arbitrary value—if you want to be a bit more responsive, you can choose a shorter interval. If you want to consume fewer CPU cycles, you can choose a longer interval.

At lines 58 and 59, you initialize an `fd_set` structure. An `fd_set` is a data structure that represents a set of file (or, in our case, socket) descriptors. When you call `select()`, you must tell it which file descriptors (or socket descriptors) you are interested in. You want to listen for data on the socket you retrieved from `PQsocket()`, so you turn on the corresponding entry in the `fd_set`[5].

At line 61, you call the `select()` function. This function waits until any of the following occurs:

- Data is ready on one of the file descriptors indicated in the `read_mask`.
- The timer expires (that is, 1 second elapses).
- A Unix signal is intercepted.

5. This description might sound a bit mysterious. We programmers aren't supposed to know *how* an `fd_set` is implemented. The developers of the socket library want to hide the implementation so they can change it without our permission. We are only supposed to use a prescribed set of macros and functions to manipulate an `fd_set`. Think of an `fd_set` as a big set of bits. Each bit corresponds to a file/socket descriptor. When you call `PQsocket()`, it gives you back a number—you want to turn on the bit corresponding to that number to tell `select()` that you are interested in activity on that socket. The `FD_SET()` macro turns on one bit. FD_ZERO() turns off all the bits. Now, if anyone asks, pretend that you don't know any of this stuff.

In other words, the `select()` function returns after waiting one second for data to become available on the `my_socket` socket. If data is ready before the timer expires, `select()` will return immediately.

When `select()` finally returns, you have to figure out which of the three previously-mentioned events actually occurred.

If `select()` returns zero, it's telling you that the timer expired without any activity on `my_socket`. In that case, you know that a result set can't possibly be ready so you return `FALSE` to your caller.

If `select()` returns something other than zero, you know that one of the file descriptors specified in `read_mask` has some data available. We'll be good little programmers here and use the `FD_ISSET()` macro to make sure that data is available on the `my_socket` socket. Practically speaking, there is only one descriptor enabled in `read_mask`, so you know that if any of the descriptors has data, it must be your descriptor.

At line 66, you know that *some* data is available from the server, but don't know if an entire result set is ready so you call `PQconsumeInput()`. `PQconsumeInput()` reads all data available from the server and stuffs that data into the result set that is being accumulated.

After that's done, you can call `PQisBusy()` again. `PQisBusy()` tells you whether a complete result set has been assembled. If `PQisBusy()` returns `0` (meaning, no, the connection is not busy), you tell the caller that a result set is ready for processing. Otherwise, you return `FALSE` to indicate that more data is needed.

Lines 74 through 77 handle the case where a Unix signal interrupted the call to `select()`. There really isn't much to do in this case, so you just tell the caller that a result set is *not* ready for processing.

If you want to try this code, you will find it in the `client4c.c` source file. Here is a sample session:

```
$ ./client4c dbname=movies
-->SELECT COUNT(*) FROM pg_class, pg_attribute;
.........
count
-----
96690
(1 rows)
-->
```

Notice that it took nine seconds to execute this query (nine dots printed while we were waiting for the result set to come back from the server).

Besides the asynchronous command processing functions, libpq offers a way to make asynchronous connection attempts. I find that the asynchronous connection functions are overly complex for the limited benefits that they offer. In general, database connections are established in such a short period of time that I am willing to wait for the attempt to complete. If you find that a connection attempt is taking an excessive amount of time, you probably have a name server problem and I would rather fix that problem. If you do find that you need to make asynchronous connection attempts, see the PostgreSQL Programmer's Guide.

Summary

The libpq library is very well designed. I've used many other database APIs (OCI from Oracle, DBLibrary and OpenClient from Sybase, and ODBC) and none have compared to the simplicity offered by libpq. Other database APIs may offer a few more features, but these generally come at the cost of greatly increased complexity.

I encourage you to try the sample applications in this chapter. Feel free to experiment. I haven't covered all the libpq functions in this chapter, only the ones you are most likely to need in your own applications. Explore the library; as you will see in the next few chapters, libpq is the foundation on which most of the other PostgreSQL APIs are built. The better you understand libpq, the easier it will be to work with other APIs.

9

A Simpler C API—libpgeasy

THE LIBPQ LIBRARY IS VERY POWERFUL. In fact, libpq is the basis for most of the other PostgreSQL APIs—the other APIs translate a high-level request into a set of calls to the libpq library. The power behind libpq comes at the price of complexity. libpgeasy lets you avoid that complexity by acting as a lightweight wrapper around the more commonly used libpq functions. The simplicity afforded by the use of libpgeasy often comes at the expense of functionality.

The functions provided by the libpgeasy library use the same data structures used by libpq. For example, when you connect to a database using libpgeasy, you get back a `PGconn * ;` that's the same data type that you get when you connect to a database using libpq. This means that you can mix and match calls to libpq and libpgeasy, taking advantage of the power of libpq and the simplicity of libpgeasy.

Although the data types of libpq and libpqeasy may be similar, the design philosophies of libpq and libpgeasy are very different. libpq is designed to provide access to all the features of the PostgreSQL server. Libpgeasy, on the other hand, is designed to provide a simple interface to the most commonly used PostgreSQL features.

Prerequisites

As mentioned previously, libpgeasy is a wrapper around libpq. The basic requirements for building a libpq client were described in Chapter 8, "The PostgreSQL C API—libpq (Client Applications)," and so I won't repeat them here.

Besides the libpq header files and object libraries, you will need to `#include` the `libpgeasy.h` file and link to the libpgeasy object library (`-lpgeasy`).

Client 1—Connecting to the Server

Connecting to a database using libpgeasy is simple. libpgeasy provides a single connection function:

```
PGconn * connectdb( char * options );
```

The single argument to `connectdb()` is a connection string in the same form expected by the libpq `PQconnectdb()` function. An example connection string might look like this:

```
char * connectString = "dbname=movies user=sheila";
```

Let's look at a simple client that uses the `connectdb()` function:

```
/* client1.c */

#include <stdlib.h>
#include <libpq-fe.h>
#include <libpgeasy.h>

int main( int argc, char * argv[] )
{
  connectdb( argv[1] ? argv[1] : "" );
  disconnectdb();
  exit( EXIT_SUCCESS );

}
```

This example shows the minimum required code for a libpgeasy application. You must `#include` two files: `libpq-fe.h` and `libpgeasy.h`, and you must `#include` them in that order[1].

In the call to `connectdb()`, I've passed in the first command-line argument (or an empty string if there are no command-line arguments). When you run this program, you should provide a connection string as the only argument. If you need to specify more than one connection property, enclose the list in double quotes and separate the properties with a space. Here are two examples:

```
  $ ./client1 dbname=movies
$ ./client1 "dbname=movies user=sheila"
```

After the `connectdb()` function returns, I call `disconnectdb()`. The function prototype for `disconnectdb()` is

```
void disconnectdb( void );
```

Notice that `disconnectdb()` does *not* expect any arguments. You may have also noticed that I did not capture any return value from the call to `connectdb()`.

How does libpgeasy know which connection I want to terminate? In keeping with the goal of simplicity, libpgeasy remembers the database connection for me. When I call `connectdb()`, libpgeasy stores (in a private variable) the PGconn pointer. When I call `disconnectdb()`, it uses the stored connection pointer. Although libpgeasy has the capacity to remember the database connection, it will remember only one connection at a time. This is one example of the tradeoffs made when using libpgeasy versus libpq—you have gained simplicity, but lost some flexibility.

1. libpqeasy refers to items in `libqp-fe`, so they must be `#included` in that order.

If you want, you can capture the return value from `connectdb()` in a `PGconn` pointer variable and use it in the same ways that you could use a `PGconn *` through libpq.

Now let's run this client application to see what it does:

```
$ ./client1 dbname=movies
$
```

Exciting, don't you think? Let's try that again, feeding it an erroneous database name this time:

```
$ ./client1 dbname=foofoo
Connection to database using 'dbname=foofoo' failed.
FATAL 1:  Database "foofoo" does not exist in the system catalog.
$
```

This time, you can see that libpgeasy produced an error message. The `client1.c` source code doesn't include any error handling at all—you didn't include any code to check for errors or to print error messages. Again, this is consistent with the goal of simplicity. Of course, in a sophisticated application, you probably want a little more control over the handling of error conditions.

Client 2—Adding Error Checking

Now let's add a little error-handling code to the client:

```
/* client2a.c   */

#include <stdlib.h>
#include <libpq-fe.h>
#include <libpgeasy.h>

int main( int argc, char * argv[] )
{
  PGconn *  connection;

  connection = connectdb( argv[1] ? argv[1] : "" );

  if( PQstatus( connection ) != CONNECTION_OK )
    printf( "Caught an error: %s\n", PQerrorMessage( connection ));
  else
    printf( "connection ok\n" );

  disconnectdb();

  exit( EXIT_SUCCESS );
}
```

This time around, I captured the `PGconn *` returned by `connectdb()`. Remember that this `PGconn *` is the same type of object that you would find in a libpq application. Call the `PQstatus()` function to determine whether the connection attempt succeeded or failed. If a failure occurs, print an error message; otherwise, print "connection ok."

Let's run this a couple of times to see how it behaves:

```
$ ./client2a dbname=movies
connection ok
```

As expected, you see a friendly little confirmation that the connection attempt was successful. Now let's feed in an error and see what happens:

```
$ ./client2a dbname=foofoo
Connection to database using 'dbname=foofoo' failed.
FATAL 1:  Database "foofoo" does not exist in the system catalog.
```

This time, you see an error message. But look closely and you'll see that the error message doesn't match your source code—the error message should start with the text `Caught an error:`.

What happened? If you don't make any other arrangements, `connectdb()` will print an error message and terminate the calling program if it encounters a failure. So, this program didn't even get to the point where it could call `PQstatus()`—the program terminated before `connectdb()` ever returned.

So, how do you make these "other arrangements?" libpgeasy provides two functions that you can use to control the error-handling mode:

```
void on_error_stop( void );
void on_error_continue( void );
```

The `on_error_stop()` function tells libpgeasy that you want *it* to handle error conditions. Calling `on_error_continue()` tells libpgeasy that you want to handle error conditions yourself. `on_error_stop()` is the default error-handling mode.

I should point out here that calling `on_error_continue()` has no effect on the `connectdb()` function. If the connection attempt fails, `connectdb()` will terminate the program regardless of which error-handling mode is in effect.

In the next section, you will see that libpgeasy does in fact let you construct your own error-handling code once a connection has been established.

Client 3—Processing Queries

Query processing is simple in libpgeasy. To execute a SQL command, you call the `doquery()` function. The function prototype for `doquery()` is

```
PGresult * doquery( char * query );
```

Notice that `doquery()` does not expect a `PGconn *`—libpgeasy can deal with only a single database connection and it implicitly uses the one returned by `connectdb()`. `doquery()` returns a `PGresult *`. This is the same data structure you saw in the previous chapter—it represents the result set of the query.

After you have executed a command, you will need to process the result set. libpgeasy provides a number of functions for dealing with a result set—of course, you can use any of the libpq functions as well.

If you are reasonably sure that your query succeeded, you can use the `fetch()` function to retrieve a single row from the result set. Here is the function prototype for `fetch()`:

```
int fetch( void * param, ... );
```

The `fetch()` function returns the index of the row that you just fetched. The first row returned is row 0, the second row is row 1, and so on. When the result set is exhausted, `fetch()` will return `END_OF_TUPLES`. If the query returns zero rows, the first call to `fetch()` will return `END_OF_TUPLES`. When you call `fetch()`, you pass a list of pointers. Each argument should point to a buffer large enough to hold the corresponding field from the result set. You must pass one pointer for each column returned by the query. If you aren't interested in the value of a column, you can pass a `NULL` pointer.

This might be a good point to see an example:

```
/* client3a.c */

#include <stdlib.h>
#include <libpq-fe.h>
#include <libpgeasy.h>

int main( int argc, char * argv[] )
{
  char      tape_id[8+1];
  char      title[80+1];
  char      duration[80+1];
  PGconn *  connection;

  connection = connectdb( argv[1] ? argv[1] : "" );

  on_error_stop( );

  doquery( "SELECT * FROM tapes" );

  while( fetch( tape_id, title, duration ) != END_OF_TUPLES )
  {
    printf( "%s - %-40s - %s\n", tape_id, title, duration );
  }

  disconnectdb();

  exit( EXIT_SUCCESS );

}
```

In client3a.c, I select all columns (and all rows) from the tapes table. Here is the definition of tapes:

```
movies=# \d tapes
                Table "tapes"
 Attribute |         Type          | Modifier
-----------+-----------------------+----------
 tape_id   | character(8)          | not null
 title     | character varying(80) | not null
 duration  | interval              |
```

I've allocated three buffers; one for each column in the table. The tape_id column is eight characters long. The buffer that I allocated for tape_id is 8+1 bytes[2] long—the extra byte is for the null terminator (remember that C strings are terminated with a zero, or null, byte). title is a varchar with a maximum of eighty characters; my buffer is 80+1 bytes long. The duration column is an interval; it will be automatically converted into a null-terminated character string. You don't know exactly how long the text form of an interval will be, but 80+1 bytes should be enough.

I haven't included any error-handling code in this program, so I'll ask libpgeasy to intercept any error conditions by calling on_error_stop(). As I mentioned earlier, on_error_stop() is the default error-handling mode, but including an explicit call makes the behavior obvious to anyone reading your code.

Next, I'll call doquery() to send the command to the server.

When doquery() returns, it has assembled the result set and I can call fetch() repeatedly to process each row. When I call the fetch() function, I pass in three addresses. fetch() matches each buffer that I provide with a column in the result set. The tape_id column is placed in my tape_id buffer, the title column is placed in my title buffer, and the duration column is placed in my duration buffer. If I am not interested in retrieving a field, I can pass in a NULL pointer for that field.

Some readers might find my call to fetch() a little confusing at first. It may clarify things to rewrite the call to fetch() as follows:

```
while( fetch( &tape_id[0], &title[0], &duration[0] ) != END_OF_TUPLES )
```

Writing the code this way makes it a little more obvious that I am passing the address of the first byte of each buffer to fetch().

After fetch() returns, I print the row. In case you aren't too familiar with the syntax, "%-40s" tells printf() to print the title within a left-justified 40-character column[3].

2. I tend to declare my string buffers using this *n+1* format. I could obviously declare the tape_id variable as "char tape_id[9];". When I see [9], I wonder if I forgot to include space for the null-terminator. When I see [8+1], I know I did the right thing.

3. The title column is 80 characters wide but I am only printing the first 40 characters to conserve screen real estate.

Let's run this program:

```
$ ./client3a dbname=movies
AB-12345 - The Godfather                          -
AB-67472 - The Godfather                          -
MC-68873 - Casablanca                             -
OW-41221 - Citizen Kane                           -
AH-54706 - Rear Window                            -
OW-42200 - Sly                                    - 01:36
KJ-03335 - American Citizen, An                   -
OW-42201 - Stone Cold                             - 01:52
```

There is one very important point to understand when you use the `fetch()` function. When you call `fetch()`, you are passing in buffer pointers—`fetch()` has no way to know how large those buffers are. If you give `fetch()` a pointer to a four-byte buffer, but you really need 80 bytes to hold a value, `fetch()` will happily copy 80 bytes. The most likely effect of this is that your program will immediately crash—if you are lucky. If you aren't lucky, your program will exhibit random failures that are really hard to track down. Sometimes, ignorance is *not* bliss.

Working with Binary Cursors

You can use the libpgeasy library to retrieve binary[4] data as well as text-form data. Using binary data can give you a performance boost in a few cases, but you usually use binary cursors to retrieve, well...binary data (such as JPEG files, audio files, and so on). Let's modify this simple application a little to see how binary data is handled (the examples are getting a little longer now, so I'll start including line numbers):

```
1 /* client3b.c */
 2
 3 #include <stdlib.h>
 4 #include <libpq-fe.h>
 5 #include <libpgeasy.h>
 6
 7 int main( int argc, char * argv[] )
 8 {
 9   int       customer_id;
10   char      customer_name[80+1];
11   PGconn *  connection;
12
13   connection = connectdb( argv[1] ? argv[1] : "" );
14
15   on_error_stop( );
```

4. *Binary* is really a misnomer. Declaring a binary cursor really means that you will get results in the form used to store the data in PostgreSQL. If you don't use a binary cursor, PostgreSQL will convert all values into null-terminated strings.

```
16
17    doquery( "BEGIN WORK" );
18    doquery( "DECLARE customer_list BINARY CURSOR FOR "
19             "SELECT id, customer_name FROM customers" );
20
21
22    doquery( "FETCH ALL FROM customer_list" );
23
24    while( fetch( &customer_id, customer_name ) != END_OF_TUPLES )
25    {
26      printf( "%d: %-40s\n", customer_id, customer_name );
27    }
28
29    doquery( "COMMIT" );
30
31    disconnectdb();
32    exit( EXIT_SUCCESS );
33 }
```

This example is a little more complex than the previous one. To retrieve binary values, I have to DECLARE a BINARY CURSOR within the context of a transaction block. At line 17, I create a new transaction; the transaction will end at line 29. At line 18, I declare a binary cursor. Rather than processing the (direct) results of a SELECT statement, I loop through the results of a FETCH ALL.

In the previous example (client3a.c), I used the fetch() function to retrieve the text form for each value. In client3b.c, I am retrieving binary values. The fetch() function doesn't know anything about data types—it just copies bytes from the result set into the buffer that was provided.

If you compare the call that I made to printf() in client3b to the corresponding call in client3a, you will see that the difference between text and binary form is reflected in the format string. With text format data, you can always use %s to print result values. With binary data, the format string depends on the underlying column types.

The id column is defined as an int. You want fetch() to copy the id column into the customer_id variable. Because this is a binary cursor, the id column will come to us in binary (or int) form; therefore, customer_id is declared as an int. The customer_name column is defined as a varchar(50)—a character column comes to you as a null-terminated string regardless of whether you are retrieving from a binary or text-form cursor.

Now let's run this client:

```
$ ./client3b dbname=movies
1: Jones, Henry
2: Rubin, William
3: Panky, Henry
4: Wonderland, Alice N.
5: Funkmaster, Freddy
7: Gull, Jonathon LC
8: Grumby, Jonas
```

Byte Ordering and NULL Values

There are two more things you have to worry about when working with a binary cursor.

If the client application is not on the same host as the server, you must be concerned about byte ordering. As I mentioned in the previous chapter, different processors (CPUs) order the bytes within numeric data types in different ways. If the client is running on a big-endian host and the server is running on a little-endian host (or vice versa), the non-character data that you receive through a binary cursor will require byte-order conversion.

The next problem that you will encounter when using a binary cursor is the `NULL` value. If you are using a text-form cursor, PostgreSQL simply returns an empty string whenever it encounters a `NULL` value in the result set. That won't work if you are retrieving an `int` value (or any of the noncharacter data types). You should really use the `fetchwithnulls()` function whenever you use a binary cursor. The function prototype for `fetchwithnulls()` is

```
int fetchwithnulls( void * param, ... );
```

When you call `fetchwithnulls()`, you provide two buffers for each field in the result set. The first buffer receives the field value; the second receives a `NULL` indicator (in the form of an `int`). If the field in question contains a `NULL` value, the `NULL` indicator will be set to `1` and the value returned (in the first buffer) is meaningless. If the field contains a non-`NULL` value, the `NULL` indicator is set to `0` and you can use the value returned in the first buffer.

```
 1 /* client3c.c */
 2
 3 #include <stdlib.h>
 4 #include <libpq-fe.h>
 5 #include <libpgeasy.h>
 6
 7 int main( int argc, char * argv[] )
 8 {
 9   int       id;             /* customer_id column   */
10   char      name[80+1];     /* customer_name column */
11   float     balance;        /* balance column       */
12   int       nulls[3];       /* NULL indicators      */
13   PGconn *  connection;
14
15   connection = connectdb( argv[1] ? argv[1] : "" );
16
17   on_error_stop( );
18
19   doquery( "BEGIN WORK" );
20
21   doquery( "DECLARE customer_list BINARY CURSOR FOR "
22            "SELECT "
23            "id, customer_name, CAST(balance AS real) "
```

```
24           "FROM customers" );
25
26   doquery( "FETCH ALL FROM customer_list" );
27
28   while( fetchwithnulls( &id,       &nulls[0],
29                          &name[0], &nulls[1],
30                          &balance, &nulls[2] )
31          != END_OF_TUPLES )
32   {
33     if( nulls[2] )
34       printf( "%4d: %-40s   NULL\n", id, name );
35     else
36       printf( "%4d: %-40s %6.2f\n", id, name, balance );
37   }
38
39   doquery( "COMMIT" );
40
41   disconnectdb();
42   exit( EXIT_SUCCESS );
43 }
```

In this client application (`client3.c`), you are retrieving data using a binary cursor. At line 12, you allocate an array of three null indicators. At lines 28[nd]31, you pass a pointer to each null indicator (and the value buffers) to the `fetchwithnulls()` function.

By the time `fetchwithnulls()` has returned, it has set each of the null indicators—`1` if the corresponding field is `NULL`, `0` if the corresponding field is non-`NULL`.

In this example, you know that the `customer_id` and `customer_name` columns cannot be `NULL`; when you created the customers table, you specified that these two columns were *`not null`*. You must provide `fetchwithnulls()` with the address of a null indicator, even if a result field cannot possibly contain a `NULL` value.

Working with Result Sets in libpgeasy

In this chapter, you may have noticed that I never bother to free any of the query result sets when I have finished with them. When you use the libpq API, you have to be sure to call `PQclear()` when you are finished processing a result set—if you don't, your application will have a memory leak. The libpgeasy library manages the result set for you. Each time you execute a new query (by calling `doquery()`), the previous result set is cleared.

libpgeasy provides a few functions that you can use to manipulate the result set. If you call the `reset_fetch()` function, the result set will be "rewound" to the beginning. If you fetch after calling `reset_fetch()`, you will find yourself back at the first row in the result set.

libpgeasy provides three more (poorly documented) functions that you can use to manage multiple result sets.

The `get_result()` function returns a pointer to the current result set (that is, `get_result()` returns a `PGresult *`). When you call `get_result()`, you are telling libpgeasy that you are going to manage the result set and it will not be automatically cleared the next time you call `doquery()`. When you want to use a result set that you have saved, pass the `PGresult *` to `set_result()`. After calling `set_result()`, any calls to `fetch()` (or `fetchwithnulls()`) will use the new result set.

When you want libpgeasy to manage its own result sets again, call `unset_result()` with the pointer you got from the first call to `get_result()`. Don't forget to clear the other result sets using `PQClear()`.

Client 4—An Interactive Query Processor

To wrap up this chapter, you'll convert the interactive query processor from the previous chapter into a libpgeasy client.

Most of the code remains the same, so I'll point out only the differences. The most important change is that you no longer have to pass the `PGconn *` (connection handle) to every function—libpgeasy is managing the connection handle for you.

```
 1 /*
 2 ** File: client4.c
 3 */
 4
 5 #include <stdlib.h>
 6 #include <string.h>
 7 #include <libpq-fe.h>
 8 #include <libpgeasy.h>
 9 #include <readline/readline.h>
10 #include <readline/history.h>
11
12 typedef enum { FALSE, TRUE } bool;
13
14 #define MAX_PRINT_LEN40
15
16 static char separator[MAX_PRINT_LEN+1];
17
18 void print_result_set( PGresult * result )
19 {
20   int          col;
21   int          row;
22   int        * sizes;
23
24 /*
25 ** Compute the size for each column
26 */
27   sizes = (int *)calloc( PQnfields( result ), sizeof( int ));
28
29   for( col = 0; col < PQnfields( result ); col++ )
30   {
```

```
31     int   len = 0;
32
33     for( row = 0; row < PQntuples( result ); row++ )
34     {
35       if( PQgetisnull( result, row, col ))
36         len = 0;
37       else
38          len = PQgetlength( result, row, col );
39
40       if( len > sizes[col] )
41          sizes[col] = len;
42     }
43
44     if(( len = strlen( PQfname( result, col ))) > sizes[col] )
45       sizes[col] = len;
46
47     if( sizes[col] > MAX_PRINT_LEN )
48       sizes[col] = MAX_PRINT_LEN;
49   }
50
51 /*
52 ** Print the field names.
53 */
54   for( col = 0; col < PQnfields( result ); col++ )
55   {
56     printf( "%-*s ", sizes[col], PQfname( result, col ));
57   }
58
59   printf( "\n" );
60
61 /*
62 ** Print the separator line
63 */
64   memset( separator, '-', MAX_PRINT_LEN );
65
66   for( col = 0; col < PQnfields( result ); col++ )
67   {
68     printf( "%*.*s ", sizes[col], sizes[col], separator );
69   }
70
71   printf( "\n" );
72
73 /*
74 ** Now loop through each of the tuples returned by
75 ** our query and print the results.
76 */
77   for( row = 0; row < PQntuples( result ); row++ )
```

```
 78     {
 79       for( col = 0; col < PQnfields( result ); col++ )
 80       {
 81         if( PQgetisnull( result, row, col ))
 82            printf( "%*s", sizes[col], "" );
 83         else
 84            printf( "%*s ", sizes[col], PQgetvalue(result, row, col));
 85       }
 86
 87       printf( "\n" );
 88
 89     }
 90     printf( "(%d rows)\n", PQntuples( result ));
 91
 92     free( sizes );
 93   }
```

You can't use the `fetch()` or `fetchwithnulls()` in the `print_result_set()` function. There is no way to construct a call to these functions because you can't know (at the time the program is compiled) how many columns will be returned by a query.

The `process_query()` function is very simple. The call to `doquery()` sends the command to the server and returns a pointer to the result set.

```
 95 void process_query( char * buf )
 96 {
 97   PGresult *  result;
 98
 99   result = doquery( buf );
100
101   if( PQresultStatus( result ) == PGRES_TUPLES_OK )
102   {
103     print_result_set( result );
104   }
105   else if( PQresultStatus( result ) == PGRES_COMMAND_OK )
106   {
107     printf( "%s", PQcmdStatus( result ));
108
109     if( strlen( PQcmdTuples( result )))
110       printf( " - %s rows\n", PQcmdTuples( result ));
111     else
112       printf( "\n" );
113   }
114   else
115   {
116       printf( "%s\n", PQresultErrorMessage( result ));
117   }
118 }
```

The main() function is largely unchanged. I don't bother to save the connection handle returned by connectdb() because libpgeasy remembers it for me. The only other change in main() is that you set the error-handling mode calling on_error_continue(). If you don't set the error-handling mode, libpgeasy assumes that it should terminate your application if an error is encountered.

```
120 int main( int argc, char * argv[] )
121 {
122   char    * buf;
123
124   connectdb( argc > 1 ? argv[1] : "" );
125
126   on_error_continue();
127
128   using_history();
129   read_history( ".pg_history" );
130
131   while(( buf = readline( "->" )) != NULL )
132   {
133     if( strncmp( buf, "quit", sizeof( "quit" ) - 1  ) == 0 )
134     {
135       break;
136     }
137     else
138     {
139       if( strlen( buf ) != 0 )
140       {
141          add_history( buf );
142          process_query( buf );
143       }
144       free( buf );
145     }
146   }
147
148   write_history( ".pg_history" );
149
150   disconnectdb();
151
152   exit( EXIT_SUCCESS );
153 }
```

Summary

The libpgeasy library is a nice addition to libpq. You can mix and match libpgeasy and libpq functions. libpgeasy makes it easy to write simple utility applications, but it is not well suited to writing applications that need a lot of user input. If your application needs to execute commands that are not known at compile time, you should probably use libpq instead—libpgeasy won't offer you many advantages.

The source code for libpgeasy is available in the PostgreSQL source distributions. I recommend that you read through the code—you'll see some good sample code that will help in your libpq programming efforts. You will also gain a better understanding of some of the limitations of libpgeasy.

10

The PostgreSQL C++ API—libpq++

YOU CAN BUILD POSTGRESQL CLIENT APPLICATIONS USING a variety of programming languages. In Chapter 8, "The PostgreSQL C API—libpq (Client Applications)," and Chapter 9, "A Simpler C API—libpgeasy," you looked at two of the APIs that you can conveniently use from a C program (libpq and libpgeasy). This chapter introduces you to the libpq++ API. libpq++ is an API designed for use from within a C++ client application. To demonstrate the capabilities provided by libpq++, you'll build a number of client applications in this chapter:

- client1—A simple example that shows how to connect a C++ application to a PostgreSQL database.
- client2—Next I'll show you how to catch runtime errors that might occur when you are using libpq++.
- qt-query—After you know how to intercept and respond to error conditions, you'll build a graphical client (using the Qt GUI toolkit) that will process a single SQL command and display the results in a form that is (hopefully) more attractive than a simple text-based interface.
- qt-sql—The last client presented in this chapter combines Qt and libpq++ to provide a graphical interactive query processor.

I mentioned in the previous chapter that the libpgeasy API is a wrapper around libpq. The same is true for libpq++—libpq++ is implemented using libpq.

When you use the libpq or libpgeasy APIs, you use a collection of data types (`PGresult *`, `PGconn *`, and so on) and functions (`PQconnectdb()`, `PQexec()`, and so on) to perform server operations and obtain results. In contrast, when you use the libpq++ API, you use a small collection of classes. The difference between the two approaches can affect the way you think about solving a particular problem. In a function+data type architecture (such as libpq or libpgeasy), you are working with data types that are somewhat independent from the functions that operate on those types. When you use a class- (or more precisely object-) oriented architecture, you define a set of classes that contain both state and behavior. An object is an instance of a class. Its data members represent the state of an object and the behavior is supplied by its member functions[1].

Prerequisites

I'll assume that you have a working knowledge of general C++ programming. All the examples in this chapter were tested using the GNU C++ compiler and GNU `make`. Some of the examples use the version 2.3.0 of the Qt user-interface library. If you don't already have Qt installed on your computer (you probably do if you are running a Linux system), you can find it at `http://www.trolltech.com`.

Client 1—Connecting to the Server

To start, let's look at a simple example that will make a libpq++ connection to a database server (see Listing 10.1).

Listing 10.1 `client1.cpp`

```
/* client1.cpp */

#include <libpq++.h>
#include <iostream.h>

int main( int argc, char * argv[] )
{
    PgConnection conn( "" );
}
```

That's all you need to do to make a connection to the default database server.

There are only two lines of code here that are specific to a libpq++ application. You first include the `libpq++.h` header file to include libpq++ class definitions (and declarations). Inside the `main()` function, you instantiate a `PgConnection` object. The `PgConnection` constructor uses the connection string that you provide to establish a database connection.

1. If you are a die-hard C programmer (like me), think of a class as a `typedef`, an object as a variable whose type is the class; data members as...well, data members; and member functions as function pointers stored within a structure. The analogies aren't perfect, and a C++ purist would probably condemn my ancestors and descendants for suggesting them, but I found the comparisons useful when I cut my first C++ teeth.

In this example, I provided the `PgConnection` constructor with an empty connection string—that means that you will make a connection with a default set of connection options. If you want, you can provide a connection string such as

```
PgConnection conn( "dbname=accounting user=korry password=cows" );
```

The connection string format may look familiar—the `PgConnection` constructor accepts the same set of connection options that are used by libpq's `PQconnectdb()` function, which was discussed in Chapter 8, "The PostgreSQL C API—libpq (Client Applications)."

Notice that I don't have any cleanup code in `client1.cpp`. The `PgConnection` constructor takes care of tearing down the server connection when the `PgConnection` object goes out of scope (at the end of the `main()` function).

Client 2—Adding Error Checking

You may have noticed (in `client1.cpp`) that I did not wrap the definition of the conn variable inside a `try{} catch{}` block. The `PgConnection` constructor does not throw any exceptions. If the `PgConnection` constructor doesn't throw an exception on failure and it doesn't return a status value, how do you tell whether the connection attempt failed?

The next code example (see Listing 10.2) shows you how to detect a connection failure.

Listing 10.2 `client2.cpp`

```
/* client2.cpp */

#include <libpq++.h>
#include <iostream.h>

int main( int argc, char * argv[] )
{
    PgConnection connect( "" );

    if( connect.ConnectionBad())
    {
        cout << "Connection was unsuccessful..." << endl
             << "Error message returned: "
             << connect.ErrorMessage() << endl;

        return( 1 );
    }
}
```

After the `connect` object is initialized, you can call either the `PgConnection::ConnectionBad()` or `PgConnection::Status()` member functions to determine the success or failure of the connection attempt.

The `PgConnection::ConnectionBad()` member function returns a non-zero value if the connection attempt failed. You could instead use the `PgConnection::Status()` member function, which returns either `CONNECTION_OK` or `CONNECTION_BAD`. You can use whichever of these two functions you find more convenient—they are completely interchangeable.

If the connection attempt has failed, you probably want to know what went wrong. The `PgConnection::ErrorMessage()` function returns an error message in the form of a `NULL`-terminated string. The error messages returned by `PgConnection::ErrorMessage()` are the same as those returned by the `PQerrorMessage()` function provided by libpq.

Besides the constructor that takes a connection string, `PgConnection` also provides a protected default constructor (that is, a constructor that takes zero arguments). The default constructor does *not* connect to a database. Instead, the default constructor simply initializes the `PgConnection` object. You would use the `PgConnection::Connect()` function later to create a connection. Using the default constructor gives you more control over the timing of the connection process—you may want to allocate a `PgConnection` object in one function, but defer the connection attempt until a later time. Notice that the default constructor is "protected"—you can't use that constructor unless you create a new class that inherits from `PgConnection`.

The Relationship Between libpq and libpq++

I mentioned earlier that libpq++ is a wrapper around the libpq API. The `PgConnection` class is a wrapper around a `PgConn *`. If you were to look at the source code for the `PgConnection::ErrorMessage()` function you would see

```
const char* PgConnection::ErrorMessage()
{
    return (const char *)PQerrorMessage(pgConn);
}
```

Each `PgConnection` object contains a `PgConn *`. The member functions provided by `PgConnection` correspond closely to the set of libpq functions requiring a `PgConn *`.

If the `PgConnection` class doesn't provide a function that you need, you can get to the embedded `PgConn *`, even though it is declared as `protected`, by creating your own class that inherits from PgConnection.

Now that you know how to attempt a database connection and how to tell whether the connection succeeded, let's look at the code required to process a simple query.

Client 3—Processing Queries

For the rest of the examples in this chapter, I will use the Qt library to build the user interface. Qt is a toolkit that you can use to build complete, attractive GUI applications for Unix (Linux) and Windows systems. Using Qt complicates the code, but I hope you find that the results are worth it. To use any of these examples, you must be running in a GUI environment (either the X Window System or Microsoft Windows). The resulting applications are graphical in nature and cannot be executed without a windowing environment.

The `PgConnection` class doesn't really provide much functionality. Using a `PgConnection` object, you can make a connection attempt, determine whether the connection attempt succeeded or failed, and execute a simple command. You can't use a `PgConnection` object to retrieve result set information. To do that, you need a different kind of object—a `PgDatabase`. The `PgDatabase` class inherits directly from `PgConnection`. Anything that you can do with a `PgConnection` object, you can also do with a `PgDatabase` object (but the reverse is not true). The `PgDatabase` class exposes member functions that you can use to process result set information. In the discussion that follows, I'll be talking about member functions exposed by `PgConnection` and `PgDatabase`. Keep in mind that because `PgDatabase` inherits from `PgConnection`, you can call `PgConnection` member functions using a `PgDatabase` object.

`PgDatabase` (and the `PgConnection` base class) provide three different member functions that you can use to execute a query.

First, `int PgConnection::ExecTuplesOk(const char *query)` sends a query to the backend and waits for a result set to be accumulated. `ExecTuplesOk()` should be used when you need to execute a query that returns rows (as opposed to a command, such as `INSERT`, that returns a simple result: the `OID` of the new row). `ExecTuplesOk()` returns a non-zero value if the given string was a query and the query was successful.

Next, `int PgConnection::ExecCommandOk(const char *query)` is identical to `ExecTuplesOk()`, except that it should be used for commands (rather than queries that can return rows). You would use `ExecCommandOk()` to execute commands such as `INSERT`, `DELETE`, or `CREATE TABLE`—those commands that return a simple result, rather than an arbitrary number of rows. `ExecCommandOk()` returns a non-zero value if the given string was a command and the command executed successfully.

`ExecStatusType PgConnection::Exec(const char* query)` is a general-purpose function that can execute either a command or a query. The `Exec()` member function returns a value that is equal to one of the enumeration members shown in Table 10.1.

Table 10.1 `PgConnection::Exec()` **Return Values**

Return Value	Meaning
`PGRES_EMPTY_QUERY`	The given string did not contain a command
`PGRES_COMMAND_OK`	The given string contained a command and the command succeeded
`PGRES_TUPLES_OK`	The given string contained a query and the query succeeded
`PGRES_COPY_OUT`	A copy out operation has started
`PGRES_COPY_IN`	A copy in operation has started
`PGRES_BAD_RESPONSE`	A bad response was received from the server
`PGRES_NONFATAL_ERROR`	A non-fatal error has occurred
`PGRES_FATAL_ERROR`	A fatal error has occurred

The first five values in Table 10.1 indicate success.

If any of these query execution member functions indicates that an error (PGRES_BAD_RESPONSE, PGRES_NONFATAL_ERROR, or PGRES_FATAL_ERROR) has occurred, you can call the `const char *PgConnection::ErrorMessage()` function to retrieve the text of the error message.

Now, let's see how some of the query execution functions in a real application. The next client application that we'll look at, `qt-query` (see Listing 10.3), executes a single query and, if successful, displays the results in tabular form. When you run this program, you supply a query and an optional connection string on the command line—for example:

```
./qt-query "SELECT * FROM tapes" "dbname=movies"
```

`qt-query` attempts to connect to the specified database or the default database if you don't include the second command-line argument. If the connection attempt fails, you'll see an error message similar to the one shown in Figure 10.1.

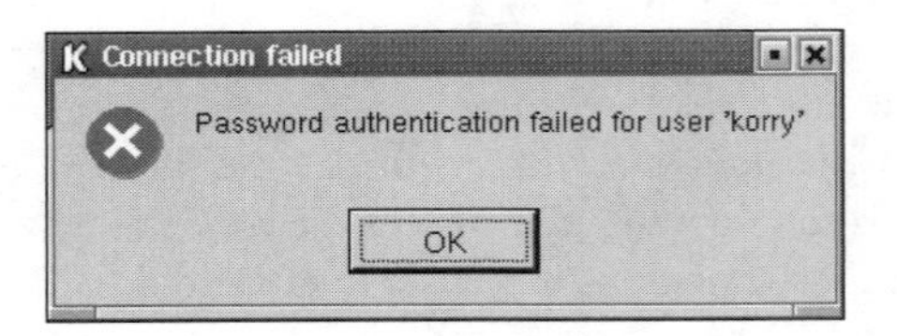

Figure 10.1 qt-query error message.

If the connection attempt is successful, qt-query will send the query string (from the first command-line argument) to the server and display the results. If the query fails, you will see a message similar to the one shown in Figure 10.1 (although the message will be different). If the query is successful, you will see the results in a window similar to that shown in Figure 10.2.

qt-query

	tape_id	title	box
1	AB-12345	The Godfather	27356
2	AB-67472	The Godfather	27356
3	MC-68873	Casablanca	27343
4	OW-41221	Citizen Kane	27350
5	AH-54706	Rear Window	27361
6	AA-1234	Casablanca2	27642

Quit

Figure 10.2 qt-query results.

(Note: As in previous chapters, I'll start adding line numbers as the code listings become longer.)

Listing 10.3 qt-query.h

```
 1 /* qt-query.h */
 2
 3 class MyTable : public QTable
 4 {
 5 public:
 6
 7   MyTable( QWidget * parent, const char* connect, const char* query );
 8
 9   PgDatabase * db;
10
11
12 };
13
14 class MyMain : public QWidget
15 {
16
17 public:
18   MyMain( const char * connect, const char * query );
19
20 private:
21
22   MyTable    * table;
23
24 };
```

I've declared two classes: `MyTable` and `MyMain`.

The `MyTable` class inherits from Qt's `QTable` widget. `QTable` is a class that displays data in a tabular format—you can see an example in Figure 10.2.

`MyMain` inherits from `Qwidget`—a basic widget control that you will use to contain the other controls (a Quit button and the QTable widget) that you create.

Next, let's look at the implementation of these two classes. In Listings 10.4a and 10.4b, I've included the source code for three functions. The first two, `main()` and the `MyMain::MyMain()` constructor, are dealing primarily with Qt. The last function, `MyTable::MyTable()`, is where you start using the libpq++ classes to connect to a database, execute a query, and display the results.

If you aren't interested in the details of building a Qt application, you can skip ahead to Listing 10.4b.

Listing 10.4a qt-query.cpp

```
1 /* qt-query.cpp */
2
3 #include <qapplication.h>    // QT Basic application classes
4 #include <qwidget.h>         // QT Basic widget class
5 #include <qtable.h>          // QT Table widget
```

Listing 10.4a **Continued**

```
 6 #include <qmessagebox.h>      // QT MessageBox widget
 7 #include <qlayout.h>          // QT Layout manager
 8 #include <qpushbutton.h>      // QT Pushbutton widget
 9
10 #include <libpq++.h>          // PostgreSQL libpq++ API
11 #include <iostream.h>         // Standard C++ io library
12
13 #include "qt-query.h"
14
15 int main( int argc, char * argv[] )
16 {
17   QApplication app( argc, argv );
18   MyMain       win( app.argv()[2], app.argv()[1] );
19
20   app.setMainWidget( &win );
21
22   win.show();
23   app.exec();
24   return( 0 );
25 }
26 MyMain::MyMain( const char * connect, const char * query )
27 {
28   QVBoxLayout *  vbox    = new QVBoxLayout( this );
29
30   table = new MyTable( this, connect ? connect : "", query );
31
32   QPushButton * quit = new QPushButton( "Quit", this );
33
34   connect( quit, SIGNAL( clicked()), qApp, SLOT( quit()));
35
36   vbox->addWidget( table );
37   vbox->addWidget( quit );
38
39 }
```

The first few lines of `qt-query.cpp` are used to `#include` various Qt header files. Each Qt class that you use is declared in a separate header file.

The `main()` function is purely concerned with setting up a Qt application. You start by defining a `QApplication` object—every Qt application must have a QApplication. Next, you define a `MyMain` object (I'll explain this class in a moment). When you run this program, you have to provide at least one command-line argument. The first argument is a query string. The second argument, if present, should be a connection string (something like `dbname=movies password=cows`). The second argument is a query string. The `QApplication` object examines the command line before you get a chance to parse it apart (`QApplication` may remove Qt-specific arguments from the command line).

To gain access to the post-processed command line, I use the `app->argv()` function to pass the first two arguments to the `MyMain` constructor. Line 20 tells the Qt library that you want to use the `MyMain` widget as the main application window. Lines 22 and 23 are used to start the Qt application.

Next, let's examine the `MyMain` constructor. Because you are writing a GUI application, there is a little bit of scaffolding that you have to include in your code to handle screen layout. You will use a layout manager to handle screen layout. The `QVBoxLayout` manager class gives you an easy way to arrange components within a vertical box (in other words, the widgets that you add to the layout manager are stacked vertically).

You can see the layout that you are trying to generate in Figure 10.3. The thick black line surrounding the `QTable` and `QPushButton` shows the `QVBoxLayout` (it will actually be invisible when you run the client; I'm just showing it here so you have some idea of its function). The `QPushButton` widget appears at the bottom of the `QVBoxLayout` and the `QTable` consumes the remaining real estate.

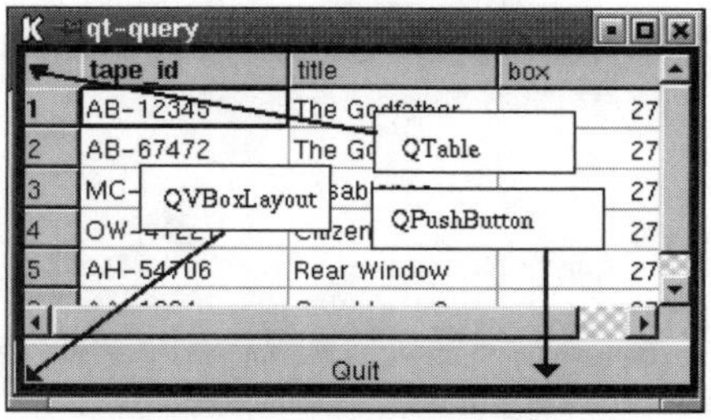

Figure 10.3 qt-query widget layout.

Line 30, defines a new `MyTable` object, sending it the connection string and query text. Most of the interesting stuff happens in the `MyTable` constructor, and I'll describe that function next.

Line 32 creates a pushbutton (with the label Quit), and line 34 arranges for the button to do something useful when you press it (in this case, you connect the `clicked()` signal with the applications `quit()` slot).

Signals and Slots—The Qt Event Handling Architecture

In this context, *signal* and *slot* refer to the way that you wire together an action and a behavior in a Qt application. A widget fires a signal whenever an event occurs that affects that widget; for example, a `QPushButton` widget fires the `clicked()` signal when the user clicks on the button. A slot is a member function that can be connected to a signal. You are wiring the `click()` signal from your `QPushButton` widget to the `quit()` slot of the qApp object. When the user clicks on the `QPushButton`, it fires a `click()` signal, which is intercepted by the qApp's `quit()` function. The `quit()` function causes the application to exit. That's pretty much all you need to know about signals and slots.

Lines 36 and 37 add the table widget and the pushbutton to your layout manager. Because you add the table widget first, it is at the top of the window and the pushbutton appears at the bottom of the window.

Now let's see the interesting code—the `MyTable` constructor (shown in Listing 10.4b) is where you get back to interacting with libpq++.

Listing 10.4b `qt-query.cpp`

```
41 MyTable::MyTable( QWidget * parent,
42      const char * connect,
43      const char * query )
44   : QTable( parent )
45 {
46   db = new PgDatabase( connect ? connect : "" );
47
48   if( db->ConnectionBad())
49   {
50     QMessageBox::critical( 0, "Connection failed",
51       db->ErrorMessage());
52     exit( 1 );
53   }
54
55   if( db->ExecTuplesOk( query ? query : "" ))
56   {
57     setNumRows( db->Tuples());
58     setNumCols( db->Fields());
59
60     for( int col = 0; col < db->Fields(); col++ )
61     {
62       horizontalHeader()->setLabel( col, db->FieldName( col ));
63     }
64
65     for( int row = 0; row < db->Tuples(); row++ )
66     {
67       for( int col = 0; col < db->Fields(); col++ )
68       {
69         setText( row, col, db->GetValue( row, col ));
70       }
71     }
72   }
73   else
74   {
75     QMessageBox::critical( 0, "Query failed", db->ErrorMessage());
76     exit( 1 );
77   }
78 }
```

Line 46 creates a new PgDatabase object—the connection string that comes from the command-line argument one passes through. Recall that there are two constructors for a PgDatabase object—the one that you are using expects a connection string and actually attempts to make a connection. If the connection attempt fails, a message displays and exits the entire application. Note that you use the PgDatabase::ErrorMessage() function to retrieve the error text and then display the reason for failure.

Line 55 executes the query text. If the query succeeds, you start filling our table widget with the result set. (If the query fails, line 75 displays the reason for failure and exit.)

The QTable widget makes it easy to build a nicely formatted table. Start by defining the number of rows and columns that you want in your table. How many rows do you want? The PgDatabase::Tuples() member function tells you how many rows in the result set. The PgDatabase::Fields() member function tells you how many columns that you need. After the table is properly sized, you want to build the column headers. PgDatabase::FieldName() returns the name of each field in the result set, and you just pass along that information to the horizontalHeader() component of our QTable.

Finally, you fill the table with the result set. The PgDatabase::GetValue() member function returns one field (within a given row) in the form of a NULL-terminated string. The QTable::setText() member function fills a given cell with a string. It can't get much easier than that.

When you run this program and click the Quit button, you may notice an ugly error message (Unexpected EOF on client connection)—if you don't see the error, it will appear in your PostgreSQL server log. The database server generates this error message if you forget to close the database connection before your program ends. When you use the PgDatabase (or PgConnection) class, the database connection is established by the class constructor and torn down by the class destructor. In this client application (qt-query), the destructor won't execute when you click the Quit button—the Qt library calls exit() and doesn't give your C++ objects a chance to clean up themselves. I'll show you how to take care of this problem a little later in this chapter (see Listing 10.9e for more information).

Working with Transactions

The libpq++ library provides a class that makes it easy to work with transactions: PgTransaction. A *transaction* is a group of one or more SQL commands that have a handy property: Either all the commands complete, or none of the commands complete. This is important in many applications in which you don't want to leave the database in an unknown state because some modification (or modifications) did not run to completion. When you wrap the modifications within a single transaction, PostgreSQL guarantees that the modifications are treated *atomically*; that is, all the modifications persist, or none of them persists.

The PgTransaction class inherits directly from PgDatabase (which means that all the public member functions exposed by PgDatabase are available through a PgTransaction object as well). You can use the PgDatabase or PgConnection classes to manage transactions, but you have to execute the BEGIN WORK, COMMIT, and ROLLBACK commands yourself. The PgTransaction class provides an interesting alternative: It uses the lifetime of a C++ object to mark the beginning and ending points of a transaction.

Recall that when you create a PgDatabase object, the constructor expects a connection string and uses that string to establish a database connection. The constructor for a PgTransaction works the same way. Here is a code snippet that shows how to instantiate a PgTransaction object:

```
int main( int argc, char * argv[] )
{
    PgTransaction  tran( argv[1] ? argv[1] : "" );

    if( tran.ConnectionBad())
    {
        cout << "Connection failed" << endl
             << tran.ErrorMessage() << endl;
    }
    else
    {
        cout << "Connection ok" << endl;
    }
}
```

When the constructor for tran executes, it attempts to establish a database connection and then executes a BEGIN WORK command—this starts a new transaction. You can now use the PgTransaction object in the same way that you would use a PgDatabase object (remember that PgTransaction inherits from PgDatabase).

When the PgTransaction is destroyed (in this case, it goes out of scope at the end of main()), the PgTransaction destructor closes out the transaction. In PostgreSQL releases prior to 7.2, the PgTransaction destructor executes an END (or COMMIT) command. Starting in version 7.2, PgTransaction destructor will ABORT (or ROLLBACK) the transaction if you have not committed it.

So you can see that all the operations that you perform using a PgTransaction object are executed within a transaction block. The constructor starts a transaction and the destructor ends the transaction.

PgTransaction defines two protected member functions: BeginTransaction() and EndTransaction(). Because these member functions are protected (rather than private), you can manage the transaction yourself from a derived class. You might, for example, extend the PgTransaction class to execute a ROLLBACK command if a fatal error occurs.

One important note here: You probably won't use the PgTransaction class in complex applications. Each time you instantiate a PgTransaction object, you establish a new database connection. Each time a PgTransaction object is destroyed, the database connection is torn down. Those are expensive operations. Most likely, you will want to use a stripped-down `PgDatabase` object and execute `BEGIN`, `COMMIT`, and `ROLLBACK` commands yourself.

Another alternative is to create your own class to solve the connection/teardown performance problem. Listing 10.5 is a short example that shows how you might construct such a class.

Listing 10.5 `persist-tran.cpp`

```
 1 /* persist-tran.cpp */
 2 #include <libpq++.h>
 3 #include <iostream.h>
 4
 5 class Transaction
 6 {
 7 public:
 8
 9   Transaction( PgDatabase & db );
10   ~Transaction();
11
12   PgDatabase & db;
13 };
14
15 Transaction::Transaction( PgDatabase & myDb )
16   : db( myDb )
17 {
18   if( db.Status() == CONNECTION_OK )
19   {
20     (void)db.Exec( "BEGIN" );
21   }
22 }
23
24 Transaction::~Transaction()
25 {
26   if( db.Status() == CONNECTION_OK )
27   {
28     (void)db.Exec( "COMMIT" );
29   }
30 }
31
32 void do_transaction( PgDatabase & db )
33 {
34   Transaction  tran( db );
35
36   tran.db.Exec( "update customers set balance = balance * 1.10::numeric" );
37
38 }
39
```

Listing 10.5 **Continued**

```
40 int main( int argc, char * argv[] )
41 {
42   PgDatabase db( argv[1] ? argv[1]: "" );
43
44   if( db.Status() != CONNECTION_OK )
45   {
46     cout << "Connection failed" << endl << db.ErrorMessage() << endl;
47   }
48   else
49   {
50     do_transaction( db );
51   }
52 }
```

The `Transaction` class encapsulates a transaction, much as a `PgTransaction` would. The difference between the two is that a `Transaction` object works with an existing database connection, rather than creating a new one.

The `main()` function starts by creating a `PgDatabase` object. If the `PgDatabase` object is connected to a database, you pass that object to the `do_transaction()` function.

`do_transaction()` starts by creating a `Transaction` object—the constructor for a `Transaction` requires a `PgDatabase` reference. At this point, the `Transaction` object has access to a database connection. Take a look at the constructor function for `Transaction`: When a `Transaction` object is created, it immediately begins a new transaction. Likewise, the destructor function will `COMMIT` the transaction (on the server) when the transaction goes out of scope.

Working with Cursors

Now that you know how to work with a transaction using `PgTransaction`, let's look at a class that extends `PgTransaction` to provide an easy-to-use cursor interface: `PgCursor`.

A *cursor* is a mechanism that allows an application to process the rows in a result set in smaller chunks, rather than having to deal with the entire result set at once. SQL is a set-oriented language, but programmers using procedural languages (such as C++) find it easier to deal with one row at a time.

The `PgCursor` class encapsulates cursor operations. `PgCursor` inherits from `PgTransaction` (which inherits from `PgDatabase`, which inherits from `PgConnection`), so you can do anything with a `PgCursor` object that you can do with the base classes.

The constructor for a `PgCursor` object requires two arguments: a connection string and a cursor name. When you instantiate a `PgCursor` object, the constructor will establish a database connection and remember the cursor name (the cursor isn't active at this point; you still have to provide the query for the cursor).

After the database connection is successfully established (remember that you still need to check for connection success yourself), you can use the `PgCursor::Declare()` member function to create the cursor. `Declare()` expects two arguments: the query text and an indicator that specifies whether the cursor should be a binary cursor. (Remember from Chapter 8 that a binary cursor returns data in PostgreSQL-internal form and a non-binary cursor returns data in the form of `NULL`-terminated strings.)

```
int main( int argc, char * argv[] )
{
    PgCursor  cursor( "dbname=accounting", "next_record");

    if( cursor.ConnectionBad())
    {
        cout << "Connection failed" << endl
             << cursor.ErrorMessage() << endl;
    }
    else
    {
        cout << "Connection ok" << endl;
    }

    if( !cursor.Declare( "select * from returns", 0 ))
    {
        cout << "DECLARE failed:" << endl
             << cursor.ErrorMessage() << endl;
    }
}
```

The call to `cursor.Declare()` sends the following command to the server:

```
DECLARE next_record CURSOR FOR select * from returns
```

If the `DECLARE` command fails, the `Declare()` function will return `0`.

Now that you have established a cursor, there are three member functions that you can use to control the cursor:

```
int Fetch( const char* dir = "FORWARD" )
int Fetch( unsigned num, const char* dir = "FORWARD" );
int Close();
```

Each of the `Fetch()` functions sends a `FETCH` command to the server. The first `Fetch()` function sends a `FETCH ALL` command to the server. You can use the second `Fetch()` function to fetch a specific number of rows. By default, each `FETCH` command is a `FORWARD` fetch, and you can specify other options using the `dir` parameter.

Now let's look at a sample that shows how to use the `Fetch()` functions with a Qt Table widget. When you run this program, you provide two command-line arguments: a connection string and a `select` statement. For example, if you invoke the application as

```
$ ./qt-cursor "select * from pg_tables" "dbname=movies"
```

you will see a screen similar to that shown in Figure 10.4.

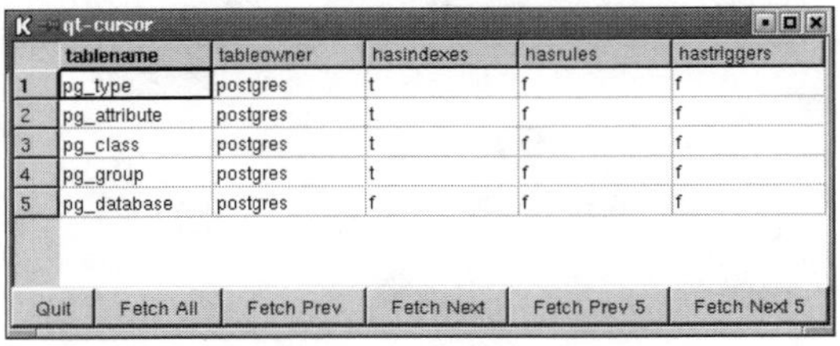

qt-cursor

	tablename	tableowner	hasindexes	hasrules	hastriggers
1	pg_type	postgres	t	f	f
2	pg_attribute	postgres	t	f	f
3	pg_class	postgres	t	f	f
4	pg_group	postgres	t	f	f
5	pg_database	postgres	f	f	f

Quit | Fetch All | Fetch Prev | Fetch Next | Fetch Prev 5 | Fetch Next 5

Figure 10.4 Sample qt-cursor display.

You can press any of the Fetch buttons at the bottom of the window to experiment with the various cursor operations.

Like the previous example, this application uses the Qt toolkit to construct the user interface. Also like the previous example, there is some extra setup work that you have to do in order to build a Qt application. Let's start by looking at the class declarations (see Listing 10.6).

Listing 10.6 `qt-cursor.h`

```
 1 /* qt-cursor.h */
 2
 3 class MyTable : public QTable
 4 {
 5   Q_OBJECT
 6
 7 public:
 8
 9   MyTable( QWidget * parent, const char * connect, const char * query );
10
11   PgCursor * cursor;
12
13 public slots:
14  void fetch( int id );
15
16 private:
17  void buildTable( void );
18
19 };
20
```

Listing 10.6 **Continued**

```
21 class MyMain : public QWidget
22 {
23
24 public:
25   MyMain( const char * connect, const char * query );
26
27 private:
28  MyTable   * table;
29
30 };
```

Listing 10.6 shows the `qt-cursor.h` file. This file declares the two classes that you will need to build: `MyTable` and `MyMain`. If you look ahead to Listing 10.7 (`qt-cursor.cpp`), you may notice that I don't `#include "qt-cursor.h"`; instead, I `#include "qt-cursor.moc"`. Why? The `MyTable` class (at lines 13 and 14)declares a new slot. You might remember (from the initial discussion of Qt earlier in this chapter) that a slot is a member function that can be connected to a signal (a signal is an even, such as a mouse click). If you tried to `#include` the `qt-cursor.h` file as written, your C++ compiler would complain about the word "slots" at line 13. Instead, any header file that defines a new Qt slot must be processed by the moc preprocessor. When you run a header file through moc, the preprocessor will produce an equivalent `.moc` file that can be compiled by a C++ compiler. The `makefile` included with the sample code for this book takes care of running the moc preprocessor for you.

Listing 10.7 `qt-cursor.cpp`

```
 1 /* qt-cursor.cpp */
 2
 3 #include <qapplication.h>     // QT Basic application classes
 4 #include <qwidget.h>          // QT Basic widget class
 5 #include <qtable.h>           // QT Table widget
 6 #include <qmessagebox.h>      // QT MessageBox widget
 7 #include <qlayout.h>          // QT Layout manager
 8 #include <qpushbutton.h>      // QT Pushbutton widget
 9 #include <qhbuttongroup.h>    // QT Button group widget
10
11 #include <libpq++.h>          // PostgreSQL libpq++ API
12 #include <iostream.h>         // Standard C++ io library
13
14 #include "qt-cursor.moc"
15
16 void main( int argc, char * argv[] )
17 {
18   QApplication app( argc, argv );
19   MyMain       win( app.argv()[2], app.argv()[1] );
```

Listing 10.7 **Continued**

```
20
21   app.setMainWidget( &win );
22
23   win.show();
24   app.exec();
25 }
26
27 MyMain::MyMain( const char * connect, const char * query )
28 {
29   QVBoxLayout   * vbox  = new QVBoxLayout( this );
30   QHButtonGroup * group = new QHButtonGroup( this );
31
32   table = new MyTable( this, connect ? connect : "", query );
33
34   new QPushButton( "Quit", group );        // id = 0
35   new QPushButton( "Fetch All", group );   // id = 1
36   new QPushButton( "Fetch Prev", group ); // id = 2
37   new QPushButton( "Fetch Next", group ); // id = 3
38   new QPushButton( "Prev 5", group );      // id = 4
39   new QPushButton( "Next 5", group );      // id = 5
40
41   vbox->addWidget( table );
42   vbox->addWidget( group );
43
44   connect( group, SIGNAL( clicked( int )),
45   table, SLOT( fetch( int )));
46 }
47
48 void MyTable::fetch( int id )
49 {
50   int result;
51
52   switch( id )
53   {
54     case 0:
55       QApplication::exit( 0 );
56       break;
57
58     case 1:  // Fetch All
59       result = cursor->Fetch();
60       break;
61
62     case 2:  // Fetch Previous
63       result = cursor->Fetch( 1, "backward" );
64       break;
65
```

Listing 10.7 **Continued**

```
 66     case 3:  // Fetch Next
 67       result = cursor->Fetch( 1, "forward" );
 68       break;
 69
 70     case 4:  // Fetch Previous 5
 71       result = cursor->Fetch( 5, "backward" );
 72       break;
 73
 74     case 5:  // Fetch Next 5
 75       result = cursor->Fetch( 5, "forward" );
 76       break;
 77   }
 78
 79   if( result == 0 )
 80   {
 81     QMessageBox::critical( 0, "fetch failed",
 82     cursor->ErrorMessage());
 83   }
 84   else
 85   {
 86     buildTable();
 87   }
 88 }
 89
 90 void MyTable::buildTable( void )
 91 {
 92   setNumRows( cursor->Tuples());
 93   setNumCols( cursor->Fields());
 94
 95   for( int col = 0; col < cursor->Fields(); col++ )
 96   {
 97      horizontalHeader()->setLabel( col, cursor->FieldName( col ));
 98   }
 99
100   for( int row = 0; row < cursor->Tuples(); row++ )
101   {
102     for( int col = 0; col < cursor->Fields(); col++ )
103     {
104       setText( row, col, cursor->GetValue( row, col ));
105     }
106   }
107 }
108
109 MyTable::MyTable( QWidget * parent,
110   const char * connect,
```

Listing 10.7 **Continued**

```
111     const char * query )
112     : QTable( parent )
113 {
114     cursor = new PgCursor( connect, "my_cursor" );
115
116     if( cursor->ConnectionBad())
117     {
118       QMessageBox::critical( 0, "Connection failed",
119       cursor->ErrorMessage());
120       exit( -1 );
121     }
122
123     if( !cursor->Declare( query ))
124     {
125       QMessageBox::critical( 0, "Query failed",
126       cursor->ErrorMessage());
127       exit( -1 );
128     }
129 }
```

Let's start by looking at the `MyMain::MyMain()` constructor This function creates the bulk of your user interface. The main window has a table positioned at the top and a row of buttons at the bottom. The `QVBoxLayout` object stacks the table over the buttons, and the `QHButtonGroup` arranges the buttons in a horizontal row.

Line 32 creates a new `MyTable` object, which I'll discuss in a moment.

Next, you create the buttons. Because you are looking at the `PgCursor::Fetch()` methods, I've created a button for each of the major operations.

The remainder of the `MyMain::MyMain()` constructor is devoted to wiring the buttons and the table into the Qt API. Rather than managing each button individually, you create a `QHButtonGroup` object that manages the entire group. When you create each button, you specify that the parent of the button is a `QHButtonGroup`. Each button is assigned an `id`, starting at 0 (the buttons are automatically assigned an `id` based on the order of creation). The call to `connect()` arranges for the Qt library to call `MyTable::fetch( int )` whenever you press one of the buttons within the button group. Qt passes the `id` of the selected button as the one and only parameter.

Next, let's look at the `MyTable` constructor. You start building a `MyTable` object by creating a new `PgCursor` object. As usual, pass a connection string to the `PgCursor` constructor and provide a cursor name. At this point, the `PgCursor` object has connected to the database, but it hasn't actually executed any commands yet. It remembers the name of the cursor, but it won't actually create the cursor until you call the `Declare()` member function.

When you call the `Declare()` function, you are executing a command on the server. In this example, you send the following command:

```
DECLARE my_cursor CURSOR FOR SELECT * FROM pg_tables;
```

If anything goes wrong with the DECLARE ... CURSOR command, the Declare() function will return 0.

After the MyTable constructor completes, the Qt library displays the (empty) table to the user and waits for a button press.

When you press one of the Fetch buttons, Qt will call the MyTable::fetch() function, giving you the button id as a parameter. Inside of MyTable::fetch(), you examine the button id and decide which of the PgCursor::Fetch() functions to call. Table 10.2 shows you the correspondence between button labels and calls to Fetch():

Table 10.2 **PGCursor::Fetch() Function Examples**

Button Label	Calls
Fetch All	Fetch()
Fetch Prev	Fetch(1, "backward")
Fetch Next	Fetch(1, "forward")
Fetch Prev 5	Fetch(5, "backward")
Fetch Next 5	Fetch(5, "forward")

Let's look at what happens the first time you press one of the Fetch buttons, say Fetch Next 5. Before calling PgCursor::Fetch(), the PgCursor object has just processed a DECLARE ... CURSOR command. The result set for this object reflects the status of the DECLARE ... CURSOR command. If you were to call cursor->Tuples() or cursor->Fields() at this point, you would find that the DECLARE ... CURSOR statement returns 0 rows and 0 columns. When you call the PgCursor::Fetch() function, the result set for the DECLARE ... CURSOR command is replaced by the result set for a FETCH command. At this point, a call to cursor->Tuples() would return 5 (or fewer if there are fewer than five rows left in the cursor). After the result set has been assembled, you call buildTable() to actually populate the table control.

The buildTable() function (that follows) makes use of the PgDatabase::FieldName(), PgDatabase::GetValue(), PgDatabase::Tuples(), and PgDatabase::Fields() functions to create the table column headers and the table cells.

```
void MyTable::buildTable( void )
{
  setNumRows( cursor->Tuples());
  setNumCols( cursor->Fields());

  for( int col = 0; col < cursor->Fields(); col++ )
  {
      horizontalHeader()->setLabel( col, cursor->FieldName( col ));
  }

  for( int row = 0; row < cursor->Tuples(); row++ )
  {
```

```
    for( int col = 0; col < cursor->Fields(); col++ )
    {
      setText( row, col, cursor->GetValue( row, col ));
    }
  }
}
```

Working with Large-Objects

Most of the tables that you create are defined in terms of simple data types. You already know that PostgreSQL provides numeric, textual, date-time, geometric, and logical data types. But what data type should you use to store photographs? Or .MP3 audio files?

One answer is a *large-object* (you might also see the term *BLOB*, or *binary-large-object*). A large-object is just an entry in the pg_largeobject system table. PostgreSQL provides a few predefined functions that make it reasonably easy to work large-objects.

A second alternative is the `BYTEA` data type. A column of type `BYTEA` can store an arbitrarily sized string of octets (also known as bytes). The `BYTEA` data type is similar to the `VARCHAR` data type but there are some important differences. First, a `VARCHAR` value cannot hold a character whose value is `0`–I'm not talking about the character '0' whose value is actually 48 (see `http://www.asciitable.com`); I mean the character often called `NULL`. A `BYTEA` value can hold any 8-bit character. Second, a `VARCHAR` value is defined in terms of some specific character set (usually US ASCII). This means that the collation sequence that is used when you compare two `VARCHAR` values may be based on something other than just the numeric value of each byte. When you compare two `BYTEA` values, the relationship between the two values is determined by comparing the numeric value of each character.

Whether you choose to use the large-object interface or the `BYTEA` data type depends mostly on how large your data is and what you need to do with it. A `BYTEA` column can hold up to 1GB—a large-object can hold values larger than 1GB. PostgreSQL provides a few functions that make it easy to load binary data from an external file into a large-object. Loading external data into a `BYTEA` column isn't quite so easy. When you insert data into a `BYTEA` column, you must translate the data into a quoted (also called escaped) form (see Chapter 2, "Working with Data in PostgreSQL"). When you `SELECT` data from a `BYTEA` column, it comes back in quoted form and that's not always easy to work with (you have to parse through the result and unquote it yourself). When you retrieve data from a large-object, you get the same binary data that you put into it, but you have to get at the data using some special functions, described in this section.

For more information on the `BYTEA` data type, refer to Chapter 2. In this section, I'll describe how to work with large-objects using libpq++.

Let's say that you want to add a picture to the tapes table—for each tape, you want to store a photograph of the box that was shipped with the tape. Currently, the tapes table looks like this:

```
CREATE TABLE tapes
(
    tape_id     character(8),
    title       character varying(80)
);
```

Because you aren't actually storing a photograph in this table (remember that large-objects are stored in the pg_largeobject table), you add a large-object identifier instead. A large-object identifier has a data type of OID. Here's what the new tapes table looks like after adding the row reference:

```
CREATE TABLE tapes
(
    tape_id    character(8),
    title      character varying(80),
    photo_id   oid
);
```

It's important to remember that the photo_id column doesn't actually hold a photograph—it holds the address of a row in the pg_largeobjects table.

To store a photo in PostgreSQL, you might use the lo_import() function. lo_import() takes a filename as an argument and returns an oid as a result—for example:

```
INSERT INTO tapes VALUES
(
       'AA-55892',
       'Casablanca',
       lo_import('/tmp/casablanca.jpg' )
);
```

The call to lo_import() opens the /tmp/Casablanca.jpg file, imports the contents of that file into the pg_largeobjects table, and returns the oid of the new large-object—we insert the oid into the photo_id column.

After you have a photo in your database, what can you do with it? It doesn't make a lot of sense to SELECT the photo from a text-based client—you would just see a lot of binary garbage.

You could use the lo_export() function to copy a photo back out to the filesystem. For example:

```
SELECT lo_export( photo_id, '/tmp/casa2.jpg' )
WHERE tape_id = 'AA-5892';
```

If you are using the libpq++ class library, you can use the PgLargeObject class. PgLargeObject inherits from the PgConnection class—anything that you can do with a PgConnection object you can do with a PgLargeObject object.

PgLargeObject offers a few member functions specifically designed for working with large-objects. The PgLargeObject::Import() function imports a file and returns the oid. Of course, there is an Export() function as well.

The other interesting members of the PgLargeObject class are the Open(), Read(), and LSeek() functions. After you Open() a large-object, you can use the LSeek() and Read() functions to read the binary data into your application.

Here is a snippet of code that shows how you might use a PgLargeObject to read a photo (or audio file or whatever) into your application:

```
oid   photo_id = 27642;

PgLargeObject  photo( photo_id, "dbname=movies" );

int size = photo.LSeek( 0, SEEK_END );

void * photo_bits = malloc( size );

photo.LSeek( 0, SEEK_SET );
photo.Read( photo_bits, size );
photo.Close();
```

When you create a PgLargeObject object, you specify a large-object identifier as the first constructor argument and an optional connect string as the second argument. The PgLargeObject constructor connects to the database and opens the specified large-object.

The first call to LSeek() tells you how many bytes you need to allocate to hold the entire picture. The second call to LSeek() positions back to the beginning of the large-object. The call to Read() fills your buffer (photo_bits) with the actual contents of the large-object.

After you have read the large-object into your application, you can take whatever action is appropriate to the object. For example, if the large-object contains an audio file, you might want to play it for the user; if the large-object contains a photograph, you may want to display it. You can't do either of those things using a text-mode user interface (such as psql), but if you are creating your own client application, you can process large-objects however you need.

PgLargeObject exports other member functions to create and delete large-objects from memory (the Import() function creates a large-object based on the contents of a file).

Like the PgTransaction class, you aren't likely to use PgLargeObject directly within a sophisticated application. Each time you create a PgLargeObject, you are spawning a new backend database process (this is expensive). If you need to work with large-objects in a C++ application, you'll probably want to implement your own large-object class that doesn't spawn and then close a new database process for each large-object. I would recommend reading the source code for the `PgLargeObject` class as a starting point for building your own large-object manager class.

Client 4—An Interactive Query Processor

At this point, you should be familiar with the five basic libpq++ classes: `PgConnection`, `PgDatabase`, `PgTransaction`, `PgLargeObject`, and `PgCursor`. The `PgDatabase` class probably forms the basis of most of your libpq++ applications, so I'd like to explore it a bit more for the final application in this chapter.

The `PgDatabase` class exposes all the member functions that you need to process a result set. The following member functions return the number of rows and columns (respectively) returned by a `SELECT` statement:

```
int PgDatabase::Tuples();
int PgDatabase::Fields();
```

The `PgDatabase::CmdTuples()` member function returns the number of rows affected by an `INSERT`, `UPDATE`, or `DELETE` command. If the most recent command was not an `INSERT`, `UPDATE`, or `DELETE`, `PgDatabase::CmdTuples()` will return–1.

```
int CmdTuples();
```

The `PgDatabase::FieldName()` member function returns the name of a field, given a field number.

`PgDatabase::FieldNum()` returns a field number given a field name (or –1 if the given field name is not a member of the result set).

```
const char * PgDatabase::FieldName( int field_num );
int PgDatabase::FieldNum( const char* field_name );
```

`PgDatabase::FieldType()` returns the OID (object ID) of the data type for a given field (you can use the following query to see a list of data types and their OIDs: `select oid, typename from pg_type;`). Notice that you can identify the field in which you are interested by providing either a field name or a field number. This is true for the remainder of the member functions in this section.

```
Oid FieldType( int field_num );
Oid FieldType( const char* field_name );
```

`PgDatabase::PgFieldSize()` returns the size (in bytes) of the given field. The size returned by `PgFieldSize()` represents the amount of space required to store the field on the server; it returns –1 if the field is defined by a variable sized data type.

```
int FieldSize( int field_num );
int FieldSize( const char* field_name );
```

The `PgDatabase::GetValue()`, `PgDatabase::GetIsNull()`, and `PgDatabase::PgGetLength()` member functions return information about a given field within a given row.

```
const char* GetValue( int row_num, int field_num );
const char* GetValue( int row_num, const char* field_name );
bool        GetIsNull( int row_num, int field_num );
bool        GetIsNull( int row_num, const char* field_name );
int         GetLength( int row_num, int field_num );
int         GetLength( int row_num, const char* field_name );
```

Now, let's put the `PgDatabase` class to use in an interactive query program (see Listing 10.8). I'll use the Qt library to build the user interface. In this application, you can enter arbitrary SQL commands; the result set for `SELECT` statements appear in a table, and the results for other commands display in a status bar. Figure 10.5 shows a sample of what you are going to build.

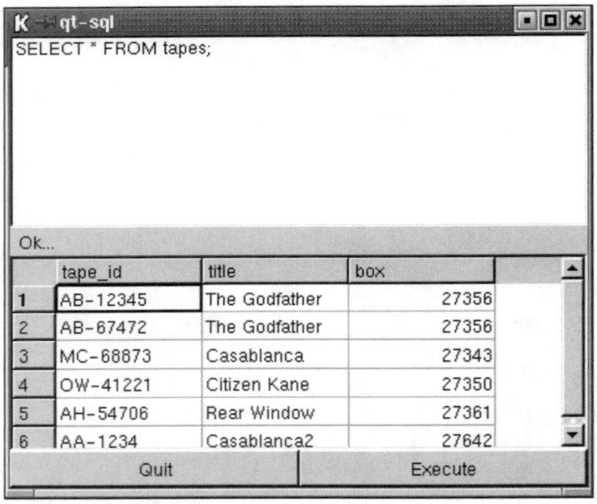

Figure 10.5 qt-query Results.

Listing 10.8 `qt-sql.h`

```
1 /* qt-sql.h */
2
3 class MyTable : public QTable
4 {
5 public:
6
7     MyTable( QWidget * parent, const char * connect );
8
```

Listing 10.8 **Continued**

```
 9      PgDatabase * db;
10
11      void buildTable( void );
12
13 };
14
15 class MyMain : public QWidget
16 {
17   Q_OBJECT
18 public:
19   MyMain( const char * connect );
20
21 public slots:
22   void execute( void );
23   void quit( void );
24
25 private:
26
27 // These are our user-interface components:
28   QMultiLineEdit * edit;
29   QStatusBar     * status;
30   MyTable        * table;
31
32 };
```

You should be familiar with the `MyTable` class by now. `MyTable` is a `QTable` that knows how to work with a `PgDatabase` object. The MyMain class defines the bulk of the user interface for your application. A `MyMain` object is a `QWidget` (container) that contains a table, status bar, and multiline editor.

Listing 10.9a `qt-sql.cpp`

```
 1 /* qt-sql.cpp */
 2
 3 #include <qapplication.h>    // QT Basic application classes
 4 #include <qwidget.h>         // QT Basic widget class
 5 #include <qtable.h>          // QT Table widget
 6 #include <qmessagebox.h>     // QT MessageBox widget
 7 #include <qlayout.h>         // QT Layout manager
 8 #include <qpushbutton.h>     // QT Pushbutton widget
 9 #include <qmultilineedit.h>  // QT MultiLineEdit widget
10 #include <qstatusbar.h>      // QT Statusbar widget
11
12 #include <libpq++.h>         // PostgreSQL libpq++ API
13 #include <iostream.h>        // Standard C++ io library
14
```

Listing 10.9a **Continued**

```
15 #include "qt-sql.moc"
16
17 int main( int argc, char * argv[] )
18 {
19
20   QApplication a( argc, argv );
21   MyMain       w( a.argv()[1] ? a.argv()[1] : "" );
22
23   a.setMainWidget( &w );
24
25   w.show();
26   a.exec();
27  return( 0 );
28 }
```

The `main()` function defines a prototypical Qt application. You start by creating a `QApplication` object and a `MyMain` object and then wire together the two objects by calling the `QApplication::setMainWidget()` function.

Listing 10.9b `qt-sql.cpp`

```
29 MyMain::MyMain( const char * connectStr )
30 {
31   // Establish a reasonable size for our main window
32   resize( 640, 450 );
33
34   // Create two layout helpers -
35   //   the vbox layout object will stack things vertically
36   //   the buttons layout object will hold a row of buttons
37
38   QVBoxLayout *  vbox    = new QVBoxLayout( this );
39   QHBoxLayout *  buttons = new QHBoxLayout();
40
41   //
42   //  Create the user-interface components
43   //
44   edit   = new QMultiLineEdit( this );
45   status = new QStatusBar( this );
46   table  = new MyTable( this, connectStr );
47
48   // remove the resize-grip from the statusbar,
49   // it looks kinda strange in the middle of a
50   // window.
51
52   status->setSizeGripEnabled( FALSE );
53
```

Listing 10.9b **Continued**

```
54  //
55  //  give the keyboard focus to the editor control
56  //
57  edit->setFocus();
58
59  connect( edit, SIGNAL( returnPressed()), this, SLOT( execute()));
60
61  vbox->addWidget( edit );
62  vbox->addWidget( status );
63  vbox->addWidget( table );
64
65  // And finally create the row of buttons at
66  // the bottom of the main window (quit, execute)
67  //
68  vbox->addLayout( buttons );
69
70  QPushButton * quit = new QPushButton( "Quit", this );
71  connect( quit, SIGNAL( clicked()), this, SLOT( quit()));
72
73  QPushButton * exec = new QPushButton( "Execute", this );
74  connect( exec, SIGNAL( clicked()), this, SLOT( execute()));
75
76  buttons->addWidget( quit );
77  buttons->addWidget( exec );
78
79 }
```

The `MyMain` constructor is where you build most of the user interface. You use two layout managers (a `QHBoxLayout` and a `QVBoxLayout`) to take care of widget positioning. The layout managers also reposition and resize the component widgets if you resize the main window—that's a lot of code that you don't have to write. After the editor, status bar, and table have been created, you add each one to the vertical layout manager (the ordering is important—you want the editor on top, the status bar in the middle, and the table control at the bottom, so you have to add them in that order).

You may want to remove the call to `connect()` (on line 59). That particular function call wires the `Return` key to the `MyMain::execute()` function. If you leave that function call in your code, your query will be sent to the server every time you press Return. Some of you will prefer to use multiple lines to structure your queries and you will probably be in the habit of using the Return key to move to the next line of the editor. If you remove the call to `connect()`, you will have to use the `Execute` button.

Listing 10.9c qt-sql.cpp

```
 81 MyTable::MyTable( QWidget * parent, const char * connect )
 82   : QTable( parent )
 83 {
 84   //
 85   //  Create a database connection...
 86   //
 87   db = new PgDatabase( connect );
 88
 89   if( db->ConnectionBad())
 90   {
 91     QMessageBox::critical( 0, "Connection failed",
 92     db->ErrorMessage());
 93     exit( -1 );
 94   }
 95
 96   //  We don't have any table-oriented results to
 97   //  show yet, so hide the table.
 98   //
 99   setNumRows( 0 );
100   setNumCols( 0 );
101 }
```

The `MyTable` constructor creates a database connection and then hides the table control. You display the table whenever you have some results to show to the user.

Listing 10.9d qt-sql.cpp

```
103 void MyMain::execute( void )
104 {
105   //  This function is called whenever the user
106   //  presses the 'Execute' button (or whenever
107   //  the user presses the Return key while the
108   //  edit control has the keyboard focus)
109
110   PgDatabase    * db = table->db;
111   ExecStatusType  result;
112
113   //  Execute whatever the user has entered into
114   //  the edit control
115   //
116   result = db->Exec(( const char *)edit->text());
117
118   //
119   //  Now process the results...
120   //
121   switch( result )
122   {
```

Listing 10.9d **Continued**

```
123     case PGRES_EMPTY_QUERY:
124       status->message( "That was fun..." );
125       break;
126
127     case PGRES_COMMAND_OK:
128       status->message( "Ok" );
129       break;
130
131     case PGRES_TUPLES_OK:
132       status->message( "Ok..." );
133       table->buildTable();
134       break;
135
136     default:
137       status->message( db->ErrorMessage());
138       break;
139   }
140 }
```

The `MyMain::execute()` function is called whenever you want to execute the query string that the user has entered. The `PgDatabase::Exec()` function returns one of the values described in Table 10.1. If the user enters an empty command or a command that will not return any rows (`INSERT` for example), you just add a message to the status bar. If you enter a command that can return rows (for example, `SELECT`), you call `buildTable()` to fill the table control with the result set.

Listing 10.9e `qt-sql.cpp`

```
142 void MyTable::buildTable( void )
143 {
144   //  This function is called to fill in
145   //  the table control.  We want to fill
146   //  the table with the result set.
147
148   setNumRows( db->Tuples());
149   setNumCols( db->Fields());
150
151   //
152   //  First, populate the column headers...
153   //
154   for( int col = 0; col < db->Fields(); col++ )
155   {
156       horizontalHeader()->setLabel( col, db->FieldName( col ));
157   }
158
159   //
```

Listing 10.9e **Continued**

```
160   //  Now, put the data into the table...
161   //
162   for( int row = 0; row < db->Tuples(); row++ )
163   {
164     for( int col = 0; col < db->Fields(); col++ )
165     {
166       setText( row, col, db->GetValue( row, col ));
167     }
168   }
169 }
```

You've already seen `buildTable()` (see Listing 10.7). This function copies the result set into the table control. The `PgDatabase::Fields()` member function tells you how many fields are in the result set, and `PgDatabase::Tuples()` tells you how many rows to expect. `PgDatabase::FieldName()` returns the name of a given field (identified by its field number). And finally, `PgDatabase::GetValue()` returns a pointer to the value (in the form of a `NULL`-terminated string) for a given row and column.

Listing 10.9f shows the `MyMain::quit()` function. This function is called whenever you click the Quit button. You may remember that the `qt-query` client left a nasty message in the server log (and/or on the screen) each time you exited. The `qt-query` application was not closing the database connection properly.

The `PgDatabase` class closes its database connection whenever the destructor function executes. Normally, the destructor function is executed when an object goes out of scope. You allocated the `PgDatabase` object from the heap, which means that it will never go out of scope (until the program ends, which is too late). To ensure that the destructor for `PgDatabase` is executed, you intercept a mouse click on the Quit button and call the `MyMain::quit()` function (see Listing 10.9b, line 71). You can see (at line 177) that we are forcing the *db destructor to execute by using the `delete` operator. When the destructor executes, it closes the database connection, so no more nasty error message.

Listing 10.9f `qt-sql.cpp`

```
171 void MyMain::quit( void )
172 {
173   PgDatabase * db = table->db;
174
175   if( db != NULL )
176   {
177     delete db;
178     db = NULL;
179   }
180
181   qApp->quit();
182
183 }
```

Summary

The libpq++ API provides five related classes that you can use to build client applications written in C++:

- `PgConnection`—Provides a minimal object that can manage a database connection.
- `PgDatabase`—Extends `PgConnection` with a set of member functions that provide access to a result set.
- `PgTransaction`—Extends `PgDatabase` to provide an automatic transaction context.
- `PgCursor`—Extends `PgTransaction` with member functions that manage a cursor.
- `PgLargeObject`—Extends `PgConnection` with member functions for dealing with large-objects.

You are most likely to use the `PgDatabase` and `PgLargeObject` classes in your applications. You might extend the `PgConnection` class if you want to control the connection process more closely. I recommend that you view the `PgTransaction` and `PgCursor` classes as sample code. You probably won't use either of those classes, but you can certainly learn from their implementations.

libpq++ is a wrapper around the libpq C API. If you build your own C++ classes based on `PgConnection`, you can use the entire libpq API because a `PgConnection` object contains a `PGconn *` (and you need a `PGConn *` to use the libpq API).

At the time I am writing this chapter, another C++ API is appearing in the PostgreSQL community. The libpqxx library is a STL-friendly class library that seems to be much more complete than libpq++. libpqxx provides individual classes for dealing with database connections, transactions, cursors, triggers, and result sets. The classes exported by libpqxx provide a number of convenience features. For example, you can iterate through a result set using array indexing (rather than using explicit member functions).

You can find more information about libpqxx at `http://members.ams.chello.nl/j.vermeulen31/proj-libpqxx.html`. By the time this book is published, libpqxx may be an official part of the PostgreSQL distribution.

11

Embedding SQL Commands in C Programs—ecpg

IN THE THREE PREVIOUS CHAPTERS, YOU'VE SEEN how to connect a C or C++ application to a PostgreSQL database by making function calls into a PostgreSQL API. Now you're going to look at a different method for interfacing C applications with PostgreSQL. The ecpg preprocessor and runtime library enable you to embed SQL commands directly into the source code of your application. Rather than making explicit function calls into PostgreSQL, you include specially tagged SQL statements in your C code. The ecpg preprocessor examines your source code and translates the SQL statements into the function calls needed to carry out the operations that you request. When you run the ecpg preprocessor, you feed it a source file that includes both C source code and SQL commands; the preprocessor produces a file that contains only C source code (it translates your SQL commands into function calls) and you then compile the new C file. Using ecpg, you can retrieve PostgreSQL data directly into C variables, and the ecpg runtime library takes care of converting between PostgreSQL data types and C data types.

The ecpg package is great for developing static applications—applications whose SQL requirements are known at the time you write your source code. ecpg can also be used to process *dynamic SQL*. Dynamic SQL is an accepted standard (part of the ANSI SQL3/SQL99 specification) for executing SQL statements that may not be known until the application is actually executing. I'll cover the dynamic SQL features at the end of this chapter, but I don't think that ecpg offers many advantages (over libpq) when dealing with ad hoc queries.

Prerequisites

Because an ecpg application is written in C, you will need a C compiler, the GNU `make` utility, and the ecpg preprocessor and library on your system before you can try the examples in this chapter.

The makefile for this chapter follows:

```
 1 #
 2 # Filename: makefile
 3 #
 4 INCLUDES   = -I/usr/include/pgsql
 5
 6 CFLAGS    += $(INCLUDES) -g
 7 LDFLAGS   += -g
 8 LDLIBS    += -lecpg -lpq
 9 ECPGFLAGS += -c $(INCLUDES)
10 ECPG       = /usr/bin/ecpg
11
12 .SUFFIXES: .pgc
13 .pgc.c:
14         $(ECPG) $(ECPGFLAGS) $?
15
16 ALL  = client1a client1b client2a client2b client2c
17 ALL += client3a client3b client3c client3d client3e client3f
18 ALL += client4.pgc
19
20 all: $(ALL)
21
22 clean:
23         rm -f $(ALL) *~
```

The examples in this chapter follow the normal PostgreSQL convention of naming ecpg source files with the extension .pgc. The makefile rules on lines 11 through 13 tell make that it can convert a .pgc file into a .c file by running the ecpg preprocessor.

For the examples in this chapter, I have used a version of the ecpg package that has not been released in an official distribution at the time of writing. You need to use a version of PostgreSQL later than version 7.2.1 to compile some of the sample applications. (Version 7.2.1 did not include the -c flag that I will discuss later, but releases after 7.2.1 should include that feature.) This feature is not required for most ecpg applications.

Assuming that you have the prerequisites in place, let's start out by developing a simple client that will connect to a database using ecpg.

Client 1—Connecting to the Server

If you have read the previous three chapters, you know that there are two schemes for managing PostgreSQL connections.

In libpq and ODBC, you ask the API to create a connection object (a handle) and then your application keeps track of the connection. When you need to interact with the database, you call an API function and pass the connection object to the API. When you are finished interacting with the database, you ask the API to tear down the connection and destroy the connection object. When you use libpgeasy, the API keeps track of the connection object for you. You still have to ask the API to create a connection and, when you are finished, you must ask the API to tear down the connection, but libpgeasy stores the connection object itself and you never need to worry about it.

The ecpg interface gives you a mixture of these two schemes. Most ecpg applications use a single database connection. If you only need one connection, ecpg will keep track of it for you. If your application needs to work with multiple connections, you can switch between them.

In the libpq and ODBC APIs, a database connection is represented by a handle of some type. In an ecpg application, a database connection is simply a name[1].
Let's start by building a simple client application that connects to a database and then disconnects:

```
/* client1a.pgc */

int main( )
{
    EXEC SQL CONNECT TO movies AS myconnection;

    EXEC SQL DISCONNECT myconnection;

    return( 0 );
}
```

In `client1a`, you create a database connection named `myconnection`. Assuming that the connection attempt is successful, `myconnection` can be used to access the `movies` database. You will notice that you did not have to declare any C variables to keep track of the connection; the ecpg API does that for you—all you have to do is remember the name of the connection. Just like normal C statements, `EXEC SQL` statements are terminated with a semicolon.

If your application doesn't need more than one database connection, you can omit the `AS` *`database`* clause when you create the connection. You can also omit the name in the `DISCONNECT` statement:

```
/* client1b.pgc */

int main( )
{
    EXEC SQL CONNECT TO movies;

    EXEC SQL DISCONNECT;

    return( 0 );
}
```

1. Later in this chapter, I'll show you how to use C variables (called *host* variables in ecpg) within `EXEC SQL` statements. If you use a host variable to specify a connection name, the variable should be a pointer to a null-terminated string.

`client1a.pgc` and `client2a.pgc` are functionally equivalent applications.

You can associate a SQL statement with a named connection using an extended form of the `EXEC SQL` prefix:

```
EXEC SQL AT connection_name sql_statement;
```

If you don't specify an `AT connection_name` clause, ecpg will execute statements using the current connection. When you create a new connection, that connection becomes the current one. You can change the current connection using the `SET CONNECTION TO` command:

```
SET CONNECTION TO connection_name;
```

When you close a connection, you can specify any of the statements shown in Table 11.1.

Table 11.1 **Various Approaches to *DISCONNECT***

Statement	Explanation
`EXEC SQL DISCONNECT connection-name;`	Closes the named connection
`EXEC SQL DISCONNECT;`	Closes the current connection
`EXEC SQL DISCONNECT CURRENT;`	Closes the current connection
`EXEC SQL DISCONNECT ALL;`	Closes all connections

The ecpg Preprocessor

The C compiler obviously won't understand the `EXEC SQL` statements that you must include in an ecpg application. To fix this problem, you have to run the source code for your applications through a preprocessor named `ecpg`.

You can view the syntax expected by the ecpg preprocessor using the `--help` option:

```
$ ecpg --help
ecpg - the postgresql preprocessor, version: 2.8.0
Usage: ecpg:  [-v] [-t]
              [-I include path]
              [ -o output file name]
              [-D define name]
             file1 [file2] ...
```

Let's take a quick peek under the hood to see what the ecpg preprocessor is doing with our source code. I'll run the `client1b.pgc` program through ecpg:

```
$ ecpg client1b.pgc
$ cat client1b.c
/* Processed by ecpg (2.8.0) */
/* These three include files are added by the preprocessor */
#include <ecpgtype.h>
```

```
#include <ecpglib.h>
#include <ecpgerrno.h>
#line 1 "client1b.pgc"

/* client1b.pgc */

int main( )
{
    { ECPGconnect(__LINE__, "movies" , NULL,NULL , NULL, 0); }
#line 5 "client1b.pgc"


    { ECPGdisconnect(__LINE__, "CURRENT");}
#line 7 "client1b.pgc"


    return( 0 );
}
```

The ecpg preprocessor converts `client1b.pgc` into `client1b.c`. You can see that ecpg has inserted quite a bit of code into our application.

First, `ecpg` has inserted some comments and a few `#include` statements. You can usually ignore the `#include` files—they declare the functions and data types that are required by the ecpg library.

Following the `#includes`, ecpg has inserted a C preprocessor directive that you might not have seen before. The `#line` directive tells the C compiler to pretend that it is compiling the given line (and source file)—ecpg inserts these directives so that any error messages produced by the C compiler correspond to the correct line numbers in your original source file. For example, consider what would happen if you had a syntax error in your declaration of the `main()` function. In your original source file (`client1b.pgc`), `main()` is declared at line 4. In the post-processed file, `main()` is declared at line 10. Without the `#line` directives, the C compiler would tell you that an error occurred at line 10 of `client1b.c`. With the `#line` directives, the C compiler will report the error at line 4 of `client1b.pgc`.

Debugging ecpg Applications

Unfortunately, the `#line` directives inserted by the ecpg preprocessor can really confuse most source-level debuggers. If you find that you need to debug an ecpg application, you should run the ecpg preprocessor over your source code, strip the #line directives from the resulting `.c` file, and then compile the `.c` file into an executable. At that point, you will have a program in which the debug symbols correspond to the `.c` file and your debugger should behave properly.

The interesting part of `client1b.c` starts where the preprocessor translated

```
EXEC SQL CONNECT TO movies;
```

into

```
{ ECPGconnect(__LINE__, "movies" , NULL,NULL , NULL, 0); }
```

You can see that ecpg parsed out the EXEC SQL CONNECT command into a simple function call. This is really what ecpg is all about—translating EXEC SQL statements into function calls. The resulting code calls functions defined in the ecpg library.

Connection Strings

When you create a client application using libpq or libpgeasy, you specify a connection string as a series of keyword=value properties. Connecting to a database using ecpg is a bit different. When you connect to a database using ecpg, you can use any of three forms. The first form is considered obsolete but is still accepted by the most recent releases of PostgreSQL:

```
database[@host][:port][AS conn-name][USER username]
```

In this form, you must specify the name of the database to which you want to connect. You can also specify the hostname (or network address), port number (as an integer value), connection name, and username. The username can be in any of the following formats:

```
userid
userid/password
userid IDENTIFIED BY password
userid USING password
```

Each of the next two forms is similar to a URL (Uniform Resource Locator):

```
TCP:POSTGRESQL://host [:port] /database [AS conn-name] [USER username]
UNIX:POSTGRESQL://host [:port] /database [AS conn-name] [USER username]
```

In each of these forms, you specify the type of socket to which you want to connect (either TCP or Unix). If you specify a Unix socket type, the only valid value for the *host* component is localhost, or 127.0.0.1.

The documentation distributed with PostgreSQL says that the */database* component is optional. In releases 7.1 and 7.2, an apparent bug in the preprocessor makes the */database* component mandatory. The 7.1 and 7.2 documentation also suggests that you can specify DEFAULT or USER after EXEC SQL CONNECT TO; these features do not seem to be implemented.

Here are a few sample connection strings, first in the old (obsolete) format:

```
EXEC SQL CONNECT TO movies;

EXEC SQL CONNECT TO movies AS movie_conn;

EXEC SQL CONNECT TO movies USER bruce/cows;

EXEC SQL CONNECT TO movies@arturo:1234 AS remote_movies USER sheila;
```

and now in the new (URL-based) format:

```
EXEC SQL CONNECT TO UNIX:POSTGRESQL://localhost/movies;

EXEC SQL CONNECT TO UNIX:POSTGRESQL://localhost/movies AS movie_conn;

EXEC SQL CONNECT TO UNIX:POSTGRESQL://localhost/movies USER bruce/cows;

EXEC SQL CONNECT TO TCP:POSTGRESQL://arturo:1234/movies
             AS remote_movies USER sheila;
```

Client 2—Adding Error Checking

Now let's move on to see how you can detect and respond to errors. When you create an application that works by calling API functions, you can usually tell whether an operation succeeded or failed by examining the return value. In an ecpg application, your program is not calling PostgreSQL functions (at least at the source code level), so you can't just examine a return code.

The sqlca Structure

Instead, the ecpg library uses a special data structure, the `sqlca`, to communicate failure conditions. Here is the definition of the `sqlca` structure (from `sqlca.h`):

```
struct sqlca
{
   char       sqlcaid[8];
   long       sqlabc;
   long       sqlcode;
   struct
   {
      int    sqlerrml;
      char   sqlerrmc[SQLERRMC_LEN];
   } sqlerrm;
   char       sqlerrp[8];
   long       sqlerrd[6];
   char       sqlwarn[8];
   char       sqlext[8];
};
```

You don't `#include` this file as you would with most header files. The ecpg preprocessor offers a special directive that you should use[2]:

```
EXEC SQL INCLUDE sqlca;
```

2. Starting with PostgreSQL release 7.2, `sqlca` is automatically included in every ecpg program. You don't have to include it yourself.

The difference between a #include and an EXEC SQL INCLUDE is that the ecpg preprocessor can see files that are included using the second form—ecpg ignores #includes. That doesn't mean that you can't use #include files, just remember that the inclusion occurs *after* the ecpg preprocess has finished its work.

The contents of the sqlca structure might seem a bit weird. Okay, they don't just seem weird—they *are* weird.

Let's walk through the members of the sqlca structure. PostgreSQL won't use many of the fields in the sqlca structure—that structure was inherited from the SQL standard.

First, we'll look at the fields that never change. The sqlaid array always contains the string 'SQLCA'. Why? I don't know—history, I suppose. The sqlabc member always contains the size of the sqlca structure. sqlerrp always contains the string 'NOT SET'.

Now let's look at the interesting parts of a sqlca.

The sqlcode member is an error indicator. If the most recent (ecpg library) operation was completely successful, sqlcode will be set to zero. If the most recent operation succeeded, but it was a query that returned no data, sqlcode will contain the value ECPG_NOT_FOUND[3] (or 100). sqlcode will also be set to ECPG_NOT_FOUND if you execute an UPDATE, INSERT, or DELETE that affects zero rows. If an error occurs, sqlcode will contain a negative number.

If sqlca.sqlcode contains a non-zero value, the sqlerrm structure will contain a printable error message. sqlerrm.sqlerrmc will contain the null-terminated text of the message and sqlerrm.sqlerrml will contain the length of the error message.

The sqlerrd array also contains useful information. After executing a SELECT statement, sqlerrd[2] will contain the number of rows returned by the query. After executing an INSERT, UPDATE, or DELETE statement, sqlerrd[1] will contain the oid (object ID) of the most recently affected row, and sqlerrd[2] will contain the number of rows affected.

The sqlwarn array is used to tell you about warnings. When you retrieve data from PostgreSQL, sqlwarn[1] will be set to W if any of the data has been truncated. Truncation can occur, for example, when you retrieve a varchar column into a buffer too small to contain the actual value. sqlwarn[2] is set to W whenever a non-fatal error (such as executing a COMMIT outside of the context of a transaction) occurs. If any member of the sqlwarn array contains a W, sqlwarn[0] will contain a W.

I've modified the previous client application (client1b.pgc) so that it prints an error message if the connection attempt fails. Here is client2a.pgc:

```
1  /* client2a.pgc */
2
3  EXEC SQL INCLUDE sqlca;
4
5  #include <stdio.h>
6
```

3. The symbolic names for sqlcode values (such as ECPG_NOT_FOUND) are automatically #defined for you by the ecpg preprocessor.

```
 7 int main( )
 8 {
 9     EXEC SQL CONNECT TO movies;
10
11     if( sqlca.sqlcode == 0 )
12         printf( "Connected to 'movies'\n" );
13     else
14         printf( "Error: %s\n", sqlca.sqlerrm.sqlerrmc );
15
16     EXEC SQL DISCONNECT;
17
18     return( 0 );
19 }
```

At line 11, check `sqlca.sqlcode`. If it contains a zero, your connection attempt was successful. If `sqlca.sqlcode` contains any other value, an error has occurred and you find the error message in `sqlca.sqlerrm.sqlerrmc`. If you want to try this code, you can induce an error by shutting down your PostgreSQL server and then running `client2a`.

Now let's modify this client slightly so that you can experiment with different error-processing scenarios:

```
 1 /* client2b.pgc */
 2
 3 EXEC SQL INCLUDE sqlca;
 4
 5 #include <stdio.h>
 6
 7 void dump_sqlca( void )
 8 {
 9     int     i;
10
11     printf("sqlca\n" );
12     printf("sqlaid                    - %s\n",sqlca.sqlcaid );
13     printf("sqlabc                    - %d\n",sqlca.sqlabc );
14     printf("sqlcode                   - %d\n",sqlca.sqlcode );
15     printf("sqlerrml                  - %d\n",sqlca.sqlerrm.sqlerrml);
16     printf("sqlerrmc                  - %s\n",sqlca.sqlerrm.sqlerrmc);
17     printf("sqlerrp                   - %s\n",sqlca.sqlerrp );
18     printf("sqlerrd[1] (oid)          - %d\n",sqlca.sqlerrd[1] );
19     printf("sqlerrd[2] (rows)         - %d\n",sqlca.sqlerrd[2] );
20     printf("sqlwarn[0]                - %c\n",sqlca.sqlwarn[0] );
21     printf("sqlwarn[1] (truncation)   - %c\n",sqlca.sqlwarn[1] );
22     printf("sqlwarn[2] (non-fatal)    - %c\n",sqlca.sqlwarn[2] );
23 }
24
```

```
25 int main( int argc, char * argv[] )
26 {
27     EXEC SQL BEGIN DECLARE SECTION;
28     char * url;
29     EXEC SQL END DECLARE SECTION;
30
31     url = argv[1] ? argv[1] : "";
32
33     EXEC SQL CONNECT TO :url;
34
35     if( sqlca.sqlcode == 0 )
36         printf( "Connected to '%s'\n", url );
37     else
38     {
39         printf( "Error: %s\n", sqlca.sqlerrm.sqlerrmc );
40         dump_sqlca( );
41     }
42
43     EXEC SQL DISCONNECT;
44
45     return( 0 );
46 }
```

In `client2b.pgc`, I've added a new function, `dump_sqlca()`, which simply prints the contents of the `sqlca` structure. I've also changed the `main()` function so that you can include a connection URL on the command line. We haven't talked about the `EXEC SQL BEGIN DECLARE SECTION` and `EXEC SQL END DECLARE SECTION` directives yet, so don't worry if they aren't familiar—I'll cover that topic in a moment. I'll also show you how to refer to host variables (that `:url` thing in line 33) in `EXEC SQL` statements.

Compile this program and run it a few times, feeding it connection URLs that will result in errors. Here is an example of what you might see:

```
$ ./client2b foo
Error: Could not connect to database foo in line 32.
sqlca
sqlaid                      - SQLCA   O
sqlabc                      - 140
sqlcode                     - -402
sqlerrml                    - 45
sqlerrmc                    - Could not connect to database foo in line 32.
sqlerrp                     - NOT SET
sqlerrd[1] (oid)            - 0
sqlerrd[2] (rows)           - 0
sqlwarn[0]                  -
sqlwarn[1] (truncation) -
sqlwarn[2] (non-fatal)  -
```

Table 11.2 shows some of the error messages you might encounter. This list is not exhaustive. Some of the messages in this table may not make sense to you until later in this chapter.

Table 11.2 **EPCG Runtime Errors**

Error	Explanation
`ECPG_NOT_FOUND`	No data found
`ECPG_OUT_OF_MEMORY`	Out of memory
`ECPG_UNSUPPORTED`	Unsupported type `typename`
`ECPG_TOO_MANY_ARGUMENTS`	Too many arguments
`ECPG_TOO_FEW_ARGUMENTS`	Too few arguments
`ECPG_TOO_MANY_MATCHES`	You selected more rows than will fit into the space you allocated
`ECPG_INT_FORMAT`	Incorrectly formatted int type `typename`
`ECPG_UINT_FORMAT`	Incorrectly formatted unsigned type `typename`
`ECPG_FLOAT_FORMAT`	Incorrectly formatted floating point type `typename`
`ECPG_CONVERT_BOOL`	Unable to convert to `bool`
`ECPG_EMPTY`	Empty query
`ECPG_MISSING_INDICATOR`	`NULL` value without indicator
`ECPG_NO_ARRAY`	Variable is not an array
`ECPG_DATA_NOT_ARRAY`	Data read from backend is not an array
`ECPG_NO_CONN`	No such connection `connection_name`
`ECPG_NOT_CONN`	Not connected to `'database'`
`ECPG_INVALID_STMT`	Invalid statement name `statement_name`
`ECPG_UNKNOWN_DESCRIPTOR`	Descriptor name not found
`ECPG_INVALID_DESCRIPTOR_INDEX`	Descriptor index out of range
`ECPG_UNKNOWN_DESCRIPTOR_ITEM`	Unknown descriptor item `item`
`ECPG_VAR_NOT_NUMERIC`	Variable is not a numeric type
`ECPG_VAR_NOT_CHAR`	Variable is not a character type
`ECPG_TRANS`	Error in transaction processing
`ECPG_CONNECT`	Could not connect to database `database_name`
`ECPG_PSQL`	Generic PostgreSQL error

The ecpg preprocessor provides an alternative method for detecting and handling errors: the `EXEC SQL WHENEVER` directive. The general form for a `WHENEVER` directive is

```
EXEC SQL WHENEVER condition action;
```

where *condition* can be any of the following:

- SQLERROR—Occurs whenever sqlca.sqlcode is less than zero
- SQLWARNING—Occurs whenever sqlca.sqlwarn[0] contains W
- NOT FOUND—Occurs whenever sqlca.sqlcode is ECPG_NOT_FOUND (that is, when a query returns no data)

When you use the EXEC SQL WHENEVER directive, you are telling the ecpg preprocessor to insert extra code into your program. Each time ecpg emits an ecpg library call that might raise a *condition* (at runtime), it follows that function call with code to detect and handle the *condition* that you specify. The exact format of the error-handling code depends on the *action* that you use. You can specify any of the following *actions*:

- SQLPRINT—Calls the sqlprint() function to display an error message to the user; the sqlprint() function simply prints "sql error " followed by the contents of the sqlca.sqlerrm.sqlerrmc string
- STOP—Calls exit(1); this will cause your application to terminate whenever the specified *condition* arises
- GOTO *label-name*—Causes your application to goto the label specified by *label-name* whenever the specified *condition* arises
- GO TO *label-name*—Same as GOTO
- CALL *function-name(arguments)*—Causes your application to call the given *function-name* with the given *arguments* whenever the specified *condition* arises
- DO function-name(arguments)—Same as CALL
- CONTINUE—Causes your application to execute a continue statement whenever the specified *condition* arises; this should be used only inside of a loop
- BREAK—Causes your application to execute a break statement whenever the specified *condition* arises; this should be used only inside loops or a switch statement

You may find it useful to examine the sqlca structure, even when you use EXEC SQL WHENEVER to intercept errors or warnings. EXEC SQL WHENEVER is a convenient way to detect error conditions, but sometimes you will find it overly broad—different error conditions can produce the same result. By interrogating the sqlca structure, you can still use EXEC SQL WHENEVER to trap the errors, but treat each condition differently.

Here is client2c.pgc. I've modified the first client in this section (client2a.pgc) so that it uses the EXEC SQL WHENEVER directive to intercept a connection error.

```
1
2 /* client2c.pgc */
3
4 EXEC SQL INCLUDE sqlca;
```

```
 5
 6 #include <stdio.h>
 7
 8 int main( int argc, char * argv[] )
 9 {
10     EXEC SQL BEGIN DECLARE SECTION;
11       char * url;
12     EXEC SQL END DECLARE SECTION;
13     url = argv[1] ? argv[1] : "";
14
15     EXEC SQL WHENEVER SQLERROR SQLPRINT;
16
17     EXEC SQL CONNECT TO :url;
18
19     EXEC SQL DISCONNECT;
20
21     return( 0 );
22 }
```

Let's run this program in such a way that a connection error occurs:

```
$ ./client2c foo
sql error Could not connect to database foo in line 17.
sql error No such connection CURRENT in line 19.
```

Notice that I received two error messages. The first error occurred when my connection attempt failed; the second occurred when I tried to tear down a nonexistent connection. That's an important thing to remember—the `EXEC SQL WHENEVER` directive continues to affect your epcg code until you change the *`action`* associated with a given *`condition`*.

It's important to understand that `EXEC SQL WHENEVER` is a preprocessor directive, not a true statement. A directive affects the actions of the ecpg preprocessor from the point at which it is encountered in the source code. This means, for example, that if you include an `EXEC SQL WHENEVER` directive within an `if` statement, you probably won't get the results you were hoping for. Consider the following code:

```
if( TRUE )
{
EXEC SQL WHENEVER SQLERROR SQLPRINT;
}
else
{
EXEC SQL WHENEVER SQLERROR STOP;
}

EXEC SQL CONNECT TO movies;
```

Looking at this code, you might expect that a connection failure would result in a call to the `sqlprint()` function. That's not what you'll get. Instead, the ecpg preprocessor will arrange for the `exit()` function to be called if the connection attempt fails. Preprocessor directives are not executable statements; they affect the code produced by the preprocessor. As the preprocessor reads through your source code, it keeps track of the *action* that you choose for each *condition*. Each time the preprocessor encounters an `EXEC SQL WHENEVER` directive, it remembers the new *action* and applies it to any `EXEC SQL` statements further down the source code. So, with `EXEC SQL WHENEVER`, the order of appearance (within the source file) is important, but the order of execution is not.

I recommend compiling a few ecpg programs that include the various `EXEC SQL WHENEVER` directives and then examining the resulting C code to better understand how they will affect your programs.

Client 3—Processing SQL Commands

Now let's turn our attention to the task of executing SQL commands and interpreting the results. To start with, I'll show you how to execute simple SQL statements in an ecpg application:

```
 1
 2 /* client3a.pgc */
 3
 4 EXEC SQL INCLUDE sqlca;
 5
 6 #include <stdio.h>
 7
 8 int main( )
 9 {
10
11   EXEC SQL WHENEVER SQLERROR   SQLPRINT;
12   EXEC SQL WHENEVER SQLWARNING SQLPRINT;
13   EXEC SQL WHENEVER NOT FOUND  SQLPRINT;
14
15   EXEC SQL CONNECT TO movies;
16
17   EXEC SQL
18     INSERT INTO tapes
19       VALUES
20       (
21         'GG-44278',
22         'Strangers On A Train',
23         '1 hour 3 minutes'
24       );
25
26   EXEC SQL
```

```
27       DELETE FROM tapes WHERE tape_id = 'GG-44278';
28
29     EXEC SQL
30       DELETE FROM tapes WHERE tape_id IS NULL;
31
32     EXEC SQL DISCONNECT;
33
34       return( 0 );
35 }
```

You can see from this example that executing simple SQL statements with ecpg is easy—you just insert the text of the statement after `EXEC SQL`. I've used the `EXEC SQL WHENEVER` statement that you saw in the previous section to show how easy it can be to handle errors. The `DELETE` command on lines 29 and 30 will produce an error message; and at the beginning of the program, I told ecpg to `SQLPRINT` whenever a `NOT FOUND` condition occurs.

The three SQL statements executed in `client3a.pgc` are considered simple for two reasons:

- They don't require any data to be provided at runtime (the values involved are hard-coded).
- No data is returned to the client application (other than error conditions).

Things get a bit more complex if you need to provide (or process) data at runtime. The first thing that changes when you need to provide C data to ecpg is that you have to tell the ecpg preprocessor about the variables in your code. You may remember from earlier in this chapter that I used the `EXEC SQL BEGIN DECLARE SECTION` and `EXEC SQL END DECLARE SECTION` directives. These ecpg directives tell the preprocessor that it should pay close attention to the variable declarations in between because you will use those variables when interacting with ecpg. A quick example should make this a little clearer:

```
 1 /* client3b.pgc */
 2
 3 EXEC SQL INCLUDE sqlca;
 4
 5 #include <stdio.h>
 6
 7 int main( int argc, char * argv[] )
 8 {
 9   EXEC SQL BEGIN DECLARE SECTION;
10     char  * tape_id  = argc > 1 ? argv[1]  : NULL;
11     char  * title    = argc > 2 ? argv[2]  : NULL;
12     char  * duration = argc > 3 ? argv[3]  : NULL;
13   EXEC SQL END DECLARE SECTION;
14
15   EXEC SQL WHENEVER SQLERROR   SQLPRINT;
16   EXEC SQL WHENEVER SQLWARNING SQLPRINT;
```

```
17   EXEC SQL WHENEVER NOT FOUND  SQLPRINT;
18
19   EXEC SQL CONNECT TO movies;
20
21   EXEC SQL
22     INSERT INTO tapes
23       VALUES
24       (
25         :tape_id,
26         :title,
27         :duration
28       );
29
30   EXEC SQL DISCONNECT;
31
32   return( 0 );
33 }
```

At line 9, I've included an `EXEC SQL BEGIN DECLARE SECTION` directive. This tells the ecpg preprocessor that I will declare one or more variables—the variable declarations end with an `EXEC SQL END DECLARE SECTION` directive. Once I have told ecpg about my variables, I can use them in future `EXEC SQL` commands.

At lines 25, 26, and 27, I've told ecpg that it should find the values that I want to insert in the `tape_id`, `title`, and `duration` variables. When you want ecpg to substitute a C variable within a SQL statement, you prefix the variable name with a colon (`:`).

When you run this program, you should provide three strings on the command line (enclose each string in double quotes). For example:

```
$ ./client3b "SP-00001" "Young Einstein" "91 minutes"
```

If you run this program with fewer than three command-line arguments, it will crash because one (or more) of the substitution variables will be set to `NULL`. To handle `NULL` values correctly, you must pair each substitution variable with an *indicator variable*. An indicator variable is a value that determines whether the related substitution variable is `NULL`. Indicator variables can be any of the following types: `unsigned short`, `unsigned int`, `unsigned long`, `unsigned long long`, `short`, `int`, `long`, or `long long`. As you'll see a little later, you should avoid using the `unsigned` variants because PostgreSQL uses negative values to return useful information to your application.

You match the substitution variable to its indicator by appending a colon and then the indicator name to the substitution variable name. I've rewritten `client3b.pgc` a bit (now `client3c.pgc`) to handle `NULL` values better:

```
1 /* client3c.pgc */
2
3 EXEC SQL INCLUDE sqlca;
```

```
 4
 5 EXEC SQL WHENEVER SQLERROR   SQLPRINT;
 6 EXEC SQL WHENEVER SQLWARNING SQLPRINT;
 7 EXEC SQL WHENEVER NOT FOUND  SQLPRINT;
 8
 9 #include <stdio.h>
10
11 int main( int argc, char * argv[] )
12 {
13   EXEC SQL BEGIN DECLARE SECTION;
14
15     char  * tape_id  = argc > 1 ? argv[1]  : "ignored";
16     char  * title    = argc > 2 ? argv[2]  : "ignored";
17     char  * duration = argc > 3 ? argv[3]  : "ignored";
18
19     short   tape_id_ind  = argc > 1 ? 0 : -1;
20     short   title_ind    = argc > 2 ? 0 : -1;
21     short   duration_ind = argc > 3 ? 0 : -1;
22
23   EXEC SQL END DECLARE SECTION;
24
25   EXEC SQL CONNECT TO movies;
26
27   EXEC SQL INSERT INTO tapes
28     VALUES
29     (
30       :tape_id  :tape_id_ind,
31       :title    :title_ind,
32       :duration :duration_ind
33     );
34
35   EXEC SQL DISCONNECT;
36
37   return( 0 );
38 }
```

You can see that at lines 19, 20, and 21, I've created three indicator variables—one for each substitution variable. If I want to tell the ecpg library that a column value should be set to NULL, I set its corresponding indicator variable to a negative number (0 means NOT NULL, any other value means NULL). Notice that if an indicator variable is set to indicate a NULL value, the matching substitution variable is completely ignored.

Indicator variables are also used when you request data from the database. The following client application (client3d.pgc) requests a single row from the tapes table and displays the values:

```
1 /* client3d.pgc */
2
```

```
 3 EXEC SQL INCLUDE sqlca;
 4
 5 EXEC SQL WHENEVER SQLERROR   SQLPRINT;
 6 EXEC SQL WHENEVER SQLWARNING SQLPRINT;
 7 EXEC SQL WHENEVER NOT FOUND  SQLPRINT;
 8
 9 #include <stdio.h>
10
11 int main( int argc, char * argv[] )
12 {
13   EXEC SQL BEGIN DECLARE SECTION;
14
15     char  * desired_tape = argv[1];
16
17     char    tape_id[8+1];
18     varchar title[80+1];
19     varchar duration[30+1];
20
21     short   duration_ind;
22
23   EXEC SQL END DECLARE SECTION;
24
25   EXEC SQL CONNECT TO movies;
26
27   EXEC SQL
28     SELECT * INTO
29       :tape_id,
30       :title,
31       :duration :duration_ind
32     FROM tapes
33     WHERE
34       tape_id = :desired_tape;
35
36   printf( "tape_id  = %s\n", tape_id );
37   printf( "title    = %s\n", title.arr );
38   printf( "duration = %s\n", duration_ind < 0
39                                ? "null" : duration.arr );
40
41   EXEC SQL DISCONNECT;
42
43   return( 0 );
44 }
```

At line 21, I've declared a single indicator—I don't need an indicator variable for `tape_id` or `title` because those columns are declared as `NOT NULL`. In the `SELECT` command that starts at line 27, I've asked ecpg to return the value of the tape_id column into the tape_id variable, the title column into the title variable, and the duration column into the duration variable and duration_ind indicator. If you SELECT a row where the duration column is NULL, the duration_ind variable will be set to a negative number.

Take a close look at the definitions of the title and duration variables—each is defined as an array of type varchar. varchar has special meaning to the ecpg preprocessor. Whenever the preprocessor sees a variable defined as varchar (within the declaration section), it translates the variable into a structure. The title variable is defined as varchar title[80+1]; the ecpg preprocessor will translate that definition into

```
struct varchar_title { int len; char arr[80+1]; } title;
```

When you SELECT a column into a varchar variable, ecpg will set the len member to the length of the data actually retrieved (the array is also null-terminated if the null character will fit).

You might be wondering what happens if the data that you ask for won't fit into the space that you have allocated. This is the second use for an indicator variable. Whenever ecpg has to truncate a value, it sets the indicator to the number of bytes actually retrieved.

So, when you retrieve a value from the database, an indicator variable can hold any of the values shown in Table 11.3.

Table 11.3 **Indicator Variable Values**

Indicator Value	Meaning
indicator < 0	Value was NULL
indicator = 0	Value was NOT NULL and fit into the associated substitution variable without being truncated
indicator > 0	Value was NOT NULL, but was truncated

ecpg Data Types

I mentioned the varchar data type earlier, but what other data types are understood by ecpg? The ecpg preprocessor needs to know some basic information about each of the data types that you use. When you interact with a database using ecpg, the ecpg library can convert between the C data types used in your application and the PostgreSQL data types stored in the database. When you supply data *to* the database, the ecpg library will convert from your C data type into the format required by the database. When you retrieve data *from* the database, the ecpg library will convert from PostgreSQL format into the format required by your application.

The ecpg library includes implicit support for the C data types shown here:

- `unsigned`
- `unsigned short`
- `unsigned int`
- `unsigned long`
- `unsigned long int`
- `unsigned long long`
- `unsigned long long int`
- `unsigned char`
- `short`
- `short int`
- `int`
- `long`
- `long int`
- `long long`
- `long long int`
- `bool`
- `float`
- `double`
- `char`
- `varchar`
- `struct`
- `union`
- `enum`

Note that the `char` and `varchar` data types will be null-terminated if the null character will fit within the allotted space. If the null terminator will *not* fit, the indicator variable will *not* reflect the fact that the string was truncated.

Sometimes, we C programmers find that it's a good idea to introduce artificial data types. For example, if your application must deal with account numbers, you might introduce an `acct_no` data type that is defined in terms of one of the basic C data types:

```
typedef unsigned int acct_no;
```

You can use the contrived data type with ecpg, but you must use the `EXEC SQL TYPE` directive. Here's a code snippet that shows how you might use `EXEC SQL TYPE`:

```
EXEC SQL TYPE acct_no IS unsigned int;
typedef unsigned int acct_no;

EXEC SQL BEGIN DECLARE SECTION;
    acct_no payroll_acct;
EXEC SQL END DECLARE SECTION;

EXEC SQL
    SELECT payroll_acct
    INTO :payroll_acct
    FROM employees
    WHERE employee_id = 133;
```

Notice that you must tell both ecpg and the C compiler what an `acct_no` is (in other words, you need both the `EXEC SQL TYPE` and the `typedef`). In later releases of ecpg (newer than 7.2), you can use the `-c` flag to tell the ecpg preprocessor to generate the `typedefs` for you.

In the preceding list you saw that the ecpg preprocessor supports the `struct` data type. When you ask ecpg to retrieve data into a `struct`, it will place each result column in a separate member of the structure. Let's modify client3d.pgc to `SELECT` into a structure:

```
 1 /* client3e.pgc */
 2
 3 EXEC SQL INCLUDE sqlca;
 4
 5 EXEC SQL WHENEVER SQLERROR   SQLPRINT;
 6 EXEC SQL WHENEVER SQLWARNING SQLPRINT;
 7 EXEC SQL WHENEVER NOT FOUND  SQLPRINT;
 8
 9 #include <stdio.h>
10
11 int main( int argc, char * argv[] )
12 {
13   EXEC SQL BEGIN DECLARE SECTION;
14
15     char  * desired_tape = argv[1];
16
17     struct
18     {
19         char    tape_id[8+1];
20         varchar title[80+1];
21         varchar duration[30+1];
22     } tape;
23
24     struct
25     {
26         short   tape_id_ind;
27         short   title_ind;
28         short   duration_ind;
29     } tape_ind;
30
31   EXEC SQL END DECLARE SECTION;
32
33   EXEC SQL CONNECT TO movies;
34
35   EXEC SQL
36     SELECT * INTO
37       :tape :tape_ind
38     FROM tapes
39     WHERE
40       tape_id = :desired_tape;
41
42   printf( "tape_id  = %s\n", tape_ind.tape_id_ind < 0
43                             ? "null" : tape.tape_id );
```

```
44    printf( "title    = %s\n", tape_ind.title_ind < 0
45                               ? "null" : tape.title.arr );
46    printf( "duration = %s\n", tape_ind.duration_ind < 0
47                                 ? "null" : tape.duration.arr );
48
49    EXEC SQL DISCONNECT;
50
51    return( 0 );
52 }
```

At lines 17–22, I've defined a structure to hold a single row from the `tapes` table. At lines 24–29, I've defined a structure that holds the indicator variables for a `tapes` row.

When I `SELECT` a row from the `tapes` table, I've asked ecpg to place the resulting data into the `tape` structure and to set the indicators in the `tape_ind` structure.

If the data that you retrieve into a structure cannot be matched up with the structure members, you will receive a runtime error. For example, if you `SELECT` four columns of data into a structure that contains three members, you will receive an `ECPG_TOO_FEW_ARGUMENTS` error (at runtime). Likewise, if your indicator structure doesn't match the data returned by the query, you may get an `ECPG_MISSING_INDICATOR` error if you run into a `NULL` value.

To wrap up this discussion of ecpg data types, I should mention that you can ask ecpg to retrieve multiple rows into an array of substitution (and indicator) variables. I've modified the previous client application to show you how to use arrays with ecpg:

```
 1 /* client3f.pgc */
 2
 3 #include <stdio.h>
 4
 5 EXEC SQL INCLUDE sqlca;
 6
 7 EXEC SQL WHENEVER SQLERROR   SQLPRINT;
 8 EXEC SQL WHENEVER SQLWARNING SQLPRINT;
 9 EXEC SQL WHENEVER NOT FOUND  SQLPRINT;
10
11 EXEC SQL TYPE tape IS
12     struct tape
13     {
14         char    tape_id[8+1];
15         varchar title[80+1];
16         varchar duration[10+1];
17     };
18
19 EXEC SQL TYPE ind IS
20     struct ind
21     {
22         short   id_ind;
23         short   title_ind;
24         short   duration_ind;
```

```
25     };
26
27 int main( )
28 {
29   EXEC SQL BEGIN DECLARE SECTION;
30
31     tape    tapes[5];
32     ind     inds[5];
33
34   EXEC SQL END DECLARE SECTION;
35
36   int       r;
37
38   EXEC SQL CONNECT TO movies;
39
40   EXEC SQL
41     SELECT * INTO :tapes:inds
42     FROM tapes
43     LIMIT 5;
44
45   for( r = 0; r < 5; r++ )
46   {
47     printf( "tape_id  = %s\n", inds[r].id_ind < 0
48                               ? "null" : tapes[r].tape_id );
49     printf( "title    = %s\n", inds[r].title_ind < 0
50                               ? "null" : tapes[r].title.arr );
51     printf( "duration = %s\n\n",inds[r].duration_ind < 0
52                                ? "null" : tapes[r].duration.arr );
53   }
54
55   EXEC SQL DISCONNECT;
56
57   return( 0 );
58 }
```

At line 30 and 31, I've defined an array of five `tape` structures and five indicator structures.[4] When I `SELECT` data into these variables, the ecpg library will place the first row in the first array element, the second row in the second array element, and so on. Likewise, the indicators for the first row will be placed in the first member of the `inds` array, the second set of indicators will be placed in the second member, and so on. In this example, I've allocated enough space to hold five rows and I've limited the query to return no more than five rows. If you try to retrieve more rows than will fit into the space you've allocated, ecpg will trigger an `ECPG_TOO_MANY_MATCHES` error.

4. In this example, I've taken advantage of the `-c` flag to let the ecpg preprocessor generate structure `typedefs` for me. The `-c` flag offers more than mere convenience—it lets you include `varchar` members in a structure. Without the `-c` flag, you can't include `varchar` members with a structure; the ecpg preprocessor can't handle it.

Client 4—An Interactive Query Processor

Following the pattern set in the previous few chapters, I'll wrap up the discussion of ecpg by developing an interactive query processor. Because of the complexity of using ecpg to handle dynamic queries, I'll take a few shortcuts in this client, and I'll try to point to them as I go.

Let's start by looking at the `main()` function for the final client application in this chapter:

```
 1 /* client4.pgc */
 2
 3 #include <stdio.h>
 4 #include <stdlib.h>
 5
 6 EXEC SQL INCLUDE sql3types;
 7 EXEC SQL INCLUDE sqlca;
 8
 9 EXEC SQL WHENEVER SQLERROR DO print_error();
10
11 static int  is_select_stmt( char * stmt );
12 static void process_other_stmt( char * stmt_text );
13 static void process_select_stmt( char * stmt_text );
14 static void print_column_headers( int col_count );
15 static void print_meta_data( char * desc_name );
16 static void print_error( void );
17 static int  usage( char * program );
18
19 char * sep = "----------------------------------------";
20 char * md1 = "col field                data              ret";
21 char * md2 = "num name                 type              len";
22 char * md3 = "--- -------------------- ----------------- ---";
23
24 int    dump_meta_data = 0;
25
26 int main( int argc, char * argv[] )
27 {
28   EXEC SQL BEGIN DECLARE SECTION;
29     char * db   = argv[1];
30     char * stmt = argv[2];
31   EXEC SQL END DECLARE SECTION;
32
33   FILE * log = fopen( "client4.log", "w" );
34
35   ECPGdebug( 1, log );
36
37   if( argc < 3 )
38     exit( usage( argv[0] ));
```

```
39    else if( argc > 3 )
40      dump_meta_data = 1;
41
42    EXEC SQL CONNECT TO :db;
43
44    if( is_select_stmt( stmt ))
45      process_select_stmt( stmt );
46    else
47      process_other_stmt( stmt );
48
49    exit( 0 );
50 }
```

You've already seen most of this code. I've included an extra `EXEC SQL INCLUDE` statement: `sql3types` provides symbolic names for the data types returned by a dynamic SQL statement. I'll show you where to use these a little later.

The only other new feature in `main()` is the call to `ECPGdebug()`. Debugging dynamic SQL can be pretty tricky, and it's always helpful to have a record of the sequence of events that your application follows. When you call `ECPGdebug()`, you provide an integer and a `FILE *`: a 0 means to turn off logging and any other value means to turn on ecpg library logging.

Here is the first shortcut that I've taken (for clarity). Rather than prompting you for multiple commands, you provide a single command (on the command line) for this application. This client expects either two or three command-line arguments. The first argument should be the name of the database to which you want to connect. The second argument is a SQL command. The third argument is optional. If you provide a third command-line argument (it doesn't matter *what* you provide), `client4` will print out meta-data for a `SELECT` command. A typical invocation of this application might look like this:

```
$ ./client4 movies "select * from tapes" true
```

Notice that at line 44, I am calling the `is_select_stmt()` function. The processing required to handle a `SELECT` statement is considerably different from that required to handle other command types, so let's defer it for a while and first look instead at the code required execute commands other than `SELECT`:

```
52 static void process_other_stmt( char * stmt_text )
53 {
54   EXEC SQL BEGIN DECLARE SECTION;
55     char  * stmt = stmt_text;
56   EXEC SQL END DECLARE SECTION;
57
58   EXEC SQL EXECUTE IMMEDIATE :stmt;
59
60   if( sqlca.sqlcode >= 0 )
61   {
```

```
62     printf( "ok\n" );
63     EXEC SQL COMMIT;
64   }
65 }
```

The `process_other_stmt()` function is actually pretty simple. You define a variable to hold the statement text (inside of a `DECLARE SECTION` so that you can use it as a substitution variable). At line 50, you execute the command using the substitution variable. Using this form of the `EXEC SQL EXECUTE` command, you don't get back any result information other than what's found in the `sqlca` structure. In the next section, I'll show you how to get more result information.

If the command succeeds, execute a `COMMIT` command to commit any changes.

ecpg and Autocommit

When you compile this program, you do *not* use the `-t` flag. The `-t` flag tells the `ecpg` preprocessor to arrange for each statement to be committed as soon as it completes (in other words, the `-t` flag enables `autocommit`). Because you aren't using `autocommit` in this example, you must `COMMIT` or `ROLL-BACK` your changes to complete the transaction. If you forget to `COMMIT` your changes (and you don't use the `-t` flag), your changes will automatically be rolled back when your application completes. If you invoke the ecpg preprocessor with the `-t` flag, each change will be committed as soon as it completes.

Now let's look at the `process_select_stmt()` function—it is much more complex.

```
67 static void process_select_stmt( char * stmt_text )
68 {
69   EXEC SQL BEGIN DECLARE SECTION;
70     char  * stmt = stmt_text;
71   EXEC SQL END DECLARE SECTION;
72     int      row;
73
74     EXEC SQL ALLOCATE DESCRIPTOR my_desc;
75     EXEC SQL PREPARE query FROM :stmt;
76
77     EXEC SQL DECLARE my_cursor CURSOR FOR query;
78     EXEC SQL OPEN my_cursor;
79
80     for( row = 0; ; row++ )
81     {
82       EXEC SQL BEGIN DECLARE SECTION;
83         int      col_count;
84         int      i;
85       EXEC SQL END DECLARE SECTION;
86
87       EXEC SQL FETCH IN my_cursor INTO SQL DESCRIPTOR my_desc;
88
89       if( sqlca.sqlcode != 0 )
```

```
 90         break;
 91
 92       EXEC SQL GET DESCRIPTOR my_desc :col_count = count;
 93
 94       if( row == 0 )
 95       {
 96         print_meta_data( "my_desc" );
 97         print_column_headers( col_count );
 98       }
 99
100       for( i = 1; i <= col_count; i++ )
101       {
102         EXEC SQL BEGIN DECLARE SECTION;
103           short   ind;
104         EXEC SQL END DECLARE SECTION;
105
106         EXEC SQL GET DESCRIPTOR my_desc VALUE
107           :i :ind = INDICATOR;
108
109         if( ind == -1 )
110         {
111           printf( "null " );
112         }
113         else
114         {
115           EXEC SQL BEGIN DECLARE SECTION;
116             varchar val[40+1];
117             int     len;
118           EXEC SQL END DECLARE SECTION;
119
120           EXEC SQL GET DESCRIPTOR my_desc VALUE
121             :i :len = RETURNED_LENGTH;
122
123           EXEC SQL GET DESCRIPTOR my_desc VALUE :i :val = DATA;
124
125           if( len > 40 )
126             len = 40;
127
128           printf( "%-*s ", len, val.arr );
129         }
130       }
131
132       printf( "\n" );
133
134     }
135
136     printf( "%d rows\n", row );
137
138 }
```

If you've read the previous few chapters, you know that the most stubborn problem in ad-hoc query processing is that you don't know, at the time you write the program, what kind of data will be returned by any given query. The bulk of the code that you need to write involves discovering and interpreting the meta-data associated with a query.

When you use ecpg to process dynamic SQL commands, the meta-data comes back in the form of a descriptor (or, more precisely, a group of descriptors). A *descriptor* is a data structure, much like libpq's PGresult, that contains information about the data returned by a SQL command.

Before you can use a descriptor, you must tell the ecpg library to allocate one. The following statement will create a new descriptor named `my_desc`:

```
EXEC SQL ALLOCATE DESCRIPTOR my_desc;
```

At line 75, you prepare your command for execution. When you prepare a command, you are giving ecpg a chance to peek at the command and do whatever bookkeeping it needs to do to execute it. After a command has been prepared, ecpg will remember it for you and you can refer to that statement by name (`query`, in this case).

After you have a prepared the statement, you will declare a cursor (named `my_cursor`) for the statement and then open the cursor. (You can execute singleton[5] `SELECT`s without preparing them, but there is a no way to tell that a dynamic query is a singleton `SELECT`.)

At line 80, you enter a loop to process all the rows returned by the cursor.

Line 87 shows the magic that occurs in a dynamic SQL application. When you execute the `EXEC SQL` statement at line 87, you are fetching the next row from `my-_cursor` and putting the results into the `my_desc` descriptor. The `my_desc` descriptor now contains all the meta-data for this SQL command (`FETCH`).

I mentioned earlier that a descriptor is a data structure. Although that is a true statement, you can't access the members of the data structure using the normal C structure reference syntax. Instead, you use the `EXEC SQL GET DESCRIPTOR` directive. The general form of the `GET DESCRIPTOR` directive is

```
EXEC SQL GET DESCRIPTOR
descriptor_name [column_number] substitution_variable = item;
```

The *`item`* specifies what kind of information you want to retrieve from the descriptor. The returned information is placed into the *`substitution_variable`*. The *`column_number`* is optional, but there is only one item that you can specify if you omit the *`column_number`*—a count of the columns in the result set.

To retrieve the column count, ask ecpg to place the `COUNT` into the `col_count` variable.

After you know how many columns are in the result set, (optionally) print the meta-data and the column headers. I'll show you those functions in a moment.

5. A singleton `SELECT` is a `SELECT` command that returns either zero rows or one row, never more.

At line 100, you enter a loop that processes each column from the most recently fetched row.

The first thing you need to know is whether a given column is NULL. Each column in the result set has an associated indicator variable, and you can retrieve the value of that indicator through the descriptor. Notice (at line 107) that you have to tell ecpg in which column you are interested: for any descriptor item other than count, you have to include a column number after the word VALUE.

If the column contains NULL, just print null. This is another shortcut that I've taken in this client; to properly maintain the alignment of the columns when you print the result set, you have to know the maximum length of each value within a column and that information is not available using dynamic SQL and ecpg. So, instead of printing null and then padding it with spaces to the proper length, just print null. This means that you lose vertical alignment of the columns if your data includes NULL values.

If a column contains a value other than NULL, you will print the value (or at most the first 40 characters of the value).

At line 120, you retrieve the length of the character form of the value from the RETURNED_LENGTH member of the my_desc descriptor. I say the "length of the character form" here because there are other length-related items that you can retrieve from a descriptor. I'll include a description of all the descriptor items a little later.

Finally, at line 123, I retrieve the actual data value from the descriptor. When I ask for a DATA item, I have to provide a substitution variable where ecpg can return the value. If the data value that I retrieve is longer than 40 bytes, ecpg will truncate the value and set sqlca.sqlwarn[1] to tell me that truncation has occurred.

After you have processed all the columns for all rows, you print a message indicating how many rows were retrieved.

Now let's move on to the print_meta_data() function. The first thing I'll point out about this function is that it expects the descriptor name to be passed in as the one and only argument. This isn't really important to the structure of this particular application, but I wanted to point out that you can use a substitution variable to specify a descriptor.

```
140 static void print_meta_data( char * desc_name )
141 {
142   EXEC SQL BEGIN DECLARE SECTION;
143     char  * desc = desc_name;
144     int     col_count;
145     int     i;
146   EXEC SQL END DECLARE SECTION;
147
148   static char * types[] =
149   {
150     "unused           ",
151     "CHARACTER        ",
152     "NUMERIC          ",
153     "DECIMAL          ",
```

```
154     "INTEGER           ",
155     "SMALLINT          ",
156     "FLOAT             ",
157     "REAL              ",
158     "DOUBLE            ",
159     "DATE_TIME         ",
160     "INTERVAL          ",
161     "unused            ",
162     "CHARACTER_VARYING",
163     "ENUMERATED        ",
164     "BIT               ",
165     "BIT_VARYING       ",
166     "BOOLEAN           ",
167     "abstract          "
168   };
169
170   if( dump_meta_data == 0 )
171     return;
172
173   EXEC SQL GET DESCRIPTOR :desc :col_count = count;
174
175   printf( "%s\n", md1 );
176   printf( "%s\n", md2 );
177   printf( "%s\n", md3 );
178
179   for( i = 1; i <= col_count; i++ )
180   {
181     EXEC SQL BEGIN DECLARE SECTION;
182       int     type;
183       int     ret_len;
184       varchar name[21];
185     EXEC SQL END DECLARE SECTION;
186     char *  type_name;
187
188     EXEC SQL GET DESCRIPTOR :desc VALUE
189       :i :name = NAME;
190
191     EXEC SQL GET DESCRIPTOR :desc VALUE
192       :i :type = TYPE;
193
194     EXEC SQL GET DESCRIPTOR :desc VALUE
195       :i :ret_len = RETURNED_OCTET_LENGTH;
196
197     if( type > 0 && type < SQL3_abstract )
198       type_name = types[type];
199     else
200       type_name = "unknown";
201
```

```
202         printf( "%02d: %-20s %-17s %04d\n",
203           i, name.arr, type_name, ret_len );
204     }
205
206     printf( "\n" );
207 }
```

In this function, you are pulling a few more meta-data items out of the descriptor. The first thing you do in this function is to check the `dump_meta_data` flag—if you don't want to see meta-data, this function will simply return without printing anything. The `dump_meta_data` flag will be set to `TRUE` if you include a third argument on the command line when you run this program.

At line 173, you (again) retrieve a count of the number of columns in the descriptor. Lines 175 through 177 print column headers for the meta-data (`md1`, `md2`, and `md3` are defined at the top of `client4.pgc`).

At line 179, you enter a loop that prints the meta-data for each column. Lines 188 through 195 retrieve the `NAME`, (data) `TYPE`, and `RETURNED_OCTET_LENGTH` for each column.

The `TYPE` item returns an integer that *may* correspond to one of the data type names defined in the `sql3types.h` header file. Not all data types are defined in `sql3types.h`—there are many PostgreSQL data types that don't exactly map to a SQL3 data type. If you encounter an unknown data type, just print unknown instead of a real type name.

This is probably a good place to show you all the descriptor items that you can retrieve using ecpg (see Table 11.4).

Table 11.4 **Descriptor Item Types**

Item Type	Meaning
`CARDINALITY`	Number of rows in result set (usually one and therefore not particularly useful)
`DATA`	Actual data value
`DATETIME_INTERVAL_CODE`	`SQL3_DDT_DATE`, `SQL3_DDT_TIME`, `SQL3_DDT_TIMESTAMP`, `SQL3_DDT_TIMESTAMP_WITH_TIME_ZONE`, `SQL3_DDT_TIME_WITH_TIME_ZONE`
`DATETIME_INTERVAL_PRECISION`	Not currently used
`INDICATOR`	Indicator variable
`KEY_MEMBER`	Always returns `FALSE`
`LENGTH`	Length of data as stored in server
`NAME`	Name of field
`NULLABLE`	Always returns `TRUE`
`OCTET_LENGTH`	Length of data as stored in server
`PRECISION`	Precision (for numeric values)

Table 11.4 **Continued**

Item Type	Meaning
RETURNED_LENGTH	Length of actual data item
RETURNED_OCTET_LENGTH	Synonym for RETURNED_LENGTH
SCALE	Scale (for numeric values)
TYPE	SQL3 data type or PostgreSQL data type

The rest of `client4.pgc` is pretty mundane; I'll include the remainder of the source code here and offer a few quick explanations:

```
209 static void print_column_headers( int col_count )
210 {
211   EXEC SQL BEGIN DECLARE SECTION;
212     char    name[40];
213     int     len;
214   EXEC SQL END DECLARE SECTION;
215   int     i;
216
217   for( i = 1; i <= col_count; i++ )
218   {
219     EXEC SQL GET DESCRIPTOR my_desc VALUE
220       :i :name = NAME;
221
222     EXEC SQL GET DESCRIPTOR my_desc VALUE
223       :i :len  = RETURNED_OCTET_LENGTH;
224
225     if( len > 40 )
226       len = 40;
227
228     printf( "%-*s ", len, name );
229   }
230
231   printf( "\n" );
232
233   for( i = 1; i <= col_count; i++ )
234   {
235     EXEC SQL GET DESCRIPTOR my_desc VALUE
236       :i :len  = RETURNED_OCTET_LENGTH;
237
238     if( len > 40 )
239       len = 40;
240
241     printf( "%*.*s ", len, len, sep );
242   }
```

```
243
244   printf( "\n" );
245 }
```

The `print_column_headers()` function does a half-hearted job of trying to print properly aligned column headers. This function can't do a perfect job because ecpg doesn't expose enough information. For example, to properly align column headers, you have to know the longest value in any given column. Because you process `SELECT` statements one record at a time, you would have to do a lot of work to be able to find this information. If you are not a purist, you can mix ecpg and libpq code in the same application.

```
247 static int is_select_stmt( char * stmt )
248 {
249   char * token;
250
251   for( token = stmt; *token; token++ )
252     if( *token != ' ' && *token != '\t' )
253       break;
254
255   if( *token == '\0' )
256     return( 0 );
257
258   if( strncasecmp( token, "select", 6 ) == 0 )
259     return( 1 );
260   else
261     return( 0 );
262 }
```

The `is_select_stmt()` function represents another shortcut—you have to look at the first word of a SQL command to determine whether it is a `SELECT` statement or some other command. With other dynamic SQL packages (such as Oracle's Pro*C product), you can obtain this information from the descriptor, but not with PostgreSQL.

```
264 static void print_error()
265 {
266   printf( "#%ld:%s\n", sqlca.sqlcode, sqlca.sqlerrm.sqlerrmc );
267 }
268
269 static int usage( char * program )
270 {
271   fprintf( stderr, "usage: %s <database> <query>\n", program );
272   return( 1 );
273 }
```

The `print_error()` and `usage()` functions are simple utility functions. `print_error()` is called whenever a SQL error occurs. The `usage()` function is called by `main()` if there is an improper number of arguments on the command line.

Summary

This chapter should have given you a good feel for how to build C applications using ecpg. Don't let the last section throw you off too much—ecpg isn't all that well suited to processing dynamic SQL (at least in comparison to libpq or libpgeasy).

The ecpg preprocessor and library are remarkably well designed for building complete PostgreSQL applications quickly.

If you don't need to process dynamic queries, I think that ecpg is the quickest and easiest way to connect a C application to a PostgreSQL database. If you do need to handle dynamic queries, you should consider coding the static parts of your application using ecpg and using libpq (or libpgeasy) for the dynamic parts.

Most of the features in ecpg come from the SQL3 standard and you should find that it is reasonably easy to move embedded SQL applications among various databases (assuming that you haven't used too many "special" features).

12

Using PostgreSQL from an ODBC Client Application

ODBC (OPEN DATABASE CONNECTIVITY) IS AN API (application programming interface) that provides an application with a consistent database interface. To understand the architecture of ODBC, it helps to understand the problem that ODBC was designed to solve.

Let's say that you are an independent software vendor and you have just finished developing an accounting package that you intend to sell to as many users as possible. Your accounting application was designed to store its data in Sybase. Your original application uses the Sybase OpenClient interface to interact with the database. One day, a potential customer tells you that he is very interested in buying your application, but his corporate standard mandates that all data must be stored in PostgreSQL. If you want to sell your product to this customer, you have two options.

First, you could add a second interface to your application and somehow arrange things so that your application would use whichever database is available. That would leave you with a Sybase-specific interface and a PostgreSQL-specific interface. The downside to this approach is that you now have twice as much code to maintain (not to mention having to learn both interfaces). If you encounter another customer who requires Oracle support, you'll have to learn and maintain three interfaces.

Your other choice is to use a database-independent interface from the start. That's ODBC. ODBC gives your application a single API that can interact with PostgreSQL, Oracle, Sybase, SQL Server, MySQL, and many other databases.

The ODBC interface is based on the X/Open CLI (call-level interface) standard. The X/Open CLI standard is compatible with the ISO/IEC SQL/CLI standard. This means that an application that is written to use the ODBC standard API will also be compatible with the X/Open CLI standard and the ISO/IEC SQL/CLI standard. There are two important consequences to all this: An ODBC application can interact with many databases, and the standard is not likely to change at the whim of a single database vendor.

ODBC won't solve all your database portability problems. It provides an industry-standard API for establishing database connections, sending commands to a server, and retrieving the results. ODBC does *not* provide a standard language. If your application sends commands that are specific to PostgreSQL, that application won't automatically work with an Oracle backend. For example, in PostgreSQL, `END WORK` is a synonym for the more common `COMMIT`. If you are trying to build a portable application, you should use `COMMIT` rather than `END WORK`. In practice, most applications can use a common subset of SQL to achieve database portability. ODBC provides API portability, and SQL provides language portability. With this combination, your application can be *very* portable.

In this chapter, I'll focus on using ODBC from an application written in C or C++. ODBC would be a very useful API if it only provided a consistent database interface to C programs. However, ODBC offers another important feature—you can use ODBC to access databases from languages such as Visual Basic, Microsoft Access, FoxPro, Delphi, and others. You can also use ODBC to connect a web server to an ODBC-compliant database. I'll talk more about the PostgreSQL/Web server connection in Chapter 15, "The PHP API."

ODBC Architecture Overview

In a typical ODBC application, there are five components: the client application, the ODBC driver manager, a database-specific driver, an ODBC-compliant database server, and a data source.

The ODBC Client Application

The client application is the component that you have to write. Typically, an ODBC client is written in C or C++. The client interacts with a database by opening a data source (which I will describe in a moment), sending requests to the data source, and processing results.

The ODBC Driver Manager

The ODBC driver manager gets involved when the client application opens a data source. The driver manager is responsible for converting a data source name into a data source handle. After the client has provided the name of a data source, the driver manager searches a configuration file for the definition of that data source. One of the properties contained in a data source is the name of an ODBC driver.

The ODBC Driver

An ODBC driver is a shared library (or DLL on the MS Windows platform). A driver provides access to a specific type of database (for example, PostgreSQL or Oracle). The driver is responsible for translating ODBC requests into whatever form is expected by the backend database. The driver also translates database-specific results back into ODBC form for the client application.

The ODBC-Compliant Database

The backend database processes requests and provides results. By the time the database receives a request from the client application, the driver has already translated the request from ODBC form into a form understood by the server. In the case of PostgreSQL, the PostgreSQL ODBC driver translates requests into libpq function calls.

The Data Source

A *data source* is a named set of connection properties.

Each data source has a unique name (in the following examples, I use a data source named `MoviesDSN`). This name is used by a client application to represent the connection properties needed to connect to a particular database.

Here is a simple data source definition (later, I'll tell you how to actually build a data source definition):

```
[MoviesDSN]
Driver                 = PostgreSQLDriver
Description            = Movie Database
```

(Don't worry—you rarely have to build a data source definition by hand. In most cases, you construct a data source using a nice graphical user interface.)

The first line specifies the name of the data source (in this case, the data source is named `MoviesDSN`). The data source name is followed by a set of "keyword=value" pairs—each pair defines a connection property. The `Driver` property tells the ODBC driver manager which driver should be used to connect to this particular data source. The `Description` property is a human-friendly description of the data source (this property is displayed in ODBC configuration utilities).

Each ODBC driver supports a different set of connection properties (the `Driver` and `Description` properties are used by the driver manager, not by the driver). The PostgreSQL driver enables you to specify the database name, host address, port number, and a number of other properties.

Why does ODBC use a data source instead of letting you specify the connection properties each time you connect? It is much easier for an application (and a human) to work with a data source name than with a huge set of connection properties (I've shown you two properties here—most drivers support 10 or more properties). Separating the connection properties from the application also makes it much easier for a client to achieve database portability. Rather than embedding the properties in each client, you can use an external configuration tool to define a data source for each database that you might want to use.

Setting Up a Data Source on Unix Systems

Many people think that ODBC exists only in the world of Microsoft Windows—that's not the case at all. If you are working in a Linux or Unix environment, there are two open-source ODBC implementations: unixODBC (`www.unixODBC.org`) and iODBC (`www.iodbc.org`). You can also find commercially supported ODBC implementations for Unix, Linux, and other environments.

Installing unixODBC and the PostgreSQL ODBC Driver

Before you can use unixODBC, you must ensure that it is installed on your system. You'll also need the PostgreSQL ODBC driver. As in previous chapters, I'll assume that you are running a Red Hat Linux host. You'll need two RPM (Red Hat Package Manager) files: `unixODBC` and `unixODBC-kde`. Assuming that your host is connected to the Internet, you can use the `rpmfind` program to download the latest versions:

```
# rpmfind --latest --auto unixODBC unixODBC-kde
Installing unixODBC will require 2345 KBytes
Installing unixODBC-kde will require 244 KBytes

### To Transfer:
ftp://ftp.redhat.com/pub/.../RPMS/unixODBC-kde-2.2.0-5.i386.rpm
ftp://ftp.redhat.com/pub/.../RPMS/readline-4.2a-4.i386.rpm
ftp://ftp.redhat.com/pub/.../RPMS/unixODBC-2.2.0-5.i386.rpm
transferring ...
```

The `rpmfind` utility has located and downloaded all the packages that you need and saved them in the `/tmp` directory. Notice that you asked for two packages, but `rpmfind` downloaded three. The `rpmfind` utility checks for dependencies: It found that `unixODBC` requires the `readline` package and downloaded that for you as well.

Now that you have the packages downloaded, let's install them:

```
# cd /tmp
# rpm -ihv *.rpm
Preparing...     ########################### [100%]
1: readline      ########################### [ 33%]
2: unixODBC      ########################### [ 66%]
3: unixODBC-kde ########################### [100%]
```

If you want to view the list of files installed for a given package, you can use the `rpm` command in query mode. For example:

```
$ rpm -q -l unixODBC-kde
/etc/X11/applnk/System/DataManager.desktop
/etc/X11/applnk/System/ODBCConfig.desktop
/usr/bin/DataManager
/usr/bin/ODBCConfig
```

The `unixODBC` package includes the PostgreSQL ODBC driver.

If you install `unixODBC` from the Red Hat package files, `unixODBC` will store configuration information in the `/etc` directory. If you decide to build and install unixODBC from source, the default configuration will store information in the

`/usr/local/etc` directory, but you can override the location at compile time. The remainder of this discussion assumes that you installed from the Red Hat package files and will expect configuration files to be located in `/etc`.

The unixODBC implementation stores data source information in a set of configuration files (in Windows, ODBC configuration information is stored in the Registry). For any given user, there are three configuration files: a systemwide list of data sources, a systemwide list of drivers, and a user-specific list of data sources.

Each configuration file is organized as a flat text file, divided into sections, starting with a name surrounded by square brackets (`[]`). Each section contains a list of *`property = value`* pairs.

The `/etc/odbcinst.ini` file contains a list of ODBC drivers that are available on your system. Here is a sample `odbcinst.ini` entry:

```
[PostgreSQLDriver]
Description      = PostgreSQL driver
Driver           = /usr/local/lib/libodbcpsql.so
Setup            = /usr/local/lib/libodbcpsqlS.so
FileUsage        = 1
```

The first line defines a driver named `PostgreSQLDriver`. When you define a data source, you use this name to connect a data source to a driver. An ODBC driver is usually composed of two shared libraries: a setup library and the driver itself. The ODBC administrator (`ODBCConfig`) uses the setup library to prompt the user for driver-specific configuration information. The driver library contains a set of functions that provide a client application with access to the database. The `Driver` property contains the name of the driver-shared library. The `Setup` property contains the name of the setup-shared library. The final property (`FileUsage`) is an enumerated value that describes how a driver maps files into relational tables.[1] See the ODBC reference documentation (`msdn.microsoft.com/library`) for more information.

The `/etc/odbc.ini` file contains a list of ODBC data sources. Remember that a data source is a named set of properties. Here is a sample entry:

```
[PostgreSQL]
Description          = PostgreSQL Accounting Database
Driver               = PostgreSQLDriver
```

1. The `FileUsage` property can be set to one of three predefined values: `0`, `1`, or `2`. `FileUsage` provides a *hint* to the client application about how the database stores data in the OS file system. Some databases, such as Oracle, can store an entire installation in a single file or in a collection of files—the actual organization of the data is not important (and is not discernable) to the client application. An Oracle data source has a `FileUsage` value of `0`. Other databases, such as Paradox, store each table in a separate file. A Paradox data source has a `FileUsage` value of `1`. Finally, a data source whose `FileUsage` is set to `2` stores an entire database in a single file. This is different from type `0` in that a type `0` data source can store multiple databases in a single file.

The first line defines a data source named PostgreSQL. The Description property provides a human-friendly description of the data source (you will see both the description and the data source name in the ODBCConfig program). The Driver property contains the name of an ODBC driver, as defined in the /etc/odbcinst.ini file. Most of the entries in /etc/odbc.ini are more complex than this example. The unixODBC driver manager understands a few more properties, and each driver supports its own set of properties.

Fortunately, you don't have to edit any of the configuration files by hand. The unixODBC package includes a GUI configuration tool named ODBCConfig. When you first run ODBCConfig, you will see a list of all the data sources defined on your system (see Figure 12.1).

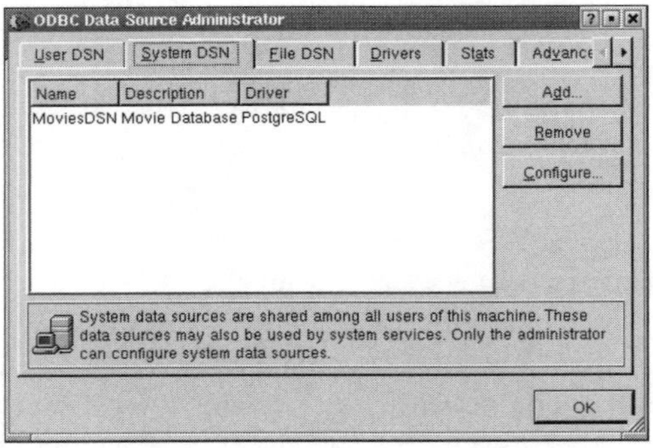

Figure 12.1 unixODBC Data Source Administrator.

If you installed unixODBC from the unixODBC and unixODBC-kde packages as previously described, you should find the ODBCConfig application on the KDE Start menu in the System folder. Click the ODBCConfig entry to invoke the program, or run ODBCConfig from a command line. The first time you run this program, you may get a warning that you don't have an .ODBCConfig subdirectory in your home directory—you can just click the OK button and ignore this warning: ODBCConfig creates the required configuration files automatically.

To add a new data source, press the Add button and you will see a list of installed drivers (see Figure 12.2).

Select one of the drivers and press OK (Note: If you're like me, you'll press the Add button by mistake. If you do that, ODBCConfig will assume that you want to add a new driver.)

After you have selected a driver, you will be asked to define the rest of the connection properties (see Figure 12.3). Remember that each driver understands a different set of connection properties, so the Data Source Properties dialog will look different if you are using a different driver.

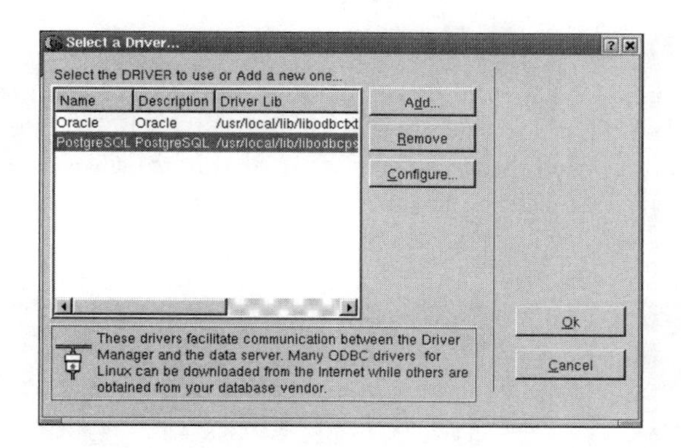

Figure 12.2 Adding a new data source.

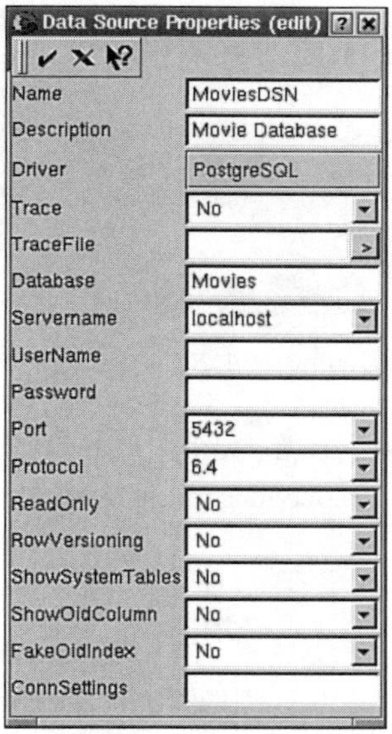

Figure 12.3 PostgreSQL Data Source Properties.

You can leave most of these properties set to their default values—you really need to provide only the `Name`, `Description`, and `Database` properties. (This dialog is a little confusing. Where's the OK button? To accept the changes that you have made, click the check mark in the upper-left corner of the window. To cancel, click the X.)

You can see that using the `ODBCConfig` utility is much easier than configuring a data source by hand. When you create a new data source using `ODBCConfig`, the data source properties are stored in the odbc.ini file.

Setting Up a Data Source in Windows

MS Windows also provides a graphical configuration tool, almost identical to `ODBCConfig`. On most Windows systems, you will find the ODBC administrator in the Control Panel or in the Administrative Tools applet within the Control Panel. Double-click whichever ODBC icon is present on your system, and you should see something similar to what is shown in Figure 12.4.

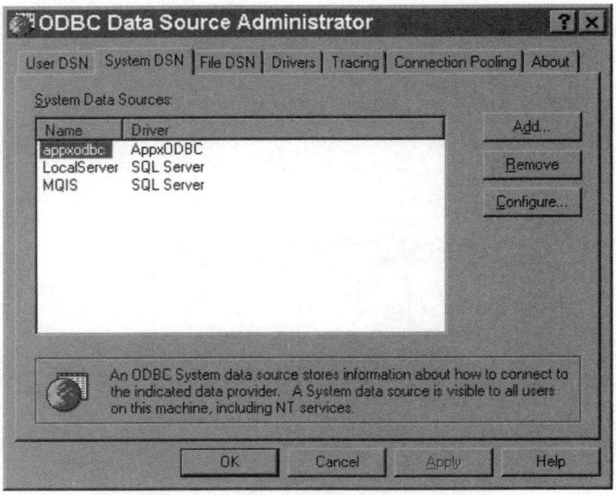

Figure 12.4 Windows ODBC Data Source Administrator.

The procedure for creating a data source using the Windows ODBC Data Source Administrator is identical to the procedure you would following using the unixODBC Data Source Administrator.

Prerequisites

The examples in this chapter assume that you have installed and configured the unixODBC or iODBC driver manager. I'll also assume that you have installed the PostgreSQL ODBC driver and created an ODBC data source.

Most of the examples in this chapter were developed with the GNU C/C++ compiler and GNU `make`. The final example uses the Qt library described in Chapter 10, "The PostgreSQL C++ API—`libpq++`."

Client 1—Connecting to the Server

Now that you understand the basic architecture of the ODBC API and you have defined a PostgreSQL data source, let's look at some sample code. This first client application connects to a database and then exits. Listing 12.1 provides an example that is much more complex than the sample clients in earlier chapters—ODBC is a complex API.

Listing 12.1 odbc/client1.c

```
 1 /* client1.c */
 2 
 3 #include <sql.h>
 4 #include <sqlext.h>
 5 
 6 #include <stdio.h>
 7 
 8 typedef enum { FALSE, TRUE } bool;
 9 
10 int main( int argc, char * argv[] )
11 {
12   SQLRETURN   result;
13   SQLHENV     envHandle;
14   SQLHDBC     conHandle;
15 
16   SQLAllocHandle( SQL_HANDLE_ENV,
17                   SQL_NULL_HANDLE,
18                   &envHandle );
19 
20   SQLSetEnvAttr( envHandle,
21                  SQL_ATTR_ODBC_VERSION,
22                 (SQLPOINTER)SQL_OV_ODBC2,
23                  0 );
24 
25   SQLAllocHandle( SQL_HANDLE_DBC,
26                   envHandle,
27                   &conHandle );
28 
29   result = SQLConnect( conHandle,  // connection handle
30                 argv[1], SQL_NTS,   // data source name
31                 argv[2], SQL_NTS,   // user name
32                 argv[3], SQL_NTS ); // password
33 
34 
35   if( result == SQL_SUCCESS || result == SQL_SUCCESS_WITH_INFO )
36   {
37     printf( "connection ok...\n" );
38     return( 0 );
39   }
40   else
41   {
42     printf( "connection failed...\n" );
43     return( -1 );
44   }
45 }
```

If you want to run this program, you will need to provide three arguments: the name of a data source, a valid username, and a password. Here is an example:

```
$ ./client1 MoviesDSN korry cows
connection ok...
```

Now, let's look through the code.

The first thing you'll notice when you work with ODBC is that you have to create a lot of handles. Remember that a handle is an opaque data type—there is a data structure behind a handle, but you can't get to it. There are only three things that you can do with a handle: You can create it, you can destroy it, and you can pass it to a function.

ODBC Handle Types

ODBC defines four different types of handles:

- A `SQLHENV` is an environment handle—it functions as the top-level handle to the ODBC API. You must create an environment handle before you can do anything else with ODBC.
- A `SQLHDBC` is a handle to a database connection. When you connect to a database, you initialize a `SQLHDBC` handle. After you have a valid database connection handle, you can allocate a statement handle.
- A statement handle has the type `SQLHSTMT`. You must create a statement handle before you can send a command to the database. Result set information is returned through a `SQLHSTMT` handle.
- The last handle type defined by ODBC is `SQLHDESC`. A SQLHDESC handle is a descriptor handle. Descriptor handles are used when you are writing an ODBC driver (as opposed to a client application) and may be used in sophisticated error-handling code. I've never needed to allocate a SQLHDESC myself; you probably won't need to either.

You create an environment handle at line 13 and initialize it by calling `SQLAllocHandle (SQL_HANDLE_ENV, ...)`. There are three arguments to the `SQLAllocHandle()` function. The first argument specifies what type of handle you are trying to create. The second argument specifies the parent of the new handle. The final argument is a pointer to the handle that you want to initialize. Table 12.1 shows how to allocate different types of handles using `SQLAllocHandle()`. Notice that an environment handle doesn't have a parent, so you pass `SQL_NULL_HANDLE` as the second argument.

Table 12.1 **SQLAllocHandle() Arguments**

Symbolic Name	Data Type of New Handle	Type of Parent	Description
SQL_HANDLE_ENV	SQLHENV	No parent	Environment handle
SQL_HANDLE_DBC	SQLHDBC	SQLHENV	Database connection handle
SQL_HANDLE_STMT	SQLHSTMT	SQLHDBC	Statement handle
SQL_HANDLE_DESC	SQLHDESC	SQLHDBC	Descriptor handle

After you have an initialized environment handle, you need to tell the ODBC library what version of ODBC you expect to find. Use the `SQLSetEnvAttr()` function to tell ODBC that you are going to interact using the ODBC 2.x protocol. The PostgreSQL ODBC driver is written to the ODBC 2.5 specification, so you can't call any of the driver-supplied functions that were added in ODBC 3.0. (Note: The driver manager translates many 3.0 functions into 2.x requests, but I find that the results generally are not reliable.)

At line 25, you allocate a connection handle (a `SQLHDBC`). Compare this function call with your earlier call to `SQLAllocHandle()`:

```
SQLAllocHandle( SQL_HANDLE_ENV, SQL_NULL_HANDLE, &envHandle );
SQLAllocHandle( SQL_HANDLE_DBC, envHandle,       &conHandle );
```

You can see in Table 12.1 that an environment handle does not have a parent. When you allocate an environment handle, you pass `SQL_NULL_HANDLE` instead of a parent. When you allocate a connection handle, you allocate it within the context of an environment; you provide an environment handle as the second parameter to `SQLAllocHandle()`.

At this point in the example code, you have allocated an environment handle, declared which ODBC protocol you want to use, and allocated a connection handle. You still have not connected to a data source. There are three functions that we can use to connect to a data source: `SQLConnect()`, `SQLDriverConnect()`, and `SQLBrowseConnect()`. The simplest connection function is `SQLConnect()`. Here is the function prototype for `SQLConnect()`:

```
SQLRETURN SQLConnect( SQLHDBC       ConnectionHandle,
                      SQLCHAR     * DataSourceName,
                      SQLSMALLINT DataSourceLength,
                      SQLCHAR     * UserName,
                      SQLSMALLINT UserNameLength,
                      SQLCHAR     * Password,
                      SQLSMALLINT PasswordLength );
```

When you call `SQLConnect()`, you provide a connection handle, a data source name, a username, and a password. In this sample code, you use command-line arguments for the data source name, username, and password. Notice that you don't actually compute the length of each string that you pass to `SQLConnect()`—instead, you pass SQL_NTS to tell ODBC that you are sending NULL-terminated strings.

The other connection functions—(`SQLDriverConnect()` and `SQLBrowseConnect()`—are more complex. I'll show you how to use `SQLDriverConnect()` in a later example, but the PostgreSQL ODBC driver does not support `SQLBrowseConnect()`.

`SQLConnect()` returns a `SQLRETURN` value. One of the things that complicates ODBC programming is that ODBC defines two different `SUCCESS` values, `SQL_SUCCESS` and `SQL_SUCCESS_WITH_INFO`, and you have to check for either of these values. I'll discuss the difference between these two values in the next section.

In the sample code, you just print a message to tell the user whether he could connect to the requested data source. I'm cheating a little in this example—a well-behaved application would tear down the database connection and properly discard the environment and connection handles. In this case, the application exits immediately after finishing its interaction with the database. If you still had more work to do and no longer needed the database connection, it would be a good idea to free up the resources required to maintain the connection.

Client 2—Adding Error Checking

In the previous example, I omitted a lot of code that would normally appear in a real-world application. In this section, I'll add some simple error-handling functions and show you how to properly free up the resources (handles) that you create. I'll also use a more complex and more flexible connection function: `SQLDriverConnect()`.

In the previous section, I mentioned that most ODBC functions return two different values to indicate a successful completion: `SQL_SUCCESS` and `SQL_SUCCESS_WITH_INFO`. To make your ODBC programming life a little easier, you can use the following function to check for success or failure:

```
static bool SQL_OK( SQLRETURN result )
{
  if( result == SQL_SUCCESS || result == SQL_SUCCESS_WITH_INFO )
    return( TRUE );
  else
    return( FALSE );
}
```

A typical call to `SQL_OK()` might look like this:

```
if( SQL_OK( SQLAllocHandle( SQL_HANDLE_ENV, SQL_NULL_HANDLE, &handle ))
{
    ...
}
```

So what's the difference between `SQL_SUCCESS` and `SQL_SUCCESS_WITH_INFO`? The simple answer is that `SQL_SUCCESS` implies that a function succeeded; `SQL_SUCCESS_WITH_INFO` also means that a function succeeded, but more information is available. For example, if you try to `REVOKE` a privilege from a user, but the user did not have the privilege to begin with, you'll get a `SQL_SUCCESS_WITH_INFO` result. The request is completed successfully, but you might want to know the extra information.

In an ODBC 2.x application, you call the `SQLError()` to retrieve any extended return information. If you call `SQLError()` after receiving a `SQL_SUCCESS` result, the `SQLError()` function will fail. Here is the function prototype for the `SQLError()` function:

```
SQLRETURN SQLError(
    SQLHENV        envHandle,
    SQLHDBC        conHandle,
    SQLHSTMT       stmtHandle,
    SQLCHAR      * sqlState,
```

```
SQLINTEGER  * nativeError,
SQLCHAR     * messageText,
SQLSMALLINT   messageTextLength,
SQLSMALLINT * requiredLength );
```

Notice that the `SQLError()` function can accept three different handles—when you call `SQLError()`, you provide only one of the three. For example, if you receive an error status on a statement handle, you would call `SQLError()`, as follows:

```
SQLError( SQL_NULL_HENV, SQL_NULL_HDBC, stmtHandle, ... );
```

Table 12.2 shows how you would call `SQLError()` given each handle type.

Table 12.2 **Handle Types and SQLError() Parameters**

Handle Type	SQLError() Parameters
`SQLHENV`	`envHandle`, `SQL_NULL_HDBC`, `SQL_NULL_HSTMT`, ...
`SQLHDBC`	`SQL_NULL_HENV`, `conHandle`, `SQL_NULL_HSTMT`, ...
`SQLHSTMT`	`SQL_NULL_HENV`, `SQL_NULL_HDBC`, `stmtHandle`, ...

If the `SQLError()` function succeeds[2], it returns three pieces of status information.

The first is called the `SQLSTATE`. The `sqlState` parameter should point to a six-byte `SQLCHAR` array. `SQLError()` will fill in the `sqlState` array with a five-character code (and a NULL-terminator). ODBC uses the `SQLSTATE` as a way to provide status information in a database-independent format. A `SQLSTATE` code is composed of a two-character *class* followed by a three-character *subclass*. `SQLSTATE` code '`00000`' means 'successful completion' and is equivalent to `SQL_SUCCESS`. `SQLSTATE` values that begin with the class '01' are warnings. Any other `SQLSTATE` class indicates an error. Table 12.3 shows a few common `SQLSTATE` values.

Table 12.3 **Common SQLState Values**

SQLState	Meaning
`00000`	Successful completion
`01004`	Warning-string data, right truncation (that is, you tried to select 20 bytes into a 10-byte buffer)
`23000`	Integrity constraint violation (for example, you tried to add a duplicate key value into a unique index)
`42000`	Syntax error or access rule violation
`HY010`	Function sequence error
`42S02`	Base table (or view) not found

2. The `SQLError()` will fail if you give it a bad handle or if there are no more messages to report to the application.

The second piece of information returned by `SQLError()` is a native error number. The driver returns the native error number—you have to know what kind of database your application is connected to before you can make sense of the native error numbers. Not all drivers return native error numbers.

The most useful information returned by `SQLError()` is the text of an error message. The last three parameters to `SQLError()` are used to retrieve the error message. The `messageText` parameter points to an array of `SQLCHAR`s. This array should be `SQL_MAX_MESSAGE_LENGTH+1` bytes long. `messageTextLength` tells `SQLError()` how many bytes it can write into `*messageText`. `SQLError()` writes the number of bytes required to contain the message text into the `SQLSMALLINT` pointed to by the `requiredLength`[3] parameter.

Listing 12.2 shows the `client1.c` example, fleshed out with some error-handling code.

Listing 12.2 `odbc/client2.c`

```
 1 /* client2.c */
 2
 3 #include <sql.h>
 4 #include <sqlext.h>
 5 #include <sqltypes.h>
 6 #include <stdio.h>
 7
 8 typedef enum { FALSE, TRUE } bool;
 9
10 static bool SQL_OK( SQLRETURN result )
11 {
12   if( result == SQL_SUCCESS || result == SQL_SUCCESS_WITH_INFO )
13     return( TRUE );
14   else
15     return( FALSE );
16 }
17
```

3. Many API functions need to return variable-length information—somehow, the caller must know how much space to allocate for the return information. A common solution to this problem is to call a function twice. When you make the first call, you tell the function that you allocated 0 bytes for the variable-length information. The function tells you how much space is required by setting something like the `requiredLength` parameter described previously. After you know how much space is required, you allocate the required number of bytes and call the function a second time. In the case of `SQLError()`, the `requiredLength` parameter is pretty pointless. We can't call `SQLError()` more than once per diagnostic because the diagnostic is discarded as soon as `SQLError()` retrieves it from the given handle.

You've already seen the `SQL_OK()` function—it simply checks for the two success codes returned by ODBC.

```
18 static bool printErrors( SQLHENV  envHandle,
19                          SQLHDBC  conHandle,
20                          SQLHSTMT stmtHandle )
21 {
22   SQLRETURN   result;
23   SQLCHAR     sqlState[6];
24   SQLINTEGER  nativeError;
25   SQLSMALLINT requiredLength;
26   SQLCHAR     messageText[SQL_MAX_MESSAGE_LENGTH+1];
27
28   do
29   {
30     result = SQLError( envHandle,
31                        conHandle,
32                        stmtHandle,
33                        sqlState,
34                        &nativeError,
35                        messageText,
36                        sizeof( messageText ),
37                        &requiredLength );
38
39     if( SQL_OK( result ))
40       {
41         printf( "SQLState     = %s\n", sqlState );
42         printf( "Native error = %d\n", nativeError );
43         printf( "Message text = %s\n", messageText );
44       }
45   } while( SQL_OK( result ));
46 }
47
```

The `printErrors()` function is new. You call `SQLError()` until it returns a failure code. Why would you call `SQLError()` multiple times? Because each ODBC function can return multiple errors. Remember, each time `SQLError()` returns successfully, it removes a single diagnostic from the given handle. If you don't retrieve all the errors from a handle, they will be discarded (and lost) the next time you use that handle.

```
48 int main( int argc, char * argv[] )
49 {
50   SQLRETURN   res;
51   SQLHENV     env;
52   SQLHDBC     con;
53   SQLCHAR     fullConnectStr[SQL_MAX_OPTION_STRING_LENGTH];
54   SQLSMALLINT requiredLength;
```

```
 55
 56   res = SQLAllocHandle( SQL_HANDLE_ENV, SQL_NULL_HANDLE, &env );
 57
 58   if( SQL_OK( res ))
 59   {
 60     res = SQLSetEnvAttr( env,
 61                          SQL_ATTR_ODBC_VERSION,
 62                          (SQLPOINTER)SQL_OV_ODBC2,
 63                          0 );
 64     if( !SQL_OK( res ))
 65     {
 66       printErrors( env, SQL_NULL_HDBC, SQL_NULL_HSTMT );
 67       exit( -1 );
 68     }
 69
 70     res = SQLAllocHandle( SQL_HANDLE_DBC, env, &con );
 71     if( !SQL_OK( res ))
 72     {
 73       printErrors( env, SQL_NULL_HDBC, SQL_NULL_HSTMT );
 74       exit( -2 );
 75     }
 76
 77     res = SQLDriverConnect( con,
 78                             (SQLHWND)NULL,
 79                             argv[1], SQL_NTS,
 80                             fullConnectStr,
 81                             sizeof( fullConnectStr ),
 82                             &requiredLength,
 83                             SQL_DRIVER_NOPROMPT );
 84
 85
 86     if( !SQL_OK( res ))
 87     {
 88       printErrors( SQL_NULL_HENV, con, SQL_NULL_HSTMT );
 89       exit( -3 );
 90     }
 91
 92     printf( "connection ok...disconnecting\n" );
 93
 94     res = SQLDisconnect( con );
 95     if( !SQL_OK( res ))
 96     {
 97       printErrors( SQL_NULL_HENV, con, SQL_NULL_HSTMT );
 98       exit( -4 );
 99     }
100
101     res = SQLFreeHandle( SQL_HANDLE_DBC, con );
```

```
102      if( !SQL_OK( res ))
103      {
104        printErrors( SQL_NULL_HENV, con, SQL_NULL_HSTMT );
105        exit( -5 );
106      }
107
108      res = SQLFreeHandle( SQL_HANDLE_ENV, env );
109      if( !SQL_OK( res ))
110      {
111        printErrors( env, SQL_NULL_HDBC, SQL_NULL_HSTMT );
112        exit( -6 );
113      }
114    }
115
116    exit( 0 );
117
118 }
```

There are three new features in the `main()` function.

First, you'll notice that I have littered the code with calls to `printErrors()`. You call `printErrors()` any time an ODBC function returns a failure status. You could also call `printErrors()` when you get a `SQL_SUCCESS_WITH_INFO` status, but in most cases, the extra information is uninteresting.

Notice that you exit as soon as an error is encountered. Each call to `exit()` specifies a different value: If the program succeeds, you return `0`; in all other cases, you return a unique negative number. The return value is given to the calling program (usually a shell) and is used to check for success or failure.

The other thing that's different between this version of `main()` and the version that I included in `client1.c` is that you use the `SQLDriverConnect()` function instead of `SQLConnect()`. The `SQLDriverConnect()` function is a more powerful version of `SQLConnect()`. Whereas `SQLConnect()` allows you to specify three connection properties (the data source name, user id, and password), `SQLDriverConnect()` can accept an arbitrary number of properties. In fact, the following two calls are (roughly) equivalent:

```
SQLConnect( con, "MoviesDSN", SQL_NTS, "korry", SQL_NTS, "cows", SQL_NTS );
SQLDriverConnect( con, (SQLHWND)NULL,
                  "DSN=MoviesDSN;UID=korry;PWD=cows", SQL_NTS, ... );
```

Here is the function prototype for `SQLDriverConnect()`:

```
SQLRETURN SQLDriverConnect(
    SQLHDBC        connectionHandle,
    SQLHWND        windowHandle,
    SQLCHAR      * connectStrIn,
    SQLCHAR      * connectStrOut,
    SQLSMALLINT    connectStrOutMax,
    SQLSMALLINT  * requiredBytes,
    SQLUSMALLINT   driverCompletion )
```

The purpose of the first argument is pretty obvious—you provide the connection handle that you want to connect.

The second argument might seem a bit mysterious—what's a `SQLHWND`, and why would I need one to connect to a database? One of the differences between `SQLDriverConnect()` and `SQLConnect()` is that `SQLDriverConnect()` can prompt the user for more connection parameters. If you are running a graphical client application, you would expect to see a pop-up dialog if the database that you are connecting to requires more information. The `SQLHWND` parameter is used to provide a parent window handle that the driver can use to display a dialog. Under Windows, a `SQLHWND` is really a window handle (that is, a `HWND`). There is no clear winner in the Unix GUI wars, so there is no standard data type that represents a window handle. The driver manager ignores the `windowHandle` parameter and just passes it along to the driver. Very few Unix-hosted ODBC drivers support a connection dialog when using `SQLDriverConnect()`. One driver that *does* support a connection dialog is the IBM DB2 driver If you are calling `SQLDriverConnect()` to connect to a DB2 database, you would pass in a Motif widget handle as the `windowHandle` parameter (if you are connecting to a DB2 database under Windows, you would pass in a HWND). Drivers that don't provide a connection dialog return an error if the `connectStrIn` parameter doesn't contain all the required information.

The third argument to `SQLDriverConnect()` is an ODBC connection string (this is *not* the same as a libpq connection string). An ODBC connection string is a semicolon-delimited collection of keyword=value properties. The ODBC driver manager looks for the `DSN` property to determine which data source you want to connect to. After the driver is loaded, the driver manager passes all the properties to the driver. The PostgreSQL driver understands the following properties shown in Table 12.4.

Table 12.4 **PostgreSQL/ODBC Connection String Properties**

Property	Description
`DSN`	Data source name
`UID`	User ID
`PWD`	Password
`SERVER`	Server's IP address or hostname
`PORT`	TCP port number on server
`DATABASE`	PostgreSQL database name

(The PostgreSQL ODBC driver supports other connection properties. See the documentation that comes with the driver for a complete list.)

The next three arguments (`connectStrOut`, `connectStrOutMax`, and `requiredBytes`) are used to return a complete connection string to the client application. If you successfully connect to a database, the driver will populate `*connectStrOut` with a null-terminated string that contains all the connection properties that the driver used. For example, if you call `SQLDriverConnect()` with the following connection string:

```
"DSN=MoviesDSN; UID=korry; PWD=cows"
```

the driver will return a string such as

```
DSN=MoviesDsn;
DATABASE=movies;
SERVER=localhost;
PORT=5432;
UID=korry;
PWD=;
READONLY=No;
PROTOCOL=6.4;
FAKEOIDINDEX=No;
SHOWOIDCOLUMN=No;
ROWVERSIONING=No;
SHOWSYSTEMTABLES=No;
CONNSETTINGS=';
```

This is assuming that the `video-store` data source uses a PostgreSQL driver. You may have noticed that the complete connection string is composed from the set of connection properties that this driver understands—most of the properties are defaulted from the data source.

If the buffer that you provide is too short for the entire connection string, `SQLDriverConnect()` will truncate the string and will return the required length in `*requiredBytes`.

You use the final parameter to `SQLDriverConnect()` to indicate how much assistance you want if the connection string is incomplete. Acceptable values for `driverCompletion` are shown in Table 12.5.

Table 12.5 **Values for SQLDriverConnect().driverCompletion**

Value	Description
`SQL_DRIVER_PROMPT`	The user sees a connection dialog, even if it is not required.
`SQL_DRIVER_COMPLETE`	The user sees a connection dialog if the connection string does not contain all required information. The connection dialog prompts the user for required and optional connection properties.
`SQL_DRIVER_COMPLETE_REQUIRED`	The user sees a connection dialog if the connection string does not contain all required information. The connection dialog only prompts the user for required connection properties.
`SQL_DRIVER_NOPROMPT`	If the connection string does not contain all required information, `SQLDriverConnect()` will return `SQL_ERROR`, and the user will not be prompted (by the driver).

Most open-source ODBC drivers support only the `SQL_DRIVER_NOPROMPT` option. If you ask for a different completion type, it will be treated like `SQL_DRIVER_NOPROMPT`.

The last thing that I'll explain about this client is the teardown code. To properly clean up the client application, you have to disconnect the connection handle (using `SQLDisconnect()`) and then free the connection and environment handles using `SQLFreeHandle()`. The order in which you tear down connections is important. You won't be able to free the connection handle until you disconnect it. You won't be able to free an environment handle until all the connection handles have been disconnected and freed.

If you want to run this program, the single command-line argument is a `SQLDriverConnect()` connection string. For example:

```
$ ./client2 "DSN=MoviesDSN; UID=korry; PWD=cows"
```

In the next section, I'll introduce a new handle type—the `SQLHSTMT` statement handle. The parent of a `SQLHSTMT` is a connection handle. You must free all child statement handles before you can free a connection handle.

This section was rather long, but now you know how to connect to a database, how to detect errors, and how to properly tear down an ODBC connection. The next section describes how to process a simple query in an ODBC client.

Client 3—Processing Queries

When you execute a query using ODBC, your client will first send the query to the server, and then process the results.

The ODBC result-processing model is more complex than other PostgreSQL APIs. In the libpq, libpq++, and libpgeasy APIs, you send a query to the server and then call a function to access each field (in each row) in the result set.

An ODBC application generally uses a different scheme. After you send the query to the server, you *bind* each field in the result set to a variable in your application. After all the result fields are bound, you can fetch the individual rows in the result set—each time you fetch a new row, the bound variables are populated by ODBC.

Listing 12.3 shows you how to execute a query and display the results.

Listing 12.3 `odbc/client3.c`

```
 1 /* client3.c */
 2
 3 #include <sql.h>
 4 #include <sqlext.h>
 5 #include <sqltypes.h>
 6 #include <stdio.h>
 7
 8 typedef enum { FALSE, TRUE } bool;
 9
10 typedef struct
```

Listing 12.3 **Continued**

```
11 {
12   char          name[128+1];
13   SQLSMALLINT   nameLength;
14   SQLSMALLINT   dataType;
15   SQLUINTEGER   fieldLength;
16   SQLSMALLINT   scale;
17   SQLSMALLINT   nullable;
18   SQLINTEGER    displaySize;
19   int           headerLength;
20   SQLINTEGER    resultLength;
21   char        * value;
22 } resultField;
23
24 static void printResultSet( SQLHSTMT stmt );
25
```

The only thing that is new here is the `resultField` structure. I'll use an array of `resultFields` to process the result set. A note on terminology here: PostgreSQL documentation makes a minor distinction between a field and a column. Column refers to a column in a database, whereas field can refer to a column or a computed value. ODBC does not make this distinction. I tend to use the terms interchangeably.

```
26 static bool SQL_OK( SQLRETURN result )
27 {
28   if( result == SQL_SUCCESS || result == SQL_SUCCESS_WITH_INFO )
29     return( TRUE );
30   else
31     return( FALSE );
32 }
33
34 static bool printErrors( SQLHENV  envHandle,
35                          SQLHDBC  conHandle,
36                          SQLHSTMT stmtHandle )
37 {
38   SQLRETURN   result;
39   SQLCHAR     sqlState[6];
40   SQLINTEGER  nativeError;
41   SQLSMALLINT requiredLength;
42   SQLCHAR     messageText[SQL_MAX_MESSAGE_LENGTH+1];
43
44   do
45   {
46     result = SQLError( envHandle,
47                        conHandle,
48                        stmtHandle,
49                        sqlState,
```

```
50                            &nativeError,
51                            messageText,
52                            sizeof( messageText ),
53                            &requiredLength );
54
55      if( SQL_OK( result ))
56        {
57          printf( "SQLState     = %s\n", sqlState );
58          printf( "Native error = %d\n", nativeError );
59          printf( "Message text = %s\n", messageText );
60        }
61    } while( SQL_OK( result ));
62 }
63
```

You've already seen SQL_OK() and printErrors() in the previous example, so I won't bother explaining them here.

```
64 static void executeStmt( SQLHDBC con, char * stmtText )
65 {
66   SQLHSTMT  stmt;
67
68   SQLAllocHandle( SQL_HANDLE_STMT, con, &stmt );
69
70   if( SQL_OK( SQLExecDirect( stmt, stmtText, SQL_NTS )))
71     printResultSet( stmt );
72   else
73     printErrors( SQL_NULL_HENV, SQL_NULL_HDBC, stmt );
74 }
```

The executeStmt() function is responsible for sending a query to the server. You start by allocating a new type of handle—a SQLHSTMT. A SQLHSTMT is a statement handle. The parent of a statement handle is always a connection handle (or a SQLHDBC).

After you have a statement handle, send the query to the server using SQLExecDirect(). SQLExecDirect() is pretty simple—you provide a statement handle, the text of the query that you want to send to the server, and the length of the query string (or SQL_NTS to indicate that the query text is a null-terminated string).

If SQLExecDirect() returns a success value, you call printResultSet() to process the result set.

```
75
76 static void printResultSet( SQLHSTMT stmt )
77 {
78   SQLSMALLINT   i;
79   SQLSMALLINT   columnCount;
80   resultField * fields;
81
82   //  First, examine the metadata for the
```

```
 83  //  result set so that we know how many
 84  //  fields we have and how much room we need for each.
 85
 86  SQLNumResultCols( stmt, &columnCount );
 87
 88  fields = (resultField *)calloc( columnCount+1,
 89              sizeof( resultField ));
 90
 91  for( i = 1; i <= columnCount; i++ )
 92  {
 93    SQLDescribeCol( stmt,
 94          i,
 95          fields[i].name,
 96          sizeof( fields[i].name ),
 97          &fields[i].nameLength,
 98          &fields[i].dataType,
 99          &fields[i].fieldLength,
100          &fields[i].scale,
101          &fields[i].nullable );
102
103    SQLColAttribute( stmt,
104           i,
105           SQL_DESC_DISPLAY_SIZE,
106           NULL,
107           0,
108           NULL,
109           &fields[i].displaySize );
110
111
112    fields[i].value = (char *)malloc( fields[i].displaySize + 1 );
113
114    if( fields[i].nameLength > fields[i].displaySize )
115      fields[i].headerLength = fields[i].nameLength;
116    else
117      fields[i].headerLength = fields[i].displaySize;
118  }
119
120  //  Now print out the column headers
121
122  for( i = 1; i <= columnCount; i++ )
123  {
124    printf( "%-*s ", fields[i].headerLength, fields[i].name );
125  }
126  printf( "\n" );
127
128  //  Now fetch and display the results...
129
130  while( SQL_OK( SQLFetch( stmt )))
```

```
131    {
132      for( i = 1; i <= columnCount; i++)
133      {
134        SQLRETURN result;
135
136        result = SQLGetData( stmt,
137             i,
138             SQL_C_CHAR,
139             fields[i].value,
140             fields[i].displaySize,
141             &fields[i].resultLength );
142
143        if( fields[i].resultLength == SQL_NULL_DATA )
144           printf( "%-*s ", fields[i].headerLength, "" );
145        else
146           printf( "%-*s ", fields[i].headerLength, fields[i].value );
147      }
148      printf( "\n" );
149    }
150
151    for( i = 1; i <= columnCount; i++ )
152      free( fields[i].value );
153
154    free( fields );
155
156 }
157
```

The `printResultSet()` function is somewhat complex. It starts by building up an array of `resultField` structures to keep track of the metadata for the query that was just executed.

You first call `SQLNumResultCols()` to determine how many fields (or columns) will appear in the result set. After you know how many fields you will be processing, you allocate an array of `resultField` structures—one structure for each field (and one extra to simplify the code).

Next, you call two metadata functions so that you know what kind of information is being returned for each field. The `SQLDescribeCol()` function returns the column name, data type, binary field length, scale (used for numeric data types), and nullability for a given field. Notice that field indexes start with `1`, not `0`—so, the loop goes from `1` to `columnCount` rather than the usual `0` to `columnCount-1`; you don't use `fields[0]` for simplicity.

The `SQLColAttribute()` function returns a specific metadata attribute for the given column (`i`). You will retrieve each field in the form of a null-terminated string, so you need to know the maximum display length for each field. The `SQL_DESC_DISPLAY_SIZE` attribute is just what you need.

The `SQLDescribeCol()` and `SQLColAttribute()` functions both return column-related metadata. `SQLDescribeCol()` is a convenient function that returns the most commonly used metadata properties. Calling `SQLDescribeCol()` is equivalent to

```
SQLColAttribute( stmt, column, SQL_DESC_NAME, ... );
SQLColAttribute( stmt, column, SQL_DESC_TYPE, ... );
SQLColAttribute( stmt, column, SQL_DESC_LENGTH, ... );
SQLColAttribute( stmt, column, SQL_DESC_SCALE, ... );
SQLColAttribute( stmt, column, SQL_DESC_NULLABLE, ... );
```

After you have retrieved and stored the metadata for a column, you allocate a buffer large enough to contain the data for the column in the form of a null-terminated string. You also compute the header length. You want to print each column in a horizontal space large enough to hold either the column name or the column contents, whichever is longer.

After printing out the column headings (lines 122–126), we start processing the contents of the result set. The `SQLFetch()` function will fetch the next row within the result set associated with the given `SQLHSTMT`. `SQLFetch()` will return the value `SQL_NO_DATA` when you have exhausted the result set.

ODBC Metadata Types

So far, we have looked only at metadata that describes a result set. Because ODBC is designed as a portability layer between your application and the backend database, ODBC provides a rich set of metadata functions. First, you can retrieve a list of the data sources defined on your system using the `SQLDataSources()` function. The `SQLDrivers()` function will retrieve a list of installed drivers.

After you have connected to a data source, you can retrieve a list of supported data types by calling `SQLGetTypeInfo()`. This function returns the list as a result set—you use `SQLFetch()` and `SQLGetData()` (described later) to obtain the list.

You can use `SQLFunctions()` to determine which of the ODBC API functions are supported by a given driver. The PostgreSQL ODBC Driver is (currently) an ODBC 2.5 driver and does not directly support ODBC 3.0 functions. The PostgreSQL driver does not support a few of the ODBC 2.5 functions (such as `SQLProcedures()`, `SQLProcedureColumns()`, and `SQLBrowseConnect()`).

You can also ask the driver whether it supports various SQL syntax features. For example, if you call `SQLGetInfo( ..., SQL_CREATE_TABLE, ... )`, you can determine which `CREATE TABLE` clauses are supported by the database's `CREATE TABLE` statement. The `SQLGetInfo()` function also returns version information, as shown in Table 12.6.

Table 12.6 **Version Information Returned by** `SQLGetInfo()`

`SQLGetInfo()` **InfoType Argument**	**Return Information**
SQL_DBMS_VER	Database version (for example, PostgreSQL 7.1.3)
SQL_DM_VER	Driver manager version
SQL_DRIVER_NAME	Driver name
SQL_DRIVER_ODBC_VER	ODBC version that driver conforms to
SQL_DRIVER_VER	Driver version
SQL_SERVER_NAME	Name of server

You can use `SQLGetInfo(..., SQL_TXN_CAPABLE, ...)` to find out about the transaction-processing capabilities of a database.

By my count, `SQLGetInfo()` can return more than 150 different pieces of information about a data source!

If `SQLFetch()` succeeds, you retrieve each column in the current row using the `SQLGetData()` function, which has the following prototype:

```
SQLRETURN SQLGetData( SQLHSTMT stmtHandle,
                      SQLUSMALLINT columnNumber,
                      SQLSMALLINT  desiredDataType,
                      SQLPOINTER   destination,
                      SQLINTEGER   destinationLength,
                      SQLINTEGER * resultLength );
```

When you call `SQLGetData()`, you want ODBC to put the data into your `fields[i].value` buffer so you pass that address (and the `displaySize`). Passing in a `desiredDataType` of `SQL_C_CHAR` tells ODBC to return each column in the form of a null-terminated string. `SQLGetData()` returns the actual field length in `fields[i].resultLength`—if the field is NULL, you will get back the value `SQL_NULL_DATA`.

Lines 143–146 print each field (left-justified within a `fields[i].headerLength` space).

Finally, clean up after yourself by freeing the value buffers and then the `resultField` array:

```
158 int main( int argc, char * argv[] )
159 {
160   SQLRETURN   res;
161   SQLHENV     env;
162   SQLHDBC     con;
163   SQLCHAR     fullConnectStr[SQL_MAX_OPTION_STRING_LENGTH];
164   SQLSMALLINT requiredLength;
165
166   res = SQLAllocHandle( SQL_HANDLE_ENV, SQL_NULL_HANDLE, &env );
167
168   if( SQL_OK( res ))
169   {
170     res = SQLSetEnvAttr( env,
171                          SQL_ATTR_ODBC_VERSION,
172                          (SQLPOINTER)SQL_OV_ODBC2,
173                          0 );
174     if( !SQL_OK( res ))
175     {
176       printErrors( env, SQL_NULL_HDBC, SQL_NULL_HSTMT );
177       exit( -1 );
178     }
179
180     res = SQLAllocHandle( SQL_HANDLE_DBC, env, &con );
181     if( !SQL_OK( res ))
182     {
183       printErrors( env, SQL_NULL_HDBC, SQL_NULL_HSTMT );
```

```
184        exit( -2 );
185      }
186
187      res = SQLDriverConnect( con,
188                              (SQLHWND)NULL,
189                              argv[1], SQL_NTS,
190                              fullConnectStr,
191                              sizeof( fullConnectStr ),
192                              &requiredLength,
193                              SQL_DRIVER_NOPROMPT );
194
195
196      if( !SQL_OK( res ))
197      {
198        printErrors( SQL_NULL_HENV, con, SQL_NULL_HSTMT );
199        exit( -3 );
200      }
201
202      printf( "connection ok\n" );
203
204      executeStmt( con, argv[2] );
205
206      res = SQLDisconnect( con );
207      if( !SQL_OK( res ))
208      {
209        printErrors( SQL_NULL_HENV, con, SQL_NULL_HSTMT );
210        exit( -4 );
211      }
212
213      res = SQLFreeHandle( SQL_HANDLE_DBC, con );
214      if( !SQL_OK( res ))
215      {
216        printErrors( SQL_NULL_HENV, con, SQL_NULL_HSTMT );
217        exit( -5 );
218      }
219
220      res = SQLFreeHandle( SQL_HANDLE_ENV, env );
221      if( !SQL_OK( res ))
222      {
223        printErrors( env, SQL_NULL_HDBC, SQL_NULL_HSTMT );
224        exit( -6 );
225      }
226    }
227
228    exit( 0 );
229
230 }
```

The main() function for client3.c is identical to that in client2.c.

When you run this program, the single command-line argument should be a SQLDRIVERCONNECT() connection string:

```
$ ./client3 "DSN=MoviesDSN; UID=korry; PWD=cows"
```

This example has shown you the easiest way to execute a query and process results in an ODBC application, but using SQLExecDirect() and SQLGetData() will not always give you the best performance. The next client shows a method that is more complex, but performs better.

Client 4—An Interactive Query Processor

I'll finish this chapter by developing a general-purpose, interactive query processor. In this example, I'll describe the SQLPrepare()/SQLExec() query execution method. Finally, I'll show you a way to process result sets more efficiently.

This example is based on the libpq++/qt-sql.cpp client from Chapter 10. Rather than showing you the entire application again, I'll just explain the differences—refer to Chapter 10 for a complete explanation of the original application.

In this application, you can enter arbitrary SQL commands; the result set for SELECT statements appears in a table and the results for other commands displays in a status bar.

The first thing that you need to change in this client is the MyTable class. The new MyTable class includes an environment handle (env) and a connection handle (db).

```
 1 /* qt-sql.h */
 2
 3 class MyTable : public QTable
 4 {
 5 public:
 6
 7     MyTable( QWidget * parent );
 8
 9     SQLHDBC     db;
10     SQLHENV     env;
11
12     void buildTable( SQLHSTMT stmt );
13     void displayErrors( SQLSMALLINT type, SQLHANDLE handle );
14
15 };
```

Next, I'll borrow the resultField structure from the previous example. This structure contains metadata for a field and a pointer to a buffer (value) that holds the field data as you retrieve each row.

```
// File qt-sql.cpp (partial listing - see downloads for complete text)
22 typedef struct
23 {
```

```
 24   char          name[128+1];
 25   SQLSMALLINT   nameLength;
 26   SQLSMALLINT   dataType;
 27   SQLUINTEGER   fieldLength;
 28   SQLSMALLINT   scale;
 29   SQLSMALLINT   nullable;
 30   SQLINTEGER    displaySize;
 31   int           headerLength;
 32   SQLINTEGER    resultLength;
 33   char        * value;
 34 } resultField;
```

Now let's look at the MyTable constructor:

```
// File qt-sql.cpp (partial listing - see downloads for complete text)
109 MyTable::MyTable( QWidget * parent )
110   : QTable( parent )
111 {
112   //
113   //  Create a database connection...
114   //
115   SQLRETURN  res;
116
117   res = SQLAllocHandle( SQL_HANDLE_ENV,
118           SQL_NULL_HANDLE,
119           &env );
120   if( !SQL_OK( res ))
121   {
122     displayErrors( SQL_HANDLE_ENV, env );
123     exit( -1 );
124   }
125
126   SQLSetEnvAttr( env,
127        SQL_ATTR_ODBC_VERSION,
128        (SQLPOINTER)SQL_OV_ODBC2,
129        0 );
130
131   res = SQLAllocHandle( SQL_HANDLE_DBC,
132          env,
133          &db );
134
135   if( !SQL_OK( res ))
136   {
137     displayErrors( SQL_HANDLE_ENV, env );
138     exit( -1 );
139   }
140
```

```
141   res = SQLConnect( db,
142           (SQLCHAR *)qApp->argv()[1], SQL_NTS,
143           (SQLCHAR *)qApp->argv()[2], SQL_NTS,
144           (SQLCHAR *)qApp->argv()[3], SQL_NTS );
145
146   if( !SQL_OK( res ))
147   {
148     displayErrors( SQL_HANDLE_DBC, db );
149     exit( -1 );
150   }
151
152
153   //  We don't have any table-oriented results to
154   //  show yet, so hide the table.
155   //
156   setNumRows( 0 );
157   setNumCols( 0 );
158 }
```

The `MyTable` constructor should be familiar by now. You initialize an environment handle, inform ODBC that you are an ODBC version 2 (`SQL_OV_ODBC2`) application, and then try to connect to the database identified on the command line. When this application is invoked, it expects three command-line arguments: a data source name, a username, and a password. The `qApp->argv()` function returns a pointer to the array of command-line arguments. If the connection attempt fails, you call the `displayErrors()` function to display any error messages. `displayErrors()` is shown here:

```
// File qt-sql.cpp (partial listing - see downloads for complete text)
160 void MyTable::displayErrors( SQLSMALLINT type, SQLHANDLE handle )
161 {
162   SQLHDBC    dbc  = SQL_NULL_HDBC;
163   SQLHENV    env  = SQL_NULL_HENV;
164   SQLHSTMT   stmt = SQL_NULL_HSTMT;
165
166   switch( type )
167   {
168     case SQL_HANDLE_ENV:  env  = (SQLHENV)handle; break;
169     case SQL_HANDLE_DBC:  dbc  = (SQLHENV)handle; break;
170     case SQL_HANDLE_STMT: stmt = (SQLHSTMT)handle; break;
171   }
172
173   SQLRETURN   result;
174   SQLCHAR     sqlState[6];
175   SQLINTEGER  nativeError;
```

```
176     SQLSMALLINT requiredLength;
177     SQLCHAR     messageText[SQL_MAX_MESSAGE_LENGTH+1];
178
179     QDialog     * dlg  = new QDialog( this, 0, TRUE );
180     QVBoxLayout * vbox = new QVBoxLayout( dlg );
181     QPushButton * ok   = new QPushButton( "Ok", dlg );
182
183     setCaption( "Error" );
184     QMultiLineEdit * edit = new QMultiLineEdit( dlg );
185
186     vbox->addWidget( edit );
187     vbox->addWidget( ok );
188
189     connect( ok, SIGNAL( clicked()), dlg, SLOT( accept()));
190
191     edit->setReadOnly( TRUE );
192
193     do
194     {
195       result = SQLError( env,
196                          dbc,
197                          stmt,
198                          sqlState,
199                          &nativeError,
200                          messageText,
201                          sizeof( messageText ),
202                          &requiredLength );
203
204       if( SQL_OK( result ))
205       {
206         edit->append((char *)messageText );
207         edit->append( "\n" );
208       }
209     } while( SQL_OK( result ));
210
211     dlg->adjustSize();
212     dlg->exec();
213
214 }
```

The `displayErrors()` function is complicated by the fact that you may get multiple error messages from ODBC—you can't use the usual QT `MessageBox` class to display multiple errors. Instead, we construct a dialog that contains an edit control (to contain the error messages) and an OK button. Figure 12.5 shows a typical error message.

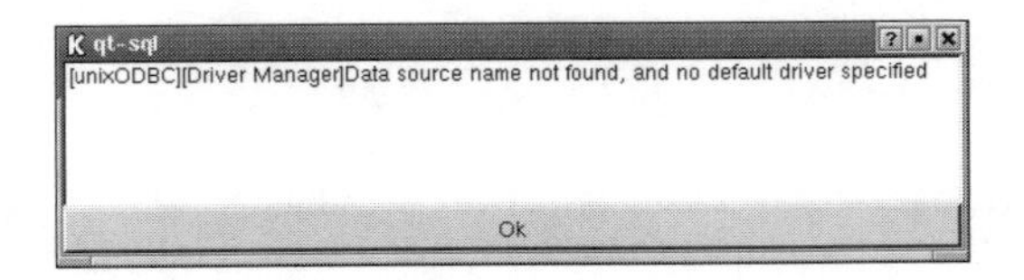

Figure 12.5 Sample error message.

After the dialog object has been built, you call `SQLError()` to retrieve the error messages and append each message into the edit control. When you have retrieved the final error message, you display the dialog by calling the `dlg->exec()` function.

Now let's look at the code that used to execute a command:

```
// File qt-sql.cpp (partial listing - see downloads for complete text)
216 void MyMain::execute( void )
217 {
218   //  This function is called whenever the user
219   //  presses the 'Execute' button (or whenever
220   //  the user presses the Return key while the
221   //  edit control has the keyboard focus)
222   SQLHDBC    db = table->db;
223   SQLHSTMT  stmt;
224   SQLRETURN res;
225   QString    qcmd = edit->text();
226   SQLCHAR * cmd;
227
228   // Convert the query command from Unicode
229   // into an 8-bit, SQLCHAR format
230
231   cmd = (SQLCHAR *)qcmd.latin1();
232
233   SQLAllocHandle( SQL_HANDLE_STMT, db, &stmt );
234
235   res = SQLPrepare( stmt, (SQLCHAR *)cmd, SQL_NTS );
236
237   if( !SQL_OK( res ))
238   {
239     table->displayErrors( SQL_HANDLE_STMT, stmt );
240   }
241   else
242   {
243
244     if( SQL_OK( SQLExecute( stmt )))
245     {
246       SQLSMALLINT  columnCount;
247
248       SQLNumResultCols( stmt, &columnCount );
```

```
249
250         if( columnCount == 0 )
251         {
252            SQLINTEGER  rowCount;
253            SQLRowCount( stmt, &rowCount );
254
255            if( rowCount == -1 )
256              status->message( "Ok" );
257            else
258            {
259              QString m( "Ok, %1 rows affected" );
260
261              status->message( m.arg((int)rowCount ));
262            }
263         }
264         else
265         {
266            status->message( "Ok..." );
267            table->buildTable( stmt );
268         }
269       }
270       else
271         table->displayErrors( SQL_HANDLE_STMT, stmt );
272
273     }
274
275     SQLFreeHandle( SQL_HANDLE_STMT, stmt );
276 }
```

`MyMain::execute()` starts by making a copy of the query (`edit->text()`) and converts the string from Unicode (Qt's native character encoding) into ASCII (the format expected by ODBC).

Next, you initialize a statement handle.

In the previous example (`client3.c`), I used the `SQLExecDirect()` function to execute a SQL command. In this function, I am using a different execution model—the Prepare/Execute model.

You should use the Prepare/Execute model if you are expecting to execute the same SQL command multiple times, possibly substituting different values for each execution. Some ODBC-compliant databases support "parameter markers" within a SQL command. You generally use parameter markers when you are using the Prepare/Execute model. Here is an example of a command that contains parameter markers:

```
insert into customers values ( ?, ?, ? );
```

Each question mark in this command represents a parameter whose value is provided each time the command is executed. (The parameters are numbered—the leftmost question mark is parameter number 1, the next mark is parameter number 2, and so on.)

The advantage to the Prepare/Execute model is that you send the command to the server only once, but you can execute the command as many times as needed. Most ODBC-compliant databases parse the command and create an execution plan when you call `SQLPrepare()`. When you want to execute the statement, you *bind* each parameter to a memory address, place the appropriate value at that address, and then call `SQLExecute()` to execute the command. When you use the Prepare/Execute model with a database that supports parameter markers, you can gain a huge performance boost.

It's not really appropriate to use the Prepare/Execute model to process ad hoc queries. Prepare/Execute is useful when you plan to execute the same SQL command multiple times. You can also use Prepare/Execute to simplify your code: Factor the code that generates a command into a function separate from the code that generates data.

PostgreSQL and the Prepare/Execute Model

PostgreSQL does not support parameter markers directly. The PostgreSQL ODBC driver performs parameter substitution and sends the translated command to the database each time you call `SQLExecute()`. You will *not* see a performance boost using Prepare/Execute when your application is connected to a PostgreSQL database, but you should be aware of the technique anyway. If you are building an ODBC application, you are probably concerned with portability (and performance) issues.

After you have successfully prepared and executed the command entered by the user, you are ready to process the results.

The first thing you need to know is whether the command could have returned any rows. (In other words, was this a `SELECT` command.) ODBC version 2.x does not provide a function that tells you what kind of SQL command you just executed, but you can use the `SQLNumResultCols()` to infer that information. If `SQLNumResultCols()` tells you that there are no columns in the result set, you can assume that you have not executed a `SELECT` command. In that case, you use `SQLRowCount()` to determine how many rows (if any) were affected by the command. For `UPDATE`, `INSERT`, and `DELETE` statements, `SQLRowCount()` returns a value (greater than or equal to zero) indicating how many rows were affected. For other types of statements (such as `BEGIN WORK` or `CREATE TABLE`), `SQLRowCount()` returns `-1`. Use the value returned by `SQLRowCount()` to determine how to update the status bar.

When you execute a `SELECT` command, you call the `MyTable::buildtable()` function to copy the result set into a table:

```
// File qt-sql.cpp (partial listing - see downloads for complete text)
278 void MyTable::buildTable( SQLHSTMT stmt )
279 {
280   //  This function is called to fill in
281   //  the table control.  We want to fill
282   //  the table with the result set.
```

```
283   SQLSMALLINT   i;
284   SQLSMALLINT   columnCount;
285   resultField * fields;
286
287   setNumRows( 0 );
288   setNumCols( 0 );
289
290   //  First, examine the metadata for the
291   //  result set so that we know how much
292   //  room we need for each column.
293
294   SQLNumResultCols( stmt, &columnCount );
295
296   fields = new resultField[ columnCount+1 ];
297
298   setNumCols( columnCount );
299
300   for( i = 1; i <= columnCount; i++ )
301   {
302     SQLDescribeCol( stmt,
303            i,
304            (SQLCHAR *)fields[i].name,
305            sizeof( fields[i].name ),
306            &fields[i].nameLength,
307            &fields[i].dataType,
308            &fields[i].fieldLength,
309            &fields[i].scale,
310            &fields[i].nullable );
311
312     SQLColAttribute( stmt,
313             i,
314             SQL_DESC_DISPLAY_SIZE,
315             NULL,
316             0,
317             NULL,
318             &fields[i].displaySize );
319
320     fields[i].value = (char *)malloc( fields[i].displaySize+1 );
321
322     // Build the column headers as we go
323     horizontalHeader()->setLabel( i-1, fields[i].name );
324
325   }
326
327   //  Bind the fields to our buffers
```

```
328    for( i = 1; i <= columnCount; i++ )
329    {
330      SQLRETURN res;
331
332      res = SQLBindCol( stmt,
333                        i,
334                        SQL_C_CHAR,
335                        fields[i].value,
336                        fields[i].displaySize+1,
337                        &fields[i].resultLength );
338
339      if( !SQL_OK( res ))
340        displayErrors( SQL_HANDLE_STMT, stmt );
341    }
342
343    //
344    //  Now, put the data into the table...
345    //
346    int         row = 0;
347    SQLRETURN res;
348
349    while( SQL_OK(( res =  SQLFetch( stmt ))))
350    {
351      if( res == SQL_SUCCESS_WITH_INFO )
352        displayErrors( SQL_HANDLE_STMT, stmt );
353
354      setNumRows( row+1 );
355
356      for( int col = 1; col <= columnCount; col++ )
357      {
358        setText( row, col-1, fields[col].value );
359      }
360
361      row++;
362
363    }
364 }
```

`buildTable()` starts by initializing the table to zero rows and zero columns. Next, you use `SQLNumResultCols()` to determine how many columns are in the result set. You allocate a `resultField` structure for each column.

Then, you build an array of `resultField` structures (the same way you did in the `odbc/client3.c example`) using `SQLDescribeCol()` and `SQLColAttribute()`. You also populate the table's column headers as you process the metadata.

Rather than using `SQLGetData()` to retrieve field values, I'm going to bind each column to a memory buffer. Then, as you fetch each row from the server, ODBC automatically copies the data values into your bind buffers. Here is the function prototype for SQLBindCol():

```
SQLRETURN SQLBindCol( SQLHSTMT      stmtHandle,
                      SQLUSMALLINT columnNumber,
                      SQLSMALLINT  bindDataType,
                      SQLPOINTER   bindBuffer,
                      SQLINTEGER   bindBufferLength,
                      SQLLEN     * resultLength )
```

When you call SQLBindCol(), you are binding a column (columnNumber) to a memory address (bindBuffer and bindBufferLength) and asking ODBC to convert the field data into a specific data type (bindDataType). You can also provide a pointer to a result length—after you fetch a row, the result length will contain the length of the data value (or SQL_NULL_DATA if the field is NULL). In general, you will get better performance results if you bind each column rather than using SQLGetData(). You have to call SQLGetData() for each column in each row, but you have to bind each column only once.

After you have bound all the columns in the result set, you can start fetching. For each row that you fetch, you increase the table size by one row (this isn't very efficient, but ODBC does not give you a way to determine the size of the result set without fetching each row).

Finally, use the QTable::setText() member function to insert each column into the table.

Figure 12.6 shows you an example of what you would see when you run the odbc/qt-sql sample.

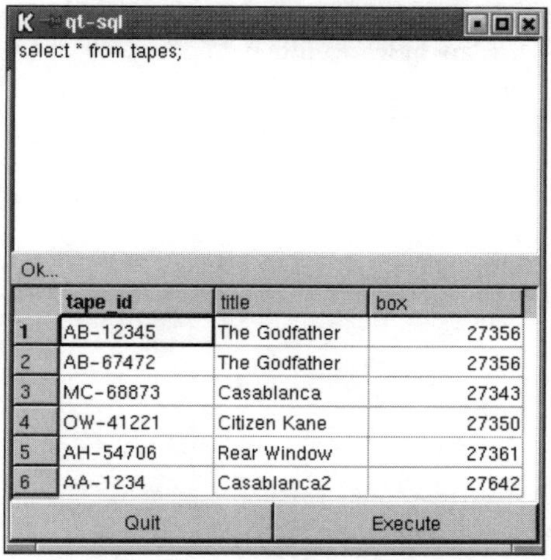

Figure 12.6 Running the qt-sql application.

That's it! The rest of the qt-sql application is explained in Chapter 10.

Summary

ODBC is a complex API. I have covered only the basics of ODBC programming in this chapter. If you decide to write a client application using ODBC, I strongly recommend that you obtain one (or more) of the books in the "Resources" section that follows. Several of these books are devoted entirely to ODBC programming, whereas this chapter gives a short introduction aimed at writing simple applications against the PostgreSQL ODBC driver.

Resources

1. Stinson, Barry. *PostgreSQL Essential Reference*. New Riders Publishing, 2002.

   Chapter 13 provides a brief description of how to install unixODBC and create a PostgreSQL data source.

2. Gulutzan, Peter and Pelzer, Trudy. *SQL-99 Complete, Really*. R&D Books, 1999.

   The ODBC standard is paralleled by the SQL-99 standard. This book provides a complete description of SQL-99. Most of the information in this book applies directly to an ODBC application.

3. Sanders, Roger E. *DB2 Universal Database Call Level Interface Developer's Guide*. McGraw-Hill, 1999.

   The DB2 Call Level Interface is nearly identical to the ODBC API; as in the previous reference, this book translates almost entirely into ODBC.

4. Geiger, Kyle. *Inside ODBC*. Microsoft Press, 1995.

   This book is currently out of print, but if you can find a copy, I highly recommend it. *Inside ODBC* includes an interesting history of ODBC development within Microsoft and describes how ODBC works from the inside.

13

Using PostgreSQL from a Java Client Application

IF YOU READ THE PREVIOUS CHAPTER, YOU KNOW THAT ODBC is a technology that can connect a single application to multiple databases without making any changes to the application. ODBC is popular in the C, C++, Visual Basic, and VBA worlds. The folks at Sun Microsystems developed a similar technology for Java applications: JDBC. Many people will tell you that JDBC is an acronym for "Java Database Connectivity," but according to Sun, "*...JDBC is the trademarked name and is not an acronym.*"

JDBC is an API that makes it easy for Java applications to connect to a database, send commands to the database, and retrieve the results. JDBC is packaged as a collection of classes[1]. To start working with JDBC, you use the `DriverManager` class to obtain a `Driver` object. After you have a `Driver`, you make a connection to the database, which results in a `Connection` object. Using a `Connection`, you can create `Statement`. When you execute a command (using a `Statement` object), you get back a `ResultSet`. JDBC also provides classes that let you retrieve `ResultSetMetaData` and `DatabaseMetaData`.

In this chapter, I won't try to explain all the features of Java's JDBC technology—covering that topic thoroughly would easily require another book. Instead, I'll show you how to use the PostgreSQL JDBC driver. I'll briefly discuss each of the classes I mentioned earlier and show you how to use them.

1. I use the term *class* rather loosely in this chapter. JDBC is actually a collection of classes and *interfaces*. The distinction is not important to JDBC application developers—we use interfaces as if they were classes. Programmers who are building new JDBC drivers will need to understand the distinction.

JDBC Architecture Overview

JDBC is similar in structure to ODBC. A JDBC application is composed of multiple layers, as shown in Figure 13.1.

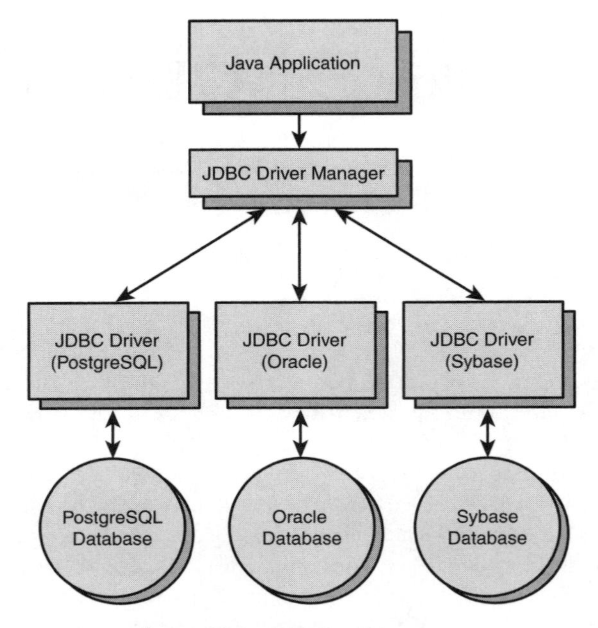

Figure 13.1 JDBC architecture.

The topmost layer in this model is the Java application. Java applications are portable—you can run a Java application without modification on any system that has a Java runtime environment installed. A Java application that uses JDBC can talk to many databases with few, if any, modifications. Like ODBC, JDBC provides a consistent way to connect to a database, execute commands, and retrieve the results. Also like ODBC, JDBC does not enforce a common command language—you can use Oracle-specific syntax when connected to an Oracle server and PostgreSQL-specific syntax when connected to a PostgreSQL server. If you stick to a common subset, you can achieve remarkable portability for your applications.

The JDBC DriverManager

The JDBC `DriverManager` class is responsible for locating a JDBC driver needed by the application. When a client application requests a database connection, the request is expressed in the form of a URL (Uniform Resource Locator). A typical URL might look like `jdbc:postgresql:movies`. A JDBC URL is similar to the URLs that you use with a web browser (`http://www.postgresql.org`, for example). I'll explain the JDBC URL syntax in detail a bit later.

The JDBC Driver

As each driver is loaded into a Java Virtual Machine (VM), it registers itself with the JDBC `DriverManager`. When an application requests a connection, the `DriverManager` asks each `Driver` whether it can connect to the database specified in the given URL. As soon as it finds an appropriate `Driver`, the search stops and the `Driver` attempts to make a connection to the database. If the connection attempt fails, the `Driver` will throw a `SQLException` to the application. If the connection completes successfully, the `Driver` creates a `Connection` object and returns it to the application.

The JDBC 2.0 architecture introduced another method for establishing database connections: the `DataSource`. A `DataSource` is a named collection of connection properties that can be used to load a `Driver` and create a `Connection`. I do not discuss the `DataSource` class in this chapter because it is not yet part of the J2SE (Java 2 Standard Edition) standard; the DataSource class is a component of J2EE (Java 2 Enterprise Edition). The PostgreSQL JDBC driver does support the `DataSource` class.

The JDBC-Compliant Database

The bottom layer of the JDBC model is the database. The PostgreSQL Driver class (and other JDBC classes) translates application commands into PostgreSQL network requests and translates the results back into JDBC object form.

Prerequisites

If you want to build the sample applications in this chapter, you will need a Java compiler and a Java runtime environment. If you are using Windows, Linux, or Solaris, you can obtain the Java SDK (software development kit) and runtime environment from Sun Microsystems (`http://java.sun.com`). For other environments, search the web or contact your vendor.

I'll use a simple `makefile` to build the JDBC sample applications, so you will need the `make` utility as well.

Listing 13.1 shows the `makefile` that I'll use:

Listing 13.1 `makefile`

```
#
# Filename: makefile
#
JAVAC      = javac
JFLAGS     = -g

.SUFFIXES: .class .java


.java.class:
        $(JAVAC) $(JFLAGS) $<
```

This makefile states that, to turn a .java (Java source code) file into a .class (Java executable) file, you must run the javac compiler. I like all my applications to be debuggable, so I set JFLAGS to -g (the -g flag tells the compiler to include symbolic debugger information in the .class file); you can replace -g with -O if you want better performance and less debugability.

The last piece that you will need is the PostgreSQL JDBC driver itself. You can find a precompiled version of the PostgreSQL JDBC driver at http://jdbc.postgresql.org. The Java runtime environment will need to know where your driver is located. The driver is typically named postgresql.jar, and the easiest way to tell Java about the driver is to add the jar file's location to the end of your CLASSPATH environment variable. For example, if you are connected to a Unix/Linux host and find postgresql.jar in the /usr/local/pgsql/share directory, execute the following command:

```
$ export CLASSPATH=$CLASSPATH:/usr/local/pgsql/share/postgresql.jar
```

If you are connected to a Windows host and find postgresql.jar in the C:\WINDOWS\CLASSES directory, use the following command:

```
C:\>  set CLASSPATH=%CLASSPATH%;C:\WINDOWS\CLASSES\postgresql.jar
```

Client 1—Connecting to the Server

Before you can connect to a database, you have to tell JDBC to which server you want to connect. JDBC uses a paradigm that you are undoubtedly already familiar with: A database is identified using a URL (Uniform Resource Locator). Every time you use your web browser, you use URLs.

A URL is composed of at least two parts, sometimes more. For example, the URL http://www.postgresql.org has two components. The http part specifies the protocol to use (in this case, hypertext transport protocol). Everything following the colon is used by the protocol to find the resource you want.

JDBC URLs

A JDBC URL is composed of three parts. We'll be using the URL jdbc:postgresql:movies in many of the examples for this chapter.

The protocol component for a JDBC URL is always jdbc. Following the protocol (and the : delimiter), is the *subprotocol*. The subprotocol is usually the name of a JDBC driver, but it can also identify a naming service that will provide a specific name, given an alias[2]. In the case of PostgreSQL, the subprotocol is postgresql. Finally, you can include a string that identifies a specific data source that the driver should use (Sun's JDBC documentation calls this the *subname*). In our example, the subname is movies.

2. See the JDBC documentation for more information about naming services.

The format of the subname string is determined by the author of the JDBC driver. In the case of the PostgreSQL JDBC driver, the URL can take any of the following forms:

```
jdbc:postgresql:database
jdbc:postgresql://host/database
jdbc:postgresql://host:port/database
jdbc:org.postgresql://host:port/database?param1=val1&...
```

You don't provide a port—the standard PostgreSQL port (`5432`) is assumed. Notice that in all cases, you must provide the database name. Unlike the other PostgreSQL APIs, JDBC will not look for any environment variables when you omit required connection parameters, so you must include the database name in the URL. In the last form, you can include other connection parameters. For example:

```
jdbc:org:postgresql?user=korry&password=cows
```

You can include any of the following connection parameters following the question mark in the URL:

```
user=user-name
password=password
loglevel={0|1|2}
```

The `loglevel` parameter determines how much driver debugging information is written to the standard error stream. The default value is `0`, meaning that no debugging information is logged. Setting `loglevel` to `1` (informational) or `2` (debug) will produce more debugging information.

Listing 13.2 shows a simple JDBC client application. This application connects to a database (using a URL), prints a completion message, disconnects, and then exits.

Listing 13.2 `client1.java`

```
 1 //
 2 // File: client1.java
 3 //
 4
 5 import java.sql.*;
 6
 7 public class client1
 8 {
 9   public static void main( String args[] )
10     throws ClassNotFoundException, SQLException
11   {
12     String  driver = "org.postgresql.Driver";
13     String  url    = "jdbc:postgresql:movies";
14     String  user   = "korry";
15     String  pwd    = "cows";
16
```

Listing 13.2 **Continued**

```
17       Class.forName( driver );
18
19       Connection con = DriverManager.getConnection( url, user, pwd );
20
21       System.err.println( "Connection complete" );
22
23       con.close();
24
25   }
26 }
```

At line 5, you import the `java.sql` package. Most of the JDBC interface is defined in this package, with a few extensions residing in the `javax.sql` package[3]. You don't do any error checking in this client, so you have to declare that your `main()` method can throw two exceptions (at line 10). In the next client application (client2.java), you will intercept these exceptions and handle them a bit more gracefully.

Lines 12 through 15 define a few `String` objects that should make the code more descriptive. The `driver` string tells the JVM the fully qualified name of the driver class. The JDBC driver distributed with PostgreSQL is named `org.postgresql.Driver`[4]. The `url` string specifies the URL to which you want to connect. The `user` and `pwd` (password) strings will be passed to the `DriverManager` and then to the `Driver` when you actually get around to making a connection attempt.

Line 17 loads the PostgreSQL `Driver` class. A lot of things happen with this simple method call. First, the `Class.forName()`[5] method locates and loads the object file that implements the `org.postgresql.Driver` class. Normally, a reference to another class is compiled into your class. Using `Class.forName()`, you can dynamically load classes into your VM at runtime. This is roughly equivalent to

```
org.postgresql.Driver Driver = new org.postgresql.Driver();
```

The important difference between this method (creating an instance of an `org.postgresql.Driver` object) and using `Class.forName()` is that you can use the latter method to select the driver that you want at *runtime*, rather than at compile time. If you

3. The javax.sql package was an optional feature introduced in the JDBC 2.0 specification. In the JDBC 3.0 specification, javax.sql has been moved from the JDBC 2.0 Optional Package (included in the J2EE) into J2SE.

4. If you use a JDBC driver obtained from another source, the driver name will be different. For example, the PostgreSQL driver from the jxDBCon project is named org.sourceforge.jxdbcon.JXDBConDriver.

5. In some versions of Java, you may need to call `Class.forName().newInstance()` to load the driver correctly. If you have trouble with `Class.forName()`, append `.newInstance()` to the end of the string.

arrange the code properly, you can load different drivers based on an external value, such as a command-line parameter or an environment variable. That might not be important if you simply want code that can talk only to PostgreSQL, but JDBC was designed to provide database portability. After `Class.forName()` loads the `Driver` class into your VM, the `Driver`'s static initializer is invoked to register the driver with the JDBC `DriverManager` class.

After the `DriverManager` knows about the PostgreSQL JDBC driver, you can ask it to create a `Connection` object for you.

There are three `DriverManager.getConnection()` methods:

```
getConnection( String url, String user, String password );
getConnection( String url, Properties props );
getConnection( String url );
```

Each form uses a different strategy for getting the username and password to the driver. In the first form, the username and password are passed as extra parameters. In the second form, the user name and password are expected to be in the `props` property list. In the last form, the URL should contain the user name and password as separate properties.

In the following code fragment, the three calls to `getConnection()` are equivalent:

```
...
Properties    connectionProps;
String        url = "jdbc:postgresql:movies";

connectionProps.put( "user", "korry" );
connectionProps.put( "password", "cows" );

DriverManager.getConnection( url, "korry", "cows" );
DriverManager.getConnection( url, connectionProps );
DriverManager.getConnection( url + "?user=korry&password=cows" );
...
```

Looking back at `client1.java`, you use the first form of `getConnection()`. If `getConnection()` returns successfully, you print a message, close the connection (at line 23), and run to completion. If `getConnection()` fails to connect to the database, it will throw an exception. You'll see how to intercept errors in the next section.

Let's compile and run this client:

```
$ make client1.class
javac -g client1.java

$ java client1
Connection complete
$
```

Sorry, that's not very exciting is it? Shut down the `postmaster` just so you know what an error might look like:

```
$ pg_ctl stop
waiting for postmaster to shut down......done
postmaster successfully shut down

$ java client1
Exception in thread "main" Connection refused. Check that the
hostname and port is correct, and that the postmaster is
running with the -i flag, which enables TCP/IP networking.
        at org.postgresql.Connection.openConnection(Unknown Source)
        at org.postgresql.Driver.connect(Unknown Source)
        at java.sql.DriverManager.getConnection(DriverManager.java:517)
        at java.sql.DriverManager.getConnection(DriverManager.java:177)
        at client1.main(client1.java:19)
$
```

You can almost feel the heat as `client1` crashes and burns. That error message isn't very friendly. Let's move on to `client2`, in which we will try to intercept the failure and provide a little insulation to the end users.

Client 2—Adding Error Checking

In the previous section, I mentioned that the `DriverManager.getConnection()` method will throw an exception whenever it fails. Listing 13.3 shows the second JDBC client. This version is nearly identical to `client1.java`, except that in `client1`, you ignored any exceptions and in `client2`, you will intercept them and produce friendlier error messages.

Listing 13.3 `client2.java`

```
 1 //
 2 // File: client2.java
 3 //
 4
 5 import java.sql.*;
 6
 7 public class client2
 8 {
 9   public static void main( String args[] )
10   {
11     String driver = "org.postgresql.Driver";
12     String url    = "jdbc:postgresql:movies";
13     String user   = "korry";
14     String pwd    = "cows";
15
16     try
```

Listing 13.3 **Continued**

```
17      {
18        Class.forName( driver );
19      }
20      catch( ClassNotFoundException e )
21      {
22        System.err.println( "Can't load driver" + e.getMessage());
23        System.exit( 1 );
24      }
25
26      try
27      {
28        Connection con = DriverManager.getConnection(url, user, pwd);
29
30        System.out.println( "Connection attempt successful" );
31
32        con.close();
33
34      }
35      catch( Exception e )
36      {
37        System.err.println( "Connection attempt failed" );
38        System.err.println( e.getMessage());
39      }
40    }
41 }
```

The first difference between `client1` and `client2` appears at line 10. In the client1 version, you had to declare that `main()` could throw `ClassNotFoundException` and `SQLException`. You'll be intercepting those exceptions now, so `main()` should not throw any exceptions.

At lines 17 through 24, you wrap the call to `Class.forName()` in a `try/catch` block. Remember that `forName()` dynamically loads the implementation of a class into your VM—it is entirely possible that `forName()` may not be able to load the class file that you need. You may have misspelled the class name, or the class file might not be in your `$CLASSPATH` search path. You could also find that you don't have the permissions required to load the class file, or you could even find that the class file has been corrupted. If you catch an exception, print a suitable error message and exit.

After the `Driver` class has been loaded into your VM, you can attempt to make a connection. Wrap the connection attempt in a `try/catch` block so that you can intercept any exceptions. The call to `DriverManager.getConnection()` throws a `SQLException` if something goes wrong. Let's compile this application and give it a try:

```
$ make client2.class
javac -g client2.java
```

```
$ java client2
Connection attempt failed
Connection refused. Check that the hostname and port is correct,
and that the postmaster is running with the -i flag, which
enables TCP/IP networking.
$
```

I haven't restarted the `postmaster` yet, so I encounter the same error as before, but this time the error message is less intimidating.

`DriverManager.getConnection()` can throw two kinds of exceptions: `SQLException` and `PSQLException` (`PSQLException` is derived from `SQLException`). `PSQLExceptions` are specific to the PostgreSQL driver; `SQLExceptions` indicate errors that might be common to many drivers. Let's modify `client2.java` so that you can see which type of exception you catch. The new client is shown in Listing 13.4.

Listing 13.4 `client2a.java`

```
 1 //
 2 // File: client2a.java
 3 //
 4
 5 import java.sql.*;
 6 import org.postgresql.util.PSQLException;
 7
 8 public class client2a
 9 {
10   public static void main( String args[] )
11   {
12     String  driver = "org.postgresql.Driver";
13
14     try
15     {
16       Class.forName( driver );
17     }
18     catch( ClassNotFoundException e )
19     {
20       System.err.println( "Can't load driver " + e.getMessage());
21       System.exit( 1 );
22     }
23     catch( Exception e )
24     {
25       System.err.println( "Can't load driver " + e.toString());
26       System.exit( 1 );
27     }
28
29     try
```

Listing 13.4 **Continued**

```
30      {
31        Connection con = DriverManager.getConnection( args[0] );
32
33        System.out.println( "Connection attempt successful" );
34
35        con.close();
36
37      }
38      catch( PSQLException e)
39      {
40        System.err.println( "Connection failed(PSQLException)" );
41        System.err.println( e.getMessage());
42      }
43      catch( SQLException e )
44      {
45        System.err.println( "Connection failed(SQLException)" );
46        System.err.println( e.getMessage());
47      }
48    }
49 }
```

I've made a few minor changes in `client2a.java`. You want to distinguish between `SQLException` and `PSQLException`, so at line 6, import the appropriate package. I've also removed most of the `String` variables used in the previous version. In this version, you supply a URL on the command line rather than hard-coding the connection parameters. At line 31, you call a different flavor of the `getConnection()` method; this one expects a single argument (the URL to which you want to connect). Notice that I have removed the hard-coded URL from this client. When you invoke `client2a`, you provide a connection URL on the command line (see the next example). Finally, you will catch `PSQLException` explicitly.

Compile this client and reproduce the same error that you saw earlier:

```
$ make client2a.class
javac -g client2a.java

$ java client2a "jdbc:postgresql:movies?user=korry&password=cows"
Connection failed(PSQLException)
Connection refused. Check that the hostname and port is correct,
and that the postmaster is running with the -i flag, which
enables TCP/IP networking.
$
```

Okay, that message comes from a `PSQLException`. Now, let's restart the `postmaster` and try connecting with an invalid password:

```
$ pg_ctl start -l /tmp/pg.log -o -i
postmaster successfully started
$ java client2a "jdbc:postgresql:movies?user=korry&password=oxen"
Connection failed(PSQLException)
Something unusual has occurred to cause the driver to fail.
Please report this exception:
Exception: java.sql.SQLException:
  FATAL 1:  Password authentication failed for user "korry"

Stack Trace:

java.sql.SQLException: FATAL 1:  Password authentication failed
for user "korry"

        at org.postgresql.Connection.openConnection(Unknown Source)
        at org.postgresql.Driver.connect(Unknown Source)
        at java.sql.DriverManager.getConnection(DriverManager.java:517)
        at java.sql.DriverManager.getConnection(DriverManager.java:199)
        at client2a.main(client2a.java:31)
End of Stack Trace
```

We're back to the intimidating error messages again. This is still a `PSQLException`, but the PostgreSQL JDBC Driver feels that an invalid password is unusual enough to justify this kind of error. You can see the importance of catching exceptions—you may want to translate this sort of message into something a little less enthusiastic rather than attacking your users with the raw error message text, as we've done here.

It's a little harder to generate a `SQLException` when the only thing you are doing is connecting and disconnecting. If you try hard enough, you can break just about anything:

```
$ java client2a "jdbc:postgres:movies?user=korry&password=cows"
Connection failed(SQLException)
No suitable driver
```

In this example, I've misspelled the subprotocol portion of the connection URL (`postgres` should be `postgresql`).

Now, let's move on to the next topic: command processing.

Client 3—Processing Queries

The next client executes a hard-coded query, intercepts any errors, and prints the result set. I've factored most of the code into separate methods to make it easier to follow. Listing 13.5 shows `client3.java`.

Listing 13.5 `client3.java` **(Part 1)**

```
 1 //
 2 //  File: client3.java
 3 //
 4
 5 import java.sql.*;
 6
 7 public class client3
 8 {
 9   public static void main( String args[] )
10   {
11     Class driverClass = loadDriver( "org.postgresql.Driver" );
12
13     if( driverClass == null )
14       return;
15
16     if( args.length != 1 )
17     {
18       System.err.println( "usage: java client3 <url>" );
19       return;
20     }
21
22     Connection con = connectURL( args[0] );
23
24     if( con != null )
25     {
26       ResultSet result = execQuery( con, "SELECT * FROM tapes;" );
27
28       if( result != null )
29         printResults( result );
30     }
31   }
```

The `main()` method for `client3` should be much easier to read now that the details have been factored out (see Listing 13.6). Start by loading the `Driver` class. If that fails, the call to `loadDriver()` will print an error message and you exit. Next, verify that the user provided a URL on the command line, and connect to the database using that URL. If the connection succeeds, execute a hard-coded query and print the result set.

Listing 13.6 `client3.java` **(Part 2)**

```
33   static Class loadDriver( String driverName )
34   {
35     try
36     {
37       return( Class.forName( driverName ));
38     }
```

Listing 13.6 **Continued**

```
39      catch( ClassNotFoundException e )
40      {
41        System.err.println( "Can't load driver - " + e.getMessage());
42        return( null );
43      }
44    }
45
46    static Connection connectURL( String URL )
47    {
48      try
49      {
50        return( DriverManager.getConnection( URL ));
51      }
52      catch( SQLException e )
53      {
54        System.err.println( "Can't connect - " + e.getMessage());
55        return( null );
56      }
57    }
```

You should be familiar with most of the code in the `loadDriver()` and `connectURL()` methods[6].
In `loadDriver()`, you use `Class.forName()` to load the named `Driver` into your VM. If the load is successful, you return the Class object for the `Driver`; otherwise, you print an error message and return `null` to inform the caller that something went wrong.

The `connectURL()` method is similar in structure. It attempts to connect to the requested URL, returning a `Connection` object or `null` if the connection attempt fails (see Listing 13.7).

Listing 13.7 `client3.java` **(Part 3)**

```
59    static ResultSet execQuery( Connection con, String query )
60    {
61      try
62      {
63        Statement stmt = con.createStatement();
64
65        System.out.println( query );
66
```

6. These methods show a personal design preference. I try to intercept exceptions as early as possible rather than throwing them back up the call stack. I find the resulting mainline code a little easier to read without the `try/catch` blocks.

Listing 13.7 **Continued**

```
67        return( stmt.executeQuery( query ));
68      }
69      catch( SQLException e )
70      {
71        System.err.println( "Query failed - " + e.getMessage());
72        return( null );
73      }
74 }
```

`execQuery()` shows how to execute a query using JDBC. When this method is invoked, the caller gives you a `Connection`. Before you can execute a query, you have to create a `Statement` object. A `Statement` object gives you a way to send a command to the server. After the command has been sent to the server, you can ask the `Statement` for a `ResultSet`. Some database servers (PostgreSQL included) support multiple `Statement` objects for each `Connection`. This means that you can execute multiple commands and process the results concurrently.

The `Statement.executeQuery()` method throws a `SQLException` if something (a syntax error, for example) goes wrong.

If the call to `executeQuery()` succeeds, you return the `ResultSet` to the caller, which passes it to `printResults()` to be displayed to the user.

The final method (see Listing 13.8) in this application is `printResults()`.

Listing 13.8 `client3.java` **(Part 4)**

```
76   static void printResults( ResultSet res )
77   {
78     System.out.println( " tape_id | title" );
79     System.out.println( "---------+------------------------" );
80
81     try
82     {
83       while( res.next())
84       {
85         System.out.print( res.getString( 1 ));
86         System.out.print( " | ");
87         System.out.print( res.getString( 2 ));
88         System.out.println( "" );
89       }
90     }
91     catch( SQLException e )
92     {
93       System.err.println( "Fetch failed: " + e.getMessage());
94     }
95   }
96 }
```

The `printResults()` method fetches every row in the given `ResultSet` and prints each column. Lines 78 and 79 print the column headings for the result set. Because you are working with a hard-coded query in this client, you can take a few shortcuts—if you didn't know the shape of the result set, you would have to interrogate the metadata for this `ResultSet` to find the column headings. You'll do that in the next client (`client4.java`).

The loop at lines 83 through 89 iterates through each row in the result set. Each `ResultSet` maintains a pointer[7] to the current row. `ResultSet` offers a number of methods for navigating through a result set. The `ResultSet.next()` method moves you forward through the result set. Table 13.1 lists all the navigation methods.

Table 13.1 `ResultSet` **Navigation Methods**

Navigation Method	Related Accessor Method	Description
`absolute(n)`	`getRow()`	Moves to the *n*th row in the result set if *n* is positive or to the last |*n*| row if *n* is negative
`afterLast()`	`isAfterLast()`	Moves past the last row in the result set
`beforeFirst()`	`isBeforeFirst()`	Moves to just before the first row
`first()`	`isFirst()`	Moves to the first row
`last()`	`isLast()`	Moves to the last row
`next()`	`getRow()`	Moves to the next row
`previous()`	`getRow()`	Moves to the previous row
`relative(n)`	`getRow()`	Moves forward *n* rows if *n* is positive or back *n* rows if *n* is negative

The first column in Table 13.1 lists the methods you can call to move through the result set. Each entry in the second column shows the related accessor method. The `isAfterLast()`, `isBeforeLast()`, `isFirst()`, and `isLast()` methods return `true` or `false` to indicate whether you are pointed to the named position within the result set. The `getRow()` function returns the current row number with the result set.

`first()` differs from `beforeFirst()` in that you can retrieve column values if you are positioned on the first row, but not if you are positioned before the first row. Similarly, you can retrieve column values if you are positioned on the last row, but not if you are positioned after the last row.

7. The JDBC documentation refers to this pointer as a *cursor*; to avoid confusion with database cursors (a similar concept), I'll use the term *pointer*.

You use the `ResultSet.getString()` method to retrieve a column from the current row. When you call `getString()`, you provide an integer argument that specifies which column you are interested in; column numbers start at 1.

After printing the two column values, you continue looping until `res.next()` returns `false` (meaning that there are no more rows in the result set).

This example shows that it's easy to process a query and a result set using JDBC. Now, let's go back and fill in a few of the details that I avoided.

Statement Classes

In client3.java, you used the `Statement.executeQuery()` method to execute a query. `Statement` is one of three interfaces that you can use to execute a SQL command. `Statement` is the most general interface and can be used to execute any SQL command. Let's look at the other `Statement` interfaces.

PreparedStatement

The `PreparedStatement` interface provides a way to *precompile* a command and execute it later. `PreparedStatement` inherits from (extends) `Statement`, so anything that you can do with a `Statement`, you can also do with a `PreparedStatement`. If you read the previous chapter, you may recognize `PreparedStatement` as the JDBC implementation of the ODBC Prepare/Execute execution model. When you use a `PreparedStatement`, you can parameterize your SQL commands. Let's say you are writing an application that repeatedly queries the `tapes` table, providing a different tape_id for each query. Rather than constructing a new command for each query, you can create a `PreparedStatement` like this:

```
...
PreparedStatement stmt;

stmt = con.prepareStatment( "SELECT * FROM tapes WHERE tape_id = ?" );
...
```

Notice that the text of this query doesn't specify an actual `tape_id` in the `WHERE` clause; instead, you include a parameter marker (`?`). Using a parameter marker, you can substitute different values each time you execute the `PreparedStatement`. You can include as many parameter markers as you like[8].

8. The JDBC documentation suggests that you can include a parameter marker *anywhere* within a SQL command. For example, the following command is allowed `SELECT ? FROM customers`, implying that you could substitute a list of column names at runtime. I recommend that you only use parameter markers where *values* are expected (and use one marker for each value). The PostgreSQL driver and many other drivers will not function correctly if you try to use a parameter marker in a context in which a value is not allowed.

The PreparedStatement object returned by prepareStatement() can be executed many times. Each time you execute the query, you can provide a different substitution value for each parameter marker. For example, to substitute a tape_id value in the previous query:

```
...
PreparedStatement stmt;

stmt = con.prepareStatment( "SELECT * FROM tapes WHERE tape_id = ?" );

stmt.setString( 1, "AA-55281" );

ResultString result = stmt.executeQuery();
...
```

The call to setString() substitutes the value "AA-55281" in place of the first parameter marker (parameter markers are numbered starting with 1). The net effect is that executeQuery() executes the string "SELECT * FROM tapes WHERE tape_id = 'AA-55281'". Notice that setString() automatically includes the single quotes required around a string literal, so you don't have to include them in the string.

PreparedStatement supports a number of parameter-substitution methods. We've used the setString() method in this example, but there are also methods for setting Boolean values (setBoolean()), numeric values (setInt(), setFloat(), setDouble(), setLong(), setBigDecimal()), temporal values (setDate(), setTime(), setTimestamp()), large objects (setBlob(), setClob()), and generic objects (setObject()). Each of these methods expect a parameter number and a value of the appropriate type. You can use the setNull() method to substitute a null value.

Each time you execute a PreparedStatement, you can substitute new values for some or all the parameter markers. If you don't supply a new value for a given marker, the previous value is retained.

Why would you want to use a PreparedStatement instead of a Statement? The Prepare/Execute model makes it easy to factor the code required to generate a command into a separate method. You may also experience a performance boost by preparing a command and then reusing it many times. The current version of the PostgreSQL JDBC driver will not show increased performance using the Prepare/Execute model, but other drivers (for other databases) will. It is also possible that a future release of PostgreSQL will provide complete support for this execution model.

CallableStatement

The CallableStatement interface inherits from PreparedStatement, so anything that you can do with a PreparedStatement, you can also do with a CallableStatement. The CallableStatement provides a way to call a function or stored-procedure using a database-independent syntax.

The following code fragment illustrates `CallableStatement`:

```
...
CallableStatement stmt;
boolean           result;

stmt = con.prepareCall( "{?= call has_table_privilege(?,?)}");

stmt.registerOutParameter( 1, Types.BIT );

stmt.setString( 2, "customers" );
stmt.setString( 3, "UPDATE" );

stmt.execute();

result = stmt.getBoolean( 1 );
...
```

This example calls PostgreSQL's `has_table_privilege()` function. `has_table_privilege()` expects two parameters: a table name and an access type. It returns a Boolean value that indicates whether the current user holds the given privilege on the named table. The query string contains three parameter markers. The first marker tells JDBC that the function that you want to call will return a value. The second and third markers specify the `IN` parameters. Each function parameter can be an input value (`IN`), a return value (`OUT`), or both (`IN/OUT`).

Before you can execute the `CallableStatement`, you use the `setString()` method (inherited from `PreparedStatement`) to substitute the two input parameters. You also have to tell JDBC about the type of all `OUT` parameters; the call to `registerOutParameter()` does that for you. After executing the statement, you can retrieve the result using `getBoolean()`.

Metadata

Metadata is another issue that I glossed over in describing client3. There are two types of metadata that you can retrieve using JDBC: database metadata and result set metadata.

The `DatabaseMetaData` interface provides information about the database at the other end of a `Connection`. To access a `DatabaseMetaData` object, you call the `Connection.getMetaData()` method. Here is a snippet that shows how to retrieve the JDBC driver name and version information:

```
...
Connection       con  = DriverManager.getConnection( args[0] );
DatabaseMetaData dbmd = con.getMetaData();

System.out.println( "Driver name:    " + dbmd.getDriverName());
System.out.println( "Driver version: " + dbmd.getDriverVersion());
...
```

At last count, `DatabaseMetaData` exposes more than 120 items of database information. The sample source code for this chapter (`http://www.conjectrix.com/pgbook/jdbc`) includes an application (`printMetaData`) that displays most of the metadata exposed by `DatabaseMetaData`.

In most applications, you will probably be more interested in the other type of metadata. The `ResultSetMetaData` interface exposes information about the data contained within a result set. You obtain a `ResultSetMetaData` object by calling the `ResultSet.getMetaData()` method. For example:

```
...
ResultSet           rs   = stmt.executeQuery();
ResultSetMetaData   rsmd = rs.getMetaData();
...
```

After you have a `ResultSetMetaData` object, you can query it for all sorts of information. The `getcolumnCount()` method returns the number of columns in the result set. Because all `ResultSetMetaData` methods (except `getColumnCount()`) return information about a given column, you will probably want to process metadata in a loop:

```
...
int    colCount = rsmd.getColumnCount();

for( int column = 1; column <= colCount; column++ )
{
  System.out.println( "Column #" + column );
  System.out.println( "  Name: " + rsmd.getColumnName( column ));
  System.out.println( "  Type: " + rsmd.getTypeName( column ));
}
...
```

This code snippet uses `getColumnName()` to retrieve the name of each column and `getTypeName()` to retrieve the type of each column.

Client 4—An Interactive Query Processor

Now, let's move on to the final JDBC client. As in previous chapters, we'll wrap up by looking at an application that processes arbitrary commands entered by the user.

Listing 13.9 shows the `client4.main()` method.

Listing 13.9 `client4.java` **(Part 1)**

```
 1 //
 2 //  File: client4.java
 3 //
 4
```

Listing 13.9 **Continued**

```
 5 import java.sql.*;
 6 import java.io.*;
 7
 8 public class client4
 9 {
10   static String blanks = "                                    ";
11   static String dashes = "------------------------------------";
12
13   public static void main( String args[] )
14     throws SQLException
15   {
16     Class driverClass = loadDriver( "org.postgresql.Driver" );
17
18     if( driverClass == null )
19       return;
20
21     if( args.length != 1 )
22     {
23       System.err.println( "usage: java client4 <url>" );
24       return;
25     }
26
27     Connection con = connectURL( args[0] );
28
29     if( con != null )
30     {
31       DatabaseMetaData dbmd = con.getMetaData();
32
33       System.out.print( "Connected to " );
34       System.out.print( dbmd.getDatabaseProductName());
35       System.out.println( " " + dbmd.getDatabaseProductVersion());
36
37       processCommands( con );
38
39       con.close();
40     }
41   }
```

`client4.main()` is similar to `client3.main()`; you load the PostgreSQL driver and then connect to the database using the URL provided by the user. At line 31, you obtain a `DatabaseMetaData` object, so you can print a welcome message that includes the product name and version.

`main()` finishes by calling `processCommands()`. Now, let's look at the `processCommands()` method (Listing 13.10).

Listing 13.10 `client4.java` **(Part 2)**

```
43   static void processCommands( Connection con )
44   {
45     try
46     {
47       Statement      stmt = con.createStatement();
48       String         cmd  = "";
49       BufferedReader in;
50
51       in = new BufferedReader( new InputStreamReader( System.in ));
52
53       while( true )
54       {
55         System.out.print( "--> ");
56
57         cmd = in.readLine();
58
59         if( cmd == null )
60             break;
61
62         if( cmd.equalsIgnoreCase( "quit" ))
63           break;
64
65         processCommand( stmt, cmd );
66
67       }
68
69       System.out.println( "bye" );
70
71     }
72     catch( Exception e )
73     {
74         System.err.println( e );
75     }
76   }
```

The `processCommands()` method prompts the user for a command and then executes that command. Because this is not a graphical application, you need a way to read input from the user. Java's `BufferedReader` class lets you read user input one line at a time, so you create a new `BufferedReader` object at line 51.

Lines 53 through 67 comprise the main processing loop in this application. At the top of the loop, you print a prompt string and then read the user's response using `BufferedReader`'s `readline()` method.

Three things can cause you to break out of this loop. First, one of the methods that you call can throw an exception. You catch exceptions at line 72 and simply print any error message contained in the exception. Next, the user can close the input stream (usually by pressing Ctrl+D). In that case, readline() returns a null String reference and you break out of the loop at line 60. Finally, you break out of this loop if the user enters the string quit.

When you reach line 65, you call the processCommand() method to execute a single command. Listing 13.11 shows the processCommand() method.

Listing 13.11 client4.java **(Part 3)**

```
78   static void processCommand( Statement stmt, String cmd )
79     throws SQLException
80   {
81
82     if( stmt.execute( cmd ))
83         printResultSet( stmt.getResultSet());
84     else
85     {
86       int count = stmt.getUpdateCount();
87
88       if( count == -1 )
89         System.out.println( "No results returned" );
90       else
91         System.out.println( "(" + count + " rows)" );
92     }
93   }
```

The processCommand() method is a little difficult to understand at first. Here's some background information that might help.

There are three[9] ways to execute a command using a Statement object. I've used the executeQuery() method in most of the examples in this chapter. Calling executeQuery() is only appropriate if you know that you are executing a SELECT command. executeQuery() returns a ResultSet. If you know that you are executing some other type of command (such as CREATE TABLE, INSERT, or UPDATE), you should use the executeUpdate() method instead of executeQuery(). executeUpdate() returns the number of rows affected by the command (or 0 for DDL commands).

If you don't know whether you are executing a query or a command, which is the case in this client, you can call the execute() method. execute() returns a Boolean value: true means that the command returned a result set; false means that the

9. Actually, there is a fourth way to execute a SQL command. You can call the addBatch() method repeatedly to build up a batch of commands, and then execute the whole batch using executeBatch().

command returned the number of rows affected by the command (or 0 for DDL commands)[10].

Because you don't know what kind of command the user entered, you use `execute()`. If the command returns a result set (that is, if `execute()` returns `true`), you call `printResultSet()` to display the results. If the command does not return a result set, you have to call `getUpdateCount()` to determine whether the command modified any rows. Note that the 7.2 version of the PostgreSQL JDBC driver seems to contain a small bug: the `getUpdateCount()` method returns 1, even for commands such as `CREATE TABLE`, `GRANT`, and `CREATE INDEX`.

Now let's look at the methods that display result sets to the user. The first one is `pad()`, shown in Listing 13.12.

Listing 13.12 `client4.java` **(Part 4)**

```
 95   static String pad( String in, int len, String fill )
 96   {
 97       String result = in;
 98
 99       len -= in.length();
100
101       while( len > 0  )
102       {
103           int l;
104
105           if( len > fill.length())
106               l = fill.length();
107           else
108               l = len;
109
110         result = result + fill.substring( 0, l );
111
112         len -= l;
113       }
114
115       return( result );
116   }
```

The `pad()` method is a helper method used by `printResultSet()`. It returns a string padded with `fill` characters to the given length.

Next, let's look at the `printResultSet()` method, shown in Listing 13.13.

10. This is not entirely accurate. Some JDBC drivers (but not the PostgreSQL driver) can execute multiple commands in a single call to `execute()`. In that case, the return code from `execute()` indicates the type of the *first* result. To get subsequent results, you call the `getMoreResults()` method. See the JDBC documentation for more information.

Listing 13.13 `client4.java` **(Part 5)**

```
118   static void printResultSet( ResultSet rs )
119     throws SQLException
120   {
121     int[]             sizes;
122     ResultSetMetaData rsmd     = rs.getMetaData();
123     int               colCount = rsmd.getColumnCount();
124     int               rowCount = 0;
125
126     sizes = new int[colCount+1];
127
128     //
129     // Compute column widths
130     //
131     while( rs.next())
132     {
133       rowCount++;
134
135       for( int i = 1; i <= colCount; i++ )
136       {
137         String val = rs.getString(i);
138
139         if(( rs.wasNull() == false ) && ( val.length() > sizes[i] ))
140           sizes[i] = val.length();
141       }
142     }
143
144     //
145     // Print column headers
146     //
147     for( int i = 1; i <= colCount; i++ )
148     {
149       if( rsmd.getColumnLabel(i).length() > sizes[i] )
150         sizes[i] = rsmd.getColumnLabel(i).length();
151
152       System.out.print( pad( rsmd.getColumnLabel( i ),
153                              sizes[i],
154                              blanks ));
155
156       if( i < colCount )
157         System.out.print( " | " );
158       else
159         System.out.println();
160     }
161
162     for( int i = 1; i <= colCount; i++ )
```

Listing 13.13 **Continued**

```
163       {
164         if( i < colCount )
165           System.out.print( pad( "", sizes[i], dashes ) + "-+-" );
166         else
167           System.out.println( pad( "", sizes[i], dashes ));
168       }
169
170       //
171       // Rewind the result set and print the contents
172       //
173       rs.beforeFirst();
174
175       while( rs.next())
176       {
177         for( int i = 1; i <= colCount; i++ )
178         {
179           String val = rs.getString(i);
180
181           if( rs.wasNull())
182             val = "";
183
184           if( i < colCount )
185             System.out.print( pad( val, sizes[i], blanks ) + " | " );
186           else
187             System.out.println( pad( val, sizes[i], blanks ));
188         }
189       }
190     }
```

The `printResultSet()` method is easily the most complex method in this application.

Start by computing the width of each column header. Each column is as wide as the widest value in that column. You have to read through the entire result set to find the widest value. At lines 147 through 168, print the column headers. If `getColumnLabel()` returns a string longer than the widest value in the column, adjust the width to accommodate the label.

After you have printed the column headers, you have to rewind the result set so that you are positioned just before the first row. Remember, you processed the entire result set earlier when you were computing column widths.

The loop covering lines 175 through 189 processes every row in the result set. For each column in the result set, you retrieve the value in `String` form. Line 181 shows an oddity in the JDBC package: There is no way to determine whether a value is `NULL` without first retrieving that value. So, first call `rs.getString()` to retrieve a column from the current row and then call `rs.wasNull()` to detect `NULL` values. You may be wondering what the `getXXXX()` methods will return if the value is `NULL`. The answer depends on which `getXXXX()` method you call. In this chapter, you have retrieved most result values in the form of a Java `String`, but you can also ask for values to be returned in other data types. `getString()` returns a `null` reference if the column value is `NULL`. `getBoolean()` will return `false` if the column value is `NULL`. Of course, `getBoolean()` will also return `false` if the column value is `false`. Likewise, `getInt()` returns `0` if the value is `NULL` or if the value is `0`. You *must* call `wasNull()` to detect `NULL` values.

After you have detected `NULL` values, print the result, padded to the width of the column.

The last two methods in `client4.java` are identical to those included in `client3.java`. `loadDriver()` is shown in Listing 13.14.

Listing 13.14 `client4.java` **(Part 6)**

```
192    static Class loadDriver( String driverName )
193    {
194      try
195      {
196        return( Class.forName( driverName ));
197      }
198      catch( ClassNotFoundException e )
199      {
200        System.err.println( "Can't load driver - " + e.getMessage());
201        return( null );
202      }
203    }
204
205    static Connection connectURL( String URL )
206    {
207      try
208      {
209        return( DriverManager.getConnection( URL ));
210      }
211      catch( SQLException e )
212      {
213        System.err.println( "Can't connect - " + e.getMessage());
214        return( null );
215      }
216    }
217 }
```

The `loadDriver()` method tries to load the named JDBC driver, and `connectURL()` attempts to connect to the given JDBC URL.

Now, let's compile and run this application:

```
$ make client4.class
javac -g client4.java
```

```
$ java client4 "jdbc:postgresql:movies?user=korry&password=cows"
Connected to PostgreSQL 7.2.1

--> SELECT * FROM tapes
tape_id  | title
---------+--------------
AB-12345 | The Godfather
AB-67472 | The Godfather
MC-68873 | Casablanca
OW-41221 | Citizen Kane
AH-54706 | Rear Window

--> SELECT * FROM customers
id | customer_name        | phone    | birth_date
---+----------------------+----------+-----------
1  | Jones, Henry         | 555-1212 | 1970-10-10
2  | Rubin, William       | 555-2211 | 1972-07-10
3  | Panky, Henry         | 555-1221 | 1968-01-21
4  | Wonderland, Alice N. | 555-1122 | 1969-03-05
5  | Funkmaster, Freddy   | 555-FUNK |
7  | Gull, Jonathan LC    | 555-1111 | 1984-02-05
8  | Grumby, Jonas        | 555-2222 | 1984-02-21
```

Now, I'd like to show you a problem with this application:

```
--> SELECT * FROM tapes; SELECT * FROM customers
Cannot handle multiple result groups.
```

In this example, I tried to execute two SQL commands on one line. As the message suggests, the PostgreSQL JDBC driver cannot handle multiple result groups (this message comes from an exception thrown by the PostgreSQL driver). Note that this is not a limitation of the JDBC package, but of this particular driver. The PostgreSQL source distribution includes an example application (`src/interfaces/jdbc/example/psql.java`) that gets around this problem by parsing user input into individual commands.

Summary

The JDBC package is a large piece of technology. This chapter described the basic techniques for connecting a Java application to PostgreSQL using JDBC and the PostgreSQL JDBC driver. It does not cover a few of the more advanced JDBC topics.

The `Connection` class includes methods that can commit and roll back transactions—of course you can do that yourself by executing `COMMIT` and `ROLLBACK` commands.

The examples in this chapter intercept database errors by catching exceptions. JDBC also throws exceptions for database *warnings*.

One of the more interesting features added to the JDBC 2.0 specification is the updateable `ResultSet`. This feature lets you update, insert, and delete rows in a result set by directly modifying the `ResultSet`, rather than executing the corresponding commands yourself. As of PostgreSQL release 7.2.1, updateable result sets are not fully implemented.

Finally, JDBC gives you a way to map PostgreSQL data types into Java data types. In this chapter, you used `String` values (and an occasional Boolean) to communicate between Java and PostgreSQL, but JDBC can map between other data types as well. You can even map user-defined PostgreSQL types into Java.

JDBC is a powerful and well-designed technology. If you are interested in Java programming, you will want to learn more about JDBC. Sun has done a great job of documenting the JDBC package. For more information, I suggest reading the "JDBC Technology Guide: Getting Started" at `http://java.sun.com/j2se/1.3/docs/guide/jdbc/`.

14

Using PostgreSQL with Perl

THE PERL LANGUAGE HAS BEEN CALLED THE "toolbox for Unix." If you are an experienced Perl programmer, you already know three things about the language: It's extremely useful, it's notoriously difficult to master, and it gives you a new way to write completely incomprehensible code. If you are *not* already a Perl programmer, you should be forewarned that I won't try to teach you the basics of Perl programming in this chapter. But that doesn't mean that you won't be able to get anything useful from this chapter. If you don't already know Perl, read this chapter once without paying too much attention to the syntactical details—they won't make a lot of sense the first time through. Then, read through the client applications again, trying them out as you go. You'll be surprised at how quickly you can make sense of the examples if you don't get too hung up on the unusual syntax.

There are two ways to connect to a PostgreSQL database from a Perl application[1]: pgsql_perl5 (also known as the Pg module) and the DBI module.

The pgsql_perl5 interface is a Perl binding for the libpq API. If you are already comfortable with the libpq API, you will find pgsql_perl5 very familiar.

In this chapter, I'll focus on the DBI module. DBI provides a portable interface to a variety of database systems. When you use the DBI module within a Perl application, you can move from database to database with few if any changes to your code. The architecture of the DBI module is similar in structure to JDBC (the Java database API) and ODBC.

1. I'll use the terms *application*, *script*, and *program* interchangeably in this chapter. They all mean the same thing in Perl: a series of statements that does something—hopefully something useful.

DBI Architecture Overview

The DBI module, like other portable database interfaces, is layered. Figure 14.1 shows the structure of a Perl/DBI application.

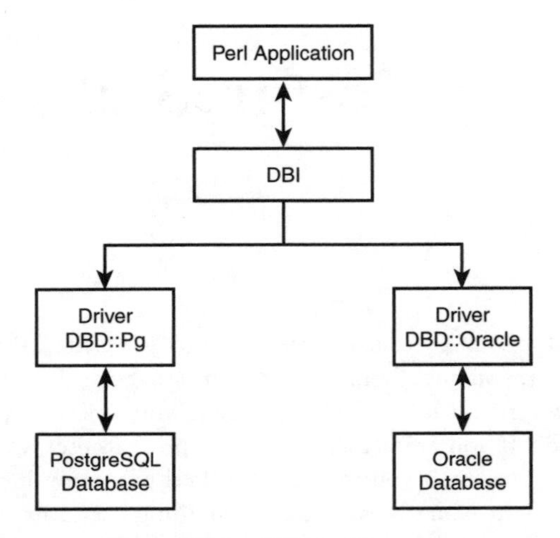

Figure 14.1 DBI architecture.

The topmost layer is the Perl application. A Perl application uses the DBI module to interact with one or more database drivers in a driver-independent (and therefore, database-independent) fashion. *DBI* is an acronym for "database interface." *DBD* is an acronym for "database driver." You can think of the DBI module as "database independent" and the DBD module as "database dependent."

The DBI

The DBI class is responsible for loading DBI drivers into the Perl runtime. The DBI can return a list of available drivers as well as a list of data sources available through a given driver. The DBI class is also responsible for creating database connections.

The DBD Driver

The DBD driver is the component that interfaces with the database. Notice that I've changed spelling here: DBI is the interface seen by the application; DBD is the interface seen by DBI.

The PostgreSQL DBI driver is known as DBD::Pg. DBD::Pg is a combination of Perl code and C code. In the future, you may see a pure Perl driver for PostgreSQL. Pure Perl drivers are much easier to install because you don't have to worry about finding a binary (that is, precompiled) distribution or compiling the driver yourself.

The DBI-Compliant Database

At the bottom of the heap, you'll find the actual database. The DBD driver translates client requests into the form required by the backend database and translates results into the form expected by the client application. The PostgreSQL driver connects to a PostgreSQL database using the libpq API.

Prerequisites

If you want to try out the examples in this chapter, you will need to install and configure the following components (in addition to a running PostgreSQL installation):

- Perl5 or later (`www.perl.org`)
- The DBI module (`www.cpan.org/modules/by-module/DBI`)
- The DBD::Pg driver (`www.cpan.org/modules/by-module/DBI`)

Client 1—Connecting to the Server

Before you try to connect to a PostgreSQL server, take a moment to examine the basic components of a typical Perl/DBI script.

Listing 14.1 shows a Perl script that will print the list of available DBD drivers.

Listing 14.1 `get_drivers.pl`

```
 1 #!/usr/bin/perl -W
 2 #
 3 #  Filename: get_drivers.pl
 4 #
 5 use strict;
 6 use DBI;
 7
 8 # Get the list of drivers from the DBI
 9 #
10 my @driver_names = DBI->available_drivers();
11
12 # Print the name of each driver
13 #
14 foreach my $driver ( @driver_names ) {
15     print( "Driver: $driver\n" );
16 }
```

The first line of the script identifies this file as an executable. When you run a program on Unix/Linux systems, or if you are using Cygwin in the Windows environment, a script file is (directly) executable when the first line of the file contains the characters `#!` followed by the name of the script interpreter (of course, you must hold *execute* privileges for the script, too). For example, a `bash` shell script would start with the line

`#!/bin/bash`. For Perl scripts, the interpreter is named `perl` and is usually found in the `/usr/bin` directory. So, the first line of each of our Perl scripts will be `#!/usr/bin/perl -W`[2]. The `-W` flag is passed to the `perl` interpreter and tells `perl` to display all warnings—this is useful when you are trying to debug new scripts.

The next feature common to all our Perl applications is seen at line 5. If you don't include `use strict`, Perl will be happy to let you misspell variable names and it will just assume that a misspelled name is a variable that it has never seen before. The `use strict` directive tells the Perl interpreter to catch this kind of mistake by requiring that you declare all variables before they are used.

The `use DBI` directive (at line 6) tells Perl that you want to use features defined in the DBI module. You must include a `use DBI` directive in every application that uses the DBI module.

In this application, you call the `DBI->available_drivers()` method to retrieve the names of all drivers currently installed on our host. `available_drivers()` returns an array of driver names. The loop at lines 14 through 16 iterates through the array and prints each driver name.

To run this script, you first have to be sure that its "x" (executable) permission is turned on:

```
$ chown a+x get_drivers.pl
$ ./get_drivers.pl
Driver: ExampleP
Driver: Pg
Driver: Proxy
```

You can see that there are three DBD drivers installed on my system: `ExampleP`, `Pg`, and `Proxy`.

The DBI class also can give you a list of the data sources accessible through a driver. Let's pick one of these drivers (`Pg` is the PostgreSQL driver) and print the list of data sources. Listing 14.2 shows the required code:

Listing 14.2 `get_datasources.pl`

```
 1 #!/usr/bin/perl -W
 2 #
 3 #  Filename: get_datasources.pl
 4 #
 5 use strict;
 6 use DBI;
 7
 8 foreach my $data_source ( DBI->data_sources( "Pg" )) {
 9     print $data_source . "\n";
10 }
```

2. You can also run a Perl script without including the magic first line—just type `perl` followed by a space and then the name of the script file. So you can invoke this program as `./get_drivers.pl` or as `perl get_drivers.pl`.

This script calls the DBI->data_sources() method to obtain a list of the data sources accessible through the Pg driver. Each driver is free to define a data source however it sees fit; the PostgreSQL driver considers a data source to be equivalent to a database. The PostgreSQL driver connects to the template1 database to obtain a list of valid database names. When you run this program, you will see a list of all databases in your database cluster:

```
$ ./get_datasources.pl
dbi:Pg:dbname=movies
dbi:Pg:dbname=perf
dbi:Pg:dbname=template0
dbi:Pg:dbname=template1
```

If you don't see a list of database names when you run this program, you may have to define the DBI_USER and DBI_PASS environment variables. DBI_USER should hold your PostgreSQL user name, and DBI_PASS should hold your PostgreSQL password. In the next two sections, you'll see a better way to supply a username and password to PostgreSQL.

The list returned by get_datasources.pl shows the same set of databases that would be returned using the psql -l command:

```
$ psql -l
       List of databases
   Name    | Owner | Encoding
-----------+-------+-----------
 movies    | bruce | SQL_ASCII
 perf      | bruce | SQL_ASCII
 template0 | bruce | SQL_ASCII
 template1 | bruce | SQL_ASCII
```

Notice that these two lists are not identical. The list produced by psql includes the owner and encoding[3] of each database. The list produced from DBI->data_sources() is actually a list of data source names, or DSNs. A DSN is similar in concept to the connection strings that you have seen in earlier chapters.

DBI URLs

A DBI data source name is encoded in the form of a URL (Uniform Resource Locator). A DBI URL is composed of three parts: a protocol (always dbi), a driver name, and a driver-specific string of connection options. For example, the URL for the movies database is dbi:Pg:dbname=movies. The PostgreSQL driver can work with connection URLs of the following form:

dbi:Pg:*option=value*[;*option=value*]...

3. You won't see the Encoding column on your system if you have not enabled multibyte support.

Where option=value can be any of the values shown in Table 14.1.

Table 14.1 **PostgreSQL DBI URL Options**

Option	Environment Variable Used as Default
dbname=*database_name*	PGDATABASE
host=*host_name*	PGHOST
port=*port_number*	PGPORT
options=*options*	PGOPTIONS
tty=*tty*	PGTTY

To connect to the movies database, you could use any of the following URLs:

```
dbi:Pg:dbname=movies
dbi:Pg:dbname=movies;host=arturo;port=8234
dbi:Pg:
```

The final URL doesn't include any connection options. DBD::Pg uses the environment variables shown in Table 14.1 to default any values missing from the connection URL.

At this point, you know how to obtain the list of installed drivers, how to get the list of data sources accessible through a given driver, and how to construct a connection URL. Now, let's try to connect to a database (see Listing 14.3).

Listing 14.3 client1.pl

```
1 #!/usr/bin/perl -W
2 #
3 #  Filename: client1.pl
4 #
5
6 use strict;
7 use DBI;
8
9 my $dbh = DBI->connect( "dbi:Pg:" );
```

The DBI->connect() method tries to connect to the URL that you provide (dbi:Pg:). If successful, connect() will return a database handle. If connect() fails, things get complicated. The connect() method can perform a number of different actions, depending on the attributes that you specify. In client1.pl, you didn't supply any attributes—I'll get to attributes in a moment.

Let's run this script to see how it reacts to error conditions:

```
$ chmod a+x client1.pl  # Make sure the script is executable
$ ./client1.pl
DBI->connect() failed: FATAL 1:  Database "korry" does not exist
    in the system catalog. at ./client1.pl line 9
```

This error is telling you that `client1` tried to connect to a database named `korry` and you don't have a database named `korry`. Why did you try to connect to that database? Take a look at line 9 in Listing 14.3. When you asked DBI to create a connection, you didn't provide a database name. According to Table 14.1, the DBD::Pg driver looks to the `PGDATABASE` environment variable if you don't specify a database name in the connection URL. If you don't supply a database name in the connection URL and you haven't defined `PGDATABASE`, how does DBD::Pg decide which database to connect to? To find this answer, you have to look to libpq (the PostgreSQL C API); DBD::Pg is implemented using the libpq library. It's actually libpq that looks for the environment variables shown in Table 14.1. If you don't supply an explicit database in the connection URL and you didn't define `PGDATABASE`, libpq will try to connect to a database whose name matches your username; I'm logged-in as user `korry` so libpq (and therefore DBD::Pg) tries to connect to a database named `korry`.

Now let's run this script again, supplying a value for `PGDATABASE`:

```
$ PGDATABASE=movies ./client1.pl
Database handle destroyed without explicit disconnect.
```

That's a little better (take my word for it). This message means that you did make a successful connection, but you didn't clean up after yourself as the script ended. Fixing that problem is easy—you need to call the `$dbh->disconnect()` function before you exit. You'll do that in the next client.

Client 2—Adding Error Checking

In client1.pl, you didn't do any error checking at all. The error messages that you saw were produced by DBI or DBD::Pg, not by your script. For simple applications, it might be sufficient to let DBI handle errors, but in more complex cases, you probably want some other options.

Let's start by modifying the previous client so that it prints its own error message if something goes wrong. Listing 14.4 shows the resulting code.

Listing 14.4 `client2a.pl`

```
 1 #!/usr/bin/perl -W
 2 #
 3 #  Filename: client2a.pl
 4 #
 5
 6 use strict;
 7 use DBI;
 8
 9 my $dbh = DBI->connect( "dbi:Pg:" )
10   or die "Can't connect to PostgreSQL: $DBI::errstr ($DBI::err)\n";
11
12 $dbh->disconnect();
```

This script detects `connect()` failures by examining the return value. `DBI::connect()` returns `undef` (instead of a database handle) when it fails. The error message that you print at line 10 includes an error message (`$DBI::errstr`) and an error number (`$DBI::err`).

At line 12, you disconnect the database handle if the connection attempt was successful. This should avoid the error message that you saw with client1 (`Database handle destroyed without explicit disconnect`). Notice that you will never reach line 12 if the connection attempt fails because you `die` (at line 10) if `connect()` encounters an error.

Now, let's run this client:

```
$ chmod a+x client2a.pl
$ ./client2a.pl
DBI->connect() failed: FATAL 1:  Database "korry" does not exist
    in the system catalog. at ./client2a.pl line 9
Can't connect to PostgreSQL: FATAL 1:  Database "korry" does not
    exist in the system catalog. (1)
```

There's the error message, but you are still getting the automatic error message delivered by DBI and/or DBD::Pg. Listing 14.5 shows how to turn off DBI's automatic error messages.

Listing 14.5 `client2b.pl`

```
 1 #!/usr/bin/perl -W
 2 #
 3 #  Filename: client2b.pl
 4 #
 5
 6 use strict;
 7 use DBI;
 8
 9 my $dbh = DBI->connect( "dbi:Pg:", undef, undef, {PrintError => 0} )
10   or die "Can't connect to PostgreSQL: $DBI::errstr ($DBI::err)\n";
11
12 $dbh->disconnect();
```

In client2b, you are using another form of the `DBI->connect()` method (actually, it's the same method, just a different number of arguments). The full prototype for the `DBI->connect()` method is

```
DBI->connect( $url, $username, $password, \%attributes )
```

The `$url` parameter specifies to which data source you want to connect. The `$username` and `$password` parameters specify the username and password, respectively (I'll come back to those in a moment). The final parameter is a list of attributes. Every DBI-related handle has a set of attributes that control how the handle behaves.

There are two attributes that control how a handle responds when an error occurs. `client2b.pl` sets the `PrintError` attribute to `0`. `PrintError` controls whether error messages should be printed by the driver (or the DBI class). When `PrintError` is enabled (which is the default), the driver (or DBI) prints an error message any time an error is encountered—that's where the extra message came from when you ran `client2a.pl`. If `PrintError` is disabled (by setting it to `0`), the driver will not print any error messages. In either case, the DBI will set `$DBI::err` and `$DBI::errstr`. The next error-control attribute is `RaiseError`. When `RaiseError` is enabled, the DBI or driver throws an exception (by calling the `die()` method) whenever an error is encountered. Unless you catch the exception (using `eval{}`), your application will terminate when an error is raised. `RaiseError` is disabled by default. If you want a really quick way to handle DBI-related errors, enable `RaiseError` (that is, set it to `1` using `{RaiseError => 1}`), and your application will `die` if any errors occur. We'll leave `RaiseError` disabled in the examples shown in this chapter.

When you run this client, you'll see that you have disabled the automatic error messages and intercepted any error conditions with your own code:

```
$ chmod a+x client2b.pl
$ ./client2b.pl
Can't connect to PostgreSQL: FATAL 1:  Database "korry" does not
    exist in the system catalog. (1)
```

This time, you only see the error message that you explicitly printed.

Client 3—Processing Queries

Now, let's turn our attention to query processing. DBI treats `SELECT` commands and non-`SELECT` commands differently. Commands other than `SELECT` require less-complex processing, so let's look at those first. Listing 14.6 shows the source code for `client3a`:

Listing 14.6 `client3a.pl`

```
 1 #!/usr/bin/perl -W
 2 #
 3 #  Filename: client3a.pl
 4 #
 5
 6 use strict;
 7 use DBI;
 8
 9 my $dbh = DBI->connect( "dbi:Pg:", undef, undef, {PrintError => 0} )
10   or die "Can't connect to PostgreSQL: $DBI::errstr ($DBI::err)\n";
11
12 my $rows = $dbh->do( $ARGV[0] );
13
14 if( !defined( $rows )) {
15     print( $dbh->errstr."(".$dbh->err().")\n" );
```

Listing 14.6 **Continued**

```
16 }
17 else {
18     print( "Ok: $rows rows affected\n" );
19 }
20
21 $dbh->disconnect();
```

After successfully connecting to the database (lines 9 and 10), use the `$dbh->do()` method to execute a command. In this example, the command that you execute is specified on the command line. The `do()` method executes a single SQL command and returns *something*. I know that sounds a little vague, but `do()` encodes a lot of information in its return value—let's see what kinds of information you can discern from the return code.

If the command fails, `do()` returns `undef`, and you can interrogate the `$dbh->errstr` and `$dbh->err` values to find out what went wrong.

If you execute a command such as `CREATE TABLE`, `ANALYZE`, or `GRANT`, `do()` will return `-1` to indicate success.

If you use `do()` to execute a command such as `DELETE` or `UPDATE`, `do()` will return the number of rows affected by the command. However, if the command affects zero rows, `do()` will return the string `0E0`. I'll tell you why in just a moment. First, let's run this program and see what happens when you execute a few commands:

```
$ chmod a+x ./client3a.pl
$ ./client3a.pl "GRANT SELECT ON tapes TO bruce"
Ok: -1 rows affected
```

That behaves as advertised. No data rows were affected, so `do()` returns `-1`.

If you are following along with me, be sure you have a backup before you execute the next command—it deletes all rows from the `tapes` table.

```
./client3a.pl "DELETE FROM tapes"
Ok: 5 rows affected
```

In this case, you deleted five rows from the `tapes` table, so `do()` returned `5`. Now, let's see what happens when an error occurs:

```
./client3a.pl "DELETE FROM ship"
ERROR:  Relation "ship" does not exist(7)
```

This time, the table name is misspelled, so the `do()` method returned `undef`. We caught this condition at line 14 of `client3a.pl`, and print the error message (and error code) at line 15.

Now, let's see what the `0E0` business is all about:

```
./client3a.pl "DELETE FROM tapes where tape_id <> tape_id"
Ok: 0E0 rows affected
```

This time, I've fed do() a command that can't possibly affect any rows (it is impossible for tape_id to not be equal to tape_id in any given row). It is not considered an error for a DELETE command (or an UPDATE command) to affect zero rows, so we don't want do() to return undef. Instead, do() returns the mysterious string 0E0. If you haven't figured it out yet, 0E0 is the same thing as 0x10^0. In other words, 0E0 is 0 written in Perl's dialect of exponential notation. Why doesn't do() just return 0? Because the string 0 is interpreted as False in a logical expression. If you wrote code like this:

```
...
$row_count = $dbh->do("DELETE * FROM tapes WHERE tape_id <> tape_id");

if( $row_count ) {
  print( "Ok, $row_count rows affected\n" );
}
else {
  print( "Yeow! Something bad just happened\n" );
}
...
```

you would be reporting an error if the command affected zero rows. So instead, do() returns 0E0, which is not interpreted as False. In this way, do() returns False only when an error occurs. Perl programmers think a *little* differently....

It's easy to translate the 0E0 into a more palatable 0: just add 0. For example:

```
...
$row_count = $dbh->do("DELETE * FROM tapes WHERE tape_id <> tape_id");

if( $row_count ) {
  print( "Ok, " . $row_count+0 . " rows affected\n" );
}
else {
  print( "Yeow! Something bad just happened\n" );
}
...
```

Be sure that you add 0 *after* checking for undef (undef+0 equals 0).

Enough of that. Let's move on to SELECT execution now.

Executing a SELECT command is more complex than executing other commands because you need a way to process the result set. The DBI package uses a two-step, prepare/execute model for processing SELECT commands. Listing 14.7 shows the basic steps required to process a SELECT command.

Listing 14.7 client3b.pl

```
1 #!/usr/bin/perl -W
2 #
3 #  Filename: client3b.pl
4 #
```

Listing 14.7 **Continued**

```
 5 use strict;
 6 use DBI;
 7
 8 my $dbh = DBI->connect("dbi:Pg:", undef, undef, {PrintError => 1})
 9  or die "Can't connect to PostgreSQL: $DBI::errstr ($DBI::err)\n";
10
11 my $sth = $dbh->prepare( $ARGV[0] );
12
13 if( defined( $sth )) {
14     if( $sth->execute()) {
15         $sth->dump_results();
16     }
17 }
18
19 $dbh->disconnect();
```

Line 11 prepares a command for execution (the command is taken from the first command-line argument). The `prepare()` method returns a statement handle, or `undef` if an error is encountered. Note that I have enabled `PrintError` in this example to simplify the code a little. If the command is successfully prepared, you call the `$sth->execute()` method to actually carry out the query. At line 15, you take a real short shortcut. The `dump_results()` method prints the result set associated with your statement handle. I call this a shortcut because you probably won't want to use this method except in quick-and-dirty programs or as an aid to debugging. If you run this application, I think you'll see what I mean:

```
$ chmod a+x client3b.pl
$ ./client3b.pl "SELECT * FROM customers"
'1', 'Jones, Henry', '555-1212', '1970-10-10'
'2', 'Rubin, William', '555-2211', '1972-07-10'
'3', 'Panky, Henry', '555-1221', '1968-01-21'
'4', 'Wonderland, Alice N.', '555-1122', '1969-03-05'
'5', 'Funkmaster, Freddy', '555-FUNK', undef
'7', 'Gull, Jonathan LC', '555-1111', '1984-02-05'
'8', 'Grumby, Jonas', '555-2222', '1984-02-21'
7 rows
```

All the data shows up, but `dump_results()` didn't do a very nice job of formatting the results. I'll show you how to fix that a little later. For now, let's go back and talk about some of the things that you can do between the call to `prepare()` and the call to `execute()`.

The Prepare/Execute Model

In earlier chapters, I explained that the prepare/execute model is useful for two different reasons: performance and simplicity.

Some database systems (but not PostgreSQL) gain a performance boost by using prepare/execute. In the prepare phase, the client application constructs a query (or other command) that includes placeholders[4] for actual data values. For example, the command `INSERT INTO tapes VALUES( ?,? )` contains two placeholders (the question marks). This parameterized command is sent to the server. The server parses the command, prepares an execution plan, and returns any error messages to the client.

Before a prepared command can be executed, you must *bind* each placeholder. Binding a parameter creates a connection between a placeholder and a value—in other words, binding gives a value to a placeholder. After all the placeholders have been bound, you can execute the command.

The performance gain is realized from the fact that you can execute a prepared command over and over again, possibly providing different placeholder values each time. The server may not have to parse the command and formulate an execution plan once the command has been prepared.

Currently, PostgreSQL does not gain any performance advantage from the prepare/execute model (it parses and plans the prepared command each time it is executed). This may not be the case in the future.

The second advantage offered by the prepare/execute model is applicable to PostgreSQL. By splitting command processing into multiple pieces, you can factor your code for greater simplicity. For example, you may want to place the code that *generates* a command into one method, the code to compute and bind parameter values in a second method, and the code to process results in a third method—for example:

```
...

prepare_insert_tapes_command( $sth );

while( defined( $line = <STDIN> )) {
  bind_tape_values( $sth, chomp( $line ));
  execute_insert_tapes( $sth );
}
...
```

In this code snippet, you prepare an `INSERT` command once, and bind and execute it multiple times.

Listing 14.8 shows `client3c.pl`. When you run this client, you can include a parameterized command on the command line, and you will be prompted to supply a value for each placeholder.

4. Placeholders are also known as *parameter markers*.

Listing 14.8 client3c.pl

```
 1 #!/usr/bin/perl -W
 2 #
 3 #  Filename: client3c.pl
 4 #
 5 use strict;
 6 use DBI;
 7
 8 my $dbh = DBI->connect("dbi:Pg:", undef, undef, {PrintError => 1})
 9   or die "Can't connect to PostgreSQL: $DBI::errstr ($DBI::err)\n";
10
11 $dbh->do( "SET TRANSFORM_NULL_EQUALS TO ON" );
12
13 my $sth = $dbh->prepare( $ARGV[0] );
14
15 if( defined( $sth )) {
16
17     get_params( $sth );
18
19     if( $sth->execute()) {
20         $sth->dump_results();
21     }
22 }
23
24 $dbh->disconnect();
25
26 #
27 #  subroutine: get_params( $sth )
28 #
29 sub get_params
30 {
31     my $sth             = shift;
32     my $parameter_count = $sth->{NUM_OF_PARAMS};
33     my $line            = undef;
34
35     for( my $i = 1; $i <= $parameter_count; $i++ ) {
36         print( "Enter value for parameter $i: " );
37
38         chomp( $line = <STDIN> );
39
40         if( length( $line )) {
41             $sth->bind_param( $i, $line );
42         }
43         else {
44             $sth->bind_param( $i, undef );
45         }
46     }
47 }
```

After connecting to the database, you execute the command `SET TRANSFORM_NULL_EQUALS TO ON`. This command allows you to write `WHERE ... = NULL` when you should really write `WHERE ... IS NULL`. I know that sounds a little mysterious right now, but I'll show you why you want to do that in a moment. At line 13, you prepare the statement entered on the command line. If that succeeds, you call the `get_params()` method (described next) to prompt the user for parameter values. Then, you wrap up by executing the prepared command and dumping the results.

The `get_params()` method (line 29) prompts the user for a value for each placeholder in the command. How do you know how many placeholders appear in the command? The statement handle has a number of attributes that you can query once the command has been prepared. One of these attributes (`NUM_OF_PARAMS`) contains the number of placeholders on the command. The `for` loop starting at line 35 executes once for each placeholder. After printing a prompt, you read one line from `STDIN` and strip off the terminator (`new-line`). If the user enters something, you call `bind_param()` to bind the string entered by the user to the current parameter. If the user doesn't enter anything (that is, he just presses the `Return` key), you bind `undef` to the current parameter. When you bind `undef` to a placeholder, you are effectively setting the parameter to `NULL`.

Let's run this script a few times. First, execute a command that does not include any placeholders:

```
$ chmod a+x client3c.pl
$ $ ./client3c.pl "SELECT * FROM customers WHERE id = 2"
'2', 'Rubin, William', '555-2211', '1972-07-10'
1 rows
```

Now, try one that includes a parameter marker:

```
$ ./client3c.pl "SELECT * FROM customers WHERE id = ?"
Enter value for parameter 1: 2
'2', 'Rubin, William', '555-2211', '1972-07-10'
1 rows
```

Finally, see what happens when you *don't* enter a parameter value:

```
$ ./client3c.pl "SELECT * FROM customers WHERE birth_date = ?"
Enter value for parameter 1:
'5', 'Funkmaster, Freddy', '555-2132', undef
1 rows
```

Because you bind `undef` to this parameter (see line 44), you are executing the command `SELECT * FROM customers WHERE birth_date = NULL`. Normally, that would not be considered a valid command (`NULL` is never *equal* to anything), but at the beginning of this script, you enable PostgreSQL's `TRANSFORM_NULL_EQUALS` runtime parameter.

Metadata and Result Set Processing

Now, I'd like to revisit the issue of result set processing. In earlier examples, you have been using `dump_results()` to avoid dealing with too many details at once.

After you call the `execute()` method, you can access the result set and metadata about the result set through the statement handle.

You can use any of three methods to process individual rows within the result set: `fetchrow_arrayref()`, `fetchrow_array()`, or `fetchrow_hashref()`. A fourth method, `fetchall_arrayref()`, returns a reference to an array that contains a reference to each row.

Let's look at each of these methods in detail.

`fetchrow_arrayref()` returns a reference to an array containing the values for the next row in the result set. If you reached the end of the result set, `fetchrow_arrayref()` returns `undef`. `fetchrow_arrayref()` will also return `undef` if an error occurs—you have to check `$sth->err()` to distinguish between an error and the end of the result set.

Each element of the array returned by `fetchrow_arrayref()` contains a value that corresponds to a column in the result set. If a row contains `NULL` values, they are represented by `undef` values in the array. Listing 14.9 shows a script that processes a result set using the `fetchrow_arrayref()` method.

Listing 14.9 `client3d.pl`

```
 1 #!/usr/bin/perl
 2 #
 3 #  Filename: client3d.pl
 4 #
 5 use strict;
 6 use DBI;
 7
 8 my $dbh = DBI->connect("dbi:Pg:", undef, undef, {PrintError => 1})
 9   or die "Can't connect to PostgreSQL: $DBI::errstr ($DBI::err)\n";
10
11 my $sth = $dbh->prepare( $ARGV[0] );
12
13 if( defined( $sth )) {
14     if( $sth->execute()) {
15         print_results( $sth );
16     }
17 }
18
19 $dbh->disconnect();
20
21 #
22 #  subroutine: print_results( $sth )
23 #
```

Listing 14.9 **Continued**

```
24 sub print_results
25 {
26     my $sth = shift;
27
28     while( my $vals = $sth->fetchrow_arrayref()) {
29         foreach my $val ( @$vals ) {
30             print( $val . "\t" );
31         }
32         print( "\n" );
33     }
34 }
```

The interesting part of this script is the `print_results()` subroutine (lines 24 through 34). This method loops through the result set by calling `fetchrow_arrayref()` to retrieve one row at a time. You loop through each value in the array and print the contents. When you run this script, you will see the result set printed in a format similar to that produced by the `dump_results()` method:

```
$ chmod a+x client3d.pl
$ ./client3d.pl "SELECT * FROM customers"
1       Jones, Henry    555-1212        1970-10-10
2       Rubin, William  555-2211        1972-07-10
3       Panky, Henry    555-1221        1968-01-21
4       Wonderland, Alice N.    555-1122        1969-03-05
7       Gull, Jonathan LC       555-1111        1984-02-05
8       Grumby, Jonas   555-2222        1984-02-21
```

It's important to understand that `fetchrow_arrayref()` does *not* return an array; it returns a reference to an array. In fact, `fetchrow_arrayref()` happens to return a reference to the same array each time you call it. This means that each time you call `fetchrow_arrayref()`, the values from the previous call are overwritten by the next row.

You can see this by modifying the `print_results()` subroutine to save each reference returned by `fetchrow_arrayref()`, as shown in Listing 14.10.

Listing 14.10 `print_results_and_saved_references`

```
...
sub print_results_and_saved_references
{
    my $sth = shift;
    my @saved_refs;

    while( my $vals = $sth->fetchrow_arrayref()) {
        foreach my $val ( @$vals ) {
```

Listing 14.10 **Continued**

```
            print( $val . "\t" );
        }
        print( "\n" );

        push( @saved_refs, $vals );
    }

    print( "Saved References:\n" );

    foreach my $vals ( @saved_refs ) {
        foreach my $val( @$vals ) {
            print( $val . "\t" );
        }
        print( "\n" );
    }
}
...
```

In this version of `print_results()`, you add each reference returned by `fetchrow_arrayref()` to your own `@saved_refs` array. After you finish processing the result set, go back and print the contents of `@saved_refs`. Now the output looks like this:

```
1       Jones, Henry    555-1212        1970-10-10
2       Rubin, William  555-2211        1972-07-10
3       Panky, Henry    555-1221        1968-01-21
4       Wonderland, Alice N.    555-1122        1969-03-05
7       Gull, Jonathan L        1984-02-05
8       Grumby, Jonas   555-2222        1984-02-21
Saved References:
8       Grumby, Jonas   555-2222        1984-02-21
8       Grumby, Jonas   555-2222        1984-02-21
8       Grumby, Jonas   555-2222        1984-02-21
8       Grumby, Jonas   555-2222        1984-02-21
8       Grumby, Jonas   555-2222        1984-02-21
8       Grumby, Jonas   555-2222        1984-02-21
```

You can see that there were six rows in this result set, so you saved six references in `@saved_refs`. When you print the contents of `@saved_refs`, you can see that all prior results have been overwritten by the last row in the result set. This is because `fetchrow_arrayref()` uses a single array *per statement handle*, no matter how many rows are in the result set.

In contrast, `fetchrow_array()` returns a new array each time you call it (except, of course, when you encounter an error or the end of the result set; then `fetchrow_array()` returns `undef`). Listing 14.11 shows how to process a result set using the `fetchrow_array()` method.

Listing 14.11 `print_results_using_fetchrow_array`

```
...
sub print_results_using_fetchrow_array
{
    my $sth = shift;

    while( my @vals = $sth->fetchrow_array()) {
        foreach my $val ( @vals ) {
            print( $val . "\t" );
        }
        print( "\n" );
    }
}
...
```

In some circumstances, it's easier to work with a hash than with an array. The `fetchrow_hashref()` method fetches the next result set row into a hash and returns a reference to the hash. Listing 14.12 shows how to process a result set using `fetchrow_hashref()`.

Listing 14.12 `print_results_using_fetchrow_hashref`

```
...
sub print_results_using_fetchrow_hashref
{
    my $sth = shift;

    while( my $vals = $sth->fetchrow_hashref()) {
        foreach my $key ( keys( %$vals )) {
            print( $vals->{$key} . "\t" );
        }
        print( "\n" );
    }
}
...
```

Each key in the hash is a column name. For example, if you execute the command `SELECT * FROM` customers, you will find the following keys:

customer_name

`birth_date`

`id`

phone

There are a couple of points to be aware of when using `fetchrow_hashref()`. First, the order of the column names returned by `keys()` is random[5]. If you feed the same result set to `print_results_using_fetchrow_hashref()` and print_results_using_fetchrow_array(), you will see the same values, but the columns are not likely to be displayed in the same left-to-right order. Second, if a result set contains two or more columns with the same name, all but one value will be discarded. This makes a lot of sense because a hash cannot contain duplicate keys. You might encounter this problem when a query includes computed columns and you forget to name the columns (using AS). This problem can also occur when you join two or more tables and SELECT the common columns. For example:

```
./client3d_hashref.pl "
> SELECT
>   datname, blks_read*8192, blks_hit*8192
> FROM
>   pg_stat_database"
0          perf
0          template1
0          template0
235732992  movies
```

Notice that you requested three values, but you see only two of them. The column name for blks_read*8192 and blks_hit*8192 is the same:

```
?column?
```

So, one of the columns is discarded by fetchrow_hashref(), and you can't predict which one will be thrown out. If you give a unique name to each column, you will see all three results:

```
./client3d_hashref.pl "
> SELECT
>   datname, blks_read*8192 AS Read, blks_hit*8192 AS Hit
> FROM
>   pg_stat_database"
perf    0         0
template1         0       0
template0         0       0
movies  243728384         3661824
```

That fixes one bug, but now you have a new problem. This table is difficult to read; it doesn't have column headers and there is no vertical alignment. Let's fix both of those problems.

Listings 14.13 through 14.18 show the client3e.pl script. This client is (almost) capable of executing an arbitrary query and printing a nicely formatted result set. There's still one problem left in this client, and I'll show you how to fix it in a moment.

Listing 14.13 shows the mainline code for client3e.pl:

5. Random, but consistent. It is extremely likely that the column names will appear in the same order during the processing of the entire result set. If the ordering is important, you should really be using an array in the first place, not a hash.

Listing 14.13 client3e.pl

```
 1 #!/usr/bin/perl
 2 #
 3 #  Filename: client3e.pl
 4 #
 5 use strict;
 6 use DBI;
 7
 8 my $dbh = DBI->connect("dbi:Pg:", undef, undef, {PrintError => 1})
 9   or die "Can't connect to PostgreSQL: $DBI::errstr ($DBI::err)\n";
10
11 my $sth = $dbh->prepare( $ARGV[0] );
12
13 if( defined( $sth )) {
14   if( $sth->execute()) {
15     my($widths, $row_values) = compute_column_widths( $sth );
16     print_column_headings( $sth, $widths );
17     print_results( $row_values, $widths );
18   }
19 }
20
21 $dbh->disconnect();
```

After connecting to the database, preparing the command, and executing it, you are ready to print the results. First, call `compute_column_widths()` (see Listing 14.14) to figure out how wide each column should be. Next, print the column headings, and finally print the results.

Listing 14.14 client3e.pl—compute_column_widths

```
23 #
24 #  subroutine: compute_column_widths( $sth )
25 #
26 sub compute_column_widths
27 {
28   my $sth   = shift;
29   my $names = $sth->{NAME};
30   my @widths;
31
32   for( my $col = 0; $col < $sth->{NUM_OF_FIELDS}; $col++ ) {
33     push( @widths, length( $names->[$col] ));
34   }
35
36   my $row_values = $sth->fetchall_arrayref();
37
38   for( my $col = 0; $col < $sth->{NUM_OF_FIELDS}; $col++ ) {
```

Listing 14.14 **Continued**

```
39      for( my $row = 0; $row < $sth->rows(); $row++ ) {
40        if( defined( $row_values->[$row][$col] )) {
41          if( length( $row_values->[$row][$col] ) > $widths[$col] ) {
42            $widths[$col] = length( $row_values->[$row][$col] );
43          }
44        }
45      }
46    }
47
48    return( \@widths, $row_values );
49 }
```

Listing 14.14 shows the `compute_column_widths()` subroutine. There's a lot of new stuff going on in this subroutine. First, you use the statement handle to retrieve two pieces of metadata. At line 29, you use the `{NAME}` attribute to find column names. `{NAME}` is a reference to an array of column names[6]. DBI also provides the `{NAME_lc}` and `{NAME_uc}` attributes, in case you want the column names to appear in lowercase or uppercase, respectively. The `{NUM_OF_FIELDS}` attribute returns the number of columns (or fields, if you prefer) in the result set. `{NUM_OF_FIELDS}` will return 0 for commands other than SELECT.

At lines 32 through 34, you loop through each column in the result set and insert the length of the column name into the widths array. When you finish the loop, you have an array with `{NUM_OF_FIELDS}` entries, and each entry in this array contains the length of the corresponding column name.

I mentioned earlier that there are four methods that you can use to walk through a result set. The first three, `fetchrow_array()`, `fetchrow_arrayref()`, and `fetchrow_hashref()`, process a result set one row at a time. The fourth method, `fetchall_arrayref()`, gives us access to the entire result set at once. We use `fetchall_arrayref()` at line 36. This method returns a reference to an array of references: one reference for each row in the result set. Think of `fetchall_arrayref()` as returning a two-dimensional array. For example, to get the value returned in the fourth column of the third row, you can use the syntax `$row_values->[3][4]`.

After you have a reference to the entire result set, you loop through every row and every column (lines 38 through 46), finding the widest value for each column.

There's another piece of metadata buried in this loop. At line 39, you call `$sth->rows()` method to determine how many rows are in the result set.

6. Some database drivers may include `undef` column names in the `{NAME}` array. The `DBD::Pg` never includes undefined column names.

Calling `$sth->rows()`

The DBI reference guide discourages calls to `$sth->rows()`, except in cases where you know that you have executed a command *other than* `SELECT`. The DBD::Pg driver always returns a meaningful value when you call `$sth->rows()`. If you are concerned with the portability of your Perl application, you should compute the number of rows in a result set using some other method (such as finding the size of the array returned by `fetchall_arrayref()`).

`compute_column_widths()` returns two values. The first value is a reference to the `@widths` array. The second value returned by this method is the reference to the result set.

You may be thinking that it's kind of silly to return the result set reference from this subroutine; why not just call `fetchall_arrayref()` again when you need it? You can't. After a command has been executed, you can *fetch* the results only once. Of course, you can *access* the result set as many times as you like; you just can't fetch any given row more than once.

Now, let's look at the `pad()` subroutine (see Listing 14.15).

Listing 14.15 `client3e.pl—pad`

```
51 #
52 #  subroutine: pad( $val, $col_width, $pad_char )
53 #
54 sub pad
55 {
56   my( $val, $col_width, $pad_char ) = @_;
57   my $pad_len;
58
59   $val      = "" if ( !defined( $val ));
60   $pad_char = " " if( !defined( $pad_char ));
61   $pad_len  = $col_width - length( $val );
62
63   return( $val . $pad_char x $pad_len . " " );
64
65 }
```

The `pad()` subroutine simply pads the given value (`$val`) to `$col_width` characters. If the given value is `undef`, meaning that it is a `NULL` value from the result set, you translate it into an empty string for convenience. The optional `$pad_char` parameter determines the pad character. If the caller does not provide a `$pad_char`, you can pad with spaces.

Listing 14.16 shows the `print_column_headings()` subroutine.

Listing 14.16 `client3e.pl—print_column_headings`

```
67 #
68 #  subroutine: print_column_headings( $sth )
69 #
70 sub print_column_headings
```

Listing 14.16 **Continued**

```
 71 {
 72   my $sth    = shift;
 73   my $widths = shift;
 74   my $names  = $sth->{NAME};
 75
 76   for( my $col = 0; $col < $sth->{NUM_OF_FIELDS}; $col++ ) {
 77     print( pad( $names->[$col], $widths->[$col] ));
 78   }
 79
 80   print( "\n" );
 81
 82   for( my $col = 0; $col < $sth->{NUM_OF_FIELDS}; $col++ ) {
 83     print( pad( "-", $widths->[$col], "-" ));
 84   }
 85
 86   print( "\n" );
 87 }
```

The `print_column_headings()` subroutine prints properly aligned column headings. The first loop (lines 76 through 78) prints each column name, padded with spaces to the width of the column. The second loop (lines 82 through 84) prints a string of dashes under each column name.

The `print_results()` subroutine is shown in Listing 14.17.

Listing 14.17 `client3e.pl—print_results`

```
 89 #
 90 #  subroutine: print_results( )
 91 #
 92 sub print_results
 93 {
 94   my( $rows, $widths ) = @_;
 95
 96   for( my $row = 0; $row < $sth->rows(); $row++ ) {
 97     for( my $col = 0; $col < $sth->{NUM_OF_FIELDS}; $col++ ) {
 98       print( pad( $rows->[$row][$col], $widths->[$col] ));
 99     }
100     print( "\n" );
101   }
102 }
```

Finally, `print_results()` prints the entire result set. Use the widths array (constructed by `compute_column_widths()`) to pad each value to the appropriate width.

Now let's run this script a few times:

```
$ chmod a+x ./client3e.pl
$ ./client3e "SELECT * FROM customers";
id customer_name        phone    birth_date
-- -------------------- -------- ----------
1  Jones, Henry         555-1212 1970-10-10
2  Rubin, William       555-2211 1972-07-10
3  Panky, Henry         555-1221 1968-01-21
4  Wonderland, Alice N. 555-1122 1969-03-05
8  Grumby, Jonas        555-2222 1984-02-21
7  Gull, Jonathan LC             1984-02-05
```

That looks much better; all the columns line up nicely and you can finally see the column names.

Now how does this client react when you give it a bad table name?

```
$ ./client3e.pl "SELECT * FROM ship"
DBD::Pg::st execute failed: ERROR:  Relation "ship" does not
exist at ./client3e.pl line 14.
```

That's not the prettiest error message, but it certainly does tell you what's wrong and even where in your code the error occurs.

What happens if you try to execute a command other than `SELECT`?

```
$ ./client3e.pl "INSERT INTO tapes VALUES( 'JS-4820', 'Godzilla' )"
DBD::Pg::st fetchall_arrayref failed: no statement executing at
 ./client3e.pl line 36.
```

That's not so good. You can't use `fetchall_arrayref()` or any of the `fetch()` methods, unless the command that you execute returns a result set. Notice that you got all the way to line 36 before you ran into an error. That's an important point—you can still use `prepare()` and `execute()` to executed non-`SELECT` commands, you just can't fetch from a nonexistent result set.

Listing 14.18 presents a new version of the `client3e.pl` mainline that fixes the problem.

Listing 14.18 **`client3e.pl`—modified mainline**

```
 1 #!/usr/bin/perl -W
 2 #
 3 #  Filename: client3e.pl
 4 #
 5 use strict;
 6 use DBI;
 7
 8 my $dbh = DBI->connect("dbi:Pg:", undef, undef, {PrintError => 1})
 9   or die "Can't connect to PostgreSQL: $DBI::errstr ($DBI::err)\n";
10
```

Listing 14.18 **Continued**

```
11 my $sth = $dbh->prepare( $ARGV[0] );
12
13 if( defined( $sth )) {
14   if( $sth->execute()) {
15     if( $sth->{NUM_OF_FIELDS} == 0 ) {
16         print($sth->{pg_cmd_status} . "\n" );
17     }
18     else {
19       my($widths, $row_values) = compute_column_widths( $sth );
20       print_column_headings( $sth, $widths );
21       print_results( $row_values, $widths );
22     }
23   }
24 }
25
26 $dbh->disconnect();
```

You distinguish between `SELECT` commands and other commands by interrogating `$sth->{NUM_OF_FIELDS}`. If `{NUM_OF_FIELDS}` returns `0`, you can safely assume that you just executed some command other than `SELECT`. If `{NUM_OF_FIELDS}` returns anything other than `0`, you know that you just executed a `SELECT` command.

You can't use `$sth->rows()` to determine the command type. When you execute a `SELECT` command, `$sth->rows()` returns the number of rows in the result set. When you execute an `INSERT`, `UPDATE`, or `DELETE` command, `$sth->rows()` returns the number of rows affected by the command. For all other command types, `$sth->rows()` will return `-1`.

Other Statement and Database Handle Attributes

At line 16, you use a nonstandard extension to the DBI statement handle: `pg_cmd_status`. The PostgreSQL DBI driver adds four PostgreSQL-specific attributes to the statement handle. `pg_cmd_status` returns the standard PostgreSQL command status. For example, when you `INSERT` a new row, the command status is the word `INSERT`, followed by the OID of the new row, and then the number of rows affected:

```
$ psql -d movies
movies=# INSERT INTO tapes VALUES
movies-# (
movies(#   'KL-24381', 'The Day The Earth Stood Still'
movies(# );
INSERT 510735 1
```

Now, when you run client3e.pl (with the new code in place), you see that non-SELECT commands are handled properly:

```
$ ./client3e.pl "INSERT INTO tapes VALUES( 'JS-4820', 'Godzilla' )"
INSERT 510736 1

$ ./client3e.pl "DELETE FROM tapes WHERE tape_id = 'JS-4820'"
DELETE 1
```

The other three statement handle extensions are pg_size, pg_type, and pg_oid_status.

The pg_size attribute returns a reference to an array that contains the size of each column in the result set. The size of a variable-length column is returned as -1. In most cases, this information is not terribly useful because it represents the size of each column *on the server*, not the actual amount of data sent to the client. If you need to know the width of a column, you'll have to compute it by hand as you did in the compute_column_widths() function.

pg_type is a little more useful than pg_size. pg_type returns a reference to an array that contains the name of the data type of each column in the result set. Note that pg_type does not understand user-defined data types and will return the string "unknown" for such columns.

The pg_oid_status attribute returns the OID (object-ID) of the new row after an INSERT command is executed. This attribute uses the libpq PQoidstatus() function and has the same limitations (namely, pg_oid_status returns a meaningful value only when an INSERT command creates a single new row).

The DBI API supports a few more statement handle attributes that are not well-supported (or not supported at all) by the PostgreSQL driver.

The {TYPE} attribute returns a reference to an array containing data type codes (one entry per result set column). The values returned by {TYPE} are intended to provide database-independent data type mappings. Currently, the DBD::Pg module maps PostgreSQL data types into the symbolic values shown in Table 14.2. All other PostgreSQL data types map to a number—the OID (object id) for the type as defined in the pg_type system table. For example, the OID for the BOX data type is 603—the {TYPE} value for a BOX column is 603.

Table 14.2 {TYPE} **Mappings**

PostgreSQL Data Type	Symbolic Name
BYTEA	SQL_BINARY
INT8	SQL_DOUBLE
INT2	SQL_SMALLINT
INT4	SQL_INTEGER
FLOAT4	SQL_NUMERIC
FLOAT8	SQL_REAL

Table 14.2 **Continued**

BPCHAR	SQL_CHAR
VARCHAR	SQL_VARCHAR
DATE	SQL_DATE
TIME	SQL_TIME
TIMESTAMP	SQL_TIMESTAMP

The {PRECISION}, {SCALE}, and {NULLABLE} attributes are not supported by DBD::Pg. {PRECISION} returns the same value as {pg_size}, {SCALE} will return undef, and {NULLABLE} will return 2 (meaning *unknown*).

Another statement handle attribute not supported by DBD::Pg is {CursorName}. Other drivers return the name of the cursor associated with statement handle (if any): the {CursorName} attribute in DBD::Pg returns undef. You *can* use cursors with the PostgreSQL driver, but you must do so explicitly by executing the DECLARE ... CURSOR, FETCH, and CLOSE commands.

As you know, PostgreSQL cursors can be used only within a transaction block. By default, a DBI database handle starts out in AutoCommit mode. When the {AutoCommit} attribute is set to 1 (meaning *true*), all changes are committed as soon as they are made. If you want to start a transaction block, simply set {AutoCommit} to 0 (meaning *false*), and the DBD::Pg driver will automatically execute a BEGIN command for you. When you want to complete a transaction block, you can call $dbh->commit() or $dbh->rollback(). You should not try to directly execute COMMIT or ROLLBACK commands yourself—the DBD::Pg driver will intercept those commands and reward you with an error message. The next client (client4.pl) lets you explore DBI transaction processing features interactively.

Client 4—An Interactive Query Processor

The final client application for this chapter will be a general-purpose interactive command processor. Perl makes it easy for you to create a feature-rich application with a minimum of code: You don't need a lot of scaffolding just to use the basic DBI features. Accordingly, I'll use this application as a way to explain some of the remaining DBI features that haven't really fit in anywhere else.

client4.pl (see Listing 14.19) accepts two kinds of commands from the user. Commands that start with a colon are meta-commands and are processed by the application. Commands that don't begin with a colon are PostgreSQL commands and are sent to the server.

Listing 14.19 **client4.pl—mainline**

```
1 #!/usr/bin/perl -W
2 #
3 #  Filename: client4.pl
```

Listing 14.19 **Continued**

```
 4 #
 5
 6 use DBI;
 7 use Term::ReadLine;
 8
 9 my $dbh = DBI->connect("dbi:Pg:", undef, undef, {PrintError => 1})
10   or die "Can't connect to PostgreSQL: $DBI::errstr ($DBI::err)\n";
11
12 my $term = new Term::ReadLine( 'client4' );
13
14 print( "\nEnter SQL commands or :help for assistance\n\n" );
15
16 while( my $command = $term->readline( "--> " )) {
17     if( $command =~ /^:(\w+)\s*(.*)/ ) {
18         eval {
19             my $subr_name = "do_$1";
20             my @args      = split '\s', $2||'';
21
22             &$subr_name( $dbh, @args );
23         }
24     }
25     else {
26         do_sql_command( $dbh, $command );
27     }
28 }
29
30 do_quit( $dbh );
```

The mainline code for this client is a little different from the earlier clients in this chapter. Because this client is interactive, you will need to accept queries and other commands from the user. The `Term::ReadLine` module (which you `use` at line 7) offers the Perl equivalent of the GNU ReadLine and History libraries.
The main loop in this application (lines 16 through 28) prompts the user for a command, executes the command, and displays the results (if any).

When you call the `$term->readline()` method (at line 16), the user is presented with the prompt (`-->`) and can compose a command string using the editing and history features offered by the `Term::ReadLine` module. `$term->readline()` returns the fully composed command string.

This client application handles two different command types. If a command starts with a colon character (`:`), it is treated as a meta-command and is handled by subroutines that I'll explain in a moment. If a command does *not* start with a colon, assume that it is a PostgreSQL command, and call the `do_sql_command()` method to execute the command and display the results.

We will support the following meta-commands:

- `:help`
- `:autocommit [0|1]`
- `:commit`
- `:rollback`
- `:trace [0|1|2|3|4] [`*`tracefile`*`]`
- `:show_tables`
- `:show_table` *`table-name`*
- `:show_types`

Meta-commands are detected and dispatched starting at line 17. If you're not used to reading Perl regular expression strings, the `if` command at line 17 can look pretty daunting. The `=~` operator determines whether the string on the left side (`$command`) matches the regular-expression on the right side. I'll interpret the regular-expression for you: You want to match a pattern that starts at the beginning of the string (`^`) and is immediately followed by a colon (`:`). Next, you expect to see one or more *word* characters (`\w+`). A *word* character is an alphanumeric character or an underscore. I'll explain the extra parenthesis in a moment. Following the leading word, you expect zero or more white space characters (that is, tabs or spaces). Anything else on the command line is gobbled up by the last subpattern (`.*`).

Two of these subpatterns (`\w+` and `.*`) are enclosed in parentheses. Enclosing a subpattern like this tells Perl that you want it to *remember* the characters that match that subpattern in a special variable that you can use later. We have two enclosed subpatterns: the characters that match the first subpattern will be remembered in variable `$1` and the characters that match the second subpattern will be remembered in `$2`.

The effect here is that you detect meta-commands by looking for strings that start with a colon immediately followed by a word[7]. If you find one, the first word (the meta-command itself) will show up in `$1`, and any arguments will show up in `$2`. That regular-expression operator is pretty powerful, huh?

After you have parsed out the meta-command and the optional arguments, use a little more Perl magic to call the subroutine that handles the given command. If the user enters the meta-command `:help`, you want to call the subroutine `do_help()`. If the user enters the meta-command `:commit`, you want to call the subroutine `do_commit()`. You probably see a pattern developing here; to find the subroutine that handles a given meta-command, you simply glue the characters `do_` to the front of the command name. That's what line 19 is doing. At line 19, you are splitting any optional arguments (which are all stored in `$2`) into an array.

7. You could, of course, change the regular-expression to look for a string that starts with a colon, followed by optional white space, followed by a word.

Now to call the appropriate command handler, you call the subroutine, *by name*, at line 22. Don't let the funky looking expression at line 22 confuse you. This is just a plain-old subroutine call, but Perl determines *which* subroutine to call by evaluating the contents of the `$subr_name` variable. Note that you can't defer the name resolution until runtime like this if you are in `strict` mode—I have omitted the `use strict` directive from this script. Another approach that you can take is to `use strict` in most of your code, but specify `no strict` in the cases that would otherwise cause an error.

I have wrapped the subroutine invocation in an `eval{}` block. This is roughly equivalent to a `try{}/catch{}` block in Java—it catches any errors thrown by the code inside of the block. If the user enters an invalid meta-command (that is, a command that starts with a colon but doesn't match any of the `do_xxx()` subroutines), the `eval{}` block will silently catch the exception rather than aborting the entire application.

All your command handler subroutines expect to receive a database handle as the first parameter, and then an array of optional parameters.

If the command entered by the user does not match your meta-command regular expression, you assume that the command should be sent to the PostgreSQL server and call the `do_sql_command()` subroutine (see Listing 14.20).

Listing 14.20 `client4.pl—do_sql_command`

```
32 sub do_sql_command
33 {
34   my $dbh     = shift;
35   my $command = shift;
36
37   my $sth = $dbh->prepare( $command );
38
39   if( defined( $sth )) {
40       if( $sth->execute()) {
41           process_results( $dbh, $sth );
42       }
43   }
44 }
```

The `do_sql_command()` subroutine is called whenever the user enters a PostgreSQL command. We expect two arguments in this subroutine: a database handle and the text of the command. There are no surprises in this subroutine: you simply prepare the command, execute it, and call `process_results()` to finish up.

```
46 sub do_ping
47 {
48   my( $dbh, @args ) = @_;
49
50   print( $dbh->ping() ? "Ok\n" : "Not On" );
51 }
```

This subroutine, do_ping(), is called whenever the user enters the command :ping. The $dbh->ping() subroutine is designed to test the validity of a database handle. The DBD::Pg implementation of this method executes an empty query to ensure that the database connection is still active.

Listing 14.21 client4.pl—do_autocommit

```
53 sub do_autocommit
54 {
55   my( $dbh, @args ) = @_;
56
57   $dbh->{AutoCommit} = $args[0];
58
59 }
```

The do_autocommit() subroutine shown in Listing 14.21 is used to enable or disable AutoCommit mode. By default, every command executed through DBI is committed as soon as it completes. If you want to control transaction boundaries yourself, you must disable AutoCommit mode. To disable AutoCommit, execute the command :autocommit 0. To enable AutoCommit, use :autocommit 1. The $dbh->{AutoCommit} attribute keeps track of the commit mode for a database handle.

Listing 14.22 shows the do_commit() and do_rollback() subroutines.

Listing 14.22 client4.pl—do_commit, do_rollback

```
61 sub do_commit
62 {
63   my( $dbh, @args ) = @_;
64
65   $dbh->commit();
66 }
67
68 sub do_rollback
69 {
70     my( $dbh, @args ) = @_;
71
72     $dbh->rollback();
73 }
```

After you have disabled AutoCommit mode, you can commit and roll back transactions using :commit and :rollback. If you try to :commit or :rollback while AutoCommit is enabled, you will be rewarded with an error message (commit ineffective with AutoCommit enabled.).

Next, you have the do_quit() subroutine (see Listing 14.23).

Listing 14.23 `client4.pl—do_quit`

```
75 sub do_quit
76 {
77     my( $dbh, @args ) = @_;
78
79     if( defined( $dbh )) {
80         $dbh->disconnect();
81     }
82
83     exit( 0 );
84 }
```

The `do_quit()` subroutine is simple—if the database handle is defined (that is, is not `undef`), disconnect it. The call to `exit()` causes this application to end.

In Listing 14.24, you see the `do_trace()` subroutine.

Listing 14.24 `client4.pl—do_trace`

```
86 sub do_trace
87 {
88     my( $dbh, @args ) = @_;
89
90     $dbh->trace( @args );
91
92 }
```

This subroutine gives you a way to adjust the DBI tracing mechanism. The `$dbh_trace()` method expects either one or two arguments: a trace level (0 through 4) and an optional filename. Every DBI application starts at trace level 0, meaning that no trace output is generated. If you don't supply a trace filename, trace output is sent to `STDOUT` (your terminal).

If you want a *little* information about what's going on under the hood, set the trace level to 1. Here's an example of what you'll see:

```
--> :trace 1
    DBI::db=HASH(0x8208020) trace level set to 1 in DBI 1.30-nothread

--> SELECT * FROM customers LIMIT 1;
dbd_st_prepare: statement = >SELECT * FROM customers LIMIT 1;<
dbd_st_preparse: statement = >SELECT * FROM customers LIMIT 1;<
    <- prepare('SELECT * FROM customers LIMIT 1;')= DBI::st=HASH(0x82081a0) at
➥client4.pl line 37
dbd_st_execute
    <- execute= 1 at client4.pl line 39
...
```

Okay, you actually get a *lot* of information at trace level 1, but not as much as you do for higher trace levels. Tracing is useful for debugging and for understanding how DBI and the PostgreSQL driver are carrying out your requests.

Listing 14.25 shows the `do_help` subroutine.

Listing 14.25 `client4.pl—do_help`

```
 94 sub do_help
 95 {
 96     print( "Commands\n" );
 97     print( "  :help\t\t\tShow help text\n" );
 98     print( "  :autocommit [0|1]\t\tSet AutoCommit\n" );
 99     print( "  :commit\t\t\tCOMMIT TRANSACTION\n" );
100     print( "  :rollback\t\t\tROLLBACK TRANSACTION\n" );
101     print( "  :trace [0|1|2|3|4] [tracefile]\tSet Trace level\n" );
102     print( "  :show_tables\t\t\tShow all table names\n" );
103     print( "  :show_table table_name\tDescribe table\n" );
104     print( "  :show_types\t\t\tList Data Types\n" );
105 }
```

`do_help()` is called whenever the user enters the command `:help`.

This subroutine (`do_show_tables()`, Listing 14.26) shows how to call the `$dbh->table_info()` method.

Listing 14.26 `client4.pl—do_show_tables`

```
107 sub do_show_tables
108 {
109   my( $dbh, @args ) = @_;
110
111   process_results( $dbh, $dbh->table_info());
112
113 }
```

`$dbh->table_info()` returns a result set containing a list of tables accessible through the database handle. Here is an example:

```
--> :show_tables
TABLE_CAT TABLE_SCHEM TABLE_NAME TABLE_TYPE REMARKS
--------- ----------- ---------- ---------- -------
          bruce       customers  TABLE
          bruce       rentals    TABLE
          bruce       returns    TABLE
          bruce       tapes      TABLE
```

The author of each DBD driver can interpret the `$dbh->table_info()` request in a different way. The DBD::Pg driver returns all table and view definitions owned by the current user; other drivers may give different results. In some cases, you may find it easier to call the `$dbh->tables()` method, which returns an array of table names rather than a result set.

The `do_show_types()` subroutine, shown in Listing 14.27, displays a list of server data types.

Listing 14.27 `client4.pl—do_show_types`

```
115 sub do_show_types
116 {
117   my( $dbh, @args ) = @_;
118
119   print("Type            Type         SQL  Col.  Prefix  \n");
120   print("Name            Parameters   Type Size    Suffix\n");
121   print("--------------- ------------ ---- ----- - ------\n" );
122
123   foreach my $type ( $dbh->type_info( undef )) {
124       printf( "%-15s %-12s %-3d  %-5d %s %s\n",
125               $type->{TYPE_NAME},
126               $type->{CREATE_PARAMS} || "",
127               $type->{DATA_TYPE},
128               $type->{COLUMN_SIZE},
129               $type->{LITERAL_PREFIX} || " ",
130               $type->{LITERAL_SUFFIX} || " " );
131   }
132 }
```

At line 123, you call the `$dbh->type_info()` method: This method returns an array of hash references. Each hash corresponds to a single data type and contains a number of key/value pairs. You print the `{TYPE_NAME}`, `{CREATE_PARAMS}`, `{DATA_TYPE}`, and `{COLUMN_SIZE}` attributes as well as the prefix and suffix characters. Here is an example:

```
--> :show_types

Type            Type         SQL  Col.  Prefix
Name            Parameters   Type Size    Suffix
--------------- ------------ ---- ----- - ------
bytea                        -2   4096  ' '
bool                         0    1     ' '
int8                         8    20
int2                         5    5
int4                         4    10
text                         12   4096  ' '
float4          precision    6    12
float8          precision    7    24
abstime                      10   20    ' '
reltime                      10   20    ' '
tinterval                    11   47    ' '
```

```
money                          0    24
bpchar           max length   1    4096  ' '
bpchar           max length   12   4096  ' '
varchar          max length   12   4096  ' '
date                           9    10    ' '
time                           10   16    ' '
datetime                       11   47    ' '
timespan                       11   47    ' '
timestamp                      10   19    ' '
```

You may notice that this list is not a complete list of PostgreSQL data types. It is also not entirely accurate. For example, you know that a `VARCHAR` column has no maximum length, but it is reported to have a length of 4096 bytes.

The `$dbh->type_info()` method is implemented by the DBD::Pg driver, not by the DBI package, so the DBD::Pg author chose the data types that he used most often. My recommendation would be to ignore the information returned by this method, at least when you are connected to a PostgreSQL database. You may find this method more useful if you are exploring *other* database systems.

Listing 14.28 shows the `do_show_table()` subroutine.

Listing 14.28 `client4.pl—do_show_table`

```
134 sub do_show_table
135 {
136     my( $dbh, @args ) = @_;
137
138     my $sth = $dbh->prepare( "SELECT * FROM $args[0] WHERE 1 <> 1" );
139
140     if( defined( $sth )) {
141         if( $sth->execute()) {
142             print_meta_data( $dbh, $sth );
143             $sth->finish();
144         }
145     }
146 }
```

I wanted to include a subroutine that would display the layout of a named table, similar to the `\d` meta-command in `psql`. The DBI package does not provide a method that exposes this information, but you can certainly trick it into providing enough metadata that you can build such a method yourself.

The `do_show_table()` method is called whenever the user enters a command such as `:show_table customers`. The trick is to construct a query that returns all columns, but is guaranteed to return 0 rows. At line 138, you create and execute a query of the following form:

```
SELECT * FROM table-name WHERE 1 <> 1;
```

The WHERE clause in this command can never evaluate to True so it will never return any rows. When you execute this query, you get a result set, even though no rows are returned. You can examine the metadata from this result set to determine the layout of the table. After you have displayed the metadata, call $sth->finish() to tell DBI that you are finished with this result set.

The print_meta_data subroutine is shown in Listing 14.29.

Listing 14.29 client4.pl—print_meta_data

```
148 sub print_meta_data
149 {
150   my $dbh = shift;
151   my $sth = shift;
152
153   my $field_count = $sth->{NUM_OF_FIELDS};
154   my $names       = $sth->{NAME};
155   my $pg_types    = $sth->{pg_type};
156
157   print( "Name                          | Type    \n" );
158   print( "------------------------------+--------\n" );
159
160   for( my $col = 0; $col < $field_count; $col++ ) {
161     printf( "%-30s| %-8s\n", $names->[$col], $pg_types->[$col] );
162   }
163 }
```

This subroutine prints the metadata associated with a result set. Call print_meta_data() from do_show_table().

This subroutine shows how to obtain the number of fields in a result set ($sth->{NUM_OF_FIELDS}), the name of each column ($sth->{NAME}), and the PostgreSQL data type name for each column ($sth->{pg_type}).

As I mentioned earlier, the DBD::Pg driver adds three PostgreSQL-specific attributes to a statement handle: {pg_type}, {pg_oid_status}, and {pg_ctl_status}.

Here is a sample showing print_meta_data() in action:

```
--> :show_table customers
Name                          | Type
------------------------------+--------
id                            | int4
customer_name                 | varchar
phone                         | bpchar
birth_date                    | date
```

The process_results() subroutine (see Listing 14.30) prints the result of a PostgreSQL command.

Listing 14.30 `client4.pl—process_results`

```
165 sub process_results
166 {
167   my $dbh = shift;
168   my $sth = shift;
169
170   if( defined( $sth )) {
171       if( $sth->{NUM_OF_FIELDS} == 0 ) {
172         print( $sth->{pg_cmd_status} . "\n" );
173       }
174       else {
175         my($widths, $row_values) = compute_column_widths( $sth );
176         print_column_headings( $sth, $widths );
177         print_results( $sth, $row_values, $widths );
178     }
179   }
180 }
```

You've already seen most of this code in earlier clients. Start by deciding whether you are processing a `SELECT` command or some other type of command. If the number of fields in the result set is 0 (that is, this is a non-`SELECT` command), you simply print the `$sth->{pg_cmd_status}` attribute. If you decide that you *are* processing a `SELECT` command, you compute the column widths, print the column headings, and then print the entire result set.

The `compute_column_widths()`, `print_column_headings()`, and `print_results()` subroutines are identical to those used in `client3e.pl` earlier in this chapter, so I won't describe them here.

Let's run this client and exercise it a bit:

```
$ chmod a+x client4.pl
$./client4.pl

Enter SQL commands or :help for assistance

--> :help
Commands
  :help                         Show help text
  :autocommit [0|1]             Set AutoCommit
  :commit                       COMMIT TRANSACTION
  :rollback                     ROLLBACK TRANSACTION
  :trace [0|1|2|3|4] [filename] Set Trace level
  :show_tables                  Show all table names
  :show_table table_name        Describe table
  :show_types                   List Data Types
```

So far, so good. This help text was generated by the `do_help()` subroutine. Now, let's see a list of the tables in this database:

```
--> :show_tables
TABLE_CAT TABLE_SCHEM TABLE_NAME TABLE_TYPE REMARKS
--------- ----------- ---------- ---------- -------
          bruce       customers  TABLE
          bruce       rentals    TABLE
          bruce       returns    TABLE
          bruce       tapes      TABLE
```

Next, I'll turn off `AutoCommit` mode, create a new table, and show the layout of the new table:

```
--> :autocommit 0

--> CREATE TABLE foobar( pkey INTEGER, data VARCHAR );
CREATE TABLE

--> :show_table foobar
Name                          | Type
------------------------------+--------
pkey                          | int4
data                          | varchar
```

Now, let's roll back this transaction and try to view the table layout again:

```
--> :rollback
--> :show_table foobar
DBD::Pg::st execute failed: ERROR:  Relation "foobar" does not exist at
➥./client4.pl line 141.
```

The `:rollback` meta-command apparently worked (we don't see any error messages), but the `:show_table` meta-command has failed. We expect this `:show_table` command to fail because we have rolled back the `CREATE TABLE` command.

You may have noticed that I haven't included any error-handling code in this application. When you make the initial connection to the database (way back at line 9 of this script), you set the `{PrintError}` attribute to `1` so DBI and the DBD::Pg driver print any error messages that you may encounter.

Summary

The first time I looked at a Perl program, my reaction was "that is some *ugly* code." I still think Perl is an ugly language, but it sure is useful! I am amazed at how quickly you can construct a useful application with Perl.

After reading this chapter, you may think that Perl is great for quick-and-dirty programs, but not for serious applications. I would disagree—like any programming language, you can write incomprehensible code in Perl. But you can also write Perl scripts that are easy to understand and not too difficult to maintain. Include comments in your code. Avoid constructs that are difficult to understand. Perl often offers many ways to do any one thing: Use the most descriptive form, not the most cryptic.

One of the real benefits to the combination of Perl and PostgreSQL is that you can execute Perl scripts (accessing a PostgreSQL database) from within a web server. When you write Perl scripts intended to run within a web server, the script produces a new web page each time it executes. Because a Perl script can interface with PostgreSQL, you can generate dynamic web content on-the-fly.

I haven't covered web interfacing in this chapter, but Chapter 15, "Using PostgreSQL with PHP," shows you how to use PostgreSQL with the PHP web server scripting language.

15

Using PostgreSQL with PHP

PHP IS A GENERAL-PURPOSE PROGRAMMING LANGUAGE. The most common use of PHP is for building dynamic web pages. A *dynamic* web page is a document that is regenerated each time it is displayed. For example, each time you point your web browser to `cnn.com`, you see the latest news. PHP is useful for building dynamic web pages because you can embed PHP programs within HTML documents. In fact, you can *produce* HTML documents from a PHP script.

PHP Architecture Overview

The job of a web server (such as Apache or Microsoft's IIS) is to reply to requests coming from a client (usually a web browser). When a browser connects to a web server, it requests information by sending a URL (Uniform Resource Locator). For example, if you browse to the URL `http://www.postgresql.org/software.html`, your web browser connects to the server at `www.postgresql.org` and requests a file named `software.html`.

After the web server has received this request, it must decide how to reply. If the requested file cannot be found, you'll see the all too familiar `HTTP 404 - File not found`. Most web servers will choose a response based on the extension of the requested file. A filename ending with `.html` (or `.htm`) is usually associated with a text file containing a HTML document.

Occasionally, you'll see a URL that ends in the suffix `.php`. A `.php` file is a script that is executed by a PHP processor embedded within the web server. The script is executed each time a client requests it. The web *browser* never sees the `.php` script; only the web server sees it. As the `.php` script executes, it sends information back to the browser (usually in the form of an HTML document).

Listing 15.1 shows a simple PHP script.

Listing 15.1 Simple.php

```
1  <?php
2    # Filename: Simple.php
3    echo "Hey there, I'm a PHP script!";
4  ?>
```

When you run this script (I'll show you how in a moment), the PHP interpreter will send the string "Hey there, I'm a PHP script!" to the browser.

PHP syntax might look a little strange at first, so here's a quick explanation. The script starts with the characters <?php: This tells the web server that everything that follows, up to the next ?>, is a PHP script and should be interpreted by the PHP processor. The next line is treated as a comment because it starts with a # character (PHP understands other comment characters, such as "//" as well). The third line is where stuff happens—this is a call to PHP's echo() function. echo() is pretty easy to understand; it just echoes a string to the web server. The characters on line 4 (?>) mark the end of the script.

Web *browsers* don't understand how to interpret PHP scripts; they prefer HTML documents. If you can use PHP to send textual data from the server to the browser, you can also send HTML documents (because an HTML document is textual data). This next PHP script (see Listing 15.2) will create an HTML document (and send it to the browser) as it executes.

Listing 15.2 SimpleHTML.php

```
 1 <?php
 2   # Filename: SimpleHTML.php
 3   echo "<HTML>\n";
 4   echo   "<HEAD>\n";
 5   echo     "<TITLE>SimpleHTML</TITLE>\n";
 6   echo   "<BODY>\n";
 7   echo     "<CENTER>I'm another simple PHP script</CENTER>\n";
 8   echo   "</BODY>\n";
 9   echo "</HTML>";
10 ?>
```

When you use a web browser to request this file (SimpleHTML.php), the server will execute the script and send the following text to the browser:

```
<HTML>
<HEAD>
<TITLE>SimpleHTML</TITLE>
<BODY>
<CENTER>I'm another simple PHP script</CENTER>
</BODY>
</HTML>
```

The web browser interprets this as an HTML document and displays the result, as shown in Figure 15.1.

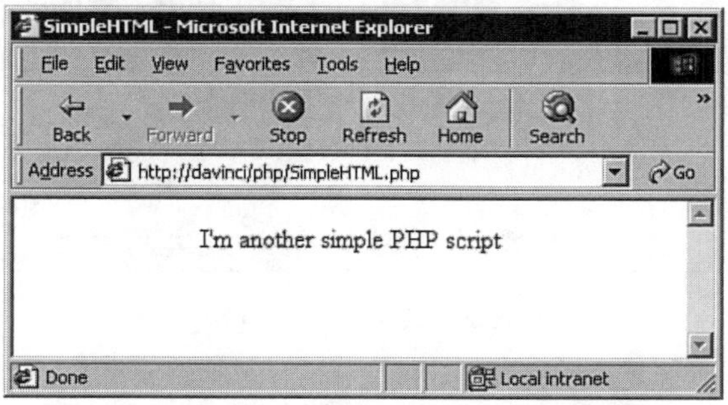

Figure 15.1 `SimpleHTML.php` in a browser.

Of course, if you want to display static HTML pages, PHP doesn't really offer any advantages—we could have produced this HTML document without PHP's help. The power behind a PHP script is that it can produce different results each time it is executed. Listing 15.3 shows a script that displays the current time (in the server's time zone).

Listing 15.3 `Time.php`

```
 1 <?php
 2   //Filename: Time.php
 3
 4   $datetime = date( "Y-m-d H:i:s (T)" );
 5
 6   echo "<HTML>\n";
 7   echo   "<HEAD>\n";
 8   echo     "<TITLE>Time</TITLE>\n";
 9   echo   "<BODY>\n";
10   echo     "<CENTER>";
11   echo       "The current time " . $datetime;
12   echo     "</CENTER>\n";
13   echo   "</BODY>\n";
14   echo "</HTML>";
15 ?>
```

Line 4 retrieves the current date and time, and assigns it to the variable `$datetime`. Line 11 appends the value of `$datetime` to a string literal and echoes the result to the browser. When you request this PHP script from within a browser, you see a result such as that shown in Figure 15.2.

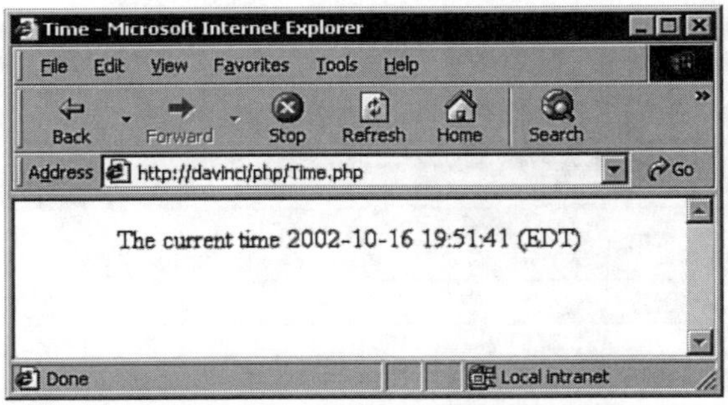

Figure 15.2 `Time.php` in a browser.

If you request this document again (say by pressing the `Refresh` button), the web server will execute the script again and display a different result.

Prerequisites

To try the examples in this chapter, you will need access to a web server that understands PHP. I'll be using the Apache web server with PHP installed, but you can also use PHP with Microsoft's IIS, Netscape's web server, and many other servers.

I'll assume that you are comfortable reading simple HTML documents and have some basic familiarity with PHP in general. Most of this chapter focuses on the details of interacting with a PostgreSQL database from PHP. If you need more information regarding general PHP programming, visit `http://www.zend.com`.

Client 1—Connecting to the Server

The first PHP/PostgreSQL client establishes a connection to a PostgreSQL server and displays the name of the database to which you connect. Listing 15.4 show the `client1a.php` script.

Listing 15.4 `client1a.php`

```
 1 <?php
 2   //Filename: client1a.php
 3
 4   $connect_string = "dbname=movies user=bruce";
 5
 6   $db_handle = pg_connect( $connect_string );
 7
 8   echo "<HTML>\n";
 9   echo   "<HEAD>\n";
10   echo     "<TITLE>client1</TITLE>\n";
11   echo   "<BODY>\n";
```

Listing 15.4 **Continued**

```
12    echo      "<CENTER>";
13    echo        "Connected to " . pg_dbname( $db_handle );
14    echo      "</CENTER>\n";
15    echo    "</BODY>\n";
16    echo "</HTML>";
17 ?>
```

This script connects to a database whose name is hard-coded in the script (at line 4). At line 6, you attempt to make a connection by calling the `pg_connect()` function. `pg_connect()` returns a database handle (also called a database *resource*). Many of the PostgreSQL-related functions require a database handle, so you need to capture the return value in a variable (`$db_handle`).

PHP's `pg_connect()` function comes in two flavors:

```
$db_handle = pg_connect( connection-string );
$db_handle = pg_connect( host, port [,options [, tty ]], database );
```

In the first form (the one you used in `client1.php`), you supply a connection string that contains a list of *`property=value`* pairs[1]. Table 15.1 lists the properties that can appear in a `pg_connect()` connection string. In `client1.php`, you specified two properties: `dbname=movies` and `user=bruce`.

Table 15.1 **Connection Attributes**

Connect-string Property	Environment Variable	Example
user	PGUSER	user=korry
password	PGPASSWORD	password=cows
dbname	PGDATABASE	dbname=accounting
host	PGHOST	host=jersey
hostaddr	PGHOSTADDR	hostaddr=127.0.0.1
port	PGPORT	port=5432

If you don't specify one or more of the connect-string properties, default values are derived from the environment variables shown in Table 15.1. If necessary, `pg_connect()` will use hard-coded default values for the `host(localhost)` and `port(5432)` properties. The second form for the `pg_connect()` function is a bit more complex. In this form, you can provide three, four, or five parameters. The first two parameters are always treated as a hostname and port number, respectively. The last parameter is always treated as a database name. If you pass four or five parameters, the third parameter is assumed to be a list of backend (server) options. If you pass five parameters, the fourth one is expected to be a

1. When you call `pg_connect()` with a single argument, PHP calls the `PQconnectdb()` function from PostgreSQL's libpq API. PHP is yet another PostgreSQL API implemented in terms of libpq.

tty name or filename to which the PostgreSQL server will write debugging information. Just in case you find that a little hard to follow, here are the valid combinations:

```
$db_handle = pg_connect( host, port, database );
$db_handle = pg_connect( host, port, options, database );
$db_handle = pg_connect( host, port, options, tty, database );
```

You might have noticed that you can't specify the username and password using the multiparameter form of `pg_connect()`—you have to use the `PGUSER` and `PGPASSWORD` environment variables. The tricky thing about using environment variables with PHP is that the variables come from the web server's environment. In other words, you have to set `PGUSER` and `PGPASSWORD` before you start the web server. Another option is to use the PHP's `putenv()` function:

```
...
putenv( "PGUSER=korry" );
putenv( "PGPASSWORD=cows" );

$db_handle = pg_connect( NULL, NULL, NULL, NULL, "movies" );
...
```

I'm not very comfortable with the idea of leaving usernames and passwords sitting around in the web server's document tree. It's just too easy to make a configuration error that will let a surfer grab your PHP script files in plain-text form. If that happens, you've suddenly exposed your PostgreSQL password to the world.

A better solution is to factor the code that establishes a database connection into a separate PHP script and then move that script outside the web server's document tree. Listing 15.5 shows a more secure version of your basic PostgreSQL/PHP script.

Listing 15.5 `client1b.php`

```
 1 <?php
 2   //Filename: client1b.php
 3
 4   include( "secure/my_connect_pg.php" );
 5
 6   $db_handle = my_connect_pg( "movies" );
 7
 8   echo "<HTML>\n";
 9   echo   "<HEAD>\n";
10   echo     "<TITLE>client1</TITLE>\n";
11   echo   "<BODY>\n";
12   echo     "<CENTER>";
13   echo       "Connected to " . pg_dbname( $db_handle );
14   echo     "</CENTER>\n";
15   echo   "</BODY>\n";
16   echo "</HTML>";
17 ?>
```

If you compare this to client1a.php, you'll see that you replaced the call to pg_connect() with a call to my_connect_pg(). You've also added a call to PHP's include() directive. The include() directive is similar to the #include directive found in most C programs: include(*filename*) inlines the named file into the PHP script (.php). Now let's look at the my_connect_pg.php file (see Listing 15.6).

Listing 15.6 connect_pg.php

```
 1 <?php
 2   // File:  my_connect_pg.php
 3
 4   function my_connect_pg( $dbname )
 5   {
 6     $connect_string  = "user=korry password=cows dbname=";
 7     $connect_string .= $dbname;
 8
 9     return( pg_connect( $connect_string ));
10   }
11 ?>
```

This script defines a function, named my_connect_pg(), which you can call to create a PostgreSQL connection. my_connect_pg() expects a single string argument, which must specify the name of a PostgreSQL database.

Notice that the username and password are explicitly included in this script.Place this script outside the web server's document tree so that it can't fall into the hands of a web surfer. The question is: Where should you put it? When you call the include() directive (or the related require() function), you can specify an absolute path or a relative path. An absolute path starts with a / (or drive name or backslash in Windows). A relative path does not. The PHP interpreter uses a search path (that is, a list of directory names) to resolve relative pathnames. You can find the search path using PHP's ini_get() function:

```
...
echo "Include path = " . ini_get( "include_path" );
...
```

The ini_get() function returns a variable defined in PHP's initialization file[2]; in this case, the value of include_path. On my system, ini_get("include_path") returns ".:/usr/local/php". PHP searches for include files in the current directory (that is, the directory that contains the including script), and then in /usr/local/php. If you refer back to Listing 15.5, you'll see that I am including secure/my_connect_pg.php. Combining the search path and relative pathname, PHP will find my include file in /usr/local/php/secure/my_connect_pg.php. The important detail here is that /usr/local/php is outside the web server's document tree (/usr/local/htdocs).

2. You can find the PHP's initialization file using echo get_cfg_var("cfg_file_path").

The `my_connect_pg.php` script not only secures the PostgreSQL password, it also gives you a single connection function that you can call from any script—all you need to know is the name of the database that you want.

If everything goes well, the user will see the message "Connected to movies."

Let's see what happens when you throw a few error conditions at this script. First, try to connect to a nonexistent database (see Figure 15.3).

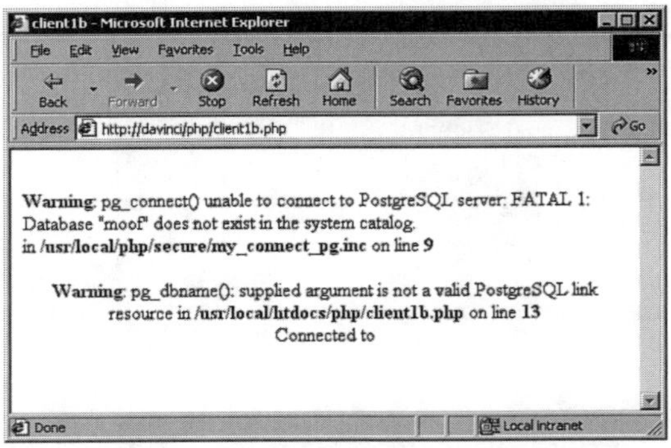

Figure 15.3 Connecting to a nonexistent database.

That's not a friendly error message. Let's see what happens when you try to connect to a database that *does* exist, but where the PostgreSQL server has been shut down (see Figure 15.4).

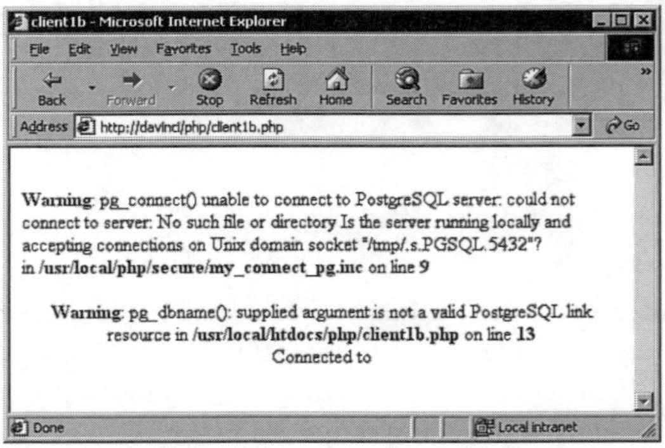

Figure 15.4 Connecting to a database that has been shut down.

Again, not exactly the kind of message that you want your users to see. In the next section, I'll show you how to intercept this sort of error and respond a little more gracefully.

Client 2—Adding Error Checking

You've seen that PHP will simply dump error messages into the output stream sent to the web browser. That makes it easy to debug PHP scripts, but it's not particularly kind to your users.

There are two error messages displayed in Figure 15.4. The first error occurs when you call the `pg_connect()` function. Notice that the error message includes the name of the script that was running at the time the error occurred. In this case, `my_connect_pg.php` encountered an error on line 9—that's the call to `pg_connect()`. The second error message comes from line 13 of client1b.php, where you try to use the database handle returned by `my_connect_pg()`. When the first error occurred, `pg_connect()` returned an invalid handle and `my_connect_pg()` returned that value to the caller.

Listing 15.7 shows a new version of the client script that intercepts both error messages.

Listing 15.7 `client2a.php`

```
 1 <?php
 2   //Filename: client2a.php
 3
 4   include( "secure/my_connect_pg.php" );
 5
 6   $db_handle = @my_connect_pg( "movies" );
 7
 8   echo "<HTML>\n";
 9   echo   "<HEAD>\n";
10   echo     "<TITLE>client1b</TITLE>\n";
11   echo   "<BODY>\n";
12   echo     "<CENTER>";
13
14   if( $db_handle == FALSE )
15     echo "Sorry, can't connect to the movies database";
16   else
17     echo "Connected to " . pg_dbname( $db_handle );
18
19   echo     "</CENTER>\n";
20   echo   "</BODY>\n";
21   echo "</HTML>";
22 ?>
```

If you compare this script with `client1b.php`, you'll see that they are very similar. The first change is at line 6—I've added a `@` character in front of the call to `my_connect_pg()`. The `@` character turns off error reporting for the expression that follows. The next change is at line 14. Rather than blindly using the database handle returned by `my_connect_pg()`, you first ensure that it is a valid handle. `pg_connect()` (and therefore `my_connect_pg()`) will return `FALSE` to indicate that a connection could not be established. If you find that `$db_handle` is `FALSE`, you display a friendly error message; otherwise, you display the name of the database to which you are connected (see Figure 15.5).

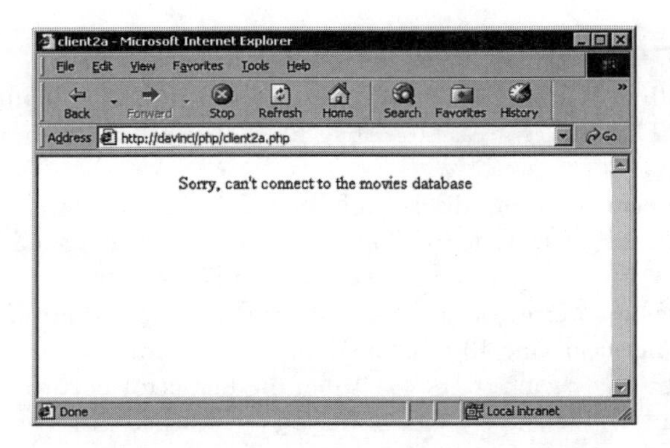

Figure 15.5 A friendlier error message.

This looks much nicer, but now we've lost the details that we need to debug connection problems. What we really want is a friendly error message for the user, but details for the administrator.

You can achieve this using a custom-written error handler. Listing 15.8 shows a custom error handler that emails the text of any error messages to your administrator.

Listing 15.8 `my_error_handler.php`

```
 1 <?php
 2
 3   // Filename: my_handler.php
 4
 5   function my_handler( $errno, $errmsg, $fname, $lineno, $context )
 6   {
 7     $dt =
 8
 9
10     $err_txt  = "At " . date("Y-m-d H:i:s (T)");
11     $err_txt .= " an error occurred at line " . $lineno;
12     $err_txt .= " of file " . $fname . "\n\n";
13     $err_txt .= "The text of the error message is:\n";
14     $err_txt .= $errmsg;
15

16     main( "bruce@virtual_movies.com", " Website error", $err_txt );
17   }
18 ?>
```

In a moment, you'll modify the `client2a.php` script so that it installs this error handler before connecting to PostgreSQL.

An error handler function is called whenever a PHP script encounters an error. The default error handler writes error messages into the output stream sent to the web browser. The custom error handler builds an email message from the various error message components and then uses PHP's `mail()` function to send the error to an address of your choice.

Now, let's modify the client so that it uses `my_handler()` (see Listing 15.9).

Listing 15.9 `client2b.php`

```
 1 <?php
 2   //Filename: client2b.php
 3
 4   include( "secure/my_connect_pg.php" );
 5   include( "my_handler.php" );
 6
 7   set_error_handler( "my_handler" );
 8
 9   $db_handle = my_connect_pg( "movies" );
10
11   echo "<HTML>\n";
12   echo   "<HEAD>\n";
13   echo     "<TITLE>client2b</TITLE>\n";
14   echo   "<BODY>\n";
15   echo     "<CENTER>";
16
17   if( $db_handle == FALSE )
18     echo "Sorry, can't connect to the movies database";
19   else
20     echo "Connected to " . pg_dbname( $db_handle );
21
22   echo     "</CENTER>\n";
23   echo   "</BODY>\n";
24   echo "</HTML>";
25
26   restore_error_handler();
27 ?>
```

You've made four minor changes to `client2a.php`. First, you `include()` `my_handler.php`. Next, you call `set_error_handler()` to direct PHP to call `my_handler()` rather than the default error handler (see line 7). Third, you've removed the `@` from the call to `my_connect_pg()`—you want errors to be reported now; you just want them reported through `my_handler()`. Finally, at line 26, you restore the default error handler (because this is the last statement in your script, this isn't strictly required).

Now, if you run client2b.php, you'll see a user-friendly error message, *and* you should get a piece of email similar to this:

```
From daemon  Sat Jan 12 09:15:59 2002
Date: Sat, 12 Jan 2002 09:15:59 -0400
From: daemon <daemon@davinci>
To: bruce@virtual_movies.com
Subject: Website error

At 2002-02-12 09:15:59 (EDT) an error occurred at line 9
of file /usr/local/php/secure/my_connect_pg.php

The text of the error message is:
   pg_connect() unable to connect to PostgreSQL server: could
   not connect to server: No such file or directory

   Is the server running locally and accepting
   connections on Unix domain socket "/tmp/.s.PGSQL.5432"?
```

Now, you know how to suppress error messages (using the @ operator) and how to intercept them with your own error handler.

In the remaining samples in this chapter, I will omit most error handling code so that you can see any error messages in your web browser; that should make debugging a little easier.

Now, it's time to move on to the next topic—query processing.

Client 3—Query Processing

The tasks involved in processing a query (or other command) using PHP are similar to those required in other PostgreSQL APIs. The first step is to execute the command; then you can (optionally) process the metadata returned by the command; and finally, you process the result set.

We're going to switch gears here. So far, we have been writing PHP scripts that are procedural—one PHP command follows the next. We've thrown in a couple of functions to factor out some repetitive details (such as establishing a new connection). For the next example, you'll create a PHP *class*, named my_table, that will execute a command and process the results. You can reuse this class in other PHP scripts; and each time you extend the class, all scripts automatically inherit the changes.

Let's start by looking at the first script that uses the my_table class and then we'll start developing the class. Listing 15.10 shows client3a.php.

Listing 15.10 client3a.php

```
1 <HTML>
2   <HEAD>
3     <TITLE>client3a</TITLE>
4   <BODY>
```

Listing 15.10 **Continued**

```
 5
 6 <?php
 7   //Filename: client3a.php
 8
 9   include( "secure/my_connect_pg.php" );
10   include( "my_table_a.php" );
11
12   $db_handle = my_connect_pg( "movies" );
13
14   $table = new my_table( $db_handle, "SELECT * FROM customers;" );
15   $table->finish();
16
17   pg_close( $db_handle );
18
19 ?>
20
21   </BODY>
22 </HTML>
```

I rearranged the code in this client so that the static (that is, unchanging) HTML code is separated from the PHP script; that makes it a little easier to discern the script.

At line 10, I `include()` the `my_table_a.php` file. This file contains the definition of the `my_table` class, and we'll look at it in greater detail in a moment. Line 14 creates a new `my_table` object named `$table`. The constructor function for the `my_table` class expects two parameters: a database handle and a command string. `my_table()` executes the given command and formats the results into an HTML table. At line 15, you call `my_table->finish()` to complete the HTML table. Finally, you call `pg_close()` to close the database connection; this is not strictly necessary, but it's good form.

Listing 15.11 shows `my_table_a.php`.

Listing 15.11 `my_table_a.php`

```
 1 <?php
 2
 3   // Filename: my_table_a.php
 4
 5   class my_table
 6   {
 7     var $result;
 8     var $columns;
 9
10     function my_table( $db_handle, $command )
11     {
12       $this->result  = pg_query( $db_handle, $command );
13       $this->columns = pg_num_fields( $this->result );
14       $row_count     = pg_num_rows( $this->result );
```

Listing 15.11 **Continued**

```
15
16        $this->start_table();
17
18        for( $row = 0; $row < $row_count; $row++ )
19            $this->append_row( $this->result, $row );
20      }
21
22      function start_table()
23      {
24        echo '<TABLE CELLPADDING="2" CELLSPACING="0" BORDER=1>';
25        echo "\n";
26      }
27
28      function finish()
29      {
30        print( "</TABLE>\n" );
31
32        pg_free_result( $this->result );
33      }
34
35      function append_row( $result, $row )
36      {
37        echo( "<TR>\n" );
38
39        for( $col = 0; $col < $this->columns; $col++ )
40        {
41          echo "  <TD>";
42          echo pg_fetch_result( $result, $row, $col );
43          echo "</TD>\n";
44        }
45
46        echo( "</TR>\n" );
47      }
48    }
49
50 ?>
```

`my_table.php` defines a single class named `my_table`. At lines 7 and 8, you declare two instance variables for this class. `$this->$result` contains a handle to a result set. `$this->columns` is used to store the number of columns in the result set.

The constructor for `my_table` (lines 10 through 20) expects a database handle and a command string. At line 12, you call the `pq_query()` function to execute the given command. `pg_query()` returns a result set handle if successful, and returns `FALSE` if an error occurs. You'll see how to intercept `pg_query()` errors in a moment. After you have a result set, you can call `pg_num_fields()` to determine the number of columns in the result set and `pg_num_rows()` to find the number of rows.

pg_query() in Earlier PHP Versions

In older versions of PHP, the `pg_query()` function was named `pg_exec()`, `pg_num_fields()` was named `pg_numfields()`, and `pg_num_rows()` was named `pg_numrows()`. If you run into complaints about invalid function names, try the old names.

At line 16, you call the `start_table()` member function to print the HTML table header. Finally, at lines 18 and 19, you iterate through each row in the result set and call `append_row()` to create a new row in the HTML table. We'll look at `append_row()` shortly.

The `start_table()` and `finish_table()` member functions create the HTML table header and table footer, respectively. `finish_table()` also frees up the resources consumed by the result set by calling `pg_free_result()`.

The `append_row()` member function starts at line 35. `append_row()` expects two parameters: a result set handle (`$result`) and a row number (`$row`). At line 37, you write the HTML table-row tag (`<TR>`). The loop at lines 39 through 44 processes each column in the given row. For each column, you write the HTML table-data tag (`<TD>`) and the table-data closing tag (`</TD>`). In-between these tags, you call `pg_fetch_result()` to retrieve a single value from the result set. When you call `pg_fetch_result()`, you provide three parameters: a result set handle, a row number, and a column number. `pg_fetch_result()` returns `NULL` if the requested value is `NULL`[3]. If not `NULL`, `pg_fetch_result()` will return the requested value in the form of a string. Note that the PHP/PostgreSQL documentation states numeric values are returned as `float` or `integer` values. This appears not to be the case; all values are returned in string form.

Now if you load `client3a.php` in your web browser, you'll see a table similar to that shown in Figure 15.6.

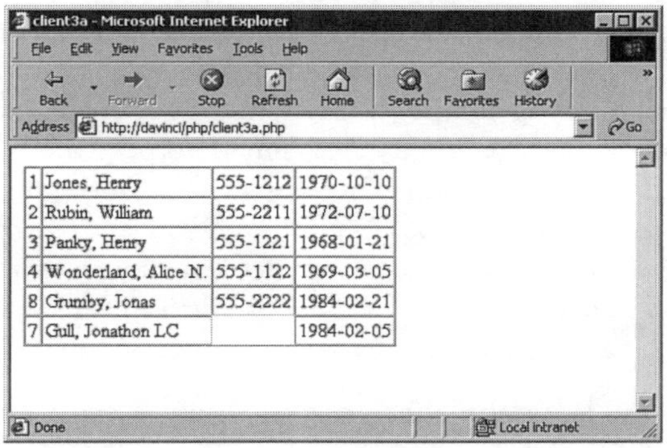
client3a - Microsoft Internet Explorer
File Edit View Favorites Tools Help
Back Forward Stop Refresh Home Search Favorites History
Address http://davinci/php/client3a.php
Go
1 Jones, Henry 555-1212 1970-10-10
2 Rubin, William 555-2211 1972-07-10
3 Panky, Henry 555-1221 1968-01-21
4 Wonderland, Alice N. 555-1122 1969-03-05
8 Grumby, Jonas 555-2222 1984-02-21
7 Gull, Jonathon LC 1984-02-05
Done
Local intranet

Figure 15.6 `client3a.php` loaded into your web browser.

3. In PHP 4.0 and above, `NULL` is equal to `FALSE`, but not identical to `FALSE`. This means that `NULL == FALSE` evaluates to `TRUE`, but `NULL === FALSE` does not.

Other Ways to Retrieve Result Set Values

Besides pg_fetch_result(), PHP provides a number of functions that retrieve result set values.

The pg_fetch_row() function returns an array of values that correspond to a given row. pg_fetch_row() requires two parameters: a result resource (also known as a result set handle) and a row number.

```
pg_fetch_row( resource result, int row_number )
```

Listing 15.12 shows the my_table.append_row() member function implemented in terms of pg_fetch_row().

Listing 15.12 append_row() **Using** pg_fetch_row()

```
...
 1 function append_row( $result, $row )
 2 {
 3   echo( "<TR>\n" );
 4
 5   $values = pg_fetch_row( $result, $row );
 6
 7   for( $col = 0; $col < count( $values ); $col++ )
 8   {
 9     echo "  <TD>";
10     echo $values[$col];
11     echo "</TD>\n";
12   }
13   echo( "</TR>\n" );
14 }
...
```

In this version, you fetch the requested row at line 5. When the call to pg_fetch_row() completes, $values will contain an array of column values. You can access each array element using an integer index, starting at element 0.

The next function, pg_fetch_array(), is similar to pg_fetch_row(). Like pg_fetch_row(), pg_fetch_array() returns an array of columns values. The difference between these functions is that pg_fetch_array() can return a normal array (indexed by column *number*), an associative array (indexed by column *name*), or both. pg_fetch_array() expects one, two, or three parameters:

```
pg_fetch_array( resource result [, int row [, int result_type ]] )
```

The third parameter can be PGSQL_NUM, PGSQL_ASSOC, or PGSQL_BOTH. When you specify PGSQL_NUM, pg_fetch_array() operates identically to pg_fetch_row(); the return value is an array indexed by column number. When you specify

PGSQL_ASSOC, pg_fetch_array() returns an associative array indexed by column name. If you specify PGSQL_BOTH, you will get back an array that can be indexed by column number as well as by column name. An array constructed using PGSQL_BOTH is twice as large as the same array built with PGSQL_NUM or PGSQL_ASSOC. Listing 15.13 shows the append_row() function rewritten to use pg_fetch_array().

Listing 15.13 append_row() **Using** pg_fetch_array()

```
...
 1  function append_row( $result, $row )
 2  {
 3    echo( "<TR>\n" );
 4
 5    $values = pg_fetch_array( $result, $row, PGSQL_ASSOC );
 6
 7    foreach( $values as $column_value )
 8    {
 9      echo "  <TD>";
10      echo $column_value;
11      echo "</TD>\n";
12    }
13
14    echo( "</TR>\n" );
15    }
...
```

You should note that this version of append_row() misses the point of using PGSQL_ASSOC. It ignores the fact that pg_fetch_array() has returned an *associative* array. Associative arrays make it easy to work with a result set if you know the column names ahead of time (that is, at the time you write your script), but they really don't offer much of an advantage for ad hoc queries. To really take advantage of pg_fetch_array(), you would write code such as

```
...
  $result   = pg_query( $dbhandle, "SELECT * FROM customers;" );

  for( $row = 0; $row < pg_num_rows( $result ); $row++ )
  {
      $customer = pg_fetch_array( $result, $row, PGSQL_ASSOC );

      do_something_useful( $customer["customer_name"] );

      do_something_else( $customer["id"], $customer["phone"] );
  }
...
```

Another function useful for static queries is pg_fetch_object(). pg_fetch_object() returns a single row in the form of an object. The object returned has one field for each column, and the name of each field will be the same as the name of the column. For example:

```
...
  $result   = pg_query( $dbhandle, "SELECT * FROM customers;" );

  for( $row = 0; $row < pg_num_rows( $result ); $row++ )
  {
      $customer = pg_fetch_object( $result, $row, PGSQL_ASSOC );

      do_something_useful( $customer->customer_name );

      do_something_else( $customer->id, $customer->phone );
  }
...
```

There is no significant difference between an object returned by pg_fetch_object() and an associative array returned by pg_fetch_array(). With pg_fetch_array(), you reference a value using $array[$column] syntax. With pg_fetch_object(), you reference a value using $object->$column syntax. Choose whichever syntax you prefer.

One warning about pg_fetch_object() and pg_fetch_array(..., PGSQL_ASSOC)—if your query returns two or more columns with the same column name, you will lose all but one of the columns. You can't have an associative array with duplicate index names, and you can't have an object with duplicate field names.

Metadata Access

You've seen that pg_fetch_object() and pg_fetch_array() expose column names to you, but the PHP/PostgreSQL API lets you get at much more metadata than just the column names.

The PHP/PostgreSQL interface is written using libpq (PostgreSQL's C-language API). Most of the functions available through libpq can be called from PHP, including the libpq metadata functions. Unfortunately, this means that PHP shares the limitations that you find in libpq.

In particular, the pg_field_size() function returns the size of a field. pg_field_size() expects two parameters:

```
int pg_field_size( resource $result, int $column_number )
```

The problem with this function is that the size reported is the number of bytes required to store the value *on the server*. It has nothing to do with the number of bytes seen by the client (that is, the number of bytes seen by your PHP script). For variable-length data types, pg_field_size() will return –1.

The pg_field_type() function returns the name of the data type for a given column. pg_field_type() requires two parameters:

```
int pg_field_type( resource $result, int $column_number )
```

The problem with pg_field_type() is that it is not 100% accurate. pg_field_type() knows nothing of user-defined types or domains. Also, pg_field_type() won't return details about parameterized data types. For example, a column defined as NUMERIC(7,2) is reported as type NUMERIC.

Having conveyed the bad news, let's look at the metadata functions that are a little more useful for most applications.

You've already seen pg_num_rows() and pg_num_fields(). These functions return the number of rows and columns (respectively) in a result set.

The pg_field_name() and pg_field_num() functions are somewhat related. pg_field_name() returns the name of a column, given a column number index. pg_field_num() returns the column number index of a field given the field's name.

Let's enhance the my_table class a bit by including column names in the HTML table that we produce. Listing 15.14 shows a new version of the start_table() member function.

Listing 15.14 my_table.start_table()

```
 1 function start_table()
 2 {
 3   echo '<TABLE CELLPADDING="2" CELLSPACING="0" BORDER=1>';
 4
 5   for( $col = 0; $col < $this->columns; $col++ )
 6   {
 7     echo "  <TH>";
 8     echo pg_field_name( $this->result, $col );
 9     echo "</TH>\n";
10   }
11  echo "\n";
12 }
```

I used the <TH> tag here instead of <TD>, so that the browser knows that these are table header cells (table header cells are typically bolded and centered).

Now when you browse to client3a.php, you see a nice set of column headers as shown in Figure 15.7.

Let's fix one other problem as long as we are fiddling with metadata. You may have noticed that the last row in Figure 15.7 looks a little funky—the phone number cell has not been drawn the same as the other cells. That happens when we try to create a table cell for a NULL value. If you look at the code that you built for the HTML table, you'll see that the last row has an empty <TD></TD> cell. For some reason, web browsers draw an empty cell differently.

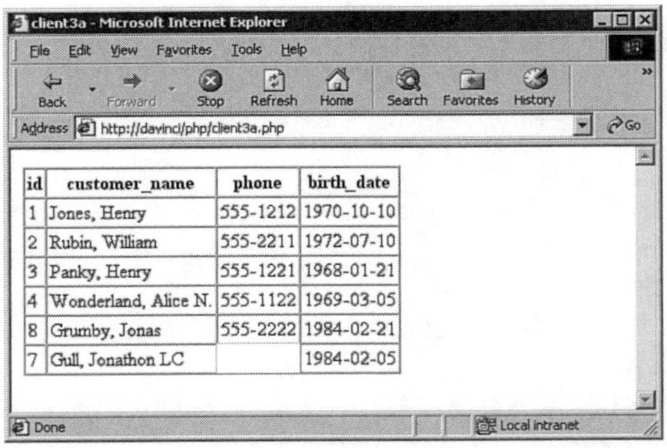
client3a - Microsoft Internet Explorer
File Edit View Favorites Tools Help
Back Forward Stop Refresh Home Search Favorites History
Address http://davinci/php/client3a.php
id customer_name phone birth_date
1 Jones, Henry 555-1212 1970-10-10
2 Rubin, William 555-2211 1972-07-10
3 Panky, Henry 555-1221 1968-01-21
4 Wonderland, Alice N. 555-1122 1969-03-05
8 Grumby, Jonas 555-2222 1984-02-21
7 Gull, Jonathon LC 1984-02-05
Done
Local intranet

Figure 15.7 `client3a.php`—with column headers.

To fix this problem, you can modify `append_row()` to detect `NULL` values (see Listing 15.15).

Listing 15.15 `my_table.append_row()`

```
 1  function append_row( $result, $row )
 2  {
 3    echo( "<TR>\n" );
 4
 5    for( $col = 0; $col < $this->columns; $col++ )
 6    {
 7      echo "  <TD>";
 8
 9      if( pg_field_is_null( $result, $row, $col ) == 1 )
10         echo " ";
11      elseif( strlen( pg_result( $result, $row, $col )) == 0 )
12         echo " "
13      else
14         echo pg_result( $result, $row, $col );
15      echo "</TD>\n";
16    }
17
18    echo( "</TR>\n" );
19  }
```

At line 9, you detect `NULL` values using the `pg_field_is_null()` function. If you encounter a `NULL`, you echo a nonbreaking space character (` `) instead of an empty string. You have the same problem (a badly drawn border) if you encounter an empty string, and you fix it the same way (lines 11 and 12). Now, when you display a table, all the cells are drawn correctly, as shown in Figure 15.8.

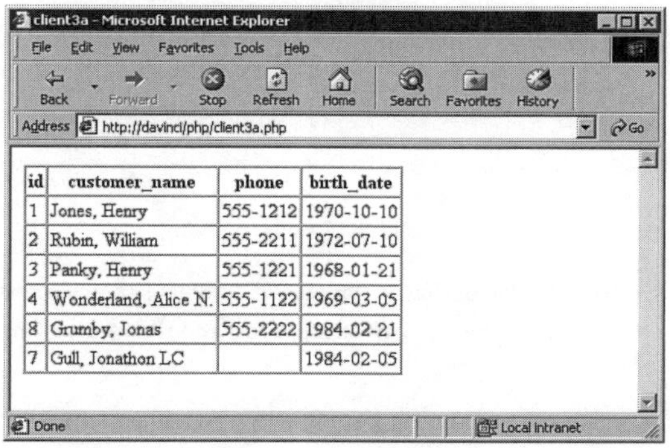

id	customer_name	phone	birth_date
1	Jones, Henry	555-1212	1970-10-10
2	Rubin, William	555-2211	1972-07-10
3	Panky, Henry	555-1221	1968-01-21
4	Wonderland, Alice N.	555-1122	1969-03-05
8	Grumby, Jonas	555-2222	1984-02-21
7	Gull, Jonathon LC		1984-02-05

Figure 15.8 `client3a.php`—final version.

There are a few more metadata functions that you can use in PHP, and you will need these functions in the next client that you write.

PHP, PostgreSQL, and Associative Functions

One of the more interesting abstractions promised (but not yet offered) by PHP and the PHP/PostgreSQL API is the *associative function*. An associative function gives you a way to execute a SQL command without having to construct the entire command yourself. Let's say that you need to `INSERT` a new row into the `customers` table. The most obvious way to do this in PHP is to build up an `INSERT` command by concatenating the new values and then executing the command using `pg_query()`. Another option is to use the `pg_insert()` function. With `pg_insert()`, you build an associative array. Each element in the array corresponds to a column. The key for a given element is the name of the column, and the value for the element is the value that you want to insert. For example, you can add a new row to the `customers` table with the following code:

```
...
$customer["id"]              = 8;
$customer["customer_name"] = "Smallberries, John";
$customer["birth_date"]     = "1985-05-14";

pg_insert( $db_handle, "customers", $customer );
...
```

In this code snippet, you have created an associative array with three entries. When you execute the call to `pg_insert()`, PHP will construct the following `INSERT` command:

```
INSERT INTO customers
  (
    id,
    customer_name,
    birth_date
```

```
)
VALUES
(
  8,
  'Smallberries, John',
  '1985-05-14'
);
```

PHP knows the name of the table by looking at the second argument to `pg_insert()`. The column names are derived from the keys in the `$customers` array, and the values come from the values in the associative array.

Besides `pg_insert()`, you can call `pg_delete()` to build and execute a `DELETE` command. When you call `pg_delete()`, you provide a database handle, a table name, and an associative array. The associative array is used to construct a `WHERE` clause for the `DELETE` command. The values in the associative array are *ANDed* together to form the `WHERE` clause.

You can also use `pg_select()` to construct and execute a `SELECT *` command. `pg_select()` is similar to `pg_delete()`—it expects a database handle, a table name, and an associative array. Like `pg_delete()`, the values in the associative array are *ANDed* together to form a `WHERE` clause.

Finally, the `pg_update()` function expects *two* associative arrays. The first array is used to form a `WHERE` clause, and the second array should contain the data (column names and values) to be updated.

As of PHP version 4.2.2, the associative functions are documented as experimental and are likely to change. In fact, the code to implement these functions is not even included in the distribution (they are documented, but not implemented). Watch for these functions in a future release.

Client 4—an Interactive Query Processor

You now have most of the pieces that you need to build a general-purpose query processor within a web browser. Our next client simply prompts the user for a SQL command, executes the command, and displays the results.

If you want to try this on your own web server, be sure that you understand the security implications. If you follow the examples in this chapter, your PHP script will use a hard-coded username to connect to PostgreSQL. Choose a user with *very* few privileges. In fact, most PHP/PostgreSQL sites should probably define a user account specifically designed for web access. If you're not careful, you'll grant John Q. Hacker permissions to alter important data.

We'll start out with a simple script and then refine it as we discover problems.

First, you need an HTML page that displays a welcome and prompts the user for a SQL command. Listing 15.16 shows the `client4.html` document.

Listing 15.16 `client4.html`

```
 1 <HTML>
 2
 3 <!-- Filename: client4.html>
 4
 5   <HEAD>
 6     <TITLE>client4a</TITLE>
 7   <BODY>
 8    <CENTER>
 9    <FORM ACTION="client4a.php" METHOD="POST">
10      <I>Enter SQL command:</I><br>
11
12      <INPUT TYPE="text"
13             NAME="query"
14             SIZE="80"
15             ALIGN="left"
16             VALUE="">
17
18      <BR><BR>
19      <INPUT TYPE="submit" VALUE="Execute command">
20   </FORM>
21 </CENTER></BODY>
22 </HTML>
```

This HTML document defines a form that will be *posted* to the server (see line 9). After the user enters a command and presses the `Execute Command` button, the browser will request the file `client4a.php`. We'll look at `client4a.php` in a moment. When you request this page in a web browser, you will see a form similar to that shown in Figure 15.9.

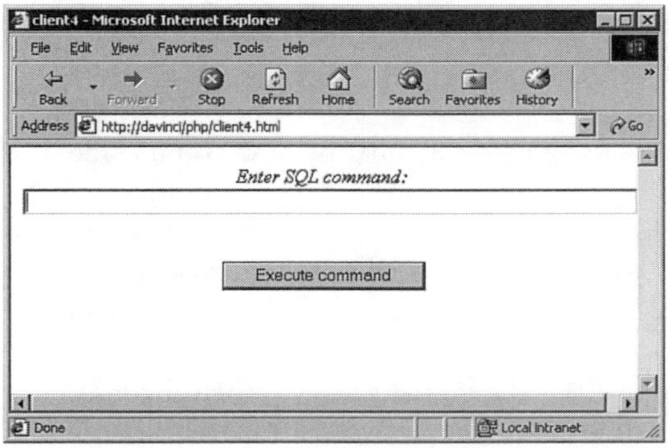

Figure 15.9 `client4.html`.

Now let's look at the second half of the puzzle—`client4a.php` (see Listing 15.17).

Listing 15.17 `client4a.php`

```
 1 <HTML>
 2   <HEAD>
 3     <TITLE>Query</TITLE>
 4   <BODY>
 5     <?php
 6
 7       # Filename: client4a.php
 8
 9       include( "secure/my_connect_pg.php" );
10       include( "my_table_e.php" );
11
12       $command_text = $HTTP_POST_VARS[ "query" ];
13
14       if( strlen( $command_text ) == 0 )
15       {
16         echo "You forgot to enter a command";
17       }
18       else
19       {
20         $db_handle = my_connect_pg( "movies" );
21
22         $table = new my_table( $db_handle, $command_text );
23         $table->finish();
24
25         pg_close( $db_handle );
26       }
27     ?>
28   </BODY>
29 </HTML>
```

Most of this script should be pretty familiar by now. You include `secure/my_connect_pg.php` to avoid embedding a username and password inline. Next, you include `my_table_e.php` so that you can use the `my_table` class (`my_table_e.php` includes all the modifications you made to the original version of `my_table_a.php`).

At line 12, you retrieve the command entered by the user from the `$HTTP_POST_VARS[]` variable. Look back at lines 12 through 16 of Listing 15.16 (`client4.html`). You are defining an `INPUT` field named `query`. When the user enters a value and presses the `Execute Command` button, the browser *posts* the `query` field to `client4a.php`. PHP marshals all the post values into a single associative array named `$HTTP_POST_VARS[]`. The key for each value in this array is the name of the posted variable. So, you defined a field named `query`, and you can find the value of that field in `$HTTP_POST_VARS["query"]`.

If you try to execute an empty command using `pg_query()`, you'll be rewarded with an ugly error message. You'll be a little nicer to our users by intercepting empty commands at lines 14 through 16 and displaying a less intimidating error message.

The remainder of this script is straightforward: You establish a database connection and use the `my_table` class to execute the given command and display the result.

Let's run this script to see how it behaves (see Figures 15.10 and 15.11).

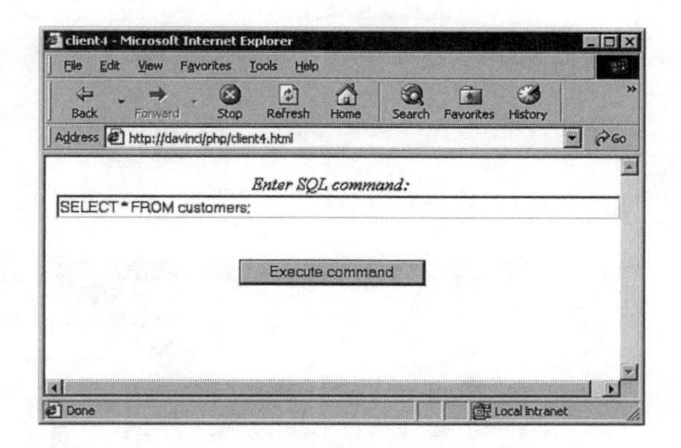

Figure 15.10 Submitting a query with `client4.html`.

id	customer_name	phone	birth_date
1	Jones, Henry	555-1212	1970-10-10
2	Rubin, William	555-2211	1972-07-10
3	Panky, Henry	555-1221	1968-01-21
4	Wonderland, Alice N.	555-1122	1969-03-05
8	Grumby, Jonas	555-2222	1984-02-21
7	Gull, Jonathon LC		1984-02-05

Figure 15.11 Submitting a query with `client4.html`—result.

That worked nicely. Let's try another query (see Figures 15.12 and 15.13).

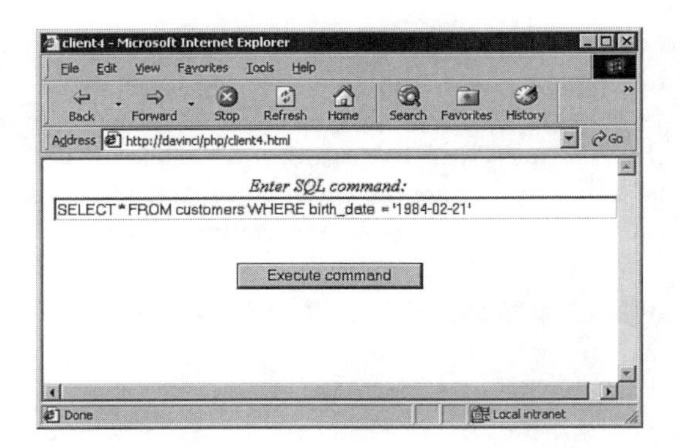

Figure 15.12 Causing an error with `client4.html`.

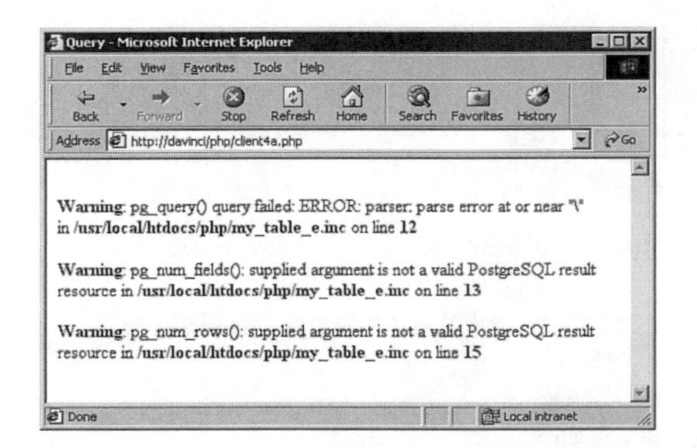

Figure 15.13 Causing an error with `client4.html`—result.

Hmmm… that's not what we were hoping for. What went wrong? Actually, there are several problems shown here. First, PHP is reporting that we have an erroneous backslash on line 12 of `my_table_e.php`. Line 12 is inside of the `my_table` constructor and it sends the following command to the server:

```
$this->result  = pg_query( $db_handle, $command );
```

There are no backslashes on that line; there are no backslashes in the command that you entered. Where are the backslashes coming from? If you echo `$HTTP_POST_VARS ["query"]`, you'll see that PHP has added escape characters to the command entered by the user. You entered `SELECT * FROM customers WHERE birth_date = '1984-02-21'`, and PHP changed this to `SELECT * FROM customers WHERE birth_date = \'1984-02-21\'`. According to the PHP manual, all single-quotes, double-quotes, backslashes, and `NULL`s are escaped with a backslash when they come from a posted value.[4]

4. You can disable the automatic quoting feature by setting the `magic_quote_gpc` configuration variable to no. I would not recommend changing this value—you're likely to break many PHP scripts.

This is easy to fix. You can simply strip the escape characters when you retrieve the command text from `$HTTP_VARS[]`. Changing `client4a.php`, line 12, to

```
if( get_magic_quotes_gpc())
    $command_text = stripslashes( $HTTP_POST_VARS[ "query" ] );
```

will make it possible to execute SQL commands that contain single-quotes.

That was the first problem. The second problem is that you don't want the end-user to see these nasty-looking PHP/PostgreSQL error messages. To fix this problem, you need to intercept the error message and display it yourself. Listing 15.18 shows a new version of the `my_table` constructor.

Listing 15.18 `my_table.my_table()`

```
 1 function my_table( $db_handle, $command )
 2 {
 3   $this->result  = @pg_query( $db_handle, $command );
 4
 5   if( $this->result == FALSE )
 6   {
 7     echo pg_last_error( $db_handle );
 8   }
 9   else
10   {
11     $this->columns = pg_num_fields( $this->result );
12     $row_count     = pg_num_rows( $this->result );
13
14     $this->start_table( $command );
15
16     for( $row = 0; $row < $row_count; $row++ )
17       $this->append_row( $this->result, $row );
18   }
19 }
```

We've restructured this function a bit. Because the goal is to intercept the default error message, you suppress error reporting by prefixing the call to `pg_query()` with an `@`. At line 5, you determine whether `pg_query()` returned a valid result set resource. If you are used to using PostgreSQL with other APIs, there is an important difference lurking here. In other PostgreSQL APIs, you get a result set even when a command fails—the error message is part of the result set. In PHP, `pg_query()` returns `FALSE` when an error occurs. You must call `pg_last_error()` to retrieve the text of the error message (see line 7).

If you have succeeded in executing the given command, you build an HTML table from the result set as before.

Now, if you cause an error condition, the result is far more palatable (see Figures 15.14 and 15.15).

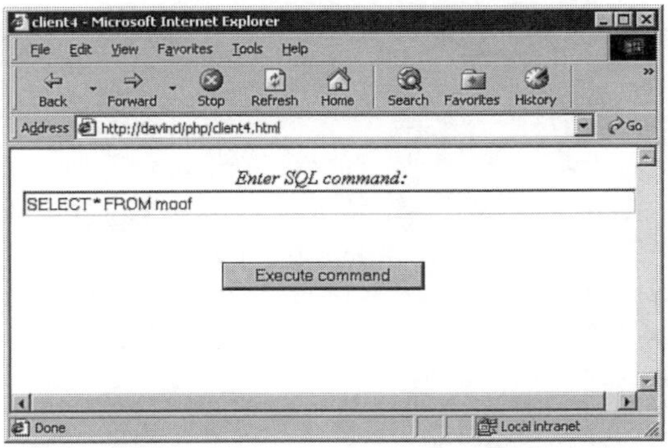

Figure 15.14 Causing an error with `client4.html`—part 2.

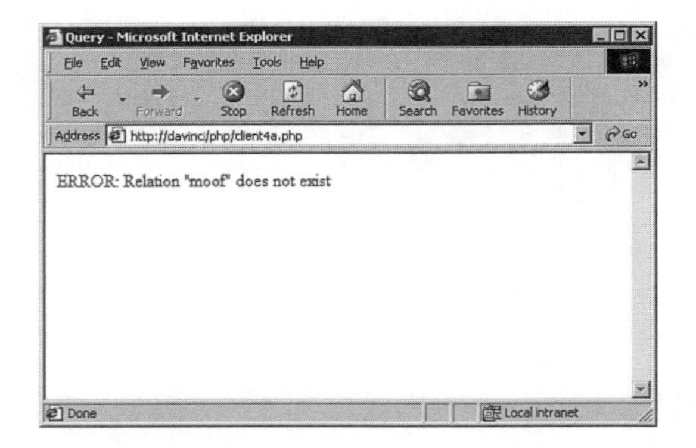

Figure 15.15 Causing an error with `client4.html`—part 2, result.

Notice that you see only one error message this time. In Figure 15.13, you saw multiple error messages. Not only had you failed to intercept the original error, but you went on to use an invalid result set handle; when you fix the first problem, the other error messages will go away.

At this point, you can execute queries and intercept error messages. Let's see what happens when you execute a command other than `SELECT`. First, enter the command shown in Figure 15.16.

After clicking on the `Execute Command` button, you see the result displayed in Figure 15.17.

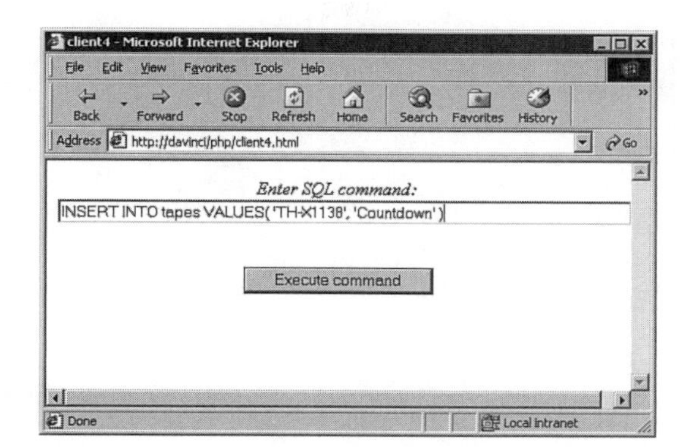

Figure 15.16 Executing an `INSERT` command.

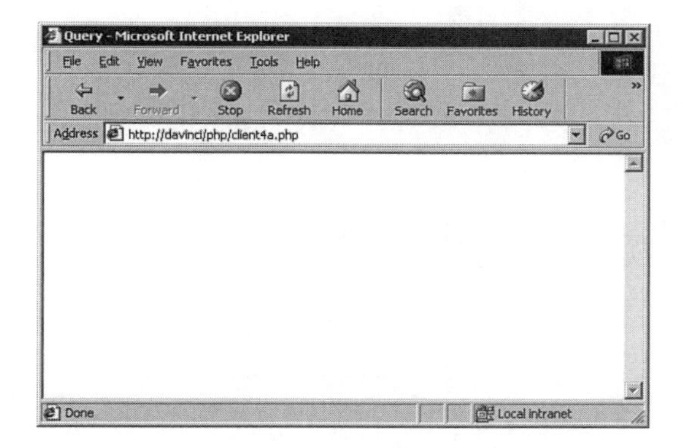

Figure 15.17 Executing an `INSERT` command—result.

Hmmm… that's a bit minimalist for my taste. You should at least see a confirmation that *something* has happened. When you execute a non-`SELECT` command, the `pg_query()` function will return a result set resource, just like it does for a `SELECT` command. You can differentiate between `SELECT` and other commands by the fact that `pg_num_fields()` always returns `0` for non-`SELECT` commands.

Let's make one last modification to the `my_table` constructor so that it gives feedback regardless of which type of command executed.

Listing 15.19 `my_table.my_table()`**—Final Form**

```
1 function my_table( $db_handle, $command )
2 {
3   $this->result  = @pg_query( $db_handle, $command );
4
```

Listing 15.19 **Continued**

```
 5    if( $this->result == FALSE )
 6    {
 7      echo pg_last_error( $db_handle );
 8    }
 9    else
10    {
11      $this->columns = pg_num_fields( $this->result );
12
13      if( $this->columns == 0 )
14      {
15        echo $command;
16        echo "<BR>";
17        echo pg_affected_rows( $this->result );
18        echo " row(s) affected";
19
20        if( pg_last_oid( $this->result ) != 0 )
21          echo ", OID =  ". pg_last_oid( $this->result );
22      }
23      else
24      {
25        $row_count     = pg_num_rows( $this->result );
26
27        $this->start_table( $command );
28
29        for( $row = 0; $row < $row_count; $row++ )
30          $this->append_row( $this->result, $row );
31      }
32    }
33 }
```

In this version, you check the result set column count at line 13. If you find that the result set contains 0 columns, echo the command text and the number of rows affected by the command. You also call the `pg_last_oid()` function. `pg_last_oid()` returns the OID (object ID) of the most recently inserted row. `pg_last_oid()` returns 0 if the command was not an `INSERT` or if more than one row was inserted.

The final results are shown in Figure 15.18.

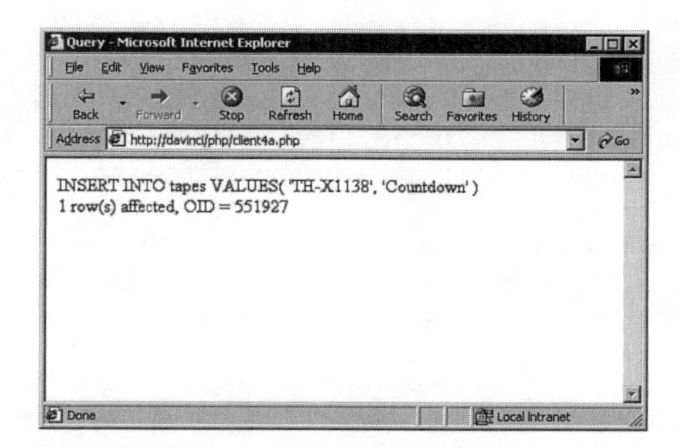

Figure 15.18 Executing an `INSERT` command—final result.

Other Features

There are a number of PostgreSQL-related PHP functions that I have not covered in this chapter.

Newer versions of PHP have added support for asynchronous query processing (see `pg_send_query()`, `pg_connection_busy()`, and `pg_get_result()`). Asynchronous query processing probably won't be of much use when you are constructing dynamic web pages, but clever coders can use asynchronous queries to provide intermediate feedback for long-running operations (sorry, I'm not that clever).

PHP offers a set of functions that can give you information about a database connection. We used the `pg_dbname()` function in the first client (see Listing 15.4) to display the name of the database to which we were connected. You can also use the `pg_port()` and `pg_options()` function to retrieve the port number and options associated with a database connection. PHP provides a `pg_host()` function that is supposed to return the name of the host where the server resides. Be very careful calling `pg_host()`; if you have established a local connection (that is, using a Unix-domain socket), calling `pg_host()` may crash your web server because of a bug in the PHP/PostgreSQL interface.

Another function offered by PHP is `pg_pconnect()`. The `pg_pconnect()` function establishes a *persistent* connection to a PostgreSQL database. Persistent connections are cached by the web server and can be reused the next time a browser requests a document that requires access to the same database. See the PHP manual for information about the pros and cons of persistent connections.

Finally, PHP supports the PostgreSQL large-object interface. You can use the large-object interface to read (or write) large data items such as images or audio files.

Summary

If you have never used PHP before, I think you'll find it a delightfully easy language to learn. As a long-time C/C++ programmer, I found PHP very familiar when I first started to explore the language. (Don't let that scare you off if you aren't a fan of C—PHP is *much* easier to learn than C.)

One of the things I like most about developing with PHP is the fact that all error messages appear in-line, right inside my web browser. This feature makes debugging easy.

PHP and PostgreSQL combine with your web server to create a system that delivers dynamic content to your users.

16

Using PostgreSQL with Tcl and Tcl/Tk

TCL IS AN INTERPRETED SCRIPTING LANGUAGE. *Tcl* is an acronym for *Tool Command Language* and is often pronounced as "tickle." The original goal of Tcl's creator (John Ousterhout) was to create an *embeddable* interpreted language that could be included in many small applications. The idea was to create a language that could be embedded in applications that might not normally justify having their own language. Another example of this sort of embeddable language is Microsoft's VBA (Visual Basic for Applications). With an embedded language, you can make any application programmable (or *scriptable*). For example, you might have a spiffy terminal emulator that you've developed for your own use. It would be nice if you could add a scripting capability to the emulator, but that would require a ton of work. This is a perfect fit for Tcl. By embedding Tcl in your terminal emulator, you are incorporating an entire programming language in your application with very little work.

Tcl is also a general-purpose programming language. In fact, I think Tcl might just be the simplest language ever invented. (But beware, a simple language doesn't *always* imply simple programs; it just means the language won't get in your way.)

There are only a few rules that you have to remember:

- Everything in Tcl is a string…*everything.*
- A variable reference (`$variable`) is replaced by the variable value anywhere it occurs within a string.
- A command reference (`[command]`) is replaced by the command value anywhere it occurs within a string.
- If you want to suppress variable and command substitution, surround a string with curly braces.
- If you don't want to suppress substitution, surround a string with double quotes.

If you remember those simple rules (and suspend your disbelief—it really is that simple), you'll be fluent in Tcl in no time. When you start writing Tcl applications, you'll probably use the Tcl shell as an execution environment. The Tcl shell (`tclsh`) is a simple shell (like `bash` or `sh`) that has been combined with the Tcl interpreter. Using `tclsh`, you can do all the things you would normally do in a Unix shell (such as run a program, change directories, redirect output, and so on) *in addition* to all the things you can do in a Tcl program.

Tcl is often combined with Tk. *Tk* is a graphical toolkit. Using Tk, you can create windows and widgets (graphical controls), and interact with the user in a graphical interface. You can use Tk with many different languages, but it was originally designed as a companion to Tcl. The Tcl/Tk environment includes a graphical shell called `wish`. The `wish` shell is similar to `tclsh`, except that it has Tk thrown in so you can build graphical shell scripts.

Tcl applications (and therefore Tcl/Tk applications) can interact with PostgreSQL database servers. The Tcl-to-PostgreSQL interface is contained in a library named libpgtcl. libpgtcl provides a small number (17) of procedures that you can call from a Tcl script. In this chapter, I'll describe each of these procedures, and you'll build a few client applications that show you how to use libpgtcl to build PostgreSQL client applications.

Prerequisites

If you want to try the examples in this chapter, you will need to install and configure Tcl/Tk (version 8.0 or later) and libpgtcl.

If you are running on a Linux host, the chances are good that you already have Tcl/Tk installed on your system. To find out whether Tcl is ready to use, enter the command `tclsh`, as shown here:

```
$ tclsh
%  exit
$
```

If you see the `%` prompt, you have Tcl installed on your system. If instead, you see an error such as "`tcl: command not found`", you may still have a copy of Tcl installed on your system, but it's not in your search path (`$PATH`) —ask your system administrator whether Tcl is available.

If you find that you need to install Tcl, you can find it at `http://tcl.activestate.com`. ActiveState distributes Tcl/Tk in binary (precompiled) form for Linux, Solaris, and Windows. You can also find the source code for Tcl/Tk at ActiveState.

The second component that you need is libpgtcl. libpgtcl is a package of Tcl extension functions that enable a Tcl script to interact with PostgreSQL. This component can be a little hard to find. If you are building your copy of PostgreSQL from source code, adding the `--with-tcl` flag to `configure` should build `libpgtcl` for you. If you have installed PostgreSQL using a RPM package, be sure to install the postgresql-tcl package. If you are using Tcl on a Windows host, the easiest way to obtain the `libpgtcl` library is to install PgAccess (`http://www.pgaccess.org`).

Finally, some of the examples in this chapter require the TkTable extension to Tk. TkTable provides a table widget that you will use to display query results. If you have already installed Tcl and Tk, you may find that TkTable came with the distribution that you loaded. If not, you can find TkTable at `http://tktable.sourceforge.net`.

PostgreSQL-Related Tcl/Tk Components

As I mentioned in the previous section, libpgtcl is a library of PostgreSQL-related functions that you can call from within a Tcl script. The libpgtcl package also includes two shell programs. `pgtclsh` is a copy of the Tcl shell (`tclsh`) that automatically loads the libpgtcl library. `pgtksh` is a copy of the `wish` shell that will automatically load libpgtcl at startup.

Client 1—Connecting to the Server

The first step to interacting with a PostgreSQL server is to establish a connection; in this section, you'll use Tcl and Tk to build a simple graphical client that establishes a connection to a PostgreSQL server. The libpgtcl library is implemented on top of the libpq, so many of the features that you see in libpgtcl will seem familiar if you've read through Chapter 8, "The PostgreSQL C API—libpq." To connect to a PostgreSQL server, use the `pg_connect` procedure. `pg_connect` comes in two flavors:

```
pg_connect -conninfo connection-string
```

or

```
pg_connect database-name
           [-host host-name]
           [-port port-number]
           [-tty tty-name]
           [-options option-string]
```

The second form is considered obsolete, and I've included it here only for completeness.

The preferred form uses a connection string similar to those used in libpq applications. A *connection string* is a list of `keyword=value` pairs, separated by whitespace. Each pair in the connection string specifies the value for a connection property. A typical connection string might look something like this:

```
host=davinci user=bruce password=koalas dbname=movies
```

This particular connection string provides four connection properties: a hostname, a username and password, and a database name. Table 16.1 lists the properties that may appear in a connection string.

Table 16.1 **Connection Properties**

Connect-String Property	Environment Variable	Example
user	PGUSER	user=korry
password	PGPASSWORD	password=cows
dbname	PGDATABASE	dbname=accounting
host	PGHOST	host=jersey
hostaddr	PGHOSTADDR	hostaddr=127.0.0.1
port	PGPORT	port=5432

The second column in Table 16.1 shows the environment variable that libpgtcl will use if you omit the property shown in the first column. For example, if you omit the host property from your connection string, libpgtcl will use the value of the PGHOST environment variable. If you don't supply a particular property in the connection string, and you haven't defined the corresponding environment variable, libpgtcl will use hard-wired default values. To see the hard-wired values, you can use the pg_conndefaults [1] procedure:

```
$ pgtclsh
% foreach prop [pg_conndefaults] { puts $prop }
authtype Database-Authtype              D 20 {}
service  Database-Service              {} 20 {}
user     Database-User                 {} 20 korry
password Database-Password              * 20 {}
dbname   Database-Name                 {} 20 korry
host     Database-Host                 {} 40 {}
hostaddr Database-Host-IPv4-Address {} 15 {}
port     Database-Port                 {} 6 5432
tty      Backend-Debug-TTY              D 40 {}
options  Backend-Debug-Options          D 40 {}
```

The first column lists property names; the last column displays the final default values that will be used if you don't provide overrides.

The pg_conndefaults procedure returns a list of sublists. The values returned by pg_conndefaults might seem a little confusing until you understand the problem that this procedure was trying to solve. From time to time, the PostgreSQL authors need to introduce new connection properties. How can you support new connection properties without rewriting every PostgreSQL client application? The client application can ask pg_conndefaults for a list of supported properties and then ask the user to provide a value for each of those properties. A robust client application will not have to be recompiled each time a new connection property is introduced; it just prompts the user for more information.

1. I've cleaned up the listing returned by pg_conndefaults to make it easier to read.

Having said that, you probably won't let me off the hook unless we build a "robust" client application (or at least make an attempt).

The first client application in this chapter does little more than connect to a PostgreSQL server, but does so using a self-adjusting login dialog box. This particular client application is rather long—building a graphical login dialog from barebones Tcl/Tk is not a trivial task. In a real-world application, you might want to explore add-on toolkits that make it easier to do this sort of work.

Let's dive into the code for client1.tcl—I'll explain the how to use `pg_conndefaults` as we go. You'll also see how to call the pg_connect procedure. Listing 16.1 shows the start of the `client1.tcl` application.

Listing 16.1 `client1.tcl—main`

```
 1 #!/usr/local/bin/wish
 2 #
 3 # Filename: client1.tcl
 4
 5 proc main { } {
 6
 7   load libpgtcl
 8
 9   wm withdraw .
10
11   set result "retry"
12
13   while { $result == "retry" } {
14     set connstr [connect_dialog]
15
16     if { [catch {pg_connect -conninfo $connstr} conn] } {
17       set result [tk_messageBox \
18                 -message $conn \
19                 -title "Connection failed" \
20                 -type retrycancel]
21     } else {
22       tk_messageBox \
23        -message "Connection is: $conn" \
24       -title "Connection Ok"
25
26      set result "ok"
27     }
28   }
29 }
```

The first line is used to specify the name of the interpreter that should be used to run this script: `wish` is the graphical Tcl/Tk shell[2]. Line 5 defines a procedure named `main`. Unlike many other languages, a function with the name of main is *not* the default entry point for Tcl script—you call this function `main` just so that it is easily recognizable. In Tcl, the entry point for a program is the first executable line of code outside of a `proc` definition. In fact, the first few executable lines of code in this program are right at the end of the script (the end of this script is *not* shown in Listing 16.1; you still have four more listings to get through).

The `main` function expects no arguments (you can tell that because the braces immediately following the function name are empty).

The first thing that you do in this function is load the libpgtcl library into the Tcl interpreter (on some systems, you may need to `load libpgtcl.so`). Before you can call *any* PostgreSQL-related functions, you must load the libpgtcl library. If you change the first line of this script to read

```
#!/usr/local/bin/pgtksh
```

you won't need to load libpgtcl; `pgtksh` is a Tk shell that automatically loads libpgtcl. Next, *withdraw* the root window. If you are not a seasoned Tk programmer, that probably sounds a little ominous. When the `wish` interpreter starts up, it automatically creates an empty window for you. That window is called a *root* window, and its name is simply the period character (`.`). You withdraw the window now so that you can make your own window a little later.

Lines 13 through 28 form a loop. Inside this loop, you create a dialog box that prompts the user for connection properties. Figure 16.1 shows the dialog box that appears when you run `client1.tcl`.

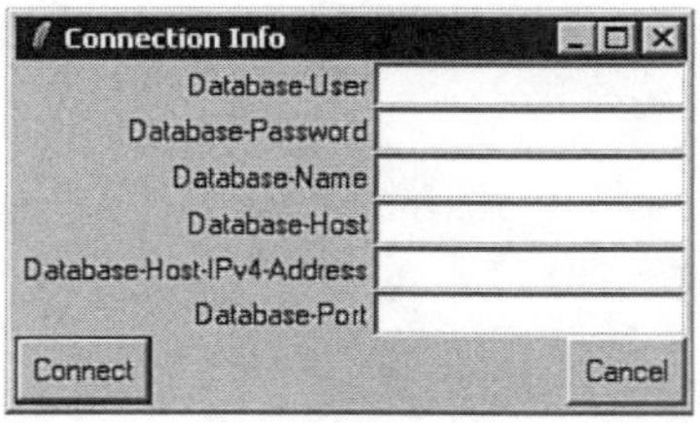

Figure 16.1 The Connection Info dialog box.

If the user clicks the `Cancel` button, the entire application will end. If the user clicks the `Connect` button, it tries to connect to a PostgreSQL server using the information provided. If the connect attempt succeeds, a message displays and the application terminates. If a connection attempt fails, you want the user to see a Retry/Cancel dialog that displays the error message and offers a chance to try again.

2. The magic string at the string at the beginning of a shell script such as this is called the shebang line: "she" is for *shell* and "bang" is how some people pronounce the exclamation point. A shebang line tells the operating system which program should be used to execute the script. Shebang lines are supported on Unix and Linux hosts, but not on Windows systems (except when using the Cygwin environment).

Repeat the loop at lines 13 through 28 until you establish a connection or until the user presses the `Cancel` button.

At line 14, call the `connect_dialog` procedure (you'll see that procedure in a moment) to display the connection dialog and wait for user input. `connect_dialog` returns a connection string, which is awfully handy because you need a connection string before you can talk to PostgreSQL.

After you have a connection string, call the `pg_connect` function to attempt a connection. When `pg_connect` is called, it either establishes a connection or it throws an error. You want to intercept any error messages, so you call `pg_connect` within a `catch{}` block. If the call to `pg_connect` succeeds, `catch{}` will return 0 (also known as `TCL_OK`). If `pg_connect` throws an error, the `catch{}` command will return a value other than zero. In either case, the `conn` variable (the third argument to the `catch{}` command) is modified. In the case of a connection failure, `conn` will contain the text of the error message. If the connection attempt is successful, `conn` will contain a connection *channel*. A channel is similar to a handle (handles are used in many programming language/API combinations). A channel is simply a unique identifier returned by the API—you give the identifier back to the API when you want to do something with that connection (like execute a command). Like everything else in Tcl, a channel is a string.

If you were not able to establish a connection, display a message to the user by using the `tk_messageBox` function (see line 17). A typical error message is shown in Figure 16.2.

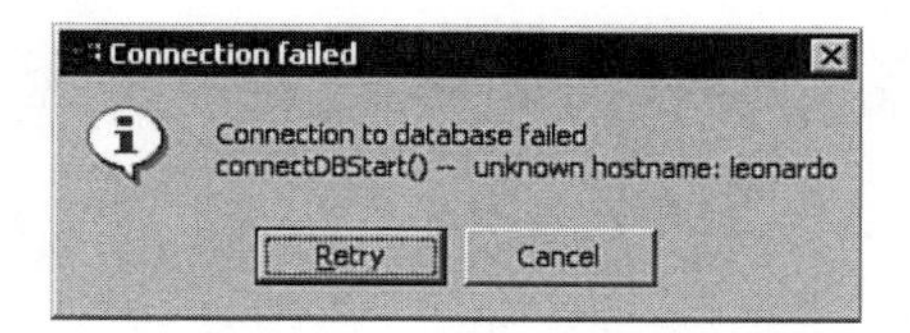

Figure 16.2 The Connection dialog, connection failed error message.

After displaying the error message, `tk_messageBox` waits for the user to click either the `Retry` button or the `Cancel` button. `tk_messageBox` returns a string telling you which option the user selected (either `retry` or `cancel`). You store that string in the `result` variable, which controls the loop. So, if the user clicks the `Retry` button, you repeat the loop; otherwise, end the loop and terminate the application.

If the connection attempt succeeds, use `tk_messageBox` again. In this case, display the channel (not really useful but mildly interesting), as shown in Figure 16.3.

Figure 16.3 The Connection dialog, Connection OK message.

That covers the `main()` function; now let's see how to build a dialog box using Tcl/Tk. (I should warn you; it's not pretty.)

Listing 16.2 shows the `connect_dialog` procedure. This procedure constructs a dialog box that prompts the user for connection properties, displays the dialog box, and assembles a connection string with the values supplied by the user.

Listing 16.2 `client1.tcl—connect_dialog`

```
31 proc connect_dialog { } {
32
33   global next_row
34
35   set next_row 0
36   set set_focus true
37
38   #  Create a new window with the title
39   #      "Connection Info"
40   #
41   set w [toplevel .dlg]
42   wm title .dlg "Connection Info"
43
44   #  Create the labels and entry fields for this dialog
45   #
46
47   foreach prop [pg_conndefaults] {
48
49      set varname    [lindex $prop 0]
50      set label_text [lindex $prop 1]
51      set type       [lindex $prop 2]
52      set length     [lindex $prop 3]
53      set default    [lindex $prop 4]
54
55      if { $type != "D" } {
56
57        global $varname
58
59        set $varname $default
60
61        set entry [add_label_field .dlg $label_text $varname]
62
63        if { $type == "*" } {
64         $entry configure -show "*"
65        }
66
67        if { $set_focus == "true" } {
68          focus -force $entry
69       set set_focus false
```

Listing 16.2 **Continued**

```
 70         }
 71       }
 72    }
 73
 74    #  Create the "Connect" and "Cancel" buttons
 75    add_button .dlg.default "Connect" {set result Ok} 1
 76    add_button .dlg.cancel  "Cancel"  {exit}          2
 77
 78    .dlg.default configure -default active
 79
 80    vwait result
 81
 82    set result ""
 83
 84    foreach prop [pg_conndefaults] {
 85
 86       set type [lindex $prop 2]
 87
 88       if { $type != "D" } {
 89
 90         set varname "$[lindex $prop 0]"
 91         set varval [subst $varname]
 92
 93         if { $varval != "" } {
 94           append result "[lindex $prop 0]=$varval "
 95         }
 96       }
 97    }
 98
 99    destroy .dlg
100
101    return $result
102 }
```

You can find Tk extension libraries that make dialog boxes easier to build, but we'll build our own so you can stick to plain-vanilla Tcl/Tk code.

Lines 33, 35, and 36 initialize a few variables that you will be using in this procedure; I'll explain the purpose of each variable as we go.

To construct the dialog shown in Figure 16.1, you will create a new `toplevel` widget named `.dlg` (at line 41). The `toplevel` widget automatically resizes as you add more widgets to it. To manage the placement of child widgets within `.dlg`, you will use the `grid` layout manager. The `grid` layout manager arranges child widgets in a grid (makes sense so far). You build a grid with two columns: A text label goes in the left column and the corresponding text entry widget goes in the right column. You use the `next_row` global variable to keep track of which grid row you are working on.

At line 47, enter a loop that iterates through each connection property returned by pg_conndefaults. Remember, pg_conndefaults returns a list of connection properties and enough information about each property so that you can construct a connection dialog. pg_conndefaults returns a list of sublists: Each sublist corresponds to a single connection property. There are five items in each sublist, and you pick apart the items at lines 49 through 53. The first item is the property name; for example, authtype, user, and password. You will create a variable that holds the value of each connection property; the name of the variable is the same as the name of the property. The second item is a descriptive name such as Database-User or Database-Name. The descriptive name displays as a prompt. The third item in the sublist is a property type. There are three possible values for the property type: an empty string, the character "D", and the character "*". If the property type is set to D, the property is meant for debugging purposes and should not normally be displayed to a casual user. If the property type is set to *, the property holds secret information (such as a password) and should not be echoed to the screen. If the property type is an empty string, it needs no special handling. You will ignore debug properties and arrange for any password fields to be displayed as * characters. The fourth sublist item returned by pg_conndefaults is the suggested length of the property value—you will ignore this item for now. The final item in each sublist is the default value for the property. The default value reflects the environment variable associated with the property, or it reflects the hard-wired value if the environment variable has not been defined.

After picking apart the property sublist, you start processing it at line 55. The if statement at line 55 ensures that you ignore debug properties. I mentioned earlier that you will create a new variable for each connection property—that happens at line 57. For example, if [lindex $prop 0] evaluates to password, you will create a new global variable named password. At line 57, you assign the default value (if any) to the new variable.

Next, add a label widget and an entry widget for each value that you want. The add_label_field procedure expects three parameters: a parent widget (.dlg), the text to display, and a variable that holds the value entered by the user.

When you call add_label_field (which you will examine next), two widgets are created. The first, a label widget, displays the text that was provided. The second, an entry widget, holds a value entered by the user. add_label_field returns the name of the new entry widget—you'll need that name to customize the widget.

At lines 63 and 64, you configure any "secret" properties (that is, passwords) to show asterisks rather than the actual characters entered by the user.

Next, at lines 67 through 70, you force the *focus* to the first entry widget in the dialog. When a widget has focus, keyboard and mouse events are sent to that widget and that widget holds the text cursor. You force the focus to the first modifiable widget on the dialog so that it lands in a useful, predictable place.

At lines 75 and 76, you create the two buttons that appear at the bottom of your dialog. When the user clicks on the first button (labeled Connect), Tcl will execute the command {set result Ok}. If the user clicks on the second button (labeled Cancel), Tcl will execute the command {exit}, terminating the entire application.

If the user presses the Return key, the default widget will be activated. You want the Return key to trigger the Connect button, so make that the default widget (see line 78).

At this point, you have created all the widgets that you want to display to the user. You have a toplevel widget that contains a collection of labels and text entry widgets, and you have a pair of buttons so the user can make something happen. Now, you want to display the complete dialog to the user and wait for him to click the Connect button or the Cancel button. That's what the vwait procedure does (line 80). The argument for vwait is the name of a variable; in this case, result. The vwait procedure waits for the result variable to change. result changes when the user clicks the Connect button because the code executed by the Connect button is {set result 1}.

Remember, if the user clicks the Cancel button, the exit procedure is invoked, terminating the entire application.

After the user has clicked the Connect button, you construct a connection string from the values the user had entered. To do this, loop through each non-debug property and extract the property name. You use the property name to reconstruct the name of the variable that holds the property value (line 90). After you know the variable name, you can extract the value (line 91). If the property value is non-null, you construct a *property=value* pair and append it to the result string.

Finally, destroy the toplevel window (.dlg) and return the connection string to the caller.

This procedure (connect_dialog) gives you a self-adjusting procedure that prompts the user for connection properties, even if you run a newer (or older) version of PostgreSQL that supports a different set of properties.

Now, let's look at the helper functions: add_label_field and add_button. The add_label_field procedure is shown in Listing 16.3.

Listing 16.3 client1.tcl—add_label_field

```
104 proc add_label_field { w text textvar } {
105
106     global next_row
107
108     set next_row    [expr $next_row + 1]
109     set label_path "$w.label_$textvar"
110     set entry_path "$w.$textvar"
111
112     label $label_path -text $text
113     grid  $label_path -row $next_row -column 1 -sticky e
114
115     entry $entry_path -textvariable $textvar
116     grid  $entry_path -row $next_row -column 2 -sticky w
117
118     bind $entry_path <Return> "$w.default invoke"
119
120     return $entry_path
121 }
```

This procedure creates two new widgets: a `label` widget and a text `entry` widget. The caller provides three arguments: a parent widget (`w`), the text to appear in the label widget (`text`), and the name of a variable that will hold the value that the user types into the entry widget (`textvar`).

We use the `next_row` global variable to determine where the `label` and `entry` widgets will be located. If you refer to line 35 of the previous listing (Listing 16.2), you'll see that `next_row` to zero was initialized before building the dialog.

Lines 109 and 110 construct the name that you will use for the `label` widget and for the `entry` widget. The widget names are constructed from the name of the text variable provided by the caller.

At line 112, you create the `label` widget and place the given text on the `label`. At line 113, you position the `label` widget using Tcl's `grid` layout manager. Always position the `label` widget in the first (leftmost) column and `entry` widget in the second (rightmost) column.

The `-sticky` option is used to position a widget within the grid cell. Specifying `-sticky e` means that the east (right) side of the widget sticks to the edge of the grid cell. The widget is right-justified within the cell.

At lines 115 and 116, you create the `entry` widget and position it within the `grid`.

Line 118 creates a *binding* for the `Return` key. If the user clicks the `Return` key while the `entry` widget is in focus, you want to trigger (or *invoke*) the `$w.default` button (that is, the `Connect` button). To accomplish this, bind the `Return` key to the code fragment `$w.default invoke`.

Finally, return the name of the `entry` widget to the caller.

The final procedure in `client1.tcl` is `add_button` (shown in Listing 16.4).

Listing 16.4 `client1.tcl—add_button`

```
123 proc add_button { path text command column } {
124
125    global next_row
126
127    if { $column == 1 } {
128      set next_row  [expr $next_row + 1]
129      set sticky "w"
130    } else { set sticky "e"   }
131
132    button $path -text $text -command $command
133    grid   $path -row $next_row -column $column -sticky $sticky
134
135    bind $path <Return> "$path invoke"
136 }
```

The caller provides four parameters: the name of the widget (`path`), the text to display on the button (`text`), a command to execute when the button is pressed (`command`), and a column number (`column`). The column number, along with the `next_row` global variable, determines which grid cell will hold the new button.

Line 132 creates and configures the button widget, and line 133 positions the button within the grid layout manager. Finally, you bind the command $path invoke to the Return key. It's a little odd, but Tk doesn't do that automatically—pressing the Return key doesn't trigger a button widget unless you explicitly configure the button to do so.

Listing 16.5 shows the mainline code for client1.tcl. When the Tcl interpreter runs this script, it begins execution at line 140 (the first command outside of a procedure body). The mainline code is simple; you invoke the procedure main (see Listing 16.1) and exit when that procedure completes.

Listing 16.5 client1.tcl—mainline

```
138 #  Mainline code follows
139 #
140 main
141 exit
```

Making the Connection Dialog Reusable

The connect_dialog procedure that you just finished turns out to be rather handy. Let's rearrange the code a little to make this procedure more reusable.

The easiest way to share code among Tcl applications is to factor the desired procedures into a separate source file and source that file into your applications. When you source a file, you are copying the contents of that file into your application at runtime. If you are familiar with C or C++, source is identical to #include.

We'll create a new file named pgconnect.tcl that contains only the code that you want to share among various applications. Listing 16.6 shows the outline of pgconnect.tcl.

Listing 16.6 pgconnect.tcl—outline

```
# Filename: pgconnect.tcl

proc connect_dialog { } {
...
}

proc add_label_field { w text textvar } {
...
}

proc add_button { path text command column } {
...
}

proc connect { } {
...
}
```

You can see that the `connect_dialog`, `add_label_field`, and `add_button` procedures are copied into `pgconnect.tcl`. I've also removed the mainline code and the `main` procedure—that code will be provided by the calling application. I've added one new procedure: `connect`. The body of the `connect` function is shown in Listing 16.7.

Listing 16.7 `pgconnect.tcl—connect`

```
 1 proc connect { } {
 2
 3  load libpgtcl
 4
 5  set result "retry"
 6
 7  while { $result == "retry" } {
 8    set connstr [connect_dialog]
 9
10    if { [catch {pg_connect -conninfo $connstr} conn] } {
11      set result [tk_messageBox \
12                 -message $conn \
13                 -title "Connection failed" \
14                 -type retrycancel]
15    } else {
16     return $conn
17    }
18  }
19  return {}
20 }
```

The `connect` procedure is similar to the `main` procedure from `client1.tcl`. After loading the libpgtcl library, `connect` enters a loop that calls the `connect_dialog` procedure until a connection is made or the user cancels. If a connection is made, `connect` will return the connection handle to the caller; otherwise, it will return an empty string.

Now that you've factored the connection dialog logic into a separate source file, you can use these procedures in multiple applications. Listing 16.8 shows a new version of the client1.tcl application, rewritten to take advantage of `pgconnect.tcl`.

Listing 16.8 `client1a.tcl`

```
 1 #!/usr/local/bin/wish
 2 #
 3 # Filename: client1a.tcl
 4
 5 proc main { } {
 6
 7   wm withdraw .
 8
 9   set conn [connect]
```

Listing 16.8 **Continued**

```
10
11   if { $conn != {} } {
12     tk_messageBox \
13         -message "Connection is: $conn" \
14             -title "Connection Ok"
15   }
16
17   pg_disconnect $conn
18
19 }
20
21 #  Mainline code follows
22 #
23
24 source pgconnect.tcl
25
26 main
27 exit
```

This new application is much shorter than the original version. I'll point out two changes that I've made to this code. First, at line 24, I replaced the `connect_dialog`, `add_label_field`, and `add_button` procedures with `source pgconnect.tcl`. Because I haven't included a pathname in the `source` command, Tcl looks for `pgconnect.tcl` in the current directory. The other change that I've made is at line 17—you call `pg_disconnect` to free up the connection handle when you are finished with it. You should call `pg_disconnect` to gracefully close a connection handle when you no longer need the connection. Closing the connection handle is not strictly required, but it is good form to free up resources as soon as you are done with them.

Now that you know how to connect to a PostgreSQL database from Tcl (and how to disconnect when you're finished), let's look at the steps required to execute an SQL command and process the results.

Client 2—Query Processing

Executing a command with libpgtcl is easy. You invoke the `pg_exec` procedure and you get back a result handle. `pg_exec` expects two parameters:

`pg_exec` *`connection_handle command`*

A typical call to `pg_exec` might look like this:

```
set result_handle [pg_exec $conn "SELECT * FROM customers"]
```

Calling `pg_exec` like this captures the result handle in the variable `result_handle`. A result handle encapsulates many items of information into a single object. You can't get at any of this information directly; instead, you have to use the `pg_result` procedure.

Result Set Processing

Let's look at some of the things that you can do with a result handle:

```
$ tclsh

% load libpgtcl

% set connstr "host=davinci user=korry password=cows dbname=movies"
host=davinci user=korry password=cows dbname=movies

% set conn [pg_connect -conninfo $connstr]
pgsql276
```

At this point, you have loaded the libpgtcl library into the Tcl interpreter and established a connection to your database. Next, you will execute a simple query using the `pg_exec` function:

```
% set result [pg_exec $conn "SELECT * FROM customers"]
pgsql276.0
```

When you call `pg_exec`, you get back a result handle. You may have noticed that the string you get back from `pg_exec` is similar to the string returned by `pg_connect`. In fact, appending a number to the connection handle forms the result handle. If you were to execute another command using the same connection handle, `pg_exec` would return `pgsql276.1`. Result handles remain valid until you clear them or close the parent connection handle. I'll show you how to clear result handles and how to close connection handles in a moment. First, let's get back to `pg_result`:

```
% pg_result $result -status
PGRES_TUPLES_OK
```

The `pg_result -status` option returns a string that tells you whether the command succeeded or failed. If a command has executed successfully, `pg_result -status` will return `PGRES_TUPLES_OK`, `PGRES_COMMAND_OK`, or `PGRES_EMPTY_QUERY`[3]. If the command fails, you will see `PGRES_NONFATAL_ERROR`, `PGRES_FATAL_ERROR`, or `PGRES_BAD_RESPONSE`.

If your command fails, you can use the `pg_result -error` option to retrieve the text of the error message. Let's execute another (erroneous) command so you can see `pg_result -error` in action:

```
% set result2 [pg_exec $conn "SELECT * FROM moof"]
pgsql276.1
```

3. You may also see `PGRES_COPY_IN` and `PGRES_COPY_OUT` if you execute the `COPY FROM` or `COPY TO` commands. I won't be covering the `COPY` command this chapter; the details vary with implementation and seem to be rather unstable.

```
% pg_result $result2 -status
PGRES_FATAL_ERROR

% pg_result $result2 -error
ERROR:  Relation "moof" does not exist
```

Of course, you could capture the error message in a variable using `set error [pg_result $result2 -error]`.

Assuming that the command succeeded, you can determine how many rows and columns are in the result set using `pg_result -numTuples` and `pg_result -numAttrs` (respectively):

```
% pg_result $result -numTuples
5

% pg_result $result -numAttrs
4
```

If you call `pg_result -numTuples` (or `-numAttrs`) using a result handle for a failed command, the row count (or column count) will be zero.

You can retrieve the column names from a result handle using `pg_result -attributes`:

```
% pg_result $result -attributes
id customer_name phone birth_date
```

`pg_result -attributes` returns a list of column names. You can pick apart this list using `lindex`:

```
% lindex [pg_result $result -attributes] 0
id

% lindex [pg_result $result -attributes] 1
customer
```

A related option is `pg_result -lAttributes`. This option returns complete metadata for a result handle. The `-Attributes` option returns a list of sublists. Each sublist contains three elements: the name of a column, the data type of a column, and the size of a column. Here is the metadata for the `SELECT * FROM customers` query that you have executed:

```
% pg_result $result -lAttributes
{id 23 4} {customer_name 1043 -1} {phone 1042 -1} {birth_date 1082 4}
```

This result set holds four columns so the `pg_result -Attributes` returns four sublists. Notice that the data type for each column is returned in numeric form. The data type values correspond to the OID (object-id) of the corresponding entry in the pg_type system table. You can find the type names using the following query (in psql):

```
$ psql -d movies -q

movies=# SELECT oid, typname FROM pg_type
movies-#   WHERE oid IN (23, 1043, 1042, 1082);
 oid  | typname
------+---------
   23 | int4
 1042 | bpchar
 1043 | varchar
 1082 | date
(4 rows)
```

Let's compare the results returned by pg_result -lAttributes with the output of the \d meta-command in psql:

```
$ psql -d movies
movies=# \d customers
                Table "customers"
   Attribute   |         Type          | Modifier
---------------+-----------------------+----------
 id            | integer               |
 customer_name | character varying(50) |
 phone         | character(8)          |
 birth_date    | date                  |
```

We see the same column names, but the column sizes and data types returned by pg_result don't look right. For example, the customer_name column is defined as a VARCHAR(50), but pg_result-lAttributes reports a length of -1 and a type of 1043. The problem is that the -lAttributes option returns the size of each column as stored *on the server*. Columns of variable size are reported as being -1 byte long. You probably won't find too many uses for -lAttributes.

One function that you *will* find useful is pg_result -getTuple. The -getTuple option returns a row from the result set in the form of a list. Let's retrieve the first row returned by our query:

```
% set tuple [pg_result $result -getTuple 0]
1 {Jones, Henry} 555-1212 1970-10-10
```

Notice that row numbers start at 0, not 1. With a result set containing five rows, you can request rows 0 through 4. If you try to retrieve an invalid row, you will see an error message:

```
% pg_result $result -getTuple 5
argument to getTuple cannot exceed number of tuples - 1
```

As with any other Tcl list, you can pick apart a row using the `lindex` operator:

```
% puts $tuple
1 {Jones, Henry} 555-1212 1970-10-10

% lindex $tuple 1
Jones, Henry
```

An empty string represents a `NULL` value. I happen to know that the last row in this result set contains a `NULL` phone number:

```
% set tuple [pg_result $result -getTuple 4]
7 {Grumby, Jonas} {} 1984-02-21

% lindex $tuple 2

%
```

Notice that `lindex` has returned an empty string when you asked for the phone number value (it's a little hard to see, but it's there).

In addition to `-getTuple`, `pg_result` gives you three other ways to get at the rows in a result set. First, and easiest to understand, is `pg_result -tupleArray`:

```
% pg_result $result -tupleArray 0 one_row

% parray one_row
one_row(birth_date)    = 1970-10-10
one_row(customer_name) = Jones, Henry
one_row(id)            = 1
one_row(phone)         = 555-1212
```

The `-tupleArray` option assigns a single tuple to an array variable. In this example, you asked `pg_result` to copy the first row (row 0) into an array variable named `one_row`. In Tcl, every array is an associative array, meaning that you can index into the array using any string value. A nonassociative array forces you to assign a unique number to each array element. Associative arrays are nice. You can see from this example that the `-tupleArray` option uses the name of each column as a key (array index). If you want to find the customer name in this array, you could write the following:

```
% puts $one_row(customer_name)
Jones, Henry
```

There is a serious *gotcha* waiting in the `-tupleArray` option. Because `-tupleArray` produces an associative array, the column names in your result set must be unique. Normally, this isn't an issue, but if you have two or more computed columns in your result set, you must give them unique names using the `AS` clause. Here is an example that shows the problem:

```
% set result2 [pg_exec $conn "SELECT 2*3, 5*3"]
pgsql276.2
```

```
% pg_result $result2 -tupleArray 0 missing_fields

% parray missing_fields
missing_fields(?column?) = 15
```

You can see the problem; unless you rename a computed column, it will be named `?column?`: If you have two columns with the same name, one of them will vanish from the associative array. Let's fix this:

```
% set result2 [pg_exec $conn "SELECT 2*4 AS first, 5*3 AS second"]
pgsql276.3

% pg_result $result2 -tupleArray 0 all_fields

% parray all_fields
all_fields(first)  = 8
all_fields(second) = 15
```

Much better—now you see both values.

The next `pg_result` option assigns all the rows in a result set to a single array—for example:

```
% pg_result $result -assign all_rows
all_rows

% parray all_rows
all_rows(0,birth_date)    = 1970-10-10
all_rows(0,customer_name) = Jones, Henry
all_rows(0,id)            = 1
all_rows(0,phone)         = 555-1212
all_rows(1,birth_date)    = 1972-07-10
all_rows(1,customer_name) = Rubin, William
all_rows(1,id)            = 2
all_rows(1,phone)         = 555-2211
all_rows(2,birth_date)    = 1968-01-21
all_rows(2,customer_name) = Panky, Henry
all_rows(2,id)            = 3
all_rows(2,phone)         = 555-1221
all_rows(3,birth_date)    = 1969-03-05
all_rows(3,customer_name) = Wonderland, Alice N.
all_rows(3,id)            = 4
all_rows(3,phone)         = 555-1122
all_rows(4,birth_date)    = 1984-02-21
all_rows(4,customer_name) = Grumby, Jonas
all_rows(4,id)            = 7
all_rows(4,phone)         =
```

`pg_result -assign` copies all rows in the result set into a two-dimensional array. After you execute the command `pg_result $result -assign all_rows`, the array variable `$all_rows` will contain 20 elements (five rows times four columns). The first array index is the row number and the second index is the column name (remember, Tcl arrays are associative; you can use any string value as an array index). If you want the phone number value from the third row, you will find it in `$all_rows(2,phone)`:

```
% puts $all_rows(2,phone)
555-1221
```

Because the array produced by `-assign` is an associative array, you must ensure that each column in the result set has a unique name.

Finally, `pg_result` can create an associative array from your result set where the key to the array is formed by the values in the first column. I think this option is best understood by looking at an example:

```
% set result3 \
[pg_exec $conn "SELECT id, phone, birth_date FROM customers"]
pgsql276.4

% pg_result $result3 -assignbyidx results
results

% parray results
results(1,birth_date) = 1970-10-10
results(1,phone)      = 555-1212
results(2,birth_date) = 1972-07-10
results(2,phone)      = 555-2211
results(3,birth_date) = 1968-01-21
results(3,phone)      = 555-1221
results(4,birth_date) = 1969-03-05
results(4,phone)      = 555-1122
results(7,birth_date) = 1984-02-05
results(7,phone)      =
```

Like `pg_result -assign`, the `-assignbyidx` option creates a two-dimensional array. The difference between `-assign` and `-assignbyidx` is in how they create the key values for the array. `-assign` uses the row number as the first index and the column name as the second dimension. On the other hand, `-assignbyidx` removes the first column from the result set and uses the first column in each row as the first index.

This result set (`$result3`) contains five rows and three columns. An array created by `-assign` would have 15 members, but an array created by `-assignbyidx` will have 10 members (five rows times two columns). The `-assignbyidx` option has removed the first column (the customer `id` column) from the array and used those values (1, 2, 3, 4, and 7) to index the first dimension in the result array.

When you use `-assignbyidx`, you have to pay attention to the order in which the columns appear in the result set. The first column is used to index the resulting array. You must also ensure that the values in the first column are unique, or you will lose entire rows from the result set.

Lazy Programmers Are Good Programmers, or pg_select

libpgtcl offers one last procedure that you can use to process the result set of a query: `pg_select`. The `pg_select` procedure gives you a quick way to execute a command (usually `SELECT`) and process the result set all at once. `pg_select` requires four parameters:

```
pg_select connection_handle command variable procedure
```

When you call `pg_select`, you supply a connection handle, the text of the command that you want to send to the server, the name of an array variable that will hold each row (one row at a time), and a procedure that will be called once for each row in the result set. Here is an example:

```
% pg_select $conn \
    "SELECT * FROM customers LIMIT 2" \
    one_row \
    {puts "" ; parray one_row }

one_row(.command)       = update
one_row(.headers)       = id customer_name phone birth_date
one_row(.numcols)       = 4
one_row(.tupno)         = 0
one_row(birth_date)     = 1970-10-10
one_row(customer_name)  = Jones, Henry
one_row(id)             = 1
one_row(phone)          = 555-1212

one_row(.command)       = update
one_row(.headers)       = id customer_name phone birth_date
one_row(.numcols)       = 4
one_row(.tupno)         = 1
one_row(birth_date)     = 1972-07-10
one_row(customer_name)  = Rubin, William
one_row(id)             = 2
one_row(phone)          = 555-2211
```

When you execute this statement, `pg_select` will send the `SELECT` command to the server. If the `SELECT` command fails, `pg_select` will throw an error. If the `SELECT` command completes successfully, `pg_select` will loop through the result set. After assigning the next row to the `one_row` variable, `pg_select` will execute the string `{puts "" ; parray one_row}`.

When `pg_select` assigns a row to the *`variable`* that you specify, it creates an associative array indexed by column name, just like `pg_result -tupleArray`. You may have noticed that there are a few extra entries reported for each row. Each time a row is processed, `pg_select` defines four extra elements in the associative array that it creates. The `.tupno` member indicates which row is currently being processed (starting at 0). The `.numcols` and `.headers` members will not change from row to row—they hold the column count and column names, respectively. The fourth special member is `.command`; this member is not only undocumented, but it appears to be wrong. Of course, we can only guess what the `.command` member is supposed to do; but in the latest release, `.command` is always set to `update`. My advice is to ignore `.command` for now.

Now that you know how to process the result set of a query, let's look at a sample application that will execute a single (hard-wired) query and display the results in tabular form.

Listing 16.9 shows the first few lines of `client2.tcl`.

Listing 16.9 `client2.tcl—main`

```
 1 #!/usr/local/bin/wish
 2 #
 3 # Filename: client2.tcl
 4
 5 proc main { } {
 6
 7   wm withdraw .
 8
 9   package require Tktable
10
11   set conn [connect]
12
13   if { $conn != {} } {
14
15      set table [build_dialog $conn]
16
17      process_command $conn $table "SELECT * FROM customers"
18
19      tkwait window .top
20
21     pg_disconnect $conn
22   }
23 }
```

In this application, you use the Tktable extension to Tk. If you don't already have this extension, you can find it at `http://tktable.sourceforge.net`. Because this is an extension, you have to explicitly load (or `package require`) the Tktable package before you can use it (see line 9).

Next, call the `connect` procedure to establish a connection to the PostgreSQL server. This is the same `connect` procedure that you developed earlier in this chapter (it's imported from `pgconnect.sql` at the bottom of this application). `connect` returns a connection handle if successful, or returns an empty string in the event of a failure.

If you connected, create a dialog box that you will use to display the results of a query. The build_dialog procedure (shown in Listing 16.10) returns the name of the table widget hosted in the dialog. Next, call the process_command procedure (shown later in Listing 16.12) to execute a simple SELECT command. process_command expects three parameters: a connection handle, the name of a table widget, and the text of a query.

After you've finished filling in the table widget, display the dialog to the user and wait for him to close that window.

Finally, play nice and disconnect from the server using pg_disconnect when you are finished.

Listing 16.10 client2.tcl—build_dialog

```
25 proc build_dialog { conn } {
26
27   toplevel .top
28
29   wm title .top "Customers"
30
31   set table [make_table .top]
32
33   button .top.close -text "Close Window" -command {exit}
34
35   scrollbar .top.sy -command [list $table yview]
36   scrollbar .top.sx -command [list $table xview] -orient horizontal
37
38   grid   $table .top.sy     -sticky news
39   grid      .top.sx         -sticky ew
40   grid     .top.close
41
42   grid columnconfig .top 0 -weight 1
43   grid rowconfig    .top 0 -weight 1
44   grid rowconfig    .top 2 -weight 0
45
46   return $table
47 }
```

Listing 16.10 shows the build_dialog procedure. This procedure creates a toplevel window that hosts a table widget, scrollbars, and a Close Window button. Figure 16.4 shows the window layout that you are constructing.

After creating a toplevel window and configuring its title bar, you call the make_table procedure (shown later in Listing 16.11). make_table creates a new table widget (whose parent is .top) and does some initial configuration work. Next you create the Close Window button and a vertical and horizontal scrollbar. Finally, arrange all the child widgets (the table widget, button, and scrollbars) using the grid layout manager.

Figure 16.4 The `client2.tcl`—results.

If you look closely at the window layout in Figure 16.4 (and use your imagination), you'll see that the child widgets are arranged in a grid containing three rows and two columns. You have to use your imagination because the grid cells are not equally sized. Be sure to look at the layout of the *child widgets*, not the data values in the table control. The top row in the grid contains a table control in the leftmost column and a vertical scrollbar in the rightmost column. The middle row contains the horizontal scrollbar in the leftmost column and the rightmost column is empty. Finally, the bottom row contains the `Close Window` button in the leftmost column and, again, the rightmost column is empty.

Now, look back to lines 38 through 40 in Listing 16.10. You'll see how the `grid` layout manager arranges everything.

Lines 42 through 44 ensure that the table widget resizes whenever the `toplevel` widget is resized. The easiest way to understand these three lines of code is to comment them out, run the application, and then stretch out the window. You'll see that the vertical scrollbar gets wider and the horizontal scrollbar gets taller. A bit too "Salvador Dali" for my taste. The `grid columnconfig` and `grid rowconfig` procedures fix up everything again.

You finish by returning the name of the table widget to our caller.

Listing 16.11 `client2.tcl—make_table`

```
49 proc make_table { parent } {
50
51   table $parent.table \
52     -titlerows 1 \
53     -titlecols 1 \
54     -roworigin -1 \
55     -colorigin -1 \
56     -variable table_data \
57     -yscrollcommand {.top.sy set} \
58     -xscrollcommand {.top.sx set} \
59     -colstretchmode last -rowstretchmode last
60
61   return $parent.table
62 }
```

This procedure (make_table) creates a new table widget and configures it so that it is ready for use.

The name of the table widget is $parent.table. You'll use the first row of the table to display column names and the first column to display row numbers: The -titlerows 1 and -titlecols 1 options tell the table widget that you want to dedicate one row and one column to hold titles.

Normally, the first row in a table is row 0 (and the first column is column 0). Change the origin of the table to -1,-1 to make it a little easier to account for the title row and column. That means that the title row is actually row –1 and the first *data* row is row zero (similar trickery is performed on the column-numbering scheme).

A table widget needs a variable to hold all its data —we'll use a variable named table_data for that purpose. We won't actually *do* anything with this variable; we just need to provide one. (If you want to see a completely pointless widget, remove the -variable table_data line and run this application—the results violate the *Principle Of Least Astonishment*).

The next two options (-yscrollcommand and -xscrollcommand) connect the table widget to the two scrollbars (.top.sx and .top.sy) that you will be creating a little later.

The final configuration options tell the table widget how to behave if the container (.top) is resized. Setting the column stretch mode to last means that the rightmost column in the table will expand to take up any extra real estate. Similarly, setting the row stretch mode to last will stretch out the bottom row in the table. See the Tktable documentation for other resizing options.

Finish up by returning the name of the table widget to the caller. Listing 16.12 shows the process_command procedure.

Listing 16.12 client2.tcl—process_command

```
64 proc process_command { conn table command } {
65
66   set result_set [pg_exec $conn $command]
67
68   load_table $table $result_set
69 }
```

This procedure is nice and short. It executes a command (passed from the caller in the command parameter) and calls the load_table procedure to load the results of the command into a table widget.

I mentioned earlier that pg_exec executes a PostgreSQL command and returns a result set handle. pg_exec returns a result set, even if something goes wrong. In the next client application, I'll show you how to handle execution errors. For now, just assume that the command will succeed.

The procedure shown in Listing 16.13 (load_table) doesn't do much by itself—it simply calls a few helper procedures in the correct order.

Listing 16.13 `client2.tcl—load_table`

```
71 proc load_table { table result_set } {
72
73   size_table $table $result_set
74
75   set_column_headers $table $result_set
76
77   fill_table $table $result_set
78
79   size_columns $table $result_set
80 }
```

`load_table` is called whenever you want to copy values from a result set into a table widget. There are four steps to this process. First, you adjust the size of the table (this is the logical size, not the physical, onscreen widget size) to contain the same number of rows and columns as the result set. Next, copy the column names from the result set into the first row of the table. After that, we copy all the data values from the result set into the individual table cells. Finally, you adjust the size of each column in the table widget. You want each column to be wide enough to display the widest value.

The `size_table` procedure (see Listing 16.14) is responsible for adjusting the number of rows and columns in the table widget to match the size of the result set. We start by extracting the number of columns (libpgtcl calls them *attributes*) and the number of rows (also known as *tuples*) from the result set.

Listing 16.14 `client2.tcl—size_table`

```
82 proc size_table { table result_set } {
83
84   set col_cnt   [pg_result $result_set -numAttrs]
85   set row_cnt   [pg_result $result_set -numTuples]
86
87   $table configure \
88     -rows [expr $row_cnt + 1 ] \
89     -cols [expr $col_cnt + 1 ]
90 }
```

Notice that you add an extra row and column to the table widget. The topmost row holds column names. The leftmost column holds row numbers.

The `set_column_headers` procedure (see Listing 16.15) performs two functions: copying column names from the result set into the title row of the given table widget and storing the width of each column name in the `col_widths` global array.

Listing 16.15 `client2.tcl—set_column_headers`

```
92 proc set_column_headers { table result_set } {
93
94   global col_widths
```

Listing 16.15 **Continued**

```
 95
 96   set col_cnt   [pg_result $result_set -numAttrs]
 97   set col_names [pg_result $result_set -attributes]
 98
 99   for {set col 0} {$col < $col_cnt} {incr col} {
100     set col_name [lindex $col_names $col]
101     $table set -1,$col $col_name
102     set col_widths($col) [string length $col_name]
103   }
104 }
```

`set_column_headers` begins by retrieving the column count and column names from the given result set. When you call `pg_result -attributes`, you get back a list of column names.

Lines 99 through 102 loop through each column in the result set. In each iteration, you extract a column name from the list, copy the column name into the first row of the table (line 101), and store the length of the column name in `col_widths`.

The `col_widths` array is used by `size_columns` to set each column to its optimal width. You want to stretch each column so that it is wide enough to display the widest value in that column. Note that you can't compute the *final* width of each column in this procedure, only the starting width. You won't know the final width for a column until you have processed every row in the result set.

The `fill_table` procedure (see Listing 16.16) copies data values from the result set into the table.

Listing 16.16 `client2.tcl—fill_table`

```
106 proc fill_table { table result_set } {
107
108   global col_widths
109
110   set col_cnt   [pg_result $result_set -numAttrs]
111   set row_cnt   [pg_result $result_set -numTuples]
112
113   for {set row 0} {$row < $row_cnt} {incr row} {
114     set tuple [pg_result $result_set -getTuple $row]
115
116     $table set $row,-1 [expr $row + 1]
117
118     for {set col 0} {$col < $col_cnt} {incr col} {
119
120       set val [lindex $tuple $col]
121
122       if { $col_widths($col) < [string length $val] } {
123         set col_widths($col) [string length $val]
```

Listing 16.16 **Continued**

```
124         }
125         $table set $row,$col $val
126       }
127     }
128 }
```

First, set up two loop invariants to help improve performance: `col_cnt` contains the number of columns in the result set and `row_cnt` contains the number of rows.

> **A Quick Word About Quick Words**[4]
>
> When we first wrote this procedure, we didn't set up any local variables to hold the row and column counts. Instead, we just plugged `[pg_result $result_set -numAttrs]` or `[pg_result $result_set -numTuples]` into the code wherever we needed it. That gave us code like this:
>
> ```
> for {set row 0} {$row < [pg_result $result_set -numTuples] } {incr row}
> ```
>
> That code works, but it's very wasteful. Each time you iterate through this loop, you have to call a procedure stored in the libpgtcl library. Worse yet, you have *nested* loops that contain multiple libpgtcl function calls. That means, for example, that a query that returns 10 rows of 20 columns each will require (let me break out my calculator here) more than 200 calls to libpgtcl. By stuffing the loop invariants into local variables, you trim this to two function calls. In a compiled C program, that might not make much of a difference, but Tcl is an interpreted language and the difference is noticeable.
>
> [4] In Tcl, each command is a *word*. This sidebar talks about writing quick code. Quick words... oh, never mind.

After computing the column count and row count, iterate through the rows in the result set. To access each row, you use `pg_result -getTuple`. You may recall from the earlier discussion that libpgtcl gives you a number of ways to get at the data values in a result set. `pg_result -getTuple` returns a single row in the form of a list of values.

At line 116, you copy the row number into the first column of the table (this is a "title" column).

Next, enter a nested loop to process each column in the current row. First, extract the data value from the list returned by `pg_result -getTuple` (line 120). Second, update the column width (stored in `$col_widths($col)`) if this value is wider than any value that you have seen in this column. Remember, you want to size each column to the width of the widest value. Finally, copy the data value into the table (line 125).

`size_columns` (see Listing 16.17) is responsible for sizing each column in the table widget. The `set_column_headers` and `fill_table` procedures built an array of column widths (`$col_widths`). We use the `table -width` option to set the size of each column.

Listing 16.17 `client2.tcl—size_columns`

```
130 proc size_columns { table result_set } {
131
132   global col_widths
133
134   set col_cnt   [pg_result $result_set -numAttrs]
135
136   for {set col 0} {$col < $col_cnt} {incr col} {
137     $table width $col $col_widths($col)
138   }
139
140   $table width -1 5
141 }
```

The final call to `table -width` adjusts the width of the first column—remember, the first column displays a row counter. A width of 5 is aesthetically pleasing (at least on my screen).

Listing 16.18 shows the mainline code for `client2.tcl`. You load the `pgconnect.tcl` source file, call the main procedure, and then exit.

Listing 16.18 `client2.tcl—mainline`

```
143 #  Mainline code follows
144 #
145 source pgconnect.tcl
146 main
147 exit
```

Try to run this application. It's not very exciting, is it? You really want to change the query and run it again, don't you?

At this point, you have enough information to write an interactive query processor in Tcl/Tk. In fact, you need only a few small changes to `client2.tcl` to process arbitrary commands.

Client 3—An Interactive Query Processor

In this section, we'll build an interactive command processor in Tcl/Tk. Fortunately, we can reuse most of the code that we developed in `client2.tcl`. I'll explain the differences and point out where we can share code with the previous client.

Figure 16.5 presents what we are trying to build.

You can see that this application is similar to the previous application. I've added a few widgets: a label at the top of the window that tells the user what to do, a text entry widget where you enter commands, and a status bar that gives feedback.

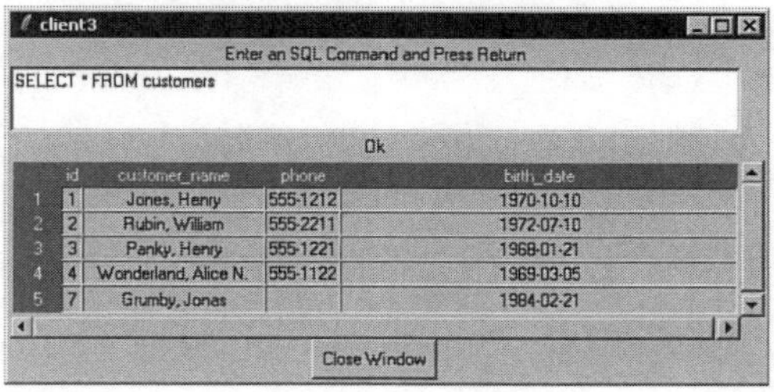

Figure 16.5 The `client3.tcl`—results.

Now, let's look at the code. We have to change three procedures to transform `client2.tcl` into `client3.tcl`. Listing 16.19 shows the `main` procedure for the third client.

Listing 16.19 `client3.tcl—main`

```
 1 #!/usr/local/bin/wish
 2 #
 3 # Filename: client3.tcl
 4
 5 proc main { } {
 6
 7   wm withdraw .
 8
 9   package require Tktable
10
11   set conn [connect]
12
13   if { $conn != {} } {
14
15     build_dialog $conn
16
17     tkwait window .top
18
19     pg_disconnect $conn
20   }
21 }
```

If you compare this to the `main` procedure from `client2.tcl` (refer to Listing 16.9), you'll see that the only difference is that I have removed the call to `process_command`. In the new application, the query is not hard-coded into the application—you prompt the user for a command string instead. So, after connecting to the server, you call `build_dialog` to construct the user interface and then wait for the dialog window to close.

Listing 16.20 shows the `build_dialog` procedure.

Listing 16.20 client3.tcl—build_dialog

```
23 proc build_dialog { conn } {
24
25   toplevel .top
26
27   wm title .top "client3"
28
29   set table [make_table .top]
30
31   button .top.close -text "Close Window" -command {exit}
32
33   label .top.label   -text "Enter an SQL Command and Press Return"
34   text  .top.command -height 3
35   label .top.status
36
37   focus -force .top.command
38
39   bind .top.command <Return> \
40       "process_command $conn $table \[.top.command get 1.0 end\]"
41
42   scrollbar .top.sy -command [list $table yview]
43   scrollbar .top.sx -command [list $table xview] -orient horizontal
44
45   grid     .top.label
46   grid    .top.command      -sticky news
47   grid     .top.status
48   grid   $table .top.sy     -sticky news
49   grid      .top.sx         -sticky ew
50   grid     .top.close
51
52   grid columnconfig .top 0 -weight 1
53
54   grid rowconfig    .top 1 -weight 0
55   grid rowconfig    .top 3 -weight 1
56   grid rowconfig    .top 5 -weight 0
57 }
```

The build_dialog procedure is a little longer than it used to be, but not any more complex. I've added a label (line 33) that displays a prompt to the user. I've also added a text widget. The text widget (named .top.command) is where you'll type in your PostgreSQL commands. A text widget is a like a multiline entry widget—you configure it to be three lines tall. We also add a second label widget (.top.status), in which, we will display the status of each command. Refer to Figure 16.5; the .top.status widget is positioned between the text entry widget and the table widget.

Line 37 forces the keyboard focus to .top.command (the text entry widget).

Next, you bind a piece of Tcl code to the Return key. This piece of code executes whenever the user presses the Return key while the .top.command widget has the focus.

Line 40 might look a bit cryptic. It might be easier to understand if you walk through the evaluation process that Tcl will use when it executes our code snippet.

When you call the bind procedure, Tcl will evaluate the code segment, performing variable substitution wherever it sees an unquoted dollar sign. So, if $conn contains pg224 and $table contains .top.table, the first iteration translates from

```
process_command $conn $table \[.top.command get 1.0 end\]
```

to

```
process_command pg224 $table \[.top.command get 1.0 end\]
```

Next, Tcl translates the second variable substitution to

```
process_command pg224 .top.table \[.top.command get 1.0 end\]
```

Finally, Tcl removes the escape characters from the string, resulting in

```
process_command pg224 .top.table [.top.command get 1.0 end]
```

At this point, Tcl stops evaluating the code snippet. It binds this final string to the Return key. When the Return key is pressed, Tk will execute this string. The last part of the string ([.top.command get 1.0 end]) extracts the contents of the text entry widget.

The net effect is that the process_command procedure is called whenever the user presses the Return key, and the text of the command is passed as the final parameter.

The rest of the code in build_dialog should be pretty familiar. We create a vertical and horizontal scrollbar and then arrange everything using the grid layout manager.

The final three lines in this procedure ensure that the text entry widget and the Close Window button remain visible if you resize the application window.

Now, let's look at the process_command procedure (see Listing 16.21).

Listing 16.21 client3.tcl—process_command

```
75 proc process_command { conn table command } {
76
77   set result_set [pg_exec $conn $command]
78
79   switch [pg_result $result_set -status] {
80
81     PGRES_EMPTY_QUERY {
82       .top.status configure -text ""
83     }
84
85     PGRES_TUPLES_OK {
86       .top.status configure -text "Ok"
```

Listing 16.21 **Continued**

```
 87         load_table $table $result_set
 88       }
 89
 90       PGRES_COMMAND_OK {
 91         .top.status configure -text "Ok"
 92       }
 93
 94       default
 95       {
 96         .top.status configure -text ""
 97
 98         tk_messageBox -title [pg_result $result_set -status] \
 99                       -message [pg_result $result_set -error] \
100                       -type ok
101       }
102     }
103 }
```

The process_command procedure has changed considerably. In the previous version (refer to Listing 16.12), a couple of assumptions were made that need to be corrected here if you want to process arbitrary commands. First, it was assumed that the command executed successfully. If you are executing something other than a hard-wired command, you must expect errors to occur (of course, you really should expect errors, even when you know which commands are going to execute). The second assumption was that you were executing only SELECT commands. Again, you have to handle any type of command if you let the user enter arbitrary text.

Like before, call the pg_exec procedure to execute the command provided by the caller.

Next, examine the value returned by pg_result -status to determine what kind of result set you have. As I mentioned earlier, pg_result -status returns values such as PGRES_TUPLES_OK, PGRES_COMMAND_OK, PGRES_FATAL_ERROR, and so on. You will handle three of these values explicitly and assume that anything else is a message that you should display to the user.

The simplest case occurs when the user presses the Return key without entering a command. When that happens, pg_result -status will return PGGRES_EMPTY_QUERY. In this case, clear the status line (.top.status) and return.

Next, handle PGRES_TUPLES_OK. pg_result -status returns PGRES_TUPLES_OK when you (successfully) execute a SELECT command. Handling the result set from a SELECT command is something you already know how to do; you set the status line to Ok and call the load_table procedure to copy the result set into the table widget. The load_table procedure is unchanged from client2.tcl.

pg_result -status returns PGRES_COMMAND_OK when you successfully execute a command other than SELECT. This one is easy—you just set the status line to read Ok.

If you were really energetic, you might also display the OID from the previous command (`pg_result -oid`).

Finally, assume that any other return code is a message that you should simply display to the user. After clearing the status line, use the `tk_messageBox` to display the status (`pg_result -status`) and error message (`pg_result -error`).

That's it. All the other procedures in `client3.tcl` are identical to those in `client2.tcl`.

Run this application a few times to see how it behaves. Be sure to feed it a few errors so you can see the error handling in action (how exciting).

I'll wrap up this chapter by describing how to access large-objects from a Tcl application.

The libpgtcl Large-Object API

The libpgtcl library provides a number of procedures that you can use to interact with PostgreSQL large-objects. A *large-object* is a value that is stored indirectly. When you create a column that will contain a large-object, the column should be of type OID (object-id). When you import a large-object into your database, the bits that make up the object are stored in the `pg_largeobject` system table and a reference is stored in your table. Large-objects are typically used to hold images, sound files, or large pieces of unstructured data.

There are two ways to create a large-object. First, you can create a large-object using the `pg_lo_creat` procedure. `pg_lo_creat` creates a new (empty) entry in the `pg_largeobject` table and returns the OID of that entry. After you have an empty large-object, you can write data into it using `pg_lo_write`.

Second, you can import an existing file (such as a JPEG-encoded photograph) into a database using `pg_lo_import`. The `pg_lo_import` manual page says that `pg_lo_import` requires two parameters (a connection handle and a filename) and returns nothing. That documentation is incorrect: `pg_lo_import` returns the OID of the new large-object.

Here is a code snippet that shows how to use the `pg_lo_import` procedure:

```
...
pg_result [pg_exec $conn "BEGIN WORK"] -clear # Start a transaction

set large_object_oid [pg_lo_import $conn "/images/happyface.jpg"]

pg_result [pg_exec $conn "COMMIT WORK"] -clear
...
```

Note that you must call `pg_lo_import` within a transaction block. In fact, *all* large-object operations must occur within a transaction block.

The inverse of `pg_lo_import` is `pg_lo_export`. `pg_lo_export` copies a large-object into a file:

```
...
pg_result [pg_exec $conn "BEGIN WORK"] -clear # Start a transaction

pg_log_export $conn $large_object_oid "/images/jocularface.jpg"

pg_result [pg_exec $conn "COMMIT WORK"] -clear
...
```

Like `pg_lo_import`, `pg_lo_export` must be called within a transaction block. You can also read the contents of a large-object using libpgtcl. To start with, you must open the desired large-object using `pg_lo_open`:

```
...
set fd [pg_lo_open $conn $large_object_oid "rw"]
...
```

When you call `pg_lo_open`, you provide a connection handle, the OID of the large-object that you want, and an access mode. libpgtcl is a little fickle when it comes to large-object access modes; `pg_lo_open` expects `"r"`, `"w"`, or `"rw"`; but `pg_lo_create` expects `"INV_READ"`, `"INV_WRITE"`, or `"INV_READ|INV_WRITE"`. The value returned by `pg_lo_open` is a large-object handle; and after you have one of those, you can read from, write to, or move around in the large-object.

First, let's talk about positioning within a large-object. Large-objects can be, well, large. Your application may not need to read (or write) an entire large-object all at once; for really big large-objects, you may want to work with small chunks. To make this possible, libpgtcl lets you *seek* your large-object handle to the part that you are interested in; then, you can read or write from there.

The `pg_lo_lseek` procedure is modeled after the Unix `lseek()` function. `pg_lo_lseek` requires three parameters:

```
pg_lo_lseek connection-handle large-object-handle offset starting-point
```

The *`connection-handle`* and *`large-object-handle`* parameters are self-explanatory. *`offset`* specifies the number of bytes you want to move. *`starting-point`* specifies which position you want to move *from*. `SEEK_CUR` means that you want to move *`offset`* bytes relative to the current position. `SEEK_SET` means that you want to move *`offset`* bytes relative to the start of the object. `SEEK_END` will position your *`offset`* bytes from the end of the object.

If you specify a *`starting-point`* of `SEEK_CUR` or `SEEK_END`, *`offset`* can be either positive or negative (a negative offset moves you toward the beginning of the object). With `SEEK_SET`, *`offset`* should always be a non-negative number. A *`starting-point`* of `SEEK_SET` and an *`offset`* of 0 position you to the beginning of the object. A *starting-point* of *SEEK_END* and an offset of 0 position you to the end of the object. If you specify a *starting-point* of SEEK_CUR and an *offset* of 0, your position within the object remains unchanged.

The pg_lo_tell procedure returns your current position within an object. pg_lo_tell requires two parameters:

```
set current_offset [pg_lo_tell connection-handle large-object-handle]
```

You can determine the number of bytes in a large-object by seeking to the end of the object and then finding the offset:

```
...
pg_lo_lseek $conn $object_handle 0 SEEK_CUR
set object_size [pg_lo_tell $conn $object_handle]
...
```

After you have established a position within a large-object, you can read from or write to the object. To write (or modify) data in a large-object, use the pg_lo_write procedure:

```
pg_lo_write connection-handle large-object-handle string length
```

For example, if you want to append a file onto an existing large-object, you would write code similar to this:

```
...
pg_exec $conn "BEGIN"
set fd [open "/images/sadface.jpg"]
set object_handle [pg_lo_open $conn $large_object_oid "rw"]

pg_lo_lseek $conn $object_handle 0 SEEK_END

while { [eof $fd] != 1 } {
  set val [read $fd 1000]
  pg_lo_write $conn $object_handle val [string length $val]
}

close $fd
pg_lo_close $object_handle
pg_exec $conn "COMMIT"
...
```

After opening the file and the large-object, seek to the end of the large-object and then copy from the file handle to the large-object handle, 1000 bytes at a time. We've also called pg_lo_close to close the large-object handle.

When you write to a large-object, you can create *holes* in the data. For example, if you start out with an empty large-object and then seek 100 bytes into it before calling pg_lo_write, you are creating a 100-byte hole at the beginning of the large-object.

Holes are treated as if they contain zeroes. In other words, when you read back this particular large-object, the first 100 bytes will contain nothing but zeroes[5].
You can also read from a large-object in a piece-by-piece manner using pg_lo_lseek and pg_lo_read:

```
...
pg_exec $conn "BEGIN"

set object_handle [pg_lo_open $conn $large_object_oid "r"]

pg_lo_lseek $conn $object_handle 0 SEEK_END
set len [pg_tell $conn $object_handle]
pg_lo_lseek $conn $object_handle 0 SEEK_SET

pg_lo_read $conn $object_handle img $len

image create photo my_photo

my_photo put $img -format gif

pg_lo_close $object_handle
pg_exec $conn "COMMIT"
...
```

As before, you must start a transaction block before using any of the large-object procedures. After opening the large-object (using pg_lo_open), compute the size of the object. The easiest way to find the size of an existing large-object is to seek to the end and then use pg_lo_tell to find the offset of the last byte. After you know the size, you can read the entire object into a string variable using pg_lo_read. In the preceding example, we read the entire large-object in one call to pg_lo_read, but that is not strictly necessary. You can use pg_lo_lseek to move around within the large-object before you read (or write).

One important point here: When you call pg_lo_read (or pg_lo_write), your position within the object is advanced by the number of bytes read (or written).

The pg_lo_read procedure requires four parameters:

```
pg_lo_read connection-handle object-handle varname length
```

5. In case you are wondering, PostgreSQL stores each large-object in a collection of blocks. Each block is typically 2048 bytes long. When you create a hole in a large-object, PostgreSQL will store the minimal number of blocks required to hold the object. If a block within a large-object contains nothing but a hole, it will not take up any physical space in the pg_largeobject table.

The *connection-handle* and *object-handle* parameters should be familiar by now. The *varname* parameter should contain the name of a variable—be careful with this parameter: You don't want to pass the *contents* of a variable; you want to pass the name. So, the following example will usually be incorrect:

```
pg_lo_read $conn $object_handle $img $len
```

This is likely to be wrong because you are passing the contents of the `$img` variable, not the name. You most likely want[6]

```
pg_lo_read $conn $object_handle img $len
```

There is one more large-object procedure that you might need to know about. If you want to remove a large-object from your database, use the `pg_lo_unlink` procedure:

```
pg_unlink $conn $large_object_id
```

Summary

Tcl is a surprisingly simple language.

Having said that, I should point out that solving complex problems is not necessarily easier in Tcl than in other languages, you just have fewer syntactic rules to remember. Tcl is not a panacea, just a really nice little language.

The libpgtcl library fits into Tcl very nicely. If you want to toss together a PostgreSQL client application quickly, explore Tcl and libpgtcl.

6. The only time you would want to pass the value of a variable (as the third parameter) would be when one variable holds the name of another.

17

Using PostgreSQL with Python

PYTHON IS AN OBJECT-ORIENTED PROGRAMMING LANGUAGE. Like Perl, Tcl, and Java, Python is an interpreted language (as opposed to being a *compiled* language such as C or C++). Python supports a number of high-level data structures (lists, tuples, and sequences) that integrate very nicely into the table-oriented world of PostgreSQL.

Python/PostgreSQL Interface Architecture

PostgreSQL usually comes packaged with a Python interface named PyGreSQL. PyGreSQL is a small collection of classes and functions that enable a Python application to interact with a PostgreSQL database. For the last several releases, PyGreSQL has included an alternate interface, which we will call the *DB-API*. The DB-API was designed to offer a portable interface between Python applications and a variety of relational databases. In the case of PostgreSQL, the DB-API is distributed as a wrapper around the PyGreSQL interface. So, when your Python application calls a DB-API function, the DB-API layer translates the request into a PyGreSQL function call. The results from each DB-API function call are translated from PyGreSQL form back into DB-API form and then returned to your application.

In addition to the PyGreSQL interface (and the PyGreSQL/DB-API wrapper), there are at least two other implementations of the DB-API written for PostgreSQL. The first, PsycoPg (isn't that a great name?), can be found at `http://initd.org/Software/psycopg`. The second, PoPy lives at `http://popy.sourceforge.net`. All three of these interfaces are DB-API-compliant—that's good news because you can switch between implementations without major changes to your application.

The alternate implementations (PyscoPg and PoPy) have been designed to maximize performance. The interface distributed with PostgreSQL (PyGreSQL) was implemented as a wrapper, so it probably won't be quite as fast as the other two; but with PyGreSQL, you can pick and choose between the two interface layers.

In this chapter, I'll describe the DB-API interface between Python and PostgreSQL, but not PyGreSQL. Applications written to the DB-API specification can connect to different databases; applications written using PyGreSQL cannot. The *PostgreSQL Programmer's Guide* contains a description of the underlying (or alternate, depending on your perspective) PyGreSQL interface.

Prerequisites

If you want to try the examples in this chapter, you'll probably need to install a few extra pieces of software. You will obviously need Python and PostgreSQL. You'll also need the PyGreSQL interface.

If you are installing PostgreSQL from RPMs, you will find the PyGreSQL interface in the `postgresql-python` RPM.

If you are building PostgreSQL from a source distribution, you must include the `--with-python` flag when you run `configure`. When you run `make install`, the following files will be installed[1]:

```
/usr/lib/python1.5/site-packages/_pgmodule.so
/usr/lib/python1.5/site-packages/pg.py
/usr/lib/python1.5/site-packages/pgdb.py
```

If you intend to use the Python-DB API (which I would recommend), you will also need the `mx` extensions package from Egenix (`http://www.egenix.com/files/python/`).

Some of the examples in this chapter make use of the Tkinter GUI toolkit (more on that later). Tkinter is usually distributed with Python, but you will also need the Tktable module. You can find Tktable.py at our web site: `http://www.conjectrix.com/pgbook/python`.

Client 1—Connecting to the Server

To interact with a PostgreSQL server using Python's DB-API, you must first import the pgdb module. This module defines a few exception classes (we'll talk about exceptions a little later), two classes (`pgdbCnx` and `pgdbCursor`), and a single module function.

The `pgdb.connect()` function returns a connection object (an instance of class `pgdbCnx`). This function actually comes in two flavors:

```
pgdb.connect( dsn )
pgdb.connect( dsn      = dsn,
              user     = user,
              password = password,
              host     = host,
              database = dbname )
```

1. The exact pathnames will depend on your configuration, but the filenames should be the same.

In the first flavor, the *dsn* is expected to be a string of the form:

```
host:database:user:password:opt:tty
```

The rules for composing a valid *dsn* are a bit complex. In the simplest case, you can specify all connection properties in the order shown:

```
"davinci:movies:bruce:cows:-fi:/dev/tty"
```

You can omit leading properties, but you must include the proper number of delimiters (that is, colons):

```
"::bruce:cows:-fi:/dev/tty"          # omit host and database
```

You can omit properties in the middle of the *dsn*, but again, you must include the proper number of colons:

```
"davinci:movies:::-fi:/dev/tty"      # omit user and password
```

You can omit trailing properties, in which case the extra delimiters are optional:

```
"davinci:movies:bruce::: "           # omit password, opt, and tty
"davinci:movies:bruce"               # ditto
```

In the second flavor, you should pass each parameter using Python's named parameter mechanism. For example:

```
pgdb.connect( host='davinci', user='bruce' )
pgdb.connect( host='davinci:5432', user='bruce' )
pgdb.connect( user     = 'bruce',
              password = 'cows',
              host     = 'davinci',
              database = 'movies' )
```

The order in which the parameters appear is unimportant when you use named parameters. Also notice, in the second example, that you can include a port number in the host parameter—just separate the hostname and port number with a colon.

You can also combine the first and second forms:

```
pgdb.connect( dsn = "davinci:movies", user='bruce', password='cows' )
```

In this case, we have used the *dsn* to specify the hostname and database, and named parameters to specify the username and password. If you have duplicate properties, the named parameters take precedence over the properties specified in the *dsn*, for example:

```
pgdb.connect( dsn      = "davinci:movies:sheila",
              user     = "bruce",
              password = "cows" )
```

In this case, we specified a username (`sheila`) in the *dsn*, but we have also supplied a username (`bruce`) with the `user` named parameter; we will connect as user `bruce`.

The PostgreSQL implementation of the DB-API eventually ends up using the libpq library (PostgreSQL's C language API) to do all the low-level communications work. If you've read some of the previous chapters, you might be thinking that you can use environment variables (such as PGDATABASE) to supply default values for connection properties (refer to Table 8.2 for a description of the connection-related environment variables). You may be able to, but for only three of the connection properties: PGHOST, PGPORT, and PGUSER. An apparent bug in Python prevents you from using PGOPTIONS, PGTTY, PGDATABASE, and PGPASSWORD. This problem may be fixed in newer versions of Python, so be sure to test the feature if you need it.

After you have successfully connected, pgdb.connect() returns a connection object. We'll look at some of the things that you can do with a connection object a bit later. For now, let's develop a simple client that establishes a connection to a PostgreSQL server.

Listing 17.1 shows the file client1.py. The first line tells the operating system which interpreter to use to run this script. If your copy of Python is stored in a different location, you should adjust this line to reflect the correct directory. If you are new to Python, you may be surprised to find that there are no block delimiters (curly braces or BEGIN/END pairs) to mark the boundaries of complex statements. Python uses indentation to indicate block boundaries.

Listing 17.1 client1.py

```
 1 #!/usr/bin/python
 2 #
 3 # Filename: client1.py
 4
 5 import pgdb
 6
 7 connection = pgdb.connect( database = "movies",
 8                            user     = "bruce",
 9                            password = "cows" )
10
11 print connection
```

At line 5, you import the pgdb module. When you import a module, all the classes and functions in that module become available for you to use. Next, at lines 7, 8, and 9 you use the pgdb.connect() function to establish a connection to the movies database. Finally, you print the connection object returned by pgdb.connect().

Let's run this client application to see what a connection object looks like:

```
$ chmod a+x client1.py
$ ./client1.py
<pgdb.pgdbCnx instance at 810dd98>
$
```

The single line of output really doesn't tell you anything useful other than your program did *something*. Now, shut down the postmaster and run `client1.py` again so you can see how an error is reported:

```
$ pg_ctl stop
waiting for postmaster to shut down......done
$ ./client1.py
Traceback (innermost last):
  File "./client1.py", line 9, in ?
    password = "cows" )
  File "/usr/lib/python1.5/site-packages/pgdb.py", line 376, in connect
    user = dbuser, passwd = dbpasswd)
    pg.error: could not connect to server: No such file or directory
        Is the server running locally and accepting
        connections on Unix domain socket "/tmp/.s.PGSQL.5432"?
```

Don't you just love being assaulted by error messages like this? If you're a programmer, you probably appreciate the level of detail and a complete context, but our users tend to get upset when they see smoke and flames. Let's clean this up.

Client 2—Adding Error Checking

If you look back to line 7 of Listing 17.1, you'll notice that you call `pgdb.connect()` to connect to a PostgreSQL server. If anything goes wrong during this function call, Python will print a stack trace and abort the program.

If you want to intercept a connection error, you must wrap the call to `pgdb.connect()` in a `try/except` block. The Python DB-API specification defines a hierarchy of exception types that a conforming implementation may throw. The most general exception type is `StandardError`. All other DB-API exceptions are derived (directly or indirectly) from `StandardError`. You might think that to catch a connection failure, you can get away with catching `StandardError` exceptions. Let's try it to see what happens. (Warning: Your *red herring alarm* should be sounding about now.)

Listing 17.2 shows `client2a.py`. Call `pgdb.connect()` inside of a try/except block and catch any exceptions derived from `StandardError` (including `StandardError`).

Listing 17.2 `client2a.py`

```
 1 #!/usr/bin/python
 2 #
 3 # Filename: client2a.py
 4
 5 import pgdb
 6
 7 try:
 8     connection = pgdb.connect( database = "movies",
 9                                user     = "bruce",
10                                password = "cows" )
```

Listing 17.2 **Continued**

```
11     print connection
12
13 except StandardError, e:
14     print str( e )
```

Now, let's run this client to see what a nice error message might look like (note: I have not restarted my Postmaster since the previous example, so I expect an error here):

```
$ chmod a+x client2a.py
$ ./client2a.py
Traceback (innermost last):
  File "./client2a.py", line 10, in ?
    password = "cows" )
  File "/usr/lib/python1.5/site-packages/pgdb.py", line 376, in connect
    user = dbuser, passwd = dbpasswd)
    pg.error: could not connect to server: No such file or directory
        Is the server running locally and accepting
        connections on Unix domain socket "/tmp/.s.PGSQL.5432"?
```

Hey, that's the same message you saw when `client1.py` failed. You are catching `StandardError` exceptions, so the only possible explanation is that `pgdb.connect()` is throwing some other type of exception. You can add a little more code to determine what kind of exception is being thrown (see Listing 17.3).

Listing 17.3 `client2b.py`

```
 1 #!/usr/bin/python
 2 #
 3 # Filename: client2b.py
 4
 5 import pgdb
 6 import sys
 7
 8 try:
 9     connection = pgdb.connect( database = "movies",
10                                user     = "bruce",
11                                password = "cows" )
12     print connection
13
14 except StandardError, e:
15     print str( e )
16
17 except:
18     exception = sys.exc_info()
19
20     print "Unexpected exception:"
21     print "  type : %s" % exception[0]
22     print "  value: %s" % exception[1]
```

In `client2b.py`, you use an untyped `except` clause, so you can catch *any* exception thrown by `pgdb.connect()`. When you catch an exception that has not been derived from `StandardError`, you use the `sys.exc_info()` function to obtain information about the exception. `sys.exc_info()` returns a tuple with three values: `exception[0]` contains the name of the exception type, `exception[1]` contains the exception parameter (usually an error message), and `exception[2]` contains a traceback object. We print the exception type and parameter:

```
$ ./client2b.py
Unexpected exception:
  type : _pg.error
  value: could not connect to server: No such file or directory
        Is the server running locally and accepting
        connections on Unix domain socket "/tmp/.s.PGSQL.5432"?
```

Looking at the results, you can see that `pgdb.connect()` throws an exception of type `_pg.error`. This seems to violate the Python DB-API specification and is most likely a bug. All other PostgreSQL/DB-API functions (other than `pgdb.connect()`)seem to throw the exceptions prescribed by DB-API.

The Python DB-API describes the exception types shown in Table 17.1.

Table 17.1 **DB-API Exception Types**

Exception Type	Derived From	Thrown By
`Warning`	`StandardError`	Not used
`Error`	`StandardError`	Not used
`InterfaceError`	`Error`	`execute()` `executemany()`
`DatabaseError`	`Error`	`execute()` `executemany()`
`DataError`	`DatabaseError`	Not used

`OperationalError`	`DatabaseError`	`execute()`
		`executemany()`
		`commit()`
		`rollback()`
		`cursor()`
		`connect()`

`IntegrityError`	`DatabaseError`	Not used
`InternalError`	`DatabaseError`	Not used
`ProgrammingError`	`DatabaseError`	Not used
`NotSupportedError`	`DatabaseError`	Not used

The first column in Table 17.1 shows the name of each exception. The middle column shows the parent type for each exception. The final column shows the name of each PostgreSQL/DB-API function that throws the exception.

It's important to remember that the DB-API functions can throw exceptions *other* than the ones listed in Table 17.1 (syntax errors, invalid data type errors, and so on). It's usually a good idea to catch specific exceptions that you expect to see with a typed `except` clause and catch unexpected exceptions with an untyped `except`. That's what we've done in `client2a.py`. The first `except` (at line 14) catches exceptions derived from `StandardError`. The second, at line 17, catches all other exceptions.

Now, you have a client application that establishes a connection or reports an error if the connection attempt fails. It's time to do something a little more interesting.

Client 3—Query Processing

To execute a SQL command with Python's DB-API, you must first create a `cursor`. Don't confuse this `cursor` with a cursor created by PostgreSQL's `DECLARE CURSOR` command; they have some similarities, but they are certainly not the same thing, as you will see in this section.

You create a `cursor` object by calling a connection's `cursor()` function[2]. For example, if you have a connection named `connect`, you would create a `cursor` like this:

```
cur = connect.cursor()
```

Notice that the `cursor()` function expects no arguments. You can create multiple `cursor` objects from the same connection; they operate independently, except that a `commit()` or `rollback()` executed on the connection will affect all `cursors` open on that connection.

The next client application (`client3.py`) shows the steps required to create a `cursor`, execute a command, and print the results (see Listing 17.4).

Listing 17.4 `client3.py—main()`

```
 1 #!/usr/bin/python
 2 #
 3 # File: client3.py
 4
 5 import pgdb
 6 import string
 7
 8 #############################################################
 9 def main( ):
10     try:
11         connection = pgdb.connect( database = "movies",
12                                    user     = "bruce",
13                                    password = "cows" )
```

2. It is possible, but extremely unlikely, that a call to `connect.cursor()` can throw a `pgOperationalError` exception. In fact, the only way that can happen is if somebody is messing around with the internals of a `connection` object; and we would *never* do that, would we?

Listing 17.4 **Continued**

```
14
15      except Exception, e:
16          print str( e )
17          exit
18
19      cur = connection.cursor()
20
21      try:
22          cur.execute( "SELECT * FROM customers" )
23          process_results( cur )
24
25      except StandardError, e:
26        print str( e )
27
28      cur.close()
29      connection.close()
30      exit
```

Listing 17.4 shows the `main()` procedure from `client3.py`. You start by calling `pgdb.connect()` to establish a connection to the `movies` database. Lines 15 through 17 take care of any exceptions thrown by `pgdb.connect()`. You take a shortcut here by defining a single exception handler that can catch proper DB-API exceptions as well as the (apparently) erroneous exception thrown by the PostgreSQL interface.

At line 19, you create a new `cursor` object by calling `connection.cursor()`. It is very unlikely that this call to `cursor()` will fail, so we won't bother catching any exceptions. If `cursor()` *does* fail, Python will print a stack trace and an error message and abort your application.

Next, use the `cursor.execute()` function to execute a simple `SELECT` command. If something goes wrong with this command, `execute()` will throw an exception. The text of the error message will be encapsulated in the exception parameter (specifically, `e.args`). If the command completes without error, call the `process_result()` function (see Listing 17.5) to display the result set.

After you have finished with the `cursor` object, close it by calling `cur.close()`. This is not strictly required because Python closes this object for you during garbage collection, but it's usually a good idea.

You also close the `connection` object when you are done with it. Even though you can ignore the `cursor.close()` function, you should get into the habit of closing `connection` objects. In fact, before you call `connection.close()`, you should call `connection.commit()`. Why? Because the PostgreSQL DB-API interface does not run in "auto-commit" mode. When you first call `pgdb.connect()` to establish a connection, the `connect()` function silently executes a `BEGIN` command for you. That means that all commands that you execute belong to a single multistatement transaction until you either `connection.commit()` or `connection.rollback()`. If you fail to commit before you close a connection, any changes made in the most recent transaction are rolled back. Watch out for this—it will bite you if you aren't careful.

Now, let's look at the process_results() function (see Listing 17.5). This function is responsible for formatting and displaying the result of the SELECT command. You don't actually do any of the grunt work in process_results(); instead, you have factored the details into three helper functions.

Listing 17.5 client3.py—process_results()

```
32 ################################################################
33 def process_results( cur ):
34
35     widths = []
36     rows   = cur.fetchall()
37     cols   = cur.description
38
39     compute_widths( cur, widths, rows, cols )
40     print_headers( cur, widths, cols )
41     print_values( cur, widths, rows )
```

Start by defining an (empty) array that holds the display width for each column in the result set. You pass this array to your helper functions, so you define it here.

Next, use the cursor.fetchall() function to retrieve all rows from the result set. The cursor.fetchall() function returns a sequence of sequences[3]. Each member of this sequence represents a single row. So, to get to the second column in the third row, you would use the following:

```
print rows[2][1] # sequence indexes start at 0, not 1
```

Besides cursor.fetchall(), there are two other functions that return all or part of a result set. The cursor.fetchone() function fetches the next row in a result set. fetchone() returns a sequence or returns None if you have exhausted the result set. The cursor.fetchmany([size=*n*]) function returns the next *n* rows in the result set. If you omit the size parameter, fetchmany() will assume that *n*=5. If there are fewer than *n* rows remaining in the result set, fetchmany() will return all remaining rows. If the result set has been exhausted, fetchmany() will return None. Like fetchall(), fetchmany() returns a sequence of one or more sequences.

Notice that there is no way to go *backward* in the result set. You can't refetch a row after you have gone past it, nor can you "rewind" the result set to the beginning. If you need to move around in the result set, use fetchall() or declare a PostgreSQL cursor (not a DB-API cursor) and execute the FETCH commands yourself.

3. If you're not familiar with Python, think of a "sequence of sequences" as "an array of arrays" or maybe as a "list of lists." They are not completely analogous, but close enough to understand that fetchall() returns a collection of collections.

After you have retrieved all the rows in the result set, nab the column metadata from `cursor.description`. Notice that `cursor.description` is a public data member, not a function. `cursor.description` is a list of seven-element lists. Table 17.2 shows the meaning of each sublist.

Table 17.2 `cursor.description` **Metadata Values**

Element	Meaning
0	Column name
1	Data type
2	Maximum display size
3	Server size (in bytes)
4	Precision (not used)
5	Scale (not used)
6	Null allowed? (not used)

Currently, the PyGreSQL DB-API implementation does not use the last three elements in the table (precision, scale, and null allowed?); they are always set to `None`. The data type member does not conform to the DB-API specification, but it's probably more useful that way. Data types are reported by their PostgreSQL names (`char`, `oid`, `float4`, and so on). The display size and server size elements are set to –1 for any variable-sized columns.

We will be using the column names a little later, so we store them in the local variable `cols`.

Now that you have access to the data (rows) and the metadata (cols), call each of your helper functions in the right order. `compute_widths()` computes the width of each column name, storing the result in the `widths` array (see Listing 17.6). Next, `print_headers()` prints column headings. Finally, `print_values()` prints the entire result set.

Listing 17.6 `client3.py—compute_widths()`

```
43 ################################################################
44 def compute_widths( cur, widths, rows, cols ):
45
46     c = 0
47
48     for col in cols:
49         widths.append( len( col[0] ))
50         c = c + 1
51
52     r = 0
53
54     for row in rows:
```

Listing 17.6 **Continued**

```
55          c = 0
56
57          for col in row:
58              if( len( str( col )) > widths[c] ):
59                  widths[c] = len( str( col ))
60              c = c + 1
61          r = r + 1
```

The `compute_widths()` function computes the width of each column in the result set.

Start by walking through the list of column names and appending the length of each name to the `widths[]` array. Remember, the caller (`process_results()`) gave you a complete metadata array in the `cols` parameter. Element 0 of each metadata list is the column name.

Next, you have to find the widest value in each column of the result set. The caller gave you a list of all the rows in the result set in the `rows` parameter. As you process each column in each row of the result set, you increase the corresponding element in the `widths[]` array to its maximum required width.

Notice (in lines 58 and 59) that you convert each data value into string form before you call the `len()` function. The result set can contain `integer` values, `string` values, `float` values, and so on. You can't invoke the `len()` function on a numeric value so convert them into string form first.

You can view the actual Python data types using the `type()` function:

```
>>> cur.execute( "SELECT * FROM pg_class" )
>>> c = 0
>>> for col in cur.fetchone():
...     print cur.description[c][0], '\t', col, '\t', type(col)
...     c = c+1
...
relname         pg_type <type 'string'>
reltype         71L     <type 'long int'>
relowner        1       <type 'int'>
relam           0L      <type 'long int'>
relfilenode     1247L   <type 'long int'>
relpages        2       <type 'int'>
reltuples       143.0   <type 'float'>
reltoastrelid   0L      <type 'long int'>
reltoastidxid   0L      <type 'long int'>
relhasindex     1       <type 'int'>
relisshared     0       <type 'int'>
relkind         r       <type 'string'>
relnatts        17      <type 'int'>
relchecks       0       <type 'int'>
reltriggers     0       <type 'int'>
relukeys        0       <type 'int'>
```

```
relfkeys        0       <type 'int'>
relrefs         0       <type 'int'>
relhasoids      1       <type 'int'>
relhaspkey      0       <type 'int'>
relhasrules     0       <type 'int'>
relhassubclass  0       <type 'int'>
relacl          None    <type 'None'>
```

Listing 17.7 shows the `print_headers()` function.

Listing 17.7 `client3.py—print_headers()`

```
63 ################################################################
64 def print_headers( cur, widths, cols ):
65
66     c = 0;
67
68     for col in cols:
69         print string.center( col[0], widths[c] ),
70         c = c + 1
71     print
72
73     c = 0;
74
75     for col in cur.description:
76         print '-' * widths[c],
77         c = c + 1
78     print
```

`print_headers()` centers each column name within the width calculated by `compute_widths()`. You may have noticed that you have a dangling comma at the end of line 69 (and again at the end of line 76). Those aren't typos—a dangling comma suppresses the new-line character that `print` would otherwise emit. You want all the column names to appear on the same line, so suppress all new-lines until you get to line 71 (or 78 in the case of the second loop).

Following the column names, print a line of separator characters (hyphens). When you apply the multiply operator (`*`) to a string, as in line 76, the result is a string of repeated characters. You create the separator strings my "multiplying" a dash by the width of each column.

Listing 17.8 shows the remaining code in `client3.py`. The `print_values()` function loops through each row and column in the result set (`rows`). At line 89, convert each value to string form, left-justify it within the proper column, and print it.

Listing 17.8 `client3.py—print_values()` **and mainline**

```
80 ################################################################
81 def print_values( cur, widths, rows ):
82
```

Listing 17.8 **Continued**

```
83     r = 0
84
85     for row in rows:
86         c = 0
87
88         for col in row:
89             print string.ljust( str(col), widths[c] ),
90             c = c + 1
91         r = r + 1
92         print
93
94
95 ############################################################
96
97 main()
```

The mainline code (that is, the entry point for your client application) is at line 97—just call the `main()` function and exit when `main()` returns.

Now, run this application:

```
$ chmod a+x client3.py
$ ./client3.py
id    customer_name        phone   birth_date
-- -------------------- -------- ----------
1  Jones, Henry         555-1212 1970-10-10
2  Rubin, William       555-2211 1972-07-10
3  Panky, Henry         555-1221 1968-01-21
4  Wonderland, Alice N. 555-1122 1969-03-05
7  Grumby, Jonas        None     1984-02-21
```

At this point, you know how to connect to a PostgreSQL server from Python, how to intercept errors, and how to process `SELECT` commands. In the next section, we'll develop an interactive command processor using Python and the Tkinter GUI module.

Client 4—An Interactive Command Processor

The next client is an interactive command processor. The basic Python language distribution does not include any tools for building graphical applications. Instead, you can add GUI toolkits to Python based on your needs. If you don't need graphics, you won't have to weigh down your application with extra code. If you *do* need graphics in your application, you can choose the toolkit best suited to your requirements.

We'll use the Tkinter toolkit for our command processor. If you read the previous chapter, you know that Tk is a portable toolkit originally designed for the Tcl language. Tkinter is a Python wrapper around the Tk graphics toolkit. Using Tkinter, you can create and manipulate Tk widgets (buttons, windows, scrollbars, and so on) from Python applications.

The application that you will build should look like Figure 17.1 when you are finished. When you run this program, you can enter an arbitrary PostgreSQL command in the text entry widget, press Return, and then view the results in the table widget below. You'll also place a status line in the middle of the window so you can show error messages and row counts.

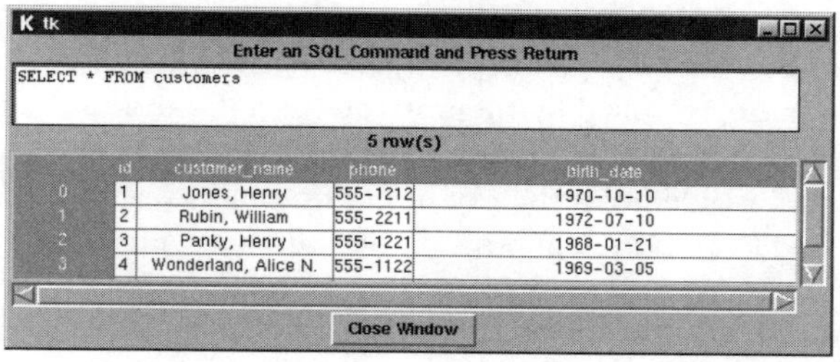

Figure 17.1 The `client4.py` application.

This application (`client4.py`) is a bit larger than the other Python clients you have seen so far (see Listing 17.9). Start by importing the `pgdb` module (as usual) and two Tk-related modules: `Tkinter` and `Tktable`. `Tkinter` is the basic Tk GUI toolkit. `Tktable` is an extension to `Tkinter` that adds a table widget. The source code for `Tktable` is a little hard to find on the Web, but you will find it with the sample code for this chapter at `http://www.conjectrix.com/pgbook`.

Listing 17.9 `client4.py—PGDialog.init()`

```
 1 #!/usr/bin/python
 2 #
 3 # File: client4.py
 4
 5 import pgdb
 6 from Tkinter import *
 7 from Tktable import Table,ArrayVar
 8
 9 class PGDialog:
10 ################################################
11     def __init__( self ):
12         self.widths  = []
13         self.conn    = None
14         # Widgets
15         self.table   = None
16         self.command = None
17         self.status  = None
```

At line 9, you declare the `PGDialog` class. You use `PGDialog` as a single container for all the variables that you would otherwise need to pass between member functions.

It may not be obvious because of the formatting requirements of this book, but all the functions defined in `client4.py` are members of the `PGDialog` class.

The `__init__()` function is called whenever you create an instance of a `PGDialog` object. C++ and Java programmers will recognize `__init__()` as a constructor. Inside of this constructor, you initialize all member variables to a known state.

You use the `self.widths[]` member variable to hold the computed width for each column. `self.widths[]` is filled by the `set_column_headers()` function, modified by `fill_table()`, and used by `size_columns()`.

The `self.conn` variable holds the `connection` object that we create in `main()`.

`self.table`, `self.command`, and `self.status` are widgets that you need to manipulate. All widgets are created in the `build_dialog()` function.

Listing 17.10 shows `PGDialog.main()`. This function is called when you want to display the dialog (refer to Figure 17.1) to the user.

Listing 17.10 `client4.py—PGDialog.main()`

```
19 ###############################################
20     def main( self ):
21
22         self.conn = pgdb.connect( database="movies" )
23
24         self.build_dialog( )
25         self.table.mainloop( )
```

At line 22, call `pgdb.connect()` to establish a connection to the PostgreSQL server. Notice that you won't catch any exceptions thrown by `pgdb.connect()`—if this call fails, your application can't do anything useful, so you just let Python print an error message and end. If you want to embed the `PGDialog` class in a larger application, you'll want to add some error checking here.

Assuming that `pgdb.connect()` returned successfully, you call the `build_dialog()` function to create all required widgets. Next, call Tk's `mainloop()` function. `mainloop()` displays the dialog and waits for user interaction. `mainloop()` does not return until the user closes the dialog window.

Listing 17.11 shows PGDialog.build_dialog().

Listing 17.11 `client4.py—PGDialog.build_dialog()`

```
28 ###############################################
29     def build_dialog( self ):
30
31         root = Tk()
32
33         self.make_table( root )
34
```

Listing 17.11 **Continued**

```
35         self.command = Text( root, height=3 )
36         self.status  = Label( root )
37
38         close = Button( root,
39                         text="Close Window",
40                         command=root.destroy )
41
42         label = Label( root,
43                        text="Enter an SQL Command and Press Return")
44
45         self.command.focus_force( )
46
47         self.command.bind( "<Return>", self.execute )
48
49         sy = Scrollbar( root,
50                         command=self.table.yview )
51
52         sx = Scrollbar( root,
53                         command=self.table.xview,
54                         orient="horizontal" )
55
56         self.table.config( xscrollcommand=sx.set,
57                            yscrollcommand=sy.set )
58
59         label.grid( row=0 )
60
61         self.command.grid( row=1, sticky='news' )
62         self.status.grid( row=2 )
63         self.table.grid( row=3, column=0, sticky='news' )
64
65         sy.grid( row=3, column=1, sticky='news' )
66         sx.grid( row=4, sticky='ew' )
67         close.grid( row=5 )
68
69         root.columnconfigure( 0, weight=1 )
70
71         root.rowconfigure( 1, weight=0 )
72         root.rowconfigure( 3, weight=1 )
73         root.rowconfigure( 5, weight=0 )
```

The `build_dialog()` function is responsible for creating and arranging the widgets in your dialog. At line 31, you construct a `Tk` object named `root`. You will use `root` as the parent window for all the widgets that you create.

Next, call the `make_table()` member function (see Listing 17.12) to create a `Tktable` widget. You won't know how many rows and columns you will need in the table until you execute a `SELECT` command, but you can configure everything else now.

Lines 35 through 42 create a few more child widgets that you will display on the dialog. `self.command` is a text entry widget that holds the command text entered by the user. `self.status` is a simple Label widget—you will display error messages and row counts in this widget (if you refer to Figure 17.1, `self.status` is the part that says "`5(rows)`").

The `close` widget is a `Button` that displays the text "`Close Window`". When the user clicks on this button, Tk will execute the command `root.destroy`, closing the application.

You create the `label` widget to display a prompt ("`Enter an SQL Command and Press Return`") to the user.

At line 45, you move the keyboard focus to the `command` (text entry) widget. That way, the cursor is positioned in the right place when this application starts running.

Next, *bind* a chunk of Python code to the `Return` key. When the command widget has the keyboard focus and the user presses `Return`, you call the `self.execute()` function (refer to Listing 17.5). The `self.execute()` function grabs any text that the user typed into the `command` widget and sends it to the PostgreSQL server.

The next few lines of code (lines 49 through 57) create a vertical scrollbar (`sy`) and horizontal scrollbar (`sx`) and connect them to the `self.table` widget. The `Tktable` widget won't automatically display scrollbars, so you have to wire them in manually.

Lines 59 through 67 arrange all the widgets using Tk's `grid` layout manager. Refer to Figure 17.1. We lay out the child widgets in a `grid` of unevenly sized cells. The `label` widget appears at the top of your dialog, so place it in row 0 (because you have only a single widget in row 0, the column is irrelevant). Next, place the `command` (text entry) widget in the second row (`row=1`). The third row (row=2) contains the `status` widget. The fourth row actually contains two widgets: the `table` widget on the left (`column=0`) and the `sy` vertical scrollbar on the right (`column=1`). The horizontal scrollbar (`sx`) and `close` button are placed in the last two rows.

The "`sticky`" stuff is taking care of widget placement *within* each grid cell. If you don't specify any `sticky` options, each widget is centered (vertically and horizontally) within its own cell. `sticky=news` means that you want the `grid` layout manager to *stick* a widget to the *n*orth (top), *e*ast (right), *w*est (left), and *s*outh (bottom) side of its cell.

The final four lines in this function tell the layout manager how to stretch or compress the widgets whenever the user resizes the `root` window. You want the `table` widget (which is positioned in column 0) to resize, but the vertical scrollbar to remain the same; so you give column 0 a resize *weight* of 1. You also want the `command` widget (row 1) and the `close` button to stay the same size, so you give those rows a weight of 0.

Give yourself a quick break—the next few functions are mercifully short.

Listing 17.12 `client4.py—PGDialog.make_table()`

```
75 ##############################################
76     def make_table( self, parent ):
77
78         var = ArrayVar( parent )
79
80         self.table = Table( parent,
81                             variable=var,
82                             titlerows=1,
83                             titlecols=1,
84                             roworigin=-1,
85                             colorigin=-1,
86                             colstretchmode='last',
87                             rowstretchmode='last' )
```

The `make_table()` function creates a `Table` widget and does some preliminary configuration work. A `Table` widget requires a variable that it can use to hold the actual data values that you stuff into the table. Fortunately, the `Tktable.py` module (remember, you imported that module at the beginning of this application) defines a data type custom-made to work with a `Tktable`. At line 78, you create an instance of `Tktable.ArrayVar()`.

Next, create the `table` widget and configure a few options. First, tell the table to use `var` as its data variable. Next, you arrange to reserve the top row for column headers and the leftmost column for row numbering. Normally, the first row in a table is row 0; likewise, the first column is usually column 0. For convenience, we will change the table origin to `-1,--1`. That way, the title row is row –1 and the first *data* row is row 0. We pull a similar trick with the column-numbering scheme.

You also set the column stretch mode and row stretch mode. `colstretchmode` and `rowstretchmode` determine how the `table` will behave when you resize it. A value of `'last'` resizes the last row (or column) to fill extra space.

The `execute()` function is called whenever the `table` widget holds the focus and the user presses the `Return` key (see Listing 17.13). You arranged for this behavior back at line 47 (refer to Listing 17.11).

Listing 17.13 `client4.py—PGDialog.execute()`

```
89 ##############################################
90     def execute( self, event ):
91
92         self.process_command( self.command.get( "1.0", "end" ))
```

This function is simple—you first retrieve the contents of the `command` widget and then call `self.process_command()` with that text. If you have trouble seeing the flow in this function, you could have written it as follows:

```
...
text = self.command.get( "1.0", "end" )

self.process_command( text )
...
```

The `process_command()` function (see Listing 17.14) is where things start to get interesting again. This function is called whenever the user wants to execute a command. Start by creating a new `cursor` object (remember, a DB-API `cursor` is *not* the same as a PostgreSQL cursor).

Listing 17.14 `client4.py—PGDialog.process_command()`

```
 94 ###############################################
 95     def process_command ( self, command ):
 96
 97         cur = self.conn.cursor()
 98
 99         try:
100             cur.execute( command )
101             self.load_table( cur )
102
103         except Exception, e:
104             from mx.TextTools import collapse
105             self.status.configure( text=collapse( str( e )))
106
```

Next, call the `cursor.execute()` function to execute the `command` provided by the caller. If the command completes without error, call the `load_table()` function (refer to Listing 17.15) to display the results. If anything goes wrong, `cursor.execute()` will throw an exception. You catch any exceptions at line 103. You want to display error messages in the `status` widget, which is only one line high. So, use the `mx.TextTools.collapse()` function to remove any new-line characters from the text of the error message before copying the message into the `status` widget.

> **A Few More Ways to Execute PostgreSQL Commands**
>
> So far, all the examples in this chapter have used a simple form of the `cursor.execute()` method to execute PostgreSQL commands. When you call `cursor.execute()`, you call it with a complete command.
>
> You can also call `cursor.execute()` with a *parameterized* command and collection of parameter values. A parameterized command contains placeholders (also known as parameter markers) in which you can

substitute values. For example, assume that you have a `dictionary` that holds two values, one named `min` and one named `max`:

```
...
>>> min_max = { 'min':2, 'max':4 }
...
```

You can execute a command such as[4]

```
...
>>> cmd="SELECT * FROM customers WHERE id >= %(min)d AND id <= %(max)d"
>>>
>>> cur.execute( cmd % min_max )
>>> cur.fetchall()
[
  [2, 'Rubin, William', '555-2211', '1972-07-10'],
  [3, 'Panky, Henry', '555-1221', '1968-01-21'],
  [4, 'Wonderland, Alice N.', '555-1122', '1969-03-05']
]
...
```

In this example, the `SELECT` command includes two placeholders: `%(min)d` and `%(max)d`. Python replaces the first placeholder with the `min` value from `dictionary min_max` and the second placeholder with the `max` value. In effect, you are executing the following command:

```
SELECT * FROM customers WHERE id >= 2 AND id <= 4
```

You can also refer to *other* variables by name in a parameterized command:

```
...
>>>  min = 2
>>>  max = 4
>>>  cmd="SELECT * FROM customers WHERE id >= %(min)d AND id <= %(max)d"
>>>  cur.execute( cmd % vars())
>>>  cur.fetchall()
[
  [2, 'Rubin, William', '555-2211', '1972-07-10'],
  [3, 'Panky, Henry', '555-1221', '1968-01-21'],
  [4, 'Wonderland, Alice N.', '555-1122', '1969-03-05']
]
...
```

I don't want to give you the impression that parameterized commands are a feature unique to the Python/PostgreSQL interface. In fact, we are simply using Python's string formatting operator. You still have to be sure that the end result (that is, the result after formatting) is a valid SQL command—you must quote strings properly, and you can't simply bind `None` where you really want `NULL` to appear.

4. The results returned by `cur.fetchall()` have been reformatted for clarity.

Note that finding documentation for Python's string formatting operator is notoriously difficult. You can find this information in the *Python Library Reference Manual*: Built-in Functions, Types, and Exceptions; Built-in Types; Sequence Types; String Formatting Operations.

Besides `cursor.execute()`, you can use the `cursor.executemany()` function to execute PostgreSQL commands. The `executemany()` function executes a command repeatedly, substituting new parameter values with each iteration. For example, let's create a list of `tuple` values that we want to `INSERT` into the `tapes` table:

```
>>> vals = \
... [
...     ( 'TH-X1138', 'This Island Earth' ),
...     ( 'MST-3000', 'Python' ),
...     ( 'B-MOVIE1', 'Frogs' ),
...     ( 'B-MOVIE2', 'Bats' )
... ]
```

Now we can `INSERT` all four tuples with a single command:

```
>>> cmd = "INSERT INTO tapes VALUES( %s, %s )"
>>> cur.executemany( cmd, vals )
```

You can use `cursor.execute()` and `cursor.executemany()` to simplify your code. Using these functions, you can factor the code that executes a command and the code that produces parameter values into two separate functions.

The function in Listing 17.15, `load_table()`,loads the result of a command into the `status` widget and the `table` widget. Start by setting the `status` widget: We query `cur.rowcount` to find the number of rows and format this value into a nice, polite message.

Listing 17.15 `client4.py—PGDialog.load_table()`

```
108 ##############################################
109     def load_table( self, cur ):
110
111         self.status.configure( text= "%d row(s)" % cur.rowcount )
112
113         self.size_table( cur )
114
115         if( cur.description == None ):
116             return
117
118         self.set_column_headers( cur )
119
120         self.fill_table( cur )
121
122         self.size_columns( cur )
```

Next, call the `size_table()` function (see Listing 17.16) to configure the `table` widget to the proper number of rows and columns.

At line 115, decide whether you are processing a `SELECT` command or some other type of command. A `SELECT` command is the only type of command that will return column metadata (`cur.description`). If you don't have metadata, you are finished. Otherwise, copy the column headers into the table (see Listing 17.17), copy the data values into the table (Listing 17.18), and size each column to match the data (Listing 17.19).

Listing 17.16 `client4.py—PGDialog.size_table()`

```
124 ##############################################
125     def size_table( self, cur ):
126
127         if( cur.description == None ):
128             self.table.configure( rows=0, cols=0 )
129         else:
130             col_cnt = len( cur.description )
131             row_cnt = cur.rowcount
132
133             self.table.configure( rows=row_cnt+1, cols=col_cnt+1 )
```

The `size_table()` function configures the `table` widget to hold the proper number of rows and columns. If you have no metadata, size the table to hold 0 rows and 0 columns (metadata is returned for only a `SELECT` command).

If you have metadata, you can look into the `cursor` object to find the number of rows and (indirectly) the number columns in the result set. Finding the row count is easy—each `cursor` object contains a data member named `rowcount`. Finding the column count is a bit more complex—you have to count the number of sequences in the metadata list.

After you know how many rows and columns are present in the result set, configure `self.table` to hold one extra row (for the column headers) and one extra column (for row numbers).

Listing 17.17 `client4.py—PGDialog.set_column_headers()`

```
135 ##############################################
136     def set_column_headers( self, cur ):
137
138         col_no = 0
139
140         for col in cur.description:
141             self.table.set( "-1," + str(col_no), col[0] )
142             self.widths.append(len( col[0] ))
143             col_no = col_no + 1
144
```

The `set_column_headers()` function tackles two different problems. First, it copies the name of each column in the result set into the first row of `self.table`. Second, it initializes the `self.widths[]` array to hold the width of each column header.

The `cur.description` data member is a `list` of `tuples`—each `tuple` corresponds to one column in the result set. The first member of each tuple contains the column name. Refer to Table 17.2 for more information on the contents of `cur.description`.

Listing 17.18 `client4.py—PGDialog.fill_table()`

```
146 ################################################
147     def fill_table( self, cur ):
148
149         rows = cur.fetchall()
150
151         r = 0
152         for row in rows:
153             c = 0
154
155             for col in row:
156
157                 self.table.set( str(r) + "," + str(c), str( col ))
158
159                 if( col != None ):
160                     if( len( str( col )) > self.widths[c] ):
161                         self.widths[c] = len( str( col ))
162
163                 c = c + 1
164
165             self.table.set( str(r) + ",-1", str(r))
166
167             r = r + 1
```

Listing 17.18 shows the `PGDialog.fill_table()` function. This function looks complicated, but it's actually very simple. You have a pair of nested loops: The outer loop iterates through each row in the result set and the inner loop iterates through each column in the current row.

In the inner loop, you convert each data value into string form and copy it into the proper cell in the `table` widget (line 157). You also use the length of each value to update the `self.widths[]` array. You'll use the `widths[]` array to set each column in the table to the proper width. You want each column to be wide enough to display the widest value in the column, so you have to measure each value as you encounter it.

After you have finished processing the data values in each row, copy the row number into the leftmost column of `self.table`.

Listing 17.19 `client4.py—PGDialog.size_columns()`

```
169 ##############################################
170     def size_columns( self, cur ):
171         col_cnt = len( cur.description )
172
173         for col in range( 0, col_cnt ):
174             self.table.width( col, self.widths[col] )
```

`size_columns()` is the last function in `client4.py`. This function is responsible for configuring each column in `self.table` to the proper width. You computed the optimal width of each column in the `fill_table()` and `set_column_headers()` functions.

Listing 17.20 shows the mainline code for `client4.py`. These are the first executable commands outside of `PGDialog`, so execution begins at line 178. Getting this program up and running is pretty easy; you create an instance of the PgDialog class and then invoke that object's `main()` function (refer to Listingv 17.9).

Listing 17.20 `client4.py`**—mainline code**

```
176 ##############################################
177
178 obj = PGDialog()
179 obj.main( )
```

Summary

In this chapter, we've shown you the Python DB-API (version 2.0). There are at least three implementations of the PostgreSQL/DB-API interface; we've used the PyGreSQL implementation because that it is the one you are most likely to have (it's distributed with PostgreSQL).

As we mentioned at the start of this chapter, you can also use the PyGreSQL interface without using the DB-API wrapper. PyGreSQL is a nifty toolkit, but the DB class offers some nice features.

You've made it through all the chapters devoted to PostgreSQL programming. In the next section, we'll be examining the administrative tasks involved in creating and maintaining a PostgreSQL environment.

III

PostgreSQL Administration

18

Introduction to PostgreSQL Administration

THIS BOOK IS DIVIDED INTO THREE PARTS. The first part of the book was designed as a guide to new PostgreSQL users. The middle section covered PostgreSQL programming. The third section is devoted to the topic of PostgreSQL administration. These three parts correspond to the real-world roles that we play when using PostgreSQL.

Users are concerned mostly with getting data into the database and getting it back out again. Programmers try to provide users with the functionality that they need. Administrators are responsible for ensuring that programmers and end-users can perform their jobs. Quite often, one person will fill two or three roles at the same time.

When you wear the hat of an administrator, you ensure that your users can store their data in a secure, reliable, high-availability, high-performance database.

Secure means that your data is safe from intruders. You must ensure that authorized users can do the things they need to do. You also need to ensure that users cannot gain access to data that they should not see.

Reliable means the data that goes into a database can be retrieved without corruption. Any data transformations should be expected, not accidental.

High-availability means that the database is available when needed. Your users should expect that the database is ready to use when they log in. Routine maintenance should follow a predictable schedule and should not interfere with normal use. High-availability may also affect your choice of operating system and hardware. You may want to choose a cluster configuration to prevent problems in the event of a single point of failure.

High-performance means that a user should be able to perform required tasks within an acceptable amount of time. A high-performance database should also feel responsive.

In this chapter, I'll introduce you to some of the tasks that a PostgreSQL administrator must perform. The remaining chapters cover each topic in greater detail.

Security

A PostgreSQL administrator is responsible for ensuring that authorized users can do what they need to do. An administrator is also responsible for making sure that authorized users can do *only* what they need to do. Another critical job is to keep intruders away from the user's data.

There are two aspects to PostgreSQL security—authentication and access. Authentication ensures that a user is in fact who he claims to be. After you are satisfied that a user has proven his identity, you must ensure that he can access the data that he needs.

Each user (or group) requires access to a specific set of resources. For example, an accounting clerk needs access to vendor and customer records, but may not require access to payroll data. A payroll clerk, on the other hand, needs access to payroll data, but not to customer records. One of your jobs as an administrator is to grant the proper privileges to each user.

Another aspect of security in general is the problem of securing PostgreSQL's runtime environment. Depending on your security requirements (that is, the sensitivity of your data), it may be appropriate to install network firewalls, secure routers, and possibly even biometric access controls. Securing your runtime environment is a problem that is not unique to PostgreSQL, and I won't explore that topic further in this book.

Chapter 21, "Security," shows you how to grant and revoke user privileges and also covers how to prevent tampering by intruders.

User Accounts

As an administrator, you are responsible for creating, maintaining, and deleting user accounts. Your first challenge will be deciding how to map real people into PostgreSQL identities. One option is to have each user connect to PostgreSQL with a unique identity. That's usually a good policy to start with, but in some circumstances may not be practical. For example, if you are running a web site that uses PostgreSQL as the backend database, you may not want to create a unique user account for every person who connects to your web site. A good way to solve this sort of problem is to create unique identities for the users who you know, and a generic (or anonymous) identity for unknown guests.

You have to know how to create user accounts and user groups. You also need to choose authentication methods. Except in the case of anonymous guest accounts, you will want a user to prove his or her identity in some fashion. PostgreSQL offers many authentication methods, ranging from `trust` (which means that you trust that the host operating system has already authenticated the user) to password-based authentication to Kerberos authentication. Which authentication method(s) you choose will depend on how sensitive your data is and how secure you feel the host environment is.

Chapter 19, "General PostgreSQL Administration," shows you how to maintain user accounts and user groups. Chapter 21, "Security" shows you how to choose authentication methods.

Backup and Restore

Okay, I'll admit it. A few years ago I lost two *months'* worth of development work when my hard drive crashed. I had not backed up my source code. That was a painful lesson. Fortunately, software is always better the second time you create it. That is not true for most data. Imagine losing two months' worth of customer transactions.

Database backups are critically important. Some types of data can be re-created, but it's usually easier to load an archive tape than to remanufacture lost data.

You may already have a backup plan in place for archiving filesystem data. That may not be a good solution for backing up data hosted in a PostgreSQL database. For one thing, you must shut down the database server if you choose to archive the filesystem.

PostgreSQL provides a set of utilities that you can use to archive and restore individual tables or entire databases. You can use these utilities on a live server (that is, you don't have to shut down the database first). Using the `pg_dump` and `pg_dumpall` utilities, you can also compress archive data on-the-fly.

Chapter 19 shows you how to use the `pg_dump` and `pg_dumpall` utilities and how to recover data from an archive.

Time for another confession. Not too long ago, I needed to recover some code from an archive that had been created the previous night. (Yes, I did something stupid, and the easiest way to undo it was to restore from backup.) I was surprised to find that, even though an archive had been made the previous night, I could not read from the tape because I had been using the wrong commands to create the archives. It's not enough to have a good backup plan—test your restore procedures as well.

Server Startup and Shutdown

There are a variety of ways to start and stop the PostgreSQL server. In earlier chapters, you used the `pg_ctl` command to perform server startup and shutdown. `pg_ctl` is a shell script that controls the `postmaster`; in some circumstances, you may want to bypass `pg_ctl` and interact directly with the `postmaster`. You'll learn how to do that in the next chapter.

In most cases, you will want the `postmaster` to start when your host system boots. You'll also want the `postmaster` to shut down gracefully whenever the host is powered down. The method you use to accomplish this varies with the host operating system. In Chapter 19, "General PostgreSQL Administration," you'll learn how to arrange for boot-time startup and graceful shutdown for a few of the more common operating systems.

Tuning

Chapter 4, "Performance," covered the basics of performance analysis and query tuning in PostgreSQL. As an administrator, you need to ensure that your users are getting the best possible performance from the database. Application developers are usually responsible for tuning the interaction between their application and the database, but the administrator is responsible for the performance of the database as a whole.

PostgreSQL provides a number of configuration parameters that control the query planner and optimizer. Starting with release 7.2, PostgreSQL also offers performance-monitoring tools that you can use to watch for poor performance before your users complain.

If you are an administrator, it's a good idea to review the material in Chapter 4. Understanding performance monitoring and tuning will help narrow your focus when you are tracking down a performance problem.

You should also formulate a plan for periodic routine maintenance. For example, you decide that you should `VACUUM` and `VACUUM ANALYZE` all tables every weekend. You may also want to `CLUSTER` important tables on a regular basis.

Installing Updates

The PostgreSQL database is constantly evolving. As a PostgreSQL administrator, you will occasionally need to upgrade an existing database to a new release. Fortunately, upgrading an existing database is usually a simple process.

In most cases, the only work required to move to a new release is to dump the entire database cluster (using `pg_dumpall`), install the new software, and restore from the dump. Installing a new release this way is nearly identical to performing a backup and restore operation. For some upgrade paths, you don't even need to dump/restore—the new release includes a `pg_upgrade` utility that upgrades your data in place.

Localization

Localization often involves the administrator. In many organizations, you will find that different users speak different languages. A user who speaks French prefers to see messages and help text in French. A user who speaks German prefers to interact with the database (as much as possible) using the German language. You also might find that you need to store data in character sets other than ASCII.

PostgreSQL can accommodate both of these issues. PostgreSQL can be *localized* into different languages and different cultural preferences. PostgreSQL can also store data using a variety of character encoding. Chapter 20, "Internationalization/Localization," provides an in-depth discussion of the issues involved in providing localized access to your users.

Summary

This short introduction to PostgreSQL administration should give you an overview of the tasks that you might have to perform as a PostgreSQL Administrator. The next few chapters fill in the details. I'll start by describing the alternatives for starting and stopping a PostgreSQL server. Next, I'll show you how to manage user accounts. Then I'll move on to the topic of backup and restore procedures. Later chapters will cover internationalization, localization, and security.

19

PostgreSQL Administration

THIS CHAPTER EXPLORES THE ROLE OF THE PostgreSQL administrator. You start by looking at the on-disk organization of a typical PostgreSQL installation. Next, you'll see how to install PostgreSQL from source code or from prebuilt binaries on Unix and Windows hosts. After that, you'll learn how to create new database clusters and new databases. We will also talk about managing user accounts and managing user groups. Then, you will see how to arrange for the database server to start up automatically when you boot your system (and how to shut down gracefully when you halt your system). We'll finish this chapter by discussing your options for backup and recovery.

Roadmap (Where's All My Stuff?)

I find it much easier to administer a product if I know where every component is located. With that in mind, let's explore the directory structure for a "standard" PostgreSQL installation.

When you install PostgreSQL, whether from an RPM (Red Hat Package Manager) or from source, it will be configured to install into a particular set of directories. The exact location for any given set of PostgreSQL files is determined when the package is built from source code.

When you build a copy of PostgreSQL from source code (more on that a little later), the `--prefix=`*`directory-name`* flag determines the installation directory. The default value for `--prefix` is `/usr/local/pgsql`. You can change this by supplying a different prefix directory when you run the `configure` program:

```
$ ./configure --prefix=/home/bruce/pg731
```

If you want more control over the location of each component, you can add some more options to the `configure` command line. Table 19.1 shows the location of each component. The leftmost column shows the name of a `configure` option, the second column lists PostgreSQL components, and the last column shows the component type.

If you want, for example, to place the PostgreSQL shared libraries in a particular directory, you would add `--libdir=`*`location`* to the `configure` command line.

Table 19.1 **PostgreSQL Executable, Library, and Header Locations**

Directory Name	Filename	File Type
bindir	clusterdb	shell script
	createdb	shell script
	createlang	shell script
	createuser	shell script
	dropdb	shell script
	droplang	shell script
	dropuser	shell script
	ecpg	executable
	initdb	shell script
	initlocation	shell script
	ipcclean	shell script
	pg_config	shell script
	pg_controldata	executable
	pg_ctl	shell script
	pg_dump	executable
	pg_dumpall	executable
	pg_encoding	executable
	pg_id	executable
	pg_resetxlog	executable
	pg_restore	executable
	postgres	executable
	postmaster	symbolic link
	psql	executable
	vacuumdb	shell script
sbindir	Not used	
libexecdir	Not used	
datadir /postgresql	conversion_create.sql	SQL script
	pg_hba.conf.sample	example
	pg_ident.conf.sample	example
	postgres.bki	server bootstrap
	postgres.description	server bootstrap
	postgresql.conf.sample	example
docdir	postgresql/html/*	Documentation in HTML form
sysconfdir	Not used	
sharedstatedir	Not used	
localstatedir	Not used	

Table 19.1 **Continued**

Directory Name	Filename	File Type
libdir	libecpg.a	ECPG - library
	libecpg.so	ECPG - shared
	libpq.a	libpq - library
	libpq.so	libpq - shared
	postgresql/plpgsql.so	PL/PGSQL - shared
	postgresql/*	Character mappings
includedir	ecpgerrno.h	CPP include file
	ecpglib.h	CPP include file
	ecpgtype.h	CPP include file
	libpq-fe.h	CPP include file
	pg_config.h	CPP include file
	pg_config_os.h	CPP include file
	postgres_ext.h	CPP include file
	sql3types.h	CPP include file
	sqlca.h	CPP include file
	libpq/libpq-fs.h	CPP include file
	postgresql/*	CPP include file
oldincludedir	Not used	
infodir	Not used	
mandir	man1/*	Manual pages
	man7/*	Manual pages

The directories marked as *not used* are described when you run `configure --help` (`configure` is a commonly used generic configuration program), but are not used by PostgreSQL.

Table 19.1 shows where PostgreSQL will install the content of a basic configuration. You also can configure PostgreSQL to install optional packages (such as PL/Perl or the Java JDBC interface). Tables 19.2 and 19.3, later in the chapter, show where PostgreSQL will install each of the optional packages.

Installing PostgreSQL

Now that you know how a typical PostgreSQL installation is arranged on disk, it's time to actually *create* a typical installation. In the next few sections, I'll show you how to install PostgreSQL on Unix/Linux hosts and on Windows hosts. In either environment, you can install PostgreSQL from prebuilt installation packages, or you can compile PostgreSQL from source code to create a fully customized installation.

Unix/Linux

PostgreSQL was originally written for Unix, so you will find that installing PostgreSQL on a Unix host is very easy. Installing PostgreSQL on a Linux host is even easier because of the availability of prebuilt distributions.

From Binaries

The easiest way to install PostgreSQL on a Unix (or Linux) system is to use a precompiled package, such as a RPM installer. You can find RPM packages for PostgreSQL at the PostgreSQL web site (`www.postgresql.org` or `ftp.postrgesql.org`).

The process of installing PostgreSQL using a RPM package is described in Chapter 1, "Introduction to PostgreSQL and SQL." Refer to the section titled "Installing PostgreSQL Using a RPM" for more information.

From Source

Given the choice between building a package (such as PostgreSQL) from source and installing a package from a precompiled package, I'll always choose to build from source. When you build from source, you have complete control over the optional features, compiler options, and installation directories for the package. When you install from a precompiled package, you're stuck with the choices made by the person who constructed the package. Of course, using a precompiled package is much simpler. If you want to get up and running as quickly as possible, install from a binary package. If you want more control (as well as a better understanding of the options), build your own copy from source code.

There are four steps to follow when you install PostgreSQL from source code. If you have built other open-source products from source, you're probably comfortable with this procedure. If not, don't be afraid to try the build procedure yourself; it's really not difficult.

We'll walk through the four steps in this section, which are

1. Downloading and unpacking the source code
2. Configuring the source code
3. Compiling the source code
4. Installing the compiled code

Downloading and Unpacking the Source Code

The first step is to load the source code onto your system. PostgreSQL source code is distributed in a set of compressed archive (`tar`) files. The exact content of each archive can vary from release to release, but since release 7.1, the PostgreSQL source code is composed of the following archives:

```
postgresql-base-7.3b2.tar.gz      6598Kb
postgresql-docs-7.3b2.tar.gz      2539Kb
postgresql-opt-7.3b2.tar.gz        451Kb
postgresql-test-7.3b2.tar.gz      1047Kb
postgresql-7.3b2.tar.gz          10642Kb
```

The file sizes shown here are for release 7.3b2 (the second beta version of release 7.3).

The "base" archive (`postgresql-base-7.3b2.tar.gz`) contains all the source code necessary to build a PostgreSQL server, the `psql` client, administrative tools, and contributed software. The "docs" archive contains the PostgreSQL documentation in HTML form (the base archive contains the PostgreSQL man pages). Optional features (that is, things that you have to specifically enable when you build from source code) are included in the "opt" archive. The "test" package contains a suite of regression tests that will ensure that your copy of PostgreSQL is functioning as expected.

The last archive (`postgresql-7.3b2.tar.gz`) contains *all* the source code combined into a single archive.

If you want to install as little software as possible, download the base package. If you want to be sure you have everything that you might need, download the combined package.

Table 19.2 shows the detailed contents of each package[1].

Table 19.2 **Source Package Contents**

Package Name	Package Contents
`base`	server (postgres, postmaster)
	contributed software (`contrib`)
	include files
	`initdb`
	`initlocation`
	`ipcclean`
	`pg_config`
	`pg_controldata`
	`pg_ctl`
	`pg_dump`
	`pg_encoding` *(7.3)*
	`pg_id`
	`pg_passwd` *(7.2)*
	`pg_resetxlog` *(7.3)*
	`psql`
	`clusterdb` *(7.3)*
	`createdb`
	`createlang`
	`createuser`
	`dropdb`
	`droplang`
	`dropuser`
	`vacuumdb`

Table 19.2 **Continued**

Package Name	Package Contents
	cli client interface ecpg client interface libpq client interface libpgeasy client interface *(7.2)* PL/pgSQL server-side language PL/Python server-side language *(7.2)*
docs	Documentation in SGML form (converted to HTML and man page format during build process)
opt	Multibyte character set support *(7.2)* src/tools (misc. tools for use by PostgreSQL authors) CORBA interface Character-set mapping data pg_encoding *(7.2)* pgaccess *(7.2)* Tutorial Tcl client interface (and Tcl/Tk shells) Python client interface JDBC client interface ODBC client interface *(7.2)* libpq++ (C++) client interface *(7.2)* Perl client interface *(7.2)* PL/Perl server-side language PL/Tcl server-side language PL/Python server-side language *(7.3)*
test	Regression tests

[1] With release 7.3, some of the optional features of PostgreSQL have been removed from the source distribution and moved to another site (http://gborg.postgresql.org). If you want to build the Perl client interface, for example, you'll have to download the base package (or combined) *and* the pgperl package from gborg.postgresql.org.

In the discussion that follows, I'll assume that you have downloaded the combined package.

Configuring the Source Code

After you have downloaded the source package that you want, you can unpack the archive with the following command[2]:

```
$ tar -zxvf postgresql-7.3b2.tar.gz
```

The source package extracts to a directory named `postgresql-7.3b2` (or, `post-gresql-`*`version`* in the more general case).

The next step is by far the most complex: configuration. Configuration is not *difficult*, it just requires a bit of thought. When you configure source code, you select the set of features that you want and define compiler and linker options. Like most open-source packages, PostgreSQL source code is configured using the `configure` command. The set of configurable features and options varies from release to release, so you should study the output from the `configure --help` command carefully. Here is a sample of the output from this command:

```
$ cd postgresql-7.3b2
$ ./configure --help=short
Configuration of PostgreSQL 7.3b2:

Optional Features:
  --disable-FEATURE       do not include FEATURE
                            (same as --enable-FEATURE=no)
  --enable-FEATURE[=ARG]  include FEATURE [ARG=yes]
  --enable-integer-datetimes  enable 64-bit integer date/time support
  --enable-recode         enable single-byte recode support
  --enable-nls[=LANGUAGES]  enable Native Language Support
  --disable-shared        do not build shared libraries
  --disable-rpath         do not embed shared library
                             search path in executables
  --enable-debug          build with debugging symbols (-g)
  --enable-depend         turn on automatic dependency tracking
  --enable-cassert        enable assertion checks (for debugging)
  --disable-largefile     omit support for large files

Optional Packages:
  --with-PACKAGE[=ARG]    use PACKAGE [ARG=yes]
  --without-PACKAGE       do not use PACKAGE (same as --with-PACKAGE=no)

  --with-includes=DIRS    look for additional header files in DIRS
  --with-libraries=DIRS   look for additional libraries in DIRS
  --with-libs=DIRS        alternative spelling of --with-libraries
```

2. The `-z` flag is an extension that is available only if you are using the GNU version of `tar`. If `tar` complains about the `-z` flag, you can achieve the same result using the command: `gunzip -c postgresql-7.3b2.tar.gz | tar -xvf -`.

```
  --with-pgport=PORTNUM   change default port number 5432
  --with-maxbackends=N    set default maximum number of connections 32
  --with-tcl              build Tcl and Tk interfaces
  --without-tk            do not build Tk interfaces if Tcl is enabled
  --with-tclconfig=DIR    tclConfig.sh and tkConfig.sh are in DIR
  --with-tkconfig=DIR     tkConfig.sh is in DIR
  --with-perl             build Perl modules (PL/Perl)
  --with-python           build Python interface module
  --with-java             build JDBC interface and Java tools
  --with-krb4[=DIR]       build with Kerberos 4 support [/usr/athena]
  --with-krb5[=DIR]       build with Kerberos 5 support [/usr/athena]
  --with-krb-srvnam=NAME  name of the service principal
                             in Kerberos postgres
  --with-pam              build with PAM support
  --with-openssl[=DIR]    build with OpenSSL support [/usr/local/ssl]
  --without-readline      do not use Readline
  --without-zlib          do not use Zlib
  --with-gnu-ld           assume the C compiler uses GNU ld default=no

Some influential environment variables:
  CC          C compiler command
  CFLAGS      C compiler flags
  LDFLAGS     linker flags, e.g. -L<lib dir> if you have libraries in a
              nonstandard directory <lib dir>
  CPPFLAGS    C/C++ preprocessor flags, e.g. -I<include dir> if you have
              headers in a nonstandard directory <include dir>
  CPP         C preprocessor
  DOCBOOKSTYLE
              location of DocBook stylesheets

Use these variables to override the choices made by `configure'
or to help it to find libraries and programs with nonstandard names/locations.

Report bugs to <pgsql-bugs@postgresql.org>.
```

If you want to configure your source code to build a plain-vanilla version of PostgreSQL, you can simply run `configure` (without any options) and watch the blinking lights. The `configure` program performs a series of tests to determine what kind of operating system you are using, what kind of CPU you have, which compilers and linkers you have installed, and so forth. `configure` creates a new set of header files and `makefiles` that reflect your configuration choices.

The most interesting configuration options are the `--with-`*`package`* options. Using the `--with-`*`package`* options, you can build optional features such as the PL/Tcl language and the libpq++ client interface library.

Table 19.3 shows the package-related `configure` options. The second column lists the set of files that result from building each package. If you ever need to know what `configure` options you need to (for example) build the libpq++ shared library or the `pgtclsh` shell, consult Table 19.3.

Table 19.3 `configure` **Options and Resulting Files**

`configure` Option	Files Added to Basic Installation
`--with-tcl` Tcl client API and PL/Tcl server-side language	`bindir/pgtclsh` `bindir/pgtksh` `bindir/pltcl_delmod` `bindir/pltcl_listmod` `bindir/pltcl_loadmod` `bindir/pgaccess` `datadir/pgaccess/*` `datadir/unknown.pltcl` `includedir/libpgtcl.h` `libdir/libpgtcl.a` `libdir/libpgtcl.so` `libdir/postgresql/pltcl.so`
`--with-CXX` `libpq++ client API (for C++ client applications)`	`includedir/libpq++/*` `includedir/libpq++.h` `libdir/libpq++.a` `libdir/libpq++.so`
`--with-java` JDBC interface	`datadir/postgresql/java/*`
`--with-python` PL/Python server-side language	`libdir/postgresql/plpython.so`
`--with-perl` PL/Perl server-side language	`libdir/postgresql/plperl.so`
`--enable-nls` Locale and multi-lingual support	`prefixdir/share/locale/*`
`--enable-multibyte` Multi-byte character set support (Unicode and others)	`bindir/pg_encoding`

I mentioned earlier that `configure` runs a number of tests to find a wealth of information about the build environment and runtime environment on your system. This can take quite awhile on a slow or heavily used system. If you want to experiment with different configuration options, you may want to enable `configure`'s cache mechanism:

```
$ ./configure --config-cache
```

This tells `configure` to record its test results in a cache file (named `config.cache`) so that the next time you run `configure`, it won't have to repeat the tests. After you have finished compiling and installing PostgreSQL, you can run the program `pg_config` to find the set of options used to configure your copy of PostgreSQL:

```
$ pg_config --configure
--prefix=/usr/local/pg73b2 --enable-debug
```

The easiest way to *add* a configuration to a previously installed copy of PostgreSQL is to feed the result from `pg_config` back into the `configure` script. For example, to add PL/Python support to your existing configuration, you can run the following command:

```
$ eval ./configure `pg_config --configure` --with-python
```

The `configure` program produces three files that you may be interested in examining.

`config.log` contains a log of the entire configuration process. This file contains a list of all the configuration tests along with the result of each test. `config.log` also shows you the changes that the `configure` program made to your source code (actually, `configure` leaves the original source code intact and constructs a working copy of each file that it needs to modify). If you run into any configuration or build errors, you may want to examine the `config.log` file to see how `configure` arrived at its decisions.

The `config.status` file is a shell script that you can run to reproduce your original configuration choices. Executing `config.status` is equivalent to running `./configure 'pg_config --configurè`. The advantage that `config.status` offers is that you can reproduce your configuration choices without having a functional copy of PostgreSQL. The advantage to the second option is that you can *add* configuration options to an existing copy of PostgreSQL.

The `src/include/pg_config.h` file is modified to reflect many of the configuration options that you select. This file contains a few extra configuration options (such as database block size, default number of buffers, and so on) that you can't adjust using the `configure` program; to change these options you must edit the `include/pg_config.h` file (or the template, `include/pg_config.h.in`) by hand. You will probably never need to change this file, but you may want to glance through it so that you know what your options are.

Compiling the Source Code

After you have configured the PostgreSQL source code, compiling it is easy; just execute the `make` command:

```
$ make
```

The `make` program compiles only those portions of the source code requiring recompilation. If you are building PostgreSQL for the first time, `make` will compile everything. If you have already compiled PostgreSQL a few times, `make` will compile only the source files that you have changed, or that depend on changes that you have made. If you have made configuration changes, `make` is likely to recompile everything. If you want to be absolutely sure that `make` builds *everything*, execute the following command[3]:

```
$ make clean && make
```

After several minutes (or several hours, depending on the speed of your system), the build will complete.

If an error occurs during compilation, you might be able to fix the problem yourself by examining the error message and correcting the cause of the problem. If you're not comfortable wading through the PostgreSQL source code, search for specific error messages at the PostgreSQL web site; you will usually find an answer there.

Installing the Compiled Code

The final step is installation. In most cases, you should be logged into your system with superuser privileges (that is, log in as user `root`) to ensure that you can write into the installation directories. To install the compiled code, execute the following command:

```
# make install
```

The `make` utility copies the programs, shell scripts, and data files from your build directories into the install directories.

Completing the Installation Process

At this point, you should have all PostgreSQL components installed into their respective directories. Now, it's time to complete the installation process. When you install PostgreSQL from an RPM script, RPM will create a `postgres` user account for you. When you build PostgreSQL from scratch, you have to do that yourself. Consult your OS documentation for more information on how to create user accounts.

You'll also want to be sure that the PostgreSQL executables (particularly the client applications, such as `psql`) appear in your users' search path. The easiest way to accomplish this is to modify the `/etc/profile` (or equivalent) shell script.

Finally, you will want to create your initial set of databases and arrange for server startup and shutdown. Those topics are covered in other parts of this chapter.

Windows

The PostgreSQL server was not originally designed to run on a Windows host. You can run most client applications under Windows without trouble, but if you want to run a PostgreSQL server, you have to install a Unix compatibility library first and then install PostgreSQL.

3. `make clean` deletes the results from previous compilations. `make distclean` throws out the results from previous runs of the `configure` program.

From Binaries

If you want to run a PostgreSQL server on a Windows host, you will need to install the Cygwin runtime environment first. Cygwin is a package that provides a Unix-like environment that makes it (relatively) easy to port applications originally written for Unix systems to Windows hosts. In this section, I'll show you how to download and install Cygwin, as well as the PostgreSQL binary distribution for Windows.

First, point your web browser to the address `http://sources.redhat.com/cygwin`. You'll see a number of buttons scattered around this page that are labeled Install Cygwin Now, click on any of those buttons. When prompted, choose Run this program from its current location. You may see a security warning that tells you that the `setup.exe` program does not include an Authenticode signature; if you are reasonably comfortable that your net connection is secure, click on `Yes` to continue.

The setup program leads you through a series of dialog boxes that prompt for the information needed to complete the Cygwin installation. The first dialog simply introduces the Cygwin setup program (see Figure 19.1).

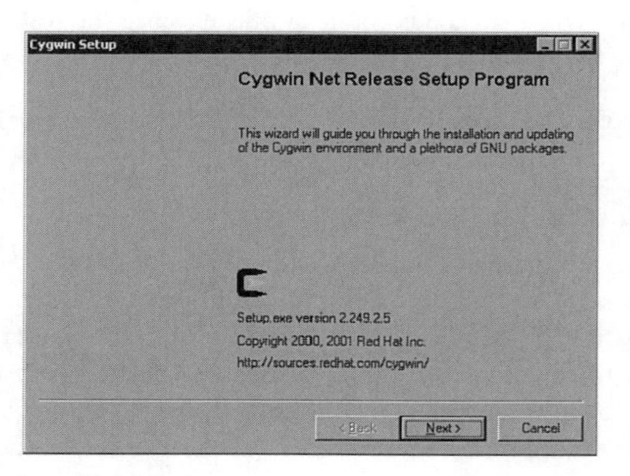

Figure 19.1 Cygwin Setup—Greeting.

On the second dialog box (see Figure 19.2), select Install from Internet to tell the setup program that you want to download the Cygwin packages from an Internet server and install them.

The third dialog box(see Figure 19.3) asks where you want to install the Cygwin package. The setup program creates a number of subdirectories in the location that you specify: `/usr`, `/bin`, `/etc`, and so on. The PostgreSQL package also installs in the directory tree that you specify, so be sure to choose a convenient location (for example, you may want to install Cygwin close to the root directory so you don't have to type really long pathnames to find your stuff).

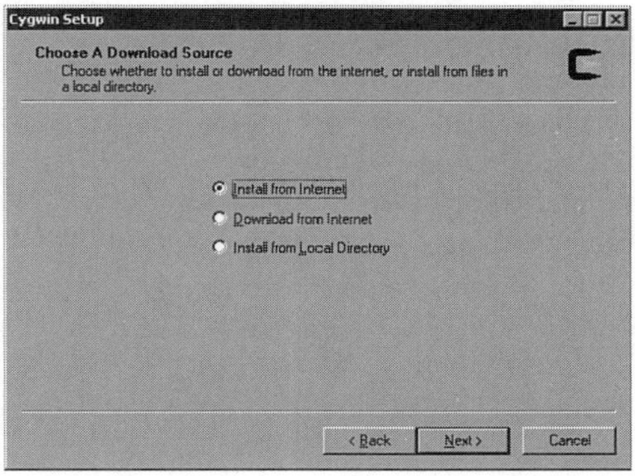

Figure 19.2 Cygwin Setup— Download Source.

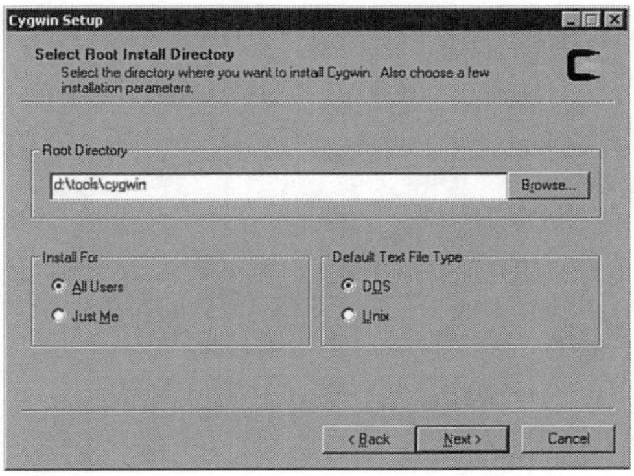

Figure 19.3 Cygwin Setup—Install Directory.

You'll also need a place to store the package archives themselves (see Figure 19.4). Each package is downloaded into the package directory and then installed to the final location. If you have limited disk space on your destination drive, you may want the package directory to reside on a different drive.

The fifth dialog box prompts for connection information (see Figure 19.5). If you're not sure whether you are connected to the Internet through a proxy server, choose Use IE5 Settings.

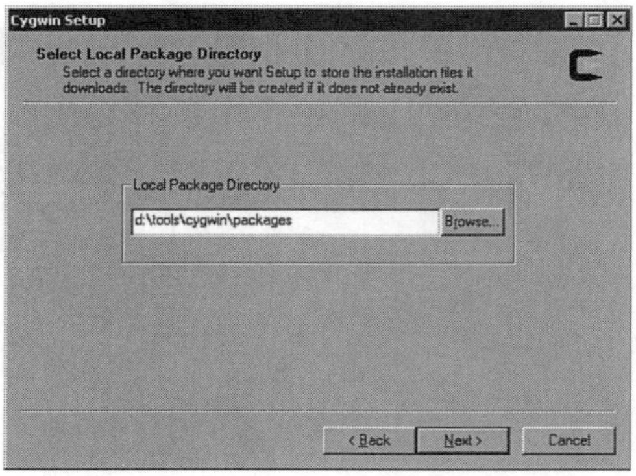

Figure 19.4 Cygwin Setup—Package Directory.

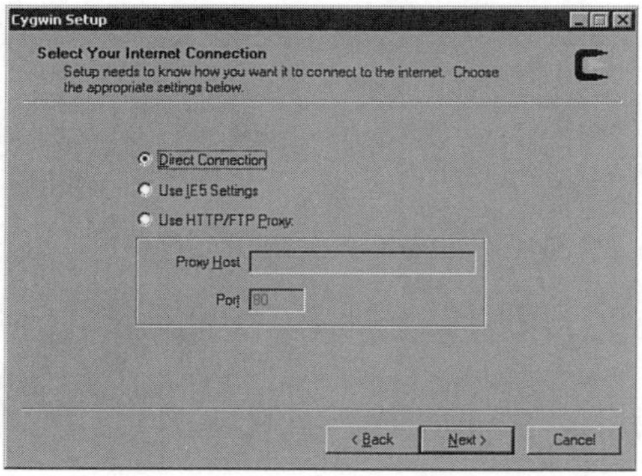

Figure 19.5 Cygwin Setup—Proxy Settings.

Next, you need to select a download site (see Figure 19.6). Cygwin is a very popular package and is mirrored at many sites throughout the world. For best performance, choose a site that is geographically close to you.

Finally, you arrive at the package selection dialog box(see Figure 19.7). I've always found this dialog box to be confusing, so I'll give you a quick tour. First, notice the button labeled View. That button rotates through three different views: `Category` (the default), `Full`, and `Partial`. In the Category view, you see a list of package categories. In Full view mode, all packages are listed in alphabetical order. Partial view mode lists the packages that you have selected to download (again, listed in alphabetical order).

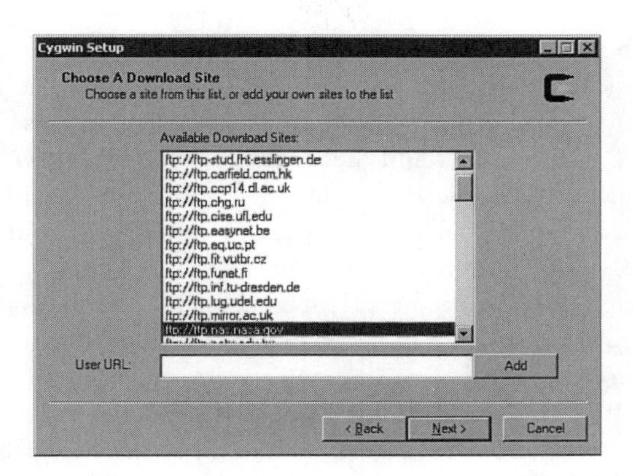

Figure 19.6 Cygwin Setup—Download Sites.

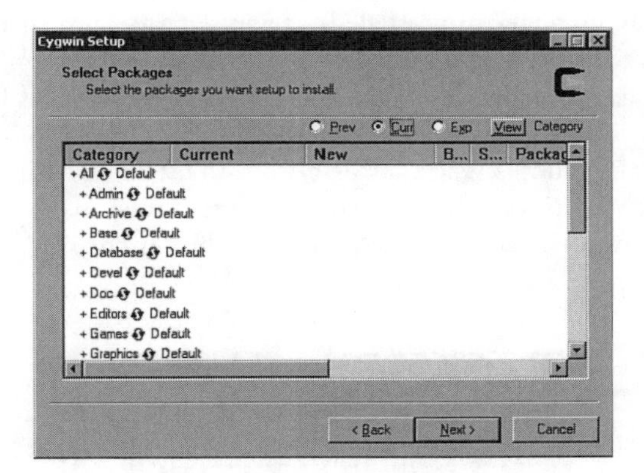

Figure 19.7 Cygwin Setup—Package Selection.

The Category view is arranged as a tree: On the left side of each category name, you'll see a plus sign (+)—click on the plus sign, and you will see a list of packages in that category. On the right side of the category name, you'll see the installation mode for the packages in that category. If you click on the installation mode (that is, click on the word Default), you'll cycle through the installation modes: Default, Install, Reinstall, and Uninstall. The Default installation mode tells the setup program to install the default set of packages in the selected category. If you choose Install, the setup program will install all packages in that category (choosing Install on the All category tells setup to install all Cygwin packages). The Reinstall mode causes setup to reinstall all previously installed packages (in that category). Uninstall removes all the packages in that category.

The three radio buttons across the top (Prev, Curr, and Exp) determine the *trust-level* that you want to achieve. The default selection is Curr, meaning that you want to use the currently released version of the packages that you select. Choose Prev if you want to install the previous (that is, older and theoretically more stable) version of a package. If you like to live dangerously, choose Exp to install experimental versions.

If you choose the Full or Partial view (or expand a category), you will see a list of packages (see Figure 19.8). There are six columns in this view: Category, Current, New, Bin?, Src?, and Package (due to space restrictions, the Bin? and Src? columns are shown as B... and S... in Figure 19.8). The Category and Package columns are self-explanatory. The Current column displays the version string for any currently installed packages (this column will be empty if you are installing Cygwin for the first time). The format of the version string varies widely from package to package. For the PostgreSQL package, the version string contains the PostgreSQL version number (7.2.2-1 for example). The New column will display Skip or a version string. If you see the word Skip, that package will not be installed (or reinstalled or uninstalled). If you see a version string, that package will be installed (or reinstalled or uninstalled) at the indicated version. If you click on the word Skip (or the version string), you can cycle through the choices for each package; you may be able to choose from multiple versions. If you choose to install a given package, the Bin? and Src? columns will transform from the string `n/a` into a pair of check boxes. If the `Bin?` check box is checked, you will install the binary (that is, executable) distribution of the given package. If the `Src?` check box is checked, you will install the source code for the given package.

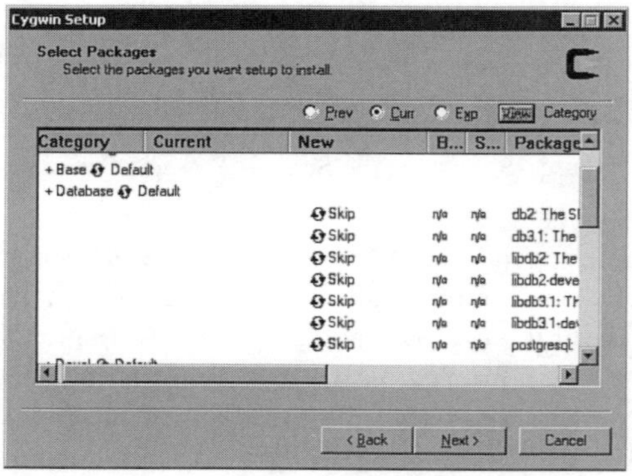

Figure 19.8 Cygwin Setup—Package Selection, Part 2.

That covers all the controls in the setup program. If you find this a bit confusing, you're not alone. In fact, I would recommend that you choose only two configurations: Install the default set of packages, or install everything. If you have plenty of room on your disk drives, choose to install everything. If not, choose the default set of packages plus the PostgreSQL package (in the `Database` category).

If you choose to roll your own configuration, be sure to select (at least) the following packages:

- Admin/cygrunsrv
- `Base/*` (do yourself a favor; choose *everything* in `Base`)
- Database/PostgreSQL

After you select the packages that you want to install and click on the `Next` button, the setup program will download and install your choices. There's not much you can do at this point; just watch the blinking lights and wait for everything to complete.

When the Cygwin setup program completes, you still have one more package to install: `cygipc`. The `cygipc` package adds shared-memory, semaphores, and message-queue support to Cygwin. PostgreSQL currently requires `cygipc`—it's likely that a future release will bundle the functionality provided by `cygipc` into the basic Cygwin package.

You can find `cygipc` at the following location:

`http://www.neuro.gatech.edu/users/cwilson/cygutils/cygipc/.`

The archive that you want is named `cygipc-1.11-1.tar.bz2`. After you have downloaded the archive, fire up the `bash` shell (included in the default Cygwin category) and execute the following commands:

```
$ cd /
$ tar -jxvf cygipc-1.11-1.tar.bz2
```

It is important to `cd` to Cygwin's root directory (/) before you unpack the `cygipc` archive; otherwise, the files that you extract will not be placed into the correct directories.

From Source

If you want to compile PostgreSQL from source code in a Windows environment, you still need the Cygwin and cygipc packages described in the previous section. You also need the GNU compiler chain (found in the `Devel` Cygwin category) and the source code for PostgreSQL. After you have installed the necessary tools, you can follow the same procedure described earlier for building PostgreSQL from source on a Unix host.

Completing the Installation Process

Arriving here, you should have all necessary PostgreSQL, Cygwin, and `cygipc` components installed on your system. To complete the installation, you'll want to make any configuration changes that you require, install PostgreSQL and `cygipc` as Windows services, create your initial databases, and create PostgreSQL user accounts. These last few steps are described elsewhere in this chapter.

Managing Databases

PostgreSQL stores data in a collection of operating system files. At the highest level of organization, you find a cluster. A *cluster* is a collection of databases (which, in turn, is a collection of schemas).

Creating a New Cluster

You create a new cluster using the `initdb` program. Note that `initdb` is an external program, not a command that you would execute in a PostgreSQL client.

When you run `initdb`, you are creating the data files that define a cluster. The most important command-line argument to `initdb` is `--pgdata=`*`cluster-location`*[4]. The `--pgdata` argument tells `initdb` the name of the directory that should contain the new cluster. For example, if you execute the command

```
$ initdb --pgdata=/usr/newcluster
```

`initdb` creates the directory `/usr/newcluster` and a few files and subdirectories within `/usr/newcluster`. It's usually a good idea to let `initdb` create the directory that contains the cluster so that all the file ownerships and permissions are properly defined. In fact, `initdb` won't create a cluster in a directory that is not empty.
So, let's see the directory structure that we end up with after `initdb` has completed its work (see Figure 19.9).

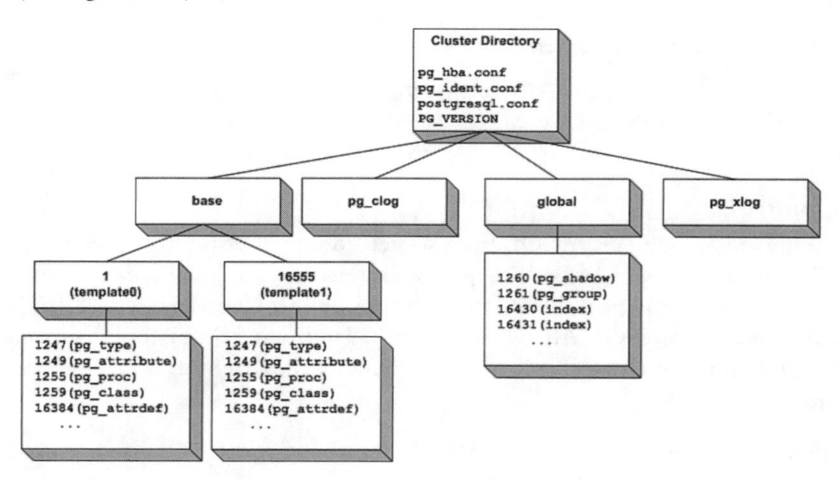

Figure 19.9 The data directory layout.

4. There are actually three ways to specify the cluster location. All the following commands are equivalent:

```
$ initdb --pgdata=/usr/newcluster
$ initdb -D /usr/newcluster
$ export PGDATA=/usr/newcluster ; initdb
```

At the top of the directory structure is the cluster directory itself—I'll refer to that as $PGDATA because that is where the $PGDATA environment variable should point.

$PGDATA contains four files and four subdirectories[5]. $PGDATA/pg_hba.conf contains the host-based authentication configuration file. This file tells PostgreSQL how to authenticate clients on a host-by-host basis. We'll look at the pg_hba.conf file in great detail in Chapter 21, "Security." The $PGDATA/pg_ident.conf file is used by the ident authentication scheme to map OS usernames into PostgreSQL user names—again, I'll describe this file in the chapter dealing with PostgreSQL security. $PGDATA/postgresql.conf contains a list of runtime parameters that control various aspects of the PostgreSQL server. The fourth file, $PGDATA/PG_VERSION, is a simple text file that contains the version number from initdb.

Now, let's look at each of the subdirectories created by initdb.

The pg_xlog directory contains the write-ahead logs. Write-ahead logs are used to improve database reliability and performance. Whenever you update a row within a table, PostgreSQL will first write the change to the write-ahead log, and at some later time will write the modifications to the actual data pages on disk. The pg_xlog directory usually contains a number of files, but initdb will create only the first one—extra files are added as needed. Each xlog file is 16MB long.

The pg_clog directory contains commit logs. A commit log reflects the state of each transaction (committed, in-progress, or aborted).

The global directory contains three tables that are shared by all databases within a cluster: pg_shadow, pg_group, and pg_database. The pg_shadow table holds user account definitions and is maintained by the CREATE USER, ALTER USER, and DROP USER commands. The pg_group table holds user group definitions and is maintained by the CREATE GROUP, ALTER GROUP, and DROP GROUP commands. pg_database contains a list of all databases within the cluster and is maintained by the CREATE DATABASE and DROP DATABASE commands. The global directory also contains a number of indexes for the pg_shadow, pg_group, and pg_database tables. global contains two other files that are shared by all databases in a cluster: pgstat.stat and pg_control. The pgstat.stat file is used by the statistics monitor (the statistics monitor accumulates performance and usage information for a database cluster). The pg_control file contains a number of cluster parameters, some of which are defined by initdb and will never change. Others are modified each time the postmaster is restarted. You can view the contents of the pg_control file using the pg_controldata utility provided in the contrib directory of a source distribution. Here's a sample of the output from pg_controldata:

```
$ pg_controldata
pg_control version number:              71
Catalog version number:                 200201121
```

5. You are looking at a cluster created with PostgreSQL version 7.2. The exact details may differ if you are using a different version.

```
Database state:                        IN_PRODUCTION
pg_control last modified:              Sat Jan 20 10:32:42 2002
Current log file id:                   0
Next log file segment:                 1
Latest checkpoint location:            0/11393C
Prior checkpoint location:             0/1096A4
Latest checkpoint's REDO location:     0/11393C
Latest checkpoint's UNDO location:     0/0
Latest checkpoint's StartUpID:         8
Latest checkpoint's NextXID:           155
Latest checkpoint's NextOID:           16556
Time of latest checkpoint:             Sat Jan 20 09:43:11 2002
Database block size:                   8192
Blocks per segment of large relation: 131072
LC_COLLATE:                            en_US
LC_CTYPE:                              en_US
```

The `initdb` utility also creates two template databases in the new cluster: `template0` and `template1`. The `template0` database represents a "stock" database—it contains the definitions for all system tables, as well as definitions for the standard views, functions, and data types. You should never modify `template0`—in fact, you can't even connect to the `template0` database without performing some evil magic. When you run `initdb`, the `template0` database is copied to `template1`. You *can* modify the `template1` database. Just as the `template0` database is cloned to create `template1`, `template1` is cloned whenever you create a new database using `CREATE DATABASE` (or `createdb`). It's useful to modify the `template1` database when you want a particular feature (like a custom data type, function, or table) to exist in every database that you create in the future. For example, if you happen to run an accounting business, you might want to define a set of accounting tables (`customers`, `vendors`, `accounts`, and so on) in the `template1` database. Then, when you sign up a new customer and create a new database for that customer, the new database will automatically contain the empty accounting tables.

You may also find it useful to create other template databases. To extend the previous example a bit, let's say that you have a core set of financial applications (general ledger, accounts payable, accounts receivable) that are useful regardless of the type of business your customer happens to run. You may develop a set of extensions that are well suited to customers who own restaurants, and another set of extensions that you use for plumbers. If you create two new template databases, `restaurant_template` and `plumber_template`, you'll be ready to sign up new restaurants and new plumbers with minimal work. When you want to create a database for a new restaurateur, simply clone the `restaurant_template` database.

After you have created a cluster (and the two default template databases), you can create the actual databases where you will do your work.

Creating a New Database

There are two ways to create a new database. You can use the CREATE DATABASE command from within a PostgreSQL client application (such as psql), or you can use the createdb shell script. The syntax for the CREATE DATABASE command is

```
CREATE DATABASE database-name
   [WITH   [TEMPLATE = template-database-name ]
      [ENCODING = character-encoding ]
         [OWNER = database-owner ]
            [LOCATION = pathname ]]
```

A *database-name* must conform to the usual rules for PostgreSQL identifiers: it should start with an underscore or a letter and should be at most 31 characters long. If you need to include a space (or start the database name with a digit), enclose the *database-name* in double quotes.

When you execute the CREATE DATABASE command, PostgreSQL will copy an existing template database. If you don't include a TEMPLATE=*template-database-name* clause, CREATE DATABASE will clone the template1 database. A few restrictions control whether or not you can clone a given database. First, a cluster superuser can clone *any* database. The owner of a database can clone that database. Finally, any user with CREATEDB privileges can clone a database whose datistemplate attribute is set to true in the pg_database system table. Looking at this in the other direction, ordinary users cannot clone a database that is not specifically marked as a template (according to the datistemplate attribute).

You can choose an *encoding* for the new database using the ENCODING=*character-encoding* clause. An encoding tells PostgreSQL which character set to use within your database. If you don't specify an encoding, the new database will use the same encoding that the template database uses. Encodings are discussed in detail in Chapter 20, "Internationalization and Localization."

If you don't include the OWNER=*username* clause or if you specify OWNER=DEFAULT, you become the owner of the database. If you are a PostgreSQL superuser, you can create a database that will be owned by another user using the OWNER=*username* clause. If you are not a PostgreSQL superuser, you can still create a database (assuming that you hold the CREATEDB privilege), but you cannot assign ownership to another user.

The final option to the CREATE DATABASE command is LOCATION=*pathname*. This clause is used to control where PostgreSQL places the files that make up the new database. If you don't specify a location, CREATE DATABASE will create a subdirectory in the cluster ($PGDATA) to hold the new database. There are some restrictions to where you can place a new database; see the "Creating New Databases" section of Chapter 3, "PostgreSQL Syntax and Use," for more information.

As I mentioned earlier, there are two ways to create a new database: CREATE DATABASE and createdb. The createdb utility is simply a shell script that invokes the psql client to execute a CREATE DATABASE, command. createdb does not offer any more functionality than `CREATE DATABASE` so use whichever you find most convenient. For more information on the `createdb` utility, invoke `createdb` with the `--help` flag:

```
$ createdb --help
createdb creates a PostgreSQL database.

Usage:
  createdb [options] dbname [description]

Options:
  -D, --location=PATH          Alternative place to store the database
  -T, --template=TEMPLATE      Template database to copy
  -E, --encoding=ENCODING      Multibyte encoding for the database
  -h, --host=HOSTNAME          Database server host
  -p, --port=PORT              Database server port
  -U, --username=USERNAME      Username to connect as
  -W, --password               Prompt for password
  -e, --echo                   Show the query being sent to the backend
  -q, --quiet                  Don't write any messages

By default, a database with the same name as the current user is created.

Report bugs to <pgsql-bugs@postgresql.org>.
```

Routine Maintenance

Compared to most relational database management systems, PostgreSQL does not require much in the way of routine maintenance, but there are a few things you should do on a regular basis.

Managing Tables (`cluster` and `vacuum`)

When you delete (or update) rows in a PostgreSQL table, the old data is *not* immediately removed from the database. In fact, unlike other database systems, the free space is not even marked as being available for reuse. If you delete or modify a lot of data, your database may become very large very fast. You may also find that performance suffers because PostgreSQL will have to load obsolete data from disk even though it won't use that data.

To permanently free obsolete data from a table, you use the `VACUUM` command. The `VACUUM` command comes in four flavors:

```
VACUUM [table-name]
VACUUM FULL [table-name]
VACUUM ANALYZE [table-name]
VACUUM FULL ANALYZE [table-name]
```

The first and third forms are the ones most commonly used.

In the first form, `VACUUM` makes all space previously used to hold obsolete data available for reuse. This form does not require exclusive access to the table and usually runs quickly. If you don't specify a *`table-name`*, `VACUUM` will process all tables in the database.

In the second form, `VACUUM` *removes* obsolete data from the table (or entire database). Without the `FULL` option, `VACUUM` only marks space consumed by obsolete data as being available for reuse. With the `FULL` option, `VACUUM` tries to shrink the data file instead of simply making space available for reuse. A `VACUUM FULL` requires exclusive access to each table and is generally much slower than a simple `VACUUM`.

The `VACUUM ANALYZE` command will first `VACUUM` a table (or database) and will then compute statistics for the PostgreSQL optimizer. I discussed optimization and statistics in Chapter 4, "Performance." If you will `VACUUM` a table (or database), you may as well update the per-table statistics as well.

The final form combines a `VACUUM FULL` with a `VACUUM ANALYZE`. As you might expect, this shrinks the database by removing obsolete data and then computes new performance-related statistics. Like `VACUUM FULL`, `VACUUM FULL ANALYZE` locks each table for exclusive use while it is being processed.

Another command that you may want to execute on a routine basis is the `CLUSTER` command. `CLUSTER` rearranges the rows in a given table so that they are physically stored in index order. This is a cheap way to get enormous performance gains—run this command occasionally and you'll look like a hero. See Chapter 4 for more information.

Managing Indexes

For the most part, indexes are self-maintaining. Occasionally, you may find that an index has become corrupted and must be rebuilt (actually, you are more likely to *suspect* a corrupted index than to find one). You can also improve performance slightly (and reduce disk space consumption) by rebuilding indexes on an occasional basis.

The easiest way to rebuild an index is with the `REINDEX` command. `REINDEX` comes in the following forms:

```
REINDEX INDEX index-name [FORCE]
REINDEX TABLE table-name [FORCE]
REINDEX DATABASE database-name [FORCE]
```

In all three forms, you can force `REINDEX` to rebuild indexes on system tables (they are normally ignored by `REINDEX`) by including the keyword `FORCE` at the end of the command. If you find you need to `REINDEX` system tables, you should consult the *PostgreSQL Reference Manual* for the gory details. (Warning—this is not for the faint-of-heart.)

Managing User Accounts

As a PostgreSQL administrator, you may be responsible for creating user accounts and groups. You may also be responsible for granting and revoking privileges.

In most environments, there is a one-to-one mapping between a user's operating system identity and his PostgreSQL identity. In fact, your PostgreSQL username is often identical to your OS username.

In some cases, other configurations are useful. For example, you may want most of your users to identify themselves uniquely while providing an anonymous account for low-privileged guests. You may also have a client application that identifies *itself* rather than identifying the user (this is useful for utility applications that can be executed by *any* user without providing any sort of authentication).

A user account is shared between all databases within a given cluster. User groups are also shared between all databases within a cluster.

CREATE USER

There are two ways to create a new user: you can execute the `CREATE USER` command from within a client application (such as psql), or you can use the `createuser` shell script.

The complete syntax for the `CREATE USER` command is

```
CREATE USER user-name
       [[WITH] option ]...

option :=  SYSID user-id-number
         | [NO]CREATEDB
         | [NO]CREATEUSER
         | IN GROUP groupname [, ...]
         | [[UN]ENCRYPTED ] PASSWORD 'password'
         | VALID UNTIL 'expiration'
```

A `user-name` must conform to the usual rules for PostgreSQL identifiers: it should start with a letter (or an underscore) and should be at most 31 characters long. If you need to start a username with a number, just enclose the name in double quotes.

User account definitions are stored in the `pg_shadow` system table. You can view the layout of the `pg_shadow` table using the `psql \d` meta-command:

```
movies=# \d pg_shadow
        Table "pg_shadow"
   Column     |  Type    | Modifiers
-------------+---------+-----------
 usename      | name    |
 usesysid     | integer |
 usecreatedb  | boolean |
 usetrace     | boolean |
 usesuper     | boolean |
```

```
 usecatupd     | boolean |
 passwd        | text    |
 valuntil      | abstime |
Unique keys: pg_shadow_usename_index,
             pg_shadow_usesysid_index
Triggers: pg_sync_pg_pwd
```

You can see the correlation between the pg_shadow table and the CREATE USER options. The *user-name* is stored in the usename column. The *user-id-number* value is stored in usesysid. The usecreatedb column reflects the [NO] CREATEDB option. usetrace is reserved for future use and is not currently used. The usesuper column reflects the value of the [NO] CREATEUSER option. (As you'll see in a moment, a user who is allowed to create new user accounts is considered to be a superuser.) The usecatupd determines whether a user can directly update PostgreSQL's system tables (using the INSERT, UPDATE, and DELETE commands). If usecatupd is false, you can update the system tables only indirectly, using other commands such as CREATE TABLE, CREATE USER, and so on. The only way to change usecatupd is to use the UPDATE command (that is, UPDATE pg_shadow SET usecatupd = true). The passwd and valuntil columns store the *password* and *expiration*, respectively.

Each of the *option* values are, well, optional. I'll describe them all here.

SYSID

Using the SYSID *user-id-number* option, you can assign a specific numeric user-id to a user. The *PostgreSQL Reference Manual* mentions that this option is useful if you want to correlate PostgreSQL user-ids with OS user-ids, but there's a more important use for the SYSID option.

When a user creates a database object (table, view, sequence, and so on), the object owner is not associated with the user's name, but with the user's SYSID. You can see this by looking at the layout of the pg_class system table:

```
movies=# \d pg_class
            Table "pg_class"
     Column     |    Type     | Modifiers
----------------+-----------+-----------
 relname        | name        |
 reltype        | oid         |
 relowner       | integer     |
 relam          | oid         |
...
...
 relhassubclass | boolean     |
 relacl         | aclitem[]   |
Unique keys: pg_class_oid_index,
             pg_class_relname_index
```

Notice that the relowner column is defined as an integer, not as a name. What happens if you delete a user that happens to own a database object? Let's see. First, we'll log in as user bruce and create a new table:

```
$ psql -d movies -q -U bruce
movies=> create table bruces_table ( pkey integer );
CREATE
movies=> SELECT * FROM pg_tables WHERE tablename = 'bruces_table';
  tablename    | tableowner | hasindexes | hasrules | hastriggers
--------------+------------+------------+----------+-------------
 bruces_table | bruce      | f          | f        | f
(1 row)
movies=# \q
```

Notice that bruces_table is owned by user bruce. Now, let's remove bruce's account:

```
$ psql -q -d movies
movies=# DROP USER bruce;
movies=# SELECT * FROM pg_tables WHERE tablename = 'bruces_table';
  tablename    |     tableowner      | hasindexes | hasrules | hastriggers
--------------+-------------------+------------+----------+-------------
 bruces_table | unknown (UID=105) | f          | f        | f
(1 row)
```

Now, bruces_table is owned by an unknown user (whose SYSID is 105). That's not really a problem in itself, but it can certainly lead to confusion. If you *don't* assign a specific SYSID, CREATE USER will choose the next highest number (starting at 100). That means that eventually, you may create a new user whose SYSID turns out to be 105—bruce's old SYSID. Suddenly your brand new user owns a whole mess of database objects. You can recover from this sort of problem by adding a new user with a specific SYSID[6].

Privileges (CREATEDB and CREATEUSER)

When you create a new user, you can control whether the user is allowed to create new databases. You also can control whether the user is allowed to create new users. Giving a user the right to create new databases will rarely, if ever, pose a security risk, but allowing a user to create new users can. When you grant a user CREATEUSER privileges, that user becomes a superuser in your cluster. Let me say that again in a slightly different way: A user who has CREATEUSER privileges can bypass *all* security restrictions in your database cluster. You can explicitly deny CREATEUSER privileges by specifying NOCREATEUSER. NOCREATEUSER is assumed if you don't specify either value.

6. You can also fix this problem by updating the relowner value in pg_class, but that's living dangerously.

The CREATEDB option grants the user the right to create new databases (within the cluster). You can specify NOCREATEDB to prohibit the user from creating new databases. If you specify neither CREATEDB nor NOCREATEDB, CREATE USER will assume NOCREATEDB.

Group Membership (IN GROUP)

You can assign a new user to one or more groups by including the IN GROUP clause. For example, to create a user named bernard as a member of the developers and administrators groups:

```
CREATE USER bernard IN GROUP developers, administrators;
```

If you don't assign the new user to a group, he will be a member of the pseudo-group PUBLIC, but no other groups.

PASSWORD and Password Expiration

The final two options are somewhat related. You can create an initial password for a new user by including the PASSWORD, ENCRYPTED PASSWORD, or UNENCRYPTED PASSWORD option. If you don't specify a password when you create a new user (and you are using passwords to authenticate client connections), the user will not be able to log in. If you choose to create an ENCRYPTED PASSWORD, the password will be stored, in encrypted form, in the pg_shadow system table. If you choose to create an UNENCRYPTED PASSWORD, it will also be stored in pg_shadow, but in cleartext form. If you create a password without specifying ENCRYPTED or UNENCRYPTED, CREATE USER will look to the PASSWORD_ENCRYPTION server option to decide whether to store the password in cleartext or encrypted form.

Be aware that unencrypted passwords are visible to any PostgreSQL super-user.

The VALID UNTIL '*expiration*' option controls password expiration. If you omit VALID UNTIL, the initial password will never expire. If you include VALID UNTIL '*expiration*', the password will become invalid after the time and date indicated by *expiration*.

createuser

The createuser shell script is a bit easier to use than CREATE USER because it prompts you for all required information. Here is sample createuser session:

```
$ createuser
Enter name of user to add: bernard
Shall the new user be allowed to create databases? (y/n) n
Shall the new user be allowed to create more new users? (y/n) n
Password:
CREATE USER
```

There's a serious gotcha that always trips me up when I use createuser. Notice in the previous example that createuser has prompted me for a password. When you see the Password: prompt, createuser is asking for *your* password, not the password to be assigned to the new user. createuser is just a shell script that connects to the server and executes a CREATE USER command on your behalf. You must authenticate yourself to the server, so createdb needs to know your password. If you invoke createuser with the --pwprompt flag (or -P for short), createdb will also prompt you for the new user's password:

```
$ createuser --pwprompt
Enter name of user to add: bernard
Enter password for user "bernard":
Enter it again:
Shall the new user be allowed to create databases? (y/n) n
Shall the new user be allowed to create more new users? (y/n) n
Password:
CREATE USER
```

You can see the difference—when I am supposed to enter bernard's password, createuser is kind enough to use a more descriptive prompt. When I have finished answering all createuser's questions, I am prompted for *my* password.

ALTER USER

You can modify the attributes of existing user accounts with the ALTER USER command. The ALTER USER command is similar to CREATE USER:

```
ALTER USER user-name
      [[WITH] option ]...

option :=  [NO]CREATEDB
         | [NO]CREATEUSER
         | [[UN]ENCRYPTED ] PASSWORD 'password'
         | VALID UNTIL 'expiration'
```

You can use ALTER USER to change a user's privileges (CREATEDB and CREATEUSER) and password information (PASSWORD and VALID UNTIL). You *cannot* use ALTER TABLE to change a user's SYSID. You can change a user's group membership, but not with ALTER USER; you must use the ALTER GROUP command for that.

DROP USER

Removing obsolete user accounts is easy: use the DROP USER command:

```
DROP USER user-name
```

You must be a PostgreSQL superuser to use DROP USER. When you drop a user, PostgreSQL will not delete any objects (tables, views, sequences) owned by that user—they will be owned by a "mystery" owner. You cannot drop a user who owns a database.

GRANT and REVOKE

After you have created a new user, you must decide which database objects (tables, views, and sequences) that user should be able to access, and what kinds of access they should have. For each user/object combination, you can grant SELECT, INSERT, UPDATE, DELETE, REFERENCES, and TRIGGER privileges (a few new privileges will be added in release 7.3). I'll show you how to grant and revoke privileges in Chapter 21, "Security."

You can imagine that assigning individual privileges for every user of every table would be rather time-consuming and difficult to maintain. You can reduce the administrative overhead by creating user groups.

Managing Groups

You can define named groups of users to make your administrative life much easier to manage. Every group can include zero or more users. Every user can belong to one or more groups. When you grant or revoke privileges for an object, you can identify a specific user or a group of users.

Every user is automatically a member of the group PUBLIC. PUBLIC is actually a virtual group—you can't add or remove members and you can't drop this group, but you can associate privileges with PUBLIC.

Groups are much easier to manage if they correspond to usage roles in your organization. For example, you might create groups named developers, guests, clerks, and administrators. Laying out groups so that they reflect real-world user groups makes it much easier to assign access privileges to your database objects. Of course any given user can belong to many groups. For example, a member of the developers group might also be an administrator.

Group definitions are stored in the pg_group system table. Like database users, group definitions are shared by all databases within a cluster.

CREATE GROUP

A PostgreSQL superuser can create a new group using the CREATE GROUP command:

```
CREATE GROUP group-name [[WITH] option [...]]

option :=   SYSID group-id-number
          | USER username, ...
```

The *group-name* must meet the usual rules for PostgreSQL identifiers (31 characters or less, quoted, or starting with an underscore or a letter).

You can include a SYSID value if you want to assign a specific numeric ID for the new group. Like user accounts, a group is referenced by its numeric ID, not by name. We users know each group by name, but any table that refers to a group will refer to the numeric value. You might assign a specific numeric ID to a group for the same reasons that you might assign as specific ID to a user (see the previous section for more information).

You can assign group membership in three ways:

- Use the IN GROUP option in the CREATE USER command
- List the usernames in the USER option of CREATE GROUP
- Change the group membership using the ALTER GROUP command

A typical CREATE GROUP command might look something like this:

```
CREATE GROUP developers USER bernard,lefty;
```

This command creates a new group named developers that initially has two members: bernard and lefty.

ALTER GROUP

Using the ALTER GROUP command, you can add members to a group, or remove users from a group. The format of the ALTER GROUP command is

```
ALTER GROUP group-name {ADD|DROP} USER user-name [, ...]
```

Only PostgreSQL superusers can alter a group.

DROP GROUP

The DROP GROUP command deletes a group. The format of the DROP COMMAND is

```
DROP GROUP group-name
```

You can drop a group only if you are PostgreSQL superuser.

Now let's change focus from security-related issues to another important administrative concern—backup and recovery.

Configuring Your PostgreSQL Runtime Environment

After you have finished installing the PostgreSQL distribution, you may want to review the runtime configuration options.

Permanent configuration options should be defined in the file $PGDATA/postgresql.conf. The postgresql.conf file is a plain text file that you can maintain with your favorite editor (vi, emacs, and so on). When you create a new database cluster, the initdb program will create a default postgresql.conf file for you. postgresql.conf is arranged as a series of *option=value* pairs; blank lines are ignored and any text that follows an octothorpe (#) is treated as a comment. Here is a snippet from a postgresql.conf file created by initdb:

```
#
#       Connection Parameters
#
#tcpip_socket = false
#ssl = false
```

```
#max_connections = 32

#port = 5432
#hostname_lookup = false
#show_source_port = false

#unix_socket_directory = ''
#unix_socket_group = ''
#unix_socket_permissions = 0777
```

PostgreSQL supports a large number of runtime configuration options (more than 90 at last count). In the next few sections, you'll see a description of each parameter and the parameter's default value. Default values can come from four sources: a hard-wired default value that you can't adjust without changing the source code, a symbolic value that can be changed only by editing the `include/pg_config.h` header file, a compile-time configuration option, or a command-line option to the `postmaster`.

Some of the options can be modified at runtime using the `SET` command; others can be defined only before starting the `postmaster`. The sections that follow document the modification time for each parameter.

Parameters with a Modify Time of "Postmaster startup" can be changed only by modifying the `postgresql.conf` file and restarting the `postmaster`.

Parameters labeled `SIGHUP` can be modified after the `postmaster` process has started. To modify a `SIGHUP` option, edit the `postgresql.conf` configuration file and send a `SIGHUP` signal to the `postmaster` process. You can use the `pg_ctl reload` command to signal the `postmaster`.

The parameters that you can change with the `SET` command are labeled with a modification time of "`SET` command".

Connection-Related Parameters

This section looks at the connection-related configuration parameters. Notice that most of the connection-related parameters must be defined at the time that the `postmaster` starts.

`TCPIP_SOCKET`

Default Value:	`False`
Modify Time:	Postmaster startup
Override:	`postmaster -i`

This parameter determines whether the `postmaster` listens for connection requests coming from a TCP/IP socket. If `TCPIP_SOCKET` is false, the `postmaster` will listen for connection requests coming only from a Unix local domain socket. If `TCPIP_SOCKET` is true, the `postmaster` will listen for connection requests coming from a

TCP/IP socket, as well as listening for local connection requests. You can override this variable by invoking the `postmaster` with the `-i` flag.

`SSL`

Default Value:	`False`
Modify Time:	Postmaster startup
Override:	`postmaster -l`

If true, the `SSL` parameter tells the `postmaster` to negotiate with clients over the use of `SSL`-secured connections. `SSL` is a protocol that encrypts the data stream flowing between the client and the server. If `SSL` is true, and the client supports `SSL`, the data stream will be encrypted; otherwise, PostgreSQL data will be sent in clear-text form. You can override this parameter by invoking the `postmaster` with the `-l` flag.

`MAX_CONNECTIONS`

Default Value:	`32`
Modify Time:	Postmaster startup
Override:	`postmaster -n` *`connections`*

The `MAX_CONNECTIONS` parameter determines the maximum number of concurrent client connections that the `postmaster` will accept. You can increase (or decrease) the maximum number of connections by invoking the `postmaster` with the `-n` *`connections`* parameter. You also can change the default value for `MAX_CONNECTIONS` by invoking `configure` with the `--with-maxbackends=`*`connections`* option when you build PostgreSQL from source code.

`PORT`

Default Value:	`5432`
Modify Time:	Postmaster startup
Override:	`postmaster -p` *`port`*

This parameter determines which TCP/IP port the `postmaster` should listen to. When a remote client application wants to connect to a PostgreSQL server, it must connect to a TCP/IP port where a postmaster is listening for connection requests. The client and server must agree on the same port number. You can override this parameter by invoking the `postmaster` with the `-p` *`port`* parameter. You can also change the default value for `PORT` by invoking `configure` with the `--with-pgport=`*`port`* when you build PostgreSQL from source code.

`HOSTNAME_LOOKUP`

Default Value:	`False`
Modify Time:	`SIGHUP` or Postmaster startup
Override:	None

If `HOSTNAME_LOOKUP` is `False`, any connection logs that you are gathering will show the IP address of each client. If `HOSTNAME_LOOKUP` is `True`, the `postmaster` will try to resolve the IP address into a host name and will include the hostname in the log if the resolution succeeds. Warning: this can a real performance hog if your name-resolution mechanism is not configured correctly.

SHOW_SOURCE_PORT

Default Value:	False
Modify Time:	SIGHUP or Postmaster startup
Override:	None

If True, this parameter tells PostgreSQL to log the outgoing port number of all client connections. The *PostgreSQL Administrator's Manual* says that this option is "pretty useless."

UNIX_SOCKET_DIRECTORY

Default Value:	/tmp
Modify Time:	Postmaster startup
Override:	postmaster -k *directory*

The postmaster always listens for local connection requests using a Unix domain socket. The socket's device file is normally found in the /tmp directory. You can move the socket device file to a different directory by using the UNIX_SOCKET_DIRECTORY configuration parameter or by invoking the postmaster with the -k *directory* parameter. You also can change the default value for this parameter by defining the DEFAULT_PGSOCKET_DIR directory when you configure and build PostgreSQL from source code.

UNIX_SOCKET_GROUP

Default Value:	None
Modify Time:	Postmaster startup
Override:	None

This parameter determines the owning group of the Unix local domain socket (see previous entry for more information). If UNIX_SOCKET_GROUP is undefined (or empty), the socket will be created using the default group for the user that starts the postmaster. The *PostgreSQL Administrator's Manual* suggests that you can use this parameter, along with UNIX_SOCKET_PERMISSION, to restrict local connections to a specific group.

UNIX_SOCKET_PERMISSIONS

Default Value:	0777
Modify Time:	Postmaster startup
Override:	None

This parameter determines the permissions assigned to the Unix local domain socket. By default, the socket is created with permissions of 0777 (meaning readable and writable by anyone). By changing the socket permissions, you can restrict local connection requests by user ID or group ID. For example, if you create a group named postgresusers, set UNIX_SOCKET_GROUP to postgresusers, and set UNIX_SOCKET_PERMISSIONS to 0060. Only users in the postgresusers group will be able to connect through the local domain socket.

VIRTUAL_HOST

Default Value:	None
Modify Time:	Postmaster startup
Override:	postmaster -h *host*

If the `postmaster` is running on a host that supports multiple IP addresses (for example, has multiple network adapters), you can use the `VIRTUAL_HOST` parameter to tell the `postmaster` to listen for connection requests on a specific IP address. If you don't specify a `VIRTUAL_HOST`, the postmaster will listen on all network adapters.

`KRB_SERVER_KEYFILE`

Default Value:	`/etc/srvtab` or `$SYSCONFDIR/krb5.keytab`
Modify Time:	Postmaster startup
Override:	None

If you are using Kerberos to authenticate clients, the server keyfile is normally located in `/etc/srvtab` (for Kerberos 4) or `$SYSCONFDIR/krb5.keytab` (for Kerberos 5). You can specify an alternate (possibly more secure) location using the `KRB_SERVER_KEYFILE` parameter.

Operational Parameters

The next set of parameters forms a group of loosely related options that affect how the PostgreSQL server operates. Most of these options affect performance and are therefore related to the options shown in the next section.

`SHARED_BUFFERS`

Default Value:	`64` or `DEF_NBUFFERS=`*`nbuffers`*
Modify Time:	Postmaster startup
Override:	`postmaster -B` *`nbuffers`*

When PostgreSQL reads data from (or writes data to) disk, it first transfers the data into a cache stored in shared memory. This cache is shared by all clients connected to a single cluster. Disk I/O (and cache I/O) is performed in 8KB chunks (each chunk is called a page). The `SHARED_BUFFERS` parameter determines how many 8KB pages will be created in the shared cache. The default value, `64`, is usually sufficient for a small number of users, but should be increased as your user count grows. See Chapter 4 for more information. You can change the default value for `SHARED_BUFFERS` by defining the `DEF_NBUFFERS` environment variable when you configure and build PostgreSQL from source code. You can also override `SHARED_BUFFERS` by invoking the `postmaster` with the `-B` *`nbuffers`* command-line parameter.

`MAX_FSM_RELATIONS`

Default Value:	`100`
Modify Time:	Postmaster startup
Override:	None

When PostgreSQL needs to write new data into a table, it searches the table for free space. If free space cannot be found *within* the table, the file holding the table is enlarged. The free-space manager caches free-space information in shared memory for better performance. The `MAX_FSM_RELATIONS` parameter determines the maximum number of tables that the free-space manager will manage at one time. If the cache becomes full, old free-space information will be removed from the cache to make room. This parameter is related to the `MAX_FSM_PAGES` parameter.

`MAX_FSM_PAGES`

Default Value:	`1000`
Modify Time:	Postmaster startup
Override:	None

This parameter (along with `MAX_FSM_RELATIONS`) determines the size of the free-space cache used by the free-space manager. The free-space cache contains, at most, `MAX_FSM_PAGES` worth of data from, at most, `MAX_FSM_RELATIONS` different tables.

These two parameters have no effect on *read* operations, but can affect the performance of `INSERT` and `UPDATE` commands.

`MAX_LOCKS_PER_TRANSACTION`

Default Value:	`64`
Modify Time:	Postmaster startup
Override:	None

This parameter, along with `MAX_CONNECTIONS`, determines the size of PostgreSQL's shared lock table. Any given transaction can hold more than `MAX_LOCKS_PER_TRANSACTION` locks, but the total number of locks cannot exceed `MAX_CONNECTIONS * MAX_LOCKS_PER_TRANSACTION`. PostgreSQL locking is described in Chapter 9, "Multi-Version Concurrency Control," of the *PostgreSQL User's Manual*.

`SORT_MEM`

Default Value:	`512 kilobytes`
Modify Time:	per-command
Override:	`SET SORT_MEM TO` *`maximum_memory_size`*

When PostgreSQL processes a query, it transforms the query from string form into an execution plan. An execution plan is a sequence of operations that must be performed in order to satisfy the query. A typical execution plan might include steps to scan through an entire table and sort the results. If an execution plan includes a `Sort` or `Hash` operation, PostgreSQL can use two different algorithms to perform the sort. If the amount of memory required to perform the sort exceeds `SORT_MEM` KB, PostgreSQL will switch from an in-memory sort to a more expensive, disk-based sort algorithm. You can adjust `SORT_MEM` on a per-command basis using the command `SET SORT_MEM TO` *`maximum_memory`*.

`VACUUM_MEM`

Default Value:	`8192 kilobytes`
Modify Time:	per-command
Override:	`SET VACUUM_MEM TO` *`maximum_memory_size`*

This parameter determines the maximum amount of memory that will be used by the VACUUM command. You can improve the performance of the VACUUM command, particularly for tables that are frequently modified, by increasing VACUUM_MEM.

WAL_BUFFERS

Default Value: 8
Modify Time: Postmaster startup
Override: None

When a transaction makes a change to a PostgreSQL table, the change is applied to the heap (and/or index) pages that are cached in shared memory. All changes are also logged to a *write-ahead* log. The write-ahead log is also cached in shared memory. When a transaction is committed, the write-ahead log is flushed to disk, but the changes made to the actual data pages may not be transferred from shared memory to disk until some point in the future. The size of the shared write-ahead cache is determined by WAL_BUFFERS. The default value of 8 creates a shared write-ahead cache of eight 8KB pages.

CHECKPOINT_SEGMENTS

Default Value: 3
Modify Time: SIGHUP or Postmaster startup
Override: None

The write-ahead log files are divided into 6MB segments. Every so often, PostgreSQL will need to move all modified data (heap and index) pages from the shared-memory cache to disk. This operation is called a *checkpoint*. Log entries made prior to a checkpoint are obsolete and the space consumed by those stale entries can be recycled. If PostgreSQL never performed a checkpoint, the write-ahead logs would grow without bound. The interval between checkpoints is determined by the CHECKPOINT_SEGMENTS and CHECKPOINT_TIMEOUT parameters. A checkpoint will occur every CHECKPOINT_TIMEOUT seconds or when the number of newly filled segments reaches CHECKPOINT_SEGMENTS.

CHECKPOINT_TIMEOUT

Default Value: 300 seconds
Modify Time: SIGHUP or Postmaster startup
Override: None

This parameter determines the maximum amount of time that can elapse between checkpoints. You may see a checkpoint occur *before* CHECKPOINT_TIMEOUT seconds has elapsed if the CHECKPOINT_SEGMENTS threshold has been reached.

WAL_FILES

Default Value: 0
Modify Time: Postmaster startup
Override: None

This parameter determines how many 16MB log segments are preallocated at each checkpoint. The WAL manager preallocates space to improve performance. If you find that write-ahead log files are being deleted (instead of being recycled), you should increase the value of `WAL_FILES`.

`COMMIT_DELAY`

Default Value:	`0` microseconds
Modify Time:	`SET` command
Override:	`SET COMMIT_DELAY TO` *`microseconds`*

When a transaction is committed, the WAL must be flushed from shared-memory to disk. PostgreSQL pauses for `COMMIT_DELAY` microseconds so that other server processes can sneak their commits into the same flush operation. The default for this parameter is `0`, meaning that the WAL will be flushed to disk immediately after each `COMMIT`.

`COMMIT_SIBLINGS`

Default Value:	`5` transactions
Modify Time:	`SET` command
Override:	`SET COMMIT_SIBLINGS TO` *`transactions`*

The `COMMIT_DELAY` (described previously) is a waste of time if there are no other transactions active at the time you `COMMIT` (if there are no other transactions, they can't possibly try to sneak in a `COMMIT`). The WAL manager will not delay for `COMMIT_DELAY` microseconds unless there are at least `COMMIT_SIBLINGS` transactions active at the time you `COMMIT` your changes.

`WAL_SYNC_METHOD`

Default Value:	Dependent on host type
Modify Time:	`SIGHUP` or Postmaster startup
Override:	None

When the WAL manager needs to flush cached write-ahead pages to disk, it can use a variety of system calls. The legal values for `WAL_SYNC_METHOD` vary by host type. It's not very likely that you will ever need to adjust this value—the default value is chosen by the `configure` program at the time PostgreSQL is built from source code. See the *PostgreSQL Administrator's Guide* for more information.

`FSYNC`

Default Value:	`True`
Modify Time:	`SIGHUP` or Postmaster startup
Override:	`postmaster -F`

When an application (such as the PostgreSQL server) writes data to disk, the operating system usually buffers the modifications to improve performance. The OS kernel flushes modified buffers to disk at some time in the future. If your host operating system (or hardware) experiences a crash, not all buffers will be written to disk. If you set the `FSYNC` parameter to `True`, PostgreSQL will occasionally force the kernel to flush modified buffers to disk. Setting `FSYNC` to `True` improves reliability with little performance penalty.

Optimizer Parameters

This section looks at the configuration options that directly influence the PostgreSQL optimizer. The first seven options can be used to enable or disable execution strategies. Some of these options affect how the optimizer estimates execution costs. The last set of options control the PostgreSQL Genetic query optimizer (`GEQO`).

`ENABLE_SEQSCAN`

Default Value:	`True`
Modify Time:	`SET command`
Override:	`SET ENABLE_SEQSCAN TO [true|false]`

This parameter affects the estimated cost of performing a sequential scan on a table. Setting `ENABLE_SEQSCAN` to `False` does not completely disable sequential scans; it simply raises the estimated cost so that sequential scans are not likely to appear in the execution plan. A sequential scan may still appear in the execution plan if there is no other way to satisfy the query (for example, if you have defined no indexes on a table).

This parameter is most often used to force PostgreSQL to use an index that it would not otherwise use. If you are tempted to force PostgreSQL to use an index, you probably need to `VACUUM ANALYZE` your table instead.

`ENABLE_INDEXSCAN`

Default Value:	`True`
Modify Time:	`SET command`
Override:	`SET ENABLE_INDEXSCAN TO [true|false]`

Setting `ENABLE_INDEXSCAN` to `False` increases the estimated cost of performing an index scan so that it is unlikely to appear in an execution plan.

`ENABLE_TIDSCAN`

Default Value:	`True`
Modify Time:	`SET command`
Override:	`SET ENABLE_TIDSCAN TO [true|false]`

Setting `ENABLE_TIDSCAN` to `False` increases the estimated cost of performing a TID scan so that it is unlikely to appear in an execution plan. Because a TID scan is generated only when you have a `WHERE` clause that specifically mentions the `CTID` pseudo-column, this parameter is seldom used.

`ENABLE_SORT`

Default Value:	`True`
Modify Time:	`SET command`
Override:	`SET ENABLE_SORT TO [true|false]`

The `ENABLE_SORT` parameter is used to increase the estimated cost of a sort operation so that it is unlikely to appear in an execution plan (set `ENABLE_SORT` to `False` to increase the estimated cost). Sort operations are often required (in the absence of a useful index) when intermediate results must appear in a specific order. For example, both input sets to the `MergeJoin` operator must appear in sorted order. Of course, an

`ORDER BY` clause can be satisfied using a sort operation. When results are required in a specific order, the only alternative to a sort operation is to use an index scan, thus it makes little sense to disable sorts and index scans at the same time.

`ENABLE_NESTLOOP`

Default Value:	`True`
Modify Time:	`SET command`
Override:	`SET ENABLE_NESTLOOP TO [true|false]`

Setting `ENABLE_NESTLOOP` to `False` increases the estimated cost of performing a nested loop operation so that it is unlikely to appear in an execution plan. The `Nested Loop` operator, described in Chapter 4, is one of three algorithms that PostgreSQL can use to join two tables. Setting `ENABLE_NESTLOOP` to `False` makes it more likely that PostgreSQL will choose a `MergeJoin` or `HashJoin` operator over a `Nested Loop` operator.

`ENABLE_MERGEJOIN`

Default Value:	`True`
Modify Time:	`SET command`
Override:	`SET ENABLE_MERGEJOIN TO [true|false]`

Setting `ENABLE_MERGEJOIN` to `False` increases the estimated cost of performing a `MergeJoin` operation so that it is unlikely to appear in an execution plan. Setting `ENABLE_MERGEJOIN` to `False` makes it more likely that PostgreSQL will choose a `NestedLoop` or `HashJoin` operator over a `MergeJoin` operator.

`ENABLE_HASHJOIN`

Default Value:	`True`
Modify Time:	`SET command`
Override:	`SET ENABLE_HASHJOIN TO [true|false]`

Setting `ENABLE_HASHJOIN` to `False` increases the estimated cost of performing a `HashJoin` operation so that it is unlikely to appear in an execution plan. Setting `ENABLE_HASHJOIN` to `False` makes it more likely that PostgreSQL will choose a `NestedLoop` or `MergeJoin` operator over a `HashJoin` operator.

`KSQO`

Default Value:	`False`
Modify Time:	`SET command`
Override:	`SET KSQO TO [true|false]`

Setting `KSQO` to `True` (the default value for this parameter is `False`) gives PostgreSQL permission to rewrite certain `WHERE` clauses in order to optimize queries that involve many `OR` operators. The *Key Set Query Optimizer* is largely obsolete as of PostgreSQL release 7.0 so the `KSQO` parameter is rarely used. See Chapter 3, "Run-time Configuration," of the *PostgreSQL Administrator's Guide* for more information about the Key Set Query Optimizer.

`EFFECTIVE_CACHE_SIZE`

Default Value:	1000
Modify Time:	`SET command`
Override:	`SET EFFECTIVE_CACHE_SIZE TO` *`size`*

When estimating the cost of an execution plan, PostgreSQL needs to make an educated guess about the cost of reading a random page from disk into the shared buffer cache. To do so, it needs to know the likelihood of finding a given page in the OS cache. The `EFFECTIVE_CACHE_SIZE` parameter tells PostgreSQL how much of the OS disk cache is likely to be given to your server process.

This parameter is used only when estimating the cost of an `IndexScan` or `Sort` operator (when the sort will overflow `SORT_MEM` bytes and switch from an in-memory sort to an on-disk sort).

Increasing the `EFFECTIVE_CACHE_SIZE` makes the cost estimator assume that any given page is more likely to be found in the cache. Decreasing the `EFFECTIVE_CACHE_SIZE` tells PostgreSQL that any given page is less likely to be found in the cache (and will therefore incur more expense).

`RANDOM_PAGE_COST`

Default Value:	4.0
Modify Time:	`SET command`
Override:	`SET RANDOM_PAGE_COST TO` *`float-value`*

`RANDOM_PAGE_COST` specifies the cost of loading a random page into the shared buffer cache. A sequential page fetch is assumed to cost `1` unit; the default value for `RANDOM_PAGE_COST` means that PostgreSQL assumes that it is four times as expensive to load a random page than a sequentially accessed page.

`CPU_TUPLE_COST`

Default Value:	0.01
Modify Time:	`SET command`
Override:	`SET CPU_TUPLE_COST TO` *`float-value`*

`CPU_TUPLE_COST` specifies the cost of processing a single tuple within a heap (data) page. With the default value of 0.01, PostgreSQL assumes that it is 100 times more expensive to load a sequential page from disk than to process a single tuple.

`CPU_INDEX_TUPLE_COST`

Default Value:	0.001
Modify Time:	`SET command`
Override:	`SET CPU_INDEX_TUPLE_COST TO` *`float-value`*

`CPU_INDEX_TUPLE_COST` specifies the cost of processing a single index entry. With the default value of 0.001, PostgreSQL assumes that it is 1000 times more expensive to load a sequential page from disk than to process a single tuple.

`CPU_OPERATOR_COST`

Default Value:	0.0025
Modify Time:	`SET command`
Override:	`SET CPU_OPERATOR_COST TO` *`float-value`*

`CPU_OPERATOR_COST` specifies the cost of processing a single operator (such as `>=` or `!=`) in a `WHERE` clause. With the default value of 0.0025, PostgreSQL assumes that it is 2500 times more expensive to load a sequential page from disk than to process a single operator.

The planner/optimizer works in three phases. The first phase examines the query parse tree and builds a set of execution plans. The second phase assigns a cost to the execution plan by estimating the expense of each step of the plan. The final phase chooses the least expensive alternative and discards the other plans.

Many queries can be evaluated by two or more execution plans. For example, if you have defined an index on the `tape_id` column, the following query:

```
SELECT * FROM tapes ORDER BY tape_id;
```

results in at least two execution plans. One plan scans through the entire table from beginning to end and sorts the results into the desired order (this plan includes a `SeqScan` operator and a `Sort` operator). The second plan reads through the entire table using the `tape_id` index (this plan includes an `IndexScan` operator). For complex queries, especially queries involving many tables, the number of alternative plans becomes large.

The job of the Genetic Query Optimizer (or GEQO, for short) is to reduce the number of alternatives that must be evaluated by eliminating plans that are likely to be more expensive than plans already seen. The next seven parameters control the GEQO. The GEQO algorithm is too complex to try to describe in the space available, so I will include the descriptions provided in the *PostgreSQL Administrator's Guide* for each of the GEQO-related parameters.

`GEQO`

Default Value:	`True`
Modify Time:	`SET command`
Override:	`SET GEQO TO [true|false]`

If `GEQO` is set to `True`, PostgreSQL will use the Genetic Query Optimizer to eliminate plans that are likely to be expensive. If `GEQO` is set to `False`, the planner/optimizer will produce every possible execution plan and find the least expensive among the alternatives.

`GEQO_SELECTION_BIAS`

Default Value:	2.0
Modify Time:	`SET command`
Override:	`SET GEQO_SELECTION_BIAS TO` *`float-value`*

`GEQO_SELECTION_BIAS` is the selective pressure within the population. Values can be from 1.50 to 2.00; the latter is the default.

`GEQO_THRESHOLD`

Default Value:	11
Modify Time:	`SET command`
Override:	`SET GEQO_THRESHOLD TO` *`float-value`*

Use genetic query optimization to plan queries with at least `GEQO_THRESHOLD` `FROM` items involved. (Note that a `JOIN` construct counts as only one `FROM` item.) The default is 11. For simpler queries, it is usually best to use the deterministic, exhaustive planner. This parameter also controls how hard the optimizer will try to merge subquery FROM clauses into the upper query

GEQO_POOL_SIZE

Default Value:	Number of tables involved in each query
Modify Time:	SET command
Override:	SET GEQO_POOL_SIZE TO *number*

GEQO_POOL_SIZE is the number of individuals in one population. Valid values are between 128 and 1024. If it is set to 0 (the default), a pool size of 2^(QS+1), where QS is the number of FROM items in the query, is taken.

GEQO_EFFORT

Default Value:	40
Modify Time:	SET command
Override:	SET GEQO_EFFORT TO *number*

GEQO_EFFORT is used to calculate a default for generations. Valid values are between 1 and 80; 40 being the default.

GEQO_GENERATIONS

Default Value:	0
Modify Time:	SET command
Override:	SET GEQO_GENERATIONS TO *number*

GEQO_GENERATIONS specifies the number of iterations in the algorithm. The number must be a positive integer. If 0 is specified, GEQO_EFFORT * LOG2(GEQO_POOL_SIZE) is used. The runtime of the algorithm is roughly proportional to the sum of pool size and generations.

GEQO_RANDOM_SEED

Default Value:	–1
Modify Time:	SET command
Override:	SET GEQO_RANDOM_SEED TO *number*

GEQO_RANDOM_SEED can be set to get reproducible results from the algorithm. If GEQO_RANDOM_SEED is set to –1, the algorithm behaves nondeterministically.

Debugging/Logging Parameters

The next set of configuration parameters relates to debugging and logging. You may notice that the user can change most of the debugging options (using the SET command). You must be a cluster superuser to change any of the logging options.

SILENT_MODE

Default Value:	False
Modify Time:	SET command
Override:	postmaster -S

If `SILENT_MODE` is set to `True`, all logging and debugging messages are suppressed. If `SILENT_MODE` is set to `True` (the default), the `postmaster` will write log and debug messages to the log destination. You can specify where log messages will be written by invoking the `postmaster` with the `-i` *`log-file-name`* command-line option.

`LOG_CONNECTIONS`

Default Value:	`False`
Modify Time:	Postmaster startup
Override:	*none*

If `LOG_CONNECTIONS` is set to `True`, the postmaster will log each successful client connection. The log message produced by this parameter is of the form:

```
connection: host=client-address user=user database=database
```

If `HOSTNAME_LOOKUP` is `True`, the *`client-address`* will include the client's host name and IP address; otherwise, only the client's IP address is shown.

If `SHOW_SOURCE_PORT` is `True`, the *`client-address`* will also include the port number used by the client side of the connection. (Note: `SHOW_SOURCE_PORT` shows the client's port number, not the server's port number.)

`LOG_TIMESTAMP`

Default Value:	`False`
Modify Time:	`SIGHUP` or Postmaster startup
Override:	None

If `LOG_TIMESTAMP` is set to `True`, each message written to the server log will be prefixed with a timestamp. Messages sent to the client will not include the timestamp.

`LOG_PID`

Default Value:	`False`
Modify Time:	`SIGHUP` or Postmaster startup
Override:	None

If `LOG_PID` is set to `True`, each message written to the server log will be prefixed with the process ID of the server process. Messages sent to the client will not include the process ID.

`DEBUG_LEVEL`

Default Value:	0
Modify Time:	`SET command`
Override:	`SET DEBUG_LEVEL TO` *`level`* `postmaster -d` *`level`*

The DEBUG_LEVEL determines the amount of detail that PostgreSQL produces when inserting debugging messages into the server log. A value of 0 (the default value) tells PostgreSQL not to log debug-related messages. Values greater than 0 increase the amount of debugging information written to the server log.

DEBUG_PRINT_QUERY

Default Value:	False
Modify Time:	SET command
Override:	SET DEBUG_PRINT_QUERY TO [true|false]

If DEBUG_PRINT_QUERY is True, PostgreSQL will write the text of every query to the server log.

DEBUG_PRINT_PARSE

Default Value:	False
Modify Time:	SET command
Override:	SET DEBUG_PRINT_PARSE TO [true|false]

If DEBUG_PRINT_PARSE is True, PostgreSQL will write a textual representation of the parse tree of each query to the server log.

DEBUG_PRINT_REWRITTEN

Default Value:	False
Modify Time:	SET command
Override:	SET DEBUG_PRINT_REWRITTEN TO [t|f]

PostgreSQL implements views using a set of rules that rewrite queries from the point of view seen by the user to the form required to evaluate the view.

If DEBUG_PRINT_REWRITTEN is True, PostgreSQL will write the rewritten form of each query to the server log.

DEBUG_PRINT_PLAN

Default Value:	False
Modify Time:	SET command
Override:	SET DEBUG_PRINT_PLAN TO [true|false]

If DEBUG_PRINT_PLAN is True, PostgreSQL will write the execution plan of each command to the server log. Turning on DEBUG_PRINT_PLAN is similar to using the EXPLAIN command—DEBUG_PRINT_PLAN gives a much more detailed (and much less readable) plan.

DEBUG_PRETTY_PRINT

Default Value:	False
Modify Time:	SET command
Override:	SET DEBUG_PRETTY_PRINT TO [true|false]

If DEBUG_PRETTY_PRINT is True, the log entries for DEBUG_PRINT_PARSE, DEBUG_PRINT_REWRITTEN, and DEBUG_PRINT_PLAN are formatted for consumption by mere mortals. If DEBUG_PRETTY_PRINT is False, the log entries just mentioned are packed very tightly and can be very difficult to read.

SYSLOG

Default Value: 0
Modify Time: SIGHUP or Postmaster startup
Override: None

The SYSLOG parameter determines where server log messages are sent. If SYSLOG is set to 0 (the default value), server log messages are written to the standard output of the terminal that starts the postmaster. You can redirect the postmaster's standard output stream by including -i *filename* on the command line. If SYSLOG is set to 1, server log messages are written to the postmaster's standard output stream and to the OS syslog facility. If SYSLOG is set to 2, server log messages are written to the OS syslog facility.

In addition to SYSLOG, there are two other configuration parameters related to the syslog facility: SYSLOG_FACILITY and SYSLOG_IDENT.

You can use only the syslog facility if your copy of PostgreSQL was configured with --enable-syslog.

See your operating system documentation for more information about the syslog facility.

SYSLOG_FACILITY

Default Value: 'LOCAL0'
Modify Time: Postmaster startup
Override: *none*

If you are sending server log messages to syslog, you can use the SYSLOG_FACILITY parameter to classify PostgreSQL-related messages. Most syslog implementations let you redirect each message classification to a different destination (to a text file, the system console, a particular user, or a remote system). SYSLOG_FACILITY is used to specify the classification that you want PostgreSQL to use when sending messages to syslog. Your choices for this parameter are LOCAL0, LOCAL1, ... LOCAL7. You want to choose a value other than the default if you already have software that uses LOCAL0.

SYSLOG_IDENT

Default Value: Postgres
Modify Time: Postmaster startup
Override: None

If you are sending server log messages to syslog, each message is prefixed with the string specified by the SYSLOG_IDENT parameter.

TRACE_NOTIFY

Default Value: False
Modify Time: SET command
Override: SET TRACE_NOTIFY TO [true|false]

If TRACE_NOTIFY is True, the server will write debug messages regarding the NOTIFY and LISTEN commands to the server log.

TRACE_LOCKS

Default Value: False
Modify Time: SET command (cluster superuser only)
Override: SET TRACE_LOCKS TO [true|false]

If TRACE_LOCKS is True, the server will write debug messages that detail locking operations within the server. This parameter can be set only if the symbol LOCK_DEBUG was defined when your copy of PostgreSQL was built from source code. TRACE_LOCKS is rarely used except by the PostgreSQL developers, but the output can be useful if you want to understand how PostgreSQL manages locking.

TRACE_LOCK_OIDMIN

Default Value: 16384
Modify Time: SET command (cluster superuser only)
Override: SET TRACE_LOCK_OIDMIN TO *oid*

If TRACE_LOCKS is True, TRACE_LOCK_OIDMIN specifies the set of tables for which lock information is logged. If the OID (object ID) of a table's pg_class entry is less than TRACE_LOCK_OIDMIN, PostgreSQL will not log locking information for that table. The default value (16384) was chosen to prevent log messages about locking performed on system tables (system tables have OIDs less than 16384). This parameter can be set only if the symbol LOCK_DEBUG was defined when your copy of PostgreSQL was built from source code.

TRACE_LOCK_TABLE

Default Value: 0
Modify Time: SET command (cluster superuser only)
Override: SET TRACE_LOCK_TABLE TO *oid*

If TRACE_LOCKS is False, you can tell PostgreSQL that it should still log locking information for a specific table by setting TRACE_LOCK_TABLE to the OID of that table's entry in pg_class. This parameter can be set only if the symbol LOCK_DEBUG was defined when your copy of PostgreSQL was built from source code.

TRACE_USERLOCKS

Default Value: False
Modify Time: SET command (cluster superuser only)
Override: SET TRACE_USERLOCKS TO [true|false]

If TRACE_USERLOCKS is True, the server will write debug messages concerning the LOCK TABLE command to the server log. This parameter can be set only if the symbol LOCK_DEBUG was defined when your copy of PostgreSQL was built from source code.

TRACE_USERLOCKS is rarely used except by the PostgreSQL developers, but the output can be useful if you want to understand how PostgreSQL manages locking.

TRACE_LWLOCKS

Default Value:	False
Modify Time:	SET command (cluster superuser only)
Override:	SET TRACE_LWLOCKS TO [true|false]

If TRACE_LWLOCKS is True, the server will write debug messages concerning the lightweight locks that PostgreSQL uses to coordinate multiple server processes. This parameter can be set only if the symbol LOCK_DEBUG was defined when your copy of PostgreSQL was built from source code. TRACE_LWLOCKS is rarely used except by the PostgreSQL developers.

DEBUG_DEADLOCKS

Default Value:	False
Modify Time:	SET command (cluster superuser only)
Override:	SET DEBUG_DEADLOCKS TO [true|false]

If DEBUG_DEADLOCKS is True, the server will log lock queue information whenever a deadlock is detected. A deadlock occurs when two (or more) transactions need to lock two (or more) resources (such as a row or table), but the transactions are blocking each other from proceeding.

This parameter can be set only if the symbol LOCK_DEBUG was defined when your copy of PostgreSQL was built from source code.

Performance Statistics

Next, let's look at the set of configuration parameters that control how PostgreSQL computes and reports performance statistics.

SHOW_PARSER_STATS

Default Value:	False
Modify Time:	SET command
Override:	SET SHOW_PARSER_STATS TO [true|false]

If SHOW_PARSER_STATS is True, the server will write parser statistics to the server log file. For each command, PostgreSQL logs parser statistics, parse analysis statistics, and query rewriter statistics.

SHOW_EXECUTOR_STATS

Default Value:	False
Modify Time:	SET command
Override:	SET SHOW_EXECUTOR_STATS TO [true|false]

If SHOW_EXECUTOR_STATS is True, the server will write execution statistics to the server log file.

SHOW_QUERY_STATS

Default Value:	False
Modify Time:	SET command
Override:	SET SHOW_QUERY_STATS TO [true|false]

If SHOW_QUERY_STATS is True, the server will write query execution statistics to the server log file.

SHOW_BTREE_BUILD_STATS

Default Value:	False
Modify Time:	SET command
Override:	SET SHOW_BTREE_BUILD_STATS TO [t|f]

If SHOW_BTREE_BUILD_STATS is True, the server will write statistics related to building B-Tree indexes to the server log file. You can define this parameter only if the symbol BTREE_BUILD_STATS was defined at the time that your copy of PostgreSQL was built from source code. This parameter is used only by the CREATE INDEX command and is not likely to be useful to most users.

STATS_START_COLLECTOR

Default Value:	True
Modify Time:	Postmaster startup
Override:	None

Starting with release 7.2, PostgreSQL can gather on-going, clusterwide usage statistics in a set of system tables and views. These tables are described in detail in Chapter 4. You must set the STATS_START_COLLECTOR to true if you want PostgreSQL to maintain the information in these tables.

STATS_RESET_ON_SERVER_START

Default Value:	True
Modify Time:	Postmaster startup
Override:	*none*

If STATS_RESET_ON_SERVER_START is True, the statistics captured by the performance monitor will be reset (that is, zeroed out) each time the postmaster starts. If this parameter is False, the performance statistics will accumulate.

STATS_COMMAND_STRING

Default Value:	False
Modify Time:	SET command (cluster superuser only)
Override:	SET STATS_COMMAND_STRING TO [true|false]

If STATS_COMMAND_STRING is True, each PostgreSQL server will send the currently executing command string to the performance monitor. This command string is displayed in the current_query column of the pg_stat_activity view.

STATS_ROW_LEVEL

Default Value:	False
Modify Time:	SET command (cluster superuser only)
Override:	SET STATS_ROW_LEVEL TO [true|false]

If STATS_ROW_LEVEL is True, the performance monitor will gather information regarding the number of tuples processed in each table. When you gather row-level statistics, PostgreSQL records the number of sequential scans and index scans performed on each table, as well the number of tuples processed for each type of scan. The performance monitor also records the number of tuples inserted, updated, and deleted. The row-level information gathered by the performance monitor is found in the pg_stat views described in Chapter 4.

STATS_BLOCK_LEVEL

Default Value:	False
Modify Time:	SET command (cluster superuser only)
Override:	SET STATS_BLOCK_LEVEL TO [true|false]

If STATS_BLOCK_LEVEL is True, the performance monitor will gather information regarding the number of blocks (also known as pages) processed in each table. When you gather block-level statistics, PostgreSQL records the number of heap blocks read, the number of index blocks read, the number of TOAST heap blocks read, and the number of TOAST index blocks read. The performance monitor also records the number of times each type of block was found in the shared buffer cache.

The block-level information gathered by the performance monitor is found in the pg_statio views described in Chapter 4. TOAST blocks are also described in Chapter 4.

Miscellaneous Parameters

Finally, we'll look at the configuration parameters that don't fit well into the other categories.

DYNAMIC_LIBRARY_PATH

Default Value:	$libdir (configure option)
Modify Time:	SET command (cluster superuser only)
Override:	SET DYNAMIC_LIBRARY_PATH TO *search-path*

The DYNAMIC_LIBRARY_PATH determines which directories PostgreSQL searches to find dynamically loaded functions (that is, external functions defined with the CREATE FUNCTION command). This parameter should be defined as a colon-separated list of the absolute directory. The DYNAMIC_LIBRARY_PATH is consulted only when PostgreSQL needs to load a dynamic object module that does not include a directory name. If

DYNAMIC_LIBRARY_PATH is defined but empty, PostgreSQL will not use a search path, and each external function must include a directory name.

AUSTRALIAN_TIMEZONES

Default Value:	False
Modify Time:	SET command
Override:	SET AUSTRALIAN_TIMEZONES TO [true|false]

If AUSTRALIAN_TIMEZONES is True, the time zones CST, EST, and SAT are interpreted as UTC+9.5 (Central Australia Standard Time), UTC+10 (Eastern Australia Standard Time), and UTC+9.5 (Central Australia Standard Time), respectively.

If AUSTRALIAN_TIMEZONES is false, CST is interpreted as UTC-6 (Central Standard Time), EST is interpreted as UTC-5 (Eastern Standard Time), and SAT is interpreted as an abbreviation for Saturday.

PostgreSQL's support for time zones is described in Chapter 2, "Working with Data in PostgreSQL."

AUTHENTICATION_TIMEOUT

Default Value:	60
Modify Time:	SIGHUP or Postmaster startup
Override:	None

This parameter defines the maximum amount of time (in seconds) that the postmaster will wait for a client to complete the authentication process. If the timeout period expires, the postmaster will sever the connection with the client.

DEFAULT_TRANSACTION_ISOLATION

Default Value:	'READ COMMITTED'
Modify Time:	SET command
Override:	SET TRANSACTION ISOLATION LEVEL TO *level*

This parameter defines default transaction isolation level for all transactions. The valid choices for this parameter are 'READ COMMITTED' and 'SERIALIZABLE'. Transaction isolation levels are described in the section titled "Transaction Isolation" in Chapter 3.

You can modify the transaction isolation level for an individual transaction using the SET TRANSACTION ISOLATION LEVEL command. You can also change the *default* isolation level for a PostgreSQL session using the command SET SESSION CHARACTERISTICS AS TRANSACTION ISOLATION LEVEL [READ COMMITTED | SERIALIZABLE], but I've never be able focus my attention long enough to enter that command.

MAX_EXPR_DEPTH

Default Value:	1000
Modify Time:	SET command
Override:	SET MAX_EXPR_DEPTH TO *depth*

This parameter defines maximum expression depth that the parser will accept. It is very unlikely that you will ever exceed the default value.

`MAX_FILES_PER_PROCESS`

Default Value: `1000`
Modify Time: Server startup
Override: None

This parameter defines maximum number of files that PostgreSQL opens for any given server process. PostgreSQL uses a file-descriptor caching mechanism to extend the number of files that are *logically* open without having to have each file *physically* opened, so if you see any error messages suggesting that you have `Too Many Open Files`, you should *reduce* this parameter.

`PASSWORD_ENCRYPTION`

Default Value: `False`
Modify Time: `SET command`
Override: `SET PASSWORD_ENCRYPTION TO [true|false]`
`CREATE USER WITH ENCRYPTED PASSWORD...`
`CREATE USER WITH UNENCRYPTED PASSWORD...`
`ALTER USER WITH ENCRYPTED PASSWORD...`
`ALTER USER WITH UNENCRYPTED PASSWORD...`

This parameter specifies whether passwords should be stored in encrypted or cleartext form in the absence of a specific choice. See Chapter 21 for more information on password-encryption options.

`SQL_INHERITANCE`

Default Value: `True`
Modify Time: `SET command`
Override: `SET SQL_INHERITANCE TO [true|false]`

Prior to release 7.1, a `SELECT` command would not include data from descendant tables unless an asterisk was appended to the table name. Starting with release 7.1, data is included from all descendant tables unless the keyword `ONLY` is included in the `FROM` clause.

In other words, in release 7.1, the default behavior of PostgreSQL's inheritance feature was reversed. If you find that you need the pre-7.1 behavior, set `SQL_INHERITANCE` to false.

Inheritance is described in Chapter 3.

`TRANSFORM_NULL_EQUALS`

Default Value: `False`
Modify Time: `SET command`
Override: `SET TRANSFORM_NULL_EQUALS TO [t|f]`

If `TRANSFORM_NULL_EQUALS` is `True`, the PostgreSQL parser will translate expressions of the form *`expression`* `= NULL` to *`expression`* `IS NULL`. In most cases, it's a bad idea to set this parameter to true because there is a semantic difference between `= NULL` and `IS NULL`. The expression *`expression`* `= NULL` should always evaluate to `NULL`, regardless of the value of *`expression`*. The only time that you should consider setting this parameter to `True` is when you are using Microsoft Access as a client application: Access can generate queries that are technically incorrect but are still expected to function.

Arranging for PostgreSQL Startup and Shutdown

In most environments, you will probably want to arrange for your PostgreSQL server to start when you boot your operating system. You'll also want to arrange for your PostgreSQL server to terminate gracefully when you power off your system. In this section, I'll show you how to make these arrangements for Windows and Red Hat Linux—the details will vary if you are using a different operating system.

First, let's see how to start and stop a PostgreSQL server *on-demand*.

Using pg_ctl

The easiest way to start a PostgreSQL server (that is, a `postmaster`) is to use the `pg_ctl` command. `pg_ctl` is a shell script that makes it easy to start, stop, restart, reconfigure, and query the status of a PostgreSQL server.

To start a server, use `pg_ctl start`:

```
$ pg_ctl start -l /tmp/pg.log -o -i
```

`pg_ctl start` fires up a `postmaster`. You can use several options with the `pg_ctl start` command, as shown in Table 19.4.

Table 19.4 `pg_ctl` **Start Options**

Option	Parameter	Meaning
`-D`	*`data-directory`*	Look for data files in *`data-directory`*
`-l`	*`logfile-name`*	Append `postmaster` output to *`logfile-name`*
`-o`	*`postmaster-options`*	Start postmaster with *`postmaster-options`*
`-p`	*`postmaster-path`*	Find postmaster in *`postmaster-path`*
`-s`		Report startup errors, but not informational messages
`-w`		Wait for postmaster to complete

The `-D` *`data-directory`* option tells the `postmaster` where to find your database cluster. If you don't include this option, the `postmaster` will interrogate the `$PGDATA` environment variable to find your cluster. If I am starting a postmaster from a shell script, I usually define PGDATA and then use it when I invoke pg_ctl:

```
...
export PGDATA=/usr/local/pgdata
pg_ctl -D $PGDATA
...
```

Arranging things this way makes it a bit more obvious that PGDATA is defined and that the postmaster will use that variable to find the cluster.

The -l *logfile-name* option determines where the postmaster will send error and informational messages. If you include this option, the postmaster's stdout and stderr will be appended to the named file. If you don't, the postmaster will write to the controlling terminal. That can be handy if you're trying to debug a server-related problem, but it's generally a bad idea. The problem with sending server output to the controlling terminal is that the controlling terminal will disappear if you log out—any server output written after you log out is lost.

You use the -o *postmaster-options* to specify options that will be passed along to the new postmaster. Any option supported by the postmaster can be specified after the -o flag. Enclose the *postmaster-options* in single or double quotes if it contains any whitespace. For example:

```
$ pg_ctl start -o "-i -d 5"
```

You will rarely, if ever, need to use the -p *postmaster-path* option. The -p option tells pg_ctl where to find the postmaster. In the normal case, pg_ctl can find the postmaster executable by looking in the directory that contains pg_ctl. If pg_ctl doesn't find the postmaster in its own directory, it will search in the bindir directory. The bindir directory is determined at the time your copy of PostgreSQL is built from source (that is, the -bindir configuration option). You will need to use only pg_ctl's -p option if you move the postmaster away from its normal location (don't do that).

The -s option is used to tell pg_ctl to be *s*ilent. Without the -s flag, pg_ctl will cheerfully display progress messages as it goes about its work. With the -s flag, pg_ctl will tell you only about problems.

Finally, use the -w flag if you want the pg_ctl program to *w*ait for the postmaster to complete its startup work before returning. If pg_ctl has to wait for more than 60 seconds, it will assume that something has gone wrong and will report an error. At that point, the postmaster may or may not be running: Use pg_ctl status to find out. I recommend including the -w flag whenever you invoke pg_ctl from a script; otherwise, your script will happily continue immediately after the pg_ctl command completes (but before the server has booted). If you want to see what kind of problems you may run into when you don't wait for a complete boot, try this:

```
$ pg_ctl -s stop
$ pg_ctl start -l /tmp/pg.log ; psql -d movies
postmaster successfully started
```

```
psql: could not connect to server: No such file or directory
        Is the server running locally and accepting
        connections on Unix domain socket "/tmp/.s.PGSQL.5432"?
```

See what happened? The `pg_ctl` command returned immediately after spawning the `postmaster`, but the `psql` command started running before the `postmaster` was ready to accept client connections. If you were to try that inside of a shell script, the PostgreSQL client (`psql` in this case) would fail. This kind of problem (apparently random client failures) can be hard to track down and usually results in a dope slap.

Shutdown Modes

You also can use `pg_ctl` to shut down (or restart) the `postmaster`. The `postmaster` honors three different shutdown signals:

- Smart shutdown—When the postmaster receives a terminate signal (SIGTERM), it performs a *smart* shutdown. In smart shutdown mode, the server prevents new client connections, allows current connections to continue, and terminates only after all clients have disconnected.
- Fast shutdown—If the `postmaster` receives an interrupt signal (`SIGINT`), it performs a *fast* shutdown. In fast shutdown mode, the server tells each server process to abort the current transaction and exit.
- Immediate shutdown—The third shutdown mode is called *immediate*, but it might be better termed *crash*. When you shut down the `postmaster` in this mode, each server process immediately terminates without cleaning up itself. An immediate shutdown is similar to a power failure and requires a WAL (write-ahead-log) recovery the next time you start your database.

To shut down the `postmaster` using `pg_ctl`, use the command

```
$ pg_ctl stop [smart|fast|immediate]
```

If you want to restart the postmaster using `pg_ctl`, use the command

```
$ pg_ctl restart [smart|fast|immediate]
```

Now that you know how to start up and shut down a PostgreSQL server on demand, let's see how to make a server start when your computer boots.

Configuring PostgreSQL Startup on Unix/Linux Hosts

Configuring PostgreSQL to automatically start when your Unix/Linux system boots is not difficult, but it is system-specific. Systems derived from BSD Unix will usually store startup scripts in the `/etc/rc.local` directory. Systems derived from System V Unix (including Red Hat Linux) will store startup scripts in the `/etc/rc.d` directory. The PostgreSQL Administrator's Guide contains a number of suggestions for configuring automatic PostgreSQL startup for various Unix/Linux systems. In this section, I'll describe the process for Red Hat Linux systems.

First, let's see the easy way to configure startup and shutdown on a typical Red Hat Linux system. There are only three steps required if you want to do things the easy way:

- Log in as the superuser (root)
- Copy the file `start-scripts/linux` from PostgreSQL's `contrib` directory to `/etc/rc.d/init.d/postgresql`
- Execute the command `/sbin/chkconfig --add postgresql`

That's it. The `chkconfig` command arranges for PostgreSQL to start when your system boots to multiuser mode and also arranges for PostgreSQL to shut down gracefully when you shut down your host system.

Now, let's look at the more complex way to arrange for startup and shutdown. Why might you want to do things the hard way? You may find that the functionality provided by the startup script (and `chkconfig`) don't fit quite right in your environment. You may have customized run levels (described next), or you may want to change the point in time that PostgreSQL starts (or stops) relative to other services. Reading the next section will also give you a good understanding of what `chkconfig` is doing on your behalf if you decide to use it.

When a Linux system boots, it boots to a specific *runlevel*. Each runlevel provides a set of services (such as network, X Windows, and PostgreSQL). Most Linux distributions define seven runlevels:

- Runlevel 0—Halt
- Runlevel 1—Single-user (maintenance mode)
- Runlevel 2—Not normally used
- Runlevel 3—Multi-user, networking enabled
- Runlevel 4—Not normally used
- Runlevel 5—Multi-user, networking enabled, X Window login
- Runlevel 6—shutdown

In the usual case, your system is running at runlevel 3 or runlevel 5. You can add PostgreSQL to the set of services provided at a particular runlevel by adding a startup script and a shutdown script to the runlevel's directory.

Startup scripts are stored in the `/etc/rc.d` directory tree. `/etc/rc.d` contains one subdirectory for each runlevel. Here is a listing of the `/etc/rc.d` directory for our Red Hat 7.1 system:

```
$ ls /etc/rc.d
init.d  rc0.d  rc2.d  rc4.d  rc6.d     rc.sysinit
rc      rc1.d  rc3.d  rc5.d  rc.local
```

The numbers in the directory names correspond to different runlevels. So, the services provided at runlevel 3, for example, are defined in the `/etc/rc.d/rc3.d` directory. Here is a peek at the `rc3.d` directory:

```
$ ls /etc/rc.d/rc3.d
K03rhnsd     S05kudzu     S14nfslock   S55sshd        S85gpm
K20nfs       S06reconfig  S17keytable  S56rawdevices  S90crond
K20rwhod     S08ipchains  S20random    S56xinetd      S90xfs
K35smb       S08iptables  S25netfs     S60lpd         S95anacron
K45arpwatch  S10network   S26apmd      S80isdn        S99linuxconf
K65identd    S12syslog    S28autofs    S80pppoe       S99local
K74nscd      S13portmap   S40atd       S80sendmail
```

Inside a runlevel subdirectory, you will see *start* scripts and *kill* scripts. The start scripts begin with the letter `S` and are executed whenever the runlevel begins. The kill scripts begin with the letter `K` and are executed each time the runlevel ends. A start script is (appropriately enough) used to start a service. A kill script is used to stop a service.

The numbers following the `K` or `S` determine the order in which the scripts will execute. For example, `S05kudzu` starts with a lower number so it will execute before `S06reconfig`.

I'll assume that you want to run PostgreSQL at runlevels 3 and 5 (the most commonly used runlevels). The start and kill scripts are usually quite complex. Fortunately, PostgreSQL's `contrib` directory contains a sample startup script that you can use: `contrib/start-scripts/linux`. To install this script, copy it to the `/etc/rc.d/init.d` directory and fix the ownership and permissions (you'll need superuser privileges to do this):

```
# cp contrib/start-scripts/linux /etc/rc.d/init.d/postgresql
# chown root /etc/rc.d/init.d/postgresql
# chmod 0755 /etc/rc.d/init.d/postgresql
```

Notice that you are copying the startup file to `/etc/rc.d/init.d` rather than `/etc/rc.d/rc3.d`, as you might expect. Start and kill scripts are usually combined into a single shell script that can handle startup requests as well as shutdown requests. Because a single script might be needed in more than one runlevel, it is stored in `/etc/rc.d/init.d` and symbolically linked from the required runlevel directories. You want PostgreSQL to be available in runlevels 3 and 5, so create symbolic links in those directories:

```
# ln -s /etc/rc.d/init.d/postgresql /etc/rc.d/rc3.d/S75postgresql
# ln -s /etc/rc.d/init.d/postgresql /etc/rc.d/rc3.d/K75postgresql
# ln -s /etc/rc.d/init.d/postgresql /etc/rc.d/rc5.d/S75postgresql
# ln -s /etc/rc.d/init.d/postgresql /etc/rc.d/rc5.d/K75postgresql
```

The numbers that you chose (`S75` and `K75`) are positioned about three quarters through the range (00–99). You will want to adjust the script numbers so that PostgreSQL starts after any prerequisite services and ends after any services that depend upon it. Whenever we reach runlevel 3 (or runlevel 5), the `init` process will execute all start scripts numbered less than 75, then your `postgresql` script, and then scripts numbered higher than 75.

You also want to ensure that PostgreSQL shuts down gracefully when you reboot or halt your server. The contributed script can handle that for you as well; you just need to create symbolic links from the halt (`rc0.d`) and reboot (`rc6.d`) directories:

```
# ln -s /etc/rc.d/init.d/postgresql /etc/rc.d/rc0.d/K75postgresql
# ln -s /etc/rc.d/init.d/postgresql /etc/rc.d/rc6.d/K75postgresql
```

As before, you will want to review the other scripts in your `rc0.d` and `rc6.d` directories to ensure that PostgreSQL is shut down in the proper order relative to other services.

Configuring PostgreSQL as a Windows Service

Running the PostgreSQL server on a Windows host currently requires the Cygwin compatibility library. The Cygwin distribution includes an application (`cygrunsrv`) that you can use to install PostgreSQL as a Windows service.

A Windows *service* is similar to a Unix *daemon*. You create a service when you want a program (such as PostgreSQL) to run, even though a user isn't logged into the Windows console. Services are controlled by the Service Control Manager (SCM—pronounced *scum*). Using the SCM, you can create, remove, start, stop, and query a service. Creating a service with the SCM is not a simple task—use `cygrunsrv` instead. Table 19.5 shows the `cygrunsrv` options.

Table 19.5 **cygrunsrv Command-Line Options**

Option	Meaning
`--args arguments`	Command-line arguments passed to service application.
`--env env-string`	Environment variable string (can appear up to 255 times).
`--disp display-name`	Display name for service.
`--desc descriptive-name`	Descriptive name for service.
`--type [auto|manual]`	Startup type (automatic or manual).
`--user`	Username for service (the service runs with the security context of this user). Defaults to `SYSTEM`.
`--passwd`	Password for `-user`.
`--stdin filename`	The standard input stream (`stdin`) of the service application will be connected to filename.
`--stdout filename`	The standard output stream (`stdout`) of the service application will be routed to filename.
`--stderr filename`	The standard error stream (`stderr`) of the service application will be routed to filename.
`--termsig signal-name`	`cygrunsrv` sends the `signal-name` signal to the service application whenever the application should be terminated.
`--dep dependency-name`	Ensure that this service is started after the service named `dependency-name`.
`--shutdown`	Send the `--termsig` signal to this service application when the operating system is shut down.

To install PostgreSQL as a service, use the `cygrunsrv --install` command. For example:

```
$ ipc-daemon --install-as-service
$ cygrunsrv \
   --install     PostgreSQL \
   --path        /usr/bin/postmaster \
   --args          "-D /usr/local/pgdata" \
   --dep           ipc-daemon \
   --user          Postgres \
   --password      bovine \
   --termsig       INT \
   --shutdown
```

This example creates a service named `PostgreSQL` (`--install PostgreSQL`).You specify the pathname to the `postmaster`: it's a good idea to include the complete pathname here rather than relying on `$PATH` because it's hard to predict (okay, hard to *remember*) which environment variables will be available at boot time. Next, define the command-line arguments that you want to send to the `postmaster`. Notice that you had to enclose the command-line arguments in quotes because of embedded spaces. Be sure that the Cygwin IPC daemon is up and running before you start PostgreSQL, so specify `--dep ipc-daemon`. Next, specify a username and password; the SCM executes the `postmaster` within the security context of the user that you specify. Be sure that the user account that you specify holds the `Log on as a service` privilege.

Finally, tell `cygrunsrv` how to gracefully terminate the `postmaster`. The `--termsig INT` option tells `cygrunsrv` to terminate the `postmaster` by sending it an interrupt signal (`SIGINT`).

Using `--termsig INT` is a compromise. On the one hand, we want the `postmaster` to terminate as gracefully as possible — that would imply a *smart* shutdown. On the other hand, we want the `postmaster` to terminate as quickly as possible (because the termination occurs when you are shutting down your operating system). Using `--termsig INT` means that you will lose any in-progress transactions, but you won't have to wait for a WAL recovery at startup. The last `cygrunsrv` option (`--shutdown`) tells `cygrunsrv` that you want to terminate the server (using the `--termsig` signal) when the operating system is shut down. That might sound redundant, but it's still required. The `--termsig` option tells `cygrunsrv` *how* to terminate the `postmaster`; the `--shutdown` option tells `cygrunsrv` to terminate the `postmaster` as the operating system is shutting down. Using the SCM, you can terminate a service at *any* time, not just at OS shutdown.

You may also want to include the `--stdout` *`filename`* and `--stderr` *`filename`* options to capture any diagnostic messages produced by the `postmaster` or by the backend servers. Redirecting the standard output and standard error streams to the same file is *almost* equivalent to `pg_ctl`'s `-l` *`logfilename`* option. The difference is that `pg_ctl -l` *`logfilename`* appends to the given file, but `--stdout` and `--stderr` will overwrite the file.

You may be wondering why we define the service to run the postmaster rather than the more friendly pg_ctl. When you run a program as a Windows service, the SCM monitors the service application. If the service application exits, the SCM assumes that the service has terminated. The pg_ctl script spawns the postmaster and then exits. Client applications will connect to the postmaster, not to pg_ctl. That means that postmaster *is* the service: pg_ctl is just an easy way to launch the postmaster. We want the SCM to watch the postmaster, not pg_ctl.

Backing Up and Copying Databases

There are two ways to back up your PostgreSQL database. The first method is to create an archive containing the filesystem files that comprise your database. The second method is to create a SQL script that describes how to re-create the data in your database.

In the first method, you use an archiving tool, such as tar, cpio, or backup, to back up all the files in your database cluster. There are a number of disadvantages to this method. First, your entire database cluster must be shut down to ensure that all buffers have been flushed to disk. Second, the size of a filesystem archive will often be larger than the size of the equivalent script because the filesystem archive will contain indexes and partially filled pages that do not have to be archived. Finally, it is not possible to restore a single database or table from a filesystem archive. There are, however, two advantages to using a filesystem archive. First, you may already have a backup scheme in place that will backup a file system; including your database cluster in that scheme is probably pretty easy.

The second (and usually preferred) method is to create a SQL script that can reconstruct the contents of your database from scratch. Then, when you need to restore data from an archive, you simply run the script.

PostgreSQL provides two utilities that you can use to create archive scripts: pg_dump, and pg_dumpall.

Using pg_dump

The pg_dump program creates a SQL script that re-creates the data and metadata in your database. Before I get into too many details, it might help to see the kind of script that pg_dump will create[7]:

```
$ pg_dump --inserts -t customers movies
--
-- Selected TOC Entries:
--
\connect - bruce


--
```

7. I've changed the formatting of this script slightly so that it fits on a printed page.

```
-- TOC Entry ID 2 (OID 518934)
--
-- Name: customers Type: TABLE Owner: bruce
--
CREATE TABLE "customers" (
        "id" integer,
        "customer_name" character varying(50),
        "phone" character(8),
        "birth_date" date
);

--
-- TOC Entry ID 3 (OID 518934)
--
-- Name: customers Type: ACL Owner:
--
REVOKE ALL on "customers" from PUBLIC;
GRANT ALL on "customers" to "bruce";
GRANT ALL on "customers" to "sheila";

--
-- Data for TOC Entry ID 4 (OID 518934)
--
-- Name: customers Type: TABLE DATA Owner: bruce
--
INSERT INTO "customers" VALUES
      (1,'Jones, Henry','555-1212','1970-10-10');
INSERT INTO "customers" VALUES
      (2,'Rubin, William','555-2211','1972-07-10');
INSERT INTO "customers" VALUES
      (3,'Panky, Henry','555-1221','1968-01-21');
INSERT INTO "customers" VALUES
      (4,'Wonderland, Alice N.','555-1122','1969-03-05');
INSERT INTO "customers" VALUES
      (7,'Grumby, Jonas',NULL,'1984-02-21');
INSERT INTO "customers" VALUES
      (8,'Haywood, Rosemary','666-1212','1965-02-03');
```

In this example, I've asked pg_dump to produce a script that re-creates a single table (-t customers) using INSERT commands rather than COPY commands (--inserts).

If we feed this script back into psql (or some other client application), psql will connect to the database as user bruce, CREATE the customers table, assign the proper privileges to the table, and INSERT all the rows that had been committed at the time that we started the original pg_dump command. You can see that this script contains everything that we need to re-create the customers table starting from an empty database. If we had defined triggers, sequences, or indexes for the customers table, the code necessary to re-create those objects would appear in the script as well.

Now let's look at some of the command-line options for pg_dump. Start with `pg_dump --help`:

```
$ pg_dump --help
pg_dump dumps a database as a text file or to other formats.

Usage:
  pg_dump [options] dbname

Options:
  -a, --data-only          dump only the data, not the schema
  -b, --blobs              include large objects in dump
  -c, --clean              clean (drop) schema prior to create
  -C, --create             include commands to create database in dump
  -d, --inserts            dump data as INSERT, rather than COPY, commands
  -D, --column-inserts     dump data as INSERT commands with column names
  -f, --file=FILENAME      output file name
  -F, --format {c|t|p}     output file format (custom, tar, plain text)
  -h, --host=HOSTNAME      database server host name
  -i, --ignore-version     proceed even when server version mismatches
                           pg_dump version
  -n, --no-quotes          suppress most quotes around identifiers
  -N, --quotes             enable most quotes around identifiers
  -o, --oids               include oids in dump
  -O, --no-owner           do not output \connect commands in plain
                           text format
  -p, --port=PORT          database server port number
  -R, --no-reconnect       disable ALL reconnections to the database in
                           plain text format
  -s, --schema-only        dump only the schema, no data
  -S, --superuser=NAME     specify the superuser user name to use in
                           plain text format
  -t, --table=TABLE        dump this table only (* for all)
  -U, --username=NAME      connect as specified database user
  -v, --verbose            verbose mode
  -W, --password           force password prompt
                              (should happen automatically)
  -x, --no-privileges      do not dump privileges (grant/revoke)
  -X use-set-session-authorization, --use-set-session-authorization
                              output SET SESSION AUTHORIZATION commands
                              rather than \connect commands
  -Z, --compress {0-9}        compression level for compressed formats

If no database name is not supplied, then the PGDATABASE environment
variable value is used.

Report bugs to <pgsql-bugs@postgresql.org>.
```

The most basic form for the `pg_dump` command is

```
pg_dump database
```

In this form, `pg_dump` archives all objects in the given *`database`*. You can see that `pg_dump` understands quite a number of command-line options. I'll explain the most useful options here.

If you use large-objects in your database, you may want to include the `--blobs` (or `-b`) option so that large-objects are written to the resulting script. Needless to say, archiving large-objects increases the size of your archive.

You also might want to include either `--clean` (`-c`) or `--create` (`-C`) when you are using `pg_dump` for backup purposes. The `--clean` flag tells `pg_dump` to `DROP` an object before it `CREATE`s the object—this reduces the number of errors you might see when you restore from the script. The second option, `--create,` tells `pg_dump` to include a `CREATE DATABASE` statement in the resulting archive. If you want to archive and restore an entire database, use the `--create` option when you create the archive and drop the database before you restore.

In the previous example, I included the `--inserts` flag. This flag, and the related `--column-inserts` flag affect how `pg_dump` populates each table in your database. If you don't include either flag, `pg_dump` will emit `COPY` commands to put data back into each table. If you use the `--inserts` flag, `pg_dump` will emit `INSERT` commands rather than `COPY` commands. If you use the `--column-inserts` flag, `pg_dump` will build `INSERT` commands, which include column lists, such as

```
INSERT INTO "customers" ("id","customer_name","phone","birth_date")
  VALUES (1,'Jones, Henry','555-1212','1970-10-10');
```

Emitting `COPY` commands causes the restore to execute more quickly than `INSERT` commands, so you should usually omit both flags (`--inserts` and `--column-inserts`). You might want to build `INSERT` commands if you intend to use the resulting script for some other purpose, such as copying data into an Oracle, Sybase, or SQL Server database.

Because `pg_dump` is a client application, you don't have to be logged in to the server to create an archive script. A few of the `pg_dump` options (`--port`, `--host`, and `--username`) control how pg_dump will connect to your database.

One of the problems that you may encounter when you run `pg_dump` is that it can produce scripts that are too large to store as a single file. Many operating systems impose a maximum file size of 2GB or 4GB. If you are archiving a large database, the resulting script can easily exceed the file size limit, even though no single table would (remember, each table is stored in its own file).

There are two (related) solutions to this problem. First, you can decrease the size of the archive script by compressing it. The `pg_dump` program writes the archive script to its standard output so you can pipe the script into a compression program:

```
$ pg_dump movies | gzip -9 > movies.gz
```

or

```
$ pg_dump movies | bzip2 -9 > movies.bz2
```

You also can compress the archive script by telling pg_dump to create the archive in *custom* format. The custom format is compressed and is organized so that the pg_restore program (described a bit later) can avoid problems caused by order of execution. To choose the custom format, include the --format c flag:

```
$ pg_dump --format c movies > movies.bak
```

Using the custom format means that your archive script will be compressed (thus taking less space and possibly fitting within the operating system imposed file size limit). However, you can't restore a custom-format script using psql; you must use pg_restore. That's not a problem per se; it's just something to be aware of.

Unfortunately, compressing the archive script is not really a solution; it simply delays the inevitable because even in compressed form, you may still exceed your OS file size limit. You may need to *split* the archive script into smaller pieces. Fortunately, the split command (a Unix/Linux/Cygwin utility) makes this easy. You can dump an entire database into a collection of smaller archive scripts (20MB each) with the following command:

```
$ pg_dump movies | split --bytes=20m movies.bak.
```

This command causes pg_dump to produce a single script, but when you pipe the script to split, it will split the script into 20MB chunks. The end result is a collection of one or more files with names such as movies.bak.aa, movies.bak.ab, … movies.bak.zz. When you want to restore data from these archives, you can concatenate them using the cat command:

```
$ cat movies.bak.* | psql -d movies
```

See the *PostgreSQL Reference Manual* for complete details on the pg_dump command.

Using pg_dumpall

The pg_dump command can archive individual tables or all the tables in a single database, but it cannot archive multiple databases. To archive an entire cluster, use the pg_dumpall command. pg_dumpall is similar to pg_dump in that it creates SQL scripts that can be used to re-create a database cluster.

pg_dumpall is actually a wrapper that invokes pg_dump for each database in your cluster. That means that pg_dumpall supports the same set of command-line options as pg_dump. Well, almost—pg_dumpall silently ignores any attempts to produce a custom or tar format script. pg_dumpall can produce archive scripts only in plain text format. This introduces two problems. First, you cannot compress the archive script by selecting the custom format; you must pipe the script to an external compression program instead. Second, you cannot archive large-objects using pg_dumpall (pg_dump can archive only large-objects using custom format, which you can't use with pg_dumpall).

Using pg_restore

When you create an archive script using `pg_dump` or `pg_dumpall`, you can restore the archive using `pg_restore`. The `pg_restore` command processes the given archive and produces a sequence of SQL commands that re-create the archived data. Note that `pg_restore` *cannot* process plain text archive scripts (such as those produced by `pg_dumpall`); you must produce the archive using the `--format=c` or `--format=t` options. If you want to restore a plain text archive script, simply pipe it into `psql`.

A typical invocation of `pg_restore` might look like this:

```
$ pg_restore --clean -d movies movies.bak
```

The `--clean` flag tells `pg_restore` to drop each database object before it is restored. The `-d movies` option tells `pg_restore` to connect to the `movies` database before processing the archive: All SQL commands built from the archive are executed within the given database. If you don't supply a database name, `pg_restore` writes the generated SQL commands to the standard output stream; this can be useful if you want to clone a database.

Like `pg_dump`, `pg_restore` can be used from a remote host. That means that you can provide the hostname, username, and password on the `pg_restore` command line.

The `pg_restore` program allows you to restore specific database objects (tables, functions, and so on); see the *PostgreSQL Reference Manual* for more details.

Summary

This chapter is intended as a supplement to the *PostgreSQL Administrator's Guide*, not as a replacement. I've tried to cover the basic operations that a PostgreSQL administrator will be required to perform, but you may need to refer to the official PostgreSQL documentation for detailed reference material.

The next chapter covers the internationalization and localization features of PostgreSQL.

20

Internationalization and Localization

INTERNATIONALIZATION AND LOCALIZATION ARE TWO SIDES of the same coin. *Internationalization* is the process of developing software so that it can be used in a variety of locations. *Localization* is the process of modifying an application for use in a specific location. When you internationalize software, you are making it portable; when you localize software, you are actually performing a port.

In the PostgreSQL world, the topics of internationalization and localization are concerned with the following:

- Viewing PostgreSQL-generated messages in the language of your choice
- Viewing PostgreSQL-generated messages in the character set of your choice
- Viewing user data in the character set of your choice
- Getting the correct results when PostgreSQL returns data in sorted order
- Getting the correct results when PostgreSQL needs to classify characters into categories such as uppercase, punctuation, and so on

We can separate these issues into two broad categories: locales and character sets.

Locale Support

A *locale* is a named group of properties that defines culture-specific conventions. Each locale is made up of one or more categories. Each category controls the behavior of a set of features. For example, the `LC_MONETARY` category contains information about how monetary values are formatted in some specific territory. The ISO and IEEE (POSIX) standards bodies have stated that a locale should include information such as the ordering of date components, the formatting of numbers, and the language preferred for message text.

PostgreSQL makes use of the locale-processing facilities provided by the host operating system. When you log into your operating system, you are automatically assigned a locale. On a Linux host (and most Unix hosts), you can find your current locale using the `locale` command:

```
$ locale
LANG=en_US
LC_CTYPE="en_US"
LC_NUMERIC="en_US"
LC_TIME="en_US"
LC_COLLATE="en_US"
LC_MONETARY="en_US"
LC_MESSAGES="en_US"
LC_PAPER="en_US"
LC_NAME="en_US"
LC_ADDRESS="en_US"
LC_TELEPHONE="en_US"
LC_MEASUREMENT="en_US"
LC_IDENTIFICATION="en_US"
LC_ALL=
```

You can see that I am using a locale named `en_US`. Locale names are composed of multiple parts. The first component identifies a language. In my case, the language is `en`, meaning English. The second (optional) component identifies a country, region, or territory where the language is used. I am in the U.S., so my country code is set to `US`. You can think of `en_US` as meaning "English as spoken in the U.S.", as opposed to `en_AU`, which means "English as spoken in Australia." The third component of a locale name is an optional codeset. I'll talk more about codesets later in this chapter. Finally, a locale name may include modifiers, such as "`@euro`" to indicate that the locale uses the Euro for currency values.

Language IDs are usually two characters long, written in lowercase, and chosen from the ISO 639 list of country codes. Territories are usually two characters long, written in uppercase, and chosen from the ISO 3166 standard.

The POSIX (and ISO) standards define two special locales named `C` and `POSIX`. The `C` and `POSIX` locales are defined so that they can be used in many different locations.

Table 20.1 shows a few locale names taken from my Linux host.

Table 20.1 **Sample Locale Names**

Locale Name	Language	Region	Codeset	Modifier
`sv_FI`	Swedish	Finland		
`sv_FI@euro`	Swedish	Finland		Euro is used in this locale
`sv_FI.utf8`	Swedish	Finland	UTF-8	
`sv_FI.utf8@euro`	Swedish	Finland	UTF-8	Euro is used in this locale
`sv_SE`	Swedish	Sweden		

Table 20.1 **Continued**

Locale Name	Language	Region	Codeset	Modifier
sv_SE.utf8	Swedish	Sweden	UTF-8	
en_AU	English	Australia		
en_AU.utf8	English	Australia	UTF-8	
en_IE	English	Ireland		
en_IE@euro	English	Ireland		Euro is used in this locale
en_IE.utf8	English	Ireland	UTF-8	
en_IE.utf8@euro	English	Ireland	UTF-8	Euro is used in this locale

My Red Hat Linux system defines 277 locales. Each locale is broken down into a set of categories. Most locale implementations define (at least) the categories shown in Table 20.2. Some operating systems define additional categories.

Table 20.2 **Locale Information Categories**

Category	Influences	Used By
LC_MESSAGES	Message formatting and message language	Client/Server
LC_MONETARY	Monetary value formatting	Server
LC_NUMERIC	Numeric value formatting	Server
LC_TIME	Date and time formatting	Not used
LC_CTYPE	Character classifications (uppercase, punctuation, and so on)	Server
LC_COLLATE	Collating order for string values	Cluster
LC_ALL	All of the above	See all of the above

Enabling Locale Support

When you build PostgreSQL from scratch, locale support is not included unless you include `--enable-locale` when you configure the source code. If you enable locale support, you should also enable NLS (National Language Support) —without NLS, you will always see PostgreSQL messages in English. Here is an example showing how to enable both:

```
$ ./configure --enable-locale --enable-nls
```

You choose a locale by setting one or more environment variables. There are three levels of environment variables that you can use. At the bottom level, you can set the `LANG` environment variable to the locale that you want to use. For example, if you want all features to run in a French context unless overridden, set `LANG=fr_FR`. You can mix locales by defining `LC_MESSAGES`, `LC_MONETARY`, `LC_NUMERIC`, `LC_CTYPE`, and/or `LC_COLLATE`. The `LC_xxx` environment variables override `LANG`. If you are working with a database that stores French names, for example, you may still want to see PostgreSQL messages in English. In this case, you would set LANG=fr_FR and LC_MESSAGES=en_US. At the top level, LC_ALL overrides any other locale-related environment variables: If you want everything to run in German (as spoken in Germany), set LC_ALL=de_DE.

Effects of Locale Support

Let's see what happens when you change locales.

The first category in Table 20.2, LC_MESSAGES, determines the language that PostgreSQL uses when displaying message text. I've been running with LC_MESSAGES set to en_US when I run psql, so messages are displayed in English:

```
$ psql -d movies
Welcome to psql, the PostgreSQL interactive terminal.

Type:  \copyright for distribution terms
       \h for help with SQL commands
       \? for help on internal slash commands
       \g or terminate with semicolon to execute query
       \q to quit

movies=#
```

Let's try setting LC_MESSAGES to fr_CA (French as spoken in Canada):

```
$ LC_MESSAGES=fr_CA psql -d movies
Bienvenu à psql, l'interface interactif de PostgreSQL.

Tapez:  \copyright pour l'information de copyright
        \h pour l'aide-mémoire sur les commandes SQL
        \? pour l'aide-mémoire sur les commandes internes
        \g ou point-virgule pour exécuter une requête
        \q pour quitter

movies=#
```

Voilà! The client messages are now in French.

When you are running a PostgreSQL client connected to a PostgreSQL server, there are *three* locales in use: the client locale, the server locale, and the cluster locale.

Some locale properties affect the server, some affect the client, and a few are stored with the database cluster itself (see Table 20.2). The LC_MESSAGES category affects both the client and server because each can produce message text.

Now, let's try a few of the other categories.

The server uses the LC_MONETARY category to control the way in which monetary values are formatted. I've modified the customers table in my database to include a balance column (using the MONEY data type). Here is the new column, shown in the en_US locale:

```
movies=# SELECT * FROM customers;
 id |     customer_name     |  phone   | birth_date |  balance
----+-----------------------+----------+------------+------------
  4 | Wonderland, Alice N. | 555-1122 | 1969-03-05 |
  1 | Jones, Henry          | 555-1212 | 1970-10-10 |     $10.00
  2 | Rubin, William        | 555-2211 | 1972-07-10 |  $1,000.00
  3 | Panky, Henry          | 555-1221 | 1968-01-21 | $10,000.00
(4 rows)
```

Now, I'll stop my server, set the `LC_MONETARY` environment variable to `fr_FR` (French as spoken in France), and restart the server. Note that you must restart the server before a change to `LC_MONETARY` can take effect (you can't change monetary formatting on a per-connection basis):

```
$ pg_ctl stop
waiting for postmaster to shut down......done
postmaster successfully shut down

$ export LC_MONETARY=fr_FR
$ pg_ctl -l /tmp/pg.log start
postmaster successfully started
```

Now, when I query the `customers` table, the monetary values are formatted using the `fr_FR` locale:

```
movies=# SELECT * FROM customers;
 id |     customer_name     |  phone   | birth_date |  balance
----+-----------------------+----------+------------+------------
  4 | Wonderland, Alice N. | 555-1122 | 1969-03-05 |
  1 | Jones, Henry          | 555-1212 | 1970-10-10 |     F10,00
  2 | Rubin, William        | 555-2211 | 1972-07-10 |  F1 000,00
  3 | Panky, Henry          | 555-1221 | 1968-01-21 | F10 000,00
(4 rows)
```

Notice that `MONEY` values are now formatted using French preferences.

The `LC_NUMERIC` category determines which characters will be used for grouping, the currency symbol, positive and negative signs, and the decimal point. Currently, `LC_NUMERIC` is used only by the `TO_CHAR()` function. The `LC_NUMERIC` category affects the server.

PostgreSQL currently does not use the `LC_TIME` category (each date/time value can include an explicit time zone).

`LC_CTYPE` is consulted whenever PostgreSQL needs to categorize a character. The server locale determines which characters are considered uppercase, lowercase, numeric, punctuation, and so on. The most obvious uses of `LC_COLLATE` are the `LOWER()`, `UPPER()`, and `INITCAP()` string functions. `LC_COLLATE` is also used when evaluating regular expressions and the `LIKE` operator.

LC_COLLATE affects the result of an ORDER BY clause that sorts by a string value. LC_COLLATE also affects how an index that covers a string value is built. Setting LC_COLLATE ensures that strings are ordered properly for your locale.

Let's look at an example. Create two new database clusters and insert the same values into each one. The first database uses the French locale for collating:

```
$ PGDATA=/usr/local/locale_FR LC_COLLATE=fr_FR initdb
...
Success. You can now start the database server using:
    postmaster -D /usr/local/locale_FR
or
    pg_ctl -D /usr/local/locale_FR -l logfile start

$ PGDATA=/usr/local/locale_FR pg_ctl start
postmaster successfully started

$ PGDATA=/usr/local/locale_FR createdb french_locale
CREATE DATABASE

$ PGDATA=/usr/local/locale_FR psql -q -d french_locale
french_locale=# CREATE TABLE sort_test ( pkey char );
CREATE TABLE
french_locale=# INSERT INTO sort_test VALUES ('a');
INSERT
french_locale=# INSERT INTO sort_test VALUES ('ä');
INSERT
french_locale=# INSERT INTO sort_test VALUES ('b');
INSERT
french_locale=# SELECT * FROM sort_test;
 pkey
------
 a
 ä
 b
 (3 rows)
french_locale=# \q
```

Now, repeat this procedure but set LC_COLLATE=en_US before creating the database cluster:

```
$ PGDATA=/usr/local/locale_EN LC_COLLATE=en_US initdb
...
Success. You can now start the database server using:
    postmaster -D /usr/local/locale_EN
or
    pg_ctl -D /usr/local/locale_EN -l logfile start
```

```
$ PGDATA=/usr/local/locale_EN pg_ctl start
postmaster successfully started

$ PGDATA=/usr/local/locale_EN createdb english_locale
CREATE DATABASE

$ PGDATA=/usr/local/locale_EN psql -q -d locale_test
english_locale=# CREATE TABLE sort_test ( pkey char );
CREATE TABLE
english_locale=# INSERT INTO sort_test VALUES ('a');
INSERT
english_locale=# INSERT INTO sort_test VALUES ('ä');
INSERT
english_locale=# INSERT INTO sort_test VALUES ('b');
INSERT
english_locale=# SELECT * FROM sort_test;
 pkey
------
 a
 b
 ä
(3 rows)
locale_test=# \q
```

Notice that the collation sequence has, in fact, changed. With `LC_COLLATE` set to `fr_FR`, you see `a,ä,b`. With `LC_COLLATE` set to `en_US`, the `ORDER BY` clause returns `a,b,ä`.

The `LC_COLLATE` category is honored only when you run the `initdb` command. Imagine what would happen if you were trying to alphabetize a long list of customer names, but the collation rules changed every few minutes. You'd end up with quite a mess—each portion of the final list would be built with a different ordering. If you could change the collating sequence each time you started a client application, indexes would not be built reliably.

Multibyte Character Sets

Most programmers are accustomed to working with single-byte character sets. In the U.S., we like to pretend that ASCII is the only meaningful mapping between numbers and characters. This is not the case. Standard organizations such as ANSI (American National Standards Institute) and the ISO (International Standards Organization) have defined many different encodings that associate a unique number with each character in a given character set. Theoretically, a single-byte character set can encode 256 different characters. In practice, however, most single-byte character sets are limited to about 96 visible characters. The range of values is cut in half by the fact that the most-significant bit is considered off-limits when representing characters. The most-significant bit is often used as a parity bit and occasionally as an end-of-string marker. Of the remaining 127 encodings, many are used to represent *control* characters (such as tab, new-line, carriage return, and so on). By the time you add punctuation and numeric characters, the remaining 96 values start feeling a bit cramped.

Single-byte character sets work well for languages with a relatively small number of characters. Eventually, most of us must make the jump to multibyte encodings. Adding a second byte dramatically increases the number of characters that you can represent. A single-byte character set can encode 256 values; a double-byte set can encode 65536 characters. Multibyte character sets are required for some languages, particularly languages used in East Asia. Again, standards organizations have defined many multibyte encoding standards.

The Unicode Consortium was formed with the goal of providing a single encoding for all character sets. The consortium published its first proposed standard in 1991 ("The Unicode Standard, Version 1.0"). A two-byte number can represent most of the Unicode encoding values. Some characters require more than two bytes. In practice, many Unicode characters require a single byte.

I've always found that the various forms of the Unicode encoding standard were difficult to understand. Let me try to explain the problem (and Unicode's solution) with an analogy.

Suppose you grabbed a random byte from somewhere on the hard drive in your computer. Let's say that the byte you select has a value of `48`. What does that byte mean? It might mean the number of states in the contiguous United States. It might mean the character '`0`' in the ASCII character set. It could represent 17 more than the number of flavors you can get at Baskin-Robbins. Let's assume that this byte represents the current temperature. Is that 48° in the Centigrade, Fahrenheit, Kelvin, Réaumur, or Rankine scale? The distinction is important: 48° is a little chilly in Fahrenheit, but mighty toasty in Centigrade.

There are two levels of encoding involved here. The lowest level of encoding tells us that `48` represents a temperature value. The higher level tells us that the temperature is expressed in degrees Fahrenheit. We have to know both encodings before we can understand the meaning of the byte. If we don't know the encoding(s), `48` is just data. After we understand the encodings, `48` becomes information.

Unicode is an encoding system that assigns a unique number to each character. Which characters are included in the Unicode Standard? Version 3.0 of the Unicode Standard provides definitions for 49,194 characters. Version 3.1 added 44,946 character mappings, and Version 3.2 added an additional 1,016 for a total of 95,156 characters. I'd say that the chances are very high that any character you need is defined in the Unicode Standard.

Just like the temperature encodings I mentioned earlier, there are two levels of encoding in the Unicode Standard.

At the most fundamental level, Unicode assigns a unique number, called a *code point*, to each character. For example, the Latin capital 'A' is assigned the code point 65. The Cyrillic (Russian) capital *de* ('?') is assigned the value 0414. The Unicode Standard suggests that we write these values using the form 'U+xxxx' where 'xxxx' is the code point expressed in hexadecimal notation. So, we should write U+0041 and U+0414 to indicate the Unicode mappings for 'A' and '?'. The mapping from characters to numbers is called the Universal Character Set, or UCS.

At the next level, each code point is represented in one of several *UCS transformation formats* (UTF). The most commonly seen UTF is UTF-8[2]. The UTF-8 scheme is a variable-width encoding form, meaning that some code points are represented by a single byte; and others represented by two, three, or four bytes. UTF-8 divides the Unicode code point space into four ranges, with each range requiring a different number of bytes as shown in Table 20.3.

Table 20.3 **UTF-8 Code Point Widths**

Low Value	High Value	Storage Size	Sample Character	UTF8-Encoding
U+0000	U+007F	1 byte	A (U+0041)	0x41
			0 (U+0030)	0x30
U+0080	U+07FF	2 bytes	© (U+00A9)	0xC2 0xA9
			æ (U+00E6)	0xC3 0xA6
U+0800	U+FFFF	3 bytes	ج (U+062C)	0xE0 0x86 0xAC
			€ (U+20AC)	0xE2 0x82 0xAC
U+10000	U+10FFFF	4 bytes	♪ (U+1D160)	0xF0 0x8E 0xA3 0xA0
			Σ (U+1D6F4)	0xF0 0x9D 0x9B 0xB4

The Unicode mappings for the first 127 code points are identical to the mappings for the ASCII character set. The ASCII code point for 'A' is 0x41, the same code point is used to represent 'A' in Unicode. The UTF-8 encodings for values between 0 and 127 are the values 0 through 127. The net effect of these two rules is that all ASCII characters require a single byte in the UTF-8 encoding scheme and the ASCII characters map directly into the same Unicode code points. In other words, an ASCII string is identical to the UTF-8 string containing the same characters.

PostgreSQL understands how to store and manipulate characters (and strings) expressed in Unicode/UTF-8. PostgreSQL can also work with multibyte encodings other than Unicode/UTF-8. In fact, PostgreSQL understands *single-byte* encodings other than ASCII.

2. Other UTF encodings are UTF-16BE (variable-width, 16 bit, big-endian), UTF-16LE (variable-width, 16 bit, little-endian), UTF-32BE, and UTF-32LE.

Encodings Supported by PostgreSQL

PostgreSQL does not store a list of valid encodings in a table, but you can create such a table. Listing 20.1 shows a PL/pgSQL function that creates a temporary table (`encodings`) that holds the names of all encoding schemes supported by our server:

Listing 20.1 `get_encodings.sql`

```
 1 --
 2 -- Filename: get_encodings.sql
 3 --
 4
 5 CREATE OR REPLACE FUNCTION get_encodings() RETURNS INTEGER AS
 6 '
 7   DECLARE
 8     enc      INTEGER := 0;
 9     name     VARCHAR;
10   BEGIN
11     CREATE TEMP TABLE encodings ( enc_code int, enc_name text );
12     LOOP
13         SELECT INTO name pg_encoding_to_char( enc );
14
15         IF( name = '''' ) THEN
16             EXIT;
17         ELSE
18             INSERT INTO encodings VALUES( enc, name );
19         END IF;
20
21         enc := enc + 1;
22     END LOOP;
23
24     RETURN enc;
25   END;
26
27 ' LANGUAGE 'plpgsql';
```

`get_encodings()` assumes that encoding numbers start at zero and that there are no gaps. This may not be a valid assumption in future versions of PostgreSQL. We use the `pg_encoding_to_char()` built-in function to translate an encoding number into an encoding name. If the encoding number is invalid, `pg_encoding_to_char()` returns an empty string.

When you call `get_encodings()`, it will return the number of rows written to the `encodings` table.

```
movies=# select get_encodings();
 get_encodings
---------------
```

```
             27
(1 row)

movies=# select * from encodings;
 enc_code |    enc_name
----------+---------------
        0 | SQL_ASCII
        1 | EUC_JP
        2 | EUC_CN
        3 | EUC_KR
        4 | EUC_TW
        5 | UNICODE
        6 | MULE_INTERNAL
        7 | LATIN1
        8 | LATIN2
        9 | LATIN3
       10 | LATIN4
       11 | LATIN5
       12 | LATIN6
       13 | LATIN7
       14 | LATIN8
       15 | LATIN9
       16 | LATIN10
       17 | KOI8
       18 | WIN
       19 | ALT
       20 | ISO_8859_5
       21 | ISO_8859_6
       22 | ISO_8859_7
       23 | ISO_8859_8
       24 | SJIS
       25 | BIG5
       26 | WIN1250
(27 rows)
```

Some of these encoding schemes use single-byte code points: `SQL_ASCII`, `LATIN*`, `KOI8`, `WIN`, `ALT`, `ISO-8859*`. Table 20.4 lists the encodings supported by PostgreSQL version 7.2.1.

Table 20.4 **Supported Encoding Schemes**

Encoding	Defined By	Single or Multibyte	Languages Supported
`SQL_ASCII`	ASCII	S	
`EUC_JP`	JIS X 0201-1997	M	Japanese
`EUC_CN`	RFC 1922	M	Chinese
`EUC_KR`	RFC 1557	M	Korean

Table 20.4 **Continued**

Encoding	Defined By	Single or Multibyte	Languages Supported
EUC_TW	CNS 11643-1992	M	Traditional Chinese
UNICODE	Unicode Consortium	M	All scripts
MULE_INTERNAL	CNS 116643-1992		
LATIN1	ISO-8859-1	S	Western Europe
LATIN2	ISO-8859-2	S	Eastern Europe
LATIN3	ISO-8859-3	S	Southern Europe
LATIN4	ISO-8859-4	S	Northern Europe
LATIN5	ISO-8859-9	S	Turkish
LATIN6	ISO-8859-10	S	Nordic
LATIN7	ISO-8859-13	S	Baltic Rim
LATIN8	ISO-8859-14	S	Celtic
LATIN9	ISO-8859-15	S	Similar to LATIN1, replaces some characters with French and Finnish characters, adds Euro
LATIN10	ISO-8859-16	S	Romanian
KOI8	RFC 1489	S	Cyrillic
WIN	Windows 1251	S	Cyrillic
ALT	IBM866	S	Cyrillic
ISO_8859_5	ISO-8859-5	S	Cyrillic
ISO_8859_6	ISO-8859-6	S	Arabic
ISO_8859_7	ISO-8859-7	S	Greek
ISO_8859_8	ISO-8859-8	S	Hebrew
SJIS	JIS X 0202-1991	M	Japanese
BIG5	RF 1922	M	Chinese for Taiwan
WIN1250	Windows 1251	S	Eastern Europe

I've spent a lot of time talking about Unicode. As you can see from Table 20.4, you can use other encodings with PostgreSQL. Unicode has one important advantage over other encoding schemes. A character in any other encoding system can be translated into Unicode and translated back into the original encoding system.

You can use Unicode as a pivot to translate between other encodings. For example, if you want to translate common characters from ISO-646-DE (German) into ISO-646-DK (Danish), you can first convert all characters into Unicode (all ISO-646-DE characters *will* map into Unicode) and then map from Unicode back to ISO-646-DK. Some German characters will not translate into Danish. For example, the DE+0040 character ('§') will map to Unicode U+00A7. There is no '§' character in the ISO-646-DK character set, so this character would be lost in the translation (not dropped, just mapped into a value that means "no translation").

If you don't use Unicode to translate between character sets, you'll have to define translation tables for every language pair that you need.

If you need to support more than one character set at your site, I would strongly encourage you to encode your data in Unicode. However, you should be aware that there is a performance cost associated with multibyte character sets. It takes more time to deal with two or three bytes than it does a single byte. Of course, your data *may* consume more space if stored in a multibyte character set.

Enabling Multibyte Support

When you build PostgreSQL from source code, multibyte support is disabled by default. Unicode is a multibyte character set—if you want to use Unicode, you need to enable multibyte support. Starting with PostgreSQL release 7.3, multibyte support is enabled by default. If you are using a version earlier than 7.3, you enable multibyte support by including the `--enable-multibyte` option when you run `configure`:

```
./configure --enable-multibyte
```

If you did not compile your own copy of PostgreSQL, the easiest way to determine whether it was compiled with multibyte support is to invoke `psql`, as follows:

```
$ psql -l
      List of databases
   Name       | Owner | Encoding
-------------+-------+----------
 movies       | bruce | SQL_ASCII
 secondbooks | bruce | UNICODE
```

The `-l` flag lists all databases in a cluster. If you see three columns, multibyte support is enabled. If the `Encoding` column is missing, you don't have multibyte support.

Selecting an Encoding

There are four ways to select the encoding that you want to use for a particular database.

When you create a database using the `createdb` utility or the `CREATE DATABASE` command, you can choose an encoding for the new database. The following four commands are equivalent:

```
$ createdb -E latin5 my_turkish_db
$ createdb --encoding=latin5 my_turkish_db

movies=# CREATE DATABASE my_turkish_db WITH ENCODING 'LATIN5';
movies=# CREATE DATABASE my_turkish_db WITH ENCODING 11;
```

If you don't specify an encoding with `createdb` (or `CREATE DATABASE`), the cluster's default encoding is used. You specify the default encoding for a cluster when you create the cluster using the `initdb` command:

```
$ initdb -E EUC_KR
$ initdb --encoding=EUC_KR
```

If you do not specify an encoding when you create the database cluster, `initdb` uses the encoding specified when you configured the PostgreSQL source code:

```
./configure --enable-multibyte=unicode
```

Finally, if you don't include an encoding name when you configure the PostgreSQL source code, `SQL_ASCII` is assumed.

So, if you don't do anything special, your database will not support multibyte encodings, and all character values are assumed to be expressed in `SQL_ASCII`.

If you enable multibyte encodings, *all* encodings are available. The encoding name that you can include in the `--enable-multibyte` flag selects the default encoding; it does not limit the available encodings.

Client/Server Translation

We now know that the PostgreSQL server can deal with encodings other than `SQL_ASCII`, but what about PostgreSQL clients? That question is difficult to answer. The `pgAdmin` and `pgAdmin II` clients do not. `pgAccess` does not. The `psql` client supports multibyte encodings, but finding a font that can display all required characters is not easy.

Assuming that you are using a client application that supports encodings other than `SQL_ASCII`, you can select a client encoding with the `SET CLIENT_ENCODING` command:

```
movies=# SET CLIENT_ENCODING TO UNICODE;
SET
```

You can see which coding has been selected for the client using the `SHOW CLIENT_ENCODING` command:

```
movies=# SHOW CLIENT_ENCODING;
NOTICE:  Current client encoding is 'UNICODE'
SHOW VARIABLE
```

You can also view the server's encoding (but you can't change it):

```
movies=# SHOW SERVER_ENCODING;
NOTICE:  Current server encoding is 'UNICODE'
SHOW VARIABLE
movies=# SET SERVER_ENCODING TO BIG5;
NOTICE:  SET SERVER_ENCODING is not supported
SET VARIABLE
```

If the CLIENT_ENCODING and SERVER_ENCODING are different, PostgreSQL will convert between the two encodings. In many cases, translation will fail. Let's say that you use a multibyte-enabled client to INSERT some Katakana (that is, Japanese) text, as shown in Figure 20.1.

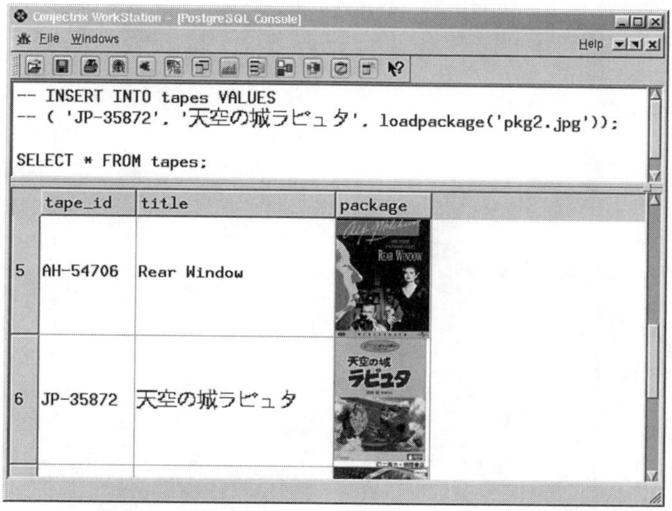

Figure 20.1 A Unicode-enabled client application.

This application (the Conjectrix™ Workstation) understands how to work with Unicode data. If you try to read this data with a different client encoding, you probably won't be happy with the results:

```
$ psql -q -d movies
news=# SELECT tape_id, title FROM tapes WHERE tape_id = 'JP-35872';
tape_id   |                  title
----------+-------------------------------------------------------
 JP-35872 | (bb)(bf)(e5)(a4)(a9)(e7)(a9)(ba)(e3)(81ae)(e5)(9f)(8e)...
(1 row)
```

The values that you see in psql have been translated into the SQL_ASCII encoding scheme. The characters in the val column can be translated from Unicode into SQL_ASCII, but most cannot. The SQL_ASCII encoding does not include Katakana characters, so PostgreSQL has given you the hexadecimal values of the Unicode characters instead.

Summary

PostgreSQL is an open-source product, and the core developers come from many different countries. PostgreSQL has been developed to be an international database system. The combination of Unicode and translated message texts mean that PostgreSQL can be used in every region of the world. The biggest challenge to using PostgreSQL in many regions will be the task of finding and installing fonts and input methods for local character sets.

21

Security

THE GOAL OF POSTGRESQL SECURITY IS to keep the bad guys out while letting the good guys in.

Security is a balancing act—it is often the case that more secure installations are less convenient for authorized users. Finding the right balance depends primarily on two factors. First, "How much do you trust the people that have access to your machine?" The answer to that question is not as obvious at it may seem—if your system is connected to the Internet, you have to extend your trust to everyone else on the Internet. The second question is "How important is it to keep your data private?" It's probably not very important to keep your personal CD catalog private, but if you are storing customer credit card numbers, you had better put in some extra effort to ensure privacy.

There are three aspects to PostgreSQL security:

- Securing the PostgreSQL data files
- Securing client access
- Granting and denying access to specific tables and specific users

The first aspect is the easiest—the rules are simple and there aren't very many decisions that you have to make. The host operating system enforces file-level security. I'll explain how to ensure that your PostgreSQL installation has the proper ownerships and permissions in the next section.

Securing client access is relatively simple if you are on a secure network and complex if you are not. The main task in securing client access is authentication. *Authentication* is proving that you are who you say you are. PostgreSQL supports a variety of authentication, ranging from complete trust (meaning, "Ok, you say your name is `bruce`, who am I to argue?") to encryption and message digest protocols. I'll describe each authentication method in this chapter.

The first two aspects of PostgreSQL security are concerned with keeping the wrong people out of your database while letting the right people in. The last aspect determines what you can do once you are allowed inside a PostgreSQL database.

Securing the PostgreSQL Data Files

The first step in securing a PostgreSQL installation is to secure the actual data files that comprise each database. PostgreSQL is typically installed in the `/usr/local/pgsql` directory. Executables (such as `psql`, `initdb`, and the `postmaster`) are often installed in the `/usr/local/pgsql/bin` directory. If you have a typical installation, you can expect to find data files: databases, configuration, and security information in `/usr/local/pgsql/data`. I'll refer to this last directory as `$PGDATA`. PostgreSQL uses the `$PGDATA` environment variable to find its data files.

Let's start by looking at the directory structure of a PostgreSQL installation. Figure 21.1 gives you a look at the structure.

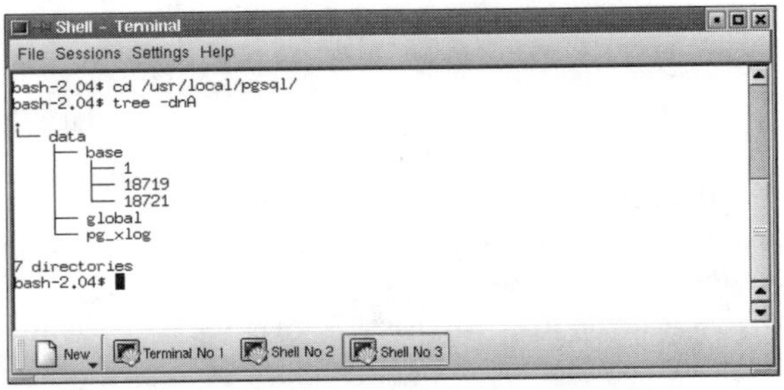

```
bash-2.04$ cd /usr/local/pgsql/
bash-2.04$ tree -dnA
.
└── data
    ├── base
    │   ├── 1
    │   ├── 18719
    │   └── 18721
    ├── global
    └── pg_xlog

7 directories
bash-2.04$
```

Figure 21.1 The directory structure of a PostgreSQL installation.

The `data` directory contains three subdirectories: `base`, `global`, and `pg_xlog`[1].

The `data/base` directory is where your databases live. Notice that I have three subdirectories underneath the base directory—that's because I have three databases. If you are curious about the directory naming scheme, the numbers correspond to the OIDs (object ids) of the corresponding rows in the `pg_database` table. You can see the correspondence by executing the following query:

```
psql> select oid, datname from pg_database;

  oid | datname
------+-----------
18721 | movies
    1 | template1
18719 | template0
```

The `data/global` directory contains information that spans all databases; in other words, the information in the `global` directory is independent of any particular

1. You may see more files and subdirectories if you are running a different version of PostgreSQL. This snapshot shows a typical installation of PostgreSQL release 7.1.3.

database. The `global` directory contains the following files: `1260`, `1261`, `1262`, `1264`, `1269`, `17127`, `17130`, `pg_control`, and `pg_pwd`.

Like the `data/base` directory, the `data/global` directory contains a few files whose names are actually OID values. Table 21.1 shows how the OID values translate into table names.

Table 21.1 **OID to Table Mapping in the global Directory**

Filename/OID	Corresponding Table
1260	pg_shadow
1261	pg_group
1262	pg_database
1264	pg_variable
1269	pg_log
17127	index (on name) for pg_group
17130	index (on sysid) for pg_group

Each of these files is explained in Chapter 19, "General PostgreSQL Administration," so I won't cover that information here.

The `data/pg_xlog` directory contains the write-ahead transaction log (also described in Chapter 19).

Unix File Permissions and Ownership

In a Unix environment, there are three aspects to file system security. Each file (or directory) has an owner, a group, and a set of permissions. You can see all three of these attributes using the `ls -l` command. Here is an example:

```
total 40
drwx------    5 postgres postgresgrp  4096 Oct 22 17:40 base
drwx------    2 postgres postgresgrp  4096 Jan 15 18:58 global
-rw-------    1 postgres postgresgrp  7482 Jan 15 19:26 pg_hba.conf
-rw-------    1 postgres postgresgrp  1118 Oct 22 17:35 pg_ident.conf
-rw-------    1 postgres postgresgrp     4 Oct 22 17:35 PG_VERSION
drwx------    2 postgres postgresgrp  4096 Oct 22 17:35 pg_xlog
-rw-------    1 postgres postgresgrp  3137 Oct 22 17:35 postgresql.conf
-rw-------    1 postgres postgresgrp    49 Jan 10 14:18 postmaster.opts
-rw-------    1 postgres postgresgrp    47 Jan 10 14:18 postmaster.pid
```

Each line of output can be divided into seven columns. Starting at the right-most column, you see the file (or directory) name. Working to the left, you'll see the modification date, file size (in bytes), group name, username, link count, and file permissions.

The file permissions column can be interpreted as follows:

```
drwxrw-r--
```

> The first character is a file type indicator and contains a "d" for directories and a "-" for normal files (other values are possible—refer to your OS documentation for more information).
>
> Following the type indicator are three groups of access permissions, and each group contains three characters. The first group (rwx in this example) specifies access permissions for the owner of the file. rwx means that the owner can read, write, and execute the file. The next three characters (rw-) specify access permissions for members of the group. rw- means that members of the group can read and write this file, but cannot execute it. The last three characters in the permissions column control access by other users (you are considered an "other" user if you are not the owner and you are not in the file's group). r-- means that other users can read the file, but cannot write or execute it.
>
> Permissions mean something a little different for directories. If you have read permissions for a directory, you can list the contents of that directory (using ls, for example). If you have write permissions for a directory, you can create files in, and remove files from, that directory. If you have execute permission, you can access the files in a directory (read permission allows you to list the contents of a directory; execute permission allows you to work with the contents of the files in that directory).

When you install PostgreSQL from a standard distribution, such as an RPM package, the installation procedure will automatically apply the correct ownership and permissions to all PostgreSQL components. In rare circumstances, you may find that you need to reset ownerships and permissions back to their correct states. Why? You may find that your system has been "hacked." You may need to recover from an error in a backup/restore procedure. You may have executed a recursive chown, chmod, or chgrp starting in the wrong directory—you're not an experienced system administrator until you have made (and recovered from) this mistake. It's a good idea to understand what the correct ownerships and permissions are, just in case you ever need to put things back the way they are supposed to be.

The entire directory tree (starting at and including the $PGDATA directory) should be owned by the PostgreSQL administrative user (this user is typically named :postgres"). It's easy to correct the file ownerships using the chown command:

```
$ chown -R postgres $PGDATA
```

You can use the following commands to find any files that are *not* owned by user postgres:

```
$ cd $PGDATA
$ find . -not -user postgres -ls
```

The $PGDATA directory tree should be readable and writable by the PostgreSQL administrative user, and should provide no access to the group and other categories. Again, setting the file permissions is easy:

```
$ cd $PGDATA
$ find . -type d -exec chmod 700 '{}' ';'
$ find . -type f -exec chmod 600 '{}' ';'
```

The first `find` command modifies the directories, and the second modifies the normal files. The numbers (`700` and `600`) are a portable way to specify access permissions. `700` is equivalent to `u=rwx,g=,o=`, meaning that the owner of the directory should have read, write, and execute permissions; other users have no rights. `600` is equivalent to `u=rw,g=,o=` meaning that the owner of the file should have read and write permissions and other users should have no access rights. You can use whichever form you prefer. The numeric form is more succinct and more portable. I prefer the symbolic form, probably because I can't do octal arithmetic in my head.

It's a good idea to verify file and directory permissions occasionally for the reasons I mentioned earlier: You may have an intruder on your system, or you might need to recover from a user mistake. You can also use the `find` command to find any files or directories with incorrect permissions:

```
$ cd $PGDATA
$ find . -type d -not -perm 700 -print
$ find . -type f -not -perm 600 -print
```

There is one more file that you should consider securing besides the files in the `$PGDATA` directory tree. When local users (meaning users who are logged in to the system that hosts your PostgreSQL database) connect to the `postmaster`, they generally use a Unix-domain socket. (A Unix-domain socket is a network interface that doesn't actually use a network. Instead, a Unix-domain socket is implemented entirely within a single Unix operating system.) When you start the `postmaster` process, it creates a Unix-domain socket, usually in the `/tmp` directory. If you have a `postmaster` running on your system, look in the `/tmp` directory and you will see the socket that your postmaster uses to listen for connection requests:

```
$ ls -la /tmp
total 8095
drwxrwxrwt    12 root     root          1024 Jan 25 18:04 .
drwxr-xr-x    21 root     root          4096 Jan 25 16:23 ..
drwxr-xr-x     2 root     root          1024 Jan 10 10:37 lost+found
srwxrwxrwx     1 postgres postgresgrp      0 Jan 25 18:01 .s.PGSQL.5432
-r--r--r--     1 root     root            11 Jan 24 19:18 .X0-lock
```

(You will likely find other files in the /tmp directory.) The postmaster's socket is named `s.PGSQL.5432`. You can tell that this is a socket because of the `s` in the left-most column. Because the name of the socket starts with a `.`, I had to use the `-a` flag on the `ls` command. Files whose names begin with a period (`.`) are normally hidden from the `ls` command.

Notice that the permissions on this socket are `rwxrwxrwx`. This means that any user (the owner, members of the group, or others) can connect to this socket. You might consider restricting access to this socket. For example, if you change the permissions to `rwxrwx---`, only user `postgres` and members of the `postgresgrp` group could connect.

Unlike normal files, you don't set the socket permissions using the chmod command (the postmaster's socket is created each time the postmaster starts). Instead, you use the UNIX_SOCKET_PERMISSION runtime-configuration option (Chapter 19 discusses runtime-configuration options in more detail).

Note that just because you can connect to the socket does not mean that the postmaster will allow you to access a database—the next section describes how to secure the postmaster.

Securing Network Access

The next step in securing a PostgreSQL installation is determining which computers are allowed to access your data.

PostgreSQL uses the $PGDATA/pg_hba.conf file to control client access (hba is an acronym for *host-based authentication*). Let's start by looking at a simple example:

```
# Allow all local users to connect without providing passwords

local   all  trust

# Allow users on our local network to connect to
# database 'movies' if they have a valid password

host movies 192.168.0.0 255.255.255.0 password
```

First, you should know that lines that begin with a # character are comments, and blank lines are ignored.

The remainder of the records in pg_hba.conf control access to one or more databases for one or most hosts.

Each record is composed of three or more fields.

The first field in each record corresponds to a type of connection. PostgreSQL currently supports three types of connections:

- local—A local connection is one that comes in over a Unix-domain socket. By definition, a client connecting via a Unix-domain socket is executing on the same machine as the postmaster.
- hostssl—A hostssl connection is a TCP/IP connection that uses the SSL (secure sockets layer) protocol.
- host—A host connection is a TCP/IP connection that does not use SSL.

TCP/IP Connections with postmaster

When you start the postmaster process, the default is to prohibit access from other systems. Unless you enable TCP/IP connections, the postmaster will listen for connection requests coming from only local clients (in other words, the postmaster will listen only on a Unix-domain socket). You can enable TCP/IP connections using the postmaster's -i flag or by setting the tcp_ip configuration variable to TRUE.

The second field in each pg_hba.conf record specifies which database (or set of databases) the record controls. You can include the name of a database in this field, or you can specify one of two special values. The string all controls access to all databases, and sameuser controls access to a database whose name is identical to the name of the user making the connection.

The remainder of the pg_hba.conf record depends on the connection type. I'll look at each one in turn.

local Connections

The format of a local record is

```
local database authentication-method [authentication-option]
```

You know that the *database* field contains the name of a database (or all or sameuser). The *authentication-method* field determines what method you must use to prove your identity. I'll explain authentication methods and authentications options in a moment.

host and hostssl Connections

The format of a host or hostssl record is

```
host    database ip-address mask authentication-method [ option ]
hostssl database ip-address mask authentication-method [ option ]
```

The *ip-address* field specifies either a TCP/IP host or a TCP/IP network (by numeric address). The *mask* field specifies how many bits in the *ip-address* are significant.

If you want to provide access to a specific host, say 192.168.0.1, you might specify

```
host all 192.168.0.1 255.255.255.255 krb5
```

The mask value of 255.255.255.255 tells PostgreSQL that all the bits in the ip-address are significant. If you want to specify that all the hosts on a network are granted some form of access, you would use a restricted mask. For example:

```
host all 192.168.0.0 255.255.255.0 krb5
```

This mask value specifies that all hosts on the 192.168.0.xxx network are granted access.

If you try to connect to a postmaster and your host address does not match any of the pg_hba.conf records, your connection attempt is rejected.

Now let's look at the authentication methods. Remember that you can specify a different authentication method for each host (or for each network). Some authentication methods are more secure than others, whereas some methods are more convenient than others.

The trust Authentication Method

When you use the trust authentication method, you allow any user on the client system to access your data. The client application is not required to provide any passwords (beyond what may be required to log in to the client system).

trust is the least secure of the authentication methods—it relies on the security of the client system.

You should never use trust to authenticate a connection attempt in an insecure network.

In most cases, you won't want to use the trust method to authenticate local connections. At first glance, it seems reasonable to trust the security on your own host; after all, I have to prove my identity to the operating system before I can start a client application. But the problem is not that I can fool the operating system; the problem is that I can impersonate another user. Consider the following scenario:

```
Welcome to arturo, please login...
login: korry
Password: cows

Last login:  Fri Jan 18 10:48:00 from marsalis

[korry]$ psql -U sheila -d movies

Welcome to psql, the PostgreSQL interactive terminal.

movies=>
```

To log in to my host (arturo) as user korry, I am required to provide an operating system-authenticated password. But, if the movies database allows local connection attempts to be trusted, nothing stops me from impersonating another user (possibly gaining elevated privileges).

Given the security problems with trust, why would you ever want to use it? The trust authentication method is useful on single-user machines (that is, systems with only one user authorized to log in). You may also use trust to authenticate local connections on development or testing systems.

You never want to use trust on a multiuser system that contains important data.

The ident Authentication Method

The ident authentication method (like trust) relies on the client system to authenticate the user.

In the previous section, I showed you how easy it is to impersonate another user using the trust authentication method. All I have to do to impersonate another user is use the -U flag when I fire up the psql client application.

ident tries to be a bit more secure. Let's pretend that I am currently logged in to host vivaldi as user korry, and I want to connect to a PostgreSQL server running on host arturo:

```
$ whoami
korry
$ psql -h arturo -d movies -U korry

Welcome to psql, the PostgreSQL interactive terminal.

movies=> select user;
 current_user
korry
```

I'll walk through the authentication process for this connection.

First, my local copy of psql makes a TCP/IP connection to the postmaster process on host arturo and sends my username (korry). The postmaster (on arturo) connects back to the identd daemon on host vivaldi (remember, I am running psql on host vivaldi). The postmaster sends the psql-to-postmaster connection information to identd and identd replies with my username (also korry).

Now, the postmaster examines the pg_hba.conf record that matches my host. Assume that it finds the following:

```
host  all  192.168.0.85 255.255.255.255 ident sameuser
```

The sameuser field tells the postmaster that if I am trying to connect using a name that matches the identd response, I am allowed to connect. (That might sound a little confusing at first. When you use the ident authentication method, the postmaster works with two different usernames: the name that I provided to the client application and the name returned by the identd daemon.)

Now let's see what happens when I try to impersonate another user. Recall from the previous section that I can fool the trust authentication method simply by lying about my username. It's a little harder to cheat with ident.

Let's say that I am logged in to host vivaldi as user sheila and I try to impersonate user korry. You can assume that because I am logged in to vivaldi, I have proven my identity to vivaldi by providing sheila's password.

```
$ whoami
sheila
$ psql -h arturo -d movies -U korry
psql: IDENT authentication failed for user 'sheila'
```

As before, my local copy of psql makes a TCP/IP connection to the postmaster process on host arturo and sends the username that I provided on the command line (korry). The postmaster (on arturo) connects back to the identd daemon on host vivaldi. This time, the identd daemon returns my real username (sheila).

At this point, the postmaster (on arturo) is working with two usernames. I have logged in to the client (vivaldi) as user sheila but when I started psql, I specified a username of korry. Because my pg_hba.conf record specified sameuser, I can't connect with two different usernames—my connection attempt is rejected.

Now that you've seen how the ident method provides a bit more security than trust, I'll show you a few more options that you can use with ident.

In the preceding examples, I used the sameuser option in my pg_hba.conf record. Instead of sameuser, I can specify the name of a map. A *map* corresponds to a set of entries in the $PGDATA/pg_ident.conf file. pg_ident.conf is a text file containing one record per line (as usual, blank lines and lines starting with a '#' character are ignored). Each record in the pg_ident.conf file contains three fields:

- mapname—Corresponds to the map field in a pg_hba.conf record
- ident-name—This is a name returned by the identd daemon on a client system
- pguser-name—PostgreSQL username

Here is an example:

```
# pg_ident.conf
#
#mapname      ident-name       pguser-name
#----------- -------------    -----------
host-wynton  Administrator    bruce
host-vivaldi Administrator    sheila
host-vivaldi sheila           sheila
host-vivaldi korry            korry

# pg_hba.conf
#
host all 192.168.0.85 255.255.255.255 ident host-vivaldi
host all 192.168.0.22 255.255.255.255 ident host-wynton
```

You can see in this example that I have defined two ident maps: host-vivaldi and host-wynton. The pg_hba.conf file specifies that any connection attempts from host 192.168.0.85 should use the ident method with the host-vivaldi ident map; any connection attempts from host 192.168.0.22 should use the host-wynton map.

Now look at the pg_ident.conf file—there are three entries in the host-vivaldi map and one entry in the host-wynton map.

The host-wynton map says that if I am logged in to my client machine (192.168.0.22) as user Administrator, I can connect to a database as PostgreSQL user bruce.

The host-vivaldi map says that I can connect as PostgreSQL user sheila if I am logged in to my host as Administrator or if I am logged in as user sheila. Also, if I am logged in as korry, I can connect as PostgreSQL user korry.

So, why is the `ident` method insecure? Think back to the `trust` method—it is insecure because you trust the user to tell the truth about his or her identity. `ident` is insecure because you are trusting the *client system*. The network protocol used by the `identd` daemon is very simple and easy to impersonate. It's easy to set up a homegrown program to respond to `identd` queries with inaccurate usernames. In fact, I recently downloaded and installed an `ident` server on my Windows laptop, and one of the command-line options allowed me to specify a *fake* username!

I would recommend against using the `ident` authentication method except on closed networks (that is, networks where you control all the connected hosts).

The password Authentication Method

The `password` authentication method provides a reasonably high level of security compared to `trust` and `ident`. When you use `password` authentication, the client is required to prove its identity by providing a valid password.

PostgreSQL authentication passwords are not related to the password that you use to log in to your operating system.

On a Unix (or Linux) host, OS passwords are usually stored in `/etc/passwd` or `/etc/shadow`. When you log in to a Unix machine, you are prompted for your OS password, and the login program compares the password that you enter with the appropriate entry in the `/etc/passwd` file.

How does PostgreSQL decide whether to look in `pg_shadow` or in a flat password file? It examines the `pg_hba.conf` record that matches your client's host IP address. Here are two sample `pg_hba.conf` entries:

```
# pg_hba.conf
#
host all 192.168.0.85 255.255.255.255 password
host all 192.168.0.22 255.255.255.255 password accounting
```

When you log in to a PostgreSQL database using password authentication, you must provide a password, but that password is stored in a separate location. By default, PostgreSQL passwords are stored (in unencrypted form) in the `pg_shadow` table. You can also store encrypted passwords in files that are external to the database (these external files are called *flat* password files).

The first record specifies that host 192.168.0.85 should use `password` authentication. Because there is nothing following the word `password`, PostgreSQL looks for passwords in the `pg_shadow` table.

The second record in this `pg_hba.conf` file specifies that host 192.168.0.22 should use `password` authentication as well. In this case, I included an `authentication-option`. Recall that the format of a `pg_hba.conf` record is

```
connect-type database authentication-method [authentication-option]
```

The *`authentication-option`* for `password` authentication specifies the name of a flat password file. The name that you provide is assumed to be the name of a file in the

$PGDATA directory. In this example, the flat password file is named $PGDATA/accounting. Note that you can define as many flat password files as you like.

Defining pg_shadow Passwords

When you store passwords in the pg_shadow table, you use the CREATE USER or ALTER USER commands to maintain passwords. For example, to create a new (password-authenticated) user, you would use the following command:

```
CREATE USER bruce WITH PASSWORD 'cricketers';
```

If you want to change bruce's password, you would use the ALTER USER command:

```
ALTER USER bruce WITH PASSWORD 'Wooloomooloo';
```

> **Are pg_shadow Passwords Encrypted?**
>
> When you store passwords in the pg_shadow table, you may be surprised to find that they are not stored in an encrypted format. If you are a PostgreSQL superuser (see Chapter 19), you can view anyone's password by selecting from the pg_shadow table. If you are a Unix superuser, you can see anyone's password by examining the $PGDATA/global/pg_pwd file (all passwords are copied from the pg_shadow table into the $PGDATA/global/pg_pwd each time you change any password using CREATE USER or ALTER USER).
>
> PostgreSQL release 7.2 gives you another option. You can choose to store md5 encrypted passwords in the pg_shadow table. md5 encrypted passwords cannot be used with either the password or crypt authentication methods. I'll describe authentication using md5 in a moment.

Defining Passwords for Flat Password Files

Remember that flat password files are stored in the $PGDATA directory (or in a subdirectory). You can't use the CREATE USER or ALTER USER commands to maintain flat password files; instead, you use an external utility program named pg_passwd.

> **Provide the Pathname When Running pg_passwd**
>
> When you run the pg_passwd command, you must provide the pathname of the flat password file. (A common mistake is to omit the path and supply only the filename—if you don't happen to be in the $PGDATA directory, you won't be editing the correct flat file.)

Here is a sample pg_passwd session:

```
$ pwd
/usr/local/pgsql/data
$ pg_passwd accounting
Username: oswald
New password:
Re-enter new password:
$
```

You'll notice that the passwords that I typed in are not echoed to the screen.

In the usual case, you must be logged in as the PostgreSQL administrative user (postgres) to edit flat password files; the files are located in the $PGDATA directory and that directory is secured.

In the preceding example, the pg_passwd program stored oswald's password in the $PGDATA/accounting file. Flat password files look very much like the /etc/passwd file:

```
$ cat $PGDATA/accounting
oswald:C63KRm.yVkrH2
```

You can see that there are two fields in this file, (separated by a colon). The first field is the name of a PostgreSQL user (oswald). The second field contains an encrypted form of oswald's password. (The /etc/passwd file contains more information than just a username and a password.) You can edit a flat password file by hand; of course, you would have trouble coming up with an encrypted password. If you remove the password (or set the password to +) for a user, the postmaster will look to the pg_shadow table to authenticate that user.

If you want each user to be able to change his own password, you can link a flat password file to the /etc/passwd file (ln -s $PGDATA/accounting /etc/passwd). When you use the /etc/passwd file to authenticate, each user can use the standard Unix passwd program to change his own password—the OS password and PostgreSQL password are then the same.

The crypt Authentication Method

The crypt authentication method is nearly identical to password. There are two features that differentiate password and crypt:

- Using the crypt method, the password is sent from the client in encrypted (rather than cleartext) form.
- The crypt method will not use an external flat password file—it will always use the pg_shadow table.

How Are Crypt Passwords Encrypted?

I mentioned in the last section that pg_shadow passwords are not stored in an encrypted form. So how is it that the crypt authentication method works with encrypted passwords?

When a client application wants to connect to a crypt-authenticating server, the server sends a random number (called a *salt* value) back to the client. After the client knows what salt value to use, it encrypts the password (entered by the user) with the salt and sends the result to the server. The server reads the cleartext password (stored in the pg_shadow table) and encrypts it with the same salt value. If the two encrypted passwords match, the client is successfully authenticated. The result is that passwords are stored in cleartext form, but encrypted passwords are sent across the network.

Now here's a tricky question: If you can store encrypted passwords in a flat password file (using the password method) and cleartext passwords are stored in $PGDATA/global/pg_pwd when you use crypt, which method is more secure? The answer depends on whom you trust. If you allow clients to connect over an untrusted network, use crypt; otherwise, network eavesdroppers might see the cleartext passwords sent by the password method. If all your clients connect over a trusted network, you might favor password authentication—that way, you are minimizing the damage that might be done if someone happens to obtain superuser access. The md5 authentication method is designed to resolve both of these problems.

The md5 Authentication Method

The third password-based authentication method is md5. With md5 authentication, passwords are stored in the pg_shadow table in encrypted form. md5 authentication was not available prior to PostgreSQL release 7.2.

You create encrypted passwords using the CREATE USER and ALTER USER commands.

```
ALTER USER bruce WITH ENCRYPTED PASSWORD 'Wooloomooloo';
```

Note the keyword ENCRYPTED.

md5 is a cryptographically secure message digest algorithm developed by Ron L. Rivest of RSA Security. A message digest algorithm takes a cleartext message (in our case, a password) and produces a long number, called a *hash* or *digest*, based on the contents of the message. The md5 algorithm is carefully designed so that no two messages are likely to produce the same digest. It is nearly impossible to recover the original password given an md5 digest.

How can a message digest be used as a password? If you feed two passwords into the md5 algorithm, you will get the same digest value if the passwords are identical. When you create an encrypted password, the password itself is not actually stored in pg_shadow. Instead, PostgreSQL computes an md5 digest over the password and stores the digest. When a client attempts to connect using md5 authentication, the client computes an md5 digest over the password provided by the user and sends the digest to the server. The server compares the digest stored in pg_shadow with the digest provided by the client. If the two digests are identical, it is *extremely* likely that the passwords match.

There are a couple of security holes in the procedure that I just described. Let's say that bruce and sheila each happened to choose the same password. Two identical passwords will produce the same message digest. If bruce happened to notice that his password had the same message digest as sheila's, he would know that he and sheila had chosen the same password. To avoid this problem, PostgreSQL combines each password with the user's name before computing the md5 digest. That way, if two users happen to choose the same password, they won't have the same md5 digests. The second problem has to do with network security. If a client sent the same message digest to the server every time a given user logged in, the message digest would essentially function as a cleartext password. A nefarious user could watch the network traffic, capture the cleartext message digest, and impersonate the real user (by providing the same cleartext message digest). Instead, PostgreSQL uses the *salt* strategy that I described earlier (see the sidebar "How Are Crypt Passwords Encrypted?"). When a client connects to an md5 authenticating server, the server sends a random *salt* to the client. The client computes an md5 digest based on the user ID and password; this digest matches the digest stored in pg_shadow. The client then combines the salt (from the server) with the first md5 digest and computes a second digest. The second digest is sent to the server. The server combines the salt with the digest stored in pg_shadow and computes a new md5 digest. The server then compares the client's digest with its (salted) own—if the digests match, the passwords match.

The pam Authentication Method

The final password-based authentication method is pam (Pluggable Authentication Module). You've probably noticed that PostgreSQL offers many methods for authenticating a user. This problem is not unique to PostgreSQL—many applications have the need to authenticate a user. The goal of pam is to separate the act of authenticating a user from each and every application by placing authentication services in a framework that can be called by any application.

A system administrator can define different authentication methods for each application, depending on how secure the application needs to be. Using pam, an administrator can create a completely open system, requiring no passwords at all, or can choose to authenticate users using passwords, challenge-response protocols, or even more esoteric biometric authentication methods. PostgreSQL can use the pam framework.

Although pam can be ported to many Unix systems, it is most commonly found in Linux and Solaris. Configuring a pam system is not for the faint-of-heart, and the topic deserves an entire book. Because of space considerations, I won't try to describe how to configure a pam installation. Instead, I recommend that you visit the Linux-PAM web site (http://www.kernel.org/pub/linux/libs/pam/) for more information.

The krb4 and krb5 Authentication Methods

The krb4 and krb5 authentication methods correspond to Kerberos version 4 and Kerberos version 5, respectively. Kerberos is a network-secure authentication service developed at MIT.

Kerberos is a complex package (particularly from the administrator's point of view), but it offers a high level of security. After Kerberos is properly installed and configured, it is easy to use.

The easiest way to understand Kerberos is to compare it with a more traditional authentication method.

Let's say that you want to use telnet to connect to another host (bach) on your network. You start by issuing the telnet command:

```
$ telnet bach
Trying bach...
Connected to bach (192.168.0.56)
Escape character is '^]'.
```

```
login: korry
Password: cows

Last login: Thu Jan 24 19:18:44
$
```

After providing your username, the login program (on bach) asks for your password. Your password is compared with the password stored on bach (in the /etc/passwd or /etc/shadow file). If the password that you provide matches, you have proven your identity and bach permits access.

If you log out of bach and log back in, you must again provide your identity and prove that you are who you say you are.

Now let's see how you perform the same operation when using Kerberos.

With Kerberos, you don't have to prove your identity to each server; instead, you authenticate yourself to a trusted server. In this case, *trusted* means that both the client (that's you) and the server will trust the Kerberos authentication agent to verify that you are who you say you are.

Before you telnet using Kerberos, you must first obtain a *ticket*.

```
$ kinit
Password for korry@movies.biz: cows
```

After you enter your password, the kinit program contacts the Kerberos authentication server (AS) and asks for a ticket. If your password was correct, the AS returns a chunk of data known as a TGT (ticket-granting ticket). The kinit program stores your TGT in a cache file inside of a temporary directory on your system.

At this point, you have proven your identity to the AS, and the AS has given back a certificate that you can use with servers that trust the AS. You can view your TGT using the klist command:

```
$ klist
Ticket cache: /tmp/krb5cc_tty1
Default principal: korry@movies.biz

Valid starting       Expires              Service principal
25 Jan 02 01:25:47   25 Jan 02 09:25:42   krbtgt/movies.bi@ movies.biz

$
```

(Notice that the ticket expires in about eight hours—I have to occasionally reauthenticate myself to the AS.)

Now, you can use that TGT by using a Kerberos-enabled `telnet` client to connect to a Kerberos-enabled `telnet` server:

```
$ telnet -a bach
Trying bach...
Connected to bach (192.168.0.56)
Escape character is '^]'.

Last login: Thu Jan 24 19:18:44
$
```

There are two things that you should notice about this login example. First, I used the -a flag when I started `telnet`—that flag asks `telnet` to use Kerberos authentication. Second, I was *not* prompted for a user or for a password. Why not? The `telnet` client (on my local machine) used my TGT to ask the AS for another ticket, specifically a ticket that allows me to connect to the `telnet` server on `bach`. The AS sent the second ticket back to my local machine, and the new ticket was stored in my ticket cache. This new ticket is specific to `telnet`. My local `telnet` client sends the new ticket to the `telnet` server. The ticket contains enough secure (encrypted) information to satisfy the `telnet` server that I have proven my identity (specifically, I have proven my identity to the AS, and the `telnet` server trusts the AS).

I can view the new ticket with the `klist` command:

```
$ klist
Ticket cache: /tmp/krb5cc_tty1
Default principal: korry@movies.biz

Valid starting      Expires             Service principal
25 Jan 02 01:25:47  25 Jan 02 09:25:42  krbtgt/movies.biz@movies.biz
25 Jan 02 03:01:25  25 Jan 02 13:01:20  host/bach.movies.biz@movies.biz
$
```

So, how does all this fit into PostgreSQL? PostgreSQL client applications (`psql`, for example) and the `postmaster` can be compiled to support Kerberos authentication.

When you specify the `krb4`- or `krb5`-authentication method, you are telling the `postmaster` that client applications must provide a valid Kerberos ticket.

When you connect to a `krb4` or `krb5` authenticated `postmaster` with a Kerberos-enabled client application, you are not required to supply a username or password—instead, the client application sends a Kerberos ticket to the `postmaster`.

The nice thing about Kerberos authentication is that it is secure and convenient at the same time. It is secure because you never send cleartext passwords over an insecure network. It is convenient because you authenticate yourself only once (using the `kinit` program).

As I mentioned earlier, setting up a Kerberos system is not a trivial project. After you have gone through the pain and mystery of installing and configuring Kerberos, you can configure PostgreSQL to use Kerberos to authenticate connection requests. Explaining how to install and configure would require a second book. If you are interested in using Kerberos authentication with PostgreSQL, I recommend you start by reading through the Kerberos web site: `http://web.mit.edu/kerberos/www/index.html`. The PostgreSQL Administrator's Guide provides the details you will need to connect a PostgreSQL database to an installed Kerberos system.

Kerberos is the second most secure authentication method.

The reject Authentication Method

The `reject` authentication method is the easiest to understand and is also the most secure. When a client tries to connect from a system authenticated by the `reject` method, the connection attempt is rejected.

If you try to connect from a system that does not match *any* of the `pg_hba.conf` records, you are also rejected.

Why might you want to use the `reject` method? Let's say that you have a reasonable amount of trust in most of the machines on your network, but you reserve one host as a demonstration machine (192.168.0.15). The demonstration machine should be allowed to access the `demo` database, but no other databases. Every other host should be allowed to access all databases (using Kerberos 5).

```
# File: pg_hba.conf
#
# Type Database Client IP address Netmask         Method
###### ######## ################# ############### ######
  host demo     192.168.0.15      255.255.255.255 trust
  host all      192.168.0.15      255.255.255.255 reject
  host all      192.168.0.0       255.255.255.0   krb5
```

Notice that there are two entries for the demo machine (192.168.0.15). The first entry allows trusted access to the `demo` database. The second entry rejects access to all other databases. This demonstrates an important point: The postmaster starts reading at the beginning of the `pg_hba.conf` file and stops as soon as it finds a record that matches on connection type, database name, and IP address/mask. When a user tries to connect to the `demo` database from the `demo` machine, the postmaster searches for a record of type `host` with a database of either `demo`, `all`, or `sameuser (and of course, a match on the IP address/Netmask combination)`. The first record matches, so the postmaster allows access without requiring any form of authentication other than the IP address of the `demo` machine. Now suppose that a user (again on the `demo` machine) tries to connect to a different database (say, `accounting`). This time, the postmaster searches for a record of type `host` and a database of `accounting`, `all`, or `sameuser`. The first record no longer matches (wrong database name), so the postmaster moves on. The second record matches and the postmaster rejects the connection attempt. If a user logged in to a different host tries to connect, the postmaster will find the third record (the first two records won't match the IP address) and allow access using Kerberos 5 authentication.

If the postmaster can't find a record that matches a connection attempt, the connection is rejected, so you may be wondering why the `reject` method is needed.

Consider what would happen if you removed the second record from this file. If a user on the `demo` machine tries to connect to the `accounting` database, the postmaster will ignore the first record (wrong database) and move on to the last record. The last record says that anyone in our local network should be allowed to connect to all databases using Kerberos 5 authentication. That is clearly the wrong answer.

Securing Tables

In the preceding sections, I showed you how to keep nefarious intruders out of your database, so you should now know how to keep unauthorized users out of your PostgreSQL data. Now let's look at a different problem: How do you secure your database in such a way that *authorized* users can manipulate database components that they need to work on without gaining access to tables that they should be kept away from?

It's important to recognize a shift in responsibilities here: The operating system enforces the first security component (data files); the postmaster enforces the second component (network access). After you have proven your identity and been granted access to a PostgreSQL database, the database starts enforcing security.

When you set up PostgreSQL internal security, you are controlling the trust relationships between users, groups, database objects, and privileges. First, let's define each of these entities.

Each user who is authorized to access a PostgreSQL database is assigned a unique username. You use the `CREATE USER` and `ALTER USER` commands to define (and alter) users. Chapter 19 explains how to maintain the list of PostgreSQL users.

A *group* is a named collection of users. You can use groups to make it easier to assign privileges to a collection of users. There is a special predefined group named `PUBLIC`—all users are members of the `PUBLIC` group. Again, see Chapter 19 for information regarding group maintenance.

There are three types of database objects that you can secure: tables, views, and sequences. Notice that you cannot secure individual rows within a table. You also cannot secure columns within a table. If you can access any part of table, you can access the entire table. You can, however, use a *view* to control access within a table.

The final piece of the internal-security puzzle is the privilege. Each privilege corresponds to a type of access. Currently, PostgreSQL allows you to control five table-related privileges: `SELECT`, `INSERT`, `UPDATE`, `DELETE`, and `RULE`. With PostgreSQL release 7.2, two new privileges were added: `REFERENCES` and `TRIGGER`.

Let's see how all those components fit together.

First, you should know that when you create a new table, you are considered to be the owner of that table. As the owner of a table, you hold all privileges—you can select, insert, update, or delete rows within that table. Unless you grant privileges to another user, you are the only person that can access that table (actually, the owner of the database can do anything he wants).

Transfering Ownership

You can transfer ownership to another user by using the command `ALTER TABLE table OWNER TO new-owner`. You must be a PostgreSQL superuser to transfer ownership. To find out who currently owns a table, `SELECT` from the `pg_tables` view.

If you want other users to have access to your tables, you need to grant one or more privileges. For example, if you want a user named `bruce` to be able to select data from the `customers` table, you would use the following command:

```
GRANT SELECT ON customers TO bruce;
```

If you change your mind, you can deny select privileges to `bruce` using the `REVOKE` command, for example:

```
REVOKE SELECT ON customers FROM bruce;
```

As I mentioned earlier, there are seven table-related privileges that you can grant to a user: `SELECT`, `INSERT`, `UPDATE`, `DELETE`, `RULE`, `REFERENCES`, and `TRIGGER`. The first four of these correspond to the command of the same name. The `RULE` privilege is used to determine which users can create *`rewrite`* rules. The `REFERENCES` privilege controls foreign key constraints. The `tapes` table in the sample database defines two foreign key constraints:

```
CREATE TABLE rentals
(
    tape_id       character(8) references tapes,
    customer_id   integer      references customers,
    rental_date   date
);
```

You must hold the `REFERENCES` privilege on the `tapes` and `customers` tables to create the `rentals` table. You are not required to hold the `REFERENCES` privilege to *use* the `rentals` table, only to create the table. This is an important distinction. If I hold the `REFERENCES` privilege for a table that you own, I can prevent you from deleting and updating records simply by creating a table that references your table.

The `TRIGGER` privilege determines which users are allowed to create a `TRIGGER`. Like the `REFERENCES` privilege, you can use the `TRIGGER` privilege to prevent users from interfering with your tables.

You can grant and revoke individual privileges for a user or a group. You can also grant or revoke `ALL` privileges:

```
GRANT ALL ON customers TO sheila;
REVOKE ALL ON customers FROM bruce;
```

Finding out which users hold privileges for a given table is simple, but the results are a bit hard to interpret. There are two ways to find the list of privilege holders for a table: You can either query the `pg_class` table, or use the `\z` command in psql—either way, you get the same results. Here is an example:

```
movies=> \z customers
  Access permissions for database "movies"
 Relation  |        Access permissions
-----------+-------------------------------
 customers | {"=","sheila=arwR","bruce=r"}
(1 row)

movies=> select relname, relacl from pg_class where relname = 'customers';
  relname  |             relacl
-----------+-------------------------------
 customers | {"=","sheila=arwR","bruce=r"}
(1 row)
```

The privileges assigned to a table are stored in an array in the `pg_class` system table (in the `relacl` column). Each member of the `relacl` array defines the privileges for a user or a group. The `relacl` column is called an *access control list,* or *ACL*. In the preceding example, user `sheila` holds four privileges and `bruce` holds three. Table 12.2 shows how the codes in a PostgreSQL `ACL` correspond to privilege names.

Table 12.2 **ACL Code to Privilege Name Mapping**

`relacl` **Code**	**Privilege Name**
a	INSERT
r	SELECT
w	UPDATE
d	DELETE
R	RULES
x	REFERENCES
t	TRIGGER
arwdRxt	ALL

You can see that user `sheila` holds all privileges for the `customers` table and user `bruce` has read-only access.

In the previous example, the ACL for `customers` (`{"=","sheila=arwR","bruce=r"}`) contains three entries. The meaning of the last two entries is obvious, but what does the first entry mean? The first entry corresponds to the `PUBLIC` group (because the username is missing)—the `PUBLIC` group has no privileges (no privileges are listed to the right of the =).

> **Versions Prior to PostgreSQL 7.2**
>
> If you are using a version of PostgreSQL older than release 7.2, you may have noticed that there is no ACL code corresponding to `DELETE` privileges. Prior to PostgreSQL release 7.2, having `DELETE` privileges was the same as having `UPDATE` privileges.

Now let's see how PostgreSQL interprets an ACL to decide whether you have privileges to access a table.

First, I'll start by creating two groups and a new user:

```
CREATE GROUP clerks;
CREATE GROUP managers;

CREATE USER monty;

ALTER GROUP clerks ADD USER bruce;
ALTER GROUP clerks ADD USER sheila;
ALTER GROUP managers ADD USER sheila;
```

Now, let's define some privileges for the `customers` table:

```
GRANT SELECT ON customers TO PUBLIC;
GRANT INSERT ON customers to GROUP clerks;
GRANT INSERT, UPDATE ON customers to GROUP managers;
```

The ACL for the `customers` table now looks like this:

```
{=r}
{bruce=r}
{group clerks=ar}
{group managers=arw}
```

Let's look at the simplest case first. User `monty` holds no explicit privileges to the `customers` table, but he is (automatically) a member of the `PUBLIC` group. He can `SELECT` from `customers`, but he can't make any changes.

Next, let's see what `sheila` is allowed to do. User `sheila` has no explicit privileges to the `customers` table, but she is a member of two groups: `PUBLIC` and `managers`. The `PUBLIC` group is allowed to `select`, but the `managers` group is allowed to modify the `customers` table. Is `sheila` allowed to insert new `customers`? The answer is yes. When deciding whether to allow a given operation, PostgreSQL uses the following set of rules:

- If there is an ACL entry that matches your username, that entry determines whether the operation is allowed.
- If there is not an ACL entry that matches your username, PostgreSQL looks through the ACL entries for all the groups that you belong to. If any of the groups hold the required privilege, you are allowed to perform the operation.

- If the PUBLIC ACL entry holds the required privilege, you are allowed to perform the operation.
- If you are not granted the required privilege by any of the preceding rules, you are prohibited from performing the operation.

So, sheila is allowed to insert new customers, not because she holds the INSERT privilege herself, but because she belongs to two groups that *do* hold that privilege.

Summary

At this point, you should know how to secure a PostgreSQL installation. There is one more important point that I need to mention. All the security mechanisms provided by PostgreSQL rely on a secure operating environment. If a nefarious user manages to gain superuser access to your system, he or she can bypass all the security measures that you have put into place. Worse yet, he or she can unravel your security in such a way that others can gain access to your private data. PostgreSQL security is not a substitute for a secure operating system.

Index

B

C

J

K

L

P

W

X-Y-Z

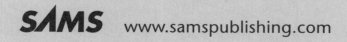

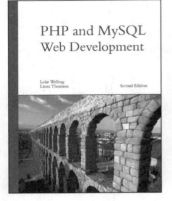

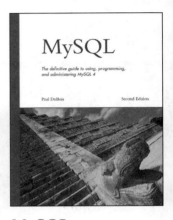